MAGILL'S
CINEMA
ANNUAL

MAGILL'S CINEMA ANNUAL

1994

A Survey of the Films of 1993

Edited by

FRANK N. MAGILL

SALEM PRESS

Pasadena, California   Englewood Cliffs, New Jersey

∞ The paper used in these volumes conforms to the American
National Standard for Permanence of Paper for Printed Library
Materials, Z39.48-1984.

LIBRARY OF CONGRESS CATALOG CARD NO. 83-644357
ISBN 0-89356-413-3
ISSN 0739-2141

First Printing

PRINTED IN THE UNITED STATES OF AMERICA

PUBLISHER'S NOTE

Magill's Cinema Annual, 1994, is the thirteenth annual volume in a series that developed from the twenty-one-volume core set, *Magill's Survey of Cinema*. Each annual covers the preceding year and follows a similar format in reviewing the films of the year. This format consists of four general sections: two essays of general interest, the films of 1993, lists of obituaries and awards, and the indexes.

In the first section, the first article reviews the career and accomplishments of the recipient of the Life Achievement Award, which is presented by the American Film Institute. In 1993, this award was given to the distinguished actress Elizabeth Taylor. Following this initial essay, the reader will find an essay that lists selected film books published in 1993. Briefly annotated, the list provides a valuable guide to the current literature about the film industry and its leaders.

The largest section of the annual, "Selected Films of 1993," is devoted to essay-reviews of ninety-eight significant films released in the United States in 1993. The reviews are arranged alphabetically by the title under which the film was released in the United States. Original and alternate titles are cross-referenced to the American-release title in the Title Index.

Each article begins with selected credits for the film. Credit categories include: Production, Direction, Screenplay, Cinematography, Editing, Art direction, and Music. Also included are the MPAA rating, the running time, and a list of the principal characters with the corresponding actors. This introductory information on a film not released originally in the United States also includes the country of origin and the year the film was released there. If the information for any of the standard categories was unavailable, the heading is followed by the phrase "no listing." Additional headings such as Special effects, Costume design, and Song have been included in an article's introductory top matter when appropriate. Also, the symbol (AA) in the top matter identifies those artists who have received an Academy Award for their contribution to the film from the Academy of Motion Picture Arts and Sciences.

The section of the annual labeled "More Films of 1993" supplies the reader with an alphabetical listing of additional feature films released in the United States during the year. Included are brief credits and short descriptions of the films. These films can be located, along with any cross-references, in the indexes.

Two further lists conclude the text of the volume. The first of these is the Obituaries, which provides useful information about the careers of motion-picture professionals who died in 1993. The second list is of the awards presented by ten different international associations, from the Academy of Motion Picture Arts and Sciences to the Cannes International Film Festival and the British Academy Awards.

The final section of this volume includes nine indexes that cover the films reviewed in *Magill's Cinema Annual*, 1994. Arranged in the order established in the introductory matter of the essay-reviews, the indexes are as follows: Title Index, Director Index, Screenwriter Index, Cinematographer Index, Editor Index, Art Director Index, Music Index, and Performer Index. A Subject Index is also provided. To assist the reader further, pseudonyms, foreign titles, and alternate titles are all cross-referenced. Titles of foreign films and retrospective films are followed by the year, in brackets, of their original release.

The Title Index includes all the titles of films covered in individual articles, in "More Films of 1993," and also those discussed at some length in the general essays. The next seven indexes are arranged according to artists, each of whose names is followed by a list of the films on which they worked and the titles of the essays (such as "Life Achievement Award" or "Obituaries") in which they are mentioned at length. The final listing is the Subject Index, in which any one film that is covered in an individual article can be categorized under several headings. Thus, a reader can effectively use all these indexes to approach a film from any one of several directions, including not only its credits but also its subject matter.

CONTRIBUTING REVIEWERS

Michael Adams
Fairleigh Dickinson University

Nalin Bakhle
Freelance Reviewer

JoAnn Balingit
Freelance Reviewer

Charles Merrell Berg
University of Kansas

Michael Betzold
Freelance Reviewer

Cynthia K. Breckenridge
Freelance Reviewer

Beverley Bare Buehrer
Freelance Reviewer

Ethan Casey
Freelance Reviewer

Richard G. Cormack
Freelance Reviewer

Jonathan David
Freelance Reviewer

George Delalis
Freelance Reviewer

Bill Delaney
Freelance Reviewer

Susan Doll
Freelance Reviewer

Rick Garman
Freelance Reviewer

Douglas Gomery
University of Maryland

Roberta F. Green
Virginia Polytechnic Institute and State University

Glenn Hopp
Howard Payne

Jim Kline
Freelance Reviewer

Patricia Kowal
Freelance Reviewer

Leon Lewis
Appalachian State University

Cono Robert Marcazzo
Upsala College

Robert Mitchell
University of Arizona

Alicia Neumann
Freelance Reviewer

Lisa Paddock
Freelance Reviewer

Pete Peterson
Freelance Reviewer

Debra Picker
Freelance Reviewer

Carl Rollyson
Baruch College, The City University of New York

Wendy Sacket
Freelance Reviewer

Catherine R. Springer
Freelance Reviewer

Gaylyn Studlar
Emory University

Kirby Tepper
Freelance Reviewer

Terry Theodore
University of North Carolina at Wilmington

James M. Welsh
Salisbury State University

Robert Yahnke
University of Minnesota

CONTENTS

CONTENTS

MAGILL'S CINEMA ANNUAL

Life Achievement Award
Elizabeth Taylor

The awarding of the American Film Institute's Life Achievement Award to Elizabeth Taylor may come as a surprise to some. In spite of the fact that Taylor has been before the public eye for more than half a century, her considerable accomplishments in the profession of acting, as well as her notable philanthropic efforts, often have been obscured by elements of her private life that seem to exert a particular fascination over the press and public. Referring to this, Taylor herself has candidly written, "Let's face it—my life seems to have lacked dignity." The continual molding of Taylor's private life as public spectacle, as well as the accompanying tendency to obscure the actress' professional triumphs, however, can be attributed to the symbolic place that Taylor holds in popular culture. She has both the good fortune and the bad luck to epitomize motion-picture stardom in the last half of the twentieth century: She is glamorous, excessive, remote and yet familiar, and, above all, human—if undignified—in her vulnerabilities.

In contrast to this pattern, Taylor's career began in the shielded atmosphere of the Hollywood studio system of the early 1940's. Elizabeth Rosemond Taylor was born in London, England, in 1932, to Sara and Francis Taylor, Americans living overseas. Anticipating the coming of war to Europe, the family (including older brother Howard) moved back to the United States in 1939. Her family took up residence in Pacific Palisades, California. Apparently prompted by her own wishes as much as proximity to Hollywood and the desires of her mother, a former stage actress, Elizabeth began her career at the tender age of nine. She signed with Universal Studios in 1941, in spite of the interest of a more prestigious studio, Metro-Goldwyn-Mayer (MGM) in her as a fledgling singer, dancer, and actress. At Universal, she was forgettably cast in an "Our Gang" comedy. The studio dropped her option with the explanation that the exquisitely featured little girl with violet eyes and coal-black hair did not look enough like a child: Her eyes were too old and she did not "have the face of a kid."

Responding to a casting call for a girl with an English accent, Elizabeth was signed by MGM for a plum role in *Lassie Come Home* (1943), which starred Lassie, of course, and child actor Roddy McDowall. With good reviews for her work in that film, Elizabeth and her formidable mother campaigned for the role of Velvet Brown in MGM's first-class production *National Velvet*. The 1944 release, costarring Mickey Rooney, was a tremendous success and garnered Academy Awards in the arenas of best supporting actress (for Anne Revere) and editing. Reviews declared the twelve-year-old to be a star and so confirmed the commercial wisdom in the powerful studio's having signed the young actress as a contract player at the beginning of production. That contract, oft-revised under the watchful eye of Elizabeth's mother, would keep Taylor under the auspices of MGM until her appearance in *Cleopatra* (1963).

Such a process of star-making would soon be coming to an abrupt end. In 1949, the U.S. Supreme Court ruled that the Hollywood studios were violating the Sherman Anti-Trust Act and had to divest themselves of interests that guaranteed their control over production, distribution, and exhibition. Never again would studios have the absolute power to create stars, as Taylor herself has described, "out of tinsel, cellophane, and newspapers." Elizabeth Taylor, child contract player and then adult actress, would be among the last superstars to be groomed, tutored, coaxed, and bullied into stardom by the studio system.

In 1946, Elizabeth appeared in *Courage of Lassie*, but her loan-out to Warner's during the same year demonstrated that she was no longer a child. Her costumes for her adolescent role in *Life with Father* (1947), starring William Powell and Irene Dunne, emphasized a blossoming figure. At the same time, Elizabeth was experiencing the first of those health problems that would become a hallmark of her accident- and illness-plagued adult life. Elizabeth was growing up fast, and both MGM and others noticed that she could scarcely play a child or an adolescent anymore. The fifteen-year-old had quickly become, in the words of one smitten novelist, "the most beautiful creature I have ever seen in my life."

In response to these changes, MGM cast her in *A Date with Judy* (1948) to begin the process of making her into a full-fledged, glamorous "starlet." Some observers thought the studio was neglecting training her rather high-pitched voice as well as overlooking the need to provide acting instruction to give her the resources to make the transition. Her films, including a remake of *Little Women* (1949) and her first adult role (as Robert Taylor's wife) in *Conspirator* (1950), did not always show her acting talent or her beauty to best advantage.

About this same time, her private life began to be used by studio publicity to solidify her screen transition to adulthood. Elizabeth became engaged and disengaged to a millionaire's son, and unceremoniously dumped a national football hero to set that process into motion. Suddenly, Elizabeth Taylor began to know the meaning of bad press at the same time that she desperately needed better film vehicles.

Soon Taylor's luck would turn. An appearance in the hit comedy *Father of the Bride* (1950) with Spencer Tracy, and at seventeen, a cover photo for *Time* magazine, confirmed her place in the public imagination as the preeminent Hollywood beauty for the 1950's. The critical success of *A Place in the Sun* (1951) would confirm that she could deliver a dramatic performance of high caliber even though some reviewers thought her successful casting as a spoiled rich girl merely a directorial exploitation of the "conceit, artificiality, and awkwardness which mar her playing in most ingenue roles."

Over the next few years, Taylor would have numerous starring roles, but in the kind of MGM vehicles that were not a challenge to her. The exception to this pattern, as reviewers enthusiastically noted, was *The Last Time I Saw Paris* (1954), directed by Richard Brooks. Taylor's private life, marked by an affair with director Stanley Donen and marriages to hotel-fortune heir Nicky Hilton and then to middle-aged English actor Michael Wilding, preoccupied the press, which gave the impression of the actress as an immature and insecure teenager who had grown up too fast physically and seemed to be burning her emotional candle at both ends. Even though Taylor's work in *The Last Time I Saw Paris* had cemented her ambition to become a good actress as well as a star, this fact seemed to escape attention.

When she was again cast in a film directed by George Stevens, Taylor had the opportunity to solidify her professional moorings. In *Giant* (1956), an epic family melodrama drawn from the Edna Ferber novel, Taylor offered a charming and convincing performance as Leslie Benedict, a Southern beauty who ages into a savvy West Texas rancher alongside her husband, Bick (Rock Hudson). This film marked the beginning of a sustained period of professional attainment, in spite of traumatic personal upheaval that was treated in the press as an ongoing three-ring circus.

During this period, Taylor's work in films such as *Raintree County* (1957), *Cat on a Hot Tin Roof* (1958), *Suddenly, Last Summer* (1959), and *Butterfield 8* (1960) brought her critical kudos, Oscar nominations for best actress for four years in a row, and finally, for the last film, an Academy Award. Nevertheless, Taylor has admitted that this particular award, for a film she hated, was probably the result of a sympathy vote. Taylor had survived the unexpected death of her third husband, producer Mike Todd, in early 1958. After his death, she became embroiled in an affair with one of his best friends, the very married Eddie Fisher. This created the biggest Hollywood sex scandal of the late 1950's, and only Taylor's brush with death from pneumonia in 1961 in the midst of filming *Cleopatra* in London regained for her a measure of public sympathy. This was short-lived once her romantic relationship to costar Richard Burton again made her the center of notoriety-provoking headlines.

Elizabeth Taylor and Richard Burton became the most highly publicized star couple in the world during the 1960's. At this time, Taylor's acting career became as mercurial in its success as the public image of her love life. In spite of the appearance of jet-setting frivolity, Taylor's work in *Who's Afraid of Virginia Woolf?* (1966) reestablished her acting credentials with another Best Actress award from the Academy. She also became a most memorable Kate in a surprisingly successful film version of Shakespeare's *The Taming of the Shrew* directed by Franco Zeffirelli in 1967. Other film choices in the late 1960's and early 1970's such as *Boom!* (1968), *The Only Game in Town* (1970), *Hammersmith Is Out* (1972), *Night Watch* (1974), and *The Blue Bird* (1976), were uniformly forgettable, however, and seemed to suggest that Taylor's excessive life-style, at least as the public conceived of it, was taking a toll on her work. Her choices for film roles seemed eccentric and self-indulgent. Her best work, as in John Huston's *Reflections in a Golden Eye* (1967) and *X, Y and Zee* (1972) seemed to be wasted in ill-conceived productions.

In 1976, after a stormy breakup with, remarriage to, and second divorce from Burton, Taylor married John Warner, a conservative U.S. senator, and settled into semiretirement. Occasional film and television appearances became the norm until her Tony-nominated appearance in a 1981 Broadway revival of *The Little Foxes*. During the 1980's, Taylor's philanthropic work of years began to be recognized. She launched a successful fragrance business. She also entered the Betty Ford Clinic in 1988 to conquer dependencies that had become addictions, and she remarried. In 1994, she continued her five-decade film career with a cameo in *The Flintstones*.

In spite of the notable distractions provided by her very public private life, Elizabeth

Taylor's work as an actress and good citizen more than justifies the accolades accompanying the AFI's Life Achievement Award. One of the last of a generation of stars whose careers were shaped by a paternalistic system, Taylor has proven that her own, self-generated attempts to become more than Hollywood star but an actress as well were worth the effort. Even as Elizabeth Taylor has become known as a "survivor," her work survives as a tribute to the actress's spirited ambitions and considerable talent.

Gaylyn Studlar

SELECTED FILM BOOKS OF 1993

Allen, Woody. *The Illustrated Woody Allen Reader*. New York: Alfred A. Knopf, 1993. Linda Sunshine has organized this collection of excerpts from Allen's screenplays, interviews, and comic routines into chapters devoted to the primary topics of the artist's work, including love, sex, death, and New York.

Ankerich, Michael G. *Broken Silence*. Jefferson, N.C.: McFarland, 1993. A collection of interview-based essays on the careers of twenty-three silent-era actors; each essay is accompanied by a filmography.

Archer, Steve. *Willis O'Brien: Special Effects Genius*. Jefferson, N.C.: McFarland, 1993. This is a survey of the career of special-effects artist O'Brien, best known for his work on *King Kong* (1933).

Attwood, Lynne, ed. *Red Women on the Silver Screen*. London: Pandora, 1993. This collection of essays examines the role of women in Soviet film, from the Russian Revolution to the fall of communism.

Balio, Tino. *Grand Design: Hollywood as a Modern Business Enterprise, 1930-1939*. New York: Scribner's, 1993. This is a detailed study of the economics of Hollywood filmmaking in the 1930's, with chapters on virtually every aspect of the industry, including production and marketing.

Basinger, Jeanine. *A Woman's View: How Hollywood Spoke to Women, 1930-1960*. New York: Alfred A. Knopf, 1993. Basinger examines the women's film genre during the studio era, arguing that these films simultaneously affirmed the traditional roles of women while showing that other options were available to them.

Behlmer, Rudy, ed. *Memo From Darryl F. Zanuck*. New York: Grove Press, 1993. Zanuck ran Twentieth Century-Fox during its heyday from 1935-1956. This is a collection of the mogul's correspondence with the studio's actors, writers, directors, and executives from that period.

Behr, Edward. *Thank Heaven for Little Girls*. London: Hutchinson, 1993. This biography of Maurice Chevalier, the celebrated French actor-singer, contains useful information on his activities during the Nazi occupation of France, when Chevalier was accused of collaborating with the enemy.

Belton, John. *American Cinema/American Culture*. New York: McGraw-Hill, 1993. Designed to accompany the PBS series *American Cinema*, this work is a history of American film and its relationship with society.

Benjamin, Ruth, and Arthur Rosenblatt. *Movie Song Catalog*. Jefferson, N.C.: McFarland, 1993. This book provides a filmography of American and British films released from 1928 to 1988 that feature singing, with special emphasis on information about the songs.

Billman, Larry. *Betty Grable: A Bio-Bibliography*. Westport, Conn.: Greenwood Press, 1993. This work surveys the life and career of Betty Grable; it includes both a filmography and a bibliography of writings about the popular actress.

Blake, Michael F. *Lon Chaney: The Man Behind the Thousand Faces*. Vestal, N.Y.:

Vestal Press, 1993. This is a comprehensive biography on the silent-film star of *The Hunchback of Notre Dame* (1923) and other films that made use of his talent for creating memorable characterizations through the application of unusual makeup and costumes.

Bondanella, Peter. *The Films of Roberto Rossellini*. New York: Cambridge University Press, 1993. This is a critical reexamination of the career of the Italian filmmaker who invented neorealism, analyzing both Rossellini's technique and his political philosophy.

Bordwell, David. *The Cinema of Eisenstein*. Cambridge, Mass.: Harvard University Press, 1993. A scholarly overview of the career of the great Russian filmmaker, incorporating newly available documents and footage.

Brewer, Gay. *David Mamet and Film: Illusion/Disillusion in a Wounded Land*. Jefferson, N.C.: McFarland, 1993. This analysis of the Pulitzer Prize-winning playwright's career focuses on his switch from the theater to screenwriting and directing.

Brode, Douglas. *The Films of Robert De Niro*. New York: Citadel Press, 1993. An illustrated film-by-film analysis of the actor's career through *This Boy's Life* (1993), featuring cast, credits, plot synopsis, and the critical reception of each film.

Carrier, Jeffrey L. *Jennifer Jones: A Bio-Bibliography*. New York: Greenwood Press, 1993. A biography of the leading lady of the 1940's, including a filmography and annotated bibliography.

Carringer, Robert L. *The Magnificent Ambersons: A Reconstruction*. Berkeley: University of California Press, 1993. Against its director's wishes, RKO Studios significantly recut Orson Welles' masterpiece. Carringer reconstructs in great detail the film Welles intended to make.

Collins, Jim, Hilary Radner, and Ava Preacher Collins, eds. *Film Theory Goes to the Movies*. New York: Routledge, 1993. This collection of scholarly essays applies various contemporary theoretical approaches to films of the 1990's.

Combs, James, ed. *Movies and Politics: The Dynamic Relationship*. New York: Garland Press, 1993. This is a collection of eight essays on a wide variety of themes illustrating the interrelationship between film and ideology.

Connelly, Marie Katheryn. *Martin Scorsese*. Jefferson, N.C.: McFarland, 1993. This survey of Scorsese's feature films from 1973 to 1992 includes a complete filmography.

Copjec, Joan, ed. *Shades of Noir: A Reader*. New York: Verso, 1993. Essays in this collection not only cover the classics of American *film noir* but also find elements of the genre in later films such as *A Rage in Harlem* (1991) and *Terminator II: Judgment Day* (1991).

Coughlan, Frank "Junior." *They Still Call Me Junior*. Jefferson, N.C.: McFarland, 1993. Coughlan was a child star in the silent era; he also played the title role in the Captain Marvel serial. This is his autobiography.

Cripps, Thomas. *Making Movies Black*. New York: Oxford University Press, 1993.

A scholarly survey of the role of blacks in Hollywood "message" films from the 1940's into the 1960's.

Curtis, Tony, and Barry Paris. *Tony Curtis: The Autobiography*. New York: Morrow, 1993. This frank, well-written autobiography of the American leading man includes both the usual behind-the-scenes anecdotes as well as an honest examination of his work as an actor.

Davis, Ronald L. *The Glamour Factory*. Dallas, Tex.: Southern Methodist University Press, 1993. Using material from the Southern Methodist University Oral History Program, Davis constructs a history of the Hollywood studio system in its glory days from the 1920's to the 1950's.

DelGaudio, Sybil. *Dressing the Part: Sternberg, Dietrich, and Costume*. Rutherford, N.J.: Fairleigh Dickinson University Press, 1993. A scholarly analysis of the function of costume in the films of Josef von Sternberg in collaboration with Paramount costume designer Travis Banton and actress Marlene Dietrich.

Desser, David, and Lester D. Friedman. *American-Jewish Filmmakers: Traditions and Trends*. Urbana: University of Illinois Press, 1993. The authors offer extended analyses of the films of Woody Allen, Mel Brooks, Sidney Lumet, and Paul Mazursky, locating in their work traditions of American Jewish art.

Diawara, Manthia, ed. *Black American Cinema*. New York: Routledge, 1993. This is a collection of nineteen scholarly essays on African American cinema, from the silent era to Spike Lee.

Dissanayake, Wimal. *Melodrama and Asian Cinema*. New York: Cambridge University Press, 1993. A collection of fourteen scholarly essays on the role of melodrama in the cinemas of China, Japan, India, Indonesia, the Philippines, and Australia.

Dixon, Wheeler Winston. *The Early Film Criticism of François Truffaut*. Bloomington: Indiana University Press, 1993. A compilation, with critical commentary by Dixon, of the early critical writings of the French filmmaker.

Doherty, Thomas. *Projections of War: Hollywood, American Culture and World War II*. New York: Columbia University Press, 1993. This is a scholarly examination of Hollywood's portrayal of World War II, and how that portrayal influenced American culture.

Eliot, Marc. *Walt Disney: Hollywood's Dark Prince*. New York: Birch Lane Press, 1993. Eliot's biography finds Disney's creativity rooted in psychosexual conflicts and alleges that the mogul was a long-time informant for the Federal Bureau of Investigation (FBI).

Eyman, Scott. *Ernst Lubitsch: Laughter in Paradise, a Biography*. New York: Simon and Schuster, 1993. This biography of the German émigré filmmaker emphasizes the connection between Lubitsch and the characters in his films.

Fairbanks, Douglas, Jr. *A Hell of a War*. New York: St. Martin's Press, 1993. Unlike many of his Hollywood contemporaries, Fairbanks saw a considerable amount of military action in World War II. This second volume of his autobiography focuses on his life during the war.

Fehr, Richard, and Frederick G. Vogel. *Lullabies of Hollywood*. Jefferson, N.C.: McFarland, 1993. This is a chronological history of the rise and fall of the Hollywood musical, emphasizing the importance of the popular song to the genre.

Fleischer, Richard. *Just Tell Me When to Cry: A Memoir*. New York: Carroll & Graff, 1993. Fleischer directed such films as *20,000 Leagues Under the Sea* (1954) and *Doctor Doolittle* (1967). This is a collection of humorous anecdotes from his nearly half century in Hollywood.

Fregoso, Rosa Linda. *The Bronze Screen*. Minneapolis: University of Minnesota Press, 1993. This is a scholarly study of the portrayal of Chicanos in American cinema, with an emphasis on recent films.

Friedberg, Anne. *Window Shopping: Cinema and the Postmodern*. Berkeley: University of California Press, 1993. Friedberg connects the visual pleasures of cinema with other cultural practices such as shopping and virtual reality in this scholarly work, permitting the viewer to partake of experience in anonymity.

Friedman, Lester, ed. *Fires Were Started: British Cinema and Thatcherism*. Minneapolis: University of Minnesota Press, 1993. This is a collection of essays that attack the Conservative government of Margaret Thatcher for its role in the decline of the British film industry in the 1980's.

Fury, David. *Kings of the Jungle*. Jefferson, N.C.: McFarland, 1993. This is an illustrated filmography of films and television programs featuring the character Tarzan.

Girgus, Sam B. *The Films of Woody Allen*. New York: Cambridge University Press, 1993. A critical reexamination of Allen's film career as an actor, writer, and director, through *Scenes from a Mall* (1991).

Goodwin, James. *Eisenstein, Cinema, and History*. Urbana: University of Illinois Press, 1993. This scholarly work examines the role of Marxist historical theory in the major films of the great Soviet filmmaker.

Greenberg, Harvey Roy. *Screen Memories: Hollywood Cinema on the Psychoanalytic Couch*. New York: Columbia University Press, 1993. Psychiatrist/film critic Greenberg describes psychoanalytic film criticism and applies its tenets to such films as *Casablanca* (1942), *Psycho* (1960), and *Alien* (1979).

Gregory, Adela, and Milo Speriglio. *Crypt 33: The Saga of Marilyn Monroe—The Final Word*. New York: Birch Lane Press, 1993. This biography of the actress alleges that she was murdered by the Mafia at the request of President Kennedy to keep secret the details of her affair with him and his brother.

Haines, Richard W. *Technicolor Movies: The History of Dye Transfer Printing*. Jefferson, N.C.: McFarland, 1993. This is a history of the Technicolor film process, complete with a list of American films using some variation of the process.

Hake, Sabine. *The Cinema's Third Machine: Writing on Film in Germany, 1907-1933*. Lincoln: University of Nebraska Press, 1993. This is a scholarly study of German film criticism and the development of a German cinema aesthetic, from the silent era to the end of the Weimar Republic.

Hecht, Herman. *Pre-Cinema History: An Encyclopaedia and Annotated Bibliography of the Moving Image Before 1896*. London: Bowker-Saur, 1993. Published in association with the British Film Institute, this important reference work annotates 4,000 publications on the subject of moving-image representations prior to the invention of cinema.

Holden, Anthony. *Behind the Oscar*. New York: Viking, 1993. A behind-the-scenes history of the Academy Awards, with an emphasis on the politicking involved in determining winners and losers.

Holston, Kim. *The English-Speaking Cinema*. Jefferson, N.C.: McFarland, 1993. Holston offers an illustrated history of British and American film since the advent of sound, documenting the major trends and genres of the past six decades.

Horton, Andrew, ed. *Inside Soviet Film Satire*. New York: Cambridge University Press, 1993. This collection of sixteen essays focuses on the origins and development of humorous and satirical films over the seventy-year existence of the Soviet Union.

Hurley, Neil P. *Soul in Suspense: Hitchcock's Fright and Delight*. Metuchen, N.J.: Scarecrow Press, 1993. Hurley argues that Hitchcock's years at a Jesuit college were to have a profound influence on his films, and this work examines the filmmaker's career in that light.

Hutchings, Peter. *Hammer and Beyond: The British Horror Film*. Manchester, England: Manchester University Press, 1993. This survey of the British horror film from 1945 into the early 1970's explores the extent to which the genre reflected aspects of the national culture.

Jackson, Kathy Merlock. *Walt Disney: A Bio-Bibliography*. Westport, Conn.: Greenwood Press, 1993. In addition to a conventional biographical essay, this book contains reprints of Disney's speeches and interviews, a reminiscence by one of his close colleagues, and a filmography.

Jenkins, David, with Sue Rogers. *Richard Burton—A Brother Remembered*. London: Century, 1993. Jenkins is the Welsh actor's older brother; this biography offers considerable detail on Burton's early life as well as on his relationship with Elizabeth Taylor.

Johnston, Ollie, and Frank Thomas. *The Disney Villain*. New York: Hyperion, 1993. The authors survey Disney's animated features and analyze the role of the villains in these films. The book includes information on production and animation techniques for these films.

Jones, James Earl, and Penelope Niven. *James Earl Jones: Voices and Silences*. New York: Charles Scribner's Sons, 1993. A thoughtful and revealing autobiography of the distinguished African American stage and film actor.

Kaleta, Kenneth C. *David Lynch*. New York: Twayne, 1993. This scholarly survey of the career of the controversial filmmaker ends with *Wild at Heart* (1990) and includes a chapter on Lynch's television series *Twin Peaks*.

Karsten, Eileen. *From Real Life to Reel Life: A Filmography of Biographical Films*. Metuchen, N.J.: Scarecrow Press, 1993. This reference work is arranged by the name of the person who is the subject of the film and covers both theatrical releases and films made for television. It includes indexes by film title, performer, and broad subject.

Kinder, Marsha. *Blood Cinema: The Reconstruction of National Identity in Spain.* Berkeley: University of California Press, 1993. A scholarly history of the Spanish cinema and its impact on Spanish culture and society during the Franco and post-Franco years.

Kolker, Robert Phillip, and Peter Beicken. *The Films of Wim Wenders: Cinema as Vision and Desire.* New York: Cambridge University Press, 1993. This critical survey of the German filmmaker's career pays special attention to issues of race, sexuality, and audience response.

Linson, Art. *A Pound of Flesh.* New York: Grove Press, 1993. Producer Linson outlines the art of producing films in contemporary Hollywood via a series of humorous cautionary tales.

Lopez, Daniel. *Films By Genre.* Jefferson, N.C.: McFarland, 1993. Lopez establishes 775 genres and subgenres of film, offers a brief definition of each style, and lists representative films in each genre.

McCarty, John. *Hollywood Gangland: The Movies' Love Affair With the Mob.* New York: St. Martin's Press, 1993. McCarty offers a popular survey of the American gangster genre, from the silent era to contemporary dramas about life in the urban ghettos.

McGrath, Patrick J. *John Garfield: The Illustrated Career in Films and on Stage.* Jefferson, N.C.: McFarland, 1993. A survey of the career of the actor best known for his leading roles in action films of the 1930's and 1940's.

Macnab, Geoffrey. *J. Arthur Rank and the British Film Industry.* London: Routledge, 1993. At the height of his influence, Rank owned more than half of the British studios, and more than 1,000 theaters. This is a survey of the film magnate's career.

Malo, Jean-Jacques, and Tony Williams. *Vietnam War Films.* Jefferson, N.C.: McFarland, 1993. This comprehensive filmography on various wars that have taken place in Vietnam covers the years 1939 to 1992 and includes not only American films but also works from Vietnam, France, and other countries.

Marcus, Millicent. *Filmmaking by the Book: Italian Cinema and Literary Adaptation.* Baltimore, Md.: Johns Hopkins University Press, 1993. Marcus utilizes a variety of critical techniques in this scholarly analysis of Italian films based on literary works.

Martin, Len D. *The Allied Artists Checklist.* Jefferson, N.C.: McFarland, 1993. This is a complete filmography of the feature films and short subjects of Allied Artists Pictures from 1947 to 1978, providing a plot synopsis as well as information on cast and credits for the studio's 452 productions.

Mayne, Judith. *Cinema and Spectatorship.* New York: Routledge, 1993. Mayne offers a feminist analysis of contemporary film scholarship and its emphasis on the role of the spectator.

Munn, Michael. *Hollywood Connection*. London: Robson Books, 1993. Munn recounts the interplay—financial and romantic—between the film world and organized-crime figures such as Lucky Luciano and Bugsy Siegel.

Naremore, James. *The Films of Vincente Minnelli*. New York: Cambridge University Press, 1993. This brief work analyzes the career of Metro-Goldwyn-Mayer's leading director of the 1940's and 1950's, and includes a detailed analysis of five of his most important films.

Neibaur, James L. *The RKO Features*. Jefferson, N.C.: McFarland, 1993. This is a comprehensive filmography of the feature films released or produced by RKO from 1929 to 1960; included is information on videocassette availability.

Nicholls, David. *François Truffaut*. London: B. T. Batsford, 1993. This is an illustrated survey of the career of the great French filmmaker, from his earliest short through his acclaimed features.

Nowlan, Robert A., and Gwendolyn W. Nowlan. *Film Quotations*. Jefferson, N.C.: McFarland, 1993. The Nowlans have culled 11,000 famous lines from cinema and arranged them by subject; the book includes an index.

Palmer, James, and Michael Riley. *The Films of Joseph Losey*. New York: Cambridge University Press, 1993. A critical survey of the blacklisted filmmaker's career, including an examination of his working relationship with writer Harold Pinter and actor Dirk Bogarde.

Parish, James Robert. *Gays and Lesbians in Mainstream Cinema*. Jefferson, N.C.: McFarland, 1993. Parish offers casts, credits, plot synopses, and brief critical commentary on 272 mainstream films (including some made for television) that contain gay or lesbian characters or themes.

Penley, Constance, and Sharon Willis, eds. *Male Trouble*. Minneapolis: University of Minnesota Press, 1993. This is a collection of scholarly essays on the cinematic representation of masculinity, written from a feminist perspective.

Portuges, Catherine. *Screen Memories: The Hungarian Cinema of Marta Meszaros*. Bloomington: Indiana University Press, 1993. This is a scholarly examination of the career of the Hungarian documentary and feature filmmaker, including an interview with its subject.

Prindle, David F. *Risky Business: The Political Economy of Hollywood*. Boulder, Colo.: Westview Press, 1993. Devoting sections to a variety of topics, including AIDS (acquired immune deficiency syndrome), political activism, and censorship, Prindle illustrates how the creative side of filmmaking is influenced by politics and economics.

Quarles, Mike. *Down and Dirty: Hollywood's Exploitation Filmmakers and Their Movies*. Jefferson, N.C.: McFarland, 1993. Quarles surveys the careers of filmmakers (including several such as Francis Ford Coppola, John Waters, and George Romero, who had mainstream hits) who specialized in low-budget exploitation films, chiefly of the horror genre.

Ray, Nicholas. *I Was Interrupted: Nicholas Ray on Making Movies*. Los Angeles: University of California Press, 1993. Susan Ray, the wife of the influential filmmaker, edited this collection of his interviews, lectures, and private writings on various topics related to Hollywood and the motion-picture industry.

Reid, Mark A. *Redefining Black Film*. Berkeley: University of California Press, 1993. Reid searches for a "black aesthetic" in American films that were made by or involved significant creative contributions from black filmmakers. The book includes a brief historical survey, but its primary emphasis is on films made in the past thirty years.

Richardson, Tony. *The Long-Distance Runner: An Autobiography*. New York: Morrow, 1993. The manuscript of this memoir was found after the British filmmaker's untimely death. It offers insights into his career and those with whom he worked.

Riefenstahl, Leni. *Leni Riefenstahl: A Memoir*. New York: St. Martin's Press, 1993. This autobiography of the controversial German filmmaker is an important addition to the body of literature about her work.

Rocks, David T. *W. C. Fields: An Annotated Guide*. Jefferson, N.C.: McFarland, 1993. This volume offers a bibliography, filmography, and chronology of the life of the great comic actor, as well as lists of other Fields memorabilia for collectors.

Rubin, Martin. *Showstoppers: Busby Berkeley and the Tradition of Spectacle*. New York: Columbia University Press, 1993. This detailed study of the filmmaker's career links his work to the traditions of minstrelsy, burlesque, and vaudeville.

Salwolke, Scott. *Nicolas Roeg Film by Film*. Jefferson, N.C.: McFarland, 1993. Salwolke presents a detailed survey of the British filmmaker's controversial career through the film *Cold Heaven* (1992).

Schneider, Kirk J. *Horror and the Holy*. Chicago: Open Court, 1993. Schneider analyzes ten classic and modern horror films in this psychological study of the genre.

Semsel, George S., Chen Xihe, and Xia Hong, eds. *Film in Contemporary China*. Westport, Conn.: Praeger, 1993. This is a collection of seventeen scholarly essays on the critical debate in China over Western influences on Chinese cinema from 1979 to 1989.

Sevastakis, Michael. *Songs of Love and Death*. Westport, Conn.: Greenwood Press, 1993. Sevastakis explores the neo-Romantic sensibilities in eleven classic American horror films of the 1930's, comparing the original work of literature with the cinematic version.

Shale, Richard, comp. *The Academy Awards Index*. Westport, Conn.: Greenwood Press, 1993. This important compilation is the most up-to-date reference work on Academy Award nominees, winners, and honorees. It is arranged in two sections: by category, and by year for all categories.

Sharrett, Christopher, ed. *Crisis Cinema: The Apocalyptic Idea in Postmodern Narrative Film*. Washington, D.C.: Maisonneuve Press, 1993. This is a collection of scholarly essays written from a variety of postmodernist viewpoints.

Simmon, Scott. *The Films of D. W. Griffith*. New York: Cambridge University Press,

1993. A brief study of the work of America's first master filmmaker, with extended analyses of his major films as well as discussions of his less well known work at Biograph.

Skal, David J. *The Monster Show: A Cultural History of Horror*. New York: W. W. Norton, 1993. Skal argues that horror films are rituals of anxiety through which Americans are able to relieve the stresses of societal tensions.

Slattery, William J., Claire Dorton, and Rosemary Enright. *The Kael Index*. Englewood, Colo.: Libraries Unlimited, 1993. This is an index to the writings of influential film critic Pauline Kael, covering her work from its beginnings in 1954 through her *New Yorker* years to her retirement in 1991.

Sloan, Jane E. *Alfred Hitchcock: A Guide to References and Resources*. New York: G. K. Hall, 1993. This outstanding one-volume reference work on Hitchcock contains a critical overview of his career, a detailed filmography (including extended plot synopses), and an annotated bibliography of writings by and about the filmmaker.

Smith, Leon. *Famous Hollywood Locations*. Jefferson, N.C.: McFarland, 1993. This book, illustrated copiously with photographs, describes 382 sites in the Los Angeles area that have been used by filmmakers since the 1920's.

Smoodin, Eric. *Animating Culture: Hollywood Cartoons from the Sound Era*. New Brunswick, N.J.: Rutgers University Press, 1993. This is a scholarly history of the American animated film; understandably, the work of Walt Disney dominates the book.

Sperling, Cass Warner, and Cork Millner. *Hollywood Be Thy Name: The Warner Brothers Story*. Rocklin, Calif.: Prima Publishing, 1993. Studio cofounder Harry Warner's granddaughter offers the family's version of the story of the brothers who built a filmmaking empire.

Stenn, David. *Bombshell: The Life and Death of Jean Harlow*. New York: Doubleday, 1993. Harlow was an early "sex symbol," an important figure in Depression-era American film who died at the age of twenty-six. This biography explicates the mysterious suicide of her husband Paul Bern, as well as her untimely death.

Sterritt, David. *The Films of Alfred Hitchcock*. New York: Cambridge University Press, 1993. A scholarly reexamination of the major themes in the works of the acclaimed director, including a detailed analysis of six films from various stages of Hitchcock's career.

Studlar, Gaylyn, and David Desser, eds. *Reflections in a Male Eye: John Huston and the American Experience*. Washington, D.C.: Smithsonian Institution Press, 1993. This collection of thirteen essays on the life and career of the American filmmaker also includes an interview, a filmography, and two of Huston's short stories.

Taves, Brian. *The Romance of Adventure*. Jackson: University Press of Mississippi, 1993. Taves analyzes the themes and narrative techniques of the Hollywood historical adventure film.

Toplin, Robert Brent, ed. *Hollywood as Mirror: Changing Views of "Outsiders" and "Enemies" in American Movies*. Westport, Conn.: Greenwood Press, 1993. This is a collection of eight scholarly essays on the evolving film role of groups such as blacks, Mexican-Americans, immigrants, and communists in American film.

Viano, Maurizio. *A Certain Realism: Making Use of Pasolini's Film Theory and Practice*. Berkeley: University of California, 1993. This is a scholarly examination of the career of the controversial Italian filmmaker, covering many films that remain unscreened in the United States.

Walker, John A. *Art and Artists on Screen*. Manchester, England: Manchester University Press, 1993. Walker examines the portrayal of artists, both real and fictional, in film, with an emphasis on Hollywood productions.

Wayne, Jane Ellen. *Clark Gable: Portrait of a Misfit*. New York: St. Martin's Press, 1993. This biography focuses primarily on Gable's romantic life, emphasizing how each relationship served to further his career.

Welch, Jeffrey Egan. *Literature and Film: An Annotated Bibliography 1978-1988*. New York: Garland, 1993. This bibliography covers books and articles published in North America and Great Britain dealing with the relationship between works of literature and the films made from those works.

Wright, Bruce Lanier. *Yesterday's Tomorrows*. Dallas, Tex.: Taylor Publishing, 1993. This colorful coffee-table volume tells the story of science-fiction cinema from 1950 to 1964, offering film synopses illustrated by posters from each picture.

Yacowar, Maurice. *The Films of Paul Morrissey*. New York: Cambridge University Press, 1993. This is a critical survey of the career of the filmmaker best known for his collaboration with Andy Warhol in the 1960's.

SELECTED
FILMS
OF 1993

THE ACCOMPANIST

Origin: France
Released: 1993
Released in U.S.: 1993
Production: Jean-Louis Livi; released by Sony Pictures Classics
Direction: Claude Miller
Screenplay: Claude Miller and Luc Beraud; based on the novel by Nina Berberova
Cinematography: Yves Angelo
Editing: Albert Jurgenson
Costume design: Jacqueline Bouchard
Music: Alain Jomy
MPAA rating: PG
Running time: 110 minutes

> *Principal characters:*
> Sophie Vasseur . . . . Romane Bohringer
> Irène Brice . . . . Elena Safonova
> Charles Brice . . . . Richard Bohringer
> Jacques Fabert. . . . . Samuel Labarthe
> Benoit Weizman . . . . Julien Rassam
> Helene. . . . . Nelly Borgeaud

The Accompanist, set in occupied France during World War II, is concerned on many levels with collaboration. Sophie Vasseur (Romane Bohringer), an accomplished young pianist, encounters the celebrated soprano, Irène Brice (Elena Safonova), when Sophie auditions with the singer as an accompanist. Sophie has the intoxicating experience of seeing and hearing Irène sing before the two actually meet, and when they do, Sophie is so overcome that she faints. Because Sophie is a poor girl who, like many Parisians during this period, suffers considerable deprivation, Irène attributes her collapse to hunger. It is clear, however, that although Sophie may be hungry, it is not for food alone, but for the beauty and grace Irène embodies.

The sumptuous feast Irène provides Sophie that night is the first of many contrasting views the film gives of the lives of the two women. The next day, before leaving for her formal audition, Sophie quarrels with her mother, Helene (Nelly Borgeaud), over who will eat the last cookie in the household. The cold, dark blues and browns director Claude Miller used in shooting Helene's apartment are quickly offset with the warm, bright pinks and yellows that color the opulent world of Irène and her wealthy businessman husband, Charles Brice (Richard Bohringer—Romane Bohringer's father), who makes his money by collaborating with the Germans and the Vichy government.

Physically and psychologically the two women present a study in contrasts: the dark, somber Sophie is twenty, but looks much younger, while the tawny-haired Irène dazzles with her sophisticated beauty and gracious self-possession. Irène's appeal is irresistible, and when she offers Sophie a position as her accompanist, the girl gratefully accepts—even though Irène stipulates that complete devotion to her is a prerequisite of the job. Irène quickly takes over Sophie's life, inviting her to move in, an offer Sophie is helpless to resist.

Sophie's commitment to her employer is tested almost immediately when Irène presses her into service, not just as a musical collaborator but as a messenger between her and her Free French lover, Jacques Fabert (Samuel Labarthe). Flattered by Irène's generosity and by her trust, Sophie eagerly agrees to do her bidding, regardless of how compromising or demeaning the task. Gradually, some resentment sets in, however, as any sign of independence on Sophie's part is immediately quashed.

Unfortunately, Charles's relations with the Germans disintegrate, and he, Irène and Sophie are forced to flee to England. While crossing the Channel, Sophie has a shipboard romance with an idealistic young French Resistance fighter, Benoit Weizman (Julien Rassam). When Benoit proposes marriage to Sophie, Irène belittles the young man, making it clear that while she can indulge in romance with a French idealist, Sophie must remain in her shadow, her devotion to her employer uncompromised. Sophie is too young and insecure to rebel and, however resentful she may feel, accepts the role of alter ego as her destiny.

Upon their arrival in London, Sophie discovers that Jacques Fabert has preceded them and that his affair with Irène continues. The accompanist, haunted by admiration and envy, trails the singer, spying on her and her lover, participating vicariously in the excitement and glamour of Irène's life, the only existence she is afforded. So fully does Sophie come to identify with Irène that she shares the singer's guilt over her betrayal of her husband. Like Irène, Sophie tries to shield Charles from knowledge of his wife's affair.

Charles, who lost everything when he fled Paris, is now forced, like Sophie, to live through Irène—in every sense. Like the accompanist, he tries to turn a blind eye to Irène's violation of his trust and devotion. Ultimately, by subsuming themselves to Irène's compelling beauty and devotion to her artistry, both of the singer's intimates are undone. Charles commits suicide, and Sophie returns to Paris, where it is by no means clear that she will be able to make a life for herself. The glimmer of hope kindled by her encounter with Benoit at the train station is quickly extinguished when she discovers that he has married another.

Irène's destructive solipsism is apparent from the first. When she initially interviews Sophie, she stresses her ambition and her complete devotion to her singing. Her narcissism is reinforced when she sings the mirror aria from Jules Massenet's opera *Thaïs*, "Dis-mois que je serai belle eternellement" ("Tell me that I will be eternally beautiful"), which becomes a musical signature for her. This song comes, however, only after Irène has removed to London. While still in France, Irène sang only German songs in public, a concession to the occupying forces that permits her career to progress even in the face of war. While her heart may belong to a Resistance fighter, she is lavishly supported by her collaborator husband. Nothing, it seems, can be permitted to stand in the way of her art—not friendship with Sophie, fidelity to Charles, love for Jacques, or allegiance to her country. In the suffocating climate of occupied France, this dedication can be seen as both trivial and admirable—the ultimate expression of freedom, the very embodiment of the Allies' reasons for fighting the war.

Clearly, Miller does not paint Irène as an evil figure. Indeed, she and her music are so transcendently beautiful that filmgoers, like Sophie and Charles, will find her a magical creature whose work is worth sacrifice. Whenever she appears on stage, Irène is clothed in shimmering white, and her face is rapturous as she sings. Miller requested that Safonova refrain from mimicking the grimaces employed by classical singers while she mimed the words sung by soprano Laurence Monteyrol, the better to convey a sense of Irène's unearthly beauty. What is more, offstage Irène customarily evinces great kindness and generosity toward others. In fact, she is no better and no worse than Sophie, who is cruel to her mother and whose general involvement with life is only that of a passive observer. She is no better or worse than Charles, who resorts to suicide as much from business failure as from his wife's infidelity.

The Accompanist deals with subtle shadings of morality that are revealed not so much through action as through camera work and sound track. As director of photography Yves Angelo's camera lingers on the faces of the actors; it communicates the subtlety of the characters' emotions with a directness like that of music. Viewers are far more focused on the deep hunger and resentment reflected in Sophie's eyes than on intricacies of story line. Furthermore, much of what passes for plot in the film is told through music. While the audience witnesses the main characters' flight from France, Miller does not emphasize the hardships and poignancy of their journey and subsequent existence as refugees, opting instead to dramatize the tragedy of the war by scoring newsreel footage of German bombing raids and Nazi parades with Wolfgang Amadeus Mozart's "Vespers." What happens to Sophie, Irène, and Charles in *The Accompanist* is, like World War II, more felt than fully articulated. The result is a film that nevertheless conveys the meaning of commitment and the awesome power of art.

Lisa Paddock

Reviews

Boston Globe. September 17, 1993, LIII, p. 3.
The Hollywood Reporter. December 23, 1993, p. 8.
Los Angeles Times. December 23, 1993, p. F3.
The New Republic. CCIX, December 13, 1993, p. 30.
The New York Times. December 23, 1993, p. B1.
Opera News. LVIII, December 25, 1993, p. 40.
Playboy. XLI, January, 1994, p. 32.
Seventeen. LIII, January, 1994, p. 63.
Time. CXLIII, January 10, 1994, p. 60.

Variety. CCCXLIX, December 21, 1993, p. 62.
The Village Voice. December 28, 1993, p. 88.
The Wall Street Journal. January 13, 1994, p. A16.
The Washington Post. March 11, 1994, p. G6.

ADDAMS FAMILY VALUES

Production: Scott Rudin; released by Paramount Pictures
Direction: Barry Sonnenfeld
Screenplay: Paul Rudnick; based on characters created by Charles Addams
Cinematography: Don Peterman
Editing: Arthur Schmidt and Jim Miller
Production design: Ken Adam
Art direction: Scott Rudin
Visual effects supervision: Alan Munro
Costume design: Theoni V. Aldredge
Choreography: Peter Anastos
Music: Marc Shaiman
MPAA rating: PG-13
Running time: 93 minutes

Principal characters:

Morticia Addams	Anjelica Huston
Gomez Addams	Raul Julia
Fester Addams	Christopher Lloyd
Debbie Jelinsky	Joan Cusack
Wednesday Addams	Christina Ricci
Granny	Carol Kane
Pugsley Addams	Jimmy Workman
Pubert Addams	Kaitlyn and Kristin Hooper
Joel Glicker	David Krumholtz
Lurch	Carel Struycken
Thing	Christopher Hart
Cousin It	John Franklin
Mr. Glicker	Barry Sonnenfeld

Charles Addams' first eccentric Addams Family cartoon ran in *The New Yorker* magazine in 1932, and for some thirty years, in some 1,300 cartoons, Addams continued to poke fun at the conformity that reigned in middle-class America. In 1964, the Addams family came to television, and at Thanksgiving 1991, to the big screen. Thanksgiving 1993 saw the return of the family and their irregular regularity to theaters everywhere with the release of *Addams Family Values*.

Addams Family Values begins with the birth of the newest Addams, Pubert, played by twin girls (Kaitlyn and Kristin Hooper), a mustachioed, infant version of Gomez Addams (Raul Julia), and a new and even happier period in Addams family life appears to have begun. With the return of Pubert and Morticia (Anjelica Huston) to the Addams mansion, however, chaos breaks out. Wednesday (Christina Ricci) and Pugsley (Jimmy Workman) suffer sibling rivalry, subjecting Pubert to guillotines, dropped anvils, and flights from the roof. Meanwhile, in another part of the mansion, Fester

(Christopher Lloyd) is suffering a bout of loneliness that can be cured only by Pubert's new nanny, Debbie Jelinsky (Joan Cusack), a murderous seductress. Before film's end, Wednesday and Pugsley are sent off to Camp Chippewa, where they suffer the wrath of "self-important blondness gone psycho"—to quote the *Baltimore Sun*—while back home, Fester is married and "murdered." All the while Morticia and Gomez tango and croon through the great romance that is their lives.

Perhaps the dominant shared feature of those who bring the Addams family to the screen is their affection and admiration for the characters created by Charles Addams. Or perhaps it is more accurate to say that the affection the characters feel for one another drives the films. Says director Barry Sonnenfeld in the film's production notes, the Addamses are "the ultimate functional family. The parents love the children. The mother and father love each other. They don't change their values based on a whim. They're a perfect family." Agrees executive producer David Nicksay, "As you get to know them, you realize that the Addamses have fantastic traditions which they pass on to each other. They love each other very much. They cherish each other's freedom to be individual, quirky, however they want to be, and so they have a really great working family unit." For example, through the connivance of Debbie the nanny, Morticia and Gomez think Wednesday and Pugsley want to go to Camp Chippewa and spend the summer "being bludgeoned into cheerfulness." Repelled by the thought and by what they see of the camp when they deposit the children, the Addamses nevertheless support their children's wishes and make camp possible for them. Further, concerned by Fester's new liaison with Debbie, Morticia and Gomez go in search of the lovebirds. Upon encountering the neo-suburbanite Fester and his consumerist love Debbie, Morticia says, "You have placed Fester under some strange sexual spell. I respect that. But Debbie, pastels?" Understanding of others' oddities, the none-too-normal Addamses work to accept everyone and everyone's none-too-normal baggage, all in the name of keeping the family together.

Anjelica Huston also sees love as the key to the characters, describing the relationship between Morticia and Gomez as "extremely loving and very passionate. If anything, I think their passion deepens with the years." Raul Julia echoes the sentiment: "Gomez is very much in love with Morticia. And he's like a swashbuckling, romantic, crazy man." While Morticia and Gomez play smaller roles in this film, their romance drives several key scenes in the film, including one in a literally mossy and cavernous French restaurant where Morticia and Gomez dance a tango. Unlike any other tango in film history, this production number involves acrobatics, weapons, high-speed action, and l'amour, toujours l'amour. While the actors worked repeatedly with a choreographer, what appears on screen is largely the actors' innovations. After all, says Julia, it is an "Addams Family tango."

All these good intentions and family values could make for a very unfunny film, however, were it not for Paul Rudnick's screenplay. Rudnick—also a novelist (*Social Disease*), playwright (*Jeffrey*), and columnist (for *Premiere*, *Spy*, and *Interview* magazines)—wrote the original version of the screenplay for *Sister Act* (1992) and also doctored the script for *The Addams Family*. Says Rudnick in the production notes,

"The best thing about writing for the Addams Family is that you don't have to be wholesome." Many of the lines he has written for these characters display just that pranksterish glee. For example, upon Debbie's arrival, Rudnick has the nanny ask, "These Addams men, where do you find them?" Answers Morticia, "It has to be damp." To the children, Debbie says, "What do we say?" Wednesday's answer: "Be afraid. Be very afraid." In a later scene, Debbie asks Fester, "Have you really never had sex?" To Fester's embarrassed silence she continues, "Well then how do you know we're not having it right now?" The screenplay is witty and fast-paced. Other great touches include Fester's reading *Strange Men and the Women Who Avoid Them* and Wednesday's scaring the other children at camp with midnight tales of the return of their pre-nose-job noses. Where *The Addams Family* was lauded for its look and lambasted for its lethargy, *Addams Family Values* moves at a quick clip, fueled largely by Rudnick's clever screenplay.

Also worth note in the film are the performances given by the three main women characters: Huston as Morticia, Ricci as Wednesday, and Cusack as Debbie. Having honed her characterization of Morticia to larger-than-large eyes, a curl of a mouth, and a whisper of a voice, Huston floats through the scenes, underplaying remarkably. To reach this point, she has given a good bit of thought to what her character would be like: "There are certain questions about Morticia, such as 'Does Morticia wake up and put that outfit on?' My feeling about her always was that this is how she wakes up in the morning. There is a question as to whether Morticia has legs." Whether delighting in her labor pains, consoling her husband, or commiserating with Debbie's unhappy childhood, Morticia is "the serene center of the film . . . almost mythical, a Circe without the attitude problem," according to the *Baltimore Sun*.

Also quite fine, and once again receiving rave reviews, Ricci has also worked on an understanding of her character: "Wednesday is very mature. She is very secure in her house and with her family, and any new person makes her very suspicious. As she grows up, she starts to look more and more like Morticia. She wants to be just like her mother." While Ricci does not have a bad scene in the film, perhaps her best work is done during the Camp Chippewa scenes. For example, after being sentenced to the Harmony Hut to watch Disney films until her attitude improves, Wednesday emerges and—gulp!—smiles to show her transformation. It is a remarkable smile. It twists slowly across her face. It is an ache as much as an expression. It is remarkable. Yet even better is when the pseudo-reformed Wednesday springs back to life and seizes control of the Thanksgiving pageant (at a summer camp?), improvising with, "We can't break bread with you. You have taken the land which is rightfully ours. Your people will wear cardigans and drink highballs. . . . And for all these reasons, I have decided to scalp you and burn your village to the ground."

In the production materials, the filmmakers discuss the need to keep the regular Addams characters unchanged and therefore the importance of casting new characters—such as Debbie the villainous nanny—absolutely correctly. Joan Cusack is just right for the role. Audience members who have followed her work from *Sixteen Candles* (1984) to *Working Girl* (1988) to *Men Don't Leave* (1990) to *Hero* (1992) to a dozen other films will be surprised at the kitsch—and the décolleté—of Cusack as Debbie. Curvacious and deadly, Debbie spins a pastel trap for Fester. Particularly fine are scenes in which Debbie and Fester spoon in the graveyard, in which Debbie shortens Fester's elaborate marriage vows to the equivalent of "Me, too," and in which a crazed Debbie holds the family hostage for her retelling of how her life ran off course. Cusack is lovely, artful, funny, and just right.

Among the other new characters who make good additions to the Addams family is David Krumholtz, who plays Wednesday's first boyfriend, Joel Glicker. As Krumholtz describes the attraction, "Joel likes the way Wednesday is not afraid to talk, because he's not very outgoing. He's very shy and nervous, and she's not at all. He loves the weirdness of Wednesday's family, and I think he fits right in and he's glad he does. He finds Wednesday beautiful. And they both think the idea of green trees and a nice, beautiful lake is their version of hell." Also memorable is Barry Sonnenfeld (the film's director) as Joel's overanxious father.

The production itself was also true to Charles Addams' vision. Details of the rooms, for example, the bed in Wednesday's bedroom, the wallpaper, the out-of-plumb walls, are pure Addams. Yet it took seven soundstages and several locations around Los Angeles to create all the different looks within the Addams world. Great attention was also paid to costuming. Gomez's attire is the same as when he made his debut—1930's-era suits. Granny is completely accessorized, right down to the dead birds in her hair. While most of the film required dressing characters to match their cartoon originals, Debbie provided an opportunity to experiment. Says costume designer Theoni V. Aldredge, "Debbie borders on really tacky taste. We tried to put in a little bad taste, but she can get away with it because she's very pretty." As for special effects, it took fifteen different puppets to create the variety of Thing scenes. The hardest scene? One in which Thing acrobatically skates on a roller skate. Remembers Alan Munro, visual effects supervisor, "It's the ultimate skateboard sequence with a detached hand."

From its November 19 release date until year's end, *Addams Family Values* grossed $59 million worldwide. Additionally, it received an Academy Award nomination for art direction.

Roberta F. Green

Reviews
Chicago Tribune. November 19, 1993, p. 7C.
The Christian Science Monitor. November 19, 1993, p. 17.
Entertainment Weekly. November 26, 1993, p. 44.
The Hollywood Reporter. November 15, 1993, p. 6.
Los Angeles Times. November 19, 1993, p. F1.
The New York Times. November 19, 1993, p. B1.
Newsweek. CXXII, November 22, 1993, p. 57.
Variety. CCCLIII, November 29, 1993, p. 31.
Washington Post. November 19, 1993, p. 50.

THE AGE OF INNOCENCE

Production: Barbara De Fina; released by Columbia Pictures
Direction: Martin Scorsese
Screenplay: Jay Cocks and Martin Scorsese; based on the novel by Edith Wharton
Cinematography: Michael Ballhaus
Editing: Thelma Schoonmaker
Production design: Dante Ferretti
Art direction: Speed Hopkins
Set decoration: Robert J. Franco and Amy Marshall
Casting: Ellen Lewis
Sound: Tod Maitland
Costume design: Gabriella Pescucci (AA)
Music: Elmer Bernstein
MPAA rating: PG
Running time: 133 minutes

Principal characters:

Newland Archer	Daniel Day-Lewis
Ellen Olenska	Michelle Pfeiffer
May Welland	Winona Ryder
Julius Beaufort	Stuart Wilson
Regina Beaufort	Mary Beth Hurt
Larry Lefferts	Richard E. Grant
Sillerton Jackson	Alec McCowen
Mrs. Welland	Geraldine Chaplin
Mrs. Mingott	Miriam Margolyes
Mrs. Archer	Siân Phillips
Janey Archer	Carolyn Farina
Henry van der Luyden	Michael Gough
Louisa van der Luyden	Alexis Smith
Rivière	Jonathan Pryce
Letterblair	Norman Lloyd
Ted Archer	Robert Sean Leonard
Narrator	Joanne Woodward

Because of the powerful content, visceral energy, and stylistic flourishes of such films as *Mean Streets* (1973), *Taxi Driver* (1976), *Raging Bull* (1980), and *Goodfellas* (1990), Martin Scorsese has been acclaimed by film critics as the most talented American director of his generation. Since several of his films depict the seedy lives of New York hustlers and criminals, many observers were surprised by his decision to film Edith Wharton's Pulitzer Prize-winning novel, *The Age of Innocence* (1920). Wharton's comedy of manners examining the snobbery of tradition-bound New York aristocrats in the 1870's hardly seems a subject of interest for Scorsese, most of whose films are brutally violent.

Those puzzled by the director's choice of material ignore that throughout his career Scorsese has refused to confine himself to one type of film. *Alice Doesn't Live Here Anymore* (1974) is a soap opera; *New York, New York* (1977), a musical melodrama; *After Hours* (1985), a black comedy; *The Last Temptation of Christ* (1988), a naturalistic version of Biblical epics; and *Cape Fear* (1991), a Southern Gothic. Given Scorsese's concern with traditional Hollywood genres, his choosing a costume drama is not surprising. Considerably much more than a genre film, *The Age of Innocence* has numerous elements in common with the typical Scorsese film, including the rituals associated with a segment of society and characters who allow others to define their roles or feel confined by such restrictions.

Newland Archer (Daniel Day-Lewis) is about to announce his engagement to May Welland (Winona Ryder) when he meets Ellen (Michelle Pfeiffer), May's cousin, now the Countess Olenska. (The characters constantly observe that everyone in New York is related, everyone, of course, excluding all those who do not give balls and spend their afternoons in well-upholstered salons.) Ellen has returned to New York after years abroad and plans to divorce her husband. Even though the influential Mrs. Mingott (Miriam Margolyes) is her grandmother, Ellen is shunned by stuffy New York society simply for contemplating divorce. Matters are made worse by her associating with the notorious adulterer Julius Beaufort (Stuart Wilson).

Newland is genuinely fond of May and comforted by the traditions of wealth, status, and social grace she embodies, but his libido, which he barely understands, is drawn to the more glamorous Ellen. He may choose the virtuous May and live a highly predictable life or the dangerous Ellen and face the unknown. At Ellen's urging, the weak Newland marries May only to find himself longing even more for her cousin. On the verge of telling his wife of his true feelings, May informs him she is pregnant, and all is lost. In a coda set more than two decades after these events, the fifty-seven-year-old Newland, now a widower, discovers that May knew about his passion all along and that both women manipulated him.

The brilliance of *The Age of Innocence* is the way the director's cinematic skills and the actors' contributions merge to tell this ironic love story. Despite his use of a voice-over narrator (Joanne Woodward) to explicate important points about this society, Scorsese presents the narrative in strongly visual terms. He uses scenes from the operas and plays the characters attend and the images in their paintings for ironic counterpoint to what is going on in their lives, as when Newland is almost overcome by emotion by a melodrama in which a woman is abandoned by her lover.

Cinematographer Michael Ballhaus' camera pauses frequently over the elaborate dishes—created by Rick Ellis, an expert in food presentation and food history—served at the characters' multicourse dinners. New York society is gently chided by these images, which suggest that the way the food is displayed on the plate is far more significant than is nourishment. The same is true for the loving re-creation of period costumes and furnishings by costume designer Gabriella Pescucci and production designer Dante Ferretti. Rather than have the audience awed by the opulence of these trappings, Scorsese uses them to emphasize the superficiality of a society defined by its material possessions. The food and clothing also underscore the overwhelming significance of ritual in this world. The tangible symbols of their class are inseparable from their trips to Newport and their archery tournaments. The exquisite arrow pin Beaufort donates as the prize for the latter confirms his status and the significance of the award over the event.

Scorsese beautifully captures the essence of *The Age of Innocence* with a sunset shot of Newland gazing at Ellen by a Newport pier as she watches a yacht sail by a lighthouse. The almost supernatural golden glow with which Ballhaus bathes Ellen suggests Newland's romantic ardor, the boat his need for escape, the phallic lighthouse his seething sexual passion, and the sunset his fading hopes of fulfilling all the above.

Scorsese's use of mattes to create this image as well as a strikingly primitive-looking Fifth Avenue shows his debt to similar manipulations of reality in the films of Michael Powell, director of *Black Narcissus* (1946) and *The Red Shoes* (1948). *The Age of Innocence* is a more subdued version of the fevered romanticism associated with Powell and with Max Ophuls, whose *Letter from an Unknown Woman* (1948) and *The Earrings of Madame de . . .* (1953) explore similar senses of loss. In a matte shot of a bustling midtown Manhattan can be seen a sign for Schoonmaker's Painters Supplies, a tribute to Scorsese's longtime editor, Thelma Schoonmaker, also Powell's widow.

Scorsese fills his film with similar touches. While Newland waits for Ellen outside a Boston hotel, the name Lily Bart, heroine of Wharton's *The House of Mirth* (1905), can be seen on a nearby window. The shot of the twist in the back of Ellen's hair, at which Newland stares while approaching her in another scene, recalls James Stewart's fascination with a similar style worn by Kim Novak in Alfred Hitchcock's *Vertigo* (1958). The latter homage is hardly frivolous since Newland is pursuing a doomed relationship, recalling that in *Vertigo*.

As Newland, Day-Lewis is not afraid to look ridiculous, as when he almost shudders with emotion at the play, caresses a leatherbound book while sniffing it, bends slowly to kiss Ellen's slipper, becomes intoxicated by the smell of a parasol he thinks is hers (that he is mistaken indicates the foolishness of his pursuit), and carefully unbuttons Ellen's glove to kiss her wrist. These gestures contrast with the character's stiff uncertainty in his scenes away from Ellen. After making *The Age of Innocence*, Scorsese served as cocurator for a James Mason series for the Film Society of Lincoln Center, and he seems to have directed Day-Lewis to emulate Mason's patented combination of suavity and weakness.

Michelle Pfeiffer, another performer of great range, also recalls an earlier star. As Ellen enters a party given for her to compensate for an earlier snub, Pfeiffer radiates with the self-assurance of the young Julie Christie. (Several aspects of Scorsese's film recall David Lean's 1965 film of *Doctor Zhivago*, starring Christie as well as Geraldine Chaplin.) Her dominance of every scene in which she appears makes clear why Newland is infatuated with Ellen. In the meeting of Newland and Ellen, Pfeiffer economically conveys all that is needed to know about these characters. Extending her hand for him to kiss, she continues to hold it out after he has merely shaken it, foreshadowing the ineptness he will bring to their unconsummated affair and the control she will exert over him. (The film overflows with images of hands, which convey different messages whether in society or in private.)

Winona Ryder's understated portrayal of May, combining youthful innocence with a wisdom beyond clumsy Newland's understanding, is one of the many subtle highlights of the film and confirmed Ryder's standing as the under-thirty performer with the brightest future in film acting.

Although highly praised by most critics, the film did not do as well commercially as some had expected, grossing $31 million by the year's end. Many viewers—and some critics—did not understand how the glamorous Pfeiffer and Day-Lewis could co-star in a love story with no erotic fireworks, and before the Academy Award nominations were announced, a prejudice against the film on the part of those in the film industry was reported. Although Scorsese was nominated for the Directors Guild of America award and a Golden Globe, he was not nominated for an Oscar. The film received Academy Award nominations for Ryder's performance, the screenplay, art direction, and musical score, with Gabriella Pescucci winning an Oscar for her costume design. Ryder won a Golden Globe, and Pfeiffer and the film received nominations for that award as well. Those who find Scorsese's *The Age of Innocence* too repressed are sadly missing the point, since subdued emotions are the film's subject.

Michael Adams

Reviews

Atlanta Constitution. September 17, 1993, p. F1.
Boston Globe. September 17, 1993, p. 49.
Chicago Tribune. September 17, 1993, p. C31.
The Christian Science Monitor. LXXXV, September 17, 1993, p. 11.
Entertainment Weekly. September 17, 1993, p. 72.
The Hollywood Reporter. August 31, 1993, p. 6.
Los Angeles Times. September 17, 1993, p. F1.
The New York Times. September 17, 1993, p. B1.
The New Yorker. LXIX, September 13, 1993, p. 121.
Newsweek. CXXII, September 20, 1993, p. 62.
Rolling Stone. September 30, 1993, p. 111.
Time. CXLII, September 20, 1993, p. 82.
Variety. CCCLII, September 13, 1993, p. 31.
The Village Voice. XXXVIII, September 21, 1993, p. 55.
The Wall Street Journal. September 16, 1993, p. A18.
The Washington Post. September 17, 1993, p. D1.

THE BALLAD OF LITTLE JO

Production: Fred Berner and Brenda Goodman for Polygram Filmed
   Entertainment; released by Fine Line Features
Direction: Maggie Greenwald
Screenplay: Maggie Greenwald
Cinematography: Declan Quinn
Editing: Keith Reamer
Production design: Mark Friedberg
Casting: Judy Claman and Jeffery Passero
Sound: Felipe Borrerro
Costume design: Claudia Brown
Music: David Mansfield
MPAA rating: R
Running time: 120 minutes

Principal characters:
Little Jo	Suzy Amis
Frank Badger	Bo Hopkins
Percy Corcoran	Ian McKellen
Tinman Wong	David Chung
Ruth Badger	Carrie Snodgrass
Streight Hollander	Rene Auberjonois
Mary Addie	Heather Graham
Jasper Hill	Sam Robards
Shopkeeper	Ruth Maleczech
Elvira	Olinda Turturro
Russian mother	Irina Pasmur
Henry Grey	Anthony Heald

   Stories of Western life on film have usually been told from a male perspective. The romantic cowboy Western with its stock versions of wild Indians, gun-toting men, and women as whores or angels has occasionally been challenged by "revisionist" Westerns. Films like the seriocomic *Little Big Man* (1970), the hip but gritty *McCabe and Mrs. Miller* (1971), and the chilling yarn *The Missouri Breaks* (1976) fascinate because they shatter at least some of the stereotypes the Hollywood Western has cherished. The true hardships men and women settlers endured in the West and the psychological wildness that the harsh, sublime landscapes encouraged are often not realistically depicted. Maggie Greenwald's *The Ballad of Little Jo* offers a revised version of frontier life in a story told from a woman's perspective. Her main character is neither saloon maid nor schoolteacher nor young mother protecting her brood from Indians and bears.

   Instead, Greenwald has created a film portrait of an idiosyncratic woman of the nineteenth century. Her bittersweet history follows a genteel young woman from the East who travels west in 1866 to find freedom from her family's scorn after she gives birth to an illegitimate son. As a woman traveling alone she confronts sexual advances, disdain, and violent attacks. She discovers right away that the only way to escape is to adopt a male disguise. So Josephine Monaghan becomes Little Jo (Suzy Amis). With a nasty, self-inflicted facial scar and ill-fitting trousers, she defies the image of femininity, even if her beardless face and slight build do not fulfill the traditional image of manhood.

Before the change, Little Jo slogs alone along a dusty road with a heavy valise, holding a parasol against the sun. Her situation invites curious stares from passersby in their buggies and wagons. Three soldiers galloping by decide she is fair game and abruptly return to harass her. She quickens her pace and remains steely-faced until they thunder off in laughter. When a traveling salesman, Streight Hollander (Rene Auberjonois), offers a lift, she accepts reluctantly. He seems fatherly and protective, but he secretly makes a deal to sell her to the soldiers. His treachery and their violence convince Josephine she needs a male disguise to help protect her.

Little Jo arrives in a boomtown called Ruby City. A rough place, it is home to outcasts and gold miners. The inhabitants do not know what to make of this young man with soft features and an adolescent-sounding voice. At first, they accuse Little Jo of being a "dude" from the East, but the newcomer's resolve and willingness to work hard soon earn her the respect of the men in town.

Little Jo befriends Percy Corcoran (Ian McKellen), a seemingly sympathetic miner who takes the novice under his wing and even offers to share his crude lodgings with her. Percy has a sadistic streak, however, that surfaces when he drinks. His misogyny is revealed when he savagely attacks a whore one night and the men fetch Jo to contain him. Jo witnesses the results of Percy's fury on the bleeding face of the mute prostitute.

She leaves Percy and takes a winter job with the rancher Frank Badger (Bo Hopkins), who has grown to respect this odd young man even if he, like everyone in town, finds Jo's aversion to sex and his hermetic life-style downright strange. Frank hires Little Jo to shepherd his flock of sheep for the winter. He is not sure Little Jo will endure the harsh winter. During her isolation in a cabin in the mountains, she teaches herself to shoot and clean a gun and to care for the flock. Evenings, she fashions a ruggedly luxurious coat from the hides of marauding wolves. When she returns in the spring, she has become a fully accepted member of the frontier community. In fact, many had wished that Little Jo would marry young Mary Addie (Heather Graham), who was sweet on the silent young man almost from the day he arrived. Instead, Mary Addie's wedding to a Texas rancher is the first social event Little Jo attends upon her return. Soon after, she is building a cabin on a homestead parcel outside of town.

The story line of *The Ballad of Little Jo* is episodic in the way of a ballad, with each sequence resembling in structure a ballad verse wherein Little Jo learns some lesson or successfully faces a great challenge. Also like the hero in a ballad, Little Jo performs noble acts. Twice she helps outcasts like herself to find a safe home. First, she leads a family of Russian immigrants to their barren homestead on a grass-covered hillside;

periodically she visits them to bring food and gifts. Then she saves a transient Chinese railroad worker whom she finds about to be lynched by a group of taunting men, Frank Badger presiding. She demands that they release him, but in return for the coolie's release Frank makes her agree to hire him as cook and housekeeper.

Tinman Wong (David Chung) performs his duties well, but at night must sleep outside his master's house, for Little Jo guards her privacy ferociously. Tinman's loyalty, and his delicate health, however, eventually melt her heart. Together they build an addition to her house for his quarters. Of course, it is not long before Tinman discovers Jo's secret, and Jo succumbs to the sort of friendship her long, lonely masquerade has denied her. The couple become lovers and recreational opium smokers. Their union seems perfect and idyllic. In fact, it is a lesson in tolerance, as well as sexual and racial politics. In their household duties, traditional gender roles have been reversed, and each accepts the other's difficulties and weaknesses without question. As in a fable, the outcasts are the enlightened ones, in stark contrast to the frontiersmen of Ruby City, who are depicted as pillagers and barbarians. Their rapaciousness and violence necessitate Jo's deception.

Little Jo is in a precarious position not only because it is illegal for a woman to dress as a man but also because the citizens of Ruby City would surely kill both her and Tinman if their secret union were discovered. The relationship is tainted by fear and sadness, therefore, since Little Jo and Tinman realize there is nowhere in the world they can live openly together undisturbed.

Except for the exploration of this tender relationship, the film avoids sentimentality. Thanks to Suzy Amis' finely tempered performance, sentimentality is not a danger. This fine actor's Jo is a woman on a hairspring, sharp-eyed and vigilant, tight-lipped and intelligent. Her surface cool radiates courage, while her eyes and expression intimate the emotional storms she is enduring. Occasional letters from her sister— always with a few words about her son—make Little Jo feel the weight of her choices. Amis' performance is a haunting study of self-discipline and courage.

Eventually big business arrives in Ruby City by way of a greedy and ambitious cattle rancher whose hired gunmen massacre homesteaders who will not sell their land. Peaceable Little Jo is forced to take up arms to protect her land. This conflict arrives at a difficult time, since she has been feeling the pressure of the townspeople to involve herself more in local politics by becoming their spokesperson. Meanwhile, Tinman's health is failing. When he is finally bedridden with pneumonia, she must fetch Frank's wife, Ruth Badger (Carrie Snodgrass). Ruth's knowledge of frontier medicine illustrates just one role pioneer women played as the West's true settlers. They cared for their communities with strength and wisdom.

The final verse of *The Ballad of Little Jo* is completed many years later, after Little Jo dies alone on her homestead. In town, her buddies gather at the saloon to drink to the memory of their friend, while the astonished undertaker becomes the first to discover the amazing truth.

Though she existed, little is known about the real Jo Monaghan. Maggie Greenwald's screenplay is wary, yet enchanting and surefooted in its exploration of the

1860's West Little Jo might have known: not the blue-sky Eden of most westerns, but the violent and gritty society evoked in memoirs and photographs of the era. It pays homage to all the brave women who were the invisible backbone within the booming new society. Above all, it offers a meditation on one of the strange yet often-documented cases of women living as day laborers, male soldiers, stagecoach drivers, performers, and doctors at a time when sexual roles were so strictly defined that just doing the things a man would do was evidence enough to establish gender identity. It is one of the first times in film the Western frontier has been observed through the eyes of a woman, moreover, a woman secretly privy to the complex interrelationships between men, men and nature, and men and women.

JoAnn Balingit

Reviews
Chicago Tribune. September 10, 1993, VII, p. 25.
The Christian Science Monitor. August 27, 1993, p. 10.
Cineaste. XX, Number 2, 1993, p. 45.
The Hollywood Reporter. August 18, 1993, p. 7.
Los Angeles Times. September 10, 1993, p. F8.
The New York Times. August 20, 1993, p. B7.
Rolling Stone. August 19, 1993, p. 83.
Sight and Sound. III, November, 1993, p. 18.
Time. August 30, 1993, p. 67.
Variety. CCCLII, August 30, 1993, p. 26. Daily August 17, p. 2.
The Wall Street Journal. September 2, 1993, p. A11.
The Washington Post. September 11, 1993, p. D2.

BEETHOVEN'S SECOND

Production: Michael C. Gross and Joe Medjuck; released by Universal Pictures
Direction: Rod Daniel
Screenplay: Len Blum
Cinematography: Bill Butler
Editing: Sheldon Kahn and William D. Gordean
Production design: Lawrence Miller
Art direction: Charles Breen
Set decoration: Cloudia
Casting: Steven Jacobs
Sound: Gene S. Cantamessa
Costume design: April Ferry
Animal Training: Glen D. Garner, April Morley, Karin McElhatton, and Paul A.
   Calabria
Music: Randy Edelman
MPAA rating: PG
Running time: 86 minutes

> *Principal characters:*
> George Newton...................... Charles Grodin
> Alice Newton .... Bonnie Hunt
> Ryce .... Nicholle Tom
> Ted .... Christopher Castile
> Emily............................. Sarah Rose Karr
> Regina................................ Debi Mazar
> Floyd................................. Chris Penn
> Taylor .... Ashley Hamilton
> Cliff............................... Maury Chaykin
> Seth.............................. Danny Masterson

In the original film, *Beethoven* (1992), a stray Saint Bernard puppy eluded the bad guys and earned a place in the heart of each member of the Newton family, including George (Charles Grodin), the punctilious father. In *Beethoven's Second*, Beethoven's back, this time to find romance.

As the film begins, life at the Newton house has fallen into disorderly order once again after the confusion that arose from saving Beethoven from the evil veterinarian (Dean Jones) in the first film. In this sequel, George is still trying to figure out how to give new life to his ailing air freshener business with the help of wife Alice (Bonnie Hunt). Fifteen-year-old daughter Ryce (Nicholle Tom) has discovered boys—or they have discovered her—causing George additional worry. Thirteen-year-old Ted (Christopher Castile) is worried about the bullies on the bus, and life has changed little for nine-year-old Emily (Sarah Rose Karr).

One day after the Newton family has left for the day, Beethoven lets himself out of the house in the usual way and heads out about his rounds of the neighborhood. He has already had a trying day, starting with dreams of pork chops that never appeared, and now his best friend Sparky has fallen in love and does not want to play. Then Missy appears, and Beethoven is in love, too. Before long, the couple has puppies. As luck would have it, however, instead of the dogs becoming a happy family, Missy becomes embroiled in her owners' nasty divorce. Regina (Debi Mazar) and her new boyfriend, Floyd (Chris Penn), dognap Missy, and try to force Regina's husband, Cliff (Maury Chaykin), to pay $50,000 to get Missy back. Soon Beethoven loses track of his new family, and the Newtons get involved in the fracas. Not unlike in *Beethoven*, chaos ensues.

Beethoven's Second has two great features: strong performances and attractive animals. Playing a role borrowed from Disney's *101 Dalmatians* (1961), Mazar creates a villainess every bit a match for Cruella De Vil. Threatening to drown the puppies, Mazar achieves a true nastiness, or as one reviewer described it, "stiletto perfection." "I played her larger than life because I wanted kids to really hate her," says Mazar in the production notes. Equally distressing is Regina's underachieving boyfriend, Floyd, who takes a good bit of guff from Regina as he stumbles along as accomplice. For example, Regina asks Floyd, "How can we have a relationship if you can't even stand right?" A deliciously diabolical pair, Mazar and Penn create villains that young viewers will love to hate.

Additionally, all the young actors in the film give strong performances. Particularly fine is Nicholle Tom's Ryce, who is eminently likable and believable as she tries out new outfits and new smiles before the mirror. Also Ryce's new beaus, Taylor (Ashley Hamilton—actor George Hamilton's son) and Seth (Danny Masterson), make good foils, ensuring that distinctions between good and evil are less apparent than with Regina and Floyd, and the rest of the cast. In one scene, Seth gives Ryce a ride to Taylor's house. While the audience watches Seth wait quietly to see if Ryce will need him, the audience also watches Taylor in the distance, wrestling with three young women in bikinis. The distinction is clear.

Yet the real star of the show is Beethoven. Beethoven was two years old when he appeared in the first film and four years old in *Beethoven's Second*. His trainer attests that "he's gained more confidence and ease on the set and in front of the cameras," and everyone agrees that the dog-biscuit consumption on the set during the filming of *Beethoven's Second* was way up from that during the production of the last film. The challenge in the sequel was to cast Missy—Beethoven's love interest— and the four puppies—Tchaikovsky, Chubby, Dolly, and Mo. Because Beethoven is a rough-coat Saint Bernard, a smooth-coat Saint Bernard was cast as Missy. Three of their offspring are rough-coat, with only Dolly being a smooth-coat like her mother.

Because puppies are like babies and have a strict nursing schedule, the trainers had to find some one hundred puppies to play the four Newton puppies at various stages. It was particularly challenging to maintain and control the puppy supply because the dogs were changing day-to-day. For example, they were growing on an average of a pound a day. Also, at any stage, puppies have their own agendas. Said producer Joe

Medjuck, "Puppies have their own priorities, and although it may say in the script, 'a puppy runs over to someone,' and it seems simple, it's difficult to do it. They have opinions and minds of their own."

They apparently have a point of view of their own, also. *Beethoven's Second* sports a good bit of doggy vision, such as when Beethoven watches Ryce rehearse her hi-thanks-for-the-ride-to-school speech before the mirror. Also, the audience spends much time viewing Beethoven's dreams, where the consuming passion is larger-than-life food.

While the original film of the series, *Beethoven*, was intended for a family audience, many portions of it were quite intense. At one point, the evil veterinarian described in detail why Beethoven's head was the right size for testing just how messy a new kind of ammunition would be. Also, the Newtons' money troubles took center stage, and the parents' bickering and marital troubles were perhaps too real for children's entertainment. In the sequel, some problems continue: There is still too little money; the air freshener business is still adrift. Furthermore, various members of the Newton family are encountering some real-world problems. For example, slick young Taylor has taken an interest in Ryce. What develops is almost date rape—rather harrowing family entertainment. The Newtons seem happier, however, and that makes parts of the second film easier to watch. The nasty bickering is gone and what has taken its place is the usual give and take of families.

Even with its December 17 release date, *Beethoven's Second* was able to finish the year with a strong box office showing: $24 million worldwide. Further, the film received an Academy Award nomination for the original song "The Day I Fall in Love." While *Beethoven's Second* received strong reviews virtually across the board, older viewers may find it drags in spots. Yet viewers of all ages will be glad to see so many cute puppies in one place. That alone may make this film just the thing for a family outing.

Roberta F. Green

Reviews

Atlanta Journal/Constitution. December 17, 1993, p. P8.
Baltimore Sun. December 24-30, 1993, p. 23.
Boston Globe. December 17, 1993, p. 97.
Chicago Tribune. December 17, 1993, Friday Section, p. 7c.
The Hollywood Reporter. December 15, 1993, p. 10.
Los Angeles Times. December 17, 1993, p. F10.
The New York Times. December 17, 1993, p. B10.
San Francisco Chronicle. December 17, 1993, p. C1.
Time. CXLII, December 20, 1993, p. 63.
Variety. CCCLIII, December 27, 1993, p. 51. Daily December 15, 1993, p. 11
The Washington Post. December 17, 1993, Weekend Section, p. 56.

BENNY AND JOON

Production: Susan Arnold and Donna Roth; released by Metro-Goldwyn-Mayer
Direction: Jeremiah Chechik
Screenplay: Barry Berman; based on a story by Berman and Leslie McNeil
Cinematography: John Schwartzman
Editing: Carol Littleton
Production design: Neil Spisak
Art direction: Pat Tagliaferro
Set decoration: Barbara Munch
Casting: Risa Bramon Garcia and Heidi Levitt
Sound: James Thornton
Costume design: Aggie Guerard Rodgers
Music: Rachel Portman
MPAA rating: PG
Running time: 100 minutes

Principal characters:

Sam	Johnny Depp
Joon	Mary Stuart Masterson
Benny	Aidan Quinn
Ruthie	Julianne Moore
Eric	Oliver Platt
Dr. Garvey	CCH Pounder
Thomas	Dan Hedaya
Mike	Joe Grifasi
Randy Burch	William H. Macy
Mrs. Smail	Eileen Ryan

The subject of mental illness is one usually treated with great seriousness by dramatists, authors, and filmmakers alike. Such films as *Spellbound* (1945), *The Snake Pit* (1948), *The Three Faces of Eve* (1957), *David and Lisa* (1963), *One Flew Over the Cuckoo's Nest* (1975), and *The Silence of the Lambs* (1991) have all presented mental illness from a grim and sobering viewpoint. When a filmmaker has attempted to portray the mentally ill as comical characters, or as people who have been labeled insane but act more sane than the normal folk—as they do in *King of Hearts* (1966)—the result is far less effective and comes very close to trivializing the subject as well as the characters.

In *Benny and Joon*, screenwriter and former circus clown Barry Berman, and director Jeremiah Chechik, whose previous directorial effort was *National Lampoon's Christmas Vacation* (1989), walk a thin line between comedy and tragedy in their efforts to dramatize the plight of a schizophrenic woman who falls in love with an illiterate young man whose role models are mimes, fools, and silent-film comedians.

The result is a somewhat schizophrenic comedy/drama, as lighthearted moments follow scenes of harrowing and dangerously unbalanced behavior.

Benny (Aidan Quinn), a Spokane, Washington, automobile mechanic, lives with and cares for his younger sister, Joon (Mary Stuart Masterson), who suffers from schizophrenia. Although he has been advised by Joon's therapist, Dr. Garvey (CCH Pounder), that his sister would be better cared for if she were institutionalized, Benny refuses even to consider the idea. He feels a deep responsibility for his younger sister, having taken on parental responsibilities ever since their parents were killed in a car crash when the two siblings were adolescents. Both Dr. Garvey and Benny are aware, however, that Joon's erratic behavior has become more severe, which has tried the patience of a string of caretakers whom Benny has hired to look after Joon while he is working. When Joon once again becomes violent around the latest caretaker, causing the woman to walk out in disgust, Benny realizes that he has no more prospects. He also realizes that, because of Joon's constant and sometimes trivial needs—interrupting him at work, for example, to inform him that they are out of peanut butter and tapioca pudding—both his professional and personal lives are suffering.

One of the few diversions in Benny's life is a weekly poker game that he attends along with his coworker Eric (Oliver Platt) and friends Thomas (Dan Hedaya) and Mike (Joe Grifasi). The gatherings, which Joon also attends on occasion, are irreverent affairs, with the men betting personal items and favors instead of money—jumper cables, clothing, and household appliances, for example. Between bets, the men poke fun at one another's habits and personal problems. When Benny announces his difficulty in finding another caretaker for Joon, Mike confesses that he is being driven to distraction by his loony cousin, who has recently moved in with him.

During a break in one of the poker gatherings, at a time when Benny and Thomas are absent, Joon sits down at the table with Mike, and the two begin making some very strange bets. At one point, as the stakes mount and the bets become increasingly eccentric, Mike wagers that if Joon loses the hand, his cousin must move in with her and Benny. When Joon loses the hand, Benny protests after learning what was at stake. Nevertheless, feeling obligated to Mike, he agrees to house the young man, thinking that he just might be competent enough to take care of Joon.

Benny's hopes are soon dashed when Mike's cousin makes his appearance. The audience has already caught glimpses of the young man in earlier scenes—sitting in a train intensely studying a book entitled *The Look of Buster Keaton* and perched in a tree watching people stroll by. When Mike introduces Benny to his cousin, Sam (Johnny Depp), the two friends watch as Sam, sporting a Keatonesque porkpie hat and a Chaplinesque bamboo cane, bangs out a tune on a series of empty bottles, then juggles hub caps. Although Benny is less than thrilled at the prospect of housing this clownish character, Joon is entranced by his comical, childlike actions, his stolid expression, and his quiet demeanor.

Although the sight of him grilling cheese sandwiches with a clothes iron and mopping the floor while riding a chair equipped with rollers is initially disconcerting, Sam proves to be a compassionate and efficient housekeeper. During a dinner outing at the local diner, Sam entertains brother and sister by mimicking Chaplin's "Dance of the Rolls" routine from *The Gold Rush* (1925), then juggles plates laden with food, and later startles the new waitress, Ruthie (Julianne Moore), by reciting dialogue from a low-budget horror film in which she appeared several years previously. Gradually, Benny realizes that he has found the perfect housekeeper in Sam.

Encouraged by his friends and inspired by Sam's unrepressed behavior, Benny asks Ruthie out on a date. The two seem to be a perfect match; however, Benny cannot ignore his feelings of responsibility for Joon and thwarts Ruthie's efforts to become more intimate. Such is not the case with Sam and Joon. Left alone with each other during the day, the two develop a special bond. Sam encourages Joon to express herself through her favorite pastime, painting, even participating in several of her artistic efforts. When Sam confesses that he is illiterate, Joon helps him write letters to his mother and later helps him complete an employment application for a part-time job as a clerk in a video store specializing in classic films, one of Sam's passions. Realizing that they have much in common, both being eccentric outcasts in their own way, Sam and Joon finally make love.

During a park outing, Sam puts on a public display of his comical talents, much to the delight of the park patrons. After witnessing Sam's routine, Benny is so impressed that he contacts a friend who works as an entertainment promoter, hoping to help Sam start a career as a comedy performer. When Benny announces his plans to Joon, however, she becomes violently opposed to the idea, not wishing to see Sam leave. She then confesses her feelings for Sam and admits that she and Sam have had sex, an admission that sends Benny into a rage. Soon afterward, Benny kicks Sam out of the house and tells him never to return—actions which do not suit Joon, who tells her brother that she hates his smothering protectiveness and constant meddling in her life.

When Sam sneaks into the house to see Joon, the two decide to run away together. After boarding a bus, however, Joon becomes extremely disoriented and creates a violent disturbance, frightening Sam, who has never had to deal with her schizophrenia. Joon's outburst is so severe that the bus is evacuated and mental health officials are called. When Benny learns of the incident, he blames Sam and physically assaults him while Joon is hauled away and institutionalized.

After Joon gets a private room in the mental hospital where Dr. Garvey works, Benny attempts to visit her, but Joon refuses to see him. Grudgingly, Benny locates Sam, who is staying with Ruthie, and asks for his help in contacting Joon. The two men improvise an effective diversionary plan that allows Benny to sneak into the private ward and meet with Joon. When Dr. Garvey suddenly appears, the three argue over what sort of treatment and care would be best for Joon. Sam, meanwhile, clambers up the side of the hospital building, attaches a painter's cable to himself, and swings in front of Joon's window. Joon is delighted at the sight of Sam and is relieved to hear that he and her brother have made amends. As Sam's cable slips, plunging him into the hospital bushes below, the siblings and Dr. Garvey agree on a plan: Joon will move into the apartment complex where Ruthie lives in order to enjoy more freedom running her own life. In the film's sentimental fade-out, Sam visits Joon in her new apartment and shows her the art of ironing cheese sandwiches while Benny and Ruthie rekindle their aborted romance.

Although at times director Chechik and screenwriter Berman come dangerously close to trivializing the plight of the mentally ill by paralleling Joon's erratic behavior with Sam's loony antics, overall the film manages to avoid becoming a cute comedy about insane people. They succeed mainly by maintaining a low-key approach to the eccentric goings-on. Chechik directs the principal cast members with an understated adeptness, slowing down the action to emphasize the interplay among his actors, injecting many quiet moments even during the scenes of horseplay.

The three principals are all extremely appealing and seem to understand the importance of remaining calm and understated in the face of the bizarre. Aidan Quinn is especially fine as Benny, playing the overly protective brother who must deal with unpredictable behavior on a daily basis as if he were beyond being shocked by anything, yet still infusing his character with a sense of urgency in his attempts to care for his erratic sister.

Of the three main characters, Mary Stuart Masterson's Joon is the most poorly developed, which is mainly the result of how Berman has written her part; the fact that she must be sympathetic, humorous, and scary all at the same time pulls her in too many conflicting directions. It could be argued that such a conflict serves to illustrate her mental condition, but it still weakens the overall effectiveness of her portrayal.

Although Johnny Depp's Sam is a simpleton, he is easily the film's most complicated and enigmatic character. Like Masterson's Joon, he is supposed to be both amusing and unpredictably strange. Unlike Joon, however, Sam can choose how he wants to behave. In other words, Depp must somehow demonstrate how acting like a mindless clown in realistic situations can be beneficial, inspiring, and believable without appearing annoyingly ridiculous. He must also avoid appearing too much like two of the greatest film comedians of the silent-screen era—Charlie Chaplin and Buster Keaton—while at the same time embodying their quiet expressiveness. Depp is hampered in his portrayal by the way his comedic behavior has been designed for him by Berman and by Dan Kamin, who choreographed Depp's physical comedy sequences. For a character who supposedly worships Chaplin and Keaton, his comedy routines are, for the most part, overly familiar mime and circus-clown routines, which ultimately weaken Depp's portrayal. Depp, however, compensates for the lack of originality in the physical routines by reproducing the look of the silent-film clown greats. Apparently, Depp trained for the part of Sam by watching Buster Keaton films, and the effort was rewarded: His stolid, childlike expression, reflecting a soulful sadness, is very much in the tradition of the Great Stone Face. This is the second time that Depp has succeeded in embodying the spirit of the silent-film comedians; his first triumph in this type of portrayal was in *Edward Scissorhands* (1990), playing the eccentric, near-silent mechanical boy as a Chaplinesque misfit.

Although the film's story line is the standard "boy meets girl, boy loses girl, boy gets girl back," the filmmakers have spiced up the formula with enough unique ingredients to hold the viewer's interest. Coupled with the fact that cast and crew manage to avoid the pitfall of presenting the mentally ill as cute eccentrics, *Benny and Joon* emerges as an extremely likable and effective comedy/drama.

Jim Kline

Reviews

Chicago Tribune. April 16, 1993, VII, p. 37.
The Christian Science Monitor. April 16, 1993, p. 14.
Entertainment Weekly. April 23, 1993, p. 36.
The Hollywood Reporter. March 29, 1993, p. 14.
Los Angeles Magazine. April, 1993, p. 106.
Los Angeles Times. April 16, 1993, p. F4.
The New York Times. April 16, 1993, p. B8.
Newsweek. April 26, 1993, p. 64.
Rolling Stone. April 26, 1993, p. 114.
The Wall Street Journal. April 15, 1993, p. A12.
The Washington Post. April 16, 1993, p. B7.

THE BEVERLY HILLBILLIES

Production: Ian Bryce and Penelope Spheeris; released by Twentieth Century-Fox
Direction: Penelope Spheeris
Screenplay: Lawrence Konner, Mark Rosenthal, Jim Fisher, and Jim Staahl; based
    on a story by Konner and Rosenthal and on the television series created by Paul
    Henning
Cinematography: Robert Brinkmann
Editing: Ross Albert
Production design: Peter Jamison
Art direction: Marjorie Stone McShirley
Set decoration: Linda Spheeris
Casting: Glenn Daniels
Sound: Thomas Causey
Costume design: Jami Burrows
Music: Lalo Schifrin
MPAA rating: PG
Running time: 93 minutes

Principal characters:

Jed Clampett	Jim Varney
Mr. Drysdale	Dabney Coleman
Granny	Cloris Leachman
Miss Hathaway	Lily Tomlin
Jethro/Jethrine	Diedrich Bader
Elly May	Erika Eleniak
Woodrow Tyler	Rob Schneider
Laura Jackson	Lea Thompson
Aunt Pearl	Linda Carlson
Margaret Drysdale	Penny Fuller
Morgan Drysdale	Kevin Connolly
Barnaby Jones	Buddy Ebsen
Zsa Zsa Gabor	Zsa Zsa Gabor
Dolly Parton	Dolly Parton

Comparisons between the 1960's television series and the film version of *The Beverly Hillbillies* are inevitable. Basing a film on a beloved and successful television series is at best a risky business. Yet, the elements that made the television show so amusing and memorable are present in the film version.

Jed Clampett (Jim Varney) is a widower of some years who lives in a little run-down shack in the Ozark mountains with his mother—Granny (Cloris Leachman)—and daughter, Elly May (Erika Eleniak). Life is simple and uncomplicated until, one day while hunting, Jed shoots at a rabbit and misses—and his wayward shot sets off an oil gush. Jed has struck oil in his own backyard. Within days, the Clampett family have signed papers that make them billionaires and, along with cousin Jethro (Diedrich Bader), head for Beverly Hills and the good life.

Being plain folk who drive a truck that appears to have been around since the Great Depression, the Clampetts are taken completely by surprise by their first glimpse of their Beverly Hills mansion. Also taken by surprise is Jane Hathaway (Lily Tomlin), the precise and punctilious secretary of toadying banker Milburn Drysdale (Dabney Coleman). Sent ahead to welcome the billionaire Clampetts, she mistakes them for intruders. During the police lineup, Drysdale and Hathaway discover to their horror that these eccentrics are the rich Clampett family. Drysdale, a spineless person who will do anything to keep the Clampetts' millions at his bank, swoons and fawns over this most atypical family.

Once the Clampetts get settled into their new mansion, Jed shares his innermost feelings about finding himself a wife and asks Jane Hathaway, of all people, if she might help. Since the Clampetts have all their money at Drysdale's bank, the Clampetts have no trouble getting whatever they want. In fact, while dining on the billiards table—a running joke from the original series—Jed suggests that Jethro become the vice president of Mr. Drysdale's bank. Almost choking with shock, Mr. Drysdale feels compelled to acquiesce.

With so much money in the Clampett account the inevitable happens—one of Drysdale's underlings has designs on stealing the billionaires' money. Woodrow Tyler (Rob Schneider) is a scheming good-for-nothing assistant who listens in on all of Drysdale's messages. Through eavesdropping on one such message, he discovers that the family is looking for a French governess to help Elly May become more refined. For Tyler this is the ideal opportunity to have his girlfriend and accomplice, Laura (Lea Thompson), sweet-talk her way into the Clampett residence and try to marry Jed herself. The unsuspecting Clampetts offer Laura the post.

Through a series of misunderstandings, Jed does ask Laura to marry him. The wedding day is set and all the Clampett kith and kin are invited. While Granny is brewing her lethal Ozark concoction in the back garden, however, she overhears Laura and Tyler's plan to swindle Jed out of his money. No sooner does she hear this than Laura and Tyler commit her to an old folks home for the chronically ill. Since Granny is known to become difficult before any wedding, her disappearance is taken lightly by the rest of the family.

Miss Hathaway thinks otherwise and hires a private investigator to find out where Granny has been taken. With only a few hours before the wedding, Miss Hathaway manages to find and then abduct Granny from the old folks home. Before Laura the impostor and Tyler the swindler can complete their scheme, Miss Hathaway ruins the wedding ceremony. Instead of a wedding celebration, the entire Clampett clan then have a rousing Blue Mountains family gathering with fiddle music and plenty of hoopla.

There is no doubt that the cast that director-producer Penelope Spheeris gathered together emulates the original Clampett family. In fact, Cloris Leachman proves to be a dead ringer for the late Irene Ryan as Granny. The striking difference between the film version and the television series, however, is the relationship within the Clampett household. Much of the success of the original "Beverly Hillbillies" was the repartee that existed among the family members. Jethro, a tall, immensely strong man, was always being set upon by the beautiful yet tomboyish Elly May. Granny and Jed continually sparred with each other. Granny had something of a drinking problem, which caused endless arguments between herself and her son. To this family dynamic was added their immense wealth. For the Clampett family, money did not change their good-heartedness nor solve the family problems that were inevitable with such a varied group of people.

Unfortunately, *The Beverly Hillbillies*, while retaining much of the charm and backwoods feeling of the original series, chooses to introduce a well-worn subplot—focusing on the scheming, underhanded plans of Drysdale's assistant Tyler—that weakens the story considerably by allowing very little time for family interaction. In fact, the Clampett family of the film was quite the opposite from its television counterparts. The original Granny always seemed to be cooking "vittles." Jethro would be out shooting flies off the wall and could never figure out the connection between the bell sounding and someone being at the door. Jed had complete faith in the less-than-reputable Mr. Drysdale. Somehow, in all the confusion and potential cheating, Miss Hathaway kept some kind of order, some kind of moral decency. The film version only hints at some of the earlier moments that made the Clampetts such a successful television show.

Much of the film was driven by the need to create a story line that would sustain a full-length feature. Given such parameters, there seems to be little time to explore individual characters. Nevertheless, Lily Tomlin was a natural choice for the part of Miss Hathaway. Tomlin re-creates to the last detail the original character. Although Jim Varney as Jed draws on all the Ozark wit and common sense, he is not the strong paterfamilias that Buddy Ebsen's Jed was. The scheming Mr. Drysdale played by Dabney Coleman manages to capture all the insincerity that was true of the original part. In fact, Coleman has almost specialized in this type of role throughout his career.

All but forgotten is the mansion where the Clampetts always seemed like fish out of water. In the film, hardly any time is spent in the actual house, observing the numerous awkward situations that the Clampetts managed to get themselves into during their weekly exploits.

Despite the obvious differences between a 1990's rendition of a 1960's television show, the Clampetts are still immortalized as one of America's most cherished families. *The Beverly Hillbillies* manages to re-create enough of the past to at least give a sense of what the old series was all about.

Nostalgia does have a place in modern cinema, and *The Beverly Hillbillies* manages to revive some of television's most cherished characters. As the Clampett family marches onto the front steps of their Beverly Hills mansion at the end of the film, Jed sums up what the "Beverly Hillbillies" stood for when he reminds the audience, "Ye-all come back now, Ye-hear."

Richard G. Cormack

Reviews

Boston Globe. October 15, 1993, p. 53.
Chicago Tribune. October 15, 1993, VII, p. 44.
The Hollywood Reporter. October 11, 1993, p. 5.
Interview. XXIII, October, 1993, p. 66.
Los Angeles Times. October 15, 1993, p. F1.
The New York Times. October 15, 1993.
Rolling Stone. November 11, 1993, p. 8.
USA Today. October 15, 1993, p. D5.
Variety. October 11, 1993, p. 3.
The Washington Post. October 15, 1993, p. D7.
Washingtonian. XXIX, November, 1993, p. 28.

BLUE

Origin: France
Released: 1993
Released in U.S.: 1993
Production: Marin Karmitz; released by Miramax Films
Direction: Krzysztof Kieslowski
Screenplay: Krzysztof Piesiewicz and Krzysztof Kieslowski
Cinematography: Slawomir Idziak
Editing: Jacques Witta
Production design: Jean-Claude Lenoir
Sound: Claude Laureux
Music: Zbigniew Preisner
MPAA rating: R
Running time: 98 minutes

Principal characters:
Julie.............................. Juliette Binoche
Olivier............................. Benoit Regent
Lucille............................ Charlotte Very
Sandrine .... Florence Pernel

Blue is the first in a trilogy of films by Polish director Krzysztof Kieslowski. The title refers to the French tricolor flag: Blue stands for liberty, white for equality, and red for fraternity. *Blue* is not a political film in the sense that it deals with public issues or the history of liberty. Rather, it is about the individual's quest for freedom, for psychological liberty, so to speak. Yet in another respect, the film is very political, because it demonstrates that there is a logical contradiction in the individual's quest for liberty. To be a person is to be connected with other individuals, who make a claim on the self and restrict or inhibit the self from attaining complete freedom to do as it chooses. This involvement with others is inescapable, even for someone such as the film's protagonist, Julie (Juliette Binoche), who does everything in her power to jettison her past and her commitment to anyone but herself.

Julie is the only survivor of a car crash. Both her daughter and her husband have died, and she is in the hospital recovering from her injuries. Finding her situation insupportable, she smashes a window at night to divert the nurse's attention, and then she tries to swallow an overdose of pills. She gags and realizes she will not be able to get them down. Although she apologizes to the nurse, her primary emotion is anger. Her smashing the glass is an expression of rage, of the individual's colossal fury at being thwarted—in this case, of having one's whole life obliterated by an accident.

Of course, Julie's whole life has not been obliterated. She has her memories, which haunt her even though she makes every effort to suppress them. There is her husband's unfinished music. A great contemporary composer, he was working on a symphony that would have expressed the quest for European unity. With the unity of her own life shattered, Julie cannot bear the theme of her husband's music—the idea that all human beings are connected. She destroys what she thinks is the only copy of his unfinished symphony. She rudely turns away an interviewer, who in exasperation taunts her with the rumor that it is Julie herself who composed her husband's music. She allows her husband's colleague, Olivier (Benoit Regent), to make love to her once in her home and then abruptly leaves, as if to say that this kind of love and need is now behind her.

Julie finds an apartment in Paris and lives by herself. Yet she cannot escape her past nor completely isolate herself from other people. A street musician plays her husband's music. When she refuses to sign a petition calling for the removal of a prostitute, Sandrine (Florence Pernel), who plies her trade in the apartment building, the prostitute introduces herself and tours Julie's apartment, spying a mobile of faceted blue glass. It is the only object Julie has preserved from her past; its beautiful, reflective quality symbolizes the futility of Julie's attempt to sever herself from humanity and a life that has hurt her.

Olivier tracks down Julie and eventually persuades her to collaborate with him on the score of her husband's unfinished symphony. Although she has tried to destroy it, a copy was saved and shown on television by Olivier, in order to entice Julie back to him and to the world in which such music was created. If Julie has not actually composed this music, she was obviously privy to her husband's creative choices, and she proves a sure guide to Olivier in his efforts to complete the score.

The television program has also shown photographs of a woman that were found in Julie's husband's papers. It suddenly occurs to Julie that he had a mistress. Through Olivier, Julie locates and meets the mistress, Lucille (Charlotte Very), finding her pregnant with her husband's child. The scene between the two women is a shocking revelation of forces and feelings that Julie had not envisioned. The very life she mourned was not quite what she thought it was.

This encounter reinforces Julie's gradual emergence into the world she has tried to reject. She begins to complete her husband's music on her own, calling Olivier to report on her progress. He now claims that the authorship of the score is his own as well as Julie's and her husband's. Her decision to join him in his apartment suggests she accepts his point—which also reinforces the film's larger point about the interconnections between human beings. The concept of liberty must in fact be mediated by a realization of how deeply committed individuals have to be to one another in order to live fully and be free. This ending confirms the words to the European concerto (from St. Paul's Letter to the Corinthians), which are put on the screen as an epigraph: "Though I have the gift of prophecy, and understand all mysteries, if I have not love, I am nothing."

Although this overview of the film's plot and themes may make it seem schematic, in fact *Blue* is most unconventional. There seems to be no plot. Indeed, for the first twenty minutes, a viewer may be puzzled as to what the film is about. There are also several scenes that apparently have no connection to the basic story. They seem accidental—as intrusive and unsettling as the car accident Julie suffers. For example, the film opens with a seemingly interminable shot of the front left wheel of the car speeding down the road. The camera, which must have been mounted just behind the tire, certainly offers an unusual angle and emphasizes the force of the car hitting the road surface, but it does not telegraph a sense that there is going to be an accident. Similarly, Julie's daughter is shown looking out the back window of the car as it goes through a tunnel. One possible reason might be that she is looking at the past, so to speak, that vanishes as soon as it is seen.

Then there is the accident, with the car smashed against a tree. Not until nearly halfway through the film is there a scene in which Julie explains to the boy who came upon the accident that just before the crash her husband was telling a joke. Even then, it is not clear whether the accident was caused by his inattention to the road or by some other factor. The director refuses to tie up such loose ends; they are fragments of reality that intrude into and break up the conventions of filmmaking. Kieslowski has admitted that in shooting his films he often allows such random incidents caught by the camera to remain—as if to remind himself of the way reality overtakes art and the plots people devise.

Consequently, Kieslowski's films have a mysterious, visceral quality. They are troubling, even scary, because the viewer cannot anticipate what is coming next. In retrospect, some of the puzzling scenes can be fitted into the film's theme; others, Kieslowski admits, continue to frustrate. Yet the frustration is of a piece with what his characters feel and allows viewers to empathize deeply with them.

The dialogue in *Blue* is spare, allowing the music and acting to dominate. Bits of composer Zbigniew Preisner's European *concerto* were played on the set during the filming, so that the music might actually shape how Julie and the other characters behave. Juliette Binoche learned to write music for her part, and it is clear from her performance that she allowed the music and the rhythm of the film—the actual mechanical process of making it—to infect her acting. Because of the many silences in the film, an interviewer asked her whether she felt lonely in front of the camera. "No," Binoche replied. "There was always an extraordinary complicity between Krzysztof and Slawomir Idziak, his director of photography who works with the camera held on his shoulder. I learned to walk with the camera, it became like my understudy."

Binoche is describing a uniquely intimate kind of filmmaking, reflected in the director's concern with close-ups, as though he wished to capture the soul, the interior liberty his characters are seeking. He has compared himself to a physicist looking at the microscopic elements of life, using a new 200mm lens, for example, to catch the reflection of someone passing by in Julie's eye. He has obviously chosen like-minded collaborators, such as his cowriter, Krzysztof Piesiewicz, who declares, "What interests us is the intimate details of people's daily lives."

Carl Rollyson

Reviews

The Christian Science Monitor. December 6, 1993, p. 16.
Los Angeles Times. December 8, 1993, p. F1.
The Nation. CCLVII, December 20, 1993, p. 778.
New Statesman and Society. VI, October 15, 1993, p. 34.
The New York Times. October 12, 1993, p. B3.
The New Yorker. December 13, 1993, p. 122.
Sight and Sound. III, December, 1993, p. 22.
Variety. CCCLII, September 20, 1993, p. 28.
The Wall Street Journal. January 20, 1994, p. A12.
The Washington Post. March 4, 1994, p. C7.

BOUND BY HONOR

Production: Taylor Hackford and Jerry Gershwin, in association with Touchwood
   Pacific Partners I; released by Hollywood Pictures
Direction: Taylor Hackford
Screenplay: Jimmy Santiago Baca, Jeremy Iacone, and Floyd Mutrux; based on a
   story by Ross Thomas
Cinematography: Gabriel Beristain
Editing: Fredric Steinkamp
Production design: Bruno Rubeo
Art direction: Marek Dobrowolski
Set decoration: Cecilia Rodarte
Costume design: Shay Cunliffe
Music: Bill Conti
MPAA rating: R
Running time: 180 minutes

Principal characters:
Miklo	Damian Chapa
Cruz	Jesse Borrego
Paco	Benjamin Bratt
Montana	Enrique Castillo
Magic Mike	Victor Rivers
Bonafide	Delroy Lindo
Red Ryder	Tom Towles
Big Al	Lanny Flaherty
Lightning	Billy Bob Thornton
Juanito	Noah Verduzco

This epic, three-hour saga about the tumultuous lives of three young Chicano men tells their story against the backdrop of the barrios of East Los Angeles and the crowded cells of San Quentin prison. Admirable in its desire to bring to life the vivid panorama of Chicano culture, *Bound by Honor* has a lot going for it: its attention to accuracy and detail, its respect for its subject, its excellent music (by Bill Conti), and Jesse Borrego's performance as Cruz. Its weakness, however, is that the film ultimately abandons its depiction of late twentieth century Chicano life, focusing instead on the tragic consequences of crime in the urban Latino community.

The story unfolds over a span of twelve years in the lives of Paco (Benjamin Bratt), Cruz (Jesse Borrego), and Miklo (Damian Chapa)—three young Chicano men in East Los Angeles, who are proudly devoted to one another and to their gang, the "Vatos Locos." Paco is a confident, handsome street fighter. His half brother, Cruz, is a brilliant artist looking forward to a successful future as a painter. Their cousin, Miklo, is a troubled youth who has found difficulty fitting into the rigid Chicano world because of his blond hair and blue eyes. Miklo's constant search for acceptance leads all three men into grave trouble as Miklo tries to prove himself by provoking a rival Chicano gang to violence.

After causing trouble with the other gang, Miklo is arrested and sent to San Quentin, where he finally achieves the acceptance he needs by becoming a powerful and dangerous prison kingpin. Paco joins the Marines and returns to the barrio as a successful police detective. Cruz, after a promising start selling paintings in a West Hollywood gallery, falls tragically into addiction and degradation because of his role in the accidental drug overdose of his youngest brother, Juanito (Noah Verduzco).

Although most of the film focuses on Miklo's rise to power in San Quentin, the interactions among the three characters are important to understanding their motivations. "Everything you did forced me into my destiny," says Miklo to Paco. By this time, Miklo and Paco find themselves on different sides of the law, and Paco has destroyed one of Miklo's legs in a shootout. Meanwhile, Cruz and Paco have become enemies because of Juanito's death and Cruz's drug use and despair. Eventually Paco and Cruz reconcile. Their well-played reconciliation scene would be even more touching, however, if the audience had sufficient time to know these characters better.

Director/producer Taylor Hackford, one of the producers of *La Bamba* (1987), used his prior experience working with the Latino community to advantage, spending considerable time and energy in creating a cinematic atmosphere that properly evokes the vivid Latino culture of East Los Angeles. For example, he asked the three leading actors to live there together for three months prior to filming. Furthermore, he employed local residents as advisers and extras to help ensure the film's authenticity. Latino poet Jimmy Santiago Baca was hired as screenwriter, with the mandate to preserve the film's cultural integrity. In addition, Hackford fills the screen with images of East Los Angeles, from busy shopping districts to crowded neighborhoods to the elaborate "Día de los Muertos" (Day of the Dead) celebration.

In fact, a crucial scene takes place during the Day of the Dead celebration that illustrates the holiday's meaning—one of the film's more thoughtful scenes. Cruz, who had been told "you are dead to me" by his father after his role in Juanito's death, returns to his family twelve years later to ask forgiveness on the Day of the Dead. On this holiday, custom dictates that living family members pray for dead relatives who sinned on Earth so that they may leave purgatory and go to heaven. Symbolically, Cruz is allowed to leave purgatory when his family accepts him once again. Embedding this scene within the context of Latino culture is a literate, intelligent choice.

Art plays an integral role in the film and is no less carefully thought out than any other aspect of the production. Artist Bruno Rubeo created the wonderful paintings that are attributed to Cruz, the artist. Because of the changes Cruz undergoes, his art also changes dramatically, from gentle representations celebrating Latino culture to tortured, violent expressionistic pieces that reveal the pain inside Cruz's soul. Cruz and Paco have two scenes involving the paintings, which are greatly enhanced by Rubeo's work. One scene involves Paco's discovery of a frightening, gory painting featuring Juanito. When Paco insists that Cruz remove Juanito from the painting, Cruz literally cuts Juanito from the middle of the canvas, handing it to Paco.

The San Quentin scenes are realistic in their detail. From the use of 350 inmates as extras and advisers, to gaining access to several areas of San Quentin as film locations, Hackford graphically depicts the gritty world of San Quentin. Warden Dan Vasquez even appears as himself.

Art also plays an important role in these scenes. In prison, art manifests itself in the form of tattoos, and once again Hackford ensures that the film's visual reality will not be compromised. In the San Quentin scenes, tattoos are ubiquitous, taking on an important thematic role in that they represent the marking of territory, the deep connections within gangs, and the willingness of an individual to deface himself physically in order to prove his loyalty and manhood. Tattoos are important to other sequences of the film as well. "Vatos Locos forever!" yells Cruz, early in the film, as the three men celebrate Miklo's new gang tattoo, just like the ones worn by Cruz and Paco. Toward the end of the film, when Paco asks, "How did everything get so f—d up?," he looks at the gang tattoo on his hand as a reminder of his past, his present, and even his future. A symbol of the inner city, the tattoos are as valid a piece of art to the denizens of San Quentin or the gangbangers of East Los Angeles as is the art created by Cruz for his wealthy gallery patrons.

Jesse Borrego, as Cruz, is the strongest of the actors, bringing realism and charisma to his role, particularly in the last scene with Paco, saying "we got something better than a rabbit's foot. . . . We got familia." He growls out the last word as he exuberantly dances around Paco. Borrego truly represents the Chicano essence of this film, and the filmmakers' failure to develop his story is ultimately one of the film's weaknesses. Benjamin Bratt as Paco and Damian Chapa as Miklo are less experienced and exciting than Borrego, but they acquit themselves well. It should be noted that Damian Chapa had no prior experience acting in film before taking on the complicated role of Miklo. Miklo is reminiscent of Al Pacino's character in *The Godfather, Part II* (1974): a young man whose life takes a cruel turn and who rises to power at the expense of morality. Miklo's prison story becomes somewhat clichéd, like a "junior Godfather."

In fact, at times, *Bound by Honor* risks becoming a film with the same simplistic prison mentality of *The Public Enemy* (1931) or *Birdman of Alcatraz* (1962). Some of the prison sequences involving complicated drug deals and prison gang war councils seem (for all their violence) no more threatening than the "rumble" scenes in *West Side Story* (1961). This is due mostly to the dialogue, which tends toward cliché, with lines such as "Inside these walls I found the strength of my raza [race]" or "Destiny is like a wave you can't stop. . . . " Chapa gamely tries to overcome these lines and for the most part remains quite believable in spite of them.

Although *Bound by Honor* tries to be an epic on the scale of *The Godfather* (1972) and its sequels, it falls short of the mark. This, combined with its length, contributed to its failure at the box office and with critics. For example, *Los Angeles Times* critic Kevin Thomas said that "Taylor Hackford . . . has been unable to translate [the film's] aspirations into believable, non-clichéd cinema." The review accompanied an article quoting several Latino civic leaders frustrated by Hollywood's inability to present

Latinos as anything but hoodlums. The few "Hollywood" Latino films have had crime, or at least juvenile delinquency, at their core: *Zoot Suit* (1981), *La Bamba*, *Stand and Deliver* (1988), and *American Me* (1992). Other Latino films, such as *The Ballad of Gregorio Cortez* (1982), *El Norte* (1983), and *El Mariachi* (1993; reviewed in this volume), found limited success in the marketplace, further frustrating the efforts of artists to make intelligent films with Latino themes. No matter what its flaws, the makers of *Bound by Honor* should be applauded for so earnestly bringing this subject matter to a mainstream film.

Kirby Tepper

Reviews
Chicago Tribune. April 30, 1993, VII, p. 23.
The Christian Science Monitor. April 30, 1993, p. 13.
Entertainment Weekly. May 14, 1993, p. 39.
Hispanic. VI, July, 1993, p. 82.
The Hollywood Reporter. April 30, 1993, p. 5.
Los Angeles Times. April 30, 1993, p. F1.
Migration World Magazine. XXII, Number 4, 1993, p. 46.
The New York Times. April 30, 1993, p. B1.
USA Today. May 6, 1993, p. D8.
Variety. CCCXLIX, January 25, 1993, p. 133.

A BRONX TALE

Production: Jane Rosenthal, Jon Kilik, and Robert De Niro for Price Entertainment, in association with Penta Entertainment and Tribeca; released by Savoy Pictures
Direction: Robert De Niro
Screenplay: Chazz Palminteri; based on his play
Cinematography: Reynaldo Villalobos
Editing: David Ray and R. Q. Lovett
Production design: Wynn Thomas
Art direction: Chris Shriver
Set decoration: Debra Schutt
Casting: Ellen Chenoweth
Sound: Tod Maitland
Costume design: Rita Ryack
Music supervision: Jeffrey Kimball
Music direction: Butch Barbella
Song: Butch Barbella, Cool Change (performer), "Streets of the Bronx"
MPAA rating: R
Running time: 122 minutes

> *Principal characters:*
> Lorenzo . . . . Robert De Niro
> Sonny . . . . Chazz Palminteri
> Calogero (seventeen years old) . . . . Lillo Brancato
> Calogero (nine years old) . . . . Francis Capra
> Jane . . . . Taral Hicks
> Rosina . . . . Kathrine Narducci
> Jimmy Whispers . . . . Clem Caserta
> Bobby Bars . . . . Alfred Sauchelli, Jr.
> Danny K. O. . . . . Frank Pietrangolare
> Carmine . . . . Joe Pesci
> Tony Toupee . . . . Robert D'Andrea
> Eddie Mush . . . . Eddie Montanaro
> JoJo the Whale . . . . Fred Fischer
> Frankie Coffeecake . . . . Dave Salerno

Based on the critically acclaimed one-man stage play written and performed by Chazz Palminteri, the film *A Bronx Tale* marks the directorial debut of Academy Award-winning actor Robert De Niro. The story is set in the colorful Bronx section of New York City during the 1960's and centers on a young boy and his relationships with his working-class father and a local gang kingpin.

Divided in half, the first part of the film deals with Calogero as a young boy (Francis Capra), whose hard-working and loving father, Lorenzo (De Niro), tries to instill the right values in his son. Lorenzo, a bus driver, often takes Calogero along on his route.

They enjoy many outings together, including New York Yankees baseball games. Despite his father's close supervision, however, Calogero daily witnesses the activities of the local mob leader, Sonny (Palminteri), who transacts his business down the street from the family's front stoop. Sonny's minions are colorful characters, such as Frankie Coffeecake (Dave Salerno) and JoJo the Whale (Fred Fischer), whose mannerisms Calogero and his buddies imitate from their perch on the stoop. Calogero is understandably attracted to the flamboyant and influential Sonny, who obviously rules the neighborhood. Sonny presides over his loyal band of men and holds court in the nearby bar, where they spend their time drinking and gambling. When Calogero witnesses a murder committed by Sonny but refuses to identify him to the police, Sonny takes the boy under his wing, despite Lorenzo's best efforts to keep them apart.

The second half of the film then concentrates on a point eight years later, when the seventeen-year-old Calogero (now played by Lillo Brancato) is controlled even more by the increasingly important Sonny. The ball games with Lorenzo have been replaced by trips to the track with Sonny and his cohorts. Added tension has come to the neighborhood as African Americans have begun to "invade" what was formerly a predominantly white Italian neighborhood. In a Romeo-and-Juliet subplot, Calogero becomes smitten with an African American girl, Jane (Taral Hicks). Fortunately, their affair does not end as tragically.

A Bronx Tale is not as predictable a morality tale as it would at first appear. Although Sonny indulges in organized crime, gambling, and other vices, he is not all bad. Some of the advice he imparts to Calogero is very sound. It is Sonny who emphasizes the importance of Calogero's going to college, who discourages Calogero from spending time with Calogero's buddies, and who reassures Calogero that it is not the color of his girlfriend's skin that matters but whether she is a good person. In the end, it is Sonny who literally saves Calogero's life when he pulls him from the car before Calogero's friends make a tragic raid on an African American neighborhood. Neither is Lorenzo all "good"; he discourages his son from dating an African American, emphasizing that people should marry their "own kind." In addition, it was because of Lorenzo that Calogero did not "rat" on Sonny all those years ago, in some sort of misguided code of neighborhood loyalty.

Although several extremely violent episodes do occur throughout the film, these scenes are significantly played down. They are filmed in almost dreamlike fashion, blurred and scattershot, so that the viewer experiences the overall effect of the violence without witnessing it in minute detail. The violence serves merely to underscore the life-style that both Calogero's father and Sonny advise him to avoid. Although the film is nominally about a young boy's fascination with gangsters and a life of crime, it is in reality a very complicated character study that operates on multiple levels.

Although most of the film takes place on the street where Calogero lives, a few scenes shot elsewhere are noteworthy. In particular, a boxing match that teenaged Calogero attends with Lorenzo both reaffirms Calogero's overriding commitment to his father and puts the entire relationship in perspective. Because Lorenzo has gone to great lengths to purchase seats for himself and his son, Calogero refuses Sonny's offer to attend the match with Sonny at his ringside seats. When Sonny later sends his right-hand man up to the "nosebleed" section to invite both Lorenzo and Calogero to come down and sit ringside with him, father and son argue and Lorenzo tells Calogero to go sit with Sonny but that he has worked hard to get the seats he has and will not relinquish them. The scene visually demonstrates Lorenzo's moral integrity as he, on one level, refuses to accept the gangster's favor, and, on a symbolic level, refuses to descend to Sonny's level and accept a seat with him below. Calogero, however, reaffirms his loyalty to his father by remaining with him above, thus foreshadowing the ending of the film.

Although *A Bronx Tale* was filmed entirely on location, Queens stood in for the 1960's Bronx. Under the artistic direction of production designer Wynn Thomas, the film crew was able to transform 30th Avenue in Astoria during the early 1990's into East 187th Street of the Bronx, vintage 1960 and 1968. The film vividly re-creates a colorful New York neighborhood both visually and aurally. Period advertisements, clothes, and doo-wop rock songs all combine to evoke an authentically appealing time and place. In fact, the sound track was repeatedly cited as one of the film's best elements. According to one interview, De Niro picked the songs himself, listening to contemporary New York City oldies stations. One hears vintage rock, from Dion and The Belmonts singing "I Wonder Why," to pop icon Frank Sinatra's version of "Same Old Song and Dance," to legendary jazzman Miles Davis, to crooner Dean Martin, to R & B stylist Jerry Butler.

Director De Niro has also captured some very winning performances, notably those of both newcomers Francis Capra as nine-year-old Calogero, who is able to tread the fine line between feistiness and obedience, and Lillo Brancato, who takes over as the seventeen-year-old Calogero. Many of the parts are played by local residents, who had little or no previous acting experience, in an attempt to maintain the realism and authenticity established by the location shooting and period music. Chazz Palminteri, who wrote and performed the original one-man stage play and also wrote the film's screenplay, plays the role of Sonny with just the right mix of menace and fatherly concern. De Niro took the less glamorous part of the responsible, uptight father who attempts at all costs to tread the straight and narrow.

A Bronx Tale is a thoughtful, in-depth character study set in the nostalgic 1960's and features several outstanding performances. Despite the subject matter and setting, the violence is kept to a minimum, and many comic moments are used throughout that help ease the tension of this very intense film. For the most part, reviewers praised the film—a moral parable in which those who live by the sword do indeed perish by the sword.

Douglas Gomery

Reviews

Atlanta Constitution. October 1, 1993, p. F1.
Baltimore Sun. October 1, 1993, Live, p. 12.

Boston Globe. October 1, 1993, p. 49.
Chicago Tribune. October 1, 1993, Take 2, p. A.
The Christian Science Monitor. October 1, 1993, p. 12.
The Hollywood Reporter. September 13, 1993, p. 5.
Interview. XXIII, October, 1993, p. 66.
Los Angeles Times. September 29, 1993, p. F1.
The New York Times. September 29, 1993, p. B1.
Newsweek. CXXII, October 4, 1993, p. 84.
Time. CXLII, October 11, 1993, p. 83.
Variety. September 13, 1993, p. 4.
The Wall Street Journal. October 7, 1993, p. A16.
The Washington Post. October 1, 1993, p. C1.

CARLITO'S WAY

Production: Martin Bregman, Willi Baer, and Michael S. Bregman for Epic
   Productions; released by Universal Pictures
Direction: Brian De Palma
Screenplay: David Koepp; based on the novels *Carlito's Way* and *After Hours*, by
   Edwin Torres
Cinematography: Stephen H. Burum
Editing: Bill Pankow and Kristina Boden
Production design: Richard Sylbert
Art direction: Gregory Bolton
Set decoration: Leslie A. Pope
Casting: Bonnie Timmermann
Sound: Les Lazarowitz
Costume design: Aude Bronson-Howard
Music supervision: Jellybean Benitez
Music: Patrick Doyle
MPAA rating: R
Running time: 144 minutes

> *Principal characters:*
> Carlito Brigante .... Al Pacino
> David Kleinfeld .... Sean Penn
> Gail .... Penelope Ann Miller
> Pachanga............................ Luis Guzman
> Benny Blanco .... John Leguizamo
> Steffie .... Ingrid Rogers
> Norwalk .... James Rebhorn
> Vinnie Taglialucci..................... Joseph Siravo
> Lalin .... Viggo Mortensen
> Pete Amadesso .... Richard Foronjy
> Saso................................. Jorge Porcel
> Frankie .... Adrian Pasdar
> Judge Feinstein..................... Paul Mazursky

The novels of New York State Supreme Court justice Edwin Torres provide the basis
for this reteaming of actor Al Pacino, director Brian De Palma, and producer Martin
Bregman. Together, these three men were the creative force behind *Scarface* (1983),
and here they have returned to similar territory. This time they tell the story about the
attempts of a former drug lord to "go straight." This is a significant change in
perspective, however, in that *Scarface* depicted the violent rise to power of mobster
Tony Montana, while *Carlito's Way* tells the tale of a softer and gentler gangster who
finds it tragically impossible to free himself from his criminal past. It is familiar

territory for the audience. Al Pacino delivers another intense performance as an otherwise honorable man caught up in drug trafficking, gangsters, and murder—similar to his performances in the groundbreaking *Godfather* series.

It is 1975, and De Palma, production designer Richard Sylbert, and costume designer Aude Bronson-Howard have re-created 1970's Spanish Harlem in a most vivid and colorful way. Carlito Brigante (Pacino) is being released from a thirty-year sentence on drug charges because evidence was illegally obtained. He has served only five years due to the loyal and unswerving service of his seedy attorney, Dave Kleinfeld (Sean Penn). From the very first scene, Carlito is bigger-than-life, pontificating to an exasperated judge and district attorney, "I have been born again . . . like the Watergaters . . . and it didn't take thirty years, like your honor expected." Yet he is telling the truth. He has changed. He wants nothing to do with drugs and crime and tells Dave that he intends to earn enough money to buy into a rental car business in the Bahamas. "You're gonna rent cars?" asks Dave incredulously. Carlito responds, "I've been stealing 'em since I was 14. . . . Car rental guys don't get killed that much."

Upon returning home, Carlito is confronted immediately with a new sense of harshness and competitiveness in his former neighborhood, telling his friend Pachanga (Luis Guzman) "mi barrio ya no existe" (my neighborhood doesn't exist anymore). He borrows money to buy a stake in a local salsa disco and begins setting aside money to escape to the Bahamas. Nevertheless, he is constantly confronted with his former life: He becomes involved in a shoot-out, during which he witnesses the death of his young cousin; he antagonizes an up-and-coming drug lord named "Benny Blanco from the Bronx" (John Leguizamo); and he faces an attempt at entrapment by the district attorney. All these events are set against the loud and turbulent nightlife of New York's Spanish Harlem.

Desiring a refuge from this turmoil, Carlito rekindles a relationship with Gail (Penelope Ann Miller), a dancer who lives in Greenwich Village and has nothing to do with his tumultuous world (she even calls him "Charlie" instead of "Carlito"). All goes well until he feels compelled to do one last favor for his crooked attorney, Dave. The results are tragic.

De Palma creates an atmosphere that has the heightened dramatic quality of grand opera such as *Tosca* or even Jacobean tragedies such as *The Duchess of Malfi*. He is known as a master of highly dramatic films, having directed *Carrie* (1976), *The Untouchables* (1987), and *Casualties of War* (1989)—also starring Sean Penn. At a point early in his career, De Palma was compared (favorably and unfavorably) to suspense pioneer Alfred Hitchcock, whose favorite plots often involved innocent men caught up in danger and terror through no fault of their own. Similarly, Carlito's predicament is tragic because he gets involved in a crime solely because of his loyalty to Dave. Several of De Palma's more Hitchcockian films include *Obsession* (1976), *Dressed to Kill* (1980), and *Blow Out* (1981).

In *Obsession*, a final scene was notable for its use of a circular shot where the camera turns 360 degrees in a tension-filled scene with Genevieve Bujold and Cliff Robertson. Many years later, that dizzying shot became more standard, and De Palma utilizes it once again to create tension in a scene where Carlito plays pool with several men, knowing they are about to try to kill him and his young cousin.

De Palma is masterful at using different camera angles, high-angle shots, and extreme close-ups to create intended effects. In the initial scene at the disco, there is a long, uninterrupted shot viewing the animated, crowded club. The doors open, and the camera takes in the scene, turning to see glimpses of action as if it were human: It looks up a winding staircase and then back down the stairs, enters the dj's booth, exits the booth to see a man being thrown out of the club, and then gazes back up the stairs, following a beautiful woman in hot pants. All of this is in one long shot, showing more influence from Hitchcock, who was noted for long, almost choreographed "takes." Late in the film, Carlito talks about the "angles" that people play; the observant audience member will then realize that throughout the film De Palma has employed dramatic camera angles to film several scenes in which Carlito has confrontations with dangerous people, such as Benny or Dave.

Most impressive is the climactic subway chase, which De Palma has dubbed a "subway ballet," in which Carlito is chased from Harlem to Grand Central Station and then through the escalators and hallways of Grand Central, leading to a climactic shoot-out on the escalators. Relentlessly exciting, the scene is made all the more so because Carlito is racing against the clock to meet Gail for the train that will take them to a new life. De Palma recognizes, however, that exciting and dynamic shots are not enough. Every interesting or exciting shot is motivated by the character's intentions or the needs of the story.

David Koepp, author of the screenplay for *Jurassic Park*, has developed a solid screenplay from two books by Judge Edwin Torres—*Carlito's Way* and *After Hours*. Torres, the judge in several sensational New York criminal trials, based his books on different characters he actually knew. Furthermore, he was reared in Spanish Harlem, only a few blocks from where some of the scenes were actually filmed.

Torres and Koepp have created a wonderful character for Sean Penn. He is virtually unrecognizable in glasses, wide ties, and huge Afro, nothing like the tough characters he played in *Bad Boys* (1983) or *Casualties of War*. He is a sniveling, coke-addicted man who has become seduced by the fake glamour of the underworld. Penn gives a performance of texture and nuance, depicting a man who is all show and no substance.

Pacino is wonderful as well, but in a different way. Although he is an actor of great intensity, he does not inhabit the character in the way that Penn does. Perhaps because of *Scarface* and the *Godfather* films, it is difficult to believe that Pacino is Puerto Rican. He speaks only a few lines of Spanish, and when he does, his accent is not authentic. He has one or two furious outbursts, which have become familiar to audiences of his films, and has a surprisingly clichéd scene where he argues with Gail about his loyalty to Dave: "I owe him. That's how I am. That's what I am, right or wrong. I can't change that." In fact, Pacino may have used these very words before, in another film. Despite a strong performance by Pacino, the familiarity of this territory may diminish the impact for some.

Some of Pacino's best scenes are the more understated, subtle ones early in the film where he reestablishes himself with his former love, Gail. He is gentle and tentative, and when Gail tells him that he is very different from when she last saw him, it is believable. The success of the relationship between Gail and Carlito is partly due to the tender performance of Penelope Ann Miller. Miller is particularly impressive in a scene in which she has no dialogue, sitting next to Carlito in the district attorney's office. She is essential to the scene, without stealing it, as her expressions reveal her character's progression from confusion to fear to anger and back to fear.

All the actors in *Carlito's Way* are excellent, but particular mention must be made of John Leguizamo as "Benny Blanco from the Bronx." He is a strutting peacock whose pride is hurt by Carlito's refusal to befriend him. When Benny says, "I'm refining my organization. I'm maximizing my potential," he is a sorry reminder of the man Carlito used to be, providing a pivotal plot point and a wonderful foil for Pacino. Leguizamo is a charismatic, energetic, and gifted actor.

There is always room for a film with excellent performances, fine direction, a good plot, and excellent music—here provided by Jellybean Benitez and Patrick Doyle. Although *Carlito's Way* may come up short in the inevitable comparisons to the *Godfather* films or even to De Palma's own *Scarface*, it is nevertheless a wonderfully crafted film and an engrossing way to spend two hours.

Kirby Tepper

Reviews
Chicago Tribune. November 12, 1993, VII, p. 19.
The Christian Science Monitor. November 12, 1993, p. 12.
Commonweal. CXX, December 17, 1993, p. 15.
Entertainment Weekly. November 12, 1993, p. 40.
Film Review. February 14, 1994, p. 53.
The Hollywood Reporter. November 8, 1993, p. 5.
Los Angeles Times. November 10, 1993, p. F1.
The New York Times. November 10, 1993, p. B1.
Newsweek. CXXII, November 15, 1993, p. 89.
Time. CXLII, November 15, 1993, p. 106.
Variety. CCCLII, November 15, 1993, p. 30.
The Washington Post. November 12, 1993, p. C6.

THE CEMETERY CLUB

Production: David Brown, Sophie Hurst, and Bonnie Palef for Touchstone Pictures,
    in association with David Manson; released by Buena Vista Pictures
Direction: Bill Duke
Screenplay: Ivan Menchell; based on his play
Cinematography: Steven Poster
Editing: John Carter
Production design: Maher Ahmad
Art direction: Nicklas Farrantello
Set decoration: Gene Serdena
Casting: Terry Liebling
Sound: Willie Burton
Costume design: Hilary Rosenfeld
Music: Elmer Bernstein
MPAA rating: PG-13
Running time: 106 minutes

Principal characters:
>Esther Moskowitz . . . . Ellen Burstyn
>Doris Silverman . . . . Olympia Dukakis
>Lucille Rubin . . . . Diane Ladd
>Ben Katz . . . . Danny Aiello
>Selma . . . . Lainie Kazan
>Larry . . . . Wallace Shawn
>Bill . . . . Robert Serbagi
>Morty . . . . Robert Constanzo
>Ed Bonfigliano . . . . Louis Guss

Ivan Menchell's play *The Cemetery Club* enjoyed a run at the Kennedy Center and
on Broadway before he turned it into this sentimental screen comedy. According to
Menchell, his play was written as a way of coping with the death of his father,
comedian Lou Menchell. His dramatic convention was simple: Three widows regularly visit the graves of their husbands, and the audience learns about them as they
speak to the headstones and to one another. Their relationship takes an unexpected
turn when one of them dates a charming widower they encounter at the cemetery.
Menchell adapted his own play for the big screen, opening up the action to show other
characters and events that affect the lives of the three heroines. It proved to be a natural
vehicle for three highly acclaimed actresses: Ellen Burstyn, Diane Ladd, and Olympia
Dukakis.

Sensible Esther Moskowitz (Burstyn), brash Lucille Rubin (Ladd), and serious
Doris Silverman (Dukakis) are widowed within four years of one another. They have
been friends for many years, and their husbands were friends as well; their bond is

strong and well established in the film's brief opening scenes.

Menchell and director Bill Duke provide a prologue which takes advantage of the opportunity that the medium of film provides to "open up" a play. The audience is introduced to the three couples as they attend yet another wedding of their wild friend Selma (Lainie Kazan). Allowing the audience to see the relationships between the couples provides texture and insight later on, as the widows struggle through the stages of grief and recovery. In particular, this is most helpful in establishing the closeness of Esther and her husband, Murray. One sees the couple dancing to the tune of the old standard "There Will Never Be Another You," symbolically underscoring the depth of their love and foreshadowing both the pain she later feels upon losing him and her fears about falling in love with another man. The opening sequence climaxes as a photographer takes the photograph of the three couples, saying "Okay, pretend you can't live without each other." A funeral sequence follows, showing all three of the husbands being buried in succession.

This prologue lays the foundation for what is to follow, and the characterization of the three women drives the plot. The three widows are seen one year after the death of Esther's husband. They visit the graves of their husbands, talking to them as if they were there, showing pictures of grandchildren, and sharing their feelings. Doris is insistent on commemorating each anniversary of her husband's death. Lucille has become tired of mourning and wants to live again; she especially wants to meet men. Into the mix comes former cop Ben Katz (Danny Aiello), who meets the ladies as he is visiting his wife's grave. Doris becomes furious with Lucille for showing interest in Ben at such an important place as her husband's graveside, and Lucille tells Esther that she will no longer be visiting the grave and that when Esther is "ready to live again, come with me."

Soon Esther runs into Ben and invites him back to her house for coffee. This scene is wonderfully awkward, painfully yet humorously depicting the challenge of beginning to date again when one is more than fifty years of age. Discomfort aside, Esther and Ben begin to see more of each other, much to the disapproval of Lucille and Doris. The relationship between shy Esther and fearful Ben tentatively develops into a romance, and the subtlety brought to the roles by Aiello and Burstyn perfectly captures both the clumsiness and apprehension of people who are falling in love again late in life.

Indeed, the issue of dating after fifty is explored quite well and in varied ways. There is an extremely amusing sequence before Ben and Esther meet, in which Lucille takes Esther to a singles' weekend. She persuades the normally mousy Esther to wear a loud-print dress, tease her hair, and wear considerable makeup. (Lucille claims that "there's no such thing as too much makeup.") The singles' weekend is a broad and comic sequence utilizing some very talented actors, especially Robert Serbagi and Robert Costanzo as Bill and Morty, two outlandish characters who attach themselves to Lucille and Esther. Burstyn is hilarious as she politely tries to have fun while listening to an endless harangue about Morty's toupee. Later, in a scene that has received much attention from the media, Esther and Ben go to a hotel and she reminds him that they should use a condom. She puts it on him in the dark; it is a tasteful and responsible scene that was improvised after Burstyn insisted that a safe-sex message be employed. This is another crowd-pleasing highlight.

Much ingenuity and good humor balance the more somber themes of loneliness and aging. This approach is the strength of the film, for rarely have mainstream films addressed the realities of sexuality and romance in the over-fifty crowd without making fun of them. *Used People* (1992) is an exception and, in fact, has much in common with *The Cemetery Club*. Both films examine widowhood and "second time around" romance for American Jewish women, and both films address the significant problem of the large numbers of women who outlive their husbands. Significantly, both *Used People* and *The Cemetery Club* also address the jealousy and anger that arise in the people around her when a mature woman who has lived under the shadow of a man for many years decides to take her life into her own hands. It is an interesting fact that both these films were written by young men. Both are admirably sensitive to the issues of these older people; it should be noted, however, that comparatively few female screenwriters have had the chance to have a screenplay produced and that a woman's perspective might bring new insight to the subject matter.

Burstyn and Ladd have been in this territory before, to great success. Burstyn won an Academy Award for Best Actress, and Ladd a Best Supporting Actress nomination, for Martin Scorsese's *Alice Doesn't Live Here Anymore* (1975), about a single woman who starts a new life with her young son. *The Cemetery Club* can be said to be a latter-day exploration of the themes explored in that film. Ladd is not as effective in *The Cemetery Club* as in her prior work, partly because she is less believable as a Jewish woman from Pittsburgh. She seems to work hard at convincing the audience that she is Jewish, thus undercutting her performance by drawing too much attention to herself. Her work is not up to her usual standards, especially when compared to the understated subtlety of Burstyn, Dukakis, and Aiello.

There are other places in which the film fails to live up to expectations. The postproduction dialogue does not always work well; there are one or two moments in which words do not match lip movements. Also, one scene clumsily tries to poke fun at the differences between Jews and Catholics. Selma is getting married again to Ed Bonfigliano (Louis Guss). He introduces his stereotypical Italian Catholic sister, who says to Esther, "you're Jewish. . . . You don't believe in the Pope?" This moment, like one or two others, seems gratuitous and not particularly amusing; yet it appears that the filmmakers saw such a scene as necessary to establish the Jewishness of the lead characters.

One other place in which the film mildly falters is in the use of the dramatic convention of the graveside talks by the three widows and Ben. They are moving as portrayed, but not established often enough as a convention to win the acceptance of the audience. These scenes appear to be a contrivance by which some touching moments can be derived rather than as a theatrical convention. This is best exemplified by the final speech by Lucille, in which she suddenly takes the role of narrator for the first time in the film.

The characters grow and change, and they learn to accept their grief, their fear, and the unexpected turns their lives take. They each learn the value of their friendships, and they learn the importance of love. Wisely, Menchell has the often-married, crazy Selma offer the film's simple message: "A Don Juan I don't need. . . . At this stage of my life, what I need is a friend, and somebody who's a good dancer." These women do dance off into the future. The film may not be profound, but its theme and its humor generally brought it critical acceptance and a warm reception from audiences. Several mixed reviews did not stop most audiences from enjoying the subtle and graceful performance by Ellen Burstyn and seeing this underused actress at the top of her form.

Kirby Tepper

Reviews
Chicago Tribune. February 12, 1993, VII, p. 29.
The Christian Science Monitor. March 12, 1993, p. 13.
The Hollywood Reporter. February 3, 1993, p. 8.
Los Angeles Times. February 3, 1993, p. F1.
The New York Times. February 3, 1993, p. B4.
San Francisco Chronicle. February 12, 1993, p. D3.
Time. CXLI, February 15, 1993, p. 67.
Variety. February 3, 1993, p. 2.
The Washington Post. February 12, 1993, p. C7.

CLIFFHANGER

Production: Alan Marshall and Renny Harlin for Mario Kassar, Carolco, Le Studio
   Canal Plus, and Pioneer, in association with RCS Video; released by TriStar
   Pictures
Direction: Renny Harlin
Screenplay: Michael France and Sylvester Stallone; based on a story by France and
   on a premise by John Long
Cinematography: Alex Thomson
Editing: Frank J. Urioste
Production design: John Vallone
Art direction: Aurelio Crugnola and Christiaan Wagener
Set decoration: Robert Gould
Casting: Mindy Marin
Visual effects production: Pamela Easley
Visual effect supervision: Neil Krepela and John Bruno
Special visual effects: Boss Film Studios
Sound: Tim Cooney
Sound design: Wylie Stateman and Gregg Baxter
Costume design: Ellen Mirojnick
Climbing coordination: Mike Weis
Music: Trevor Jones
MPAA rating: R
Running time: 118 minutes

> *Principal characters:*
> Gabe Walker . . . . Sylvester Stallone
> Eric Qualen . . . . John Lithgow
> Hal Tucker . . . . Michael Rooker
> Jessie Deighan . . . . Janine Turner
> Travers . . . . Rex Linn
> Kristel . . . . Caroline Goodall
> Kynette . . . . Leon
> Walter Wright . . . . Paul Winfield
> Frank . . . . Ralph Waite
> Delmar . . . . Craig Fairbrass
> Ryan . . . . Gregory Scott Cummins
> Heldon. . . . . Denis Forest
> Sarah . . . . Michelle Joyner

Cliffhanger may be the ultimate Saturday matinee film for 1993. It stars Sylvester
Stallone returning to the kind of action/adventure format that showcases his own acting
approach—move your body and keep your mouth shut—a formula that has, by and

large, worked well for him in the past. Nevertheless, he has on occasion strayed from it, to his regret.

Stallone was born in New York City in 1946. He grew up in the Hell's Kitchen district, was suspended from fourteen schools, began weight lifting, and studied to become a writer. In a succession of early films, from Woody Allen's *Bananas* (1971) to *Farewell, My Lovely* (1975), he performed in small roles and occasionally was credited with additional dialogue, as in *The Lords of Flatbush* (1974). His career took a significant turn when he wrote, and insisted on starring in, *Rocky* (1976), which won an Academy Award for Best Picture. In the film, he played Rocky Balboa, a Philadel-phia-born-and-reared club fighter who became heavyweight champion of the world. Stallone then wrote, starred in, and occasionally directed four *Rocky* sequels: *Rocky II* (1979), *Rocky III* (1982), *Rocky IV* (1985), and *Rocky V* (1990).

Stallone's other enduring cinematic creation is the Vietnam veteran John Rambo, a one-man avenging army whose violent character is the opposite of the peace-loving Rocky. He made three *Rambo* motion pictures, all of which became popular: *First Blood* (1982), *Rambo: First Blood Part II* (1985), and *Rambo III* (1988). Less so are some of his other film ventures. Stallone's failures include a Hoffa-style portrayal in *F.I.S.T.* (1978), a prisoner of war in *Victory* (1981), costar with Dolly Parton in *Rhinestone* (1984), and a truck driver in *Over the Top* (1987). The muscular actor did much better playing a cop in *Nighthawks* (1981), *Cobra* (1986), and *Tango and Cash* (1989).

Interested in diversifying his acting roles, Stallone spoke of writing and starring in a film about the famed writer Edgar Allan Poe. Following his successes as Rocky and Rambo, he attempted to forgo his more familiar action/adventure films to essay comedy. Surprisingly, he was quite good in the French stage farce *Oscar* (1991), playing a dapper 1930's gangster named "Snaps" Provolone. Although the actor held his own with a talented supporting cast, however, the public was not impressed. In his second comic attempt Stallone again chose a silly farce entitled *Stop! Or My Mom Will Shoot* (1992), about a tough cop henpecked by his overbearing mother, played by Estelle Getty, who turned in an obnoxious performance. The film bombed with audiences. *Cliffhanger*, therefore, represents a return to the genre with which Stallone is most comfortable and that his fans adore.

Cliffhanger opens with a chilling mountain rescue gone awry in the Colorado Rockies (actually, Italy's Dolomites were used in the film). A Rocky Mountain Rescue helicopter is searching for two climbers stranded on a mountain peak. Climbing to their aid is experienced mountain man, Gabe Walker (Sylvester Stallone). He reaches the pair and establishes a cable hookup with the helicopter, but something goes tragically wrong. The inexperienced climber, named Sarah (Michelle Joyner), be-comes unbuckled from her line and dangles thousands of feet above the valley floor. Gabe's heroic attempt to save her fails, and she plunges screaming to her death. Because he blames himself, as does his best friend, Hal Tucker (Michael Rooker), Sarah's boyfriend, Gabe quits the service.

Eight months pass. The Denver Mint is transferring by plane $100 million in thousand-dollar bills. Every safety precaution is taken. The three large suitcases containing the money have monitoring devices attached. Veteran U.S. Treasury agent Travers (Rex Linn) is assigned by his chief, Walter Wright (Paul Winfield), to supervise the money's transfer. While in flight, the plane is suddenly tracked by an approaching aircraft. Agent Travers, turned renegade, kills the three other agents guarding the suitcases and manages to transfer himself by cable aboard the pursuing plane. The three cases, however, do not cross over as planned. A dying FBI agent fires on the plane, forcing it to crash, and the suitcases fall into the Colorado Rockies. The surviving hijackers, a band of mercenary cutthroats, are led by Eric Qualen (John Lithgow), a former government operative now involved in international criminal activities. Their pilot, a clever schemer named Kristel (Caroline Goodall), radios for help, claiming that a blizzard has trapped her mountain-climbing party.

Meanwhile, Gabe has returned to his former mountain home, where he tries to persuade his estranged sweetheart, colleague, and helicopter pilot, Jessie Deighan (Janine Turner), to leave with him to start a new life. Instead, they argue about the tragedy, his leaving, and their failed relationship. She drives away, and he packs, with the intention never to return. Jessie returns quickly after the distress call. She prevails on Gabe to assist Hal, who still holds a grudge. A reluctant Gabe agrees. When the two "rescuers" reach the stranded party, they are immediately taken hostage and ordered to retrieve the three cases or die. Gabe escapes and teams with Jessie, who helps him search for the cases while Hal misleads the criminals. The greedy gang members begin quarreling, leading to violence among themselves, as well as innocent people. All the while, the U.S. Treasury is searching for Qualen, Travers, and the three cases.

All that unifies the hijackers is their greed and fear of Qualen, who is more menacing than all of them combined. Justice is served, however, as each criminal dies in a particularly violent manner: Several falling off a cliff or out of a plane, one is shot by her lover, another is trapped and drowned under ice, and the most depraved one is shoved upward into a stalactite by the hero. The deaths of two innocent people—an older helicopter rescue pilot and a young mountain sky diver—occur on-screen without sound. The effect is an eerie visual experience, as bullets silently rip into their intended victims.

The cat-and-mouse game reaches its climax when Qualen, his entire gang dead, kidnaps Jessie, forcing Gabe to give him the remaining suitcase. When Jessie is released, Gabe throws the money into the helicopter's blades and ties down the aircraft so that it crashes into the side of the mountain. The hero boards the chopper, where he and Qualen battle as the craft hangs by a thread. At the last moment, Gabe leaps free, but Qualen, trapped inside, plummets thousands of feet, a fitting conclusion to an evil life. In the final sequence, the U.S. Treasury helicopter arrives as Gabe, Jessie, and Hal reaffirm their friendship and love.

Cliffhanger is fun to watch because it employs a large cast of characters that neatly divides into the good guys and bad guys, with no shades of gray. The nasty characters try to outdo themselves at every opportunity. Nobility of deed and thought is reserved solely for the heroes. Stallone is at his best in such clearly defined roles. He is also up to the rigors of mountain climbing in a script he cowrote, which was no small challenge; the actor has publicly admitted to a fear of heights. Nevertheless, he somehow overcame his fear and was able to do many of the stunts himself. (His most dangerous stunts were performed by the late Wolfgang Gullich, and Ron Kauk performed the stunts for all the other cast members, including Janine Turner.) Stallone remains firmly in control of his character: relaxed, confident, and invoking physicality when necessary. Matching him in intensity, if not in muscularity, is Lithgow as the nefarious Qualen. Lithgow's performance is poised. He spews invective with a polish reminiscent of George Sanders and Alan Rickman. Also impressive in smaller roles are Ralph Waite as the good-hearted helicopter pilot and Michelle Joyner as the doomed climber. Most of the other performers jump into their characters with gusto.

Despite some good performances, *Cliffhanger* has obvious flaws. Chief among them is a simplistic, melodramatic plot filled with one-dimensional characters. Gabe's character is the best realized, although superheroic. Even so, his romantic relationship with Jessie lacks chemistry. Surprisingly, the film's first two hair-raising episodes outshine its climax. Furthermore, a few of the mountain settings look studio-made. Fault cannot be found in the well-designed scenery created by production designer John Vallone, but the lighting gave an unnatural theatrical glare to the sets, in contrast to the outdoor shots.

Despite these criticisms, director Renny Harlin, no stranger to big-budget action films—or snowy exteriors, terrorists, and airplanes, for that matter, as evidenced by his work in *Die Hard 2: Die Harder* (1990)—outdoes himself with *Cliffhanger*. For sheer nonstop, heart-pounding entertainment, played out atop the world, it is hard to beat. Harlin succeeded in making a film about mountain climbing that caught the death-defying, stomach-churning thrill that continually throws the filmgoer off balance. The film captures all too well the giddy, vertiginous, and gravity-challenging sport. The pacing of the many action/adventure sequences, solid performances from the cast, magnificent visualization of mountain exteriors, and blending of exteriors with studio and processing shots are all skillfully executed. Small wonder *Cliffhanger* has performed quite well at the box office, grossing well over $200 million worldwide. It also earned nominations in three important Academy Award categories: Sound, Sound Effects Editing, and Visual Effects.

The term "cliffhanger" once applied to serials shown on Saturday afternoons at moviehouses. Every week, good fought evil. No matter the genre—Western, science fiction, espionage, murder mystery, action/adventure—each episode ended with the hero or heroine's life in jeopardy. One had to return the following week to learn the outcome. So it continued for several episodes until, finally, good triumphed. With *Cliffhanger*, director Harlin has crafted a rousing, nail-biting picture that not only lives up to its name but also recalls the 1930's and 1940's, when kids lined up to see their heroes triumph over the forces of evil.

Terry Theodore

Reviews

Cinefex. May, 1993, p. 30.
Entertainment Weekly. June 11, 1993, p. 39.
Film Review. August, 1993, p. 12.
The Hollywood Reporter. May 24, 1993, p. 5.
Los Angeles Times. May 28, 1993, p. F1.
The New York Times. May 28, 1993, p. B1.
The New Yorker. LXIX, June 21, 1993, p. 69.
Newsweek. June 7, 1993, p. 66.
People Weekly. June 14, 1993, p. 21.
Sight and Sound. III, July, 1993, p. 39.
Time. CXLI, June 7, 1993, p. 69.
Variety. May 24, 1993, p. 2.
The Washington Post. May 28, 1993, p. G1.

COOL RUNNINGS

Production: Dawn Steel for Walt Disney Pictures; released by Buena Vista Pictures
Direction: Jon Turteltaub
Screenplay: Lynn Siefert, Tommy Swerdlow, and Michael Goldberg; based on a
    story by Siefert and Michael Ritchie and on a true story
Cinematography: Phedon Papamichael
Editing: Bruce Green
Production design: Stephen Marsh
Art direction: Rick Roberts
Set decoration: Lesley Beale
Casting: Chemin Sylvia Bernard and Jaki Brown-Karman
Sound: Larry Sutton
Costume design: Grania Preston
Music: Hans Zimmer
MPAA rating: PG
Running time: 97 minutes

Principal characters:
Derice Bannock	Leon
Sanka Coffie	Doug E. Doug
Yul Brenner	Malik Yoba
Junior Bevil	Rawle D. Lewis
Irv Blitzer	John Candy
Kurt Hemphill	Raymond J. Barry
Larry	Larry Gilman
Josef Grool	Peter Outerbridge
Roger	Paul Coeur

The underdog is at the center of almost every successful sports film. In *Cool Runnings*, the underdogs are the four members of the Jamaican bobsledding team who competed for the first time in the 1988 winter Olympics in Calgary, Canada.

Had it not actually happened, the concept of athletes from the Caribbean competing in a winter sport might never have been sold as a story line to a Hollywood studio. The fact that Jamaica did take a sledding crew to Alberta in 1988, however, takes care of any plausibility problems, and from the get-go this underdog of a film is a smooth ride for director Jon Turteltaub and company.

As conceived in an original story and screenplay, the unlikely sporting quest begins when sprinter Derice Bannock (Leon) gets a bad break and fails to find a spot on his country's Olympic track team. He hunts down an old friend of his sprinter father, Irv Blitzer (John Candy), an Olympic medalist ruined by his own ambition and drowning in self-pity. Derice manages to piece together a ragtag squad composed of his wisecracking soapbox derby driver friend Sanka Coffie (Doug E. Doug), a bald and dour sprinter named Yul Brenner (Malik Yoba), and a poor little rich kid, Junior Bevil

(Rawle D. Lewis), who is trying to use athletics to rebel against his autocratic father.

Candy fulfills the sports cliché of the fallen champion, but the film must work a little harder to fashion another plot mainstay: the diverse, distrustful squad that melds into a unified team. Usually this device is achieved through the old "one of each" concept: a teammate of every color and/or religion. Here the clash of cultures is intermural, not intramural, and so the writers carve out a niche for each character.

Because of the strength and genuineness of the little-known actors who play the four-headed hero role, the athletes' characters and their minor struggles are the best things in the picture. As with almost every Hollywood sports saga, *Cool Runnings* is highly didactic and each character has to learn a particular lesson. As the leader, Derice must wrestle with the meaning of responsibility and the importance of winning versus maintaining integrity. His teammates upbraid him when he tries to copy the Swiss bobsledders, teaching the standard sports lesson that athletes must remain true to their characters, or in the popular cliché, must "stay within themselves."

Sanka Coffie is the buffoon of the group, who must learn courage in the face of the icy terror of the high-speed run. Yul Brenner is the proud individualist who must learn to subordinate his ambition to the team. Junior must learn how to become a man by stepping out from under his father's shadow and asserting his independence. Blitzer, the coach, must undergo moral redemption through admitting past guilt (he cheated in a long-ago Olympics and forfeited his gold medals) and absorbing anew the purity of athletic cleansing through the fresh exploits of his unlikely squad.

In every important respect, *Cool Runnings* is a highly conventional sports film. The athletes and their coach conquer various adversities on their uphill climb: disbelief and nonsupport from their countrymen, harsh climate, poor equipment, attempts by dismayed authorities to disqualify them, taunting and contempt from their competitors.

The only thing that distinguishes this plot from scores of other sports pictures is the comedy-rich cultural clash produced by the oxymoronic central conceit: a Jamaican bobsled team. The writers and the director milk this source endlessly, as they must if they hope to capture and hold the audience.

There are certain pitfalls here to avoid: the opposing gutters of racism and political correctness. In the first part of the film, set in Jamaica, Turteltaub comes at times perilously close to a "happy natives" stereotype that is straight out of the shopworn Disney heritage. Doug E. Doug's clownish character walks that same thin line. Nevertheless, the quiet integrity of the film and its other characters eventually overcomes the early flirtation with a patronizing tone.

As the proud, defiant Brenner, Malik Yoba helps mightily. So does the single-nomered Leon, who combines a heartfelt naïveté with fierce desires and the stirrings of maturity. Rawle D. Lewis, a virtual acting novice, is fine in the Junior role.

The film, like many Disney has put out, is all about growing up. In postmodern Disney-land, however, the adults have just as much growing up to do as the youngsters. Blitzer, his betrayed-coach-turned-Olympic official (Raymond J. Barry), and the Jamaicans' haughty opponents bear the burden.

Candy is something of a surprise—the comic as straight man. Refraining from his customary scenery-chewing, Candy turns in a performance so low-key it at times becomes flat. Yet there is a charming lack of pretense to it.

In fact, the entire film's lack of pretense ultimately redeems the effort from being just another cliché-filled sports picture. Extremely formulaic, it nevertheless achieves almost flawlessly its own modest goals. At times it barely rises above the level of a cartoon, but cartoons can be among the most satisfying morality plays.

It would be an overstatement to say that *Cool Runnings* is a remarkable film, because it is not. The plot, the characters, even the very catchy music are all exactly what one would expect. What is remarkable is that there is barely a misstep in the whole picture. It is not damning with faint praise to list the traps *Cool Runnings* glides past: It is not preachy. It is not pretentious. It is not maudlin. It is not overly moralistic. It is not obsessed with athletic performance, nor does it elevate sport into religion. It degrades no one, and even saves the villains. It does not dabble in superfluous sex or violence (there is one fistfight, but it is necessary to the plot). It does not need to mock the conventions it follows in order to be thought hip. Most, if not all, of these faults can often be found in a single telecast of any major sports event or in a single episode of a standard television sitcom.

Precisely because it is so straightforward, *Cool Runnings* achieves a sense of maturity and integrity once common but becoming much rarer in an era of self-consciousness. To its highest credit, *Cool Runnings* quietly celebrates the diversity of humanity without sanctifying any sort of racial dogma. It could have bumped into the ugly edges of cultural dysfunction; instead, it barrels past with a kind of unsullied confidence.

If attitude really defines excellence in sports and if tolerance is a hallmark of maturity, *Cool Runnings* deserves at least a bronze. No one will regard it as a gold medalist among sports films, but the moral of the story is that it is fun just to be in the game. In the best senses of what is admittedly an uneven Disney tradition, it is a film at least some parents might want their children to see.

Motion pictures about sports underdogs are doomed to be compared to the very successful *Rocky* (1976). In the case of *Cool Runnings*, this is entirely unnecessary. *Rocky* is all swagger; *Cool Runnings* does not need to brag. It needs only, like its bobsledder subjects, to reach the finish line with head held high.

Michael Betzold

Reviews
Chicago Tribune. October 1, 1993, VII, p. 32.
The Hollywood Reporter. October 1, 1993, p. 8.
Los Angeles Times. October 1, 1993, p. F4.
The New York Times. October 1, 1993, p. B11.
Variety. September 21, 1993, p. 3.
The Washington Post. October 1, 1993, p. C6.
Washingtonian. XXIX, November, 1993, p. 28.

DAVE

Production: Lauren Shuler-Donner and Ivan Reitman for Northern Lights
    Entertainment; released by Warner Bros.
Direction: Ivan Reitman
Screenplay: Gary Ross
Cinematography: Adam Greenberg
Editing: Sheldon Kahn
Production design: J. Michael Riva
Art direction: David Klassen
Set decoration: Michael Taylor
Casting: Michael Chinich and Bonnie Timmermann
Sound: Gene Cantamessa
Costume design: Richard Hornung
Music: James Newton Howard
MPAA rating: PG-13
Running time: 110 minutes

> *Principal characters:*
> Dave Kovic/Bill Mitchell . . . . Kevin Kline
> Ellen Mitchell . . . . Sigourney Weaver
> Bob Alexander . . . . Frank Langella
> Alan Reed . . . . Kevin Dunn
> Murray Blum . . . . Charles Grodin
> Vice President Nance . . . . Ben Kingsley
> Duane Stevensen . . . . Ving Rhames
> Alice . . . . Faith Prince

As a satire of the mediocrity and mendacity of late twentieth century American politics, *Dave* is entertaining and charming up to a point. The screenplay's failure to develop its characters and situations to their fullest, however, undercuts the film's effectiveness as a comic portrait of the nation's capital.

As the film opens, Dave Kovic (Kevin Kline), operator of a temporary employment agency, closely resembles Bill Mitchell (Kevin Kline), the President of the United States, whom he impersonates at automobile dealerships. Because of this uncanny resemblance, the Secret Service picks Dave to pose as Mitchell at social functions while the president dallies with his latest mistress. A born showoff, Dave is overjoyed at this opportunity to be the center of attention.

When Mitchell has a stroke, Dave is enlisted by the president's chief of staff, Bob Alexander (Frank Langella), and communications director, Alan Reed (Kevin Dunn), to pretend to be Mitchell until the chief executive recovers. They explain that Vice President Nance (Ben Kingsley) cannot be trusted with the responsibility because he is mentally unstable and that First Lady Ellen Mitchell (Sigourney Weaver) is easily deceived because she hates and therefore avoids her husband.

The real goal of Alexander and Reed, reminiscent of Richard Nixon's H. R. (Bob) Haldeman and John Ehrlichman, however, is to enable the ruthless Alexander, a former senator, to maneuver his way into the presidency. To their surprise, matters do not develop as Alexander and Reed intend because the boyish, good-hearted Dave captivates the public's affection in a way the cold, aloof Mitchell never did and because Dave has a mind of his own. The hero soon devises countermoves to Alexander's machinations with the assistance of Reed, who has had a change of heart. Dave even manages to charm the First Lady.

Dave has been compared to Frank Capra's *Mr. Smith Goes to Washington* (1939)— the classic comic portrayal of an innocent abroad in Washington. While James Stewart's Senator Jefferson Smith comes to the nation's capital naïvely hoping to do good, however, Dave is seemingly apolitical, apparently oblivious to Mitchell's heartless policies. Faced by the burden of pretending to be a leader, Dave essentially grows up.

Dave is good fun as a consideration of what an ordinary person might do if given the opportunity to be president. Dave's actions are unpredictable and spontaneous. He has no idea himself of his next move. The film is also interesting as an inside view of Washington. Production designer J. Michael Riva strikingly re-creates detailed views of various rooms in the White House, as well as the tunnels beneath, where Mitchell is hidden. The film's verisimilitude is further enhanced with cameos by print journalists such as Helen Thomas and Richard Reeves, television personalities such as Jay Leno and John McLaughlin, politicians such as senators Howard Metzenbaum and Alan Simpson, and celebrities such as Arnold Schwarzenegger and Oliver Stone. The insistence of Stone, the writer and director of *JFK* (1991), to talk show-host Larry King, that a conspiracy exists in the Mitchell White House is one of the film's comic highlights.

Nevertheless, certain aspects of the film strain credibility. In the Washington imagined by the filmmakers, almost no one in the White House press corps is under fifty, and no one in the president's cabinet is. More troublesome are the satiric intentions of screenwriter Gary Ross and director Ivan Reitman. No one notices that President Dave apparently goes weeks without doing anything presidential, and his public perception improves simply because he seems, in his superficial public appearances, to be a good guy. One assumes that either Ross and Reitman are criticizing the populace for considering image more important than substance, or they themselves value appearance over reality.

Reitman, one of the most commercially successful directors, responsible for *Stripes* (1981), *Ghostbusters* (1984), *Twins* (1988), and *Kindergarten Cop* (1990), is not known for his subtlety: Slapstick, special effects, violence, crude verbal humor, and an occasional dollop of sentimentality are his trademark. For Reitman, *Dave* represents a quantum leap of sophistication because he rarely strains for effect, trusting the story and the cast to carry the burden. Reitman's gift for timing can be seen when Alexander and his supporters gather to watch Dave disgrace himself in a speech to Congress only to see the substitute triumph over evil.

The true auteur of *Dave* is Ross. A former Capitol Hill intern who wrote speeches for Michael Dukakis during the 1988 presidential campaign, Ross offers an insider's view of Washington made palatable for a mass audience. Ross is also the coscreen-writer of *Big* (1988), which *Dave* closely resembles. Both films argue that people, especially American males, are most alive when they are spontaneous and childlike. Dave impresses both the public and the First Lady with antics such as rolling around on the White House lawn with his dog. It would seem that, according to Ross, big business and big government are better left in the hands of Peter Pans.

Dave's innocent approach to running the nation leads him to consult with his best friend, Murray Blum (Charles Grodin), an accountant, to determine how to solve the nation's economic ills (in much the same way a small business would balance its books). *Dave* implies that the nation would be much improved if led by common citizens with common sense. When Dave must take a stand on an important issue, screenwriter Ross chooses for him to pledge to find jobs for all who want them, an innocuous position designed not to offend any filmgoer and one in keeping with Dave's "real-life" job as head of a temporary employment agency.

Kevin Kline is a much more accomplished performer in comic roles, such as in *A Fish Called Wanda* (1988) and *Soapdish* (1991), than in dramatic roles. Although he makes an appealing presidential stand-in, he fails to overcome the character's essential blandness. Sigourney Weaver is a wonderful actress with a deft comic touch, which she displays when, confronted by a suspicious policeman, her Ellen Mitchell awk-wardly tries to pretend to be a First Lady impersonator. Unfortunately, except for this scene, Weaver is given nothing to do other than look angry or pleased. Ben Kingsley and Faith Prince, as Dave's employment-office assistant, have even less to do.

Charles Grodin, Kevin Dunn, and Ving Rhames, as an expressionless Secret Service agent who functions as Dave's straight man, do well with similarly underwritten roles. The standout performance in *Dave* belongs to Frank Langella, an unusual choice for a comic role. Langella finds the perfect balance between menace and the ridiculous. He is especially effective when weaving his way through a tour group on his way to expressing his outrage to the stand-in, inventing a comic walk of which John Cleese would be proud.

It is pointless to compare the lightweight *Dave* to such better, more serious political films as *Mr. Smith Goes to Washington*, *The Best Man* (1964), and *The Candidate* (1972), despite the fact that it borrows from such films or unintentionally resembles elements from them. By trying to be all things to all people, the film commits some of the same sins as real-life politicians. This approach proved commercially effective, since the film grossed over $63 million in its theatrical release in the United States and Canada, thirteenth highest for the year. Ross' screenplay was nominated for an Academy Award and the film and Kline for Golden Globes.

Michael Adams

Reviews

Atlanta Constitution. May 7, 1993, p. H1.
Boston Globe. May 7, 1993, p. 25.
The Christian Science Monitor. LXXXV, May 7, 1993, p. 113.
Chicago Tribune. May 7, 1993, VII, p. C21.
Entertainment Weekly. May 14, 1993, p. 36.
Films in Review. XLIV, July, 1993, p. 261.
The Hollywood Reporter. April 23, 1993, p. 8.
Los Angles Times. May 7, 1993, p. F1.
The New York Times. May 7, 1993, p. B2.
The New Yorker. LXIX, May 17, 1993, p. 101.
Newsweek. CXXI, May 10, 1993, p. 59.
Time. CXLI, May 10, 1993, p. 65.
Variety. April 23, 1993, p. 4.
The Washington Post. May 7, 1993, p. B1.

DAZED AND CONFUSED

Production: James Jacks, Sean Daniel, and Richard Linklater; released by
Gramercy Pictures
Direction: Richard Linklater
Screenplay: Richard Linklater
Cinematography: Lee Daniel
Editing: Sandra Adair
Production design: John Frick
Art direction: Jenny C. Patrick
Set decoration: Deborah Pastor
Production management: Alma Kuttruff
Casting: Don Phillips
Sound: Jennifer McCauley
Makeup: Jean Black
Costume design: Katherine (K. D.) Dover
Stunt coordination: Fred Lerner
Music: Richard Linklater
MPAA rating: R
Running time: 97 minutes

Principal characters:
Pink	Jason London
Simone	Joey Lauren Adams
Michelle	Milla Jovovich
Pickford	Shawn Andrews
Slater	Rory Cochrane
Mike	Adam Goldberg
Tony	Anthony Rapp
Don	Sasha Jenson
Cynthia	Marissa Ribisi
Shavonne	Deena Martin
Jodi	Michelle Burke
Benny	Cole Hauser
Kaye	Christine Harnos
Mitch	Wiley Wiggins
O'Bannion	Ben Affleck
Melvin	Jason O. Smith
Sabrina	Christin Hinojosa
Darla	Parker Posey

Similar to *American Graffiti* (1973), *Dazed and Confused* is an ensemble film
following a group of high school students through a single day. Unlike *American*

Graffiti, however, *Dazed and Confused* is not about leaving high school and dispelling the illusions of youth; rather, it is about life in the middle of high school.

The film opens at 1:05 p.m. on the last day of school in 1976 in Austin, Texas, and concludes at dawn the following day. During these eighteen hours, screenwriter/ director Richard Linklater focuses on a group of high school students, their hazing rituals, and their nearly continuous partying that culminates in a beer bust at a local forest clearing. Before school lets out for the afternoon, Linklater presents the principal characters, who include "stoners," jocks, brains, and incoming freshmen. Interestingly, all the characters possess an irreverent attitude that makes this film very realistic, if not universally appealing.

Linklater immediately establishes this theme: At school, projects in wood shop include paddles for hazing freshmen, and a bong, which, according to Slater (Rory Cochrane), does not draw correctly and needs work. Other classes include history, where Jodi (Michelle Burke) and her friends Kaye (Christine Harnos) and Shavonne (Deena Martin) list episodes of *Gilligan's Island* on the blackboard while the teacher dozes and then smoke in the bathroom where Kaye expresses her disgust with the show's male-fantasy aspect.

Neither do the jocks respect authority. Throughout the film, one of the central characters, Randy "Pink" Floyd (Jason London), and his friends Don (Sasha Jenson), Melvin (Jason O. Smith), and Benny (Cole Hauser), confront an issue raised by their football coach. Next year's players are being required to sign a pledge swearing off drugs and alcohol. Although none of the boys has any intention of obeying the restrictions, the attitudes toward signing the pledge vary. Don, who is easygoing and takes nothing personally, believes the coaches will not enforce any of the rules. Melvin and Benny, who drink heavily, above all want the team to stay together. Pink resents the pledge and resists signing. In fact, standing up for one's self and one's beliefs is another recurring theme. Conventional morality, however, such as laws against destruction of property, drinking-age limits, and sexual abstinence, is not upheld by any of these kids.

Hazing rituals play a major role in *Dazed and Confused*. They include paddling for the boys and humiliation for the girls. Among the seniors, both boys and girls, there are those who indulge most wholeheartedly in the hazing, such as flunked senior O'Bannion (Ben Affleck) and Darla (Parker Posey). Juxtaposed to these two are Pink and Jodi, who befriend two of the beleaguered freshmen, Mitch (Wiley Wiggins) and Sabrina (Christin Hinojosa). Both of these freshmen grapple with the pain and humiliation of adolescence, enduring a difficult hazing, but both stand up to an abusive senior and assimilate into an environment of sex, drugs, and rock and roll.

Senior Tony (Anthony Rapp) and his brainy friends Mike (Adam Goldberg) and Cynthia (Marissa Ribisi) primarily function throughout the film as a Greek chorus, analyzing events and their own lives. Their analysis, however, criticizes the society to which they belong. During the hazing of the freshmen girls, Mike disapprovingly comments that society condones this behavior (although his disgust does not stop him from watching). While driving around with Mike and Tony before hearing of the beer bust, Cynthia argues against living her life as only preparation for the future, and she decides to start appreciating visceral experiences, as Mike calls them.

Linklater has said that his memories of high school include feeling trapped, but he also remembers an innocence and tremendous energy. Although many of the teenagers drink throughout the film, smoke pot, and vandalize property, and most of the guys seek sex continuously, many of the characters are also introspective, creative, and caring. These kids may not be focused on a career track, but they are not bad souls, and their innocence shines through consistently.

Toward the end of the film, Pink asks to be reminded to kill himself if he ever refers to these as the best years of his life. His date for the night, Simone (Joey Lauren Adams), responds by reminding him that his life as a "big man on campus" is privileged. This seems Linklater's final analysis: These are not the best years because of the confinement of school and rules, but there can be a lot of good times if the moment is not completely ignored in preparation for the future or ignored in regard for the law.

Unlike *Fast Times at Ridgemont High* (1982), another film featuring an ensemble of high school students, *Dazed and Confused* is not a parody. Linklater's film—his second, following his critically acclaimed feature-film debut, *Slacker* (1991)—is a realistic portrayal of life in high school among an irreverent, partying crowd of kids. These teenagers are rowdy, funny, and primarily interested in what is happening right now. Some think more than others, but Don best conveys the characters' common attitude toward high school when he says that he just wants to have as many good times as possible.

Linklater's attention to the details of the 1970's is impressive, evidenced in the clothing, cars, continuous use of pot and beer, and especially the music. Linklater personally selected all the songs that track throughout the film—including cuts by such 1970's mainstays as Alice Cooper, Aerosmith, Bob Dylan, ZZ Top, and Kiss— and by filming the characters nodding in time, Linklater pulls his audience into the middle of the action. The camera technique throughout *Dazed and Confused* also places the audience in the middle of the action. When Pink, Don, Mitch, and Pickford (Shawn Andrews) are out driving, Linklater's camera is in the car with them, and then out the window, with Don grabbing a garbage can to hurl at a mailbox. When Pickford, Slater, and Mitch climb the tall light tower at the site of the beer bust, Linklater's camera is inside the tower with them, hanging on the bars with Pickford and Slater.

Linklater thus synchronizes his subject, setting, camera, and direction throughout *Dazed and Confused*. His characters are in the middle of high school, in the middle of the 1970's, in the middle of the United States, and his camera and sound track pull his audience into the middle of the action. Also, the film is refreshing given that these characters are neither the early career-track yuppies nor the mass murderers portrayed in many other films and on television. Linklater's characters are middle-class, and middle-of-the-road in terms of their reckless behavior. They are not saints, but neither are they monsters. How refreshing to see such ambiguity.

Alicia Neumann

Reviews

Chicago Tribune. September 24, 1993, VII, p. 36.
Entertainment Weekly. September 24, 1993, p. 68.
The Hollywood Reporter. September 13, 1993, p. 7.
Los Angeles Times. September 24, 1993, p. F1.
The New York Times. September 24, 1993, p. B6.
The New Yorker. LXIX, October 4, 1993, p. 214.
Newsweek. CXXII, October 4, 1993, p. 85.
Playboy. October, 1993, p. 20.
Rolling Stone. September 16, 1993, p. 17.
Spin. IX, October, 1993, p. 59.
Variety. June 9, 1993, p. 13.
The Washington Post. October 22, 1993, p. C7.

DEMOLITION MAN

Production: Joel Silver, Michael Levy, and Howard Kazanjian for Silver Pictures; released by Warner Bros.
Direction: Marco Brambilla
Screenplay: Daniel Waters, Robert Reneau, and Peter M. Lenkov; based on a story by Lenkov and Reneau
Cinematography: Alex Thomson
Editing: Stuart Baird
Production design: David L. Snyder
Art direction: Walter Paul Martishius
Set decoration: Robert Gould and Etta Leff
Casting: Joy Todd and Ferne Cassel
Visual effects: Michael J. McAllister and Kimberly K. Nelson
Sound: Tim Cooney
Costume design: Bob Ringwood
Music: Elliot Goldenthal
MPAA rating: R
Running time: 114 minutes

Principal characters:
John Spartan	Sylvester Stallone
Simon Phoenix	Wesley Snipes
Lenina Huxley	Sandra Bullock
Dr. Raymond Cocteau	Nigel Hawthorne
Alfredo Garcia	Benjamin Bratt
Chief George Earle	Bob Gunton
Associate Bob	Glenn Shadix
Edgar Friendly	Denis Leary

The full-page ads supporting the release of *Demolition Man* set up the narrative as well as generic expectations of this quirky yet entertaining action-adventure yarn. On the left-hand side of the ad, just below the boldly printed "STALLONE," is a profile of the actor facing right; beneath the star is the caption, "The 21st Century's Most Dangerous Cop." On the right-hand side of the ad, just below "SNIPES," is a profile of the actor facing left; beneath the star is the caption, "The 21st Century's Most Ruthless Criminal." At the bottom of the ad is the film's title plus another caption, "The Future Isn't Big Enough for the Both of Them."

The ad's brilliant distillation of *Demolition Man*'s critical selling points signals that this Warner Bros. release is a star vehicle for Sylvester Stallone, the creator and eponymous embodiment of the box-office successes in the *Rocky* and *Rambo* series. It also signals the arrival of noted African American actor Wesley Snipes, whose credits include *Jungle Fever* (1991) and *White Men Can't Jump* (1992), as a young superstar deserving of co-billing with Stallone. By referencing the twenty-first century, the film's futuristic science-fiction setting is spelled out clearly. Finally, by situating the film's central characters in a confrontational configuration, it is equally clear that the narrative structure springs from the template of the classic Western. In *Demolition Man*, Stallone's tough cop, John Spartan, is fated for a mortal showdown with Wesley Snipes' archvillain, Simon Phoenix.

The film begins with a tumultuous precredit sequence set in Los Angeles in 1996, a noisy prelude that immediately establishes the conflict between Spartan, an LAPD sergeant, and his nemesis. Nicknamed "Demolition Man" because of his no-holds-barred approach to law enforcement, Spartan is dispatched to an eerie warehouse, a veritable armed camp, to rescue thirty hostages held captive by the psychopathic Phoenix. In the wake of the bloody but cinematically spectacular firestorm that leaves the hostages dead, Spartan is convicted on a trumped up charge of involuntary manslaughter and sentenced to seven decades of "rehabilitation" as a frozen prisoner in the California CryoPenetentiary. Phoenix has been similarly incarcerated.

The story then jumps to the year 2032, and an Edenic society called San Angeles, a new political-social entity comprising Southern California, formed after a cataclysmic 2011 earthquake provided humankind with the opportunity to start over. The new, kinder, gentler society presided over by the enigmatic Raymond Cocteau (Nigel Hawthorne) is in reality, however, a fascist, although serene, state. Here, the film's gritty action-adventure dynamics give way, at least for a moment, to a parodistic send-up of 1990's standards of political correctness. Indeed, San Angeles' citizens are prohibited from smoking, drinking, and having sex, except for electronically-induced virtual-reality trysts that recall the delightful man-caught-out-of-time hilarities of Woody Allen's comic science-fiction film, *Sleeper* (1973).

In *Demolition Man*'s future world, even caffeine and red meat are banned. When a fit of petulance leads to the utterance of a four-letter word, a buzzer sounds and a prissy British voice informs the offender that a fine of one credit has been levied for violating the "verbal morality code." By extending the left-of-center canons of the 1990's into a future where incorrect thoughts and bad habits have been purged, *Demolition Man*'s scriptwriters—Daniel Waters, Robert Reneau, and Peter M. Lenkov—reveal a kind of right-wing nostalgia for the good old days of the Reagan administration when, as *The New York Times*' Vincent Canby puts it, "government regulators kept quiet and red-blooded American men could exchange body fluids with the women of their choice without being hectored by public health nuts."

After this comparative idyll, the action again picks up when Phoenix is thawed from his icy crypt for a mandatory parole hearing. With what is later revealed as aid from the henchmen of Dr. Cocteau, Phoenix manages an elaborate escape. Cocteau's motivation is simple. He has resuscitated Phoenix to quell the growing menace of the Scraps, a ragtag band of social outcasts. Like the proletarian workers of Fritz Lang's classic science-fiction film *Metropolis* (1926), the rebellious nonconformists inhabit an underground maze of dark tunnels known in *Demolition Man* as the Wasteland. For Cocteau, the defiant Scraps, who swig beer and grill hamburgers (really, ratburgers)—

but whose threat to San Angeles' mind-controlled autocracy is more symbolic than actual—need to be expunged. It is a task best left to an anachronistic yet still useful thug from the previous age of barbarism such as Phoenix.

When the flamboyant, showboating Phoenix begins to run amok with acts of gratuitous mischief committed for the pure pleasure of creating mayhem, San Angeles' police force proves ill-equipped to deal with this killing machine from the past. Because the police do not know that Phoenix is in league with Cocteau, and they are handicapped by having been programmed with the same wimpish attitudes and behaviors of the general populace, the crisis quickly escalates. In desperation, Lenina Huxley (Sandra Bullock), a young police officer and connoisseur of 1990's popular culture and its testosterone-driven heroes, becomes convinced that only "barbarian savage" John Spartan has the right stuff to go toe-to-toe with Phoenix. With Spartan revived from his block of ice, and with his own 1996 score to settle, the chase is on.

The last forty-five minutes of the film is a nonstop tour de force of high-tech, cinematic shoot-outs and explosions. An exemplar of the everything-goes-boom school of action-adventure previously exploited by producer Joel Silver in his *Lethal Weapon* and *Die Hard* series, *Demolition Man*'s own lethal loaf is leavened by the engaging antics of its principal players. Indeed, Stallone and Snipes often seem to wink at their cartoon-like action characters as they banter and brawl. It seems obvious that they had great fun in bringing their roles to life. Similarly, Sandra Bullock's take on the naïvely bookish yet ultimately brave policewoman has the right resonance to make her romantic scenes with Stallone both credible and funny. As expected, after the heavy weapons have been set aside and Phoenix has been dispatched to his just reward, *Demolition Man* delivers a typically Hollywood happy ending. Cocteau, like his cryogenic enforcer, has been vanquished. This allows the Scraps to emerge from the underground and commingle happily with the now psychologically liberated abovegrounders. Final closure is signaled by Spartan' and Huxley's curtain-dropping romantic embrace.

In spite of *Demolition Man*'s attempt to appeal to all audience segments, and the contradictions in tone and style that result, the film has moments to savor. The future celebration of late twentieth century jingles such as Alka Seltzer's "Plop, Plop, Fizz, Fizz" and "Good Things from the Garden (of the Jolly Green Giant)" clicks with postmodern irony. So, too, does the gag about the Arnold Schwarzenegger Presidential Library as the future's archive of choice. Also ironic, and an effective promotional tie-in for the film, is the designation of Taco Bell as the future's sole survivor of the "franchise wars."

Demolition Man's compelling *mise-en-scène* is bolstered by the handsomely slick direction of Marco Brambilla, making his feature-film debut after a successful tenure as a director of commercials. The settings by designer David L. Snyder, who created the indelible look of another futuristic Los Angeles for Ridley Scott's *Blade Runner* (1982), are similarly critical to the film's visual credibility. A further embellishment is provided by sleek prototype "concept cars" from General Motors' Research Division. Finally, the blonde peroxide coiffure provided Phoenix adds just the right absurdist touch to help cap Snipes's menacing yet comically nuanced scenery-chewing performance.

At the box office, *Demolition Man* handily broke the fall record for opening weekend grosses. In part, its success was the result of Stallone's momentum from his 1993 summer hit, *Cliffhanger*. It was also a matter of Warner Bros. learning a lesson from the hyperinflated expectations and promotion for Columbia's *The Last Action Hero*, the 1993 action-adventure vehicle starring Arnold Schwarzenegger deemed a flop by industry insiders. Wishing to avoid the perception of similarly unrealistic expectations, Warner Bros. created the perception as well as the fact of a hit by "underselling" *Demolition Man*. Of course, the appearance of Stallone—nude, toned, and contemplative—on the cover of the November 1993 issue of *Vanity Fair* did not hurt the film's appeal to women, a slice of the demographic pie usually discounted in the promotion of action-adventure films. Indeed, Warner's decision to pitch the film directly to women is itself something of an innovation in that conventional industry wisdom associates the genre with an essentially young and male audience.

Charles Merrell Berg

Reviews
Chicago Tribune. October 8, 1993, I, p. 28.
Cinefantastique. XXIV, December, 1993, p. 16.
Entertainment Weekly. October 22, 1993, p. 54.
Film Review. December, 1993, p. 40.
The Hollywood Reporter. October 8, 1993, p. 6.
Los Angeles Times. October 8, 1993, p. F1.
The New York Times. October 8, 1993, p. B2.
Time. October 18, 1993, p. 98.
Variety. October 8, 1993, p. 2.
USA Today. October 8, 1993, p. 5D.
The Washington Post. October 9, 1993, p. D5.

DENNIS THE MENACE

Production: John Hughes and Richard Vane; released by Warner Bros.
Direction: Nick Castle
Screenplay: John Hughes; based on characters created by Hank Ketcham
Cinematography: Thomas Ackerman
Editing: Alan Heim
Production design: James Bissell
Art direction: Michael Baugh and Steve Wolff
Set decoration: Eve Cauley
Casting: Jane Jenkins and Janet Hirshenson
Sound: Jim Alexander
Costume design: Ann Roth and Bridget Kelly
Music: Jerry Goldsmith
MPAA rating: PG
Running time: 97 minutes

Principal characters:

Mr. Wilson	Walter Matthau
Dennis Mitchell	Mason Gamble
Martha Wilson	Joan Plowright
Switchblade Sam	Christopher Lloyd
Alice Mitchell	Lea Thompson
Henry Mitchell	Robert Stanton
Chief of police	Paul Winfield
Margaret Wade	Amy Sakasitz
Joey	Kellen Hathaway

Based on the long-running Hank Ketcham comic strip, *Dennis the Menace*, loaded with lots of physical pranks and cute little faces, will appeal primarily to small children. Although producer/screenwriter John Hughes was also the genius behind the very successful *Home Alone* (1990), *Dennis the Menace* falls far short of that blockbuster. Long on gags and short on story, this film exhausts its little legs almost immediately, when the next prank becomes painfully predictable. Viewers must sit through the entire series of mishaps, hoping some semblance of story will materialize.

At the film's opening, it is a slow, sunny morning in suburbia for grumpy old, retired mail carrier Mr. Wilson (Walter Matthau) as he retrieves his newspaper. All of a sudden he realizes that it is "too quiet." Then he hears the high, shrill voice of seven-year-old Dennis Mitchell (Mason Gamble) and the ominous clanging of his red bike and wagon approaching. Panicked, Mr. Wilson runs to his bedroom and feigns sleep, hoping to avoid "the little terror." Dennis, however, enters the Wilson house and innocently entertains himself over Mr. Wilson's seemingly sleeping body. After a few typical mishaps, Dennis becomes convinced that his elderly neighbor must be sick. "Poor Mr.

Wilson," Dennis quietly mutters to himself as he retrieves a jar of aspirin. When Dennis is unable to insert an aspirin in Mr. Wilson's mouth with his tiny fingers, he tries the next best thing—a slingshot. Mr. Wilson bolts up, howling in pain. Thus begins the first of a series of comic-strip gags involving poor Mr. Wilson. With each new prank, Mr. Wilson's anger increases. First, Dennis unknowingly shoots paint onto Mr. Wilson's barbecuing food. Then, after Dennis loses the two front teeth of Mr. Wilson's dentures, he replaces them with oversized Chiclets resembling buckteeth. Unsuspecting, Mr. Wilson inserts his dentures and has his picture taken for the local newspaper.

This is only the beginning. When Dennis' parents (Lea Thompson and Robert Stanton) are both called out of town on business over the same weekend, they exhaust an entire telephone book trying to get a baby-sitter for Dennis. In one last, desperate attempt, they ask Mrs. Wilson (Joan Plowright) for help. Missing the presence of children in her life, she is only too happy to take care of the boy.

As expected, what follows is a new series of tortures for the jaded old Wilson—such as Dennis putting cleaning fluid in Wilson's nose drops and toilet cleanser in his mouthwash. It all comes to a head at Mr. Wilson's garden party in honor of the once-in-a-lifetime, ten-second opening of his prized night-blooming orchid. Mr. Wilson has been growing this flower for forty years in order to experience this ten seconds of glory. Because he wants the reception to go smoothly, Mr. Wilson begs Dennis to sit in a chair and not cause any problems.

In a departure from typical Dennis the Menace fare, the filmmakers introduce a villainous stranger, named Switchblade Sam (Christopher Lloyd). He breaks into the Wilson house during the ill-fated garden party and steals Mr. Wilson's prized gold coin collection. Dennis is the first to discover the theft and immediately yells the news across the yard, diverting everyone's attention during those few precious seconds when the orchid is in bloom. In a fit of rage, Mr. Wilson snaps at Dennis, "You're a pest and a menace. I don't want to see you. I don't want to know you." Hurt, Dennis runs away.

While a neighborhood search is conducted, Dennis encounters Switchblade, who decides to take him hostage. In what is the most amusing sequence in the film, Switchblade replaces Mr. Wilson as Dennis' victim. By the time the police arrive, Switchblade is barely conscious. As he is carried away, the police chief remarks, "You can tell everyone in the big house you met Dennis Mitchell." Feeling guilty for snapping at Dennis, and grateful for the retrieval of his coins, Mr. Wilson finally decides to befriend him—a touching ending that pulls the whole script together.

Unfortunately, director Nick Castle's playful film suffers from too many shortcomings to be saved by a quaint, sugar-coated ending. From the opening sequence, there is the problem of believability. Most thinking people will not understand why Mr. Wilson would allow the menacing kid from next-door into the sanctity of his home or why he would allow himself to be physically violated. He could lock the door or simply tell the child to leave. The film's lame explanation is that Mr. Wilson does not want to be thought of as an ogre. After telling Dennis' father to keep the kid on a leash, Mr. Wilson says, "I'm not the bad one here . . . that kid has to be controlled."

A much bigger problem is the script's lack of story progression. The introduction of Switchblade Sam is an unsuccessful attempt to enliven a flat story. The script is merely a distillation of forty years of comic-strip gags, with no story in the conventional sense. Although the outrageous gags often hit their mark, they become old and repetitive relatively quickly. For this reason, most viewers, school-age and older, will eventually grow tired as nothing new unfolds.

The film's one saving grace is the acting. Mason Gamble has the look and feel of the Dennis of the 1960's television series. Although he is an adequate casting selection, however, he lacks the charisma of fellow John Hughes prodigy Macaulay Culkin. He does have some cute lines, nevertheless, such as when he tells Mrs. Wilson about the only time his father is happy—on Sundays, "When Mom and he wrestle . . . take off their shirts and make funny noises."

Less perfunctory is Walter Matthau's performance as the irascible Mr. Wilson, the man perpetually plagued by the mischievous boy next-door. Matthau captures the essence of the character—the scowl, the squint, the crotchetiness, the outrage. This is an actor who can overcome even such limiting material. Joan Plowright, a queen of actresses, embodies the kind, child-loving Mrs. Wilson. According to Dennis, she is the nicest "old gal" on the block. She is the polar opposite of her cranky husband. Matthau and Plowright complement each other beautifully.

Christopher Lloyd brings some zany energy to the screen as the villain who drops out of a passing freight car at night. With twisted features and tattered clothing, he has fun as the incarnation of evil: He steals purses outside schoolyards, takes food from little children, and even snatches their baby dolls. He lacks the screen time, however, to add significant energy to the film.

In addition, child star Amy Sakasitz, who plays fellow tyke-terror Margaret Wade, is convincing as a seven-year-old feminist who enjoys making little boys' lives difficult. Also, Lea Thompson and Robert Stanton turn heads as Dennis' parents. They bring an old-fashioned retro-1950's innocence to the screen that captures the essence of what the film was meant to be.

Despite these good performances, however, the film suffers. For some, especially young children, the brainless gags and quirky characters may be enough. Unfortunately, truly comic moments are few and far between. For the average filmgoer, *Dennis the Menace* will prove to be a disappointment.

Jonathan David

Reviews
Boston Globe. June 25, 1993, p. 51.
Chicago Tribune. June 25, 1993, VII, p. 22.
The Christian Science Monitor. June 25, 1993, p. 14.
The Hollywood Reporter. June 21, 1993, p. 6.
Los Angeles Times. June 25, 1993, p. F1.

New York. XXVI, July 12, 1993, p. 53.
The New York Times. June 25, 1993, p. B2.
USA Today. June 25, 1993, p. D2.
Variety. June 21, 1993, p. 4.
The Washington Post. June 25, 1993, p. C1.
Washingtonian. XXVIII, August, 1993, p. 19.

ETHAN FROME

Production: Stan Wlodkowski for American Playhouse Theatrical Films; released
   by Miramax Films
Direction: John Madden
Screenplay: Richard Nelson; based on the novel by Edith Wharton
Cinematography: Bobby Bukowski
Editing: Katherine Wenning
Production design: Andrew Jackness
Art direction: David Crank
Set decoration: Joyce Anne Gilstrap
Casting: Billy Hopkins and Suzanne Smith
Sound: Paul Cote
Costume design: Carol Oditz
Music: Rachel Portman
MPAA rating: PG
Running time: 105 minutes

Principal characters:
Ethan Frome	Liam Neeson
Mattie Silver	Patricia Arquette
Zeena Frome	Joan Allen
Reverend Smith	Tate Donovan
Mrs. Hale	Katharine Houghton
Ned Hale	Stephen Mendillo
Young Ruth Hale	Debbon Ayer
Jotham	George Woodard
Denis Eady	Jay Goede
Young Ned Hale	Rob Campbell

Edith Wharton's novella *Ethan Frome*, published in 1911, reflected the societal restraints she saw present in the countryside in and around Lenox, New York. Telling a variant of an age-old story—the tragic fate of forbidden love—Wharton's novella relies on the spareness of the landscape and the seeming endlessness of winter in the far northeast to convey her themes of claustrophobia and hopelessness. *Ethan Frome* entered the public domain in 1989, and the filmmakers jumped at the chance to film it. As executive producer Lindsay Law noted, "four other companies announced plans to film it. We kept pushing on with it, and the others fell by the wayside." To make this film happen, Law brought together writer Richard Nelson and director John Madden, both of whom rose to prominence with Broadway projects. The result is, in the words of one reviewer, a "sad and somber little film."

When the new minister Reverend Smith (Tate Donovan) arrives in Starkfield, Massachusetts, he sees a disfigured, misshapen man moving slowly, tortuously down the empty white road. As the story unfolds, that man is identified as Ethan Frome (Liam Neeson), whose story is then told in flashback. As a tall and sturdy young man, Ethan had married Zeena (Joan Allen), who had cared for his ailing mother. While the newlyweds were initially happy, Zeena's hypochondria and bitterness soon became the largest feature of their life. The chill and barren landscape of their home soon paralleled that of Starkfield. The ailing Zeena sent for her cousin's daughter, Mattie Silver (Patricia Arquette), to help around the house.

While Mattie arrived looking even more sickly than Zeena, she soon blossomed. Full of life and with an inner fire that warmed Ethan's heart, Mattie soon became the center of Ethan's meager existence, and he of hers. One fateful evening, while Zeena traveled overnight to consult a new physician, Ethan and Mattie declared undying love for each other and spent the night together. With Zeena's unexpectedly early return, however, came the end of the lovers' dreams. Zeena had arranged for a different helper, and Mattie was to be sent packing. To delay the separation, Mattie and Ethan climbed a dangerous slope towing a sled, surveyed the world around them, and made a pact to die there together.

While the story of the three central characters—Ethan, Zeena, and Mattie—is narrated by those around them, perhaps the most telling reflection of all is the landscape of Starkfield (actually Peacham, Vermont) and the Frome farm, located on a frozen, barren hilltop. The filmmakers searched New York, New Hampshire, and Maine looking for rugged mountains and unending snow and avoiding all the locations that offered the cheery warmth of a Christmas-card, Currier-and-Ives New England. Peacham offered a more rustic, mountainous setting, and because of a town ordinance restricting the renovation of historic structures, the perfect homestead. The farmhouse had been uninhabited since the early 1900's: The walls had never been repainted, and the layers of dirt and grime were vintage and authentic. "It's hard to imagine it being any more perfect for the story than it is," said director Madden. "We had horrendous problems trying to film in a space the size of the farm, but I believe that on screen you feel the claustrophobia and restriction depicted in Wharton's novel."

Added to that authentic location, however, were the realities of a shoot in subzero temperatures, resulting in frostbitten crew members, frozen equipment, and multiple transportation woes. While the hill for the fateful sledding accident aptly represented the moral isolation described by Wharton, it was also a significant peak, accessible only by sled and snowmobile.

With a cast as spare as the landscape, casting decisions took on crucial importance. Irishman Liam Neeson, star of *Darkman* (1990), *Shining Through* (1992), and Woody Allen's *Husbands and Wives* (1992), may initially seem too strong and full of life to play the broken farmer Ethan Frome. Neeson brings more reality, however, to the fallen Frome than to the young lover Ethan. Throughout the scenes of growing attraction between Mattie and Ethan, Neeson so underplays the role that audience members who know the story will despair of it ever reaching the point of passion. One clear example of this restraint is the fateful scene in which Ethan watches from his shivery post outside a window as Mattie dances and laughs, surrounded by other young people, all before a roaring fire. In this scene, Ethan is to discover the depth of his feelings for Mattie. Patricia Arquette as Mattie does an admirable job of reflecting warmth and life, but Neeson looks largely cold and alone. A clearer sense of the events to come arises during the dinner eaten during Zeena's absence. Here Wharton's characters are described as awkward but love-stricken. The awkwardness is palpable, and before the end of the scene, the couple's attraction is palpable as well.

In the spirit of true tragedy, the accident on the hill maims Ethan and Mattie. Neeson changes shape completely, becoming like a wizened piece of driftwood. In fact, in his interviews concerning *Ethan Frome*, Neeson commented on his attempts to look a part of the pitiless landscape, to become a permanent fixture within the endless winter of his character's world. Not unlike Quasimodo, Ethan Frome comes to reflect externally the imperfection of his world, even as internally he is nearing peace. Late in the film, Joan Allen's withered Zeena also adds startling reality to this tale of unrelenting loss and woe.

It would be inaccurate to describe *Ethan Frome* as entertaining. It is much more accurate to describe it as a beautiful film, although a stark one. Director Madden commented that he worked to create a visual environment showing a lack of possibility combined with awesome beauty and integrity. This is what he has accomplished overall with his faithful presentation of Wharton's American classic.

Roberta F. Green

Reviews
The Atlanta Journal and Constitution. March 25, 1993, p. F7.
Boston Globe. March 12, 1993, p. 29.
Chicago Tribune. March 12, 1993, Take 2, p. C.
The Christian Science Monitor. March 12, 1993, p. 13.
Los Angeles Times. March 12, 1993, p. F14.
The New Republic. CCVIII, April 12, 1993, p. 28.
The New York Times. March 12, 1993, p. B4.
The New Yorker. LXIX, March 29, 1993, p. 103.
Newsweek. March 15, 1993, p. 74.
Variety. CCCXLIX, January 18, 1993, p. 78.
The Washington Post. March 19, 1993, p. F7.

FALLING DOWN

Production: Arnold Kopelson, Herschel Weingrod, and Timothy Harris for Le
  Studio Canal Plus, Regency Enterprises, and Alcor Films; released by Warner
  Bros.
Direction: Joel Schumacher
Screenplay: Ebbe Roe Smith
Cinematography: Andrzej Bartkowiak
Editing: Paul Hirsch
Production design: Barbara Ling
Art direction: Larry Fulton
Set decoration: Cricket Rowland
Casting: Marion Dougherty
Sound: David MacMillan
Costume design: Marlene Stewart
Music: James Newton Howard
MPAA rating: R
Running time: 112 minutes

Principal characters:

D-Fens	Michael Douglas
Prendergast	Robert Duvall
Beth	Barbara Hershey
Sandra	Rachel Ticotin
Mrs. Prendergast	Tuesday Weld
Surplus store owner	Frederic Forrest
D-Fens' mother	Lois Smith

The entire action of *Falling Down* covers about ten hours of a hot summer day in
Los Angeles. Most motion pictures that adhere to the unity of time that strictly—such
as *High Noon* (1952), *Twelve Angry Men* (1957), and *Die Hard* (1988)—acquire a
level of tension almost from the start. By selecting only one key day in a character's
life, a film or a play can become nearly all climax. Plays that adopt such an approach
to time (the works of Henrik Ibsen, for example) are sometimes called "dramas of ripe
conditions." That term fits *Falling Down*. In the film, events have been ripening in the
lives of the two main characters for years. D-Fens (Michael Douglas)—so-named for
his personalized license plate—has lost his job at a defense plant, and his former wife,
Beth (Barbara Hershey), tells him to stay away from her home on their young
daughter's birthday. Police detective Martin Prendergast (Robert Duvall) reluctantly
works his last day before taking an early retirement, a change forced on him by his
overbearing wife (Tuesday Weld). Both D-Fens and Prendergast feel the pressures of
their lives swelling to some sort of bursting point. The structure of the film, alternating
between the stories of the unemployed defense worker and the cop staring into

retirement, shows how the ripening tensions send D-Fens over the edge but allow Prendergast to find himself.

If a tight, suspenseful structure is one of the benefits of observing the unity of time, one drawback can sometimes be implausibility. Whatever happens to the character on this significant day must not seem too contrived, too conveniently arranged by the writer and director. Moreover, if the character's actions are to be believed, the filmmakers usually need to reveal enough about the protagonist's personality and background to suggest a cause for these actions, a reason for his behavior.

This is where *Falling Down* may be faulted. The filmmakers show D-Fens' violent responses to the mounting stress of urban life during one pivotal day, but they delay revealing nearly everything about him that could serve as an explanation. The audience only learns his name (Bill) at the very end of the film, when the police question his mother, and the end credits simply refer to him as D-Fens. This approach makes it easier to regard him more as a type than as a person—literally, the harried man on the street lashing out at the world. Having been set up to identify with someone who is about to crack under the pressure, most viewers will at some point pull back their sympathies as they see D-Fens' increasingly extreme behavior and transfer loyalty to Prendergast, who uses his last working day to piece together the trail of clues left by D-Fens in an effort to capture this urban vigilante. Some of the tantalizing questions posed by the film are, at what point in D-Fens' day do viewers withhold their identification with the character? When do viewers perceive Bill to have crossed the line? Put more bluntly, how much does the film intend to make its audience into vicarious vigilantes?

D-Fens' first departure from the norm occurs when he abandons his car in a morning traffic jam on the freeway. Though dressed for his job and carrying his briefcase, he is only going through the motions by driving to work, information that is revealed much later in the film. His stated plan in leaving the car is to go home—to his daughter's birthday party. Needing change to call Beth, he is told by the Korean proprietor of a small market that he must buy something to get change. A can of soda costs eighty-five cents, the merchant tells him, too much to leave enough change for his phone call. D-Fens lectures the store owner about his inflated pricing and his broken English; the two scuffle, and D-Fens pries a baseball bat away from the owner. Insulted at being taken for a thief, he tours the small grocery shelf by shelf, asking the owner the price of selected items and smashing each aisle of goods as he hears a price higher than he prefers. Finally, he pays fifty cents for the soda, takes his change and the bat, and leaves.

Like the baseball bat, every other weapon that D-Fens acquires on his journey comes from those who initially trouble him. Resting in an abandoned lot, he is threatened by two gang members who demand his briefcase as a toll. He uses the baseball bat to run them off and takes their switchblade. The gang members retaliate by attempting to kill him in a drive-by shooting, but they miss and demolish their car speeding away from the scene. D-Fens calmly takes their gym bag of automatic weapons, shoots one of them in the leg, and continues his walk home. When the workers at a fast-food restaurant refuse to sell him breakfast because lunch started three minutes earlier, he produces one of the weapons, accidentally fires a few shots at the ceiling, apologizes, and politely reorders. Shopping for boots at an army surplus store, he commits his only killing when he uses the switchblade to defend himself against the owner (Frederic Forrest), a Nazi. D-Fens' odyssey brings him into conflict with the upper class as well. He cuts across the golf course at a country club and argues with two members who demand that he leave. When he shoots at one of their golf carts, the aged club member crumples from a heart attack. D-Fens later climbs over the barbed wire surrounding the home of a plastic surgeon and disrupts the family's patio barbecue.

The film's importance and point of controversy lies in its picture of vigilantism as a tempting remedy for a failing society. Audience sympathy for D-Fens, therefore, may take the form of an attraction-repulsion response. On the one hand, the character is played by a popular actor. Douglas portrays him as a man of some dignity who has been pushed to the limit by an array of converging circumstances. Many of these incidents illustrate the stress points of urban life that audiences will recognize from the daily news or from their own experiences. On the other hand, the character is clearly out of touch with reason. When he again calls Beth from the back room of the surplus store after killing the owner, and he speaks darkly of his intentions, most viewers will have withdrawn their sympathies. Nevertheless, his sudden action of destroying a telephone booth after an angry man bellows at him for talking too long may tap into an audience's desire to rage at the system. The dangerous events of D-Fens' long trip home accumulate so rapidly that viewers may not notice the implausibilities: The unity of time manipulates by adding tension but masking contrivance.

Across town, Prendergast maps D-Fens' trail of violence and slowly closes in on him. Far from stress-free, Prendergast has transferred himself to a desk job in order to placate his high-strung wife. He sees connectedness in what others take to be a string of unrelated events and theorizes that one person may be responsible. Encouraged by the trust and friendship of his former partner, Sandra (Rachel Ticotin), Prendergast stands up to his wife, takes to the streets in pursuit of clues, and finally traces D-Fens to Beth's house.

The filmmakers encourage the audience to compare Prendergast with D-Fens through a number of parallels. Both grapple with job-related stress. Both lavish affection on unattainable daughters, D-Fens' daughter being kept from him by his wife and Prendergast's child having died years before. Their days are both dotted with tense phone conversations to their wives. Both distract themselves with the daydreams stirred by a musical paperweight that plays "London Bridge," the song that gives the film its title. The similarities even extend to their clothing, as both wear white shirts and striped ties. These pairings suggest that Prendergast functions as the opposite of D-Fens. Whereas D-Fens cracks from the accumulated pressures of his life, Prendergast manages to adapt and survive. D-Fens is surprised in the climactic scene to hear that he is thought of as "a bad guy." Prendergast reminds him that being lied to by society is nothing new: It does not excuse D-Fens' rampage of anger. Though the opposite trajectories of the two characters clarify that Prendergast represents order and control, the film may make D-Fens the more sympathetic at times. Accordingly, some critics faulted the film for its exploitative tendencies.

Glenn Hopp

Reviews

Chicago Tribune. February 26, 1993, VII, p. 19.
Commonweal. CXX, April 9, 1993, p. 21.
Entertainment Weekly. February 26, 1993, p. 38.
Films in Review. XLIV, May, 1993, p. 186.
The Hollywood Reporter. February 12, 1993, p. 7.
Los Angeles Times. February 26, 1993, p. F1.
The New York Times. February 26, 1993, p. B1.
The New Yorker. March 8, 1993, p. 98.
Newsweek. March 1, 1993, p. 80.
Sight and Sound. III, June, 1993, p. 52.
Time. March 1, 1993, p. 63.
Variety. February 12, 1993, p. 2.
The Washington Post. February 26, 1993, p. C1.

FARAWAY, SO CLOSE
(IN WEITER FERNE, SO NAH!)

Origin: Germany
Released: 1993
Released in U.S.: 1993
Production: Wim Wenders for Road Movies and Tobis Filmkunst; released by Sony
    Pictures Classics
Direction: Wim Wenders
Screenplay: Wim Wenders, Ulrich Zieger, and Richard Reitinger
Cinematography: Jurgen Jurges
Editing: Peter Przygodda
Production design: Albrecht Konrad
Sound: Gunther Kortwich
Makeup: Hasson von Hugo and Christine Atar
Costume design: Esther Walz
Music: Laurent Petitgand
MPAA rating: PG-13
Running time: 140 minutes

Principal characters:

Cassiel	Otto Sander
Raphaela	Nastassja Kinski
Peter Falk	Himself
Damiel	Bruno Ganz
Marion	Solveig Dommartin
Tony Baker	Horst Buchholz
Lou Reed	Himself
Emit Flesti	Willem Dafoe
Mikhail Gorbachev	Himself
Konrad	Heinz Ruhmann
Phillip Winter	Rudiger Vogler
Patzke	Ronald Nitschke

Faraway, So Close is a sequel to Wim Wenders' *Wings of Desire* (1987), which has often been described as a "cult classic"—a film that escaped popular notice but possesses such merit that it continues to survive in reruns because a faithful band of followers support it and spread its reputation by word of mouth. Some cult classics, such as the original *Night of the Living Dead* (1968), are overlooked because they are in a genre that appeals only to a minority; others are overlooked because they are in a foreign language and many filmgoers find it diffult to watch the faces and read the subtitles at the same time.

Wings of Desire was not only in a foreign language but in German, which is traditionally less popular with American audiences than French or Italian. The cultists are certainly right about Wenders' classic: It is a great film that deserves to be better known. Fortunately, it is available on videotape and even appears on independent television stations at off-hours. Its success inspired Wenders to make a sequel.

Otto Sander, who bears a remarkable resemblance to the British actor John Hurt, returns as Cassiel, the guardian angel who roams the streets of Berlin silently observing the suffering of humanity and sharing the pain. This is the feature of *Wings of Desire* that apparently appeals to the cultists. There is a metaphysical truth contained in this visual metaphor to which people respond. In fact, guardian angels were very much in vogue in the early 1990's, and *Wings of Desire* may have been partly responsible. Even though Wenders' guardian angels can only suffer in silence, it is touching to think that someone might understand and care.

Faraway, So Close opens in black-and-white with a stunning shot of Cassiel standing on the enormous statue of the Angel of Victory overlooking post-Cold War Berlin. The statue looks as tall as the Statue of Liberty, but Cassiel, being an angel, is not troubled by vertigo and does not even bother to hang on to anything, although many in the audience will grip their armrests.

Cassiel's sensitive face bears the marks of silent suffering. One hears his thoughts through voice-over narration, as in the original *Wings of Desire*. He is becoming frustrated with his inability to do anything but suffer along with all the misguided human beings who make themselves and others miserable because they cannot see the truth that angels see: the truth that, although everybody feels lonely and everybody suffers, each individual thinks he or she is unique and is suffering alone.

In his sequel, Wenders has had the inspiration to include a female angel; the angels in the original film were middle-aged males wrapped in drab overcoats for protection against the dour Berlin weather. Raphaela (Nastassja Kinski) is Cassiel's companion; his conversations with her throughout the film give Wenders the opportunity to do away with some of the cumbersome voice-over dialogue. Cinema connoisseurs will appreciate the technical improvements over the original version, even though they may not like the sequel as well.

One of the startling technical innovations is the use of color. When Cassiel exceeds his angelic authority by catching a little girl who has toppled over a rail and is falling from a balcony toward certain death, he automatically loses his divine status and becomes a human being. At this point, the film switches from black-and-white to full color, in a manner reminiscent of that historic moment in motion-picture history when Judy Garland as Dorothy stepped out of the house that had just blindsided the wicked witch in *The Wizard of Oz* (1939).

In *Faraway, So Close*, the transition to color represents Cassiel's sudden awareness of what it is like to be human. He is astonished by the rich sensory experiences that humans take for granted. He begins to explore Berlin with his new insight, reveling in tastes, sights, sounds, and smells. He encounters a number of colorful characters, including former angels and angels in disguise. He tries alcohol for the first time and gets drunk. When he wakes up with a bad hangover, he begins to realize the drawbacks of being human. For one thing, he is faced with the harsh necessity of earning money so that he can buy food and shelter. Instead of seeing an angel suffering with human beings, the human beings in the audience find themselves suffering with an angel.

Because of his naïveté and urgent need of money, Cassiel gets involved with bad company. To him, human beings are all alike because of their common spiritual blindness. He becomes a well-paid henchman of Tony Baker (Horst Buchholz), a crooked businessman with a likable personality. Cassiel has fun playing at being a crook until Baker shows him a huge cache of sophisticated weaponry he intends to export to fuel the fires of ethnic hatred in other parts of the world. Cassiel decides to double-cross his employer and destroy this deadly merchandise.

Peter Falk makes a cameo appearance in *Faraway, So Close*, as he did in *Wings of Desire*. Evidently, the German public has a very high regard for this actor through watching his many *Columbo* films on television. As in *Wings of Desire*, Falk looks flattered to be included in a foreign art film and seems to be having a good time. He uses his charisma to cast a spell over several guards and keep them occupied while Cassiel leads a band of men into a secret warehouse where the contraband arms are stored. This leads to an American-motion-picture-style shoot-out that is one of the most regrettable features of this uneven film. Cassiel is killed by a sinister supernatural figure named Patzke (Ronald Nitschke), who has been dogging his footsteps throughout the film like someone out of an old Jean Cocteau film and warning him against the dangers of interfering in human activities. Once again, Cassiel finds himself an angel, sadder but wiser for his mortal experiences.

Unfortunately, there seems to be an iron law of cinema forbidding sequels and remakes to be as good as the originals. It is hard to think of an exception. The 1990's have seen such a flurry of sequels and remakes that some critics wondered whether Hollywood might be running out of inspiration. Inevitably, the clones evoke comparison with the fondly remembered black-and-white originals, to the disadvantage of the former. Two examples are *Night and the City* (1992) and *Cape Fear* (1991), both featuring superstar Robert De Niro. Neither charmed audiences or critics like the originals—the 1950 version of *Night and the City* starring Richard Widmark or the 1962 version of *Cape Fear* starring the smouldering Robert Mitchum.

The remakes and sequels are almost always far more expensive than the originals, not only because of inflation but because the producers seem to want to suggest that they are offering a "new and improved" product. Such is the case with *Faraway, So Close*. Everything is bigger and better, including the use of color. The film runs for two hours and twenty minutes, which is at least a half hour too long for even the most loyal Wenders fans. There is a trapeze act in the sequel, just as in the original; but the trapeze is so enormous and oscillates so far that it has to be strung up in the middle of the street, although no explanation is offered for why the aerialists are allowed to block traffic.

The audience cannot help but be confused. There are angels who used to be mortals and mortals who used to be angels. The angel named Patzke seems to be working for the opposition or else belongs to a sort of angelic Gestapo that has never been mentioned in scripture. The touching notion of invisible guardian angels watching over all of us, which was the most attractive feature of *Wings of Desire*, gets buried under a heavy frosting of questionable supernatural improvisation.

Cinematic clones fall short of their prototypes because they lack a certain ingenuousness. With remakes and sequels, viewers often have the feeling that they are being manipulated and that the motive behind the production is the desire to exploit a proven property for residual cash profits. Such is the case with *Faraway, So Close*. It received only lukewarm reviews in the United States and was a box-office disappointment in spite of the fact that it has the distinction of having been awarded the Grand Jury Prize at the 1993 Cannes Film Festival.

Bill Delaney

Reviews

Boston Globe. January 28, 1994, p. 47.
Chicago Tribune. December 23, 1993, V, p. 10.
The Guardian. May 19, 1993, p. 5.
The Hollywood Reporter. May 19, 1993, p. 5.
Los Angeles Times. December 21, 1993, p. F6.
The Nation. CCLVI, June 21, 1993, p. 881.
The New York Times. December 22, 1993, p. B3.
San Francisco Chronicle. December 23, 1993, p. E10.
Time. CXLIII, January 10, 1994, p. 59.
Variety. May 18, 1993, p. 30.
The Washington Post. February 11, 1993, p.B7.

FAREWELL MY CONCUBINE

Origin: Hong Kong
Released: 1993
Released in U.S.: 1993
Production: Hsu Feng for Tomson Films, in association with China Film
   Coproduction Corp. and Beijing Film Studio; released by Miramax Films.
Direction: Chen Kaige
Screenplay: Lilian Lee and Lu Wei; based on the novel by Lee
Cinematography: Gu Changwei
Editing: Pei Xiaonan
Production design: Chen Huaikai
Art direction: Yang Yuhe and Yang Zhanjia
Set decoration: Wang Chunpu, Zhang Ruihe, Song Wanxiang, and Cui Xiurong
Sound: Tao Jing and Hu He
Makeup: Fan Qingshan and Xu Guangrui
Costume design: Chen Changmin
Peking Opera direction: Shi Yansheng
Peking Opera music design: Tang Jirong
Music: Zhao Jiping
MPAA rating: R
Running time: 156 minutes

> *Principal characters:*
> Cheng Dieyi (Douzi) . . . . Leslie Cheung
> Duan Xiaolou (Shitou) . . . . Zhang Fengyi
> Juxian. . . . . Gong Li
> Guan Jifa . . . . Lu Qi
> Na Kun. . . . . Ying Da
> Master Yuan. . . . . Ge You
> Laizi. . . . . Li Dan
> Red Guard . . . . David Wu
> Douzi (as a child) . . . . Ma Mingwei
> Douzi's mother . . . . Jiang Wenli
> Zhang. . . . . Tong Di

Winner of the Palme d'or at Cannes and Academy Award nominee for best foreign language film, *Farewell My Concubine* is a stunningly beautiful epic about love and betrayal, of not only individuals but a country and its culture. The story spans fifty years, as China's turbulent history parallels the complex relationship between two male opera stars.

The film opens in 1977 at a basketball stadium with two colorfully garbed actors performing the ancient opera *Farewell My Concubine*. An observer in the near-empty bleachers recognizes the two as being once-famous actors. The bulk of the film then becomes an extended flashback, beginning in 1925 in Peking, China, where young boys from the All Luck and Happiness Theater Academy perform to an unappreciative public-square crowd. An impressed prostitute (Jiang Wenli) and her young son (Ma Mingwei) are among the spectators.

After the performance, the prostitute takes her boy, Douzi, to the academy and begs them to accept him. He is too old to hang around the brothel while she services her clients. Unfortunately, Douzi is rejected when it is found he has a sixth finger on one hand. The desperate mother takes the boy into an alley and chops off the extra finger with a meat cleaver. Thus begins the difficult journey of young Douzi.

Douzi has a hard time adjusting to school life. The tough disciplinarian Master Guan Jifa (Lu Qi) and the other boys ridicule Douzi because of his prostitute mother. He does, however, find comfort with a tough yet kind student, Shitou. In the Peking Opera, actors are trained in certain types of roles, in which they specialize for life. Douzi, with a natural feminine beauty, is trained for female roles, while Shitou is given masculine military parts. Douzi, however, has difficulty accepting his role as a woman, but eventually does so so as not to disappoint his fellow students.

One day, Douzi catches the eye of a former imperial eunuch, Zhang (Tong Di), who invites him to his chambers after a show and molests the innocent child. Douzi leaves Zhang's home in a state of shock. On the way back to school, Douzi finds an abandoned baby and brings him back to the school.

The narrative then jumps forward a decade to the eve of the Japanese invasion. Douzi (Leslie Cheung) and Shitou (Zhang Fengyi) are famous stars—now called Cheng Dieyi and Duan Xiaolou—known for their performances in *Farewell My Concubine*. The ancient opera is about a great king who is about to lose his kingdom to the enemy. Against the king's wishes, his concubine refuses to flee for her life, killing herself with his sword rather than betray her king.

For Cheng (Douzi), their stage relationship crosses over to real life. He is in love with Duan (Shitou) and believes him to be his king. As in the opera, Cheng vows to stay loyal forever. His heart is broken, however, when Duan announces his engagement to a beautiful prostitute, Juxian (Gong Li). Crushed, Cheng announces that he will never sing with Duan again, then begins an illicit affair with Master Yuan (Ge You), who becomes his patron and lover. That night, Japanese troops enter the city.

One evening, while Cheng is onstage performing *The Drunken Concubine* alone, Duan is arrested for resisting a military policeman. When Cheng is invited to perform at the Japanese military headquarters, Juxian begs him to perform for Duan's life. He agrees only after she promises to return to the house of prostitution and never see Duan again. After Duan is released, instead of being grateful, he is furious that Cheng betrayed his country by performing for the enemy. In addition, Juxian breaks her promise and returns to Duan. Devastated, Cheng turns to a life of opium addiction.

When the now-ancient Master Guan invites both Cheng and Duan back to the All Luck and Happiness Theater Academy to reprimand them for not performing together, they see the mistake they made. While visiting, Cheng and Duan also discover that the abandoned baby whom they found years ago is Xaio Si, now a student at the school. Soon after, Master Guan dies and the school is disbanded. Together, the three walk the streets as the Nationalist forces take control of the city.

A year later, during a performance, Cheng is arrested as a traitor for singing to the Japanese years earlier. Juxian agrees to help Duan attempt to have him released, only after he promises to end his relationship if they succeed. They beg Master Yuan to use his influence to help. Master Yuan lies for Cheng during the trial, saying Cheng sung only because he was at gunpoint, but Cheng refuses to confirm this story. Cheng has, in essence, committed suicide. Ironically, Cheng is ultimately acquitted when a high-ranking official comes to town and wants to hear him sing. Thus, his singing was both the cause of his troubles and his saving grace.

By 1949, the Communist revolution has taken the country. Master Yuan is one of the first counterrevolutionaries executed by the Communists. Even the opera itself is changed to agree with the new ideology. Xiao Si and Cheng are at odds in their political and operatic views. One night, Cheng is replaced by Xiao Si to play the role of the concubine. Duan, not wanting to be politically persecuted, decides to go on regardless. Cheng is once again left heartbroken.

Duan and Cheng arc persecuted nevertheless in 1966 when the Great Proletarian Cultural Revolution arrives. Under pressure from a wild mob, Duan betrays Cheng by revealing his homosexual "crimes." Cheng responds by telling them about Juxian's prostitution past. To save himself, Duan declares that he is leaving her. Betrayed, Juxian then kills herself. Finally, the narrative returns to the opening basketball court scene, where Cheng performs *Farewell My Concubine* one last time with Duan, then kills himself. Duan stands contemplating above Cheng's dead body as the film fades out.

Betrayal and loyalty are by far the most prevalent themes in this film. At the film's center is Cheng's sense of betrayal when Duan marries Juxian. Yet even Cheng eventually betrays the man he loves when he reveals Duan's wife as a former prostitute. In the ultimate irony, Cheng is betrayed by the baby whose life he saved, Xiao Si. From a historical point of view, one witnesses the betrayal and raping of a country— and its culture—that was once so beautiful and innocent.

The screenwriters did a beautiful job interweaving the country's turbulent past into the story. This political and social turmoil provides a colorful backdrop against which is set a classic tale of love and betrayal. Also, in a nice change from typical motion-picture fare, very little time is spent on Cheng's homosexuality beyond the creation of sexual tension and the conflict of Cheng's more contemporary difficulty coping with it.

Leslie Cheung turns in an amazing performance as Cheng, a confused, pained, and jealous man who cannot distinguish between male or female, reality or dream. He is doomed to fail to achieve the one thing he wants, Duan's love. His movements, both on-and offstage, are careful and precise, not unlike a woman's. At times, in fact, it is hard to believe he is a man. Zhang Fengyi also does a convincing job as Duan, a man torn between friendship and love. Gong Li, as Juxian, and the rest of the supporting cast should all be applauded for fine performances. The acting is all top drawer.

Cinematically, this operatic film works equally well, if not surpassing the high level of the story and acting. The rich, colorful sets successfully evoke the past and show just how beautiful Chinese cinema can be. The cinematography, which was impressive enough to be nominated for an Academy Award in that category, is subtle and moving. The music, with its high shrill opera sound, is equally captivating, always setting the mood for what is present, and what is to come.

Everything about this film is intoxicating. Watching *Farewell My Concubine* is a visual, aural, and emotional treat that most film audiences will not want to miss.

Jonathan David

Reviews

Beijing Review. XXXVI, June 28, 1993, p. 29.
Films in Review. XLV, January, 1994, p. 49.
Los Angeles Times. October 22, 1993, p. F1.
The Nation. CCLVII, July 5, 1993, p. 38.
The New York Times. October 8, 1993, p. B1.
The New Yorker. LXIX, October 11, 1993, p. 121.
Newsweek. CXXII, November 1, 1993, p. 74.
Sight and Sound. IV, January, 1994, p. 41.
Variety. May 20, 1993, p. 19.
The Washington Post. October 27, 1993, p. C10.
World Press Review. XL, March, 1993, p. 47.

FEARLESS

Production: Paula Weinstein and Mark Rosenberg for Spring Creek; released by
   Warner Bros.
Direction: Peter Weir
Screenplay: Rafael Yglesias; based on his novel
Cinematography: Allen Daviau
Editing: William Anderson
Production design: John Stoddart
Art direction: Chris Burian-Mohr
Set decoration: John Anderson
Casting: Howard Feuer
Sound: Charles Wilborn
Costume design: Marilyn Matthews
Music: Maurice Jarre
MPAA rating: R
Running time: 122 minutes

> *Principal characters:*
> Max Klein . . . . Jeff Bridges
> Laura Klein . . . . Isabella Rossellini
> Carla Rodrigo . . . . Rosie Perez
> Brillstein . . . . Tom Hulce
> Dr. Bill Perlman. . . . . John Turturro
> Manny Rodrigo . . . . Benicio del Toro
> Nan Gordon . . . . Deirdre O'Connell
> Jeff Gordon . . . . John de Lancie
> Jonah Klein . . . . Spencer Vrooman

Director Peter Weir has fashioned an intense and moving film about life and death
that has found virtually unanimous praise. It is a beautifully wrought piece of work,
written by Rafael Yglesias—based on his novel—with resonance for anyone who has
pondered the meaning of life or who has faced death. This film is sure to take its place
as one of the most significant American films in recent memory.

A ghostly silence and a dreamlike fog engulf the screen as the film opens. Soon, the
audience discovers Max (Jeff Bridges) leading several people, all in tattered and
bloody clothes, through a cornfield. The next image is the aftermath of a huge airplane
crash. Bits of luggage, a bottle of champagne, ambulances, police, and distraught
passengers litter a highway landscape. Max and his partner (John de Lancie) had been
passengers, but Max's partner died in the crash. Max is discovered to have been the
"Good Samaritan" who helped save people from the crash. He develops a sense of
invincibility, enforced by the mythology and hero-worship of his "Good Samaritan"
identity. Nevertheless, Max returns home in a severely withdrawn and emotionally

impenetrable state. This causes deep pain and uncertainty for his son (Spencer Vrooman) and wife, Laura (Isabella Rossellini). A well-meaning but rather helpless psychiatrist, Dr. Perlman (John Turturro), introduces Max to Carla (Rosie Perez), a survivor of the same crash, whose infant son was killed. The friendship between Max and Carla, and the walls built between Max and his family, form the core of the film. Max helps the severely depressed and guilty Carla to gain perspective on her tragedy, and Carla helps Max to feel human again. It is a beautifully structured story in which character, plot, and theme are artfully interwoven by Yglesias.

Weir has extraordinary mastery of the technical aspects of the medium. He is not a director who prefers technically complex camera angles or effects unless they are valuable to the theme or story. In an early scene, Max walks into a busy intersection and, miraculously, no cars hit him. Once across the street, he lies down on a low wall and looks up at heaven, saying "You can't do it! You want to kill me but you can't." The camera looks down from high above, with Max far below, laughing and mocking God. This and another scene in which he stands on the ledge of a building are wonderfully visual ways to show Max's inner life: He is certain that, after having survived a plane crash, he is invincible.

Weir and writer Yglesias mete out the flashbacks of the crash in small increments over the course of the film. All the flashbacks leading up to the crash are bathed in bright light and have eerie synthesized sounds, like a wind tunnel. In the last flashback, however, in which the audience finally sees the crash itself, there are no sound effects. The crash is shown in harrowing detail, with brilliant special effects of people being hurled about the airplane, luggage tumbling around, passengers screaming and holding one another. The scene is edited so that the audience barely has a chance to know the image it is seeing before another one jumps on to the screen. It is a chaotic and frightening moment, captured in vivid and disturbing detail.

Light plays an important role in the technical aspect of this film. To symbolize the light seen by those who perish in the crash, and to foreshadow the symbolic "light" seen by Max, Carla, and Laura as they struggle with their inner turmoil, Weir introduces bright lights at many points throughout the film. Early in the film, Max is in a motel room, alone after the crash. When he answers the door to his room, wrapped in the bedsheets, a bright light bursts into the room from the right side of the screen, making Bridges look Christ-like. There are occasional other flashes of light during film: the lights from a passing car on Carla's face; the single street lamp shining on Max's car, alone in a parking lot; or Carla bathed in blinding light after an emotional catharsis, symbolizing her new understanding. Conversely, in the same scene, Laura enters the room from downstairs, from a hallway with no light, underscoring her powerlessness and inability to understand what is happening to her marriage.

This is a severe and introspective film, with an intensely spiritual core. The filmmakers intended to illuminate the hyperreality experienced by crash survivors, and achieved their goal. They have paid great attention to detail, capturing unique glimpses of the city (and in particular, the architecture) of San Francisco. Max's and Carla's searing experience translates into an acute awareness of their world, to the extreme that it looks like a new world. It is almost as if they have come "through the looking glass," and the audience goes with them. One particularly powerful image is of Carla approaching a woman holding an infant as they window-shop. In slow-motion, Carla approaches the baby, caresses its head lovingly, gives a warm kiss, and walks away unnoticed. "It's like I'm a ghost," she says. Bridges tells her that they are ghosts: "We died already. We passed through death."

Indeed, there is an otherworldly quality to this film. Spare use of music—Maurice Jarre did the excellent score—somber, artful cinematography by Allen Daviau, an unusually thoughtful script by Yglesias, and introspective performances are only some of the reasons why *Fearless* has such a rich and compelling atmosphere. At the helm is Weir, who has achieved this same potency in the past: *The Last Wave* (1977) and *The Year of Living Dangerously* (1982) both had a similar, spectral quality, but were far less accessible. *Fearless* achieves the ghostly quality pervasive in those films, but with the humanity found in *Witness* (1985) and *Dead Poets Society* (1989).

Bridges' Max is a man who has had life taken away and then restored, with a glazed acceptance that he is alive, if only for now. His inner turbulence is palpable even as his outward manner remains aloof and detached. He hits Perlman, the psychologist, immediately after meeting him; he drives down a highway with his body half out of the car, like a puppy, with a self-satisfied grin; he hyperventilates when situations get too sensitive, and his panic gives way to a bemused smirk when he endangers his life once again—and survives once again. The constant cycle of danger-death-redemption is evident in everything Max does. Max's tumultuous struggle is made more gripping by Bridges' astonishing ability to portray a man who is suppressing massive fear and grief, but is nevertheless ruled by his pain.

The other performances are marvelous. Isabella Rossellini is honest and regal as a woman who feels her marriage and happiness slipping away from her, powerless to do anything. Rossellini will inevitably be compared to her mother, screen legend Ingrid Bergman, and here she exceeds expectations.

Rosie Perez is similarly astonishing. She is the squeaky-voiced actress who played Woody Harrelson's girlfriend in *White Men Can't Jump* (1992) and is the Emmy-winning choreographer of television's *In Living Color*. Here, Perez establishes herself as a bona fide screen star with her powerful portrayal of a young woman immobile with grief over the loss of her baby. Two of the film's most powerful scenes are propelled by Perez as Carla. The first is an unusual scene of a group-therapy-style encounter of the crash survivors led by the innocuous Dr. Perlman. It is wrenching from the start, with one woman standing up and disclosing that she was not on the plane, but her son was killed in the crash. "I don't remember kissing him goodbye," she says to the group. Later, she tells Carla, "You're very young." Carla stoically replies, "I'm not very young," and at that moment, Perez loses her youthfulness, revealing a deep melancholy. Then she confronts the flight attendant who had told her "it would be okay," screaming "You told me it would be okay, and it wasn't! You lied to me!" Perez keeps Carla at such a high emotional pitch that she appears almost to lose control in the film's other most powerful scene. Revealing a deep secret to Max, she chants Hail Marys to relieve her unbearable guilt, building to an hysterical attack of tears. What is particularly remarkable is that Perez's intensity and her character's sorrow never cross the line into bathos or mawkishness. This is an exceptional performance.

Max says to Carla: "Life and death. They happen for no reason. People think we die because we eat red meat or rob banks. We can't accept that there is randomness, because there'd be no reason to love." The pain of the question of life's randomness haunts the characters in this heartfelt film.

Kirby Tepper

Reviews
Chicago Tribune. October 15, 1993, VII, p. 31.
The Christian Science Monitor. October 22, 1993, p. 10.
Entertainment Weekly. October 15, 1993, p. 48.
The Hollywood Reporter. October 11, 1993, p. 5.
Los Angeles Times. October 15, 1993, p. F4.
National Review. XLV, November 29, 1993, p. 69.
The New York Times. October 15, 1993, The Living Arts, P. B6.
The New Yorker. LXIX, October 25, 1993, p. 120.
Newsweek. CXXII, October 18, 1993, p. 85.
Time. CXLII, October 18, 1993, p. 98.
Variety. October 11, 1993, p. 2.
The Washington Post. October 29, 1993, p. B1.

THE FIRM

Production: Scott Rudin, John Davis, and Sydney Pollack for Mirage; released by
    Paramount Pictures
Direction: Sydney Pollack
Screenplay: David Rabe, Robert Towne, and David Rayfiel; based on the novel by
    John Grisham
Cinematography: John Seale
Editing: William Steinkamp and Fredric Steinkamp
Production design: Richard MacDonald
Art direction: John Willett
Set decoration: Casey Hallenbeck
Casting: David Rubin
Sound: David MacMillan
Costume design: Ruth Myers
Music: Dave Grusin
MPAA rating: R
Running time: 154 minutes

Principal characters:

Mitch McDeere	Tom Cruise
Abby McDeere	Jeanne Tripplehorn
Avery Tolar	Gene Hackman
Oliver Lambert	Hal Holbrook
Lamar Quinn	Terry Kinney
William Devasher	Wilford Brimley
Wayne Tarrance	Ed Harris
Tammy Hemphill	Holly Hunter
Ray McDeere	David Strathairn
Eddie Lomax	Gary Busey
F. Denton Voyles	Steven Hill
Nordic man	Tobin Bell
Kay Quinn	Barbara Garrick
Royce McKnight	Jerry Hardin
Thomas Richie	Paul Calderon
Sonny Capps	Jerry Weintraub
Barry Abanks	Sullivan Walker
Nathan Locke	John Beal
Young woman on beach	Karina Lombard
Elvis Hemphill	Tommy Matthews

Widely touted as the tale of a "yuppie Faust" seeking moral redemption from 1980's
greed, the novel *The Firm* (1991) had captivated seven million readers in twenty-nine

languages by the time of the film's release. Facing the tough job of pleasing already-pleased readers, director Sydney Pollack (who also directed *Tootsie* in 1982 and *Three Days of the Condor* in 1975) continued the 1990's trend—as depicted in such films as *The Doctor* (1991), *Regarding Henry* (1991), and *Grand Canyon* (1991)—of telling tales of life after gluttony. Said Pollack, according to the film's production notes, *"The Firm* reflects people's awareness in the '90s of the possibility of making incremental incursions into your own morality and the potential of one day waking up to realize you're not who you wanted to be."

As the film opens, Mitch McDeere (Tom Cruise), an honors graduate from Harvard Law School, is pursued by a variety of big-city, big-time law firms, a pursuit he finds pleasurable after his impoverished childhood and his years of struggle and contemptible jobs. Much to his surprise—and to the surprise of his wife, Abby (Jeanne Tripplehorn)—Mitch's best offer comes from a smaller firm located in Memphis, Tennessee: Bendini, Lambert & Locke. Bendini, Lambert & Locke has offered him everything: a huge salary, a great car, a new home. The firm will even pay his student loans. Mitch accepts.

Mitch and Abby move to Memphis, and dedicated, hardworking Mitch gets right to work, putting in long hours devising innovative solutions to clients' tax problems. Abby, however, is getting a different view of life with the firm. For example, she begins to feel the firm's iron grip when she is told that they will allow her to work, although children are encouraged. Then, with the "accidental" death of two partners, Mitch also begins to wonder about his new colleagues. Only when he is approached by FBI agent Wayne Tarrance (Ed Harris) and U.S. Department of Justice honcho F. Denton Voyles (Steven Hill), who inform him of the firm's misdeeds, is Mitch ready to believe that what looked too good to be true really is. With the help of a strong cast of minor characters (Eddie Lomax played by Gary Busey and Tammy Hemphill played by Holly Hunter, for example), Mitch wakes up and battles the powers and evils around him.

A film like *The Firm* banks on the allure of the legal profession, even as it portrays attorneys as capable of any misdeed. In Hollywood, audiences once were entertained by attorneys' astute powers of deduction and their swelling court-room soliloquies, such as in *The Caine Mutiny* (1954), *Witness for the Prosecution* (1957), *Anatomy of a Murder* (1959), or *To Kill a Mockingbird* (1962). Even more modern presentations of these officers of the court as fallen and flawed, such as *The Verdict* (1982), show that the lost can still rise to brilliance. *The Firm*, on the other hand, focuses on the wealth, privilege, and related trappings that in the 1990's were inseparable from the Hollywood version of lawyers: designer suits (the film shows Mitch being tailored for his custom suits), fancy cars (Mitch's black convertible Mercedes awaits his arrival in Memphis), leather chairs in book-lined offices. It is no accident that Tom Cruise's Mitch McDeere attends job interviews in poorly fitted suits and wrinkled shirts, only rising to tailored appeal once he is with the firm. It is no accident that the film shows the McDeeres' arrival and departure from Memphis in their old, battered—but honest—car. While the film refrains from speculating about the jobs Mitch did not take, it is clear that one of the signs of evil within this firm is lucre: condominiums in the Cayman Islands, fleets of Mercedes automobiles, opulent furnishings. Even the firm's thugs are dignified, well dressed, issuing only soft-spoken—if venomous— threats. Here the mob, the government, and felons are minor threats compared to practicing attorneys.

On the flip side, viewers will find the regular folk—plain spoken, hard-living— offering a chance of redemption. Among these are Mitch McDeere's convict brother, Ray (David Strathairn). Probably Mitch's truest friend, Ray is nevertheless an embar- rassment to upwardly mobile Mitch, who denies Ray's existence more than once. In one particularly telling scene, Mitch goes to visit Ray in prison, admitting that he has denied his brother in order to get the best job. Ray, slow-talking and gentle, forgives Mitch, countering that he too denies having Mitch as a brother, because having an Ivy League lawyer for a brother does not ingratiate one with one's colleagues in prison. Still, it is Ray and his friends Eddie Lomax and Tammy Hemphill who provide instrumental aid in Mitch's rescue. Their world is the world of prison-cell friendships and plain old street smarts. *The Firm* is clear in its lesson on how to determine who one's real friends are, citing the lowly for their steadiness, castigating the lofty for their arrogance. Quickly *The Firm* becomes a morality tale. While the form is not necessarily unpalatable, it is simplistic and not the strength of the film. *The Firm*'s bankable feature is the performances of the minor characters.

While the film received mixed reviews, most critics agreed on the power of the minor characters. Perhaps the three best performances are those given by Holly Hunter, Gary Busey, and Gene Hackman (as Mitch's mentor Avery Tolar). In John Grisham's novel *The Firm*, Tammy Hemphill is even more of a player in Mitch's escape from the firm. Even with her reduced play time in the film, however, the secretary is cagey, amiable, loyal—and fun to watch in her amusing assortment of outfits and her alarming assortment of predicaments. In one particularly fine scene, Tammy Hemphill comes to the firm to find McDeere, posing as the breakfast delivery person. Her fear is palpable, as is her grief in the next scene when she discusses the loss of her true love. Later she handles the secret handoffs and clandestine photocopying with precision, a true professional, pausing only momentarily for a worried look or to gnaw distractedly on her acrylic nails. Hunter brings to Hemphill the warm, molasses Southern accent that has put many of her other characters on the map, such as in *Miss Firecracker* (1989) and *Raising Arizona* (1987). It is a memorable performance and one for which she received an Academy Award nomination.

Gary Busey, perhaps best known for his portrayal of rocker Buddy Holly in *The Buddy Holly Story* (1978), has only two scenes as seedy, honest-when-it-counts detective Eddie Lomax. Yet he is mesmerizingly on target in both. Cowboy boots and Southern good-ol'-boy drawl in place, Busey's Lomax listens to Mitch's troubles and promises to help. If the characters in this film are developed at least in part by their surroundings, then it is no accident that Lomax's office is dark, smoky, low-rent, with a cannon of a gun strapped below the desk in case of trouble. Like his office, Lomax may not look like much, but he delivers when necessary. Busey takes his few moments on screen and builds a likable, colorful, interesting character.

Gene Hackman's last film before *The Firm* was Clint Eastwood's *Unforgiven* (1992), in which he played a sheriff who was both good and bad, and for which he received an Academy Award. In *The Firm*, Hackman's Avery Tolar is also good and bad. After all, he is part of the firm, the lawyers gone bad, who are the central menace in the film. At best, he looks the other way as certain members of the firm handle particularly seedy yet profitable business. At best, he bends the tax law to save his clients large amounts of money. At worst, he profits from it all. Tolar would be indistinguishable from the other forty-one lawyers at Bendini, Lambert & Locke except for one key scene. Pretending to believe he has successfully lured Abby to the Cayman Islands for a weekend of extramarital bliss, Tolar combines alcohol and, unknowingly, drugs, resulting in a variety of truth serum. Hackman then exposes the core of Avery Tolar, the disappointment, the lovelessness that is his life. It is a chilling, memorable scene, a true turn of the artist. In the words of one critic, "Hackman redeems this character from the simplistic moral verities that forever threaten to engulf the story, investing him with rueful tints and sad, affecting self-knowledge and self-loathing."

Among the other minor characters of interest is Wilford Brimley as the venomous William Devasher, who is in charge of the firm's security. Brimley did a series of television commercials for a hot breakfast cereal, and he brings the same grandfatherly voice to *The Firm*, adding just a slight evil edge as he blackmails. Also, Tommy Matthews gives an amusing performance as a large, jolly Elvis impersonator who is also Tammy's husband.

The main characters in the film are somehow less entertaining. Tom Cruise comes to *The Firm* from his Golden Globe-nominated portrayal of a Navy lawyer in *A Few Good Men* (1992). Unlike his character in *A Few Good Men*, however, Cruise's McDeere has no courtroom battles, no profound dialogue. He is simply an over-achiever who made a really bad career move. As an ambitious initiate seduced by wealth and power, the character of Mitch McDeere is among the most standard and is, as a result, one of the softer and flatter ones in the film. Cruise himself appears to be sleepwalking through much of the film—dazed, confused, slow to react. As his wife, Abby, Jeanne Tripplehorn serves as moral beacon and long-suffering wife. While Tripplehorn looks nice (at least one critic has compared her to Genevieve Bujold in appearance), she is given little to do in the film beyond serve as the prophet of doom. Further, little heat arises from the pairing of Cruise and Tripplehorn, although the Hackman-Tripplehorn match appears more promising. The older partners, led by Hal Holbrook (as Oliver Lambert), are more tedious than venomous. Resembling the gathered flock in *The Secret of NIMH* (1982), the middle-aged partners are little more than bad boys who plot to steal and win. With their rigid rituals (tutoring associates for the bar exam) and joyless celebrations (champagne in the library, congratulating associates who pass the bar), they are narrow in scope, minor in menace.

Even beyond the myriad characters in *The Firm*, the screenplay was challenging to construct. First the filmmakers had to decide whether to follow the book exactly or revise the text in light of the different medium; given that cuts from the five-hundred-page novel were necessary, the decisions on what to cut came next: the complicated cat-and-mouse ending? the myriad minor characters? What emerged is a compromise—for example, scaled-down minor characters and a changed ending—that in the words of Mitch McDeere is "not sexy, but . . . has teeth." A group of exceptionally well-credentialed writers accomplished this rebuilding of Grisham's novel: playwright David Rabe, author of "Streamers" and "Sticks and Bones"; Robert Towne, who won an Academy Award for *Chinatown* (1974); and David Rayfiel, who had worked with Pollack on *Three Days of the Condor* (1975) and *Havana* (1990). The result was a hit. *The Firm* grossed $125 million in its first five weeks after its release on June 30 and had grossed over $250 million worldwide by year's end. In addition to Holly Hunter's nomination, the film also received an Academy Award nomination for its original score.

Shot on location in such picturesque locations as Memphis, Boston, and the Cayman Islands, *The Firm* provides plenty of pretty scenery and several strong performances. While few surprises await viewers, *The Firm* is not an unpleasant way to spend an afternoon.

Roberta F. Green

Reviews

Boston Globe. June 30, 1993, p. 53.
Chicago Tribune. June 30, 1993, Section 2, p. 1.
The Christian Science Monitor. July 6, 1993, p. 12.
Entertainment Weekly. July 9, 1993, p. 28.
Films in Review. XLIV, September, 1993, p. 336.
The Hollywood Reporter. June 28, 1993, p. 6.
Los Angeles Times. June 30, 1993, p. F1.
National Law Journal. XV, June 28, 1993, p. 6.
The New York Times. June 30, 1993, p. C15.
Newsweek. CXXII, July 5, 1993, p. 57.
Time. CXLII, July 5, 1993, p. 58.
Variety. June 28, 1993, p. 2.
The Washington Post. June 30, 1993, p. D1.

FREE WILLY

Production: Jennie Lew Tugend and Lauren Shuler-Donner, in association with Le Studio Canal Plus, Regency Enterprises, and Alcor Films; released by Warner Bros.
Direction: Simon Wincer
Screenplay: Keith A. Walker and Corey Blechman; based on a story by Walker
Cinematography: Robbie Greenberg
Editing: O. Nicholas Brown
Production design: Charles Rosen
Art direction: Diane Yates and Charles Butcher
Set decoration: Mary Olivia-McIntosh
Casting: Judy Taylor and Lynda Gordon
Sound: Clark King
Makeup: Pamela Westmore
Costume design: April Ferry
Whale animatronics: Walt Conti
Wildlife cinematography: Bob Talbot
Music: Basil Poledouris
Song: Michael Jackson, "Will You Be There"
MPAA rating: PG
Running time: 110 minutes

Principal characters:

Jesse	Jason James Richter
Rae Lindley	Lori Petty
Annie Greenwood	Jayne Atkinson
Randolph Johnson	August Schellenberg
Glen Greenwood	Michael Madsen
Dial	Michael Ironside
Wade	Richard Riehle
Dwight Mercer	Mykelti Williamson
Perry	Michael Bacall
Gwenie	Danielle Harris
Vector	Isaiah Malone
Willy	Keiko

Free Willy, set in the Pacific Northwest, tells the story of the friendship that develops between a twelve-year-old boy, Jesse (Jason James Richter), and a seven-thousand-pound orca whale, Willy (Keiko). Both virtual orphans and alienated from their caregivers, boy and animal form a bond of friendship based on mutual need.

The film opens with gorgeous shots of several whales frolicking in the ocean, pointing up the joy of freedom and the close familial bonds that whales have. This serenity is interrupted by a whaling boat, which suddenly intrudes on this idyllic scene. Ironically, the whaling boat is named the *Pequod*—the same name as that in Herman Melville's classic 1851 novel, *Moby Dick*. This modern-day Pequod, however, is equipped with sophisticated nets instead of lethal harpoons. Willy's fate is not death, as it would have been in Melville's time, but confinement in an aquatic theme park.

As for Jesse, he is one of the thousands of children whose home is the streets and who beg for money and steal food to exist. His mother abandoned him several years earlier to the care of the local social services agency, from which Jesse has recently run away. He is soon apprehended by the police and turned over to the care of foster parents Glen (Michael Madsen) and Annie Greenwood (Jayne Atkinson). Alienated and angry, Jesse stubbornly clings to the notion that his birth mother will return for him, even though nobody has heard from her in six years. Jesse is surly with all adults, including Dwight Mercer (Mykelti Williamson), the well-meaning social worker assigned to his case.

Willy displays similar antisocial behavior with his trainer at North West Adventure Park, Rae Lindley (Lori Petty), refusing to perform in his new environment. Although Rae cares about Willy, she has been unable to gain his trust after having performed a series of medical tests on him upon his arrival at the park.

Jesse and Willy meet when Jesse is sentenced to clean up the graffiti that he and his friend Perry (Michael Bacall) applied to Willy's holding tank prior to Jesse's capture by the police. The two hit it off instantly as Willy responds to Jesse's harmonica playing. The park staff is surprised by Willy's immediate acceptance of Jesse, as Willy is considered smart, but nasty, by the staff. As Jesse's bond with Willy grows stronger, he begins to regret the near-completion of his clean-up efforts. One night, he sneaks into the park and accidentally falls into Willy's tank.

As Jesse sinks to the bottom, unconscious, Willy comes to his rescue, saving Jesse's life by forcing him back to the surface. Randolph Johnson (August Schellenberg), the park's whale keeper, is touched by the bond between these two and offers Jesse a summer job at the park. To everyone's amazement, Jesse gets Willy to do things that the trainers cannot. Soon Jesse is working with Rae as a trainer, making tremendous progress with Willy.

Just as things appear to be going well, however, Willy, intimidated by the huge crowds, refuses to perform at his first big show. As a result, the park's owner, Dial (Michael Ironside), decides that Willy is not worth keeping. In a particularly drastic move, he and the park's general manager, Wade (Richard Riehle), decide to kill Willy for the insurance money. Jesse discovers the plot and, together with Rae, Randolph, and the Greenwoods, races to save Willy's life by releasing him back into the wild.

Fortunately, *Free Willy* only occasionally lapses into the cornball clichés that are rife in most family films. Despite the fact that the filmmakers felt it necessary to include the obligatory chase scene at the end of the film, it is an otherwise satisfying motion picture.

Free Willy is a true family film, one that will entertain children and adults alike. A boy befriending a large and powerful wild animal such as a whale will appeal to the younger members of the audience. On another level, the film contains an underlying message for the adults in the audience. The filmmakers take a firm stand against whales being held in captivity for the entertainment of humans. In this respect, *Free Willy* has succeeded in stimulating awareness and debate on the subject. Articles dealing with the captivity of whales appeared in several major magazines following the film's release.

Keiko, the whale that portrays Willy in the film, is a case in point. Keiko, a huge, thirteen-year-old whale living in an amusement park in Mexico City, is confined to a tank designed for a four-year-old whale. He has been in captivity for the last eleven years, too long to be released back into the wild himself, where he would surely perish without the human care on which he has come to rely. While the awareness and interest that *Free Willy* has generated may not secure Keiko's release, the publicity surrounding his plight has created a desire by many to improve his living conditions. On a larger scale, the film may be instrumental in the future preservation of whales in the wild.

Free Willy was a seven-year labor of love for producer Lauren Shuler-Donner and her husband, the film's executive producer, Richard Donner. Together, they have compiled an impressive team that has helped create a successful film. The talents of many of the people associated with the film are suited specifically to its needs.

Director Simon Wincer had worked previously on several films dealing with animals, such as *Phar Lap* (1984) and *The Lighthorsemen* (1987), as well as the made-for-television film *Lonesome Dove* (1989), for which Wincer won an Emmy Award. Director of photography Robbie Greenberg is helped immensely by Bob Talbot, who is credited as wildlife cinematographer. Talbot, working on his first feature-length film, is a world-renowned still photographer specializing in portraits of marine animals and aquatic scenes. Talbot's footage of the whales in the wild is beautiful, awe-inspiring work.

Even more amazing is the work of Walt Conti, the whale effects supervisor. Conti built a full-size, free-swimming animatronic version of Willy that is virtually indistinguishable from the real thing. Conti's creation, known as Animatronic Willy, advances technology far beyond the days of pulleys and wires. Animatronic Willy is itself a work of art. Conti had previously built the free-swimming miniature humpback whales used in *Star Trek IV: The Voyage Home* (1986) and the underwater vehicles in *The Abyss* (1989). Adding to this already well-qualified crew is associate producer Douglas C. Merrifield, a specialist in aquatic filming.

Unfortunately, the acting and the writing are not quite as impressive as the film's technical achievements. Yet, although the screenplay is predictable, the film remains satisfying. As Willy, Keiko steals the film away from his fellow—human—actors. Keiko performs warmly and intelligently, helping greatly to establish the believability of the story. Another impressive performance is by August Schellenberg as Randolph, the Haida Indian who instructs Jesse on Native American whale mythology and the importance of the whale to the Haida. Jason James Richter, in his feature-film debut as Jesse, does a creditable job, balancing the lovability and surliness that are associated with adolescence.

Ultimately, *Free Willy* is a cross between *E. T.: The Extra-Terrestrial* (1982) and the documentary *Streetwise* (1985). Jesse's existence on the streets, however, is not nearly as gritty and desperate as that of the real homeless children depicted in *Streetwise*; it is readily apparent that Jesse's grime is applied by a makeup artist. Like *E. T.*, *Free Willy* centers on the friendship that develops between a young boy and an exotic creature, in this case one from the depths of the ocean instead of outer space. Furthermore, the climax of *Free Willy*, like that of *E. T.*, involves returning the boy's new friend to his home. Although *Free Willy* lacks the sense of magic and wonder that made *E. T.* so successful, it remains an entertaining film that carries an important message.

George Delalis

Reviews
Chicago Tribune. July 16, 1993, VII, p. 29.
The Christian Science Monitor. July 30, 1993, p. 13.
Earth Island Journal. VIII, Fall, 1993, p. 29.
Entertainment Weekly. July 23, 1993, p. 44.
Film Review. March 1, 1994, p. 53.
The Hollywood Reporter. July 2, 1993, p. 6.
Los Angeles Times. July 16, 1993, p. F1.
The New York Times. July 16, 1993, p. B7.
Time. July 19, 1993, p. 59.
Variety. July 6, 1993, p. 5.
The Washington Post. July 16, 1993, p. 38.

THE FUGITIVE

Production: Arnold Kopelson; released by Warner Bros.
Direction: Andrew Davis
Screenplay: Jeb Stuart and David Twohy; based on a story by Twohy and on
    characters created by Roy Huggins
Cinematography: Michael Chapman
Editing: Dennis Virkler, David Finfer, Dean Goodhill, Don Brochu, Richard Nord,
    and Dov Hoenig
Production design: Dennis Washington
Art direction: Maher Ahmad
Set decoration: Rick Gentz
Casting: Amanda Mackey and Cathy Sandrich
Visual effects supervision: William Mesa
Sound: Scott D. Smith
Costume design: Aggie Guerard Rodgers
Music: James Newton Howard
MPAA rating: PG-13
Running time: 127 minutes

> *Principal characters:*
> Dr. Richard Kimble . . . . Harrison Ford
> Samuel Gerard . . . . Tommy Lee Jones (AA)
> Helen Kimble . . . . Sela Ward
> Cosmo Renfro. . . . . Joe Pantoliano
> Dr. Charles Nichols . . . . Jeroen Krabbe
> Sykes. . . . . Andreas Katsulas
> Dr. Anne Eastman. Julianne Moore
> Biggs. . . . . Daniel Roebuck
> Poole . . . . L. Scott Caldwell
> Newman . . . . Tom Wood

The Fugitive is one of the many big-budget films released in the early 1990's based
on popular television shows. The reasoning behind a motion-picture studio's decision
to give the megabudget treatment to a popular television show is hardly an artistic one.
Studio executives know that, even before the film premieres, there already exists a
large, enthusiastic audience intimately familiar with the film's premise, characters,
and key ingredients, an audience that is more than likely eager to pay to see a film
adaptation of one of its favorite television programs. Obviously, it would be commercially unwise for a studio to tamper with a beloved television show's basic ingredients
since such a film would alienate the very audience that the producers hoped to capture
in the first place. *The Fugitive*, however, is a unique television-inspired film in that it
dares to use only the series' most basic premise for its inspiration, building a story

around this premise that has little to do with the program that inspired it.

The core idea for the television show was, itself, inspired by another source, Victor Hugo's classic French novel, *Les Misérables* (1862). In the novel, petty criminal Jean Valjean escapes from prison and attempts to establish a new, respectable life but is hampered in his efforts by the relentless police inspector, Javert, who is determined to return Valjean to jail. The show's creators took the novel's premise and gave it a contemporary American setting and a unique twist. Prominent and well-respected physician Dr. Richard Kimble is (Harrison Ford) falsely accused of killing his wife. Although he swears he saw a one-armed man running from his home on the night of the murder, he is convicted on circumstantial evidence and sentenced to death. En route to prison, he manages to escape when the train on which he is being transported crashes. Constantly on the move as he is pursued by obsessive police lieutenant Gerard (Tommy Lee Jones), Kimble hides, takes odd jobs, and befriends the various people with whom he comes in contact—always on the alert for his relentless pursuer as he desperately searches for the elusive one-armed man who he believes holds the key to proving his innocence.

The television show attracted a wide, faithful audience and enjoyed a successful four-year run. The final episode in which Kimble finally corners the one-armed man and proves his innocence to Gerard, captured one of the largest audiences in television history, a series record that remained untouched for more than a decade. The show's massive popularity was attributable largely to the show's universally appealing premise and its star, David Janssen, who played Kimble with a brooding, sincere vulnerability.

In adapting the television show to the big screen, the filmmakers took great liberty with some of the show's strongest assets, improving on some and muddling others. One of the most radical differences has to do with the film's structure. Instead of having Kimble involved in a series of episodical encounters, racing all over the country in his attempts to elude Gerard and track down Sykes, the one-armed man (Andreas Katsulas), screenwriters Jeb Stuart and David Twohy limit most of the action to one location, Chicago, and reduce the time over which the action takes place to a week. Given the strict time limitations inherent in a two-hour film as opposed to a multiepisode series, the decision to limit both the elapsed time and the locale resulted in one of the film's major assets. Such familiar Chicago features as Cook County Hospital, Cook County Jail, the city's elevated train system, and its elaborate St. Patrick's Day parade are used to great advantage, providing key settings and plot ingredients. Also, because of the constricted time period, the film's action becomes more relentlessly intense.

Taking advantage of the film's megabudget, the filmmakers play up the story's built-in suspense potential by staging two incredible action sequences involving Kimble eluding his pursuers. The first involves Kimble's initial escape while being transferred from county jail to a nearby penitentiary. Kimble, his arms and legs shackled, boards a bus with several other prisoners. En route, his fellow prisoners attempt an escape, resulting in the bus crashing, rolling down an embankment, and landing across a stretch of train track. As Kimble struggles to free himself and then give aid to a wounded guard, a train suddenly appears and barrels down the tracks toward the bus. At the last possible moment, Kimble escapes from the bus; then, with his legs still shackled, he frantically scuttles across muddy terrain attempting to dodge the train, which has derailed and is skidding through the mud behind him. After he jumps clear, the train crashes, explodes, and finally comes to a halt in a mangled heap of steel and debris. This scene is easily one of the most expertly staged and executed action sequences in recent memory (an actual train was used and wrecked for the sequence). It is nearly surpassed in a segment that follows only minutes later, however, in which Kimble tries to elude Gerard in a labyrinthine drainage tunnel that leads to a drop-off overlooking a massive dam. In order to escape from Gerard, Kimble makes a spectacular leap off the dam, falling hundreds of feet into the river below.

Although these two sequences are both brilliant examples of action filmmaking at its best, the filmmakers make the mistake of staging both of them in the film's first thirty minutes, thus whetting the audience's appetite for more spectacle, then failing to deliver. Most of the film is devoted to a series of near-fatal encounters between Kimble and Gerard. Although they lack the grandiose spectacle of the two earlier sequences, many of these cat-and-mouse chase scenes are also expertly staged, especially a scene involving Kimble visiting the county jail to check on a prisoner who he suspects is the one-armed murderer. As he makes his way to the lockup area, he passes dozens of police officers, wincing with each encounter. Meanwhile, Gerard and his associates are also on their way to the jail to interview the same prisoner. The crosscutting used in this scene—and throughout the entire film for that matter—first showing Kimble's movements and then Gerard's, is brilliantly handled, each edit enhancing the film's tense mood, finally leading to an explosive confrontation between the two men.

One of these types of confrontations, however, is handled extremely poorly and is an example of the film's weakest attribute. Kimble is seen walking by the side of the road in the pouring rain. A woman driver spots him, slows down, and asks him if he needs a ride. The action then immediately cuts to a scene in Gerard's office, where he and his associates have just learned that "the suspect" has taken refuge with a woman companion in a house outside town. When they stage a raid on the house, one learns that Gerard and companions are not after Kimble but another prisoner who escaped at the same time. This scene is confusing to the audience and adds little to the film; its only purpose is to show how ruthless Gerard is when it comes to apprehending escaped criminals: He endangers one of his own men when he shoots the prisoner at point-blank range; the excuse he gives is "I don't bargain." Also, the scene in which Kimble is given a ride by the woman in the middle of the night is extremely implausible. Unfortunately, these poorly conceived sequences are minor irritations when compared to the film's key plot turn, one dealing with the motive for the murder of Kimble's wife, Helen (Sela Ward).

It turns out that Sykes, the one-armed man, was actually a paid assassin hired by one of Kimble's best friends, fellow doctor Charles Nichols (Jeroen Krabbe), to kill

Helen and make it look as if Kimble killed her. Nichols' reason for masterminding the elaborate murder scheme is to prevent Kimble from ruining his plans for getting a lethal drug approved by the Food and Drug Administration, a drug manufactured by a pharmaceutical company owned in part by Nichols and one which Kimble knows is unsafe. This plot twist, one that is the most radical departure from the television show, is based on the overworked idea of the seemingly sympathetic best friend turning out to be the diabolical villain. The drug-tampering plot twist, however, is so illogical, so insulting to the audience's intelligence, that it comes close to undermining the rest of the film's sterling attributes.

What saves the film from being overwhelmed by all of its unnecessarily convoluted, conspiratorial plot shenanigans is the acting by the two principals, both of whom expand and improve upon their television-character counterparts. Tommy Lee Jones plays Gerard as a wisecracking, hyperactive control freak, obsessed not so much by apprehending Kimble but by performing his job as efficiently and as unmercifully as possible. Jones, who won the Best Supporting Actor Academy Award for his work in the film, makes it clear that his character does not care about the guilt or innocence of the criminals he pursues. He is interested only in doing his job, which he treats as a game, one he enjoys playing, especially when his relentless tactics succeed and result in the humiliation of his more conservative coworkers. The chillingly playful relentlessness he brings to the role is mesmerizing to watch and provides many of the film's best character moments.

As outstanding as Jones is, however, it is Harrison Ford who is at the core of the film's appeal. Although David Janssen made an excellent television Kimble, Ford manages to enhance the character's innate goodness while endowing Kimble with a single-minded relentlessness that surpasses even that of Jones's character. In the early scenes of the film when he is being interrogated by the police following the death of his wife, Ford quickly establishes Kimble's feelings of devastation over the events that have resulted in the death of his wife, whom he obviously loved very deeply. Then, when he realizes that the police think he is responsible for the murder, the look in his eyes, the quiver in his voice, and finally his cries of outrage overwhelmingly capture the passion and the humanity of his character. Time and again, Ford has proved that he is one of the most versatile actors currently working, able to play everything from a cocky space pilot to a bullwhip-cracking archaeologist to a vulnerable, impassioned police officer posing as an Amish farmer. With *The Fugitive*, Ford shines not only in the action scenes but also in the quieter moments when he demonstrates his character's sympathetic nature.

By radically changing the structure, content, and plot intricacies from those of the original television show, the creative artists responsible for *The Fugitive* risked alienating their huge built-in audience. Although some of the gambles severely weakened the film's overall effectiveness, the end result reflects the show's major strengths: The film resounds with heart-pounding action and suspense yet provides new twists to familiar characters as they add new dimensions to such concepts as outrage, relentlessness, and decency. Also, further proof of the filmmakers' success in not only capturing old fans familiar with the series but large audiences unfamiliar with the television show is evident in the fact that *The Fugitive* was the second-highest grossing film of the year. The film was also nominated for a Best Picture Academy Award.

Jim Kline

Reviews

Chicago Tribune. August 6, 1993, VII, p. 29.
The Christian Science Monitor. August 9, 1993, p. 13.
Entertainment Weekly. August 13, 1993, p. 52.
Film Comment. XXX, January, 1994, p. 30.
Films in Review. XLIV, September, 1993, p. 328.
The Hollywood Reporter. August 2, 1993, p. 5.
Los Angeles Times. August 6, 1993, p. F1.
The New York Times. August 6, 1993, p. B1.
The New Yorker. August 16, 1993, p. 93.
Variety. August 2, 1993, p. 3.
The Washington Post. August 6, 1993, p. D1.

GERONIMO
An American Legend

Production: Walter Hill and Neil Canton; released by Columbia Pictures
Direction: Walter Hill
Screenplay: John Milius and Larry Gross; based on a story by Milius
Cinematography: Lloyd Ahern
Editing: Freeman Davies, Carmel Davies, and Donn Aron
Production design: Joe Alves
Art direction: Scott Ritenour
Set decoration: Richard C. Goddard
Casting: Rueben Cannon
Sound: Lee Orloff
Costume Design: Dan Moore
Stunt coordination: Allan Graf
Music: Ry Cooder
MPAA rating: PG-13
Running time: 115 minutes

> *Principal characters:*
> Geronimo. . . . . Wes Studi
> Lieutenant Charles Gatewood. . . . . Jason Patric
> Brigadier General George Crook . . . . Gene Hackman
> Al Sieber . . . . Robert Duvall
> Lieutenant Britton Davis. . . . . Matt Damon
> Mangas. . . . . Rodney A. Grant
> Brigadier General Nelson Miles . . . . Kevin Tighe
> Chato . . . . Steve Reevis

Although the Western remained essentially dormant as a viable genre during the 1980's, the production of two Academy Award-winning films in the early 1990's—*Dances with Wolves* (1990) and *Unforgiven* (1992)—marked the reemergence of the form as a vibrant and significant feature of the cinematic landscape. As one critic pointed out, *Unforgiven* was especially important in that it considered both the fact and the legend of Western history without contradicting either, demonstrating the necessity for dealing with both the data as it is available and the consequences of the previous interpretations.

At the same time, *Dances with Wolves* marked the opening of an area demanding investigation but generally buried in misinformation, distortion, and racist ignorance: the world of the Native Americans who hovered on the fringes of Western films as "hostiles," simplistic savages, or Europeanized versions of local color. Aside from brief interludes of moderately enlightened portrayals, the history of the Native American in the Western film remained in a kind of stasis from John Ford's attempt to probe beyond his other presentations in *Cheyenne Autumn* (1964) until *Dances with Wolves* and *The Last of The Mohicans* (1992) began the first serious explorations of Native American cultural experience.

Working with the traditions and conventions revivified by Kevin Costner in *Dances with Wolves* and Clint Eastwood in *Unforgiven*, director Walter Hill and the screenwriters have used some of the most fundamental elements of the classic Western. Yet they have extended its scope by placing the Chiricahua Apache language at the center of *Geronimo: An American Legend*. Beginning in 1885, when the United States government was implementing the final stages of its subjugation of the last of the free native people in the Southwest, the film follows Geronimo's exploits as he eludes more than five thousand soldiers with a band of thirty-four Apaches until his final surrender in September, 1886.

The filmmakers present Geronimo (Wes Studi) as a version of a familiar Western figure—a man comfortable when alone in a vast uncharted space, beleaguered and pursued, heroically defiant and justified in his violent actions by a moral code grounded in an individualistic integrity. In an epic sense, he is an expression of his culture's values and is a leader inspiring a people who have reason to distrust a distant, insensitive government. As the film progresses, it becomes apparent that the people who are inspired are not only the Apaches Geronimo directs but also the humane, decent "White Eyes" (the Apache name for the European American settlers) and, ideally, a sympathetic audience.

Inevitably, the filmmakers were constrained by commercial expectations. Consequently, Geronimo is not the central narrative consciousness of the film. While *Dances with Wolves* starred Costner as a white Army lieutenant who grew to understand and appreciate the Sioux, and *The Last of the Mohicans* starred Daniel Day-Lewis as Hawkeye, a first-generation white American reared by the Mohicans, *Geronimo* offers two white points of view. The narration is framed by the voice-over entries of a journal written by Lieutenant Britton Davis (Matt Damon), a young officer freshly arrived from his commission at West Point. In addition, the film's most admirable soldier is Lieutenant Charles Gatewood (Jason Patric), a Virginian from a rebel family, whose growing appreciation for Geronimo turns into a partnership/friendship that leads to his ultimate disappointment as the film ends.

The multiple perspective tends to give the film a feeling of historical examination rather than specific partisanship. Furthermore, the way in which Davis and Gatewood react to Geronimo guides a response that is never eased by any reduction in the force of Geronimo's presence. At the heart of the film, Hill and his screenwriters—with the essential contribution of a truly riveting performance by Studi, seen previously as Magua in *The Last of the Mohicans*—have placed a character drawn with a mixture of hard-edged realism and a kind of mystical overlay, which imaginative cinematography and editing can generate by implication. Geronimo becomes psychologically plausible as well as mythically elusive—the man and the legend intertwined.

The three men anchor the film's generally episodic structure, and Davis's ongoing commentary permits the filmmakers to move Geronimo in and out of the action in the way he appeared to the soldiers. "At times," Davis remarks, "it seemed we were chasing a spirit more than a man." From the film's first shot of Geronimo, head-on, his upper body filling the screen in a sepia-toned, stop-action portrait, half of his figure edging toward light, the other half shading into darkness, it is clear that the largest dimensions of his character are going to be emphasized.

The sound track carries a type of rhythmic chorus that echoes and lingers throughout the film—a "song" or chant from an Apache ritual that further suggests Geronimo's connections to a civilization unfamiliar to the soldiers. Appropriately, the first words spoken are in the Apache language with subtitles, another example of the commitment to authenticity the filmmakers regarded as crucial to the development of the production's atmosphere. As the film alternates between the dark, gloomy inner recesses of the fort and the open plains and mountains where the Apaches lived for centuries, the orange-browns of Geronimo's opening image are reflected in the shades and hues of the land he inhabits. The arrival of the soldiers on Apache land introduces an element of displacement and incongruity, which is carried further by the total dismissal of Native American culture by many of the soldiers.

In the film, Geronimo is first seen surrendering to the Army in order to satisfy an agreement. The striking visual impression he makes is enhanced by a ritual performed by a medicine man and by the respect Gatewood shows and the amazement Davis registers. Geronimo's prowess as a warrior, his sardonic humor, and his sense of fairness are displayed as Gatewood escorts him to the fort and the two men jointly drive off a band of racist rabble intent on lynching the prisoner. Predictably, Geronimo is restless as a would-be farmer on useless land, but he keeps his side of the agreement until, in a scene of characteristic bureaucratic blindness, a soldier shoots an Apache shaman who refuses to stop a dance/vision. This leads to an uprising instigated by Geronimo, who asks an Apache scout in the Army's employ, "Where is your heart?"— a query central to the issue of the survival of the spirit of the Apache nation.

The clash between cultures is further emphasized by the arrival of the news of Geronimo's rebellion at the fort, while a European formal dance is taking place. The remainder of the film chronicles the Army's pursuit of Geronimo and his dwindling band, until Gatewood convinces him to surrender permanently and accept a restriction to the state of Florida, where he spends the last twenty-two years of his life. This concluding incident is wrapped in ambiguity, suggesting that Geronimo has made a kind of spiritual decision. Studi, however, has said that he regrets the cutting of a scene that explained how Geronimo's surrender guaranteed the "freedom" of Apaches held hostage—"a sacrifice for the lives of people he cared about."

Hill and screenwriter John Milius have a separate history of working on films that were not in the commercial mainstream. As Georgia Brown of *The Village Voice* points out, *Geronimo* has a "brooding, end-of-an-era, last-of-a-breed poignancy" consistent with two other films written by Milius, *The Life and Times of Judge Roy Bean* (1972) and *Jeremiah Johnson* (1972), and with Hill's haunting conception of brotherly partnership in *The Long Riders* (1980), as well as his skillful use of an unlikely friendship between Eddie Murphy as a con man and Nick Nolte as a cop in *48 Hrs.*

(1982). Among these films, only *48 Hrs.* was a notable commercial success, although the other films all have an enduring interest.

The seasoned professional technique Hill has brought to the production includes his eighth collaboration with composer Ry Cooder, whose affecting score mixing folk music and spirituals lends an elegiac tone to the film. Hill's enlistment of Sonny Skyhawk—an American Indian consultant and advocate—plus many other Native American actors provides a dimension of seriousness to what Hill called "a full social and cultural tragedy." Typically solid performances are rendered by Gene Hackman as the well-intentioned Brigadier General Crook and Robert Duvall as the professional Indian fighter, the flinty Al Sieber. Lloyd Ahern's fine photography of the Monument Valley region of Utah where John Ford made several films is also crucial to this disturbing story.

As the train carrying Geronimo and his colleagues slowly creeps across the screen as the closing credits roll—reminiscent of the train carrying Ranse Stoddard (Jimmy Stewart) back East in Ford's *The Man Who Shot Liberty Valance* (1962)—fact and legend fuse as they did in Ford's film. Questions that continue to trouble American society about territorial conflict, cultural values, and maverick individualism resonate beyond the film, centered in the weathered face, challenging gaze, explosive intensity, and psychological complexity of Wes Studi's Geronimo. Decades overdue, an American Indian joins the pantheon of heroic figures of the classic Western film.

Leon Lewis

Reviews
Chicago Tribune. December 10, 1993, VII, p. 39.
The Christian Science Monitor. December 10, 1993, p. 19.
The Hollywood Reporter. December 6, 1993, p. 8.
Los Angeles Times. December 10, 1993, p. F8.
The New York Times. December 10, 1993, p. B3.
The New Yorker. January 10, 1994, p. 81.
Rolling Stone. December 23, 1993, p. 174.
San Francisco Chronicle. December 10, 1993, p. C3.
Time. CXLII, December 13, 1993, p. 79.
Variety. December 6, 1993, p. 4.
The Village Voice. December 14, 1993, p. 65.
The Washington Post. December 10, 1993, p. B7.

GETTYSBURG

Production: Robert Katz and Moctesuma Esparza for Turner Pictures; released by New Line Cinema
Direction: Ronald F. Maxwell
Screenplay: Ronald F. Maxwell; based on the novel *The Killer Angels*, by Michael Shaara
Cinematography: Kees Van Oostrum
Editing: Corky Ehlers
Production design: Cary White
Art direction: Mike Sullivan
Casting: Joy Todd
Sound: Stephen Halbert
Costume design: Michael T. Boyd
Music: Randy Edelman
MPAA rating: PG
Running time: 258 minutes

Principal characters:

Lieutenant General James Longstreet	Tom Berenger
General Robert E. Lee	Martin Sheen
Major General George E. Pickett	Stephen Lang
Brigadier General Lewis A. Armistead	Richard Jordan
Colonel Joshua Lawrence Chamberlain	Jeff Daniels
Brigadier General John Buford	Sam Elliott
Lieutenant Thomas D. Chamberlain	C. Thomas Howell
Sergeant Buster Kilrain	Kevin Conway
Brigadier General Richard B. Garnett	Andrew Prine
Colonel Strong Vincent	Maxwell Caulfield
Major General George G. Meade	Richard Anderson
Lieutenant Colonel Arthur Freemantle	James Lancaster
Brigadier General James L. Kemper	Royce Applegate
Major General Winfield Scott Hancock	Brian Mallon
Major General J. E. B. Stuart	Joseph Fuqua

The cinematic release of *Gettysburg* represents a fortuitous intersection of pure chance and stubborn tenacity—circumstances that find curious parallels in the crossroads location of the town of Gettysburg and in the climactic military episode which occurred there. Although director Ronald F. Maxwell could not have anticipated the lengthy struggle required to bring his adaptation of the Pulitzer Prize-winning novel *The Killer Angels* (1973) to the screen, it is clear that the intervening years created the necessary environment for the film's fruition. The critical acclaim and commercial success of *Glory* (1989), with its Academy Award-winning performance by Denzel

Washington, and the overwhelming popularity of Ken Burns's documentary *The Civil War*, broadcast as a nine-part series on PBS in 1990, proved that there was an audience eager to view films that used new technology and special effects to recapture the dramatic narrative flavor of old historical epics. Originally conceived as a miniseries to be aired on Turner Network Television, *Gettysburg* became the first cinematic presentation to be released by Ted Turner's newly created film division, Turner Pictures.

The film opens with a scene in which a Confederate spy scouts out the position of the advancing Union troops and successfully negotiates his return through Confederate picket lines at night to report to Lieutenant General James Longstreet (Tom Berenger). As they become aware of the significance of the spy's findings in the absence of intelligence information from the cavalry of Major General J. E. B. Stuart (Joseph Fuqua), Longstreet and his aides take the spy to headquarters to confer with General Robert E. Lee (Martin Sheen). Next, the perspective shifts to the Union side, with cavalry commander John Buford (Sam Elliott) surveying the ground at Gettysburg and determining how to stake out the best defensive position. The scene shifts again to show the troops of the 20th Maine, under the command of Colonel Joshua Lawrence Chamberlain (Jeff Daniels), as they prepare to advance north from Maryland into Pennsylvania with the bulk of the Union Army. As the interconnecting narratives follow the activities of the key officers and their troops over the course of the days surrounding the battle, the film subtly reveals the characters' internal thoughts, motivations, and concerns.

A fine example of this film technique is demonstrated in the scenes in which Chamberlain must cope with the addition of some 120 mutineers from a disbanded Maine regiment. A former college professor faced with the daunting prospect of leading so many unwilling soldiers into battle, Jeff Daniels' Chamberlain struggles to articulate the purpose that unifies these men. In a moving speech, Chamberlain is honest and matter-of-fact in his explanation, convincing the mutineers that what they are fighting for "is something new. . . . It's the idea that we all have value," and that in the end, what they are fighting for "is each other." After the speech is over, Chamberlain is informed by his adjutant and brother, Tom (C. Thomas Howell), that all but six of the mutineers have decided to take up arms with their new regiment.

As the first of the skirmishes occurs on the outskirts of Gettysburg and as battle plans are made at the field headquarters of each army, it becomes clear that this conflict is not an encounter between anonymous opposing forces. There are close personal ties between many of the Confederate and Union officers; their perceptions of one another inform their strategic decisions and affect their ability to maintain a detached view of the war itself. In his final film role, Richard Jordan turns in a heartfelt dramatic performance that highlights this personal dimension of the war. In one scene, Jordan's Brigadier General Lewis Armistead has a lengthy conversation with Longstreet in which he fondly recalls his last encounter with his close friend, Union General Winfield Scott Hancock (Brian Mallon), who had been stationed with him in California before the war began. Armistead confesses that he had made a pledge that God should strike him dead if he took up arms against his friend Hancock and notes with gratitude that they have not yet met on the battlefield. Clinging to the hope that they may soon be reunited but knowing that he may not survive the next day's encounter, Armistead entrusts Longstreet with a package to be given to Hancock's wife in the event of his death. This knowledge heightens the audience's understanding of Armistead's behavior as he leads troops in Pickett's Charge and helps explain his reaction, upon being wounded and captured, to the news that Hancock also has been hurt.

The pressures of war create an environment in which men from different social classes and backgrounds come to depend on one another as well. In his role as Irish-born Sergeant Buster Kilrain, Kevin Conway gives a compelling performance as a battle-worn veteran who lends his wise advice and unwavering support to the inexperienced Colonel Chamberlain. Conway and Daniels together demonstrate the teamwork and mutual understanding that developed between these unlikely friends, forging a relationship that helped hold the 20th Maine firm against the onslaught of rebel troops that tried to outflank them on the Little Round Top during the second day of fighting at Gettysburg.

Perhaps the most stunning accomplishment of the film is its reenactment of the battlefield conditions at Gettysburg. More than 5,000 Civil War reenactors lent their talents to the filming of *Gettysburg*, bringing their own uniforms, horses, weapons, and other accoutrements along with their wealth of knowledge about battle conditions and living conditions as experienced by Civil War soldiers. Meticulous attention to detail led the filmmakers to employ historical consultants familiar with the period and a military choreographer to help ensure the accuracy of the battle scenes, which were shot on location in Gettysburg National Park. The full-scale re-creation of Pickett's Charge, marking the final strategic thrust of the Confederate Army, provides the film's stunning climax, while continuing to highlight the human dimension of the war. Far from being a repetition of war as seen via satellite on evening television news programs, the fine cinematography evident throughout the film lends immediacy and authenticity to the battle scenes—scenes that honor the heroic contributions of the men who fought during the Civil War without glorifying or sanitizing the horrific destruction that the war unleashed.

While the film deserves ample praise for these achievements, it also has its share of flaws. In particular, Martin Sheen seems miscast in the role of General Robert E. Lee. To be fair, Sheen does a fine job with the material he has been given and works hard to master the Virginia inflections of Lee's speaking voice. At the same time, Sheen's physical dissimilarities to Lee are evident and he does not seem to have captured the almost mystical aura of leadership and gentlemanly dignity considered to be so characteristic of one of America's most revered military figures. It also seems somewhat crass and inconsiderate, given the film's focus on the universality of the conflict and the fine performances of many unknown performers in nonspeaking roles, that media mogul Ted Turner should be singled out for a cameo death scene during the course of Pickett's Charge. The subtle cameo given to documentary filmmaker

Ken Burns, however, is more in keeping with the film's tone. Finally, while it is evident that it would have been impossible to re-create the scope of the battle and retain the flavor of the original book within the typical two-hour Hollywood format, it is clear that some judicious editing might have helped shave some minutes off the running time and eliminated the necessity for an intermission.

These criticisms aside, the film is highly entertaining while maintaining an amazing faithfulness to the text of *The Killer Angels*. New dialogue seems to be interwoven with author Michael Shaara's own words so as to be indistinguishable, and the condensing and rearrangement of some of the book's action seem only to enhance the story. With the advantage of hindsight, the audience becomes more aware of how significant each minute event, accidental encounter, and routine decision became in bringing about the ultimate conclusion at Gettysburg. Although some filmgoers may have been tempted to wait until the film is aired on television in its longer miniseries format, they will be missing out on the vivid and impressive sights and sounds that can only be conveyed, free of commercials, in the big-screen cinema format. Hollywood's renewed interest in historical epics is directly linked to box-office success—a renaissance that has allowed *Gettysburg* to be made with all the attention to detail that its story so richly deserves.

Wendy Sacket

Reviews

Chicago Tribune. October 8, 1993, VII, p. 33.
The Christian Science Monitor. October 8, 1993, p. 13.
Civil War Times Illustrated. XXXII, November, 1993, p. 40.
Commonweal. CXX, November 19, 1993, p. 27.
The Hollywood Reporter. September 24, 1993, p. 10.
Los Angeles Times. October 8, 1993, p. F6.
The New Republic. CCIX, November 8, 1993, p. 32.
The New York Times. October 8, 1993, The Living Arts, p. B2.
Time. CXLII, October 25, 1993, p. 80.
Variety. September 22, 1993, p. 2.
The Washington Post. October 8, 1993, p. D6.

GROUNDHOG DAY

Production: Trevor Albert and Harold Ramis; released by Columbia Pictures
Direction: Harold Ramis
Screenplay: Danny Rubin and Harold Ramis; based on a story by Rubin
Cinematography: John Bailey
Editing: Pembroke Herring
Production design: David Nichols
Art direction: Peter Lansdown Smith
Set decoration: Lisa Fischer
Casting: Howard Feuer
Sound: Les Lazarowitz
Costume design: Jennifer Butler
Stunt coordination: Rick LeFevour
Music: George Fenton
MPAA rating: PG
Running time: 103 minutes

Principal characters:

Phil Connors	Bill Murray
Rita Hanson	Andie MacDowell
Larry	Chris Elliott
Ned Ryerson	Stephen Tobolowsky
Buster Greene	Brian Doyle-Murray
Nancy Taylor	Marita Geraghty
Mrs. Lancaster	Angela Paton
Gus	Rick Ducommun
Ralph	Rick Overton
Doris the waitress	Robin Duke
Piano teacher	Peggy Roeder
Neurologist	Harold Ramis
Psychiatrist	David Pasquesi
Man in hallway	Ken Hudson Campbell

On February 2, according to legend, the groundhog is supposed to come out of hibernation. If it sees its shadow, there are supposed to be six more weeks of winter. This legend dates back to Pennsylvania's earliest settlers, whose answer to the European counterpart (the hedgehog) was Punxsutawney Phil. Groundhogs flourish in that state, and it is the Groundhog Club that determines if Punxsutawney Phil sees its shadow or not.

It is indeed an appropriate and superb setting for the film *Groundhog Day*, in which Phil Connors (Bill Murray), a jaded, self-centered television weatherman, reluctantly arrives in Punxsutawney to cover the festivities for his Pittsburgh station. It is his fourth time performing this assignment, and he is determined not to enjoy himself. He somehow muddles through the day with the sole intention of getting it over with and returning home. Unfortunately, an unexpected blizzard strikes the area, and the visitors, including Phil, are locked in Punxsutawney indefinitely. When he wakes up in his hotel room the next morning, it is still February 2. The radio plays the same song, the announcers speak the same lines, and when Phil steps out on the street, a little baffled, Groundhog Day as he experienced it the day before is replicated down to the smallest detail. This happens over and over again until he realizes that, by some supernatural act, he alone has been trapped in time.

A predicament of this sort does raise a number of metaphysical questions, but it is not the intention of this film to serve as a referendum on the subject. Phil's dreadful fate, and his attitude toward it, is depicted in a series of gags that present all the colors of his emotions from confusion, panic, and hedonism to resignation and hope. The visual capabilities of cinema as a medium are utilized wonderfully to create a feast for the eyes and the mind.

There are a few constants in Phil's daily experience, and it is interesting to see, for example, how he copes with having to show up at the press area every morning and say the same lines for the news segment. The producer of the news report, Rita Hanson (Andie MacDowell), and the cameraman, Larry (Chris Elliott), are the first to be affected by Phil's dilemma. In the early stages of his bewilderment, Phil fumbles over his coverage on the festivities. When the full import of his predicament is on him, however, he can no longer hide his desperation. He begins by saying, "This is the most pitiful spectacle known to civilization. With one nod from a filthy rodent, a coal mining town turns into the Lourdes of Pennsylvania." Yet, by the time that he has finally succumbed in spirit to the prospect of eternity in Punxsutawney, Phil is no longer his irreverent self. Though greatly fatigued, he is kind and courteous, and as he faces the news camera, he presents what could be considered the most thoroughly researched account of the legend of Groundhog Day.

Equally hilarious are Phil's daily encounters with Ned Ryerson (Stephen Tobolowsky), the overbearing insurance salesman who recognizes him from his high school days. All of Phil's attempts to get rid of this fast-talking pest are in vain. Finally, he has no recourse but to let down his defenses and buy the complete insurance package. The only difference is that he does it not out of malice, but with a good-hearted sense of camaraderie.

Bill Murray is largely responsible for the film's poignant moments, those that make it so enjoyable. Beneath the apparent humor in his situation is a melancholy that the actor is adept at conveying. For no matter how hard he tries during the course of the day to get help or to show his humanitarian side, Phil knows that at sunrise all of his efforts will have amounted to nothing. His good deeds will be forgotten, and he will have to perform them all over again.

The romance between Phil and Rita is the thread that runs through the film. From the moment that Phil notices Rita at the television station in Pittsburgh, he harbors an affection for her, and he decides to exploit his predicament in a variety of ways in order to win her over. He is able to use the trial-and-error method to perfection. What he learns about her likes and dislikes he uses to his advantage the following day. When he is in a position to quote her favorite French poem or to raise a toast to world peace, as she always does, it takes her by surprise. Yet he cannot win her over. It is the final hurdle of credibility that he cannot overcome, and many of their evenings end with Rita leaving the room in disgust at Phil's inherent insincerity. It is to the credit of the filmmakers that, despite the repetitive nature of these scenes, the story keeps moving forward, largely with the use of some creative editing techniques.

In films such as *Groundhog Day*, in which a supernatural occurrence plays a key role, it is often necessary to create a suspension of disbelief for the viewer. Phil's visits to the neurologist and psychiatrist provide the required sense of reality. These efforts, however, do him no good: No matter how close he comes to a revelation, he loses all momentum when the clock again reads 6 A.M.

Critics compared the film to Luis Buñuel's *El Angel Exterminador* (1962; *The Exterminating Angel*), to the metaphysical French films of Alain Resnais, and to a number of other lighthearted comedies. There is some merit to these comparisons. In *The Exterminating Angel*, a group of elite, after-opera diners find the hospitality of their host so compelling that they decide to stay the night. The next morning, they are struck by the horror of their condition: They cannot summon the willpower to leave. The doors are open, but the guests are held captive by their minds. The situation finally becomes a major crisis with reporters and friends gathering outside the house, trying to carry out a rescue operation from afar. The imaginary walls exist for them as well. It is easy to draw a parallel between the plight of the guests and that of Phil Connors. Yet, it is necessary to distinguish between the surreal and the supernatural, between being trapped in a geographical, physical space and being trapped in time. Resnais's *Hiroshima mon amour* (1959) and *L'Annee dernière à marienbad* (1961; *Last Year at Marienbad*, 1962) are two examples of films about characters who are trying to recall events in the past. The film technique is to utilize dreams, the past, the present, and the future in a complex series to demonstrate the thin line between reality and imagination. These are films about the workings of the mind: They are repetitive in structure and completely abstract.

The use of gags in *Groundhog Day* is reminiscent of Buster Keaton's comedies. A stoic disposition in the face of the absurdities of life helped Keaton's characters to survive. They had to use their wits, just as Phil Connors uses his situation to his advantage by seducing women and carrying out a simple heist of cash from an armored vehicle (he knows every move the guards are going to make). Like Buster Keaton, Phil Connors is "the square peg in society's round hole" who must determine what he has to do in order to carve a niche for himself. For a time, Phil is able to throw caution to the wind and act out his fantasies because he cannot be made to face the consequences. Yet even that pleasure wears thin, and when all else fails, he attempts to kill himself. Unfortunately for him, even death eludes him. In one scene, he makes his most heartfelt confession to Rita, telling her that he has been living the same day countless times and can prove it to her. He asks her to spend the day with him so that he can point out the immense insight that he has gained into the residents of the town. He can predict when a waiter in the diner is going to drop a tray of glasses, as well as the precise moment that Larry is going to walk in and what he is going to say. It becomes obvious to Rita that Phil could not have gathered all this information in one day, so she agrees to wait until sunrise in his room. At 6 A.M., Phil looks to his side and Rita is not there. He will have to start all over again.

The transformation in Phil's character that ultimately saves him is the finest moment in the film. Even though he is a master of his universe in a superficial sense, it is suggested that living his single day to the fullest and carrying out deeds that can be rewarding within the same twenty-four-hour span would mean a lifetime of work. Unless Phil learns to accept this fact, he cannot move on. Therefore, he must strive to improve his fundamental personality. He begins to make a serious effort to change, accumulating a reservoir of good deeds by saving a man in a restaurant from choking to death and helping some old ladies with their flat tire. Phil also learns that, in some cases, even he cannot change the course of events: An old homeless man dies every night no matter how hard Phil tries to save him.

Finally, one evening at the dinner celebration after the Groundhog Day festivities, Phil begins to experience something new. Men and women who owe him a debt of gratitude for his service walk up to him and thank him. The numbers increase, and like George Bailey in the climactic scene in *It's a Wonderful Life* (1946), Phil's nightmare comes to an end. Rita, standing by his side, is truly astonished and asks him how in one day he managed to become Punxsutawney's leading citizen. With its upbeat conclusion, *Groundhog Day* shares a number of qualities with Charles Dickens' short story, "A Christmas Carol" (1843). There is a purity to the events that bring about Phil's redemption. He changes into a better person simply because he finds it is the right thing to do.

Nalin Bakhle

Reviews
Chicago Tribune. February 12, 1993, p.23.
Entertainment Weekly. February 12, 1993, p. 37.
The Hollywood Reporter. February 8, 1993, p. 5.
Los Angeles Times. February 12, 1993, p. F1.
The New Republic. CCVIII, March 15, 1993, p. 24.
The New York Times. February 12, 1993, p. B1.
The New Yorker. February 22, 1993, p. 171.
Newsweek. CXXI, March 8, 1993, p. 52.
Sight and Sound. III, May, 1993, p. 50.
Time. CXLI, February 15, 1993, p. 61.
Variety. February 8, 1993, p. 2.

GRUMPY OLD MEN

Production: John Davis and Richard C. Berman for John Davis/Lancaster Gate; released by Warner Bros.
Direction: Donald Petrie
Screenplay: Mark Steven Johnson
Cinematography: Johnny E. Jensen
Editing: Bonnie Koehler
Production design: David Chapman
Art direction: Mark Haack
Set decoration: Clay Griffith
Casting: Sharon Howard-Field
Sound: Russell Fager
Costume design: Lisa Jensen
Music: Alan Silvestri
MPAA rating: PG-13
Running time: 104 minutes

Principal characters:

John	Jack Lemmon
Max	Walter Matthau
Ariel	Ann-Margret
Grandpa	Burgess Meredith
Melanie	Daryl Hannah
Jacob	Kevin Pollak
Chuck	Ossie Davis
Snyder	Buck Henry
Mike	Christopher McDonald

One of the most successful comedy teams in motion-picture history is that of Walter Matthau and Jack Lemmon. Unlike Abbott and Costello or Laurel and Hardy, however, they are not a pair of clowns who only perform with each other, but are two highly versatile and respected actors whose on-screen chemistry warrants continued collaborations. *Grumpy Old Men* is the most recent in what is actually a rather short but impressive list of films in which these two men have costarred. The other films include *The Fortune Cookie* (1966)—for which Matthau won an Academy Award—*The Odd Couple* (1968), *The Front Page* (1974), and *Buddy Buddy* (1981). Lemmon directed Matthau to a Best Actor Oscar nomination in *Kotch* (1971) as well.

Their on-screen charm is given ample opportunity to shine in *Grumpy Old Men*, an amusing but thin comedy about two retired widowers. These two have lived next door to each other for nearly fifty years, feuding the entire time. Their animosity is fueled by the arrival of a new neighbor, the beautiful and free-spirited Ariel (Ann-Margret). Unfortunately, the plot of this film is too predictable to be as hilarious or as touching as it aspires to be. Nevertheless, the constant bickering of these two men combined with the luminous Ann-Margret and a very funny performance by Burgess Meredith as Lemmon's ninety-four-year-old lech of a father make for a pleasant and often touching two hours.

John (Lemmon) and Max (Matthau) live in the nearly Arctic temperatures of Wabasha, Minnesota, where the only pastime appears to be the arcane sport of ice fishing. Each day, the characters greet each other in front of their homes with a cheerful "Hello, moron," "Hello, putz" as they pack their fishing rods and head for the little ice shanties they maintain on the frozen lake. They regularly stop en route to visit with shopkeeper Chuck (Ossie Davis), who tolerates their constant one-upmanship ("this fishing pole has caught more fish than you've lied about") with amusement.

They play cruel tricks on each other: John sprays water on the eaves of Max's house, waiting until it freezes so that ice will fall on Max's head when he comes out for the paper in the morning; Max rigs a remote control so that he can change channels on John's television from next door, just as John is trying to discover whether he won the lottery. The relatively benign nature of their behavior changes when Ariel moves in. She is flirtatious and available, and since neither man has been with a woman for many years, the battle is on. Ultimately, the true nature of their relationship is tested when one of them gets sick, making them realize they are truly friends.

The story superficially is augmented by a gratuitous subplot involving Daryl Hannah as John's beautiful daughter and Kevin Pollak as Max's son. This predictable and unnecessary subplot serves no purpose except to alleviate the incessant foul-mouthed squabbling of their fathers. The predictability of this secondary story reinforces the by-the-numbers feel of the entire film.

The structure is as follows: The central conflict (the bickering neighbors); disruption of the status quo (the arrival of Ariel); the secondary plot (involving the son and daughter); the sentimental revelation concerning the feud; the message of carpe diem (de rigueur in current film); and finally the moment of truth (a life-threatening illness), which leads to the resolution between the two men. Particularly in light of other films starring Lemmon and Matthau, such as Neil Simon's *The Odd Couple* or Billy Wilder's *The Fortune Cookie*, the script for *Grumpy Old Men* is simplistic indeed.

Yet the script does have tenderness, humor, and flashes of real wit amid the big-picture formula. It is the first-produced script by twenty-five-year-old writer Mark Steven Johnson, who wrote it while working as a secretary at Orion Pictures. The fact that Johnson is so young makes this an impressive debut. The idea of two cranky elderly neighbors in the harsh winter of Minnesota vying for the attention of their beautiful, sexy new neighbor is inspired. It is a welcome sight to see romance among mature people depicted without patronizing or mocking them. In that area, this film joins *The Cemetery Club* (1993; reviewed in this volume) and Public Television's *Tales of the City* (1993) in advancing the notion that seniority does not preclude sexuality.

There are some genuinely funny moments: Jack Lemmon's imitation of Tom Cruise's dance in *Risky Business* (1983); Walter Matthau in the bathtub scrubbing up for a date with Ariel; a discussion about gallstones and ulcers in a pharmacy;

Ann-Margret as Ariel rolling around in the snow after a sauna bath, wearing only a leotard; and virtually everything Burgess Meredith says. Meredith, who has played serious roles ranging from the classics (where he began on Broadway in the 1930's) to the *Rocky* series of films, is a howl as Grandpa, who can only talk about sex. Most of what he says is unprintable, but amusing.

The most telling part of the film arises out of Meredith's character and performance. The credits at the film's end are played over outtakes of the production. Meredith is prominent in these outtakes, trying to make Lemmon laugh during the shooting of a scene, and he is hilarious. These scenes, silly as they are, are much funnier than the film preceding them. Showing these outtakes makes the audience realize that it could have been a funnier film, bringing a wistful desire to see Lemmon and Matthau sparring as the odd couple or as the shyster lawyer/innocent client in *The Fortune Cookie*. Comparisons such as these will be inevitable.

Some tender scenes round out the film, with a particularly moving moment when Max's eyes well up with tears as he visits John in the hospital, realizing that they truly are friends. Jack Lemmon has a wonderful scene where his character breaks off his relationship with Ariel so that Max will not feel bad. His resignation and frustration are reminiscent of that of Lemmon's character in *The Apartment* (1960) and in *The Fortune Cookie*: a decent man trying to do the right thing and wondering why these kinds of things always happen to him. Both Lemmon and Matthau fill these moments with inner life, rendering these broadly drawn characters quite human.

Ann-Margret is a wonderful foil for both the men. Still astonishingly beautiful, she delivers an honest and interesting performance, holding her own against her scene-stealing costars. When she first arrives on the scene, both men are glued to their windows "like Garfield cats with little suction cups on their feet," according to Ariel. "Holy Moly," intones Max, as Ariel removes her helmet after a snowmobile ride. John is caught like a deer in the headlights when Ariel comes to his house with a coquettish smile to look through his bathroom, "because bathrooms tell a lot about a person." In those moments, it is hard to imagine any other actress besides Ann-Margret actually warranting the stupefied, amazed responses required of Matthau and Lemmon by the script. These charming moments make this film fun.

Director Donald Petrie, director of photography Johnny E. Jensen, and production designer David Chapman have created a wonderful look for this film, using actual winter locations in Minnesota to achieve their goals. They constructed a series of "ice shanties" (where ice-fisherman sit, sheltered as they fish on the frozen lake) on a lake outside Minneapolis, each shanty having its own idiosyncratic design. The entire film takes place in snow, echoing the cold in the hearts of these two grumps: Yet the filmmakers have given the film a storybook beauty that brings a solid foundation to the film's humorous tone. The look and feel of the film is like *Home Alone* (1990) for adults, complete with snow and Christmas trees and pranks that foil the bad guy (in this case, Buck Henry as a sniveling IRS agent). The snow and cold are used to great effect: One fight leads to Max trying to stab John with a frozen fish. From the humorous use of the song "Heat Wave," by Irving Berlin, played during the opening credits to a scene where Ariel and John lie on their backs in the snow and flap their arms to make "snow angels," Petrie has mined all the possibilities for conceptual and visual use of the snowy winter.

Grumpy Old Men was successful at the box office, winning some critical praise and bringing together several wonderful performances. Nevertheless, this is a film to be enjoyed without being too critical. Despite a weak script, the film has charm and humor, and for most audiences, that should be more than enough.

Kirby Tepper

Reviews

Chicago Tribune. December 24, 1993, VII, p. 24.
The Christian Science Monitor. January 7, 1994, p. 12.
Entertainment Weekly. January 14, 1994, p. 36.
The Hollywood Reporter. December 6, 1993, p. 6.
Los Angeles Times. December 25, 1993, p. F2.
The New York Times. December 24, 1993, p. C16.
San Francisco Chronicle. December 25, 1993, p. E1.
Time. CXLIII, January 10, 1994, p. 58.
Variety. December 6, 1993, p. 12.
The Washington Post. December 25, 1993, p. B7.
Washingtonian. XXIX, February, 1994, p. 21.

HEAVEN AND EARTH

Production: Oliver Stone, Arnon Milchan, Robert Kline, and A. Kitman Ho for Ixtlan, New Regency, and Todd-AO/TAE, in association with Regency Enterprises, Le Studio Canal Plus, and Alcor Films; released by Warner Bros.
Direction: Oliver Stone
Screenplay: Oliver Stone; based on *When Heaven and Earth Changed Places*, by Le Ly Hayslip and Jay Wurts, and on *Child of War, Woman of Peace*, by Le Ly Hayslip and James Hayslip
Cinematography: Robert Richardson
Editing: David Brenner and Sally Menke
Production design: Victor Kempster
Art direction: Alan R. Tomkins, Stephen Spence, Leslie Tomkins, Chaiyan "Lek" Chunsuttiwat, and Woods Mackintosh
Set decoration: Ted Glass and Merideth Boswell
Casting: Risa Bramon Garcia, Billy Hopkins, and Heidi Levitt
Sound: Bill Daly
Costume design: Ha Nguyen
Music: Kitaro
MPAA rating: R
Running time: 140 minutes

> *Principal characters:*
> Le Ly .... Hiep Thi Le
> Sergeant Steve Butler .... Tommy Lee Jones
> Mama................................. Joan Chen
> Papa .... Haing S. Ngor
> Eugenia .... Debbie Reynolds
> Sau................................ Dustin Nguyen
> Bernice............................ Conchata Ferrell
> Madame Lien.......................... Vivian Wu
> Anh .... Long Nguyen
> Le Ly (five years old) .... Bussaro Sanruck

Loosely based on two memoirs by Le Ly Hayslip, *Heaven and Earth* tells the epic saga of a young girl growing up in the 1960's in war-torn Vietnam and her voyage to a new life in the United States. This film is the third in a trilogy by producer-director-screenwriter Oliver Stone. His first, *Platoon* (1986), which starred Tom Berenger, Willem Dafoe, and Charlie Sheen, won Academy Awards for Best Picture and Best Director, among others. Stone again won an Academy Award for Best Director for *Born on the Fourth of July* (1989), starring Tom Cruise. Unfortunately, although *Heaven and Earth* is an extremely ambitious film, it proved less successful than the previous two.

The film begins in the 1950's when the protagonist, Le Ly (Bussaro Sanruck), is a child living in the rice-farming village of Ky La, in central Vietnam. The views of lush, verdant scenery and simple peasants working in the fields convey a bucolic life-style that had remained virtually unchanged for a thousand years despite the arrival of French colonists nearly seventy years earlier. Then the film jumps abruptly to the 1960's and the escalation of events that would come to be known in the United States as the Vietnam War.

The wartime scenes are very graphic and violent. Teenage Le Ly (now played by Hiep Thi Le) becomes enamored with the Viet Cong and their speeches about driving out the foreigners and reuniting their country. When she is caught helping them, she is taken to a South Vietnamese prison where she is brutally tortured. After her mother (Joan Chen) buys her release, Le Ly is taken by the Viet Cong, who believe that she betrayed them. They then not only torture her but rape her as well. At eighteen, Le Ly goes to Saigon with her mother, where they go to work for a wealthy man, Anh (Long Nguyen), and his wife, Madame Lien (Vivian Wu). When Le Ly becomes pregnant by Anh, her mother desperately attempts to abort the child. Unfortunately, Madame Lien finds out and banishes them from the house. From here, Le Ly's life continues its downward spiral as she attempts to support herself and her young son amid the chaos of the war-torn city.

The mood of the film changes abruptly, if only for a short time, with the appearance of a Marine sergeant, Steve Butler (Tommy Lee Jones). In an amusing scene, Le Ly is persuaded by a friend to help her trick Steve out of his money. He is not easily dismissed, however, and follows Le Ly to her home. He has only the best intentions, and the two become lovers. He at first appears to be her savior: They marry, and he eventually takes Le Ly out of Vietnam to his mother's home in San Diego. The early scenes of 1970's Southern California serve as a pleasant diversion to an otherwise sobering film. Steve's mother, Eugenia, is played by Debbie Reynolds in an all-too-brief cameo, and his overweight and very voluble sister, Bernice, is played for all its comic potential by Conchata Ferrell.

Le Ly is at first overwhelmed by these huge, enthusiastic people, who hug her and speak a mile a minute. The supreme comic moment comes when Le Ly goes with Bernice to the kitchen to help prepare dinner and confronts the largest home refrigerator ever made. In the production notes, the filmmakers admit that during the American part of the story they employed a visual style of slightly heightened realism in order to present the country from the point of view of Le Ly, a newcomer. As Bernice swings both doors open wide, Le Ly sees more food—steaks, frozen vegetables, and the like—than she has probably seen in her whole life. Another very amusing scene takes place when Steve accompanies Le Ly on her first trip to a large American grocery store. Unfortunately, these amusing scenes do not last long, and tragedy returns to plague Le Ly.

Even in this brave new world, Le Ly faces those old standbys—racism and sexism. Although she is welcomed, Le Ly must endure the unthinking remarks of Steve's middle-class family as well as the unfriendly stares of strangers. Even Steve makes a few racist remarks of his own. Her sons deny their ancestry in school by claiming to be Hispanic. Further, Steve is not as well off as he first led Le Ly to understand. When she wants to go to work to help support the family, he refuses. Le Ly, however, has worked all her life, as is expected of a Vietnamese woman. Her working, their money problems, and their past wartime traumas, (Steve's as well as Le Ly's) all come back to haunt them. Not as strong as Le Ly, Steve sucombs to alcoholism and eventually takes his own life.

Never one to give up, Le Ly successfully rears three sons, the first by Anh and the other two by Steve. Almost twenty years after she left, Le Ly returns to Vietnam with her children to see her mother once more and to reconnect with her remaining family members before once more returning to the United States. The production notes add that at the time of the film's release, Le Ly was living in California with her sons and had helped build several health clinics in Vietnam through the East Meets West Foundation.

Like a modern-day Scarlett O'Hara, Le Ly survives civil war, famine, poverty, and the breakup of her family. She proves repeatedly the validity of something her father (Haing S. Ngor) had told her years before, that "freedom is never a gift, it must be won and won again." In this epic film, Le Ly's life comes to represent more than just one woman's rise from very humble circumstances, but rather symbolizes the turmoil and hardship endured by Vietnam as a whole. Le Ly's family becomes representative of all Vietnam, divided among itself—some supporting the North, some the South. Le Ly's marriage to Steve achieves greater significance when seen as the symbolic representation of the war's outcome: Peace, but for a price—Le Ly forgoes her country and her heritage by marrying an American and moving to the United States, where she adopts a new way of life. Yet this new life is not as idyllic as was first represented and is imperiled by the past. In the end, Le Ly returns, if only for a visit, to her homeland to once more make contact with her family and with her birthplace—contact that is essential to the Vietnamese way of life.

Hiep Thi Le gives an amazing performance as Le Ly, portraying her over a period of more than thirty years, from adolescence to middle age. A college student at the University of California at Davis, Hiep Thi Le made her acting debut with this role. Interestingly, she was born in Da Nang, Vietnam, near Le Ly's own home village of Ky La. She left Vietnam in 1979 for the United States when she was nine years old as one of the famed "boat people," traveling with her seven-year-old sister. The making of the film afforded Hiep Thi Le the opportunity to return to her native land for the first time since she had left and to visit with relatives she had not seen since she was a child. Her role as Le Ly is the keystone to the entire film, as she was required to appear in virtually every scene of this long film.

Joan Chen also deserves credit for her portrayal of Le Ly's mother, a hardworking and taciturn—but loving—woman reminiscent of the Asian mothers in another 1993 release, the film adaptation of Amy Tan's novel *The Joy Luck Club*, which Stone also produced. Chen is perhaps best known for her starring role in *The Last Emperor* (1987) and her role on David Lynch's cult television series *Twin Peaks*. Noteworthy also is

Haing S. Ngor as Le Ly's father. Ngor won an Academy Award for Best Supporting Actor for his role in *The Killing Fields* (1984). Ngor, a doctor who fell victim to the cruelties exacted by the Khmer Rouge in Cambodia in the late 1970's, also escaped to the United States, where, besides his occasional acting roles, he has headed several organizations devoted to helping fellow refugees.

The filmmakers took meticulous care re-creating the village of Ky La, filming primarily in the south of Thailand. Stone did his homework, even traveling with Le Ly Hayslip, Hiep Thi Le, and Joan Chen to the real Ky La, where the actors learned firsthand about life in a traditional farming village. Stone had Ky La rebuilt from the ground up, even shipping in thousands of plants from nurseries to recapture the lush greenery of Le Ly's home. The Saigon scenes were also filmed in Thailand, many of them in Bangkok's Chinatown district.

Although Stone chose the unusual perspective of a Vietnamese woman for his third cinematic examination of the Vietnam War, his adaptation of Le Ly Hayslip's story has its problems. The Asian stars, predominantly nonprofessionals who are forced to speak English throughout, are sometimes difficult to understand. More important, the scope of Le Ly's story is so vast that two hours is not enough time to do it justice. Nearly four decades are covered, decades packed with important historical developments and personal triumphs and failures. Hence, the story goes at a lightning pace, and the rapid sequence of events may confuse viewers.

In the end, Stone's cinematographic representation does not so much present images to the viewer as burn them into the viewer's retina with a red-hot poker. Much of the film features scenes of extreme violence and cruelty, perhaps judged necessary for the emotional impact of the film, but nevertheless grueling for the audience. The coup de grace is the suicide of Le Ly's husband—a devastating development that causes the film to end on a depressing note. Although the film's production values are high, the end result is a disappointment.

Cynthia K. Breckenridge

Reviews

Chicago Tribune. December 24, 1993, VII, p. 21.
The Christian Science Monitor. December 28, 1993, p. 14.
Entertainment Weekly. December 24, 1993, p. 36.
Film Review. February, 1994, p. 40.
The Hollywood Reporter. December 20, 1993, p. 6.
Los Angeles Times. December 25, 1993, p. F1.
New Statesman and Society. VII, January 21, 1994, p. 34.
The New York Times. December 24, 1993, p. C1.
The New Yorker. LXIX, January 17, 1994, p. 87.
Newsweek. CXXII, December 27, 1993, p. 47.
Variety. December 20, 1993, p. 4.
The Washington Post. December 25, 1993, p. B1.

A HOME OF OUR OWN

Production: Dale Pollock and Bill Borden for PolyGram Filmed Entertainment and
    A & M Films; released by Gramercy Pictures
Direction: Tony Bill
Screenplay: Patrick Duncan
Cinematography: Jean Lépine
Editing: Axel Hubert
Production design: James Schoppe
Set decoration: Steven A. Lee
Casting: April Webster, Paul Ventura, and Cate Praggastis
Sound: Steven Laneri
Costume design: Lynn Bernay
Music: Michael Convertino
MPAA rating: PG
Running time: 102 minutes

Principal characters:
    Frances Lacey . . . . Kathy Bates
    Shayne Lacey. . . . . Edward Furlong
    Mr. Munimura . . . . Soon-Teck Oh
    Norman . . . . Tony Campisi
    Lynn Lacey . . . . Clarissa Lassig
    Faye Lacey. . . . . Sarah Schaub
    Murray Lacey . . . . Miles Feulner
    Annie Lacey. . . . . Amy Sakasitz
    Craig Lacey . . . . T. J. Lowther
    Father Tomlin . . . . Melvin Ward

Family dramas that come out of Hollywood can be loaded down with a certain sentimentality that evokes emotion through manipulation, rather than through identification or understanding. *A Home of Our Own*, a film from Gramercy Pictures, thankfully eludes the pitfalls of sentimentality and tells an honest, straightforward story, which allows the emotions to come through naturally.

Although *A Home of Our Own* does travel somewhat along a path of predictability, it is in the simple storytelling that the strength and warmth of this film comes through. The honesty begins with screenwriter and executive producer Patrick Duncan, who draws upon his own real-life experiences in writing the story of *A Home of Our Own*, which centers on a single mother rearing six children. Duncan comes from a family of twelve children who were reared by his single mother and this real-life experience translates vividly to the screen.

A Home of Our Own tells the story of widow Frances Lacey (Kathy Bates) and her six children, who, in 1962, barely survive on Frances' factory salary. When Frances is fired for standing up to her harassing boss, she decides, then and there, to get her family out of the city and out of their rundown apartment. The Laceys pack everything they own into their beat-up Plymouth and head East. As Shayne Lacey (Edward Furlong), the fifteen-year-old eldest son and "man of the house" narrates in a voice-over, the Laceys were going to drive until they found what they were looking for. None of them knew what that was, but they did know that they would recognize it when they saw it. Somewhere in the middle of Idaho, Frances stops the car. Across the barren Idaho landscape she sees an old house without windows or a roof. She knows, however, that it has the potential to become the home she has always promised her children. The Laceys have finally reached their destination.

Part of Frances Lacey's strength comes from the fact that once she sets her sights on something, she will not be deterred. Despite the fact that the Lacey family does not have two nickels to rub together, Frances is determined to own the house and the land it sits on. She starts by convincing the owner, Mr. Munimura (Soon-Teck Oh), a Japanese-American widower who owns his own flower shop, to trade her children's labor for the house. Frances is the type of person who makes the most of what she has rather than dwell on what she does not. She sees in Mr. Munimura a man who lives alone and runs his own business—someone who might need his laundry cleaned and chores done around the house and shop. She talks him into trading work for the land and thus begins a friendship that will transform all their lives.

Mr. Munimura knew that Mrs. Lacey was a very special woman from the moment she walked in his door, with her brood of six behind her. Her determination and strength of will inspire him to deal with his own loss—the deaths of his own wife and child. The Laceys provide him with a renewed sense of life and of living.

Although Mr. Munimura is generous in his ability and willingness to help her family and to help make their home a reality, Frances is not so willing to accept his or anybody else's help. Determined to pay for or to earn every single thing, she refuses to accept "charity" even from the local church, which has a needy children's fund, and insists on paying for everything herself, with the money she earns from her job waiting tables at a local bowling alley, or from trading her children's labor for goods or services. When the children, aged five to fifteen, are not working for other people or going to school, they are working on the house, and their home quickly gets a canvas roof, windows, and newspaper insulation, as winter rapidly approaches.

While the younger children seem to be only concerned with the trivial aspects of their poverty, like not having a television, Shayne resents having left Los Angeles and finds it difficult to accept that the ramshackle hut they live in will ever become the home of their dreams. Sleeping three to a bed, with walls created by bedsheets and an outhouse for a bathroom, their "home" is far from the stuff of fantasies. Shayne does not share his mother's idealistic vision of the potential that lies within the four walls. He longs to return to Los Angeles, but, more than that, he longs for a life of his own that does not involve sacrificing everything he has and is for the house. Even at Christmas, the children receive tools as presents instead of toys—everything for the good of the house.

Sacrifice has always been Frances' way of life—there is no way else to live with six children—but it takes its toll on the children. When Frances sees the disappointment in her children's faces at Christmas, she finally recognizes that the sacrifice may have been too much. She allows Shayne to go out on a date with a girl from school and even gives him a precious five-dollar bill to spend on the evening, a gift that Shayne knows all too well is one of the most important things his mother will ever give him.

When tragedy strikes and all that the Laceys have worked for is lost, the town rallies around them, inspired by their determination and courage. Frances finally realizes that there are some things she cannot do alone and she accepts the town's help so that the Laceys can finally have a home to call their own.

A Home of Our Own is the first solo lead role for Academy Award-winning actress Kathy Bates since *Misery* (1990), the film that earned for her the Best Actress award. Since then, she has costarred in several films, most notably *At Play in the Fields of the Lord* (1991), *Fried Green Tomatoes* (1991), and *Used People* (1992). Rob Reiner's *Misery* marked the beginning of Bates's successful film career, and Bates is now one of the most sought-after actresses. She began her career in the theater, however, where she had an equally distinguished career, which culminated with a Tony Award nomination for her critically-acclaimed performance in Marsha Norman's *'Night, Mother*. Bates certainly is the focus of *A Home of Our Own*, as the stubborn and devoted mother of six. Bates makes full use of her impressive acting talents by avoiding all the many clichés that may come with a role such as this. She avoids sentiment yet allows the audience to experience her love and total devotion to her children and to their home. Bates delivers a powerful performance, the centerpiece to this touching film.

Bates is supported by a cast that includes her real-life husband, Tony Campisi, who plays her coworker, and Soon-Teck Oh, an actor most noted for his theatrical credits, which include Stephen Sondheim's *Pacific Overtures*. Of the six Lacey children, only two come from the show-business world—Edward Furlong, best-known for his role in *Terminator II: Judgment Day* (1991), and Amy Sakasitz, who appeared in *Dennis the Menace* (1993; reviewed in this volume). The other Lacey children were selected from a massive casting call in Utah, where *A Home of Our Own* was filmed.

Much of *A Home of Our Own* feels recycled—the struggling single mother, the large, loving family overcoming adversity and tragedy—but, somehow, it all seems to work in this film. Director Tony Bill, whose directorial achievements such as *My Bodyguard* (1980) and *Untamed Heart* (1993; reviewed in this volume) have earned him praise, stays true to characters and avoids telling an all-too-familiar story. While nothing in *A Home of Our Own* can be called groundbreaking, it does allow the audience to become involved and to care about the characters. When that happens, a film is a success. Although *A Home of Our Own* may not be one of the most talked-about films of 1993, it certainly should rank as one of the most sincere.

Catherine R. Springer

Reviews

Boston Globe. November 5, 1993, p. 42.

Chicago Tribune. November 5, 1993, VII, p. 22.

Cosmopolitan. CCXV, December, 1993, p. 12.

The Hollywood Reporter. October 21, 1993, p. 6.

Interview. XXIII, October, 1993, p. 66.

Los Angeles Times. November 5, 1993, p. F10.

The New York Times. November 5, 1993, p. B8.

San Francisco Chronicle. November 5, 1993, p. C3.

USA Today. November 5, 1993, p. D4.

Variety. October 21, 1993, p. 2.

The Washington Post. November 5, 1993, p. G7.

HOMEWARD BOUND
The Incredible Journey

Production: Franklin R. Levy and Jeffrey Chernov for Walt Disney Pictures, in
    association with Touchwood Pacific Partners I; released by Buena Vista Pictures
Direction: Duwayne Dunham
Screenplay: Caroline Thompson and Linda Woolverton; based on the novel *The*
    Incredible Journey, by Sheila Burnford
Cinematography: Reed Smoot
Editing: Jonathan P. Shaw
Production design: Roger Cain
Art direction: Daniel Self
Set decoration: Nina Bradford
Casting: Susan Bluestein and Marsha Shoenman
Sound: Bayard Carey
Special animal effects and makeup: Barry Demeter
Costume design: Karen Patch
Animal training: Joe Camp, Gary Vaughn, Tammy Maples
Music: Bruce Broughton
MPAA rating: G
Running time: 84 minutes

      Principal characters:

Shadow	(voice of Don Ameche)
Chance	(voice of Michael J. Fox)
Sassy	(voice of Sally Field)
Bob	Robert Hays
Laura	Kim Greist
Kate	Jean Smart
Peter	Benj Thall
Hope	Veronica Lauren
Jamie	Kevin Chevalia

Homeward Bound: The Incredible Journey is an excellent children's film, although
it tends to tug a little hard at times on the heart strings. In order to prepare the adult
viewer adequately, one need merely describe the ending. Three children—Peter (Benj
Thall), Hope (Veronica Lauren), and Jamie (Kevin Chevalia)—play outside their
Northern California home with their new stepfather, Bob (Robert Hays), where the
family has just returned after an extended stay in San Francisco. Although happy to
be home, the children mourn the loss of their beloved pets, whom they put to board at
the ranch of a family friend, Kate (Jean Smart). The animals ran away and disappeared
into the wilderness. The family has made an exhaustive search throughout the film,
trying to locate the two dogs and the cat, a search they have been forced to abandon.

    Suddenly, Jamie hears a dog bark. "Chance!" he cries. Their mother, Laura (Kim

Greist), emerges from the house and tries to calm her excited youngest son by telling him that it could not possibly be his beloved bulldog puppy, Chance. Yet, as all the family members pause to gaze toward the horizon, a dog appears—and it is Chance! Chance charges across the open field toward Jamie; Jamie charges toward Chance. They meet in the middle and hug each other in their joy. Now Hope is on the alert; she next spies her beloved Himalayan cat, Sassy, on the horizon. "Sassy!" cries Hope. Sassy runs across the open field toward Hope; Hope runs toward Sassy. They, too, meet and hug.

Finally, the eldest boy, Peter, waits in anticipation, scanning the horizon for any sign of his beloved golden retriever, Shadow—but apparently to no avail. He was old and it was too far, declares the disheartened boy, who turns away. Nevertheless, Mom returns her gaze to the horizon and sees the familiar shape appear. Brave, loyal Shadow, who was indeed injured when the audience last saw him, limps pathetically across the field toward his beloved owner. Peter dashes toward him, and he, too, is reunited with his best friend.

Homeward Bound is a remake of Disney's 1963 drama *The Incredible Journey*, which was in turn based on the 1960 novel by Sheila Burnford. While the original focused predominantly on the three animals and their journey, employing a narrator to express the animals' thoughts, the remake alternates scenes of the animals' adventures with scenes of the concerned family as they seek to discover the whereabouts of their beloved animals. Moreover, in the newer version, the animals are given distinct human personalities: Their amusing repartee is provided by the very talented Michael J. Fox as Chance, Don Ameche as Shadow, and Sally Field as Sassy.

The film opens with the marriage of the children's mother, Laura, to their new stepfather, Bob, at their beautiful home in the Northern California wilderness. This new family arrangement is made more difficult for the children because they must all relocate temporarily to San Francisco for their stepfather's job. The animals cannot come and are to stay at friend Kate's ranch. Sadly, the animals do not understand that the arrangement is only temporary, and they panic. As Kate, too, eventually leaves to go on a cattle drive, Shadow senses that something is wrong and leaps the fence to head for home, with the other two in close pursuit. Thus begins their incredible journey through the vast Sierra Nevada.

Homeward Bound becomes essentially a buddy adventure film, with the three pets learning to work together despite their very different personalities. During the course of the film, the animals learn to overcome their differences in order to survive their current ordeal. They alternately display kindness, compassion, and courage. Fox speaks the thoughts of the wisecracking, mischievous puppy, Chance, who is very inquisitive and often gets into trouble. He has some of the best lines, as when he spies a porcupine for the first time and exclaims that it looks like a squirrel having a really bad hair day. Veteran actor Don Ameche lends his voice to the older dog, Shadow, who never doubts the family's love and who is ever faithful to his young master, Peter. It is he who decides that they must escape the ranch and return home, and he who provides the mature reassurance that they will succeed. Sally Field voices the opinions of the spoiled, finicky cat, Sassy; although a complainer at the beginning, she proves her worth by the end of their journey.

The voyage itself is full of adventure and is very well paced, thanks to the capable direction of Duwayne Dunham. The animals encounter wild animals (some benign, others not so benign), they lose Sassy at one point in a raging waterfall but are later reunited, and they protect a little girl who is lost in the woods until a search crew arrives. In fact, members of the search crew recognize the animals from their human family's description and attempt to help them by placing them at an animal shelter until their family can arrive to claim them. Again, the animals misunderstand and panic. In the most amusing sequence in the film, Sassy, who had earlier broken loose from the shelter employees and escaped, returns and enters the building to the familiar strains of television's *Mission Impossible* theme music in order to rescue "her boys." The chase and escape are very well choreographed, and the entire sequence serves to delay dramatically the final, very emotional reunion with their human family.

The cinematography is excellent, with Oregon's Eagle Cap Wilderness area doubling for the Sierra Nevada, where most of the action takes place. The views are breathtaking, with tall mountains, beautiful trees, and spectacular waterfalls. In fact, director of photography Reed Smoot also served as the cinematographer for the IMAX film *Grand Canyon: The Hidden Secrets*. The animals have numerous close encounters with wildlife, including a grizzly bear, a mountain lion, a porcupine, and a skunk. The domesticated animal actors give excellent performances, causing one to wonder which of their actions were strictly choreographed and which came naturally. The action moves quickly, helped particularly by the crosscutting of scenes of the concerned family with scenes of the three animals. Composer Bruce Broughton is also to be congratulated for his inspiring musical score.

Probably the main grievance one could venture against this otherwise fine children's film would be the overt sexism. The two dogs, the larger and stronger animals, are males, while in this newer version the cat has been rendered a female. Sassy, true to her name, is bitchy, overly concerned with her appearance, and fears trekking through the wilderness. Moreover, it is Sassy who prepares dinner—she catches fish from the river for the males. It is Shadow, the older male, who becomes leader, and Sassy, in a nursing/mothering mode, who tends to Chance when he is wounded by the porcupine.

Nevertheless, *Homeward Bound* aptly lives up to the Disney tradition of fine family entertainment. The animals' actions and the dialogue provided by the human actors are comic and entertaining, the story line and the action are swiftly paced, the scenery is gorgeous, and there are no "bad guys," only misguided humans and Mother Nature herself.

Cynthia K. Breckenridge

Reviews
Boston Globe. February 12, 1993, p. 52.
Chicago Tribune. February 12, 1993, VII, p. 27.

The Hollywood Reporter. February 3, 1993, p. 8.
Los Angeles Times. February 3, 1993, p. F6.
The New York Times. February 3, 1993, p. B1.
Sight and Sound. III, November, 1993, p. 44.
Time. CXLI, April 5, 1993, p. 60.
USA Today. February 3, 1993, p. D10.
Variety. February 3, 1993, p. 2.
The Wall Street Journal. February 4, 1993, p. A16.
The Washington Post. February 13, 1993, p. G12.

HOT SHOTS! PART DEUX

Production: Bill Badalato; released by Twentieth Century-Fox
Direction: Jim Abrahams
Screenplay: Jim Abrahams and Pat Proft
Cinematography: John R. Leonetti
Editing: Malcolm Campbell
Production design: William A. Elliott
Art direction: Greg Papalia
Set decoration: Jerie Kelter
Casting: Jackie Burch
Visual effects supervision: Erik Henry
Sound: Thomas Causey
Costume design: Mary Malin
Stunt coordination: Ernie Orsatti
Music: Basil Poledouris
MPAA rating: PG-13
Running time: 89 minutes

Principal characters:

Topper Harley	Charlie Sheen
President Tug Benson	Lloyd Bridges
Ramada Rodham Hayman	Valeria Golino
Colonel Denton Walters	Richard Crenna
Michelle Rodham Huddleston	Brenda Bakke
Harbinger	Miguel Ferrer
Dexter Hayman	Rowan Atkinson
Saddam Hussein	Jerry Haleva
Williams	Michael Colyar
Rabinowitz	Ryan Stiles

Hot Shots! Part Deux is a silly sequel of sorts to director Jim Abrahams' equally silly 1991 film *Hot Shots!* Where the first film lampooned 1986's *Top Gun*, its sequel tackles the Rambo films: *First Blood* (1982), *Rambo: First Blood Part II* (1985), and *Rambo III* (1988). The spoof even stars Richard Crenna—who played the role of Colonel Sam Trautman in the Rambo films—as Colonel Denton Walters. This name is an obvious takeoff on the name of the character he played, Walter Denton, on the 1950's television series *Our Miss Brooks.*

In the role of the Sylvester Stallone/Rambo character is a very muscular Charlie Sheen, reprising his role of Topper Harley from *Hot Shots!* Instead of a fighter pilot, however, he plays a trained killing machine, a soldier who, because of his unrequited love for Ramada Rodham Hayman (Valeria Golino), has been sequestered in a monastery with monks who are sworn to a life of silence and celibacy, as were their fathers and their fathers before them.

Like the first film, this one is set against the troubles in the Persian Gulf. Here, a decidedly incompetent and ridiculous Saddam Hussein (Jerry Naleva) is holding U.S. soldiers as prisoners of war. Following several unsuccessful rescue attempts, it is Topper's turn to try to save the men who were sent in to rescue the men who were sent in to rescue the men who were taken prisoner because, as Central Intelligence Agency operative Michelle Huddleston (Brenda Bakke) puts it, he is the best of what is left.

It is a pedestrian plot at best (" 'No originality' is our credo," states the director), but plot is never the focus of a film by one-third of the original Zucker-Abrahams-Zucker (commonly known as ZAZ) team. ZAZ elevated parody films to new heights with their films *Airplane!* (1980) and *Top Secret!* (1984) and their *Police Squad!* television series, which was later turned into two feature films, *The Naked Gun: From the Files of Police Squad!* (1988) and *The Naked Gun 2½: The Smell of Fear* (1991). Abrahams, now on his own, proves that parody is not dead, although the genre it spoofs may, indeed, be on its last legs. (On a late-night talk show, Sylvester Stallone was asked to comment about Sheen's takeoff of him in *Hot Shots! Part Deux*. Stallone thanked Sheen because the satire so thoroughly trashed the genre that he was safe from having to star in *Rambo IV*.)

In *Hot Shots! Part Deux*, plot takes a back seat to humor. In an Abrahams spoof, however, the comedy goes beyond mere slapstick and puns—although these do abound. What makes Abrahams' films so enjoyable are the layers of jokes he constructs on the screen. Astute audiences know to watch these films with an eye to the background: Iraq is found on a map next to a country called Ahardplace; Saddam Hussein's kitchen is filled with items like Saharan Wrap, Aunt Jamal pancake mix, Hungry Nomad dinners, and Old Iraqi Beer; an enemy Arab ship is named the Behn Gazzarah.

Perhaps best of all, *Hot Shots! Part Deux* excels at thievery—it steals its plot, its characters, its dialogue, and its scenes from every imaginable film and television source. From the spaghetti-eating scene in Walt Disney's animated *Lady and the Tramp* (1955), with *The Godfather* (1972) in the background, to the steamy backseat limo ride in *No Way Out* (1987), the film becomes more than a parody; it becomes a motion-picture trivia fest. Also spoofed in the film are classic scenes from *The Wizard of Oz* (1939), *Star Wars* (1977), and *Basic Instinct* (1992), as well as the television shows *Sea Hunt* (which also starred Lloyd Bridges), *Father Knows Best*, and *American Gladiators*. The best takeoff, however, is reserved for *Apocalypse Now* (1979), which starred Charlie's father, Martin, who makes a cameo appearance to great effect in *Hot Shots! Part Deux*. Another amusing cameo is by Bob Vila, who is improving the insulation at the monastery.

Even the end credits are not sacred, a legacy of Abrahams' days with the ZAZ team. All the female characters in the film have First Lady Hillary Rodham Clinton's maiden name, for example, Ramada Rodham Hayman and Michelle Rodham Huddleston. Also included are fun facts about tartar sauce and baseball player Darryl Strawberry, and even the secret to 1992's *The Crying Game* is divulged. Hidden among the song credits is "I Got a Lot of Hair for a Bald Guy and If I Wear It Like This You'll Never Notice" by Michael Bolton, and toward the end there is even a pop quiz. No one should leave one of these films before the very last frame of film has passed through the projector.

Hot Shots! Part Deux is ludicrous and preposterous. There is something for every comic bent: shallow jokes that are easily grasped, wittier jokes that require just a bit more attention, and the subtle contextual piracy from multiple sources that tests one's knowledge of popular culture. Whatever the audience, everyone is sure to find something amusing in this high-caliber parody; as one of Fox's top ten grossers for 1993, it shows that audiences were, indeed, finding it amusing.

Beverley Bare Buehrer

Reviews

Chicago Tribune. May 21, 1993, Section 7, p. B.
Entertainment Weekly. May 28, 1993, p. 47.
The Hollywood Reporter. May 21, 1993, p. 9.
Los Angeles Times. May 21, 1993, p. F8.
The New York Times. May 21, 1993, p. B6.
San Francisco Chronicle. May 21, 1993, p. C1.
Sight and Sound. III, September, 1993, p. 47.
USA Today. May 21, 1993, p. 2D.
Variety. May 21, 1993, p. 2.
The Washington Post. May 21, 1993, p. B7.
Washingtonian. XXVIII, July, 1993, p. 17.

HOUSE OF CARDS

Production: Dale Pollock, Lianne Halfon, and Wolfgang Glattes for Mario and
Vittorio Cecchi Gori, Silvio Berlusconi, and Penta Pictures, in association with
A & M Films; released by Miramax
Direction: Michael Lessac
Screenplay: Michael Lessac; based on a story by Lessac and Robert Jay Litz
Cinematography: Victor Hammer
Editing: Walter Murch
Production design: Peter Larkin
Art direction: Charley Beal
Set decoration: Leslie E. Rollins
Casting: Mali Finn
Sound: Thomas Brandau
Costume design: Julie Weiss
Music: James Horner
MPAA rating: PG-13
Running time: 107 minutes

Principal characters:

Ruth Matthews	Kathleen Turner
Jake Beerlander	Tommy Lee Jones
Sally Matthews	Asha Menina
Michael Matthews	Shiloh Strong
Adelle	Esther Rolle
Lillian Huber	Park Overall
Stoker	Michael Horse
Judge	Anne Pitoniak

House of Cards is an intelligent, low-budget picture that took years to get produced
and distributed. The story, about a young girl who withdraws into a very private world
of magical fantasy after the death of her father, was intelligently designed. In addition,
the film offers a haunting performance by Asha Menina, who plays the girl, Sally. Also
strong are Kathleen Turner as her mother, Ruth Matthews, an architect who is
determined to save her daughter, and Tommy Lee Jones as Dr. Jake Beerlander, the
child psychologist who attempts to convince Ruth that the child needs professional
help.

The releasing company, Miramax, had been successful in distributing high-quality,
low-budget films and finding an appropriate audience, but *House of Cards* was neither
so shocking as *The Crying Game* (1992) nor so elegant as *Howards End* (1992), both
previous Miramax releases. Furthermore, Miramax failed to launch a large advertising
campaign to help promote the picture. Despite East Coast premieres in Washington,
D.C., and Baltimore, where Kathleen Turner appeared in person to introduce and

promote the picture, the film did not cross over easily into the multiplex summer market, glutted with high-budget summer blockbusters such as *Jurassic Park* (1993; reviewed in this volume).

After the disastrous *V. I. Warshawski* (1991), star Kathleen Turner's box-office appeal slipped. She had seemingly reached her peak with such hits as *Body Heat* (1981), *Romancing the Stone* (1984), *Peggy Sue Got Married* (1986)—for which she was named Best Actress by the National Board of Review as well as nominated for a Golden Globe and an Academy Award—and *Prizzi's Honor* (1985), for which she earned the Best Actress Golden Globe Award. In *House of Cards* this award-winning actress gives an affecting performance as a mother who is determined to do what she believes is right for her child.

Tommy Lee Jones was brilliant as Clay Shaw in Oliver Stone's *JFK* (1991) and had done good work in other pictures, such as *Coal Miner's Daughter* (1980), the story of Loretta Lynn, starring Sissy Spacek. For the most part, Jones has worked as a character actor specializing in terrorists, villains, and psychopaths, winning an Emmy Award for his portrayal of Gary Gilmore in the television production of *The Executioner's Song* (1982). Curiously, his popularity increased with the release of *The Fugitive*, also in 1993—too late, unfortunately, to help build an audience for *House of Cards*. Despite negative criticism of the film itself, Jones is quite effective and convincing as Dr. Jake Beerlander.

The story begins with the Matthews family vacationing in Mexico. Unfortunately, tragedy strikes, and the father is killed in a fall from a pyramid at an archaeological site. Despite the fact that the whole family is grief-stricken, Sally is especially devastated by her father's death, for reasons not fully understood until later. Returning home from Mexico, Sally refuses to speak, perhaps showing symptoms of being autistic, although it is important to note that the film at no point identifies Sally as an autistic child. As the viewer alone knows, Sally has been told by a Mayan shaman in Mexico that it is easier to see without words, and for that reason, apparently, she has withdrawn into silence.

Sally, a precocious child who has learned three languages—English, Spanish, and Mayan—is told by a kindly old Mexican of Mayan descent that her father's spirit has gone to the moon. Thus Sally focuses upon an internal fantasy of getting there, too, a fantasy that is elevating and mysterious, symbolized by the intricate "house of cards" she builds in her room. This fantasy manifests itself in other odd ways, prompting her to climb trees, houses, and, in one scene, a construction crane. Following the latter incident, Dr. Beerlander accuses Ruth of child neglect and gains custody of Sally.

Ruth, however, refuses to acknowledge that the child has a problem and that Sally is putting herself into life-threatening situations. This denial makes Ruth uncooperative with Dr. Beerlander, who wants to help Sally. Ruth instead wants to enter Sally's mind and share her fantasy. To this end, Ruth attempts to find ways to communicate with Sally without speaking. When Sally builds her intricate house of cards, Ruth takes pictures of the structure and, working with a computer, fabricates a virtual nine-story structure of wood and metal—a spiral leading upward to the moon. Ruth claims that if she could meet her there, she could bring her back. The film reaches a happy conclusion after a contrived metaphysical climax between mother and daughter on the mother's life-size "house of cards."

The film indulges itself by playing with the new technology of virtual reality, stylishly rendered through special effects. It also evokes a New Age interest in Mayan mysticism. The primary achievement of the film, however, is to present a compelling parental dilemma, reduced effectively to human dimensions through the strength of the acting, not through special effects. Nevertheless, controversy arose concerning Sally's "problem." Because Sally displays symptoms of autism, such as the extreme withdrawal into her personal fantasy, as well as such physical skills as digital dexterity and climbing abilities, most viewers assumed it was a film primarily about the childhood disorder.

While Sally is undergoing treatment at the children's hospital, Ruth discovers two children "talking" to each other in prime numbers and finds that she is able to communicate with them by adapting their numerical "language." This episode gives her the idea of reaching Sally through the child's structural fantasy, a controversial therapeutic agenda. Some mothers of autistic children protested the way autism was represented in the film. Kathleen Turner was left with the unenviable task of defending the film against criticism that the film had not accurately represented autism. She emphasized the fact that no one says that Sally is autistic. In fact, Dr. Beerlander at one point speculates that Sally may be brain-damaged.

The film's emotional conflict echoes the dilemma of Dr. Dysart in Peter Shaffer's play *Equus* (1974), in which the doctor hesitates to "cure" a severely disturbed boy for fear he will destroy the wondrous, creative dream/fantasy in which the boy lives, rendering the boy merely "normal." In *House of Cards*, Ruth is impressed by the special talents of the disturbed children she sees. Sally herself demonstrates a creative talent for geometrically designed structures as part of her levitation fantasy. Her talent is awesome, but, as Dr. Beerlander asserts, "Normal is awesome!" He wants to return Sally to the normal world yet wonders whether one withdraws or rejoins the world through a creative act. In the end, Ruth succeeds in returning Sally to the ordinary world but on her own terms and by means of her own creative design. Her approach is not as commonsensical as that of the mother in *Lorenzo's Oil* (1992), but her determination and her faith in her child's ability to recover is very similar, as is the message to the medical establishment. It is unfortunate that *House of Cards* was buried in the avalanche of summer features.

James M. Welsh

Reviews
Boston Globe. July 2, 1993, p. 41.
British Medical Journal. CCCVII, November 6, 1993, p. 1218.
Chicago Tribune. July 2, 1993, VII, p. 31.

The Christian Science Monitor. July 23, 1993, p. 13.
Los Angeles Times. June 25, 1993, p. F14.
The New York Times. June 25, 1993, p. C18.
San Francisco Chronicle. July 2, 1993, p. C4.
USA Today. July 1, 1993, p. D2.
Variety. CCCL, February 15, 1993, p. 84.
The Washington Post. July 2, 1993, p. B7.

HOUSEHOLD SAINTS

Production: Richard Guay and Peter Newman for Jonathan Demme and Jones
     Entertainment Group; released by Fine Line Features
Direction: Nancy Savoca
Screenplay: Nancy Savoca and Richard Guay; based on the novel by Francine Prose
Cinematography: Bobby Bukowski
Editing: Beth Kling
Production design: Kalina Ivanov
Art direction: Charles Lagola
Set decoration: Karen Wiesel
Casting: John Lyons and Julie Madison
Sound: William Sarokin
Costume design: Eugenie Bafaloukos
Music: Stephen Endelman
MPAA rating: R
Running time: 124 minutes

Principal characters:

Catherine Falconetti	Tracey Ullman
Joseph Santangelo	Vincent D'Onofrio
Teresa Santangelo	Lili Taylor
Carmela Santangelo	Judith Malina
Nicky Falconetti	Michael Rispoli
Lino Falconetti	Victor Argo
Leonard Villanova	Michael Imperioli
Young Teresa	Rachael Bella
Evelyn Santangelo	Illeana Douglas
Frank Manzone	Joe Grifasi

Director/screenwriter Nancy Savoca received critical acclaim for her 1989 debut film *True Love*, which focused on a working-class Italian-American wedding in the Bronx. In this film, she approached the dark landscape of blue-collar American family life with humor and honesty. Her honest approach leads her to create true-to-life stories rather than fairy tales, and she avoids the sterile endings that Hollywood assumes most Americans desire in film. In fact, her ending for *True Love* was a shocker. Fed up with the jealous dependency of his bride, the irresponsible buffoonish groom announces he wants to spend his wedding night drinking with his buddies. Despite the film's critical success, Savoca had problems getting her first film distributed because she refused to change this ending to one in which everyone lived happily ever after.

Household Saints, Savoca's third film, is meticulously and lovingly wrought. The story focuses again on the world of Italian-Americans and Italian immigrants. It examines the relationships among three generations of women, how each relates to God and responds to community beliefs. Each woman interprets her role in the household differently, especially as it relates to the men's desires. Despite the dark and mystical quality of the narrative, the film is often amusing and manages to parody devout Catholicism without making fun of the believers themselves. Savoca, whose Argentinean mother was very Catholic, is interested in an intelligent exploration of the superstitions, ghosts, and saints that these worshipers cherish, and her approach to their mysticism is appropriately spiced with magical realism and humor. Nun-bashing, as the director has said, is fun but too easy.

Based on the novel by Francine Prose, *Household Saints* is a dreamily realistic fable set in New York's Little Italy in the years following World War II. Spanning more than twenty years, it charts not only America's changing culture as seen through the eyes of its protagonists but also the changing role of women in this tightly knit community. The film opens in the present day with a family luncheon on the lawn. An elderly couple tells the story of St. Therese of Mulberry Street, the young local girl who yearned to become a saint. They then proceed to take their listeners back in time.

On an unusually hot night during the festival of San Genarro, a group of sweaty men gather behind the butcher shop to wager on a few hands of pinochle. Lino Falconetti (Victor Argo) is drunk and dazed enough by the heat to wager his daughter against a blast of cool air from the butcher's walk-in freezer. The young butcher, Joseph Santangelo (Vincent D'Onofrio), has been crudely but doggedly wooing Catherine Falconetti (Tracey Ullman) for some time. Now his miraculous hand in a game of cards allows him to win her for his own.

Catherine is seventeen years old and has been growing up in post-war New York City surrounded by men, her life shaped by the dual forces of family and tradition. She cooks and cares for her widowed father, Lino, and her war-weary older brother, Nicky (Michael Rispoli), who lives in a dream world and is infatuated with Japanese women. To break the monotony of household chores, Catherine reads film magazines. After she marries Santangelo, she is initiated into a strange new world of wifely duties, dominated by her husband's lovemaking and the religious superstitions and mysterious rites of womanhood performed by her new mother-in-law, Carmela Santangelo (Judith Malina). Carmela instructs Catherine on the proper respect for saints who protect the family, and she teaches her to make the sausage for the butcher shop.

Due in part to Carmela's superstitions, Catherine's first pregnancy is spent fearfully: She believes that she will give birth to a chicken because she entered the shop pregnant and saw a fowl being butchered. The pregnancy does end in tragedy, but eventually Joseph and Catherine have another child. Meanwhile, Carmela has died. A miraculous event marks her as one of the household saints: The family's ill-kept potted plants have inexplicably grown lush on the morning of her death. Savoca's stylized suggestions here and elsewhere have a surreal, almost painterly quality that give her film a storyteller's animation and energetic strangeness.

The Santangelos name their healthy beautiful daughter after the saint of flowers and labor. Surrounded by tradition and her family's strong and quirky personalities, Teresa Santangelo (Lili Taylor) grows up devoted to her faith. She grows so certain of her special vocation, in fact, that she believes she can become a saint. As a young girl, she dedicates herself to Our Lady of Fatima and yearns to know the secret of the Virgin's letter to the world. Strongly influenced by the Catholic school myth of Saint Therese, "The Little Flower," Teresa resolves to obtain religious perfection in her life. Her parents wonder at her fervor, which seems a little extreme to them.

Apparently, a supernatural relationship of some sort exists between the dead grandmother Carmela and her granddaughter Teresa. While Carmela's religious devotion was expressed with anger and criticism, however, Teresa's religious nature expresses itself with a purity and genuine love that can only be described as saintly. Her obsession with Jesus and the Virgin does not seem at first so unusual. Her boyfriend, Leonard Villanova (Michael Imperioli), tells her that half the girls in his school wanted to be "The Little Flower." Unfortunately, Teresa's ongoing dedication to God comes at the expense of her health and family harmony. When Teresa announces her intention to join the Carmelites, her father roars that no daughter of his will be a slave to line the Pope's pockets. In response, Teresa begins a hunger strike. Her refusal to take food is patterned after the way a number of female saints found they could exert power over the patriarchal system.

Eventually she can no longer resist food, and her determination to join the nuns seems to have abated. Soon, she is in college and spending time at Leonard's apartment. When she loses her virginity, she is able to convince herself at first that it is Jesus' plan for her. Her fervent devotion continues, and Teresa goes on searching for ways to redeem herself and prove her devotion.

That opportunity arrives when she is alone in Leonard's apartment, ironing his shirts with a concentration that makes her seem deep in penance. She has a vision that Jesus has come to see her (just as her grandmother used to welcome her deceased husband's spirit into the living-room armchair for chats). In an extended scene, the two radiate knowingly at each other, and Jesus multiplies the one red checkered shirt Teresa is ironing into dozens of identical shirts. The image of all those shirts lining the closet and swirling over the apartment walls is simultaneously hilarious and very moving. It is Taylor's skilled manipulation of her character's joyous response that allows this scene to avoid seeming ridiculous. When Teresa succumbs to pure happy laughter, with Jesus smiling at her, the film has accomplished another sudden and bizarre turn successfully.

Leonard, Catherine, and Joseph, however, believe that Teresa must be having a nervous breakdown. She is taken to a sanatorium, where she continues to insist that Jesus visited her. One day, she asks her father about the legendary pinochle game in which he won her mother's hand. Joseph shows consternation and guilt, since it is a story he has tried to keep secret. Yet Teresa points out that the winning hand was a miracle. Her insistence on miracles as part of everyday life ties a number of incidents in the story together at last. The film also implies that small miracles beget more miracles, a repeated theme. In the end, the tragedy of Teresa's unexplainable death becomes a celebration of a miracle when the gardens burst into bloom all over the sanatorium. It is then that her family and the community realize that she has indeed attained sainthood.

Household Saints combines elements of parable, popular folklore, and black comedy to tell a story about how people try to determine the extent and limits of their spiritual faith. Director Nancy Savoca has said that she wants her story to show that magic happens in everyday life, in ways people often take for granted: babies being born, people falling in love, cycles of death and birth. As Catherine Santangelo points out, the miracle is when you stop and pay attention.

JoAnn Balingit

Reviews
Boston Globe. October 29, 1993, p. 53.
Chicago Tribune. October 1, 1993, VII, p. 22.
The Christian Science Monitor. September 21, 1993, p. 14.
The Hollywood Reporter. September 15, 1993, p. 7.
Los Angeles Times. October 1, 1993, p. F16.
National Catholic Reporter. October 8, 1993, p. 15.
The New York Times. September 15, 1993, p. B3.
San Francisco Chronicle. October 1, 1993, p. C3.
Variety. September 14, 1993, p. 18.
The Wall Street Journal. September 23, 1993, p. A14.
The Washington Post. October 2, 1993, p. G3.

IN THE LINE OF FIRE

Production: Jeff Apple for Castle Rock Entertainment; released by Columbia
   Pictures
Direction: Wolfgang Petersen
Screenplay: Jeff Maguire
Cinematography: John Bailey
Editing: Anne V. Coates
Production design: Lilly Kilvert
Art direction: John Warnke
Set decoration: Kara Lindstrom
Casting: Janet Hirshenson and Jane Jenkins
Sound: Willie Burton
Costume design: Erica Edell Phillips
Music: Ennio Morricone
MPAA rating: R
Running time: 123 minutes

Principal characters:
<pre>
Frank Horrigan . . . . Clint Eastwood
Mitch Leary . . . . John Malkovich
Lilly Raines. . . . . Rene Russo
Al D'Andrea . . . . Dylan McDermott
Bill Watts . . . . Gary Cole
Harry Sargent . . . . Fred Dalton Thompson
Sam Campagna. . . . . John Mahoney
</pre>

In one of 1993's ten highest grossing films, *In the Line of Fire*, Clint Eastwood plays Frank Horrigan, a veteran Secret Service agent who has the notorious distinction of being the only active agent ever to lose a president. He was once John F. Kennedy's favorite and jogged dutifully behind the Dallas motorcade on that fateful day when the president was assassinated in 1963. Thirty years later, still haunted by his hesitation and failure to react, Horrigan is a self-described "borderline burnout with questionable social skills," a man whose life and self-respect nearly collapsed under the burden of alcoholism, divorce, and self-imposed disgrace.

Responding to what is considered a routine field call, Horrigan stumbles onto the trail of a would-be presidential assassin, a dangerous man who later affectionately calls himself Booth, in reference to President Abraham Lincoln's assassin, because he had "flair, panache." Booth is actually a former CIA operative named Mitch Leary, a cold-blooded hitman, a master of disguise and an expert at deception and deceit. In a series of seductive phone calls, Leary taunts Horrigan with his plans to kill the president and his insinuations concerning Horrigan's integrity and willingness to perform the ultimate service: to step into the line of fire and take the assassin's bullet.

Leary is the perfectly crafted, textbook antagonist, one who matches the hero's strength and intelligence. When asked why he wants to assassinate the president, Leary chillingly responds: "To punctuate the dreariness." He poignantly reminds Frank that there is no cause worth fighting for; all one has is the game. Indeed, it is this seductive game of psychological cat-and-mouse between two perfectly matched opponents, cut from the same mold but with differing motivations, that places *In the Line of Fire* above other thrillers. Both Horrigan and Leary have been betrayed by the very government that once prized their cold-bloodedness.

Clint Eastwood once again plays the man on the outside, the rugged individualist who refuses to waste his time on rules and departmental procedures when instead he could be out there doing rather than being. The greater part of Eastwood's career is based on the man who "speaks softly, but carries a big stick," from his early Sergio Leone Italian "spaghetti Westerns" to Dirty Harry. He became an American film icon, one of the few actors with enduring screen presence who acted out the audience's secret right-wing fantasies. In his early sixties, the veteran actor finally seems secure enough to have fun in the midst of a very serious situation.

In the Line of Fire is a taut, rapid-fire thriller that offers Eastwood the opportunity to meld his bipolar on-screen personas from such films as *Dirty Harry* (1971) and *Bronco Billy* (1980). The result is the apex of an acting career that has spanned thirty-plus years and thirty-seven starring roles in feature films. In a rare moment of working with a director other than himself, Eastwood allows himself the opportunity to mock his on-screen tough-guy persona. In fact, the script trades heavily on the Eastwood mystique, to the point of having Horrigan proclaim with a wink, "A good glare can be just as effective as a gun."

This melding of tough guy with sensitive feminist is further accomplished effectively through the relationship with fellow agent Lilly Raines (Rene Russo), a no-nonsense careerist who slowly allows herself to see past the hard edges of Horrigan. Raines is a beautiful, sensuous woman who has obviously been challenged by countless men who attempt to dismiss her as mere "window dressing." As Frank quickly amends, however, "We're all window dressing, just here to make the President look good." The May-December romance between Horrigan and Raines works effectively to address the social issues of not only sex discrimination but age discrimination as well. Rene Russo, probably best known for the scene in *Lethal Weapon III* (1992) in which she and Mel Gibson try to top one another with their respective battle scars, offers a strong and often amusing sparring partner for Eastwood's Frank. They have a comfortable, easy rapport, and Frank's avowal that he would sacrifice his career for her reflects the dilemma more commonly faced by women in the late twentieth century.

In contrast to director Oliver Stone's typical heavy-handedness in such films as *JFK* (1991) or *Born on the Fourth of July* (1989), the polemics of writer Jeff Maguire's Academy Award-nominated original script are often subtle and used more for character development and delineation than in driving the film's narrative. While some critics believed that the character of Lilly Raines was underwritten—and therefore in itself mere "window dressing"—one can argue that the role would have been difficult to strengthen, given the confines of the script and story. Raines is, indeed, a working woman, and when Horrigan is removed from the presidential detail, Raines continues on the tour. She is one of the rare on-screen heroines who is an active character, not one who waits around for her man to return home after a tough day at the office. Furthermore, it is Raines who makes the active decision to ask for Horrigan to be on her team. She is too smart and conscientious to let personal feelings get in the way of business.

It is easy to be mesmerized by John Malkovich's performance as the would-be assassin, Mitch Leary; and, in fact, Malkovich received an Academy Award Nomination for Best Supporting Actor for his portrayal. With his impressive array of wigs and mustaches and false noses, Leary is the kid with all the fun toys, and therefore it becomes much easier for an established stage actor such as Malkovich to perform the same kind of razzle-dazzle, sleight-of-hand tricks as were afforded Anthony Hopkins in his Oscar-winning performance as Hannibal Lecter in Jonathan Demme's *The Silence of the Lambs* (1991). In many ways, it is more difficult to play the protagonist, who bears the burden of surrogate viewer. This is by no means a belittlement of Malkovich's accomplishment. He does a remarkable job giving urgency to, and insight into his character's plight. What he fails to do, however, is to grasp fully the viewer's sympathy. Ever the master thespian, Malkovich is the epitome of a Method actor's performance, with carefully thought-out line deliveries that ooze insinuating perversity.

German-born director Wolfgang Petersen, perhaps best known for his critically aclaimed World War II U-boat drama *Das Boot* (1981), the highest-grossing foreign-language film ever to be released in the United States (as of *In the Line of Fire*'s release), was Eastwood's personal choice to direct *In the Line of Fire*. Petersen has the distinction of being the first German director to be nominated for an Academy Award as Best Director, but his English-language films such as *Shattered* (1991) and *Enemy Mine* (1985), have met with far less success. Petersen focuses his taut, unadorned style on creating a quick pace (aided by the very talented Anne V. Coates, who earned an Academy Award Nomination for her editing work) that combines with brutal characterizations to distract the viewer from the predictability of the plot line. Particularly frustrating, however, is Petersen's refusal to reveal Leary's face to the audience in the beginning of the film. This stylistic technique does nothing to heighten the suspense, since audiences sense the villain's identity by the casting of certain actors in most contemporary Hollywood tales.

What was once considered to be Eastwood's greatest weakness, the terse, laconic acting style that became legendary since Leone's *A Fistful of Dollars* (1967), is now being embraced. Eastwood appears to have silenced his critics with his demythologizing Western *Unforgiven* (1992), which finally garnered both national and international artistic recognition, including nine Academy Award nominations. It went on to win four, including Best Picture and Best Director. *In the Line of Fire* was originally conceived as a directing project for Eastwood, but the actor confessed to having suffered long bouts of envy over the fun that fellow actors Gene Hackman, Richard Harris, and Morgan Freeman had while filming *Unforgiven* and vowed only to act in his next film.

One of the shortcomings of the film lies in its decision to fall victim to the "buddy cliché," that seemingly inevitable tactic of killing the partner in order to up the ante for the main character. In this case, Horrigan convinces his young partner, Al (Dylan McDermott), to remain in the service, despite Al's growing fear. When Al is killed by Leary in a thrilling chase across rooftops, Frank suffers the appropriate amount of guilt and vows revenge. This whole subplot is unnecessary and seems to exist solely to fulfill audience expectations that if something happens to a man's partner, he must do something about it.

Whereas *Unforgiven* was a story of the futility of seeking redemption, *In the Line of Fire* presents the tale of a character who ultimately finds redemption through sheer will and determination.

Patricia Kowal

Reviews

America. CLXIX, September 11, 1993, p. 24.
Chicago Tribune. July 9, 1993, VII, p. 31.
Entertainment Weekly. July 16, 1993, p. 38.
Films in Review. XLIV, September, 1993, p. 329.
The Hollywood Reporter. July 6, 1993, p. 6.
Los Angeles Times. July 9, 1993, p. F1.
The New York Times. July 9, 1993, p. B1.
Newsweek. CXXII, July 12, 1993, p. 60.
Rolling Stone. August 5, 1993, p. 71.
Time. July 12, 1993, p. 61.
Variety. July 6, 1993, p. 4.
The Wall Street Journal. July 8, 1993, p. A12.
The Washington Post. July 9, 1993, p. B1.

IN THE NAME OF THE FATHER

Origin: Ireland, Great Britain, and USA
Released: 1993
Released in U.S.: 1993
Production: Jim Sheridan for Hell's Kitchen/Gabriel Byrne; released by Universal
    Pictures
Direction: Jim Sheridan
Screenplay: Terry George and Jim Sheridan; based on the autobiography *Proved*
    Innocent, by Gerry Conlon
Cinematography: Peter Biziou
Editing: Gerry Hambling
Production design: Caroline Amies
Art direction: Rick Butler
Casting: Patsy Pollock and Nuala Moiselle
Sound: Kieran Horgan
Costume design: Joan Bergin
Music: Trevor Jones
MPAA rating: R
Running time: 127 minutes

Principal characters:

Gerry Conlon	Daniel Day-Lewis
Giuseppe Conlon	Pete Postlethwaite
Gareth Peirce	Emma Thompson
Robert Dixon	Corin Redgrave
Joe McAndrew	Don Baker
Paul Hill	John Lynch
Carole Richardson	Beatie Edney
Paddy Armstrong	Mark Sheppard
Annie Maguire	Britta Smith
Sarah Conlon	Marie Jones
Barker	John Benfield
Benbay	Paterson Joseph
Pavis	Gerard McSorley

While such Irish films of the early 1990's as *The Crying Game* (1992) and *Into the West* (1993; reviewed in this volume) dealt with terrorism and social and political problems, *In the Name of the Father* was the most overtly political. No film delved as deeply into the turmoil of the Irish dilemma and few films about any subject have blended actual events, controversial political issues, and basic human drama so acutely.

In the Name of the Father is based on *Proved Innocent* (1990), Gerry Conlon's account of his false arrest and fifteen-year imprisonment. As the film opens, Gerry (Daniel Day-Lewis) leaves his native Belfast, Northern Ireland, in 1974 after the Irish Republican Army (IRA) threatens his life. Apparently, his petty thievery threatens the security of their arms caches. In London, Gerry and his friend Paul Hill (John Lynch) join a commune. On October 5, 1974, the IRA bombs two Guildford pubs, killing five young people. Under pressure to take quick action, the police, led by Robert Dixon (Corin Redgrave), arrest Gerry, Paul, and two of their commune friends, Paddy Armstrong (Mark Sheppard) and Carole Richardson (Beatie Edney), whom they torture into confessing.

One of the sad ironies of the situation is that the four are apolitical, interested far more in drugs, sex, and rock and roll than anything else. When Gerry's bookmaker father, Giuseppe (Pete Postlethwaite), comes to England to help his son, he, Gerry's aunt, Annie Maguire (Britta Smith), her husband, and her two young sons are also charged. Alleged evidence of traces of nitroglycerin on their hands makes them suspects in the making of the bombs. Even though Gerry and Paul have an alibi in a homeless Irishman with whom they spoke in a park at the time of the bombing, all are convicted.

The film finds its true focus once Gerry and Giuseppe (named for an Italian ice-cream maker in his mother's youth) go to prison. Despised by the English prisoners, Gerry is offered companionship only by the other outsiders, the West Indians led by Benbay (Paterson Joseph). Lazy, easygoing Gerry and his timid, conformist father have never communicated well, Giuseppe never giving Gerry the recognition he craves, Gerry resenting having grown up with a sickly father. Sharing a prison cell, Giuseppe tries to reach out to his son, with Gerry sneering at his father's all-purpose clichés.

Gerry eventually finds a surrogate father in Joe McAndrew (Don Baker), the IRA terrorist who actually carried out the Guildford bombings. Joe has told the police that Gerry and his friends are innocent. As Joe quickly takes charge of their cell block, Gerry begins to assert himself. When Joe sets on fire the chief of the prison officers, Barker (John Benfield), however, Gerry is disgusted and turns against Joe and toward his father.

Sadly, Gerry's attempts to reconcile himself with his father are short-lived since the feeble Giuseppe becomes increasingly ill and dies. During this time, English lawyer Gareth Peirce (Emma Thompson), a human rights activist, tries to reopen the case and eventually stumbles upon not only evidence of the innocence of Gerry and Paul but its suppression. The four are freed in 1989 when Peirce presents the new evidence in court.

Director Jim Sheridan and Terry George alter several facts in their screenplay for dramatic effect. The Conlons never shared a cell, Peirce never appeared in court on behalf of her clients because she is a solicitor and not a barrister, and the police suppression of Gerry and Paul's alibi was never mentioned during the proceedings.

In the Name of the Father has been attacked in the English tabloid press as a piece of anti-British propaganda. While Sheridan and George are more concerned with the emotional issue of injustice than with the nationality of its perpetrators, they make clear that such injustice is inevitable given the heat of the passions over Northern Ireland. Sheridan and George can be accused of oversimplifying the issues by portraying the police as villains out of an old-fashioned melodrama. Redgrave plays the chief investigator as a twitching mass of corruption. Pavis (Gerard McSorley), a detective from Belfast, is uncertain of Gerry's guilt one moment and is threatening to kill Giuseppe, jumping around with his gun pointed at Gerry's head, the next. The film does try to attain some balance, however, by showing the IRA negatively as well. Those in Gerry's neighborhood murder one of Gerry's friends for continuing to steal despite their warnings, and Joe McAndrew is depicted as a heartless savage.

Sheridan's cinematic skills have improved since the earnest yet awkward *My Left Foot* (1989), which also starred Daniel Day-Lewis, and the ponderously melodramatic *The Field* (1990). The opening sequence is brilliantly staged by Sheridan and edited by Gerry Hambling, who also cut *The Commitments* (1991), as Gerry, stealing scrap metal from a roof, is mistaken for a terrorist and chased through Belfast by British soldiers and tanks. Sheridan also strikes an almost perfect balance between the political, legalistic, and domestic sides of the Conlon story.

The many elements of *In the Name of the Father* also coalesce through the excellence of the performances, excluding the cartoonish police. Thompson does nothing to make the audience realize she is a star playing a supporting role, subtly conveying Peirce's dedication and compassion. Baker, a singer, musician, and former juvenile offender making his acting debut, was originally to play a small role but was given the part of Joe McAndrew when Gabriel Byrne, the film's executive producer, became unavailable. Seemingly effortlessly, Baker displays both the character's charisma and his viciousness.

Best known as the cruel father in *Distant Voices, Still Lives* (1988), Postlethwaite portrays Giuseppe as a painfully decent man who comprehends little of the world's complexities. He honestly thinks that if he goes to London to speak up for his son, Gerry will be freed. Postlethwaite gives Giuseppe the stiff-legged, hunched-over shuffle of a man overburdened but still confident that justice will prevail.

As if *The Last of the Mohicans* (1992) and *The Age of Innocence* (1993; reviewed in this volume), among others, had not already proved it, Day-Lewis belongs with Alec Guinness, Laurence Olivier, Marlon Brando, Albert Finney, Dustin Hoffman, and Robert De Niro as one of the greatest film actors. Like the latter, he is adept at portraying a character almost incapable of rational thought and maturity. His Gerry grows somewhat during his years in prison, yet the change is subtle and incomplete. Gerry is just as impulsive at the conclusion as at the beginning. Day-Lewis has no peer at knowing how to underplay certain scenes to balance the more emotional ones. The scene in which Gerry, outraged at the uselessness of language, begins destroying the audiotapes he has been making for his defense, wrapping the tape around his face and body, is extremely moving.

One affirmation of the film's success was its seven Academy Award nominations. *In the Name of the Father* was nominated as Best Picture, Jim Sheridan for Best

Direction, Terry George and Jim Sheridan for Adapted Screenplay, and Gerry Hambling for Editing. Also nominated were the film's three principals: Daniel Day-Lewis for Best Actor, Pete Postlethwaite for Best Supporting Actor, and Emma Thompson for Best Supporting Actress. It also received Golden Globe nominations for best drama, actor, and supporting actress.

Comparing *In the Name of the Father* to such political thrillers as Costa-Gavras' *Z* (1969), as have many reviewers, misses the uniqueness of the film. It triumphs by emphasizing the humanity beneath the issues.

Michael Adams

Reviews

America. CLXX, February 12, 1994, p. 20.
The Christian Science Monitor. December 28, 1993, p. 11.
Entertainment Weekly. January 21, 1994, p. 34.
The Hollywood Reporter. December 20, 1993, p. 6.
Interview. XXIII, December, 1993, p. 52.
Los Angeles Times. December 29, 1993, p. F1.
The New Republic. CCX, January 3, 1994, p. 28.
New Statesman and Society. VII, February 11, 1994, p. 35.
The New York Times. December 29, 1993, p. B1.
The New Yorker. LXIX, January 24, 1994, p. 88.
Newsweek. CXXIII, January 3, 1994, p. 63.
Variety. December 20, 1993, p. 12.
The Village Voice. XXXIX, January 11, 1994, p. 56.
The Wall Street Journal. January 11, 1994, p. A10.
The Washington Post. January 14, 1994, p. G7.

INDECENT PROPOSAL

Production: Sherry Lansing; released by Paramount Pictures
Direction: Adrian Lyne
Screenplay: Amy Holden Jones; based on the novel by Jack Engelhard
Cinematography: Howard Atherton
Editing: Joe Hutshing
Production design: Mel Bourne
Art direction: Gae Buckley
Set decoration: Etta Leff
Costume design: Bobbie Read, Bernie Pollack, and Beatrix Aruna Pasztor
Music: John Barry
MPAA rating: R
Running time: 118 minutes

Principal characters:
John Gage . . . . Robert Redford
Diana Murphy. . . . . Demi Moore
David Murphy. Woody Harrelson
Mr. Shackleford . . . . Seymour Cassel
Jeremy. . . . . Oliver Platt
Day Tripper. Billy Bob Thornton
Mr. Langford. . . . . Rip Taylor
Auction emcee . . . . Billy Connolly
Realtor. . . . . Joel Brooks
Van Buren . . . . Pierre Epstein

Many films raise moral questions over which audiences love to ruminate. Many of these films strike box-office gold even when critics find them wanting. Such is the case with *Indecent Proposal*. Producer Sherry Lansing cites *Indecent Proposal* as a story of love and of what money can and cannot buy, an interesting juxtaposition of ideas. Yet the film, for audiences, columnists, and talk-show hosts everywhere, boiled down to one question: Would you sleep with someone for a million dollars? Screenwriter Amy Holden Jones, who also wrote *Mystic Pizza* (1988) and *Beethoven* (1992), adds a fine gloss to an otherwise fiscal quandary by summarizing her film as relating to "the value of love and the endurance of love in the face of temptation and over a period of time."

David and Diana Murphy (Woody Harrelson and Demi Moore) met and married as teenagers. Diana sold real estate to pay David's way through architecture school and to support them while David established his career. With both of their careers on the rise, their life together seems perfect. In fact, the Murphys' biggest problem might be David's habit of leaving his muddy shoes on the kitchen table. Buoyed by their success, they have acquired a prime piece of beach-front property upon which they intend to build David's dream house. When the recession of the late 1980's hits the real estate market, however, meaning that Diana can sell no property and David can design no buildings, the Murphys quickly come to the edge of bankruptcy. Taking the five thousand dollars loaned to them by David's father, the pair heads to Las Vegas to try to win the rest of the fifty thousand dollars that they need to save their dream house. While they eventually lose the money, they meet billionaire John Gage (Robert Redford), who embodies the Faustian bargain that made this film a box-office hit: Would David allow Diana to spend the night with Gage in return for a million dollars? After dismissing and then considering the offer, the Murphys accept. Their marriage falls apart soon after Diana's tryst with Gage, and all three must reevaluate what they feel and desire.

In many ways, *Indecent Proposal* is anachronistic, a film of the 1980's floating adrift in the 1990's. Its director, Adrian Lyne, made a name for himself in the 1980's directing slick commercial films—*Flashdance* (1983), *Nine and a Half Weeks* (1986), and *Fatal Attraction* (1987)—and in many ways his formula is at work here, too. The filmmakers themselves compare *Indecent Proposal* to *Fatal Attraction*, finding that each "explores contemporary relationships and the consequences of moral compromises." While that may be true on one level, on a much more pertinent level *Indecent Proposal* is about money and sex, as are the other Lyne films mentioned above. At one point in *Indecent Proposal*, David and Diana have parlayed their five thousand dollars into twenty-five thousand dollars. Returning to their rather seedy Las Vegas motel room, they tumble among the bills, consummating their love for money as much as, or more so than, their love for each other. The scene is quite remarkable even beyond the basic of idea of sex literally on top of money. Lyne spends significant amounts of time exploring the cash-filled crevices of his stars. While certainly a cinematic first, this union of love and money is a hollow pleasure.

Also reminiscent of the 1980's is the Murphys' yuppie look and life-style. Even when they are experiencing hard times, they are beautiful to look at, as is Gage. In this film, it is one thing to be in financial straits and quite another to be unattractively dressed or out of shape. The advertisements for the film and the glossies sent out in the press packet included large photographs of each of the three leads, golden-age-of-Hollywood star shots. Soft-focus and high-contrast, the photographs emphasize what the film offers: fame, beauty, wealth. In support of this highly stylized view of the world, Lyne creates a self-conscious, highly stylized film that draws attention to itself. For example, the film begins and ends literally in fog, Lyne's characters floating in and out of view. Additionally, he makes extensive use of voice-overs, while Jones has given her characters such lines as, "Losing Diana was like losing part of me. I thought we were invincible."

One of the strengths of the film, however, is its minor characters. Oliver Platt's performance as the Murphys' lawyer, Jeremy, is one of the high points of the film. While his role adds few nuances to the stereotypical attorney—heartless, greedy—Platt brings a comic timing and irreverence desperately needed in this ponderous and overly stylized film. For example, when negotiating the contract for the night between

Diana and Gage, Jeremy pushes for additional clauses for payment even in the event of Gage's impotence or death. It is a clever, well-played scene.

Redford, on the heels of the box-office smash *Sneakers* (1992), gives one of his standard performances here, even while drawing on other Hollywood classics. Gage is very clearly reminiscent of the title character of F. Scott Fitzgerald's 1925 novel *The Great Gatsby*, made into a film starring Redford in 1974. Gage is a tan and beautiful loner, standing apart in his lovely pastel suits. Not unlike Gatsby, he hints of a sad past and has the same tragic wish for happiness. Gage, like Gatsby, has millions of dollars and no one with whom to share them. Beyond his rendition of the romantic hero, Redford also captures the romance and pity of Orson Welles' Charles Foster Kane when he gives his girl-that-got-away speech, retelling the sighting of a beautiful woman to whom he never spoke but whose beauty continues to haunt him. Taken almost verbatim from *Citizen Kane* (1941), the speech nevertheless has a visible impact on Diana and an audible impact on audiences. To say that Redford draws on other performances is not to diminish his achievement in *Indecent Proposal*. Given little with which to work, he manages to create a likable, sympathetic handsome man.

Beyond its look, it is possible that the film carries a deeper meaning. One possible reading of the film would be to see Diana as pulled between the two worlds of art (David, the artist who designs buildings) and commerce (Gage, the billionaire who trades in them). Clearly, then, Diana's role as a real estate agent makes her the perfect go-between for art and commerce. While such a schematic may reduce the film beyond what its trappings offer, it is a kinder reading of the film than that offered by several critics. For example, Peter Travers of *Rolling Stone* thought that the film offers Gage as a "romantic paragon" and David as a suffering artist, loving the simplicity of art and beauty. In his understanding of the film, Diana becomes a hedonist, unrestrained by moral bounds. For Travers, the bottom line in this scenario, labeled a "bonbon spiked with malice," is that the men get to be noble and good while the woman gets to be beautiful and "good in bed." Additionally, the film follows on the heels of a variety of films that have shown yuppies surviving the post-1980's withdrawal from high living. *Regarding Henry* (1991) and *The Doctor* (1991) both dealt with yuppies learning to set their priorities correctly. It would be possible to see *Indecent Proposal* as trying to address a similar issue. In support of this, the production notes quote Redford as saying, "*Indecent Proposal* is a postmortem of the 1980's when greed was licensed in the United States as a way to be and a way to go." The fact that the same unlikely boy-buys-girl story is being told in other 1990's films, such as *Honeymoon in Vegas* (1992), may also show a trend.

Although described as "lethargic," "insincere," and "preposterous," *Indecent Proposal* was a certifiable box-office hit. If indeed there is a dichotomy between a film for audiences and a film for critics, this may be a classic example. For example, the film's box office—nearly $260 million worldwide—was fifth highest of the films released in 1993. *Indecent Proposal* is likely to be a landmark film, if not for its art, then for the questions it raises.

Roberta Green

Reviews

Boston Globe. April 7, 1993, Living, p. 45.
Chicago Tribune. April 7, 1993, p. C1.
Entertainment Weekly. April 16, 1993, p. 34.
Films in Review. XLIV, July, 1993, p. 263.
Los Angeles Times. April 7, 1993, p. F1.
The New York Times. April 7, 1993, p. B3.
The New Yorker. LXIX, April 26, 1993, p. 107.
Newsweek. April 19, 1993, p. 64.
Rolling Stone. April 29, 1993, p. 67.
Sight and Sound. III, June, 1993, p. 55.
Time. CXLI, April 19, 1993, p. 71.
The Washington Post. April 7, 1993, p. D1.

INTO THE WEST

Origin: Ireland
Released: 1993
Released in U.S.: 1993
Production: Jonathan Cavendish and Tim Palmer, for Majestic Films International, Film Four International, Little Bird Productions, and Parallel Films; released by Miramax Films
Direction: Mike Newell
Screenplay: Jim Sheridan; based on a story by Michael Pearce
Cinematography: Tom Sigel
Editing: Peter Boyle
Production design: Jamie Leonard
Art direction: Mark Geraghty
Casting: Ros Hubbard and John Hubbard
Sound: Peter Lindsay
Costume design: Consolata Boyle
Music: Patrick Doyle
MPAA rating: PG
Running time: 92 minutes

Principal characters:
Papa Riley . . . . Gabriel Byrne
Kathleen . . . . Ellen Barkin
Ossie . . . . Ciaran Fitzgerald
Tito . . . . Ruaidhri Conroy
Grandfather . . . . David Kelly
Superintendent O'Mara . . . . Jim Norton
Inspector Bolger . . . . Brendan Gleeson
Hartnett . . . . John Kavanagh
Barreller . . . . Colm Meaney
Tracker . . . . Johnny Murphy

Into the West is an unusual blend of several genres: children's film, animal story, family drama, fantasy, social criticism, quest adventure, and Western. That it succeeds reasonably well on all these levels is equally unusual. Screenwriter Jim Sheridan and director Mike Newell have created a unique—if difficult to classify—film that is both moving and entertaining.

The film centers on one of the last nomadic tribes in Europe, the Celtic gypsies known as the "travelers," who roam the west country of Ireland. Victims of prejudice because of their rootless ways, many travelers have been herded into urban jungles. This is where Papa Riley (Gabriel Byrne) and his two young sons, Tito (Ruaidhri Conroy) and Ossie (Ciaran Fitzgerald), find themselves at the beginning of *Into the*

West. Papa has rejected the tribal life following the death of his wife and has brought the boys to a prisonlike tower block in the slums of Dublin.

Tito and Ossie have two means of escape from this gloom. One is watching American Western films on televison. The other is the magical white horse that has followed the caravan of their maternal grandfather (David Kelly) into the city. The horse, known as Tir na nOg, is seemingly wild but surprises the grandfather by calmly allowing the boys to mount and ride it. Its name, meaning "the land of eternal youth," comes, explains the grandfather, from a Celtic myth about a land under the sea.

Soon Tir na nOg is living in the Riley apartment, riding elevators and taking showers. When neighbors complain, the police arrive to try to take it away. In the course of the struggle, the horse jumps over an automobile. An unscrupulous police officer, Inspector Bolger (Brendan Gleeson), illegally sells Tir na nOg to Hartnett (John Kavanagh), a wealthy breeder who has the horse trained as a jumper.

When Tito and Ossie see their horse performing on television, they steal it in front of thousands of spectators, initiating a nationwide search. The remainder of *Into the West* is a chase as the boys ride their horse to Ireland's western coast pursued by the police, the vengeful Hartnett, and their protective father and his friends. Papa has sensed something eerie about Tir na nOg, and its attachment to Tito and Ossie seems almost supernatural. The horse is revealed, in the climactic showdown, to be the spirit—or possessed by the spirit—of the boys' dead mother.

Sheridan, Newell, and Byrne, who served as associate producer and was instrumental in getting the film made, clearly are criticizing Irish society for its mistreatment of and intolerance toward the travelers and by extension its social inequalities in general. This message is made palatable by being embedded in a film thick with texture: the boys' desperate need for their mother, particularly Ossie, who never knew her, since she died giving birth to him; Papa's anger at his inability to improve his lot; the beauty and grace of Tir na nOg; the frequent comic touches, such as the boys' bathing the horse in an apartment's shower stall, that grow out of the material rather than being imposed upon it; and the allusions to Westerns, which represent the desire for adventure, escape, and freedom. While on the run, Ossie asks Tito if they are cowboys or Indians. With a $10,000 reward on their heads, they are outlaws, but since their way of life is threatened, they are more obviously the Indians of Ireland.

Into the West works as a children's film because Tito and Ossie are sympathetic figures with whom children can identify. Their working-class realism, moreover, makes it easy for adult viewers to feel compassion for them. They are victims of the circumstances of their birth and of a hostile society. That magic is their only apparent hope for escape adds poignance to their plight.

Into the West is most likely to work for children as a rousing adventure in which two kids run away from the bad guys on a beautiful white horse. Adults are more likely to respond to it as a quest-for-freedom story. Miramax Films attempted to emphasize this aspect of the film by changing its marketing approach in large cities a month after the initial American release, advising parents to see it as an art film and leave the children at home.

Screenwriter Sheridan is experienced with creating works about Irish youths rising above their limitations, having written and directed *My Left Foot* (1989), the story of Christy Brown's becoming a painter and writer despite severe physical handicaps. Newell, best known for *Dance with A Stranger* (1984), *The Good Father* (1987), and *Enchanted April* (1992), seems to be one of those talented directors who strive not to repeat themselves. Nevertheless, his four best films all center on protagonists who attempt to deal with harsh realities, though each does so with quite different results. *Into the West* is a logical continuation of *Enchanted April*, although the characters and situations are worlds apart, since the women on vacation in 1920's Italy in the latter film also need a touch of magic to find themselves. The subtlety of Newell's approach to his material in *Into the West* can best be seen in his decision to show the boys' rescue of Tir na nOg on a small scale as televised news highlights instead of as a melodramatic spectacle.

The visual style of *Into the West* owes much to cinematographer Tom Sigel and production designer Jamie Leonard. They make Dublin horribly oppressive, a dark, dank, and dingy hole. The countryside, in contrast, is presented not as a picturesque fairyland but as a vast space dwarfing the tiny heroes and offering both freedom and danger.

Gabriel Byrne's tormented, brooding Papa might seem too intense for this fragile story, but his unhappiness offers hints at what might await his sons. Ellen Barkin and Colm Meaney offer solid support as travelers who help Papa search for the boys. The best performances in *Into the West*, however, are those of Ciaran Fitzgerald and Ruaidhri Conroy, who make Ossie and Tito believably vulnerable and resourceful. Despite looking like nonprofessionals, both are screen veterans, Conroy having appeared in *Hear My Song* (1991) and *Far and Away* (1992), Fitzgerald having been in the latter as well as *My Left Foot* and *The Miracle* (1991). One of the many triumphs of *Into the West* is that these young actors are never cloying.

Michael Adams

Reviews

Chicago Tribune. September 17, 1993, VII, p. 36.
The Christian Science Monitor. October 29, 1993, p. 13.
Entertainment Weekly. October 1, 1993, p. 40.
The Hollywood Reporter. January 25, 1993, p. 18.
Los Angeles Times. September 17, 1993, p. F12.
The New York Times. September 17, 1993, p. B9.
Rolling Stone. May 27, 1993, p. 59.
Time. CXLII, September 27, 1993, p. 86.
Variety. CCCXLIX, December 21, 1992, p. 60.
The Village Voice. XXXVIII, September 21, 1993, p. 55.
The Wall Street Journal. September 23, 1993, p. A14.
The Washington Post. September 17, 1993, p. D7.

THE JOY LUCK CLUB

Production: Wayne Wang, Amy Tan, Ronald Bass, and Patrick Markey for
   Hollywood Pictures and Oliver Stone; released by Buena Visa
Direction: Wayne Wang
Screenplay: Amy Tan and Ronald Bass; based on the novel by Tan
Cinematography: Amir Mokri
Editing: Maysie Hoy
Production design: Donald Graham Burt
Art direction: Diana Kunce
Set decoration: Jim Poynter
Casting: Heidi Levitt
Sound: Curtis Choy
Costume design: Lydia Tanji
Music: Rachel Portman
MPAA rating: R
Running time: 138 minutes

Principal characters:

Suyuan	Kieu Chinh
Lindo	Tsai Chin
Ying Ying	France Nuyen
An Mei	Lisa Lu
June	Ming-Na Wen
Waverly	Tamlyn Tomita
Lena	Lauren Tom
Rose	Rosalind Chao
Harold	Michael Paul Chan
Ted	Andrew McCarthy
Rich	Christopher Rich
Lin Xiao	Russell Wong
Old Chong	Victor Wong
An Mei's mother	Vivian Wu
Mr. Jordan	Jack Ford
Mrs. Jordan	Diane Baker
Ying Ying (sixteen to twenty-five years old)	Yu Fei Hong
June (nine years old)	Melanie Chang
Waverly (six to nine years old)	Vu Mai
Lindo (fifteen years old)	Irene Ng

Amy Tan's best-selling novel *The Joy Luck Club* (1989) reaches the screen through
Wayne Wang's direction of a screenplay by Ronald Bass and Tan. The story is told
through flashbacks and voice-overs, charting the lives and loves of the four Chinese

immigrant women who make up the Joy Luck Club and their American-born, adult daughters. The Joy Luck Club is the name the older women gave to the regular players in their weekly mah-jongg games. Upon the death of one of the members, Suyuan (Kieu Chinh), the other three women arrange for Suyuan's daughter, June (Ming-Na Wen), to travel to China to meet two half sisters whom Suyuan abandoned decades earlier for reasons that become clear by film's end. It is the bon voyage party for June that prompts the reminiscences of the mothers and daughters—tales of hardship, despair, and self-discovery.

The eight main characters each have a dramatic past. Young June (Melanie Chang) grew up as a piano prodigy forced to succeed for the sake of her mother's pride. Afraid that she could never fulfill Suyuan's expectations, however, June gave up the piano, never to play again. Suyuan had reasons of her own for being overly involved in June's young life. During a wartime evacuation in China many years before June was born, Suyuan fell ill while fleeing with her twin daughters. She was forced to abandon the children. When Suyuan unexpectedly recovered, she was forced to live with the guilt and loneliness of having abandoned her babies, whom she never saw again.

Waverly (Tamlyn Tomita) grew up under a dysfunctional relationship with her mother, Lindo (Tsai Chin), similar to June's. Young Waverly (Vu Mai) was a chess prodigy whose talent was constantly pitted against that of June's in a game of one-upmanship by the haughty mothers. Like June, young Waverly developed a hatred for her talent, and she too abandoned it. Rather than fight Waverly, Lindo never mentioned chess again. When Waverly tried to take it up again, her spirit as well as her ability could not be found.

Like Lindo, Suyuan, too, had a difficult past in China. Young Lindo (Irene Ng) was forced into an arranged marriage that came with shrewish in-laws. Although Lindo was miserable, her spirit could not be broken, and by guile, she freed herself from the imprisoning marriage and came to America. It is this history that later caused her to want too much for and from her daughter, Waverly. Lindo's irrepressible spirit later caused Lindo to crush her daughter's more fragile spirit.

Lena (Lauren Tom) entered into a Chinese-American marriage based more on financial equality, regardless of how equal it actually was, than on love. Lena's loveless life revives painful memories for her mother, Ying Ying (France Nuyen). As a young woman, Ying Ying (Yu Fei Hong), was seduced by handsome playboy Lin Xiao (Russell Wong). The ideal romance turned into a torturous marriage. Ying Ying would wait with her child while Lin would carouse with other women for days at a time. When he was home, he was abusive both verbally and physically. Pushed to her limit, Ying Ying committed an unspeakable act. Desperate to take something from Lin, she found herself holding their baby under the bath water. When she realized what she had done, it was too late: She had drowned her own child. The event stole her spirit from her.

Since Ying Ying thereafter lived without spirit, she had none to pass on to her Americanized daughter, Lena. Lena's passionless marriage is a result of this lack of spirit. Because Ying Ying cannot bear to see her daughter live like this, she pleads with her to capture and embrace her own spirit and discover what she truly wants in life. Acting on her new bravery, Lena leaves her husband and finds happiness and a new beginning.

Rose (Rosalind Chao) allowed herself to fall into a servile relationship with her husband, Ted (Andrew McCarthy). Rose's lack of self-worth led her to devote herself entirely to tending to her husband. As a result, she became the type of wife he neither asked for nor wanted. Rose did not realize how much she took after her grandmother, the mother of An Mei (Lisa Lu). An Mei had grown up in a broken home in China. After her father died, her mother (Vivian Wu) became the fourth wife to a powerful and cruel man and was ostracized by her family. An Mei witnessed the demoralizing conditions her mother went through. When her mother committed suicide, An Mei found the strength to fight back.

An Mei cannot see this strength in her daughter Rose. Rose does not value herself highly enough and therefore devotes her efforts to pleasing her husband. Only on the brink of divorce does Rose realize how important she is, and save herself and her marriage as a result.

One of the predominant themes of this film is the idea of self-worth. Each of the older women came from a time and a place when women were not highly valued. Women at that time and in that traditional society were brought up to believe that their sole purpose in life was to cater to the needs of their husbands. Arranged marriages and bigamy on the part of the men did little to enhance the women's self-esteem.

An Mei's mother is a case in point. Her feelings of worthlessness drove her to suicide. Those feelings return to haunt her granddaughter, Rose. Ying Ying's self-esteem also received a battering from her adulterous husband Lin Xiao. His cruelty drove her to kill her own child, an act for which she can never completely forgive herself. At best, she strives to help her daughter, Lena, get out of a bad marriage. Lindo, too, found herself abused by her spoiled, immature husband and vicious mother-in-law. Fortunately, she was able to turn their superstitions and selfishness to her advantage and escape. Her pride and self-confidence surface continually in her rearing of Waverly.

The other overriding theme running throughout this film is the idea of mothers wanting something better for their children. Given the difficult pasts of Suyuan, An Mei, Lindo, and Ying Ying, it is no wonder. Although given with the best intentions, their wishes for their children become burdens rather than blessings: Their hopes for their daughters turn sour when they push too hard. This theme is best illustrated in the scene in the beauty shop with Waverly and her mother, Lindo, when Waverly finally confronts her mother, lamenting the fact that she never felt that she ever pleased her. The powerful representation of the mother/daughter dynamic in this film transcends racial and cultural boundaries to speak to all women of all generations.

In the end, however, the stories of these women are not tragedies, but triumphs. The film focuses not on living under harsh circumstances, but on rising above them. Each woman displays strength and power, and each woman gains control over her life and her future. The stories are extreme, making the women's victories more incredible and fulfilling. Self-assertion and success win out over hardship and repression. The women are not victims or even survivors, they are conquerors.

The Joy Luck Club is, above all else, a group of stories about hope. Spirits triumphed over adversities, will overpowered repression, wisdom stamped out ignorance, and women found their inner strengths to overcome the unfair conditions life threw at them. The opening of the film states that the club was not about joy or luck, but about hope. It is something that all the women eventually possessed and what made them capable of the strengths they exhibited. With *The Joy Luck Club*, director Wang has successfully adapted a very complicated book, involving eight main characters and numerous jumps backward and forward in time. The acting by all the principals is superb, particularly Tsai Chin as Linda and Rosalind Chao as Rose. The film ends with the tearful reunion of June and her half sisters back in China, where all these heart-rending stories originated. It is a cause for celebration. They have one another, they have strength, and they have hope.

Pete Peterson

Reviews
Chicago Tribune. September 17, 1993, VII, p. 31.
The Christian Science Monitor. September 16, 1993, p. 11.
Entertainment Weekly. September 17, 1993, p. 74.
Films in Review. XLV, January, 1994, p. 51.
The Hollywood Reporter. September 7, 1993, p. 6.
Los Angeles Times. September 8, 1993, p. F1.
The New York Times. September 8, 1993, p. B1.
Newsweek. CXXII, September 27, 1993, p. 70.
Time. CXLII, September 13, 1993, p. 68.
Variety. September 7, 1993, p. 2.
The Wall Street Journal. September 9, 1993, p. A18.
The Washington Post. September 24, 1993, p. C1.

JURASSIC PARK

Production: Kathleen Kennedy and Gerald R. Molen for Amblin Entertainment; released by Universal Pictures
Direction: Steven Spielberg
Screenplay: Michael Crichton and David Koepp; based on the novel by Crichton
Cinematography: Dean Cundey
Editing: Michael Kahn
Production design: Rick Carter
Art direction: Jim Teegarden and John Bell
Set decoration: Jackie Carr
Casting: Janet Hirshenson and Jane Jenkins
Special visual effects: Industrial Light and Magic, Inc.
Sound: Ron Judkins (AA), Gary Summers (AA), Gary Rydstrom (AA), and Shawn Murphy (AA)
Sound effects editing: Gary Rydstrom (AA) and Richard Hymns (AA)
Women's costume supervision: Sue Moore
Men's costume supervision: Eric Sandberg
Full-motion dinosaurs: Dennis Muren (AA)
Live-action dinosaurs: Stan Winston (AA)
Dinosaur supervision: Phil Tippett (AA)
Special dinosaur effects: Michael Lantieri (AA)
Stunt coordination: Gary Hymes
Music: John Williams
MPAA rating: PG-13
Running time: 126 minutes

Principal characters:
Dr. Alan Grant	Sam Neill
Dr. Ellie Sattler	Laura Dern
Dr. Ian Malcolm	Jeff Goldblum
John Hammond	Richard Attenborough
Robert Muldoon	Bob Peck
Donald Gennaro	Martin Ferrero
Dr. Wu	B. D. Wong
Tim	Joseph Mazzello
Lex	Ariana Richards
Arnold	Samuel L. Jackson
Dennis Nedry	Wayne Knight
Jurassic Park tour voice	Richard Kiley

Jurassic Park, Steven Spielberg's frightening thriller, is best understood as a *Jaws* (1975) for the 1990's, with dinosaurs replacing great white sharks. A one-dimensional story, this film delivers where it counts, in the terrifying special effects. Technically

Jurassic Park does for the live-action monster genre what *Who Framed Roger Rabbit* (1988) did for animation. In fact, this is more a technological marvel than a great, whole piece of cinema. Not surprisingly, this monster hit earned more than $50 million during its first weekend of release, setting a record for the film business. By year's end, *Jurassic Park* had earned more than $300 million domestically and more than $800 million worldwide. It became not only the top-grossing film of the year but the highest-grossing film to date. In the summer of 1993, America was flooded with dinosaurs, as it had been with sharks in 1975.

Director Steven Spielberg surely frightens viewers. Indeed, a week or so later, one forgets that the heroes were rescued and only remembers that huge *Tyrannosaurus rex* pursuing Dr. Alan Grant (Sam Neill) and Dr. Ellie Sattler (Laura Dern) as they try to protect the frightened grandchildren of mad entrepreneur and park financier John Hammond (Richard Attenborough). Hammond, a billionaire, concocts the ultimate theme park—filled with actual dinosaurs that have been re-created from fossilized DNA. The result is Jurassic Park, built on an island off Costa Rica.

To this island Hammond brings a small group of experts, who are in the process of realizing his grandiose vision. Prior to its completion, paleontologists Grant and Sattler are brought in to inspect the park; Hammond's grandchildren are also visiting. They survive. Not so lucky are Donald Gennaro (Martin Ferrero), an attorney representing the theme park's investors, and assorted workers. Playing devil's advocate, mathematician Ian Malcolm (Jeff Goldblum) advances his Chaos Theory, a concept that states that nature is unpredictable. Not unexpectedly, nature goes out of control. When a storm strands Hammond's guests in the middle of the park at night, the audience anticipates the forthcoming death and destruction. The giant reptiles are brilliantly conceived—lifelike and natural. Even skeptics have to be amazed. *Jurassic Park* represents the ultimate ride in the ultimate theme park.

Nevertheless, in the novel, author Michael Crichton envisioned something else. For example, according to the press kit, his character John Hammond was meant to be a "dark Walt Disney." Crichton's story posed a moral and ethical question: Should human beings meddle with DNA? With life itself? The film, however, glosses over these difficult issues in favor of chills and thrills. Thus Crichton's cautionary tale of humans gone beyond their capabilities has been transformed, by Spielberg's not-so-subtle sensibilities, into a dance of threats, chills, and escapes.

Jurassic Park presents a dark and frightening look at technology gone awry. It is too tense and frightening for children less than twelve years old, as the PG-13 rating warns, but questions have been shoved aside in the end, as all the money and work paid off. The film quickly became a popular cultural phenomenon, and video distributors stocked any and all titles dealing with dinosaurs. Video-store patrons could choose from *Danny and the Dinosaur*, *Adventures in Dinosaur City*, *Land of the Lost*, and even *Dinosaur!*, a documentary narrated by Walter Cronkite. This was all in addition to the toys and memorabilia from books to bags to stuffed animals to games to any item on which a dinosaur imprint could be made.

Furthermore, *Jurassic Park* is filled with hundreds of surreptitious product plugs.

The control room for the Jurassic Park in the film, where the main characters seek refuge from the rampaging reptiles, for example, is packed with Apple computers. Other Apple equipment appears throughout. The use of these items was not accidental, as the company paid the producers well for this product placement. Many other examples abound.

The real stars of the film, however, are the dinosaurs. These were not fashioned by one individual auteur. It took hundreds of workers, many from Industrial Light and Magic, and an estimated $25 million to create the fabulous visual fantasy to be witnessed in this film. The credits at the end of *Jurassic Park* form a monster in themselves. The press kit lists thirty-eight puppeteers, thirteen stunt persons, and more names that require ten single-spaced pages to list. The film won Academy Awards in all three categories for which it was nominated: Visual Effects, Sound, and Sound Effects Editing.

Because of the vastness of this undertaking, *Jurassic Park* was a long time coming. Spielberg and his thousands of helpers began the project in 1990. Yet principal photography was not started until August, 1992, exactly two years and one month from the commencement of preproduction. The park's outdoor scenes were shot in Kauai, Hawaii, and the principal buildings and interiors were realized at Universal Studios in Los Angeles. Stage 24 at Universal became the kitchen at the Visitors Center; Stage 27 became the locus for the "T-rex" confrontation; Stage 28 housed the computer control room of Jurassic Park. The film's climactic finale was filmed on Stage 12 at Universal, in Jurassic Park's enormous Rotunda. This was to be the film to top all films.

When all is said and done, *Jurassic Park* is not so much a great motion picture as a milestone in the development and use of film technology to make millions and millions of dollars. Steven Spielberg and Universal Studios kicked off the blockbuster era in Hollywood in 1975 with *Jaws* and extended its life with *Jurassic Park*, and they will long be remembered for their ultimate skill in marketing, sales, and the creation of popular culture.

Douglas Gomery

Reviews

Baltimore Sun. June 10, 1993, p. 1E.
Boston Globe. June 11, 1993, p. 41.
Cinefex. August, 1993, p. 99.
Entertainment Weekly. June 18, 1993, p. 38.
Film Journal. July, 1993, p. 31.
Films in Review. XLIV, July, 1993, p. 259.
The Hollywood Reporter, June 7, 1993, p. 9.
Issues in Science and Technology. X, Fall, 1993, p. 92.
Los Angeles Times. June 11, 1993, p. F1.
Nature. CCCLXIII, June 24, 1993, p. 681.

New Scientist. CXXXIX, July 3, 1993, p. 43.
The New York Times. June 11, 1993, p. B1.
The Philadelphia Inquirer. June 11, 1992, Weekend, p. 3.
Time. CXLI, June 14, 1993, p. 69.
Variety. June 7, 1993, p. 3.
The Washington Post. June 11, 1993, p. G1.

JUST ANOTHER GIRL ON THE I.R.T.

Production: Erwin Wilson and Leslie Harris; released by Miramax Films
Direction: Leslie Harris
Screenplay: Leslie Harris
Cinematography: Richard Connors
Editing: Jack Haigis
Production design: Mike Green
Set decoration: Robin Chase
Costume design: Bruce Brickus
Music: Eric Sadler
MPAA rating: R
Running time: 97 minutes

> *Principal characters:*
> Chantel Mitchell . . . . Ariyan Johnson
> Tyrone . . . . Kevin Thigpen
> Natete. . . . . Ebony Jerido
> Paula . . . . Chequita Jackson
> Gerard . . . . Jerard Washington
> Debra Mitchell. . . . . Karen Robinson
> Owen Mitchell. . . . . Tony Wilkes
> Cedrick. . . . . William Badget

At the end of *Just Another Girl on the I.R.T.*, African American writer-director Leslie Harris fills the screen with the following quote: "*Just Another Girl on the I.R.T.*—The film Hollywood dared not to do." This film about a teenage African American girl who faces a crisis when she becomes pregnant in the tough world of late twentieth century Brooklyn most likely would indeed not have been made in Hollywood—for a couple of reasons. The most obvious one is that virtually no African American women had broken through the barriers of mainstream Hollywood by the mid-1990's. The only other female African American to have had a film in wide release was director Euzhan Palcy, who, at a very young age, directed Donald Sutherland and Marlon Brando in *A Dry White Season* (1989)—but it should be noted that that film was not a "Hollywood" film. When Harris says that this is a film "Hollywood dared not to do," she implies that the subject matter is somehow too intense or truthful for frivolous, commercial Hollywood. As depicted in this film, however, the subject matter is quite familiar and not at all disturbing or intense. In fact, Harris, unfortunately, takes a rather pedestrian approach to this important story, which has the odd effect of trivializing it.

Chantel (Ariyan Johnson) is a bright and clever African American teenager living in Brooklyn who dreams of becoming a doctor. She is tough, saying, "I'm a Brooklyn girl . . . lots of people think Brooklyn girls are tough. I do what I want when I want." She is also motivated, hardworking, and a good student, who also works in a gourmet food shop with her high school classmate, Natete (Ebony Jerido). She and Natete take the I.R.T. subway to work, hence the film's title. The subway is used as a theatrical device, in the beginning of the film, for the audience to get to know and understand Chantel. There are many shots of her taking the I.R.T. with Natete to and from work, and she talks directly to the audience from the subway, saying, "when I'm with my friends, I act like it don't matter. 'Cause it don't." She wants more, however, a desire that is evident on two levels: First, she wants to make more of her life than her parents, who live in the housing projects; second, she wants material things. When she meets a handsome older man outside the subway who tells her he is a model, she asks, ". . . and does the model have a car?"

Her desire to find someone with a car and money proves to be her downfall. At a party, she meets Tyrone (Kevin Thigpen) and apparently prefers him to her current boyfriend, Gerard (Jerard Washington), because he has a car and disposable income. She is elated to discover that Tyrone also has cable television. Tyrone and Chantel develop a relationship, during which Chantel becomes pregnant. The bulk of the film concerns Chantel's inability to accept her pregnancy. She at first ignores the truth, and then later cannot decide whether to accept Tyrone's offer to pay for an abortion.

Unfortunately, as *Just Another Girl on the I.R.T.* depicts Chantel's struggle to accept her pregnancy and her desire to escape the projects at all costs, it becomes unnecessarily didactic. Despite writer-director Harris' obvious and admirable fervor, her film sounds more like a high school education film than an artistic endeavor with an important message. The adults tend to sound like school textbooks, such as the principal of the school who tells Chantel to "behave more like a lady . . . going to college takes time; it's a big step." Another example is the family-planning counselor, who speaks as if she is reciting from a brochure: "no birth control method can guarantee that you won't get pregnant . . . it's illegal to have an abortion in the third trimester. . . ." In addition, most of the adults recite their lines by rote. The characters are not fully developed but rely instead on familiar stereotypes: the unwed teenager; her wisecracking, heavy-set friend; the thoughtful social worker (who eventually helps Chantel and Tyrone); and the absent and overworked parents.

The character of Chantel, as written by Harris and acted by Johnson, is a little more layered than the other characters, but not much. Johnson has a lively smile and a sharp tongue. For the most part, she does a good job of being a bubbly, talkative teenager; when she is required to handle serious dialogue, however, she appears to be less able to maintain that personality and occasionally appears self-conscious. Unquestionably, however, she does capture the terror of the birth scene. She creates a believable character who has so denied the truth of her pregnancy that she seems genuinely and frighteningly unable to cope with the inexorable labor and birth of her baby. If the rest of the film were as good as this scene, and the rest of the actors were as successful in their scenes as Johnson is in this one, it would have been the powerful film that it set out to be.

As it stands, however, some significant inconsistencies diminish the impact. Chantel talks directly to the audience throughout approximately the first third of the film, which helps reveal her character's desire to be different and helps the audience appreciate her sense of humor and pain. Then, inexplicably, after she becomes pregnant, she begins to speak in the past tense. This discrepancy undermines Harris' intent of getting the audience emotionally involved in Chantel's dilemma, because audience members are instead distracted by the inconsistency of the theatrical device. An additional and striking inconsistency is Chantel herself, who is supposedly a straight "A" student and at the top of her class, yet who handles her pregnancy in a most irresponsible and ignorant way. Perhaps the film is trying to make the point that even the smartest of young girls in the inner city lacks adequate information concerning birth control and pregnancy. Nevertheless, Chantel's capability in the classroom (she thoroughly re-searches a paper on Africa and passionately argues complex moral questions with a teacher) is at odds with her foolish approach to her pregnancy.

The production values of the film are simple and functional. Harris uses her low budget to advantage. The film's verisimilitude is enhanced by the use of real locations, simple lighting, and a handheld camera during the birth scene. Harris also employs some clever quick-cutting techniques that work well, especially in a humorous scene in which Chantel decides what to wear.

Just Another Girl on the I.R.T. is loaded with the pressing issues facing the American inner city in the late twentieth century, such as teen pregnancy, racism, AIDS (acquired immune deficiency syndrome), abortion, and devastating economic and personal hardship. It is also a notable achievement to present a realistic African American perspective in a medium in which such a perspective is rare. When a film has the power to galvanize people to work for change, as *Boyz 'n the Hood* (1991) did, then it can truly be called a milestone. Unfortunately, equating these two films would diminish the achievement and skill of *Boyz 'n the Hood* director John Singleton. *Just Another Girl on the I.R.T.* is simply a film with a winning leading lady and considerable commitment to its subject matter. For these two aspects, it is to be applauded. One hopes that director Harris can parlay this breakthrough into bigger-budget films that are just as passionate but more textured and cinematic than this first effort. One also hopes that the talents of Leslie Harris, not to mention those of other African American women filmmakers, begin to be nourished and utilized.

Kirby Tepper

Reviews
The Christian Science Monitor. March 15, 1993, p. 14.
Essence. XXIII, April, 1993, p. 50.
The Hollywood Reporter. February 22, 1993, p. 8.
Los Angeles Times. April 2, 1993, p. F4.
Ms. III, March, 1993, p. 70.
The New York Times. March 19, 1993, p. B2.
Variety. CCCXLVIII, September 21, 1992, p. 84.
The Wall Street Journal. March 18, 1993, p. A10.
The Washington Post. April 2, 1993, p. D1.

KING OF THE HILL

Production: Albert Berger, Barbara Maltby, and Ron Yerxa for Wildwood/Bona
    Fide; released by Gramercy Pictures
Direction: Steven Soderbergh
Screenplay: Steven Soderbergh; based on the memoir by A. E. Hotchner
Cinematography: Elliot Davis
Editing: Steven Soderbergh
Production design: Gary Frutkoff
Art direction: Bill Rea
Set decoration: Claire Bowin
Casting: Deborah Aquila
Sound: Larry Blake
Costume design: Susan Lyall
Music: Cliff Martinez
MPAA rating: PG-13
Running time: 109 minutes

Principal characters:

Aaron Kurlander	Jesse Bradford
Mr. Kurlander	Jeroen Krabbe
Mrs. Kurlander	Lisa Eichhorn
Miss Mathey	Karen Allen
Mr. Mungo	Spalding Gray
Lydia	Elizabeth McGovern
Ben	Joseph Chrest
Lester	Adrien Brody
Sullivan	Cameron Boyd
Billy Thompson	Chris Samples
Christina Sebastian	Katherine Heigl
Ella McShane	Amber Benson
Patrolman Burns	John McConnell
Mr. Desot	Ron Vawter
Mr. Sandoz	John Durbin
Arletta	Lauryn Hill
Front desk clerk	David Jensen

    Based on the memoirs of writer A. E. Hotchner, this drama centers on twelve-year-old Aaron Kurlander (Jesse Bradford), a young boy growing up during the Great Depression. Aaron, his loving mother (Lisa Eichhorn), his self-absorbed immigrant father (Jeroen Krabbe), and his little brother, Sullivan (Cameron Boyd), live in a single claustrophobic room in a cheap hotel, desperately trying to survive. The Empire Hotel is both a blessing and a curse for Aaron. He enjoys the people, from Lester (Adrien

Brody)—the local hood who kindly watches over him—to the eerie Mr. Mungo (Spalding Gray) and his girlfriend/prostitute, Lydia (Elizabeth McGovern). There is a constant sense of isolation and danger, however, as one by one the tenants are forced to leave because they are unable to pay their rent.

Though not episodic, Aaron's story is defined by a series of abandonments, as his family and friends disperse over the course of the film. Throughout, Aaron watches dispassionately as yet another person drives away in a car or walks away down a hall. These recurring scenes would be heartbreaking for the audience if not for Aaron's indomitable spirit, captured on screen by Jesse Bradford's winning and assured performance as Aaron.

Aaron's parents, like so many others during the Depression, break up the family in a futile attempt to make ends meet: Thus younger brother Sullivan is sent to live with an uncle. Then, his mother—in a serene and understated performance by Eichhorn—who is suffering from consumption (tuberculosis), returns to a sanatorium. Finally, his ever-optimistic and egocentric father blithely decides to leave Aaron alone at the hotel while he leaves town to become a traveling salesman. Aaron has no choice but to stay there, face his school graduation alone, and fend off creditors and starvation. He is resourceful and imaginative, two qualities that serve him well in his attempts to stave off eviction. Unfortunately, a bank has taken possession of the hotel and is systematically and unethically evicting its low-income tenants in order to make way for new and more profitable ones. The resonance for the 1980's and 1990's is astonishing: The hotel's callous foreclosure on its tenants acts (for a modern-day audience) as a metaphor for the big-business downsizing that has characterized and precipitated much of the hardship, both globally and individually, affecting Americans.

King of the Hill, though not highly entertaining, succeeds in depicting the personal growth of its young protagonist as he becomes increasingly isolated. The film is ultimately a melancholy coming-of-age piece without the excessive sentimentality common to such films. In fact, *King of the Hill* is more the dark and serious cousin to the immensely successful comedy *Home Alone* (1990). While the young boy's abandonment in *Home Alone* was completely absurd, Aaron's situation is based in reality, on the memoirs of A. E. Hotchner. As such, even with its upbeat ending, *King of the Hill* remains a dark and gloomy film.

Nevertheless, the film has its lighter moments. With Aaron's resourcefulness comes comic relief, mostly from his amusing attempts to portray his family as successful and happy. In one scene, Aaron visits the huge home of a wealthy classmate, Billy (Chris Samples). When Billy's mother asks Aaron a series of questions about what his father does for a living, Aaron takes a huge swig of bottled soda before each answer, eyes rolling to the side, searching for a good lie. He tells a whopper about his parents being aviators flying a government mission.

King of the Hill masterfully transports its audience back to the darkest parts of the 1930's. Director Steven Soderbergh and his designers do a splendid job of evoking this era. Costumer Susan Lyall has an extraordinary ability to re-create the detail of 1933 clothing, from Mr. Kurlander's jaunty straw hats and light-colored suits to the pale dress worn by a dowdy adolescent neighbor girl who tries in vain to win Aaron's affection. The bow in the back of her dress is tied in such a way as to demonstrate her character's lack of style and confidence—such is Lyall's and Soderbergh's attention to detail.

In addition, the production design of Gary Frutkoff, art direction of Bill Rea, set design by Erik Olson, and set decoration by Claire Bowin combine to present a vivid cinematic picture of the Depression. From the authentic billboards promising happiness in cigarettes, which loom over the "Hooverville" (homeless camp) across the street, to the schoolroom table filled with lunch baskets, the creators of this film miss no detail in re-creating 1930's Middle America. Combined with the sepia tones achieved throughout the film by the consistently amber lighting and a grainy quality to the cinematography, *King of the Hill* looks like a series of somber variations on Norman Rockwell paintings. Indeed, when the camera catches Patrolman Burns (John McConnell) grabbing a shabbily dressed little boy by the ear in the middle of a busy intersection, for a split second some audience members will think it is a re-creation of a Rockwell painting. There is quite a difference, however, between Rockwell's America and the increasingly dire situation in which Aaron finds himself.

The character of Mr. Mungo (Spalding Gray) is emblematic of the intrinsic irony of the Depression. He is a dapper, well-dressed man who lives across the hall from Aaron, drinking all day and pretending that he is perfectly fine. He shows Aaron a beautiful handmade cane that he "bought years ago, when people like me were using hundred dollar bills to light our cigars." Unfortunately, he still tries to maintain an appearance that he is above it all, with tragic consequences.

One disappointment of the film is that several wonderful actors such as Gray are used in roles so small that they are almost cameos. Karen Allen as Aaron's adoring teacher, Miss Mathey, appears in a completely thankless role that promises more than it delivers. At first, it seems that Miss Mathey will be Aaron's rescuer, but she ultimately proves not to be. Though this failure underscores the general powerlessness to help even a child in need in those troubled times, some of Allen's actions—and her dewy-eyed adoration of Aaron—make it implausible that she would not do more to assist him.

Likewise, Elizabeth McGovern is underused as Lydia, Mr. Mungo's "girlfriend" (prostitute). It is surprising to see McGovern in such a small role, but her throaty deep voice and her caustic worldliness make her a welcome addition. When Aaron enters Mungo's room when Lydia is half-dressed, Mungo tells her to "put something on." "He likes it," she growls, as she turns back to her beauty magazine. McGovern is particularly well suited to period films. She made her breakthrough in *Ragtime* (1981), E. L. Doctorow's account of the effect of the Industrial Revolution on the American Dream (with a knowing skepticism similar to *King of the Hill*). Since then she has not fared as well in the size of roles she has played, but she always has the same unusual screen presence and delivers a fine performance.

Jeroen Krabbe is excellent as Aaron's peacock of a father. He appears to be a one-dimensional, self-serving buffoon at first, saying "I carry a lot of influence around here," as if the ratty hotel in which they live is the White House. He is the ever-optimistic immigrant who believes in the power of the American Dream, and by film's end he seems to have achieved it. Krabbe is excellent at capturing the fear behind the facade but never letting it show. Instead, it comes out in an obsessive, insistent optimism that is pathetic. That the audience could forgive this father's abandonment of his sons is testimony to Krabbe's portrayal of a desperate man driven to do desperate things.

With *King of the Hill*, Steven Soderbergh has reaffirmed his reputation, first established with his debut film, *Sex, Lies and Videotape* (1989), which made him the darling of Cannes and Hollywood. His second effort, however, was a strange and difficult film called *Kafka* (1991), which caused many to wonder if he would ever live up to his initial potential. Although not generally appreciated by audiences, *King of the Hill* was classy and artistically executed. Soderbergh again serves as his own editor: Scenes in which he makes a marble game into a symphony and a runaway car into a harrowing (but fun) action interlude reaffirm his considerable talents.

King of the Hill is an uncomfortable but often moving story of Depression-era America, as seen through the eyes of a smart young boy. Ironically, the film's themes of depression, unemployment, and homelessness had relevance for its 1990's audience, as well. The film's overall message is summed up in something Aaron says to his little brother early in the film: "I keep telling ya, all the important stuff can't be taught, ya just have to learn."

Kirby Tepper

Reviews

Chicago Tribune. September 10, 1993, VII, p. 23.
The Christian Science Monitor. August 20, 1993, p. 12.
Los Angeles Times. August 20, 1993, p. F4.
The New York Times. August 20, 1993, p. B1.
Rolling Stone. September 2, 1993, p. 70.
Sight and Sound. IV, January, 1994, p. 48.
Time. CXLII, August 23, 1993, p. 67.
Variety. May 20, 1993, p. 17.
The Wall Street Journal. September 2, 1993, p. A11.
The Washington Post. September 10, 1993, p. G7.

LAST ACTION HERO

Production: Steve Roth and John McTiernan for Oak; released by Columbia
   Pictures
Direction: John McTiernan
Screenplay: Shane Black and David Arnott; based on a story by Zak Penn and
   Adam Leff
Cinematography: Dean Semler
Editing: John Wright
Production design: Eugenio Zanetti
Art direction: Marek Dobrowolski, Rick Heinrichs, and John Wright Stevens
Set decoration: Cindy Carr and Debra Shutt
Casting: Jane Jenkins and Janet Hirshenson
Visual effects consulting: Richard Greenberg
Visual effects supervision: John Sullivan
Sound: Lee Orloff
Costume design: Gloria Gresham
Music: Michael Kamen
MPAA rating: PG-13
Running time: 122 minutes

   Principal characters:
   Jack Slater . . . . Arnold Schwarzenegger
   Danny Madigan . . . . Austin O'Brien
   John Practice . . . . F. Murray Abraham
   Frank . . . . Art Carney
   Benedict . . . . Charles Dance
   Dekker . . . . Frank McRae
   The Ripper . . . . Tom Noonan
   Nick . . . . Robert Prosky
   Tony Vivaldi . . . . Anthony Quinn
   Mrs. Madigan . . . . Mercedes Ruehl
   Death . . . . Ian McKellen
   Tough Asian man . . . . Professor Toru Tanaka
   Teacher . . . . Joan Plowright
   Lieutenant governor . . . . Jason Kelly
   Rookie . . . . Noah Emmerich
   Mayor . . . . Tina Turner
   Whitney . . . . Bridgette Wilson

   Unfortunately for *Last Action Hero*, this Arnold Schwarzenegger vehicle opened in
the wake of Steven Spielberg's *Jurassic Park*, which was setting box-office records
as the blockbuster of the summer of 1993. Likened by some critics to Woody Allen's

The Purple Rose of Cairo (1985), *Last Action Hero* centers on a young boy who magically enters the fictional world of his hero of motion-picture action/adventure fare.

Despite the negative press the film received at the time of its release, *Last Action Hero* was in fact a better-than-average summer film that could be enjoyed on a purely visceral level or as satire or allegory. Film buffs could find a range of allusions to films as varied as *Terminator II: Judgment Day* (1991), Ingmar Bergman's *The Seventh Seal* (1957), and Laurence Olivier's *Hamlet* (1948). The gags and the allusions were as fast as the action. Schwarzenegger himself is parodied throughout the film.

The setting of *Last Action Hero* shifts between the "real" world of New York and the fantasy world of Hollywood. Eleven-year-old Danny Madigan (Austin O'Brien), a latchkey kid, spends most of his time in a dilapidated motion-picture theater that has seen better days. Nick (Robert Prosky), the kindly projectionist at the theater who has become Danny's surrogate father, offers Danny a private, late-night screening of *Jack Slater IV*, the latest film starring Danny's favorite action hero. Danny almost misses the screening, however, when a burglar breaks into his apartment. Thus the audience becomes acquainted with Danny's need to escape the grim reality of big-city life.

At the screening, Danny is given a special "magic" ticket that Nick kept from his own childhood, given to him by the great Houdini. Once the magic ticket is ripped, it gives the bearer special privileges. As Danny watches the film, he is physically transported into the film and finds himself, suddenly, in the back seat of the convertible of his screen idol, Jack Slater (Schwarzenegger), as a car chase is in progress. Despite Slater's surprise, he accepts Danny's presence and even finds him helpful: Because Danny has already witnessed key plot points and understands the rules governing the genre perfectly, he can therefore anticipate the action and the plot turns. Danny recognizes himself as a "comic sidekick" and concludes that he cannot get hurt. Later, however, he begins to worry that his role still could be dispensable to the plot.

That plot involves a heartless Mafioso named Tony Vivaldi (Anthony Quinn), who is out to destroy a rival mob with the help of a demoniacally clever enforcer named Benedict (Charles Dance). Benedict, who seems to have been imported from a James Bond film, is found to be the real villain of the piece. He discovers Danny's uncanny knowledge about his evil doings and figures out how Danny entered the story. With Danny's ripped ticket, Benedict gains entry into Danny's world. When Danny discovers what has happened, he and Jack follow Benedict into the "real" world of New York. How Danny and Jack are able to do this without the magic ticket is not satisfactorily explained in the film, one of the many logical inconsistencies. The plot of director John McTiernan's film has more holes than even the highest-paid script "doctor" could patch.

In the "real" world, Benedict realizes that he is at an advantage, because it is a place where villainy can thrive and ideal fictive genre notions that "crime does not pay" do not apply. When Benedict uses the magic ticket to import another villain from a previous Jack Slater film, Jack is forced to reenact the conclusion of one of his earlier films where he fought a homicidal maniac called the Ripper (Tom Noonan). In that film, however, a young boy dies. Replaying the scene, this time with Danny as the boy, Jack succeeds and defeats the Ripper. Nevertheless, Benedict is still at large.

Meanwhile, the devious Benedict has discovered that action hero Jack Slater is played by an actor improbably named Arnold Schwarzenegger and that Schwarzenegger will be attending the premiere of *Jack Slater IV*. Benedict decides that he can kill Slater by killing Schwarzenegger. Thus Jack and Danny are thrust into the improbable situation of having to save Schwarzenegger's life.

Slater is fascinated by the real New York and becomes involved with Danny's mother (Mercedes Ruehl). Despite the fact that he could be injured in the real world, or even killed, he continues to play his role heroically. When Jack is seriously wounded, Danny knows that the only way his life can be saved is to get him back into the film, where he belongs. The other half of the ripped ticket is retrieved from Nick's theater and saves the day for Slater.

Although *Last Action Hero* parodies the action/adventure genre as a whole, it concentrates on ridiculing Arnold Schwarzenegger himself and the type of role he usually plays. For example, Slater is surprised to learn that he is portrayed by an Austrian actor with a nearly unpronounceable name, which Jack can remember only as "Braunschweiger." Further, when Schwarzenegger as Jack meets the "real" Schwarzenegger with wife Maria Shriver on his arm at the premiere, the confrontation makes the fictive one seem far more engaging and likable than the stuffy and aloof businessman in a tuxedo who says that he has always hated Jack for what he has done to him.

Schwarzenegger became famous in part for his menacing one-liners, such as "Hasta la vista, baby." In *Last Action Hero*, Jack Slater's one-liner is "Big mistake!"—a line that some reviewers would use against Schwarzenegger in criticizing the film. Admittedly, some of the parody dialogue is infantile, as when Slater asks a villain, "You want to be a farmer?" Then, kicking him in the groin, he adds, "Here's a couple acres." Also parodied, however, is Spielberg's *E. T.: The Extra-Terrestrial* (1982), when at one point Danny is airborne, peddling a bicycle. Another amusing sequence takes place when Danny in the film-within-the-film recognizes F. Murray Abraham from his role as the devious Salieri in *Amadeus* (1984), but Jack is puzzled when he is told that this was the man who killed Moe Zart. One of the film's best parody sequences shows Danny in his English class, watching Olivier's *Hamlet*. His teacher is played by Joan Plowright, Laurence Olivier's widow. Danny imagines what it might be like if his hero, Jack Slater, were playing Hamlet. "To be or not to be?" Slater's Hamlet has the answer: "Not to be." He then lights a bomb with his cigar, while remarking, "There's something rotten in the state of Denmark, and Hamlet is taking out the trash"; the faux Olivier film then explodes into action. This sequence alone is worth the price of admission.

The film's production was beset with problems. It was assigned to a reliable action director, John McTiernan, who had established himself with the Schwarzenegger hit *Predator* (1987) and later turned the Bruce Willis picture *Die Hard* (1988) into a megahit. Nevertheless, the film fell behind schedule, and costs soared. Eight writers were involved on the project, four of them, including William Goldman, remaining uncredited. Shane Black and David Arnott got the screenwriting credit; Adam Leff and Zak Penn were credited for the story concept.

The mind-boggling plot owed something to Buster Keaton's *Sherlock, Jr.* (1924) as well as Allen's *The Purple Rose of Cairo*, in which a woman coaxes a handsome leading man out of a silly film and into her life. Thus, although this gimmick of "real" and "fictional" characters interacting was not new, it was totally unexpected in a Schwarzenegger film. *Last Action Hero* was a bold and daring experiment that unfortunately was not able to hold its own against the competition. Over time, however, it may prove to be one of Schwarzenegger's most interesting pictures.

James M. Welsh

Reviews

Entertainment Weekly. July 9, 1993, p. 32.
The Hollywood Reporter. June 14, 1993, p. 8.
Los Angeles Times. June 30, 1993, p. F1.
Newsweek. June 28, 1993, p. 64.
The New York Times. June 18, 1993, p. B1.
The New Yorker. LXIX, July 5, 1993, p. 94.
Time. June 21, 1993, p. 67.
Variety. June 14, 1993, p. 4.
The Wall Street Journal. June 24, 1993, p. A11.
The Washington Post. June 18, 1993, p. G1.
Washington Times. June 18, 1993, p. E1.

LÉOLO

Origin: Canada
Released: 1992
Released in U.S.: 1993
Production: Lyse Lafontaine and Aimee Danis for Les Alliance Communications
  Corporation, in association with Productions du Verseau, Flach Film and the
  National Film Board of Canada; released by Fine Line Features
Direction: Jean-Claude Lauzon
Screenplay: Jean-Claude Lauzon
Cinematography: Guy Dufaux
Editing: Michel Arcand
Art direction: François Seguin
Music: Richard Gregoire
MPAA rating: no listing
Running time: 107 minutes

Principal characters:
Narrator............................ Gilbert Sicotte
Léolo.............................. Maxime Collin
Mother.............................. Ginette Reno
Father .... Roland Blouin
Grandfather......................... Julien Guiomar
The Word Tamer..................... Pierre Bourgault
Bianca......................... Giuditta del Vecchio
Fernand....................... Yves Montmarquette

In *Léolo*, director-screenwriter Jean-Claude Lauzon has created a dreamlike, intricate, often unsettling semiautobiographical film about a young boy living in Montreal,
Quebec, Canada. This creative cinematic experience captures the rich imagination of
a child who discovers that the only escape from his family's oppressive and surreal
world is to become a dreamer and a writer. Emotionally powerful and cinematically
vivid, Lauzon's film depicts the torment of a young boy who struggles to realize his
potential as he grows up in a world where imagination and creativity are subservient
to fear and mediocrity.

The French-speaking Montreal cinema has been the birthplace of some original and
distinctive works. Denys Arcand's *Jesus of Montreal* (1989) is a notable example of
the vitality of the French-Canadian cinema. (It should be noted that Arcand plays a
cameo role as a school guidance counselor in *Léolo*.) Also, Lauzon's first film, *Night
Zoo* (1987), was the opening film at the prestigious Directors' Fortnight series at the
1987 Cannes Film Festival and went on to win numerous awards in Canada.

Léolo proves that Lauzon's success with *Night Zoo* was not a fluke. He is truly gifted
at the craft of creating a cinematic world that realistically portrays its subject while

achieving an evocative visual poetry. *Léolo* merits comparison to such classics as Federico Fellini's *Amarcord* (1974) and Francois Truffaut's *The 400 Blows* (1959). While it would be premature to claim that Lauzon is of the caliber of these legends, it is nevertheless fair to say that he has a dynamic mastery of the art of filmmaking.

Like James Joyce's classic novel *A Portrait of the Artist as a Young Man* (1916), *Léolo* has a nonlinear story line, at times difficult to follow, that traces the genesis of an artist—specifically a writer. Lauzon provides the audience with brief, impressionistic scenes: Léolo as a baby crying as he is patiently being toilet-trained by his enormous, loving mother (Ginette Reno); a round-faced father (Roland Blouin) proudly patting twelve-year-old Léolo (Maxime Collin) on the head for having a good bowel movement; Léolo reading the family's only book by the light of the inside of the refrigerator; a mentally ill sister who dresses in fancy clothing hiding with her collection of salamanders, snakes, and insects; a massive, bodybuilding brother (Yves Montmarquette) who is never without a piece of food in his mouth or a dumbbell in his hand; a grandfather (Julien Guiomar) who tries to kill Léolo by drowning him; and a beautiful Sicilian girl (Giuditta del Vecchio) next door who titillates the voyeuristic Léolo as he surreptitiously watches her undress.

These scenes are interspersed with Léolo's vivid fantasy life. For example, when he is being held underwater by his grandfather, he envisions himself discovering buried treasure. His fantasies about the neighbor girl, Bianca, take him to Taormina, Italy, and cause him to name himself Léolo (an Italian name) even though his real name is Leo (French-Canadian). Léolo claims that "Italy is too beautiful to belong to the Italians," so he adopts it as his own to escape from his crowded, poverty-stricken, rat-infested life. Director Lauzon is most concerned with Léolo's inner life, dramatized through these fantasies and through narration. Léolo says, "People who trust only their own truth call me Leo Lozean. Because I dream, I'm not."

Lauzon grew up in a home similar to Léolo's, in one of Montreal's toughest working-class districts. Furthermore, Lauzon at one time was a scuba-diving instructor—hence the underwater sequences where Léolo dives for hidden treasure. The treasures he finds may symbolize the treasure that is buried within a destructive family in the form of a creative child or may represent the creativity buried within an individual.

Lauzon was seventeen years old when Canadian teacher/filmmaker Andre Petrowski discovered some of Lauzon's writing. Struck by Lauzon's talent, Petrowski spent a year searching for him, subsequently becoming his mentor and guide. Petrowski is represented in *Léolo* by a character called "The Word Tamer," who discovers young Léolo's writing and monitors his progress. The character remains enigmatic and almost surreal; he reads Léolo's story in a strange room filled with candles and statues. In one brief scene, he and Léolo walk toward the camera at night wearing miners' caps with flashlights attached to the brims. The distance maintained by The Word Tamer, who is not a part of the action, emphasizes his role as a powerful observer, like the real-life Petrowski, who brings meaning to the young boy's life. The candles represent the clarity he brings with his objectivity, and the miner's flashlight signifies that for Léolo (and presumably in real life for Lauzon), this man led him out of the dark underground into a brightly lit and more hopeful world. Interestingly, The Word Tamer is played by Pierre Bourgault, a renowned Quebec separatist—echoing, perhaps, Léolo's rejection of his Canadian heritage.

The young actor playing Léolo, Maxime Collin, is a veteran of many television and film appearances in his native Quebec. He approaches his role with sincerity and a genuineness that is refreshing. Constantly apprehensive that someone else will torment him or threaten his creativity, the character of Léolo invites sympathy. The film jumps back and forth from reality to fantasy, and Collin's acting skill is such that it becomes difficult, at times, to differentiate between the two. This deliberate blurring of fantasy and reality is important to director-writer Lauzon's intent; Collin's performance serves his director well. Surprisingly, some amusing scenes revolving around Léolo's discovery of sex are rather bold, considering the young actor's age. He never brings embarrassment or crassness to his role, however, only a straightforward sense of truth.

One of the pleasures of *Léolo* is its uncompromising nature. Lauzon brings his own vision to the screen despite its potentially shocking content. At one point, Léolo imagines his mother being impregnated by a sperm-covered imported tomato. Although this sounds ridiculous and crass, on film it is humorous and magical. The sexual scenes, mostly involving masturbation, are realistically depicted without being explicit. Lauzon presents these scenes as a part of life, and they are refreshing. One particularly funny scene has Léolo in a diving mask, watching beautiful Bianca through a window. The camera shoots from the point of view of the mask, and as Léolo gets more excited the screen steams up just as the mask would.

Lauzon's directing style is similar to that of Fellini in that he understands the power of creating visual images which allow the audience to feel as well as to see. When Léolo hugs his huge mother and settles into her enormous breast with a contented smile, Lauzon fills the screen with the mother seen sideways from the neck down to point up the disparity in size between the fragile Léolo and his mother's vast bosom. Her warmth seems to encompass the entire audience.

Ginette Reno is perfect as the mother who, according to the narration, "had the strength of a frigate plowing through troubled waters." Incredibly, this is Reno's film debut, and she brings great warmth and gentility to her role. In fact, Léolo's mother is so kind that one assumed she could help Léolo out of his pain. Unfortunately, events conspire against her, as several tragedies take their toll on her family life. In fact, Reno is so likable that it is painful for the audience to watch her struggle. Reno is one of Canada's most popular singing stars, performing to huge crowds all over Canada. Despite the fact that she allows herself to be filmed in several visually unflattering ways, she never loses her dignity.

A special note should be made of the music Lauzon chose for this film. It ranges from sacred to popular, from The Rolling Stones to music by Arab artist Mahmoud Tabrizi Zadeh. The range of this music underscores the complexity and diversity of feelings possessed by all people. Léolo's inner journeys and his daily experiences are artfully enriched by such a well-designed array of songs.

Léolo achieves a certain dignity despite its raw and earthy content. Lauzon's at times shocking visual images serve his theme. Thus *Léolo* becomes a haunting portrait of a youngster that will stay with audiences for a long time.

Kirby Tepper

Reviews
Chicago Tribune. April 9, 1993, VII, p. 21.
The Hollywood Reporter. September 11, 1992, p. 6.
The Hudson Review. XLVI, Autumn, 1993, p. 544.
Los Angeles Times. April 28, 1993, p. F1.
Newsweek. CXXI, April 5, 1993, p. 56.
Sight and Sound. III, May, 1993, p. 51.
Time. CXLI, April 5, 1993, p. 60.
Variety. CCCXLVII, June 1, 1992, p. 67.
The Washington Post. May 6, 1993, p. D7.

LIKE WATER FOR CHOCOLATE
(COMO AGUA PARA CHOCOLATE)

Origin: Mexico
Released: 1992
Released in U.S.: 1993
Production: Alfonso Arau; released by Miramax Films
Direction: Alfonso Arau
Screenplay: Laura Esquivel; based on her novel
Cinematography: Emmanuel Lubezki and Steve Bernstein
Editing: Carlos Bolado and Francisco Chiu
Art direction: Marco Antonio Arteaga, Mauricio De Aguinaco, and Denise Pizzini
Costume design: Carlos Brown
Music: Leo Brower
MPAA rating: R
Running time: 113 minutes

Principal characters:

Tita	Lumi Cavazos
Pedro	Marco Leonardi
Mamá Elena	Regina Torné
John Brown	Mario Ivan Martínez
Nacha	Ada Carrasco
Rosaura	Yareli Arizmendi
Gertrudis	Claudette Maillé
Chencha	Pilar Aranda

Laura Esquivel has adapted her novel of passion, romance, feminism, and cooking for the screen in a highly successful collaboration with director Alfonso Arau. This enchanting story of a young woman's determinism and unrequited love in prerevolutionary Mexico, circa 1910, is brought vividly to life on film. *Like Water for Chocolate* received numerous honors, including ten Ariel Awards (the Mexican equivalent of the Academy Award), and a Golden Globe nomination as Best Foreign Film. It is considered to be one of the most widely seen and widely acclaimed Mexican films of all time.

As the youngest of three daughters living on a ranch in Mexico, Tita (Lumi Cavazos) is tragically denied marriage to the man she loves, Pedro (Marco Leonardi), because of family tradition. The rule that the youngest daughter must not marry and must stay with the mother until she dies has been carried on without question for generations, and Tita's widowed mother, Elena (Regina Torné), insists on perpetuating that tradition. "If Pedro is asking for your hand in marriage, he is wasting his time. . . . No one has questioned traditions in this family," says Mamá Elena. Pedro, desperately in love with Tita, accepts the hand in marriage of her sister Rosaura (Yreli Arezmendi) simply to be near Tita. Tita's and Pedro's passion for each other is boundless, and the tragedy of their thwarted love propels the story.

Yet something else propels the story as well, and it is here that *Like Water for Chocolate* is more than a romance, taking on the qualities of Magical Realism present in the novels of authors Gabriel García Márquez and Mario Vargas Llosa. The story revolves around the magical powers of Tita's cooking. Tita has grown up learning the recipes of the family cook, Nacha (Ada Carrasco). With Nacha, Tita is able to show her true emotions, while with her rigid and repressive mother she is forced to be stoic. At the wedding of her sister Rosaura to her beloved Pedro, she is overcome with grief as she and Nacha prepare the wedding cake. (Tita has been forced, by her mother, to prepare the wedding feast as punishment for wanting to break tradition and marry Pedro.) When the wedding cake is prepared and served, it causes the entire wedding party to weep uncontrollably and have severe indigestion because Tita's tears fell into the batter. Tita discovers that her recipes affect the person who eats the dish according to the emotion that she feels at the time of cooking. When Pedro surreptitiously gives Tita some roses, she pricks herself accidentally as she is cooking, and the blood that goes into the food she prepares causes everyone to feel the same passion that she feels. Her middle sister, Gertrudis (Claudette Maillé), runs to the bathhouse to take a cold shower, and the heat from her body starts a fire.

Passion is the center of this film. It is about the strength of the passion Tita and Pedro feel for each other; about the lack of passion in her pragmatic sister Rosaura; about the freely expressed passion of the now-wild Gertrudis, who runs off with a dashing and handsome soldier of the revolution; and about the secret, repressed passion of Mamá Elena. "Like water for chocolate" is a Mexican expression describing a person who is about to boil over with passion. Ultimately, *Like Water for Chocolate* is about a woman's ability to keep her passion alive even in the repressive, sexist culture of tradition-bound, early twentieth century Mexico. Like Nora in Henrik Ibsen's play *A Doll's House* (1879), Tita finds and courage to defy the status quo. In *A Doll's House*, Ibsen challenged the late nineteenth century view of feminine roles by ending the play with his heroine, Nora, slamming the door and leaving her family behind. Laura Esquivel similarly challenges the prevailing attitudes toward women, but Tita's victory is achieved through her ability to revise her role without abandoning it. She uses the most traditional of places, the kitchen, to express her passion, anger, and lust—all of which would be unacceptable if expressed openly. In fact, her sister Gertrudis is disowned by Mamá Elena because she openly expresses passion, boldly leaving the family and becoming a general in the revolution. Esquivel seems to be saying that Gertrudis' success in challenging tradition has validity but that she is not as much of a heroine as Tita, since she symbolically abandons her femininity by adopting a traditional male role. In other words, Gertrudis gains strength in spite of her femininity, while Tita gains strength because of it.

Amid all the symbolism, there exists in *Like Water for Chocolate* a simple and enchanting fable, beautifully told. Vivid colors and the rustic landscape of Mexico's Coahuila Desert give this film a rich beauty. Deep, dark tones predominate in the ranch house, where most of the action take place, and the food is as lovingly photographed as if it were a human character. When Tita's first recipe, the wedding cake, is served and passed to the guests at Pedro and Rosaura's wedding, the camera stops on each person as they take a bite of the beautiful yellow cake. Toward the end of the film, there is another wedding feast, and the preparation of the rich, brown walnuts, the brilliant green chilies, and the luscious pomegranate seeds could not make the food look more delicious. Early in the film, when Pedro eats the luminous dish quail in rose-petal sauce and calls it "nectar of the gods," it looks the part.

Much is expressed in terms of food. When Pedro agrees to marry Rosaura, the family's servant, Chencha (played hilariously by Pilar Aranda) comforts Tita by saying, "you just can't change tacos for enchiladas." Tita is said to have been borne as her mother was chopping onions and "literally pushed out into the world in a sea of tears." The film can be compared to *Babette's Feast* (1987), in which a heroine expresses herself and her emotions through food, and to *Heartburn* (1986), Nora Ephron's comic account of a troubled marriage, also told through a series of recipes.

Like Water for Chocolate is extremely amusing, yet it is told as if it were a serious, bittersweet love story. The humor comes from the humanity of these characters. Early in the film, when Tita decides to knit to take her mind off her pain, she creates a huge, endless afghan, which tells the audience how upset she really is. What makes the audience laugh is not only the endless length of the afghan but the humanity of the situation as well. Esquivel and Arau retain that sense of reality and truth even though the story has such unreal characteristics as magic and ghosts. This film does not try to be comic; it tries to tell a story in a unique way and is comic and touching as a result.

Lumi Cavazos' Tita is beautiful and tranquil in spite of her desperate pain. Cavazos has a wonderful ability to express her interior feelings with minimal effort and is a lovely screen heroine. Equally convincing are Regina Torné as Mamá Elena, as evil as Cinderella's stepmother, and Claudette Maillé as Gertrudis, the wild sister. Ada Carrasco as Nacha, who passes on the secrets of her kitchen to Tita, lends important grace and dignity to the story. Without Nacha, Tita would not have the courage and the strength to carry on in the face of tragedy. Carrasco's presence is felt long after she is offscreen. Marco Leonardi, as Pedro, however, is disappointing. Leonardi is an Italian actor who starred in *Cinema Paradiso* (1991) and learned Spanish for this role. His Pedro is unlikable in the latter third of the film, at a critical point in which Tita is to decide between Pedro and a kind doctor who wishes to marry her. The doctor, John Brown (Mario Ivan Martínez), seems to be more sympathetic. He tells Tita that he will accept her decision, but that if she decides to be with Pedro he will tell Pedro to give Tita the respect she deserves. It may be the fault of the screenplay, but at that moment the doctor appears much more sincere than Pedro. A preceding scene with Pedro makes him seem less caring and less concerned for Tita's feelings. Having both men show equal respect for Tita would make her decision more dramatic for the audience.

Laura Esquivel writes that "it is now being proved scientifically that food prepared with love is more nourishing than food prepared without." Her heroine Tita, every time she is asked how she prepared a dish, answers "with love." The end of the film brings Tita's recipes to the present day and shows a generation of women in her family no longer shackled by tradition, but strengthened by it. Yet this is not a "woman's film." In fact, it is a film for all people who wish to look within and learn, as Tita's kindly doctor puts it, "to discover that which triggers the explosion in all of us." *Like Water for Chocolate* is a thoroughly entertaining film fable that could touch even the coldest heart.

Kirby Tepper

Reviews
Chicago Tribune. April 2, 1993, VII, p. 42.
Films in Review. XLIV, May, 1993, p. 191.
Hispanic. VI, May, 1993, p. 80.
Los Angeles Times. February 26, 1993, p. F7.
The New York Times. February 17, 1993, p. B4.
Newsweek. February 15, 1993, p. 74.
Time. CXLI, April 5, 1993, p. 61.
The Times Literary Supplement. October 15, 1993, p. 17.
Variety. CCCXLVII, April 27, 1992, p. 82.
The Washington Post. March 6, 1993, p. B3.

MAC

Production: Nancy Tenenbaum and Brenda Goodman; released by the Samuel
   Goldwyn Company
Direction: John Turturro
Screenplay: John Turturro and Brandon Cole
Cinematography: Ron Fortunato
Editing: Michael Berenbaum
Production design: Robin Standefer
Art direction: John Magoun
Set decoration: Amelia Battaglio
Casting: Todd Thaler
Sound: Billy Sarokin
Costume design: Donna Zakowska
Music: Richard Termini and Vin Tese
MPAA rating: R
Running time: 117 minutes

Principal characters:
   Niccolo "Mac" Vitelli . . . . John Turturro
   Vico Vitelli . . . . Michael Badalucco
   Bruno Vitelli . . . . Carl Capotorto
   Alice Vitelli . . . . Katherine Borowitz
   Oona . . . . Ellen Barkin
   Nat . . . . John Amos
   Gus . . . . Steven Randazzo
   Polowski . . . . Olek Krupa
   Papa . . . . Joe Paparone

John Turturro is an accomplished and respected film actor whose credits include
roles in a spate of Spike Lee outings—*Do the Right Thing* (1989), *Mo' Better Blues*
(1990), and *Jungle Fever* (1991)—and in Joel and Ethan Coen's *Miller's Crossing*
(1990). He earned the Best Actor award at Cannes for his performance in the title role
of the offbeat film *Barton Fink* (1991).

Twelve years in the making, *Mac* is Turturro's directing debut. It is a triumphant,
fully realized labor of love and a tour de force of authorial vision and artistic subtlety.
It is also beautifully and intriguingly photographed, mostly in dark blues, grays, and
sepia shades (entirely on location in New York City), by Ron Fortunato. It is the rare
American commercial film that offers a strong moral vision—one that it earns rather
than insists on—and that forces the viewer to do his or her share of the work. It is
supremely satisfying and well worth seeing more than once.

Mac is the cinematic equivalent of a *Bildungsroman*, a coming-of-age novel based
on or inspired by the author's childhood. Turturro dedicates the film to his father, on

whom the title character is clearly based. Niccolo "Mac" Vitelli (Turturro) is one of three Italian-American brothers living in Queens, New York, in the 1950's. His brother Vico (Michael Badalucco, who appeared with Turturro in *Miller's Crossing* and *Jungle Fever*, as well as in 1980's *Raging Bull* and 1984's *Broadway Danny Rose*) is a would-be ladies' man. Bruno (Carl Capotorto), an aspiring artist, is the sensitive, college-educated youngest brother.

All three work in construction for Polowski (Olek Krupa), who is difficult, demanding, and (Mac believes) incompetent. Mac is a skilled carpenter and a perfectionist, passionately devoted to his craft. A running dispute early in the film makes this clear: Polowski insists on studs twenty-four inches apart in the walls of the house they are building. Mac's professional pride insists on a sixteen-inch margin. With a hammer, he tears out Polowski's offending studs as his coworkers look on in tacit approval. This and other incidents challenge Polowski's authority and foster enmity. Mac eventually finds working for Polowski intolerable. The feeling is mutual, and Polowski fires Mac, Vico, and Bruno. The brothers decide to start their own business.

With predictable difficulties, the three brothers and Mac's wife, Alice (a strong character, played well by Turturro's real-life wife, Katherine Borowitz), make their way. They buy land and eventually build four houses. Most of Polowski's multiethnic work force comes to work for them. Mac's relations with his employees reinforce his sense of honor, which is based on professional dignity and achievement. The four houses built, Mac spends anxious weeks trying to sell them. A gulf exists between his obsession and his brothers' more casual interest in the business. Mac is pondering buying more land. His lawyer and the owner of the hardware store where he buys supplies reassure Mac that there is a boom time ahead.

On the cusp of great success, Mac completely fails to anticipate the inevitable clash and parting of ways with his brothers. Implicitly, he has counted on their loyalty to him and to the business as a family venture. The moment at which he is poised to leap fully into the risks and satisfactions of his obsession is the very moment at which Vico and Bruno see that they must either get out or make commitments that they find themselves unable to make. In a brilliant, crucial scene in the lawyer's office, pent-up frustrations are released and things left unsaid come out. Vico compares Mac to Adolf Hitler, while Bruno tries to explain gently that he wants his money back. Mac is stunned. "It's supposed to be us, together," he pleads. In frustration, Bruno calls him a cripple. The scene is superbly acted all around and helped greatly by Fortunato's excellent photography, featuring inventive angles and quick cuts among the brothers' quietly expressive faces. It ends in bitter silence. The brothers'—mostly Mac's—failure to acknowledge their different paths and passions ends in an exquisitely predictable rupture.

Without ever becoming hackneyed, *Mac* falls squarely inside a venerable American literary and cinematic tradition of male lead characters obsessed with fulfilling grand schemes. Some, like Ahab in Herman Melville's *Moby Dick* (1851) and Thomas Sutpen in William Faulkner's *Absalom, Absalom!* (1936) go over the edge into evil and take others with them. Others, such as Willie Stark in Robert Penn Warren's *All the King's Men* (1946), meet grandly tragic ends. Yet Turturro would insist (and does, in *Mac*) that a grand vision, even an imperfect vision cherished by an imperfect man, need not be a tragically flawed one. Despite his flaws and tunnel vision, Mac's sincerity and single-mindedness carry the day. An important line underscores a crucial distinction between two kinds of ambition. "You know, Polowski, that thing about the rat race?" says Mac to his former boss. "The thing is to win, right? Well, you're still a rat."

Though the plot line eventually becomes clear enough, *Mac* is (refreshingly) not a plot-driven film; it is a film about character—in at least two senses of the word. The first half-hour is nearly devoid of plot, focusing on the characters of the three brothers; their relationships to one another and to their family, friends, and coworkers; and their memories of their father, whose funeral opens the film. The plot's first crux, the brothers' decision to go into business for themselves, does not occur until about a third of the way through the film.

Mac is a deeply moralistic and resonantly autobiographical devotional tale. "You know what I think happiness is?" asks Mac rhetorically in one scene. "To love your job. Not many people know this—that's why they take vacations—but it's the truth. If you hate your work, you hate your life. I like my work." These lines could have been spoken by Turturro himself, whose work on *Mac* began in 1980, when he began writing a screenplay based on his memories of summers working as a carpenter with his father. Over the next few years, he created several stage versions of *Mac*; then in 1987, Brandon Cole helped him rework the script for the screen. A 1990 meeting with an initially skeptical Nancy Tenenbaum (who produced 1989's *sex, lies and videotape*) set the wheels in motion.

Turturro originally wanted to find a director for his script, but he eventually decided to take the plunge and direct it himself. He was encouraged by such filmmakers as Spike Lee, Joel and Ethan Coen, and Martin Scorsese. Of the filming experience, Carl Capotorto, who plays Bruno, said, "It was difficult and grueling, but everyone felt that they were doing something real. It never felt like just another job." The sincerity of the studio's production notes (from which this quote was taken) attests the artistic integrity of Turturro and his colleagues. *Mac* will never be a box-office smash, but surely it will last. Turturro calls it "a very American film" about "a person who cares about what he does and the price he has to pay to be his own man." It says, he asserts, that "to build something means something, and that the most important thing a person can do is leave a mark on the world in a simple but significant way."

The film's final scene is set several years after the climactic confrontation among the three brothers. A well-dressed Mac walks down the street in front of those first four houses, holding his young son's hand. He built those houses, he tells his son. He points out the detail in a façade. "It's the doing that's the thing," he says.

Ethan Casey

Reviews

Chicago Tribune. March 5, 1993, VII, p. 36.
The Hollywood Reporter. February 18, 1993, p. 10.
Los Angeles Times. March 3, 1993, p. F5.
The Nation. CCLVI, February 15, 1993, p. 209.
National Catholic Reporter. April 23, 1993, p. 14.
National Review. XLV, March 29, 1993, p. 70.
The New York Times. February 19, 1993, p. B1.
Sight and Sound. IV, January, 1994, p. 49.
Variety. May 19, 1992, p. 2.
Video. XVII, October, 1993, p. 82.
The Washington Post. March 5, 1993, p. C7.

MAD DOG AND GLORY

Production: Barbara De Fina and Martin Scorsese; released by Universal Pictures
Direction: John McNaughton
Screenplay: Richard Price
Cinematography: Robby Müller
Editing: Craig McKay
Production design: David Chapman
Art direction: Mark Haack
Set decoration: Leslie Pope
Casting: Todd Thaler
Sound: James J. Sabat
Costume design: Rita Ryak
Music: Elmer Bernstein
MPAA rating: R
Running time: 96 minutes

> *Principal characters:*
> Wayne "Mad Dog" Dobie . . . . Robert De Niro
> Glory . . . . Uma Thurman
> Frank Milo . . . . Bill Murray
> Mike . . . . David Caruso
> Harold . . . . Mike Starr
> Andrew . . . . Tom Towles
> Lee . . . . Kathy Baker
> Shooter . . . . Derek Anunciation

In listing new releases in its March, 1993, issue, *Premiere* noted that Universal Pictures' release of *Mad Dog and Glory* "keeps getting pushed back," despite its stellar, talented cast, including Robert De Niro and Bill Murray. In his review in *The New Yorker*, Anthony Lane remarked that the film, originally scheduled for release in early 1992, was actually shot in 1991, suggesting that the studio must have had some doubts about marketability. *Variety* described the motion picture as being offbeat, off-center, and unsure of its audience. It is a mixed-genre film with an identity crisis that could be, as Lane noted, a police thriller, a mob drama, a comedy, or a love story. In the end, however, *Mad Dog and Glory* opened to good reviews; Bill Murray's *Groundhog Day*, released a week earlier to generally positive reviews, had set a favorable climate for a second Murray vehicle.

Mad Dog and Glory is full of surprises. Though it turns out to be a love story and not really a mob drama, it starts out as a brutal crime vehicle. It then begins to take shape as an odd comic buddy film, but the buddies have come to blows by the final reel. The biggest surprise, however, is in the casting. The conflict involves a tough and ruthless gangster and a timid police photographer, but the roles of stars Robert De Niro and Bill Murray are astonishingly reversed. Comedian Murray, who was so effective as the gentle and introverted Bob in *What About Bob?* (1991), plays the tough guy, while the always dependable De Niro, who played the brutal Jimmy Conway in *GoodFellas* (1990) and the homicidal maniac Max Cady in *Cape Fear* (1991) plays the hesitant wimpy police officer. De Niro can easily handle any role thrown his way, but Murray is just as good as the loan shark whose therapist tells him he should be grateful to De Niro's character for having saved his life through nonviolent means.

The film begins with a brutal shooting in Chicago involving drug dealers in a parked car, creating an unsettling and dangerous atmosphere. Wayne "Mad Dog" Dobie (De Niro) and his partner, Mike (David Caruso), are sent to investigate. Wayne's nickname is a joke, an ironic reversal, as it is Mike who seems to have the "Mad Dog" temperament. Wayne goes out of his way to avoid violence, as is quickly established when he steps into a neighborhood market after he finishes his investigation and encounters a robbery-in-progress involving the shooter who had murdered the two drug dealers.

The thug has a gun on Frank Milo (Murray), a loan shark with underworld connections who happened to be in the store. Wayne tells the killer that the area is crawling with cops and that, if he uses the gun, they will hear it and close in on him. The killer pistol-whips Frank and then escapes, sparing Frank's life. At first, the loan shark is more contemptuous than grateful and even refuses to call 911 for officer assistance as Wayne leaves in pursuit. Because of this delay, the killer eludes capture.

The next day, Frank sends his bodyguard Harold (Mike Starr) to invite Wayne to the nightclub that Frank owns and where he also performs as a comic. A waitress spills coffee on Wayne's hand at the club, burning it slightly. The next day, she turns up at Wayne's apartment, ostensibly to dress the wound, but in fact Frank "owns" her (she is working off a debt her suicidal brother owes Frank), and she has been sent to Wayne to offer her services for seven days. Thus, Glory (Uma Thurman) is Frank's gift of gratitude to Wayne, as she describes herself as "your thank-you present, a singing telegram for a week." While Wayne is not about to take advantage of Glory—he is too much of a gentlemen—he allows her to stay so that she will not get into trouble with Frank. Wayne shows her respect, Glory falls in love with him, and eventually he falls in love with her. When the week is up, Wayne is not willing to give Glory back to Frank. This is the complication that builds to a climax that is neatly resolved.

The acting in the film is outstanding. Murray plays Frank as a natural comedian with a hair-trigger temper—he is not a man to be crossed. When Wayne tells Frank at mid-week that "the net is closing" on the police investigation of the shooter, Frank laughs at him. The next day, the shooter's body is found in a trash can with a net over his head, and Wayne knows who is responsible. Frank tells Wayne "I am the expediter of your dreams" but warns Wayne never to lie to him and never to cross him. Frank is convincingly dangerous, with his command of an army of thugs and bodyguards. Nevertheless, Wayne undertakes his plan to protect Glory. Because he does not want to hurt Wayne, Frank offers to "sell" her for $40,000. When Wayne can raise only $27,000, he decides to fight for his love, living by the lesson he has learned: "no guts, no Glory."

The film is loaded with talent on both sides of the lens. As Martin Scorsese's second project as a producer, *Mad Dog and Glory* is as offbeat as the first film that he produced, *The Grifters* (1990). The film's director, John McNaughton, is best known for his brutal cult feature *Henry: Portrait of a Serial Killer* (1990), a fact that accounts for the toughness of the opening sequence of *Mad Dog and Glory*. Cinematographer Robby Müller is a major international talent who emerged from the New German Cinema movement of the 1970's. Müller shot the first eight films that Wim Wenders made in Germany and also worked with Hans W. Geissendorfer, Peter Handke, John Schlesinger, Barbet Schroeder, William Friedkin, Peter Bogdanovich, Alex Cox, and Jim Jarmusch. If Müller is to be credited with the film's rich look, the musical credit goes to the Oscar-winning composer Elmer Bernstein, who wrote the score.

New York novelist Richard Price shaped the concept into a screenplay which is remarkable for its punchy dialogue. As a screenwriter, Price is best known for *The Color of Money* (1986), his first script for Scorsese and one that earned an Academy Award nomination for Best Adapted Screenplay, and *Sea of Love* (1989). He also wrote Scorsese's "Life Lessons" segment for *New York Stories* (1989). Price's dialogue is sharp, witty, and notable for its use of verbal leitmotifs, such as the line first dropped by Wayne's police partner—"no guts, no glory"—that is repeated later to reinforce the double meaning. If Wayne wants Glory, he will have to earn her, and thinking about that line prepares him for his final confrontation with Frank. Equally effective as both a verbal and a musical leitmotif is the Louis Prima song "I Ain't Got Nobody," which also packs a double meaning and marks Wayne's psychological transformation, awakening the "mad dog" within him. Wayne grows and develops to the point where he will fight his own battles, and De Niro captures his character perfectly.

Mad Dog and Glory is a delightfully unconventional film. Reviewing it for *Variety*, Todd McCarthy called it "pleasurably offbeat," but warned that it was "rather off-center for a mass-market entry." Stephen Hunter of the *Baltimore Sun* praised the film for its "brilliant writing" and cast of "quirky, believable" characters. Vincent Canby of *The New York Times* also praised the film for taking risks, describing it as a "first-rate star vehicle." *The Philadelphia Inquirer*, however, dismissed the film as "a jazzy noir fantasy" filled with empty verbal "riffing." Anthony Lane of *The New Yorker* was also critical, claiming that although this motion picture "has all the right instruments ready to make sweet music, no one can remember the tune."

In fact, the jazz metaphor works best when evaluating this film. Murray plays effectively against De Niro's subdued, one-note samba, but De Niro also improvises brilliantly. After Wayne has found Glory, he is energized, as when—at an unexpected and inappropriate moment of exuberance at a bar, investigating a crime scene—he primes a jukebox and begins singing with the Louis Prima recording of "I Ain't Got Nobody."

Other critics made comparisons with both Raymond Chandler and Damon Runyon for the screenplay's verbal touches, as when the two shooting victims of the opening sequence are later described as "two dead mutts in Muttland." What makes this film work, however, is the gradual transformation that takes place in De Niro's Wayne, from a burnt-out, middle-aged, television-addicted coward to an energetic and courageous lover willing to put his life on the line to protect the woman he loves; "Mad Dog" ultimately lives up to his name. De Niro manages to make a very ordinary character—who has given up on life—interesting, and that is no small accomplishment.

James M. Welsh

Reviews
Chicago Tribune. March 5, 1993, VII, p. 27.
Entertainment Weekly. March 12, 1993, p. 40.
The Hollywood Reporter. March 2, 1993, p. 10.
Los Angeles Times. March 5, 1993, p. F1.
The New York Times. March 5, 1993, p. B1.
The New Yorker. March 15, 1993, p. 119.
Newsweek. CXXI, March 8, 1993, p. 52.
The Philadelphia Inquirer. March 5, 1993, p. 3.
Time. March 8, 1993, p. 67.
Variety. March 1, 1993, p. 4.
The Wall Street Journal. March 4, 1993, p. A12.
The Washington Post. March 5, 1993, p. C1.

MADE IN AMERICA

Production: Arnon Milchan, Michael Douglas, and Rick Bieber for Le Studio
   Canal Plus, Regency Enterprises, Alcor Films, Stonebridge Entertainment, and
   Kalola Productions, Inc.; released by Warner Bros.
Direction: Richard Benjamin
Screenplay: Holly Goldberg Sloan; based on a story by Marcia Brandwynne,
   Nadine Schiff, and Sloan
Cinematography: Ralf Bode
Editing: Jacqueline Cambas
Production design: Evelyn Sakash
Set decoration: Hilton Rosemarin
Casting: Reuben Cannon and Associates
Sound: Richard Lightstone
Costume design: Elizabeth McBride
Music: Mark Isham
MPAA rating: PG-13
Running time: 110 minutes

> *Principal characters:*
> Sarah Mathews . . . . Whoopi Goldberg
> Hal Jackson. . . . . Ted Danson
> Zora Mathews. . . . . Nia Long
> Tea Cake Walters . . . . Will Smith
> Jose . . . . Paul Rodriguez
> Stacy . . . . Jennifer Tilly
> Alberta . . . . Peggy Rea

From the moment the opening credits start rolling and the camera focuses on the reckless bicycle ride of Sarah Mathews (Whoopi Goldberg) through the streets of Berkeley, California, film director Richard Benjamin begins his comedic exploration of the erratic life-styles led by Americans in the 1990's.

Single mother Sarah Mathews, who owns and operates The African Queen, a bookstore geared toward black and African literature, culture, history, and tradition, has some explaining to do. When her only child, Zora (Nia Long), discovers in her high school biology lab that her own blood type makes it genetically impossible for her to be the biological daughter of Sarah and Sarah's deceased husband, she demands to know why. After confronting her mother, Zora learns that she was conceived with sperm that her mother purchased from a sperm bank. Sarah assures her, however, that the sperm bank provided the sperm of an intelligent black man. Upon learning this life-altering information, Zora commits herself to finding the father she has never known.

To accomplish this, Zora tricks her best friend, Tea Cake Walters (Will Smith), into accompanying her to the sperm bank where her mother was a customer eighteen years earlier. While Tea Cake poses as a sperm donor, Zora sneaks into the computer files to determine her father's identity. Successful, and bursting with curiosity, Zora cuts class to go to the home of her father, Halbert Jackson (Ted Danson). Upon finding him, Zora is shocked and distraught to learn that Hal is not only a white man but also an obnoxious car salesman who uses cheesy gimmicks to draw customers onto his car lot. Before she reveals her identity to him, he pruriently and egotistically mistakes her for a wanton whom he tries to discourage by explaining that he is "not into the whole black/white thing." When Zora finally reveals that she is his daughter, he breaks her heart by wanting nothing to do with her.

Determined to develop a relationship with Hal, Zora is hindered initially by her mother's attempt to exclude the socially disgraceful Hal from their lives and ultimately by the budding romantic relationship between her mother and Hal. Although Sarah initially detests everything associated with Hal—the faux woodwork and imitation leather furniture in his office; his cowboy attire; his television commercial spots, in which he appears with chimpanzees, grizzly bears, and other assorted wildlife; his womanizing; and his skin color—his sense of humor and burgeoning interest in and respect for Zora slowly win her over. Hal, too, is bothered by Sarah's meddling and outspokenness but soon learns to respect her for her business sense, her successful mothering of Zora, and her independence.

Sarah and Hal's newfound romantic relationship worries Zora, who fears that a breakup may jeopardize her own newly developed relationship with her father. Zora's concern causes Sarah to try to end their romance. Hal, however, has of late gone through a period of self-discovery and grown bored with his relationship with his live-in girlfriend, Stacy (Jennifer Tilly), which is one of pure sexual convenience. Stacy is the stereotypical dumb blond: Her existence revolves solely around aerobic exercise and body image; her relationship with Hal serves only to degrade Hal's character even further; and her placement in the film is a discredit to the filmmakers.

Hal, who as a young man had been bright in the sciences, feels prideful that Zora, an academic achiever and a science whiz, takes after him. In addition, he is attracted to Sarah and does not wish to end their romantic involvement. He has become emotionally connected to the Mathewses in a way he had not thought possible. His interest in the Mathewses marks a true change in his character.

When Sarah is hospitalized following a bicycle accident, the mishap at first bonds them together only to rip them apart later in the face of disappointment and confused emotions. While Sarah is comatose, the hospital requests blood donations from both Zora and Hal. After analyzing the blood, the lab technicians determine that, biologically, Hal and Zora cannot be related. Zora, who feels abandoned, flees the scene. Hal, on the other hand, is ambivalent, simultaneously feeling a sense of freedom and a loss of security. Sarah, however, feels intense remorse for both her own and her daughter's shattered sense of family.

Zora's high school graduation ceremony, already momentous because she has been rewarded with a full scholarship to the Massachusetts Institute of Technology, becomes even more special when Hal appears to reclaim his family. Zora and Sarah enthusiastically welcome him back into their lives, leading one to believe that the three will live happily ever after.

Although the story line is tidily resolved in a euphoric musical finale, the actors—throughout the film—fail to provide credibility for their characters' actions or emotions. The cast members, each successful and talented, would seem a shoo-in for a comic collaboration. Academy Award-winner Whoopi Goldberg, who delighted critics and audiences with her portrayal of an eccentric psychic in *Ghost* (1990), is one of Hollywood's well-loved funny ladies. Ted Danson, famous for his television role as the charismatic womanizer Sam Malone on *Cheers*, reprises some of Sam Malone's characteristics in his portrayal of Hal Jackson. Despite the fact that each gives a fair performance in this film, the relationship that develops between them on screen is pretentious and awkward. They merge as a remedy for loneliness and neediness; absolutely no chemistry exists between them.

Nia Long, who stunned audiences with her role as a sensitive, intelligent young woman trapped in the urban jungle of gang-ridden South Central Los Angeles in *Boyz 'n the Hood* (1991), breathes refreshing life into Zora Mathews. Although Long successfully conveys Zora's passion in her quest for a father, her excessive outbursts are discomforting because they seem irrational. Long infuses her scenes with charm and emotion, yet the choices that her character makes seem illogical. Despite the fact that Hal has scorned her, she is drawn to him for reasons that the script fails to make clear. Whereas *Made in America* should be lauded for positively portraying a young African American woman as a driven, intelligent achiever, Zora's hysterical and unfounded outbursts undercut the stability and likability of her character.

Will Smith, the star of the popular television situation comedy *The Fresh Prince of Bel Air*, adds some laughs to *Made in America*, particularly when he grudgingly poses as a sperm donor who quickly changes his attitude when he is given X-rated films and pornographic paraphernalia as aids. Although the film has its moments and did reasonably well at the box office, the actors do not live up to the potential suggested by the all-star cast list.

Debra Picker

Reviews

Chicago Tribune. May 28, 1993, VII, p. 25.
The Hollywood Reporter. May 27, 1993, p. 5.
Los Angeles Times. May 28, 1993, p. F1.
The New York Times. May 28, 1993, p. B6.
Newsweek. CXXI, June 21, 1993, p. 65.
Time. CXLI, June 14, 1993, p. 72.
USA Today. May 28, 1993, p. D4.
Variety. May 27, 1993, p. 2.
The Washington Post. May 28, 1993, p. G1.

THE MAN WITHOUT A FACE

Production: Bruce Davey for Icon; released by Warner Bros.
Direction: Mel Gibson
Screenplay: Malcolm MacRury; based on the novel by Isabelle Holland
Cinematography: Donald M. McAlpine
Editing: Tony Gibbs
Production design: Barbara Dunphy
Art direction: Marc Fisichella
Set decoration: Donald Elmblad
Casting: Marion Dougherty
Sound: Michael Evje
Special makeup effects: Greg Cannom
Costume design: Shay Cunliffe
Music: James Horner
MPAA rating: PG-13
Running time: 114 minutes

Principal characters:
McLeod . . . . Mel Gibson
Chuck. . . . . Nick Stahl
Catherine . . . . Margaret Whitton
Gloria. . . . . Fay Masterson
Megan . . . . Gaby Hoffmann
Chief Stark. . . . . Geoffrey Lewis
Carl . . . . Richard Masur
Douglas Hall . . . . Michael DeLuise

In *The Man Without a Face*, star Mel Gibson, in his directorial debut, worked to educate as well as entertain his audience. The film, based on the novel by Isabelle Holland, is a lesson about the importance of looking past appearances to test the worth of the person inside.

The Man Without a Face is the story of a twelve-year-old boy, Chuck Norstadt (Nick Stahl), who is searching for a way to escape his dysfunctional family. Neglected by his husband-hunting mother, Catherine (Margaret Whitton), and terrorized by his half sisters, Gloria (Fay Masterson) and Megan (Gaby Hoffmann), Chuck has a plan. He wants to attend the same military boarding school that his mysteriously absent father attended and thereby escape his unhappy home. His problem is that he has already flunked the school's entrance examination once and has only the summer to study before the test is given again in the fall. Chuck's need for a tutor coincides with the family's trip to Maine and with Chuck's encounter with a mysterious and disfigured recluse, McLeod (Mel Gibson), who was once a Latin teacher at a boys' school. Through a series of teen misadventures, Chuck meets McLeod and convinces him to be his tutor. What develops is a fine friendship and trouble for all involved.

The Man Without a Face is not a film without precedents. It has been cited as *The Elephant Man* (1980) meets *Dead Poets Society* (1989), and the appellation is appropriate. The combination of pity and perverse fascination that director David Lynch created in *The Elephant Man* for John Merrick (John Hurt), Mel Gibson is able to capture for McLeod. Drawing McLeod as the brooding loner, Gibson surrounds him with a "mad" dog, a raging stallion, a house that teeters on a cliff, and a voice of such low timbre that it could indeed be the voice of God. Clearly, McLeod is one of a series of literary misfits, not unlike Quasimodo in Victor Hugo's *The Hunchback of Notre Dame* (1831). The local lore surrounding McLeod parallels that surrounding Boo Radley in *To Kill a Mockingbird* (1960) in that each is thought to be crazed, dangerous, horrible to view. For example, the teenagers in *The Man Without a Face* call the beach in front of McLeod's house Freak Beach; the adults gather at cocktail parties and barbershops with wanted posters and theories of murder and mayhem.

On the other hand, however, McLeod is a talented and unorthodox teacher, one who can convey not only the content of the material but also a deep love for and understanding of it. If *Dead Poets Society* is the story of a misfit teacher who teaches Walt Whitman and life lessons, then *The Man Without a Face* is the story of an outcast teacher who teaches William Shakespeare and life lessons. In fact, perhaps the most memorable scene in the film is that in which McLeod recites Shylock's great speech from act 3, scene 3 of Shakespeare's *The Merchant of Venice*. Also mesmerizing in this scene is the set: The "stage," McLeod's house, is set with dozens of candles, giving the scene a warm orange glow. The film is worth seeing for this scene alone.

Also pleasing are the faces of the actors. Certainly Mel Gibson's rise to fame was based party on his good looks, so perhaps the only twist in this film is that only half of his handsome face appears. Gibson wears a large prosthetic device on the right side of his face that took three hours to apply each morning before shooting. While its contours appear to change through the film, it is more likely the audience's reaction to it that changes. Another pleasant face to watch is that of Nick Stahl. His fine, intent performance requires a series of close-ups, which Stahl handles well. He has an expressive, freckled face that also clearly conveys the passions of youth.

Much of this film is successful, particularly in the light of its being the product of a first-time director, Gibson. One of the dangers of a film filled with children, animals, and prosthetic devices is that they will distract from the main story, but here Gibson has managed to keep the focus on the relationship between Chuck and McLeod. For example, the scenes of breakfast at Chuck's house become vignettes, anecdotes of life in hell. One morning Chuck finds his mother and her boyfriend necking in the kitchen. The happy wedding announcement (husband number five) is interrupted as the three children have a particularly abusive fight that leaves their mother in tears and the prospective husband contemplating flight. As vivid as the scene is, it is still merely subplot. Not all of the film works so smoothly, however.

The dialogue in this film is so finely crafted as to be unrealistic. Also, certain scenes try too hard to be stylish and so draw attention from the story. For example, in one scene on Freak Beach, the young teens gather to compare notes on television shows, just as did the teens in *Stand by Me* (1986). Where the earlier film's characters focused on the identity of the Walt Disney animated character Goofy, the newer film (also set in the 1960's) contemplates the interrelationships among the castaways in the television show *Gilligan's Island* and the life-style of the beautiful witch in the television show *Bewitched*. It is a notably unsuccessful scene. Completely contrived, nothing happens before or after it to give it any credibility; no one watches television or mentions another popular-culture phenomenon from the 1960's. At times, Chuck also speaks in sentences beyond his years, and as happy as it would be to think his family totally venomous, Chuck's sister Gloria has lines so purposefully and extraordinarily evil that she very nearly destroys the balance of the film.

Technically, the film is also rough in spots. For example, in the previously mentioned kitchen scene, the camera's angle is so low that the audience spends most of the time watching chair legs and the underside of the table. Worse yet, people's heads are often bisected if not totally left out of the frame. Also, the scenes end abruptly, screeching to a halt immediately after the dialogue. The effect of this rapid-fire editing is that the film seems disjointed and rushed. Much of the film could have a dreamlike quality to it. Although the music (by James Horner) is haunting and bittersweet, it never lingers except through the credit sequences. Otherwise, the scenes end too quickly to provide space for an interlude of music and thought. Another example is McLeod's house. Selected by the filmmakers as the perfect representation of McLeod himself, the large stone house stands alone, solemn and dignified. In fact, the house is so central to the film that it was featured on the film's posters and promotional materials. If indeed the house was to be a major metaphor in the film, however, then perhaps the camera should have paused on the house, and the filmmakers allowed the haunting music to tie it all together. Instead, the audience sees the house in snippets: a driveway here, an attic there. Rarely is it shown in long shot, and even then the camera is constantly moving. The pacing of the film feels forced, and some of the best storytelling devices suffer in the process.

Despite these weaknesses, *The Man Without a Face* remains a memorable film. Beyond showcasing Mel Gibson's directing abilities, it also retells a classic story of friendship, with a new twist. It is surprising, entertaining, memorable, and worth seeing.

Roberta F. Green

Reviews
Chicago Tribune. August 27, 1993, Section 7, p. C.
The Christian Science Monitor. August 27, 1993, p. 12.
Entertainment Weekly. Fall, 1993, p. 90.
Films in Review. XLIV, November, 1993, p. 415.
The Hollywood Reporter. August 23, 1993, p. 6.

Los Angeles Times. August 25, 1993, p. F1.
The New York Times. August 25, 1993, p. B1.
Newsweek. CXXII, August 30, 1993, p. 52.
Sight and Sound. III, December, 1993, p. 48.
Time. CXLII, August 30, 1993, p. 63.
Variety. August 23, 1993, p. 4.
The Washington Post. August 27, 1993, p. 36.

MANHATTAN MURDER MYSTERY

Production: Robert Greenhut for Jack Rollins and Charles H. Joffe; released by
  TriStar Pictures
Direction: Woody Allen
Screenplay: Woody Allen and Marshall Brickman
Cinematography: Carlo Di Palma
Editing: Susan E. Morse
Production design: Santo Loquasto
Art direction: Speed Hopkins
Set decoration: Susan Bode
Casting: Juliet Taylor
Sound: James Sabat
Makeup: Fern Buchner
Costume design: Jeffrey Kurland
MPAA rating: PG
Running time: 108 minutes

Principal characters:

Larry Lipton	Woody Allen
Carol Lipton	Diane Keaton
Ted	Alan Alda
Marcia Fox	Anjelica Huston
Paul House	Jerry Adler
Lillian House	Lynn Cohen
Helen Moss	Melanie Norris
Sy	Ron Rifkin
Marilyn	Joy Behar

The opening sequence of Woody Allen's intellectual comedy should offer no
surprises to fans who have grown familiar with the trademarks of the writer and
director's twenty-three films. The camera zeros in on New York City's skyline as Cole
Porter's ode to the metropolis, "I Happen to Like New York," plays. Allen wastes no
time in introducing a conflict between protagonists Larry Lipton (Allen) and his wife,
Carol, played by Diane Keaton. Although Carol suffers through an entire hockey game
with Larry, he reneges on his part of the bargain by making her leave an opera in
mid-aria: Listening to the music of Richard Wagner, he says with a straight face, gives
him the sudden urge to conquer Poland. Once established, their contention worsens
throughout the film, providing much amusing dialogue and spurring Carol's closeness
to Ted (Alan Alda), a friend of the family.

The plot is propelled by Carol and Larry's brief acquaintance with their neighbors
Paul and Lillian House (Jerry Adler and Lynn Cohen), an older couple preparing to
celebrate their twenty-eighth wedding anniversary. Larry, a busy book editor with his

own agenda, finds Carol's congeniality toward the Houses a nuisance. He must, for example, endure Paul's enthusiasm for stamp collecting: "His favorite thing in life is to look at canceled postage," Larry complains. For her part, Carol worries that Larry no longer finds her attractive, a concern that is reinforced by Larry's business relationship with author Marcia Fox (Anjelica Huston), a tall, dark, sexy woman who clothes herself in tight black leather—in stark contrast to Carol's conservative layered look of browns, beiges, and belted suits. When Lillian House dies unexpectedly from an apparent coronary, neighborly Carol attempts to comfort the widowed Paul and in doing so finds an urn filled with ashes in his apartment. She immediately becomes suspicious, since Paul had specified that Lillian would be buried in one of their twin cemetery plots. Already dubious of the seemingly robust Lillian's sudden death and surprised by the grieving Paul's cheery attitude, Carol—now fueled by her discovery of the hidden urn—begins to suspect foul play.

Although Larry is initially uninterested in Carol's accusations, she finds a willing Sherlock in Ted, who is newly divorced and has always felt a strong attraction to Carol. The two amateur detectives theorize that Paul murdered his wife, and they devise numerous plans to uncover clues. As Carol's interest in and obsession with the case grows, her relationship with her husband becomes more strained. Larry, who is too neurotic and socially conservative to participate in Carol and Ted's shenanigans, thinks that Carol has gone overboard and, comparing her to a defective car that needs to be recalled, pleads with her to return to a therapist. He asks her to "save a little craziness for menopause." Larry, recognizing Carol's affinity for Ted, which is paralleled in Marcia Fox's interest in Larry, arranges a date between Ted and Marcia.

On the evening of Ted and Marcia's date, Larry makes a wholehearted effort to involve himself in Carol's exploits. After Carol insists that she spotted the supposedly dead Lillian House riding on a New York City bus, the skeptical Larry joins her for a stakeout. When Larry and Carol actually sight Lillian entering the Hotel Waldron, they are ecstatic. Trailing Lillian to her room, however, they find her dead upon their arrival. When they leave the body to contact the police, it mysteriously disappears, only to reappear later in the hotel's elevator shaft. Escaping from the broken elevator into the dark, labyrinthine basement, Larry and Carol finally find an exit to the street, where they spot Paul loading what appears to be a dead body into the trunk of his car. Chasing him to a steel-smelting factory, they witness his disposal of the body in a vat of flames.

Dumbfounded and insomniac, Larry and Carol—reveling in their revived relationship—take a late-night drive to the New Jersey restaurant where Ted and Marcia are dining in order to confer with them about the latest developments in the case. Though the four make progress in cracking the mystery, the meeting is a disaster for Carol, who feels that both Ted and Larry are fawning over the seductive Marcia, who has impressed the men by devising an intricate plan to blackmail Paul and bring him to justice. Using the technological expertise and equipment of Larry and Carol's friends Sy and Marilyn (Ron Rifkin and Joy Behar), the group participates in a hilariously dark and suspenseful sequence of events that eventually unravels the mystery.

The brutal murder at the heart of this comic screenplay is reminiscent of William

Shakespeare's tragicomedies and certainly does temper one's overall fondness for the film. Allen does, in fact, make reference to Shakespeare's *Macbeth*, among other literary and cultural allusions to such films as *Double Indemnity* (1944) and *Casablanca* (1942) and the novel *Finnegans Wake* (1939). Even with the dark overtones, this film is humorous throughout and much easier to swallow than some of Allen's other, more serious projects such as *Crimes and Misdemeanors* (1989) and *Husbands and Wives* (1992). Several critics likened Larry and Carol to the classic comic detective couple Nick and Nora Charles of *The Thin Man* series.

The script—cowritten by Allen and Marshall Brickman, the duo responsible for *Annie Hall* (1977) and *Manhattan* (1979)—contains a healthy collection of perfectly timed one-liners and weighty, cleverly written dialogue. The casting is superb, and Allen's command of his actors is, as usual, expert. Allen's own cranky and complaining Larry Lipton provides humor as long as he remains celluloid; a real-life encounter with querulous Larry would prove an annoyance. Alan Alda's Ted has much of the charisma associated with his role of Hawkeye Pierce in the long-running television series *M*A*S*H*. While Ted is certainly a pleasure to watch, and Huston's Marcia Fox is intriguing, it is Keaton's high-caliber performance as Carol Lipton that produces the character with the most integrity and emotional depth. Diane Keaton brings to the film a sweet impetuosity and raw energy. Interestingly, it was Mia Farrow who was originally to have played the part of Carol Lipton. Despite the abrupt ending of Allen and Farrow's relationship and well-publicized problems, Allen successfully recast the part and created a blithe comedy that belied his real-life turmoil. Altogether, *Manhattan Murder Mystery* is a filmic success.

Debra Picker

Reviews

Chicago Tribune. August 20, 1993, VII, p. 21.
The Christian Science Monitor. August 20, 1993, p. 12.
Entertainment Weekly. August 20, 1993, p. 36.
Films in Review. XLIV, November, 1993, p. 413.
The Hollywood Reporter. August 9, 1993, p. 5.
Los Angeles Times. August 18, 1993, p. F1.
The New York Times. August 18, 1993, p. B1.
The New Yorker. LXIX, August 23, 1993, p. 163.
Newsweek. CXXII, August 30, 1993, p. 53.
Time. CXLII, August 23, 1993, p. 67.
Variety. August 9, 1993, p. 2.
The Washington Post. August 20, 1993, p. D6.

EL MARIACHI

Production: Robert Rodriguez and Carlos Gallardo for Los Hooligans; released by
   Columbia Pictures
Direction: Robert Rodriguez
Screenplay: Robert Rodriguez and Carlos Gallardo; based on a story by Rodriguez
Cinematography: Robert Rodriguez
Editing: Robert Rodriguez
Music: Juan Suarez, Marc Trujillo, Alvaro Rodriguez, Nestor Fajardo, and Cecilio
   Rodriguez
MPAA rating: R
Running time: 82 minutes

> *Principal characters:*
> El Mariachi . . . . Carlos Gallardo
> Domino . . . . Consuelo Gómez
> Moco . . . . Peter Marquardt
> Azul . . . . Reinol Martinez

Twenty-three-year-old Robert Rodriguez and his partner, Carlos Gallardo, shot this film in fourteen days on a budget of seven thousand dollars. *El Mariachi*, a film in Spanish with English subtitles, is a comic action-adventure about an innocent mariachi musician in need of a job, who goes to a town wearing a black jacket and carrying only his guitar in its case. Unfortunately, at the same time, a hit man has arrived in the same town wearing a similar jacket and carrying a guitar case filled with weapons. Their mistaken identity propels the story and leads to a surprisingly serious conclusion. *El Mariachi* not only offers an inventive and fresh approach to the action genre but also represents a stunning feature film debut. It would be a terrific film had it been made with a budget in the customary million-dollar range, but for seven thousand dollars, it is one of the great triumphs in film; in fact, its background immediately began to take on mythic qualities among Hollywood insiders.

Indeed, the story behind the making of the film is as interesting as the film itself. Rodriguez, a veteran of many international film festival competitions with short films, and childhood friend Gallardo initially created this film with the intention of selling it to the lucrative Spanish-language video market. Instead, the film won critical and audience raves at the prestigious Telluride, Sundance, and Toronto film festivals, went on to successful popular release in English- and Spanish-speaking film theaters, and earned Rodriguez a lucrative deal with Columbia Pictures. Rodriguez earned three thousand dollars of the money to make the film by living at a hospital for one month and being paid to undergo tests for the purposes of medical research. The villain of the film is played by Peter Marquardt, who was a fellow guinea pig with Rodriguez at the Austin, Texas, hospital. The love interest, played by Consuelo Gómez, was the only actor in the film to be paid because she had a full-time job at a government agency and had difficulties with the production schedule.

It seems inevitable that any discussion of this film would require the repetition of the story of its origins, but the film stands alone. It is lively, comic, and touching. It is shot expertly, is acted with understated dignity and intelligence, and has something to say about the eclipse of old cultural values by a dangerous, fast-changing, and increasingly dehumanizing world.

A prologue sets up the action. A dusty jail cell in a village in Mexico becomes the site of the bloody jailbreak of a dangerous man named Azul (Reinol Martinez). He is being hunted by the villainous Moco (Marquardt) because of a financial dispute. Azul carries a guitar case filled with weapons as he leaves the jail. A rhythmic, high-tech score accompanies this prologue, giving way to the sounds of Mexican folk guitar as the audience is introduced to the innocent El Mariachi (Gallardo) with guitar in hand, on his way to a new town. He narrates the film, telling the audience, "My father, grandfather, and great-grandfather were mariachis. My plan was to die with a guitar in my hand. . . . We didn't know our time was running out." The abrupt change in the type of music heard during the prologue to the simple acoustic sound of the mariachi guitar foreshadows the struggle between gentle culture and urban-style violence that is at the film's core. This struggle is hilariously depicted in another early scene. El Mariachi has arrived in a new town and enters a bar searching for a job as a musician. The owner says he has no need for a mariachi because "I pay only one guy and I have a whole group of mariachis." Immediately, a man sitting in the back of the bar sets up a portable electronic keyboard making dreadful, prefabricated sounds, once again showing technology replacing art. El Mariachi wonders "what happened to the days when guitar was God."

His guitar *is* God to him, or at the very least it is the center of his spirituality. After unsuccessful attempts to find a job, El Mariachi goes to a hotel where he is mistaken for Azul. Moco's henchmen try to kill him in his hotel room, and he flees, leaving his guitar. As he is in the middle of a dangerous chase, however, he remembers his guitar. The camera zooms in on him and then zooms in on his guitar, back at the hotel: The guitar is virtually calling to El Mariachi, as if the man and the instrument have one and the same thought. He goes back for the guitar, outwits the villains with it, and even uses it as a weapon. It is his source of survival in every sense. The spiritual connection between this man and his instrument is portrayed quite well. Less understandable, however, are a series of dream sequences, which are not defined as well as other aspects of the film. Though a bit confusing, they do resonate within the film's atmosphere of myth and fable even if their symbolism is enigmatic.

Ultimately, however, the film works beautifully on a more commercial level; it is a lively action-adventure. El Mariachi is unwittingly thrown into a cat-and-mouse game through mistaken identity, but it is a comic game. Moco's henchmen are humorous characters, overly serious and rather inept. They are everywhere—the little town is teeming with henchmen trying to kill poor El Mariachi, thinking he is Azul. They have no luck doing so, as El Mariachi kills several of the men as they chase him. Moco is the only one who can recognize Azul, and he is far outside of town, keeping in touch with a portable phone. In fact, everyone in the little town seems to be connected to Moco in some way, and they are constantly calling him to tell of the whereabouts of Azul. In two hilarious scenes, a seedy hotel proprietor calls Moco to tell him where "Azul" is; the film is sped up as he dials to show his haste in calling Moco. Rodriguez constantly speeds up the film, uses extreme close-ups, and utilizes comic sound effects to tell his story. Time and again, he turns a familiar film convention on its head, and the result is refreshing. The effect is as if an avant-garde filmmaker had remade Alfred Hitchcock's suspenseful *North by Northwest* (1959) or as if Sam Peckinpah, the director of the violent film *The Wild Bunch* (1969) had made Peter Bogdanovich's comedy *What's Up Doc?* (1972).

El Mariachi meets and falls in love with the beautiful Domino (Consuelo Gómez), who helps him even as it puts her in danger with Moco. She gives him the job he needs, and his unpretentious interpretation of the mariachi music underscores how important the music is to him. The gentility of the scene in which El Mariachi is finally able to sing is contrasted with the film's bloodshed, which becomes more graphic and frequent as the story progresses. Had the film been made with a bigger budget, the bloodshed might have been too realistic, but here it is simply special effects. The fact that the blood does not seem real adds to the film's mythic quality, yet it keeps the audience unprepared for the serious conclusion. This decision works in favor of the film, however, which is ultimately a painful allegory about one man's need to adapt to the world around him, to his and society's detriment. El Mariachi is forced to resort to violence to protect himself, even as he is the victim of that violence. This dilemma serves as a perfect symbol for those among many Hispanics living in the United States: Rival gangs (Moco and Azul) create an atmosphere in which young men who are having difficulty finding jobs (El Mariachi) are forced to resort to the violence they abhor simply to survive.

Few Hispanic directors in the United States have found success within the studio system, and *El Mariachi* appeared to place Rodriguez at the beginning of a formidable career, with the ability to pave the way for other Hispanics. Rodriguez' rapid rise and early commercial success is reminiscent of the experience of John Singleton, the young African-American filmmaker whose first film, *Boyz 'n the Hood* (1991), was financed with credit cards and went on to earn several Oscar nominations. Ultimately, however, ethnic background is irrelevant. Talent is talent, and Rodriguez has it. The confident effervescence of El Mariachi is a welcome departure from other high-tech, high-finance action films, such as the *Lethal Weapon* series. Rodriguez has an uncanny ability to present a textured story while remembering the maxim that "less is more." Hopefully, this principle is deeply etched into his technique so that, when the budgets are bigger, his films retain the focus and simplicity of *El Mariachi*.

Kirby Tepper

Reviews

Chicago Tribune. March 12, 1993, VII, p. 38.
The Christian Science Monitor. February 26, 1993, p. 14.
The Hollywood Reporter. February 9, 1993, p. 25.
Los Angeles Times. February 26, 1993, p. F1.
New Statesman and Society. VI, August 13, 1993, p. 34.
The New York Times. February 26, 1993, p. 39.
The New Yorker. LXIX, February 22, 1993, p. 169.
Sight and Sound. III, September, 1993, p. 50.
Variety. September 10, 1992, p. 2.
The Wall Street Journal. March 11, 1993, p. A12.
The Washington Post. April 3, 1993, p. C1.

MATINEE

Production: Michael Finnell for Renfield; released by Universal Pictures
Direction: Joe Dante
Screenplay: Charlie Haas
Cinematography: John Hora
Editing: Marshall Harvey
Production design: Steven Legler
Art direction: Nanci B. Roberts
Set decoration: Frederick C. Weiler and Eric Weiler
Casting: Gretchen Rennell
Visual effects supervision: Dennis Michelson
Sound: Howard Warren
Costume design: Isis Mussenden
Mant/Ant design: James McPherson
Stunt coordination: Jeff Smolek
Music: Jerry Goldsmith
MPAA rating: PG
Running time: 99 minutes

Principal characters:

Lawrence Woolsey	John Goodman
Ruth Corday	Cathy Moriarty
Gene Loomis	Simon Fenton
Stan	Omri Katz
Sandra	Lisa Jakub
Sherry	Kellie Martin
Dennis Loomis	Jesse Lee
Anne Loomis	Lucinda Jenney
Harvey Starkweather	James Villemaire
Howard	Robert Picardo
Mr. Spector	Jesse White
Herb	Dick Miller
Jack	David Clennon
Bob	John Sayles
Rhonda	Lucy Butler
Dwight	Georgie Cranford
Mant	Mark McCracken
Dentist	William Schallert
General	Kevin McCarthy

Matinee puts a new spin on the coming-of-age tale. In *Mant,* the film within a film, director Joe Dante satirizes the cheesy monster films of the 1950's and 1960's while commenting on the real-life terror of the 1962 Cuban Missile Crisis. In *Matinee*, self-styled master of film horror Lawrence Woolsey (John Goodman) brings his show to the Strand theater of Key West, Florida, the same weekend of the Cuban Missile Crisis and, in the process, affects the lives of a score of area teens.

Believably cast as a huckster filmmaker, Goodman skillfully hawks *Mant* ("Half man, half ant—all terror! So terrifying only screams can describe it!") in the hope of impressing chain-theater owner Mr. Spector (played by veteran Hollywood actor Jesse White). He gives one of his best performances as the blustery Woolsey, a portly, cigar-chomping salesman who personally accompanies his creations to their city-by-city premieres. This is Goodman's film, and the other performances pale in comparison.

Goodman's inspiration was William Castle (1914-1977), who was known for similar macabre films, such as *Homicidal* (1961), as well as for his advertising gimmicks. In *Matinee*, Woolsey is undeterred by the threat of nuclear holocaust and proclaims: "What a perfect time to open a horror movie." Dante also pays homage to Alfred Hitchcock and *Psycho* (1960); indeed, the audience first sees Woolsey in a Hitchcockesque silhouette. A filmmaker such as Castle probably recalled for Dante his own days as an assistant to B-film director Roger Corman. It was Castle who wired seats with electricity for his 1959 production of *The Tingler*. For *House on Haunted Hill* (1958) and *Macabre* (1958), he offered insurance policies to patrons in the event that they were scared to death. In *Matinee*, Woolsey has his girlfriend, Ruth (Cathy Moriarty), dress as a nurse who asks patrons to release all rights to sue the filmmakers before they see *Mant*. *Matinee* also pays homage to Castle's sound system, Rumble-Rama, in which the theater seats shake on cue.

Aside from Goodman's performance, the other highlight of *Matinee* is *Mant* itself. In this film-within-a-film, the "Mant" begins as a normal guy named Bill (Mark McCracken) who then mutates and grows feelers after he is bitten by an irradiated ant. Bill becomes progressively bigger and more destructive. He is not consoled when his wife, Carole (played by Moriarty), exclaims "Oh, Bill, if you could just listen to the man and put the insect aside." *Mant* is wonderful satire.

Matinee was shot on location in Florida, with postproduction work done in Hollywood. The film's Key West was really Cocoa, Florida. Period songs are used, to great effect, as are authentic-looking cars and clothes. *Matinee* is at its best when it captures the look of the era, and thus the fear and innocence of the early 1960's as well. The temper of the times is reflected by the fact that there is a bomb shelter in the basement of the theater.

Director Dante, who is best known for *Gremlins* (1984) and its 1990 sequel, concocts an entirely benevolent monster in *Matinee*, his salute to B films and the innocence of the early 1960's. Yet this was also an era of mutants lurking under every bed and the apocalypse that was just around the corner, with "duck-and-cover" as one's only protection. The story is an entertaining hybrid of the classic horror tale *Them!* (1954) and the Italian film-about-filmgoing *Cinema Paradiso* (1989).

Less successful, however, is the coming-of-age story of *Matinee* in which Gene

Loomis (Simon Fenton), the fifteen-year-old son of a Navy officer, and his kid brother, Dennis (Jesse Lee), find true love. Young Gene falls for a ban-the-bomb, new girl in school, Sandra (Lisa Jakub), and they, like Woolsey and his Ruth, all seem to live happily ever after. Meanwhile, high school popularity queen, Sherry (Kellie Martin), the former girlfriend of rebellious older teenager Harvey (James Villemaire), is pursued by Stan (Omri Katz), Gene's best friend. This aspect of the plot is average at best, and sometimes tedious. Yet Gene and his friends do struggle with the real fear of the Cuban Missile Crisis. Indeed, young Gene's father is on a ship near Cuba, but the family does not know how he is involved in the crisis. One guesses that the father is participating in the United States blockade of Soviet ships trying to deliver missiles to Cuba.

Matinee contains enough in-jokes to keep film buffs happy. Independent director John Sayles portrays Bob, one of Woolsey's planted shills who is meant to create hysteria in the town—as if Key West needed it during the Missile Crisis. (Bob pretends to be an outraged conservative who demands that the film be banned.) Yet there is not enough Goodman, or *Mant*, or in-jokes to make *Matinee* a true success. Lawrence Cohn, of the film industry's key trade magazine, *Variety*, was right on the mark when he predicted good, but not great, box-office results for the film. Within a month of its premiere, *Matinee* had done mild theater business and had disappeared from screens.

Douglas Gomery

Reviews
Boston Globe. January 29, 1993, p. 24.
Chicago Tribune. January 29, 1993, VII, p. 21.
Cinefantastique. XXIII, April, 1993, p. 46.
Entertainment Weekly. February 5, 1993, p. 34.
The Hollywood Reporter. January 29, 1993, p. 8.
Los Angeles Times. January 29, 1993, p. F10.
The New York Times. January 29, 1993, p. B2.
The New Yorker. LXVIII, February 8, 1993, p. 102.
Sight and Sound. III, June, 1993, p. 59.
Time. CXLI, February 8, 1993, p. 78.
Variety. January 26, 1993, p. 18.
The Washington Post. January 29, 1993, p. C1.

MENACE II SOCIETY

Production: Darin Scott; released by New Line Cinema
Direction: Allen Hughes and Albert Hughes
Screenplay: Tyger Williams; based on a story by Allen Hughes, Albert Hughes, and
Williams
Cinematography: Lisa Rinzler
Editing: Christopher Koefoed
Production design: Penny Barrett
Set decoration: Adel A. Mazen
Casting: Tony Lee
Sound: Veda Campbell
Costume design: Sylvia Vega-Vasquez
Music supervision: Bonnie Greenberg and Jill Meyers
Music: QD III
MPAA rating: R
Running time: 107 minutes

Principal characters:

Caine Lawson	Tyrin Turner
Ronnie	Jada Pinkett
O-Dog	Larenz Tate
Tat Lawson	Samuel L. Jackson
Sharif	Vonte Sweet
Grandpapa	Arnold Johnson
Grandmama	Marilyn Coleman
Mr. Butler	Charles S. Dutton
A-Wax	MC Eiht
Stacy	Ryan Williams
Lew-Loc	Todd Anthony Shaw
Pernell	Glenn Plummer
Detective	Bill Duke
Anthony	Jullian Roy Doster
Harold Lawson	Saafir
Doc	Pooh Man
Chauncy	Clifton Powell
Karen Lawson	Khandi Alexander
Grocery Store Woman	June Kyoko Lu
Grocery Store Man	Toshi Toda

With this film, twenty-year-old twin brothers Allen and Albert Hughes have achieved one of the most impressive directorial debuts in the late twentieth century. *Menace II Society* is an unflinching, unapologetic look at life in the ghetto. It is a brutal film, much closer in spirit to *Bad Lieutenant* (1992) in its frank handling of its subject matter than it is to the cliché-riddled, overrated *Boyz 'n the Hood* (1991), which attempted to cover much of the same ground.

The themes of *Menace II Society* recall the novels and short stories of Jess Mowry, whose literature also documents the realities of growing up within the confines of the inner city. Like Mowry, the Hughes brothers see escape as the only solution. Guns, drugs, and senseless violence have become the sad reality of ghetto life. This film tells the story of those who are trapped in this way of life.

The film opens with a confrontation in a Korean grocery store. Although Caine Lawson (Tyrin Turner) and O-Dog (Larenz Tate) simply want to buy some beer, they are followed through the store by the Grocery Store Woman (June Kyoko Lu), who makes little effort to disguise her distrust of the two. This scene highlights the problems between Koreans and African Americans. The Hughes brothers do not offer any explanations or excuses; they simply present the problem. This scene sets the tone for the rest of the film.

As Caine and O-Dog are about to leave, the Grocery Store Man (Toshi Toda) makes the fatal mistake of commenting on O-Dog's mother. O-Dog pulls out a gun and kills the man. After obtaining the video surveillance tape from the man's wife, O-Dog kills her as well. O-Dog then calmly goes through the cash register and the dead man's pockets, taking whatever money he can find.

Caine is shocked by his friend's behavior and drops his beer bottle at the sound of the first shot. Caine has just finished high school and had been looking forward to an enjoyable summer, but now he finds himself unexpectedly involved in a murder/ robbery. This unpremeditated action aptly demonstrates the spontaneous violence that has become common in the ghetto, as the Hughes brothers go on to show repeatedly through the rest of the film.

The film is set in 1990's Watts, and to provide some historical background, the Hughes brothers include film footage of the 1963 Watts riots during the opening credits. The film segues into the early 1970's and the youth of five-year-old Caine (Brandon Hammond), who is being reared in an environment of drugs and violence. The audience discovers through Caine's narration that his father, Tat Lawson (Samuel L. Jackson), is a drug dealer, and his mother, Karen Lawson (Khandi Alexander), is a heroin addict. Caine's surrogate father, Pernell (Glenn Plummer)—one of his parents' friends—shows young Caine how to hold a gun and gives him his first taste of liquor. Not long afterward, Caine's parents both die in separate incidents, and Pernell is sent to prison on a life sentence. Caine is then reared by his grandparents, with whom he is still living as the film returns to the present day.

Ironically, the opening sequence in the Korean grocery store gave the impression that Caine was an innocent youth saddled with a psychopathic friend. The Hughes brothers, however, quickly dispel this notion. Caine is a drug dealer, as was his father, but unlike his mother, he is not a user. He drinks only beer, and the strongest drug any of his friends use is marijuana. While Caine is not as crazed as O-Dog, he is not far from it. In fact, Caine soon commits his first murder, in retaliation for the death of his cousin, Harold Lawson (Saafir), during a carjacking.

The main difference between Caine and O-Dog is that Caine has more common sense. Caine is horrified to learn that O-Dog has been showing the surveillance tape to people in the neighborhood. O-Dog sees himself as a film star, repeatedly playing the segment in which he shoots the Korean man. O-Dog tells people, in all seriousness, that he will be the next big action-film star. O-Dog is so delusional that he considers making copies of the tape to sell to his friends. Even after he has promised Caine not to show anyone else the tape, O-Dog continues to do so. It is like a drug to him.

Meanwhile, Caine sinks deeper into trouble. He and O-Dog are arrested for stealing a car. O-Dog is released because he is still a juvenile, but Caine is held. The charges are reduced to joyriding since it is Caine's first offense, but the police soon discover that his fingerprints match those on the broken bottle found at the Korean grocery store. Despite the fact that a detective (Bill Duke) interrogates Caine, without the surveillance tape the police have no case. In addition to this problem, Ilena (Erin Leshawn Wiley), a girl with whom Caine had a short-term affair, informs him that she is pregnant with his child. Caine denies responsibility, and soon Ilena's cousin (Samuel Monroe, Jr.) is looking for revenge.

Caine sees himself falling into the same trap as Pernell. Caine has been taking care of Pernell's girlfriend, Ronnie (Jada Pinkett), and her six-year-old son, Anthony (Jullian Roy Doster). Caine is afraid of the same thing happening to him and Ilena. To complicate matters, Caine has fallen in love with Ronnie but still feels loyalty to Pernell. Caine initially becomes a mentor to Anthony as Anthony's father, Pernell, was for him. Yet, although Caine shows Anthony how to hold a gun, he soon regrets this action and later prevents one of his friends from giving Anthony liquor, as Caine was given at a similar age by Pernell.

As events begin to spiral out of control, escape from Watts becomes the only option. Sharif (Vonte Sweet), a recently converted Muslim friend of Caine, and Sharif's father, Mr. Butler (Charles S. Dutton), ask Caine to come to Kansas with them. Also, Ronnie has accepted a job in Atlanta, and she asks Caine to come with her and Anthony. Caine decides on Atlanta, but it is too late, as his past catches up with him.

Allen and Albert Hughes, together with screenwriter Tyger Williams, have created a fascinating story that never falters. The realistic portrayal of life in Watts is far more terrifying than the scariest horror film. Adding to the film's authenticity are the locations: Much of the film was shot in the Jordan Downs Housing Project in Watts. This authenticity is vital to the film's success.

The film also succeeds because the filmmakers refrain from preaching to the audience. They merely show life in the ghetto: what it is like for its residents as well as how it is perceived by others, including Korean store owners, the police, and disreputable white businesspeople who come to the projects looking for desperate kids to do their dirty work for them.

The Hughes brothers were themselves steered away from drugs and gangs by their mother, who bought them a video camera when they were twelve years old. Their professional career began with directing rap-music videos. To have directed such a successful film, at such a young age and with no film-school background, is an astonishing feat. Their triumph is an inspiration to both fans of serious cinema and aspiring filmmakers alike.

Director of photography Lisa Rinzler provides the film with an appropriately grainy look, making sure that the Hollywood slickness of most commercial films does not contaminate the gritty nature of this film's subject matter. Costume designer Sylvia Vega-Vasquez also helps establish the realistic look of the film, as she did in *American Me* (1992).

The acting is first-rate. Tyrin Turner is impressive as Caine, effortlessly shifting from confused and caring to enraged or indifferent. All the while he manages the difficult task of keeping the audience sympathetic to his character. Without the viewer's caring what happened to Caine, the film would not have worked.

Samuel L. Jackson, in a relatively small role as Caine's father, is amazing. In *Jungle Fever* (1991), Jackson stole every scene in which he appeared, turning the subplot of his drug-addicted character into a more interesting part of the film than the interracial love story that forms the main plot line. As Tat Lawson, Samuel L. Jackson is virtually unrecognizable. His character oozes menace and the danger of a person who does not care about anything—a truly brilliant performance.

Larenz Tate, making his feature-film debut as O-Dog, and Jada Pinkett as the caring single mother Ronnie, both turn in fine performances as well.

Despite the fact that a number of films, such as *Boyz 'n the Hood* and *Juice* (1992), have dealt with similar subject matter, *Menace II Society* far surpasses and outclasses all of them. It will be remembered not only as one of the best films of 1993 but also as the film that launched the careers of its talented directors.

George Delalis

Reviews

Chicago Tribune. May 26, 1993, V, p. 3.
The Christian Science Monitor. July 9, 1993, p. 12.
Cineaste. XX, Number 2, 1993, p. 44.
Entertainment Weekly. May 28, 1993, p. 48.
The Hollywood Reporter. May 21, 1993, p. 11.
Los Angeles Times. May 26, 1993, p. F1.
The New York Times. May 26, 1993, p. B1.
The New Yorker. May 31, 1993, p. 160.
Newsweek. CXXII, July 19, 1993, p. 52.
Rolling Stone. July 8, 1993, p. 121.
Variety. May 20, 1993, p. 17.
The Washington Post. May 26, 1993, p. B1.

MRS. DOUBTFIRE

Production: Marsha Garces Williams, Robin Williams, and Mark Radcliffe for
   Blue Wolf; released by Twentieth Century-Fox
Direction: Chris Columbus
Screenplay: Randi Mayem Singer and Leslie Dixon; based on the novel *Alias
   Madame Doubtfire*, by Anne Fine
Cinematography: Donald McAlpine
Editing: Raja Gosnell
Production design: Angelo Graham
Art direction: W. Steven Graham
Set decoration: Garrett Lewis
Casting: Janet Hirschenson and Jane Jenkins
Sound: Nelson Stoll
Makeup: Greg Cannom (AA), Ve Neill (AA), Yolanda Toussieng (AA)
Costume design: Marit Allen
Music: Howard Shore
MPAA rating: PG-13
Running time: 119 minutes

> *Principal characters:*
> Daniel Hillard (Mrs. Doubtfire) . . . . Robin Williams
> Miranda Hillard . . . . Sally Field
> Stu . . . . Pierce Brosnan
> Frank . . . . Harvey Fierstein
> Gloria . . . . Polly Holliday
> Lydia Hillard . . . . Lisa Jakub
> Chris Hillard . . . . Matthew Lawrence
> Natalie Hillard . . . . Mara Wilson
> Jack . . . . Scott Capurro

   In 1982's *Victor/Victoria* Julie Andrews played an out-of-work singer who dresses
up like a man in order to get a singing job. Also in 1982 was *Tootsie*, in which Dustin
Hoffman played an out-of-work actor who dresses up like a woman in order to get an
acting job. In 1993, there was the hilarious *Mrs. Doubtfire*, in which Robin Williams
plays an out-of-work actor who dresses up like a woman in order to get a job as
housekeeper and spend more time with his own children. Call it a 1980's cross-dress-
ing premise with a 1990's family-values twist.
   Based on the novel *Alias Madame Doubtfire* by Anne Fine, *Mrs. Doubtfire* centers
on Daniel Hillard (Williams), a frequently unemployed actor and father of three, whose
idealistic nature and broad sense of humor clash with his wife's more sensible and
sedate style. Miranda Hillard (Sally Field) is a partner in a prestigious design firm,
who wears expensive suits and drives a Volvo. Daniel, on the other hand, provides the

voices for a cartoon bird and hires not just a pony for his son's birthday but an entire traveling zoo.

When Miranda decides to call it quits on their fourteen-year marriage and is awarded full custody of the children, Daniel decides he cannot possibly go a single day without them. So, with the help of his brother Frank (Harvey Fierstein), a makeup artist, Daniel transforms himself into the sixty-year-old Mrs. Doubtfire, an English nanny that Miranda unwittingly hires to take care of the kids. This is the true starting point of the film, as Daniel struggles to maintain his charade while trying to master the simple responsibilities, such as cooking and cleaning, that he lacked in the first place.

Coming off of the commercially unsuccessful *Toys* (1992), Robin Williams has found a mainstream film that is perfectly suited to his unique talents. Williams is a joy in the dual role of Daniel and Mrs. Doubtfire, and it is his uncanny comic ability that is the primary reason this film works as well as it does. Known to audiences for years as a master of voices, impressions, and improvisations, Williams knows how to make the most out of every comic moment, and the film's director, Chris Columbus, apparently knew that too.

Mrs. Doubtfire is hilarious when Williams is allowed to break free from the only occasionally funny script and do what he does best: make it up as he goes along. The best scenes in the film, such as a string of uncanny impressions delivered to a stone-faced social worker, or the riotously funny moments with Frank, as Daniel tries on a variety of women's looks, are tailor-made for Williams' versatile comic genius. He is sometimes so funny that the audience misses the next few jokes because they are still laughing at the last one.

This film is more than just an outrageous comedy, however. Despite the tendency to push a little too hard for sentimentality, there are many genuinely touching moments. As Miranda and Daniel come to the realization that their marriage is over, their pain and loss are deeply felt. Likewise, Daniel's love and devotion to his children and theirs to him seem real and unaffected. Director Columbus and screenwriters Randi Mayem Singer and Leslie Dixon deserve credit for eliciting many wonderful emotions from their talented ensemble.

As Miranda, Sally Field is warm and likable in a difficult role. It is easy, at first, to cast her as the "bad guy" in the breakup of the marriage and the resulting distress it causes everyone. Field, however, makes Miranda more than simply the shrewish wife. It becomes evident, through her performance, that Field's Miranda is a woman who loses some of the confidence she has in the halls of her design firm when she walks through the door of her own home. More to the point, by the end of the film there is the desire to root for her happiness as well as that of hero Daniel. Field is also a terrific "straight man" to Williams' antics, providing an equilibrium to the proceedings.

Pierce Brosnan and Harvey Fierstein deliver solid performances in small but pivotal roles. Brosnan, of television's *Remington Steele* fame, plays Stuart, a rich and handsome developer trying to win Miranda's heart. Again, this is a character that would be easy to dislike, and it would have been easier still for Singer and Dixon to write him that way. All involved, however, took that extra step to make Stuart into a man who finds himself surprised to be wanting the family life he has never had. Brosnan works hard at showing both sides and succeeds.

Actor-playwright Fierstein practically steals the show in his turn as Daniel's gay brother, Frank—no small feat considering he is paired against the king of scene-stealers, Robin Williams. His flamboyant performance is unfortunately limited to two short scenes, making Frank a one-note character. Fierstein is so funny, however, that it does not matter. As he and his lover, Jack (Scott Capurro), experiment with different looks for Mrs. Doubtfire, there is a hysterically funny series of one-liners, improvisations, and even a chorus of "Matchmaker, Matchmaker" from *Fiddler on the Roof*. Leave it to the brilliant Harvey Fierstein to work in some show tunes.

More solid support is given by young actors Lisa Jakub, Matthew Lawrence, and Mara Wilson as Daniel and Miranda's children. A wise decision was made not to spend much time on the emotional toil the divorce causes these three children. After all, this is not *Kramer vs. Kramer* (1979). Still, the three talented youngsters manage to layer their characters with depth without the overwhelming histrionics or unbearable cuteness akin to most films dealing with the subject.

Direction by Chris Columbus, best known for his over-the-top antics in the *Home Alone* films (1990, 1992), is, for the most part, assured and effective. He allows the cast to have their moments without getting in the way or making a production of them. The mark of truly good direction is that the performances are never burdened by the constraints imposed by the director. There are only a few brief moments where Columbus wants to linger longer than necessary—holding on Williams' watery eyes for a few beats too many, for example. Overall, however, the cast and writers were well served by Columbus' direction, and he deserves credit for having the courage to turn the camera on a few times and let Williams go crazy.

Although the script by Randi Mayem Singer and Leslie Dixon is well written, it is hard to believe that it would have been as funny without Williams in the title role. There are many wonderfully written bits and the dialogue is natural and at times even moving. Good plotting, solid characterizations, and a sense of believability in this far-out premise show a unique ability by the pair to draw in an audience. Like the director, Singer and Dixon deserve credit for allowing the star to expand on what was written on the page and for not stooping to an easy and predictable "one-big-happy-family" ending.

Technical credits are first-rate. Producers Marsha Garces Williams, Mark Radcliffe, and Robin Williams himself picked a winning crew. The beautiful cinematography of Donald McAlpine shows off the scenic San Francisco locale. Also set design, costumes, and some very funny musical choices add immeasurably to the film.

Special mention should be made of Greg Cannom, Ve Neill, and Yolanda Toussieng, the makeup team who transformed Williams into a sixty-year-old woman and won an Academy Award for their efforts. Their job was so complete as to make the actor virtually unrecognizable, lending credence to the entire premise of the film.

Mrs. Doubtfire is a perfect film for the holiday season—when it was released—and beyond. Filled with warmth and some fall-down-funny humor, this motion picture cannot be beat for its wonderful acting and valuable message. With one out of every two marriages ending in divorce in this country, it is nice to see a film that does not draw everything in black and white. All too often, in motion pictures and in life, people pick sides and cast one as the villain and one as the victim. *Mrs. Doubtfire* shows that there can be responsibility on both sides and commitment throughout, and most important, that just because two people stop loving each other, does not mean that they stop caring. That is a valuable lesson to learn, and it is so much better that it can be learned while laughing.

Rick Garman

Reviews
Boston Globe. November 24, 1993, p. 39.
Chicago Tribune. November 24, 1993, p. 3.
The Christian Science Monitor. March 18, 1994, p. 14.
Entertainment Weekly. November 26, 1993, p. 46
The Hollywood Reporter. November 22, 1993, p. 7.
L.A. Weekly. November 26-December 2, 1993, XV, p. 29.
Los Angeles Times. November 24, 1993, p. F1.
The New York Times. November 24, 1993, p. B3.
Newsweek. CXXII, November 29, 1993, p. 72.
Sight and Sound. IV, February, 1994, p. 58.
Time. CXLII, November 29, 1993, p. 74.
Variety. November 22, 1993, p. 4.
The Washington Post. November 24, 1993, p. C1.

MUCH ADO ABOUT NOTHING

Origin: USA and Great Britain
Released: 1993
Released in U.S.: 1993
Production: Kenneth Branagh, Stephen Evans, and David Parfitt for Renaissance
    Films, in association with American Playhouse Theatrical Films and BBC Films;
    released by The Samuel Goldwyn Company
Direction: Kenneth Branagh
Screenplay: Kenneth Branagh; based on the play by William Shakespeare
Cinematography: Roger Lanser
Editing: Andrew Marcus
Production design: Tim Harvey
Art direction: Martin Childs
Sound: David Crozier
Costume design: Phyllis Dalton
Music: Patrick Doyle
MPAA rating: PG-13
Running time: 110 minutes

> *Principal characters:*
> Benedick . . . . Kenneth Branagh
> Dogberry . . . . Michael Keaton
> Claudio. . . . . Robert Sean Leonard
> Don John . . . . Keanu Reeves
> Beatrice . . . . Emma Thompson
> Don Pedro . . . . Denzel Washington
> Leonato . . . . Richard Briers
> Hero. . . . . Kate Beckinsale
> Antonio . . . . Brian Blessed
> Conrade . . . . Richard Clifford
> Verges . . . . Ben Elton
> Borachio . . . . Gerard Horan
> Ursula. . . . . Phyllida Law
> Margaret. . . . . Imelda Staunton
> Friar Francis. . . . . Jimmy Yuill

    William Shakespeare's study of the mating game, *Much Ado About Nothing*, was conceived almost four hundred years ago. It is one of the playwright's "joyous comedies" (along with *As You Like It* and *Twelfth Night*), in which serious love is the source of interest and what mainly drives the plot. Shakespeare's romantic comedies have a lot of outdoor action, are filled with characters chiefly motivated by love, present at least one highly idealized heroine, and display love subjected to numerous difficulties. This formula characteristically leads to reconciliations and a happy ending: Boy gets girl, villains are punished, and the sun shines brightly.

For his work on the critically acclaimed film *Henry V* (1989), director/screen writer/actor Kenneth Branagh was nominated for Best Actor and Best Director Academy Awards. *Henry V* was followed by the romantic thriller *Dead Again* (1991) and a nostalgic look at friendship in middle age, *Peter's Friends* (1992). These last two films were fairly well received, but neither film showed the brilliance and ambition of *Henry V*, which amazed the critics and made Branagh an internationally known director on the strength of his first film. It was a difficult piece to tackle, and had already been filmed by Laurence Olivier and Orson Welles. Many critics declared it a masterpiece, and superior in many ways to Olivier's 1944 film.

In *Much Ado About Nothing*, Branagh has made a film version of Shakespeare's witty and alluring comedy that takes some textual and sexual liberties but always remains faithful to the spirit of the original play. At the heart of Branagh's version lies the same argument the Bard offered: that true love is only for those who acknowledge and accept the truth about each other. Branagh's *Much Ado About Nothing* is spirited, sexy, often campy, and always intelligent. The audience gets a generous dose of music played on the heartstrings and a wise consideration of love and its demands.

The film opens with shots of a half-dozen riders on thundering steeds as they approach a picturesque Italian villa. Don Pedro (Denzel Washington), Prince of Arragon, leads his victorious army home from war. Beside him are Benedick (Kenneth Branagh), Don John (Keanu Reeves)—Don Pedro's half brother—and Claudio (Robert Sean Leonard). "Sigh no more, ladies," quips Beatrice (Emma Thompson) with her uniquely dark sarcasm. She, the villa owner's niece, has been waiting for the men to return, especially one in particular.

Sandwiched between short close shots of the virile riders are scenes of pandemonium raging in the villa. The ladies who have been awaiting the warriors' homecoming burst into action with hurried preparations for their arrival. No sooner have the men strode through the archway of the villa of Leonato (Richard Briers) than the looks begin to fly. The lovely and innocent daughter of Leonato, Hero (Kate Beckinsale), succumbs to a glance from young count Claudio, who, in turn, is terminally smitten. Clearly theirs is love at first sight. Meanwhile Beatrice, known for her sharp tongue and nimble wit, has found her niche in sparring with her old acquaintance Benedick, a proud, avowed bachelor. "What, my dear Lady Disdain! Are you yet living?" he deadpans. "Is it possible disdain should die while she hath such meet food to feed it as Signor Benedick?" she answers sweetly.

One understands from the start that these two are made for each other. Thompson and Branagh are such brilliant, soulful Shakespeareans they are able to make whatever is implicit in the dialogue apparent with a twitch or a smile. Lines minimally amended for the film script are tossed off with the ease of everyday speech. The slaloms of slander and insult that they navigate effortlessly show Shakespeare's genius, and theirs.

The main characters and their dialogue are irresistible because they are Shakespeare's creations, but also because Branagh's cuts to the play's speeches are judicious. While he removed many of the jokes and puns that might leave a modern viewer in the dark, he kept the plot-necessitated speeches and leaves most lines as Shakespeare wrote them. The story moves rapidly, therefore, through the intrigue created by Don John and his followers; the playful matchmaking initiated by Leonato's brother, Antonio (Brian Blessed), and Don Pedro; the climactic heart-rending scenes between Beatrice and Benedick as they come to terms with love; and Claudio and Hero's love cruelly tested then restored.

The plot is chiefly driven by a desire to learn just how Beatrice and Benedick will come to terms with each other: who will suffer, who will bend, who will manufacture the most pain. Beatrice states that no man exists whom she can consider good enough. Benedick tells his mates he can trust no woman and so will always remain a bachelor. She insults him to the quick at the masked ball by hurling cruelties about him while pretending not to know who he is. He vows he would rather be sent on the most tedious or most dangerous mission than to have to face her again. These avowals change rather suddenly, however, when Benedick is told (actually meant to overhear) that Beatrice is madly in love with him. Next Hero and one of her attendants work the same trick with Beatrice. Both Benedick and Beatrice are completely moonstruck. The twin episodes are very funny, and Branagh is skilled at adding just the right amount of slapstick (a folding chair that keeps collapsing) while retaining the needed amount of gravity to remind the viewer that love is a serious quest.

Although love-making is its chief topic, this Shakespearean comedy also requires a villain and his evil plot. Don John's grudge against his brother Pedro is so strong (and it is not clear why) that he gains satisfaction from deceiving Claudio, Pedro's friend. The trick leaves Claudio believing his beloved Hero has sexually betrayed him on the eve of their wedding. The success of Don John's scheme leads to the most disturbing scene in the film, when Claudio denounces Hero before the entire wedding party, even throwing her to the ground and striking her. Hero's father Leonato similarly attacks her, while Beatrice and an attendant do their best to protect and comfort her. Beatrice, who suspects a plot, is enraged by the treatment that her cousin has had to endure at the hands of men.

The pain Beatrice feels for her cousin both steels her nerves and makes her vulnerable to the advances of Benedick. Distraught from witnessing Hero's ordeal, Benedick seeks Beatrice's company after the wedding guests have left. He finally gathers enough courage to declare, "I love nothing in the world so well as you. Is not that strange?" Although Beatrice is grieving for her cousin, she cannot resist Benedick's charm, his honesty, and his stark declaration of love. She in turn confesses, "I love you with so much of my heart that none is left to protest." This graceful scene is so moving and the dialogue so touching that it is easily the film's greatest scene, whether for Shakespeare's writing or Branagh's direction or Thompson's perfect handling of her character's enervated grief.

Benedick's offer to do his true love's bidding backfires, however, when Beatrice exhorts him to "Kill Claudio." He wavers, leading her to exclaim that were she a man, she "would eat his heart in the market place!" Beatrice's rage strikes a contemporary feminist chord. "I cannot be a man with wishing," she protests, "therefore I will die a woman with grieving." In the end, Benedick relents and agrees to challenge his friend Claudio.

Fortunately, however, Constable Dogberry (Michael Keaton) is hard at work applying his uniquely demented approach to the investigation of two drunken scoundrels who have been arrested by the night watchmen. Borachio (Gerard Horan) and Conrade (Richard Clifford) have been overheard describing how Claudio was duped and why Hero is innocent. Their judicial hearing as conspirators is a wild, funny scene, and Constable Dogberry's expert mangling of the English language adds to the foolishness. Most of all, Michael Keaton in this scene and others shows what a brilliantly crazy comedian he can be: His constable is a hilarious portrait for which he borrows mannerisms from his old friend Betelgeuse, from the film *Beetlejuice* (1990). Even when the comedy turns downright silly (as when Dogberry and his assistant enter and leave their scenes galloping on invisible horses), Keaton succeeds at playing the fool with that measure of absurd wisdom that all fools in Shakespeare possess.

Soon all the mayhem is discovered. Leonato is reconciled with his daughter, who is brought out of her tomb-as-hiding-place. Because the scandal has died, her reputation is restored. Claudio and Benedick forgive each other, and Beatrice and Benedick spar one more time, fortifying themselves for the years together they will be sharing. Finally, Claudio and Hero finish the ceremony with a dance.

Branagh's return to Shakespeare, accompanied by the same core production team that has helped him make all his films, has not caught the critics by surprise as *Henry V* did, but it has garnered similar accolades. Its fine direction and strong cast made *Much Ado About Nothing* a box office success. It came in as number 60 of the one hundred top-grossing films of 1993. Such success for a Shakespeare film speaks to Kenneth Branagh's considerable talent as a film artist and producer.

Much Ado About Nothing was shot in the Villa Vignamaggio, where the model for Leonardo da Vinci's enigmatic *Mona Lisa* lived. The old stone walls and beautiful grounds give the film a timeless look that suggests that the play's insights retain their relevance any time, any place. The women's classic peasant costumes and the men's sharply cut uniforms add to the film's contemporary feel. They were designed by Phyllis Dalton, who won an Academy Award for her costumes in *Henry V*. The props also add to the impression that Branagh's imaginary world could have existed any time between 1700 and 1900 or later. Thus the language works without awkwardness, and a kind of fairy-tale quality emerges. Kenneth Branagh's wild, earthy, and tender treatment of Shakespeare's comedy has produced a joyous film, one in which people, love, and life itself are honored and enjoyed.

JoAnn Balingit

Reviews

Chicago Tribune. May 21, 1993, VII, p. 29.
Entertainment Weekly. May 14, 1993, p. 38.
Films in Review. XLIV, July, 1993, p. 260.
The Hollywood Reporter. April 26, 1993, p. 6.
Los Angeles Times. May 14, 1993, p. F1.
The New York Times. May 7, 1993, p. B1.
The New Yorker. LXIX, May 10, 1993, p. 97.
The Philadelphia Inquirer. May 19, 1993, p. E1.
Sight and Sound. III, September, 1993, p. 50.
Time. CXLI, May 10, 1993, p. 65.
The Times Literary Supplement. September 3, 1993, p. 18.
Variety. April 26, 1993, p. 2.
The Washington Post. May 21, 1993, p. B7.

NAKED

Origin: Great Britain
Released: 1993
Released in U.S.: 1993
Production: Simon Channing-Williams, in association with Film Four
    International, with the participation of British Screen and Thin Man Films;
    released by Fine Line Features
Direction: Mike Leigh
Screenplay: Mike Leigh
Cinematography: Dick Pope
Editing: Jon Gregory
Production design: Alison Chitty
Art direction: Eve Stewart
Makeup: Chris Blundell
Costume design: Lindy Hemming
Music: Andrew Dickson
MPAA rating: no listing
Running time: 126 minutes

Principal characters:
Johnny............................ David Thewlis
Louise .... Lesley Sharp
Sophie........................... Katrin Cartlidge
Jeremy............................ Greg Cruttwell
Sandra............................. Claire Skinner

Naked, which follows a peripatetic, seemingly unprincipled drifter named Johnny (David Thewlis) for three days of his grimy and aimless life, ought by rights to be a depressing film. As director Mike Leigh has demonstrated in other feature films, such as *High Hopes* (1988) and *Life Is Sweet* (1991), however, the exploits of less privileged members of contemporary British society can be far from one-dimensional. Critically acclaimed, *Naked* won awards for both Best Director and Best Actor at the 1993 Cannes Film Festival. David Thewlis also won the 1993 New York Film Critics Circle award for Best Actor.

The opening sequence of *Naked* shows Johnny having rough, sadistic sex with a woman in a Manchester alley. When she runs away, he does too, later happening upon a car—its keys left in the trunk lock—which Johnny steals and drives to London. The ease with which he accomplishes the latter maneuver gives some sense of the combination of intelligence and sheer opportunism that allows someone like Johnny to survive on the streets. What happens next reinforces not only these qualities but also the amoral, even brutal attitude toward women introduced in the first scene of the film.

Johnny travels to London because he knows someone there—an old friend, or girlfriend, from Manchester, Louise (Lesley Sharp). Apparently, his intention is to play on Louise's sense of obligation to him, freeloading whatever he can—cigarettes, food, a bed, sex. When he discovers that Louise is working, he turns without hesitation to her drugged-out roommate, Sophie (Katrin Cartlidge), who unquestioningly provides what he wants, including rough sex.

The ease with which Johnny slips in and out of relationships with women would be incomprehensible if Leigh and Thewlis did not make him such a charming, manipulative rogue. Louise feels compassion for him, Sophie loves him, and when he leaves them for a night's ramble through the streets of London, Johnny manages to inveigle his way into the bedrooms of two other women. The first of these he rejects because she reminds him of his mother; the second tosses him out for no discernible reason after offering him beans and a bath.

Johnny's exploitative attitude toward women pales in comparison with the sadism exhibited by another male character—Jeremy (Greg Cruttwell). Jeremy is the rich, haughty young owner of the house Louise and Sophie are subletting from Sandra (Claire Skinner), a nurse who is traveling in Africa. In her absence, Jeremy shows up to collect his due by raping and beating Sophie. His abuse of Sophie and Louise, his commandeering of Louise's bed and Sandra's uniform, provides some counterpoint with Johnny's more cheerful and offhand brand of exploitation.

The comparison between Johnny and Jeremy might have become strained in other directorial hands, but *Naked* exhibits the seeming randomness and unpredictability that are hallmarks of a Mike Leigh film. Leigh is famed for his technique of developing scripts: working with actors, first individually, then collectively, while they improvise dialogue to flesh out a rough scenario. Months of such rehearsals lead finally to a polished script which nevertheless retains, in its veracity and variability, traces of its origins. Each character is unique and fully formed. This diversity of characterization makes Leigh's casual attitude toward plot seem both inevitable and naturalistic.

Leigh's technique is underscored in *Naked* by the fact that his protagonist is an inveterate vagrant who is, of necessity, prone to chance encounters. After just a brief sojourn with Louise and Sophie, Johnny feels compelled to roam the streets once more, where he meets an array of individuals. Among them are an incomprehensible, feuding Glasgow couple, a philosophic night watchman, and a shy waitress housesitting for a gay couple whose decorating taste favors Greek art featuring men in what Johnny calls "variety underpants." Seemingly inevitably, Johnny's nighttime adventures end in his being roughed up by a gang of young toughs. Although his injuries are disabling, he cannot tolerate the care and commitment—the salvation—offered him, in various forms, by Louise, Sophie, and finally Sandra, who returns just in time to minister to his wounds. *Naked* ends with a long shot of Johnny, who has slipped away from the women, limping down the middle of the road toward what is unquestionably an uncertain future.

Leigh leads up to this long shot by initially focusing on Johnny's head and torso in tight close-up, only gradually revealing his battered foot and ankle while taking in more of the protagonist's surroundings. The effect of this transition, as Johnny first stumbles and almost falls, then gains a quirky rhythmic locomotion, is to underscore Johnny's reintegration into the larger world as he fumbles his way back to his own peculiar place in it. Were it not for his ironic perspective on himself and society, Johnny would be a sad case. As it is, witnessing his nearly miraculous recovery from the physical insults he has borne, one cannot help but admire his spirit. Despite his aimlessness and anomie, Johnny retains a strong sense of self and of the will to survive—although outside normal societal constraints.

Johnny is hardly a sympathetic figure. He is far too self-destructive and exploitative to engender any real identification. Yet, like the women who surround him for much of the film, the audience enjoys its encounters with him often enough to find him appealing. Somehow, it is his very unpredictability that fascinates. For a brief while, bloodied and bone-tired he lets down his guard almost long enough for Louise to save him. After she bathes his wounds in the wake of his beating, the two wobble their way through an old song about their hometown. On the strength of this brief revival of intimacy, Louise resolves to quit her job and take him back to Manchester.

As soon as she leaves to give notice at work, however, Johnny makes his escape from the domesticity and settledness Louise threatens him with. On one hand, one can hardly believe that he can so disregard the help Louise represents and which he so badly needs. On the other, one sees that this near-capitulation represents the most serious type of surrender for Johnny, equivalent, in fact, to a kind of death. Like all people, Johnny needs others. Yet he finds these contacts ultimately constraining. So, when viewers last see Johnny, unsteadily escaping one kind of sure demise for another, they know at least this much: he is going to go out on his own terms.

Johnny's need for, and ultimate fear of, women helps to explain why he is such a successful seducer and such a cruel lover. This need also goes some way toward explaining the film's title. *Naked* is certainly about sex, but it is sex without love, without commitment—at least for this contemporary British Everyman who has nothing to give but a few moments of charming distraction. In the end, this is at least something—enough, it seems, to help Johnny move on down the road.

Lisa Paddock

Reviews

Entertainment Weekly. January 28, 1994, p. 34.
Film Comment. XXIX, November, 1993, p. 72.
The Hollywood Reporter. May 17, 1993, p. 5.
Los Angeles Times. December 16, 1993, p. F1.
The New York Times. October 15, 1993, p. B1.
Time. CXLII, December 20, 1993, p. 62.
Variety. May 17, 1993, p. 2.
The Washington Post. January 28, 1994, p. C1.

THE NIGHTMARE BEFORE CHRISTMAS

Production: Tim Burton and Denise Di Novi for Touchstone Pictures; released by
  Buena Vista Pictures
Direction: Henry Selick
Screenplay: Caroline Thompson; based on a story and characters by Tim Burton
  and adapted by Michael McDowell
Cinematography: Pete Kozachik
Editing: Stan Webb
Animation supervision: Eric Leighton
Art direction: Deane Taylor
Casting: Mary Gail Artz and Barbara Cohen
Visual effects supervision: Pete Kozachik
Music: Danny Elfman
MPAA rating: PG
Running time: 75 minutes

Voices of principal characters:
Jack Skellington .... (singing voice of Danny Elfman)
                         (speaking voice of Chris Sarandon)
Sally/Shock .... Catherine O'Hara
Evil Scientist .... William Hickey
Mayor............................... Glenn Shadix
Lock................................ Paul Reubens
Barrel.............................. Danny Elfman
Oogie Boogie........................... Ken Page
Santa .... Ed Ivory

Once again the fertile and imaginative mind of Tim Burton has developed a
whimsical fairy-tale adventure. Burton is the creator of *Edward Scissorhands*
(1990)—the strange adventures of a boy, created by a scientist, whose hands are
scissors—and of *Beetlejuice* (1988), the comedy starring Michael Keaton as a crazy
ghoul. Burton also directed the hugely popular *Batman* (1989). He brings a distinctive
style to each one of his films, a dark whimsy that appears to be half Edward Gorey
and half Walt Disney. In *The Nightmare Before Christmas*, producer Burton, director
Henry Selick, and a team of animation wizards have created a delightful film that
nearly defies description. It is a child's film, an adult's fairy tale, an adventure, a
musical, and a romance—all done in stop-motion animation.

"Stop-motion" is a style of animation whereby the characters are small puppets with
movable parts; they are arranged on miniature, highly detailed settings and filmed
frame by frame. The animators stop after each shot to manipulate the metal skeletons
of the puppets into a new pose. Just a simple arm movement is a highly technical
maneuver; in this laborious process, one minute of film can take as long as one week

to complete. Recalling the excitement generated by the live-action/animation combination of *Who Framed Roger Rabbit* (1988), this film breathes new life into the world of stop-motion animation and has received vast critical praise and audience approval.

The *Nightmare Before Christmas* is the story of Jack Skellington (speaking voice of Chris Sarandon and singing voice of Danny Elfman)—the Pumpkin King of Halloweentown—and his disastrous attempt to take over Christmas. He is aided in his innocent but destructive efforts by a hilarious, motley assortment of characters from Halloweentown: the Mayor (voice of Glenn Shadix), who has two faces—one with a smile, one with a worried frown; Lock (voice of Paul Reubens); Shock (voice of Catherine O'Hara); and Barrel (voice of Danny Elfman). These impish trick-or-treaters kidnap "Sandy Claws." Along for the ride is Sally (Catherine O'Hara), a rag doll in love with Jack, but afraid of the consequences of his Christmas takeover. Rounding out the cast are the creepy Evil Scientist (voice of William Hickey) and the villainous, lunatic Oogie Boogie (voice of Ken Page).

The vocal performances are an important part of the fun of this film. Chris Sarandon's soulful voice blends well with the rock-tinged sounds of composer Danny Elfman, who provides Jack Skellington's singing voice. Elfman retains the same sad weariness in the songs; particularly touching is Jack's first soliloquy, in which he dejectedly sings that "there's an empty place in my bones" and that he is in need of something new in his life. Also notable in the vocal department is the estimable Broadway veteran Ken Page as Oogie Boogie. He sings with demented glee and an infectious raucousness as he tortures poor Santa Claus. Impossible to miss, too, is the unmistakable voice of William Hickey—who was nominated for an Academy Award for his role in *Prizzi's Honor* (1985)—as the twisted scientist. Hickey's gnarled twang is funny and scary at the same time.

The screen is virtually stuffed with fascinating and hilarious characters: Half-human, half-bird characters with bug eyes, an enormous fat man with a hatchet in his head, a cone-shaped mayor with a spider-shaped bow tie, and a character called "The Clown with the Tear-Away Face." The Evil Scientist is a very funny takeoff on the Lionel Barrymore character in *It's a Wonderful Life* (1946), a bespectacled duck in a wheelchair who constantly removes half his head to scratch his brain. Oogie Boogie is a giant burlap sack filled with repulsive insects. Sally is a wide-eyed rag doll who continually tears off her limbs and sews them back together. Jack himself is a dapper, long-limbed wraith in a spiderweb suit.

There is a never-ending parade of fascinating characters. The film could be seen several times and there would still be new details to discover. When Jack gathers the townspeople to tell them about his Christmas discovery, barely noticeable in the foreground is a skeleton hanging from the ceiling in a noose, scratching his head. Other wonderful details catch the observant eye: Jack's bedposts are shaped like owls with huge eyes; the doorbell on Jack's house is a spider; a mailbox in front of an elf's house in Christmas town is a gift box with a bow; underneath the elves' beds are pairs of curled-up shoes. The attention to this sort of detail makes this film a visual feast.

Many bewitching images fill the screen, and not all are images of crazy characters.

Jack's soliloquy is set in a dark graveyard filled with misshapen and withered stones and branches; he walks through it like a spidery Hamlet. Another beautiful image is of his ghostly, gossamer dog, Zero, flowing behind him in silhouette. These images are less grand and less humorous in nature than the wild characters, but are essential to creating the mournful mood of the film. When Jack boards his sleigh of skeletal reindeer and flies off into a black night against the moon, there is no doubt that the filmmakers wish this to be as beautiful a film as it is phantasmagorical.

Also technically superb is the manner in which the animators achieved realistic movements from their stop-motion characters. When Sally hides in a graveyard, listening to Jack sing his lament about his empty life, her movements appear extremely realistic: Each movement of the head or hand is balanced by corresponding moves in the hair, eyes, or shoulders. This is a far cry from the stilted, simplistic movements of early stop-motion animation found in films by pioneer Ray Harryhausen or the television Christmas perennial *Rudolph the Red-nosed Reindeer* (1964).

Essential to the success of this film is the splendid contribution of composer/lyricist Danny Elfman. In addition to providing his rich voice, Elfman (who also scored Tim Burton's *Batman*) has fashioned ten wonderful songs. Each song advances the plot in the style of a Broadway musical. The musical idioms, however, are closer to Kurt Weill and Bertolt Brecht, as in their *The Threepenny Opera* (1931), than to Rodgers and Hammerstein, or for that matter, Alan Menken's *The Little Mermaid* (1989) and *Beauty and the Beast* (1991).

Elfman's long musical phrases and mournful melodies perfectly fit the melancholy of this black comedy. In fact, the melodies truly are haunting, most especially "This Is Halloween," a description of Halloweentown, and "Jack's Lament," the Hamlet-like musical soliloquy. Elfman provides other styles as well, especially the swinging "Oogie Boogie's Song" and the upbeat "What's This?" A very funny musical moment occurs when Jack tries to teach a ghoulish band how to play "Jingle Bells," and they can only play it in a minor key.

Elfman's lyrics are effective and witty, most especially when the Halloweentown people are coming up with their own version of Christmas: "This thing will never make a present/It's been dead too long."

The origins of *The Nightmare Before Christmas* date back to 1979, when Tim Burton was an animation assistant at the Walt Disney studios. His fascination with the aforementioned television specials such as *Rudolph the Red-nosed Reindeer* and his enchantment with Halloween led him to wonder what would happen if he visually mixed the two holidays. They prove to be a wonderful mix. Jack inadvertently discovers Christmas town and returns to his home to tell the residents about it. Halloweentown's inhabitants simply do not understand it, so they pervert Jack's entire presentation by asking such things as whether the Christmas stocking still has a foot in it. Then Jack decides to "give them what they want" and describes "Sandy Claws" as a fierce, "lobster-red" king who "rides on a dark, cold night, like a vulture in the sky." The misunderstanding of the nature of Christmas proves to be the turning point of the story, for once Jack and his friends decide to give "Sandy Claws" a vacation, everything goes awry. The concept of vile monsters preparing Christmas gifts as if they were elves is hilarious and is hilariously executed. Jack, in a skinny red suit and ill-fitting beard, takes over for Santa (after kidnapping him), certain that everyone will be delighted with their gifts: shrunken heads, a tree-eating snake, and live bats. They simply do not understand Christmas. Santa says to his captors: "Haven't you ever heard of peace on Earth and goodwill toward men?!" To which they reply, "No!!"

This absurd mixture keeps the story in the adult world because of its humor. Yet there is much for children to enjoy. The age-old message of Christmas, coming from the heart, is still here; it is simply filtered through the vivid and colorful imagination of Burton, Elfman, and the extraordinary animation department at the ever-reliable Walt Disney Studios. When Jack and Sally embrace in silhouette, framed by a full moon, it is clear that romance and warmth are the core of this engaging and colorful film. Burton has proven that fairy tales still can be touching without being overly sentimental.

Kirby Tepper

Reviews

Chicago Tribune. October 22, 1993, VII, p. 35.
Cinefantastique. XXIV, December, 1993, p. 32.
Cinefex. November, 1993, p. 30.
The Hollywood Reporter. October 11, 1993, p. 8.
Los Angeles Times. October 15, 1993, p. F1.
The New York Times. October 9, 1993, The Arts, p. 12.
Newsweek. CXXII, November 1, 1993, p. 72.
Rolling Stone. November 11, 1993, p. 79.
Time. CXLIII, January 3, 1994, p. 70.
Variety. October 8, 1993, p. 2.
The Washington Post. October 22, 1993, p. C7.

OLIVIER OLIVIER

Origin: France
Released: 1993
Released in U.S.: 1993
Production: Marie-Laure Reyre for Oliane Productions and Films A-2; released by
    Sony Pictures Classics
Direction: Agnieszka Holland
Screenplay: Agnieszka Holland, Yves Lapointe, and Régis Debray
Cinematography: Bernard Zitzermann
Editing: Isabelle Lorente
Art direction: Hélène Bourgy
Makeup: Françoise Chapuis-Asselin
Costume design: Ewa Biejat
Sound: Pierre Befve
Music: Zbigniew Preisner
MPAA rating: R
Running time: 110 minutes

> *Principal characters:*
> Dr. Serge Duval . . . . François Cluet
> Elisabeth Duval . . . . Brigitte Roüan
> Police Officer Druot . . . . Jean-François Stevenin
> Olivier . . . . Grégoire Colin
> Nadine . . . . Marina Golovine
> Marcel . . . . Frédéric Quiring
> Nadine (as a child). Faye Gatteau
> Olivier (as a child). . . . . Emmanuel Morozof

   The fact that *Europa, Europa* (1990), *The Secret Garden* (1993; reviewed in this volume), and *Olivier Olivier* are each internationally known and critically acclaimed films attests director Agnieszka Holland's mastery of cinematic narrative, even with widely varied material. *The Secret Garden* is based on Frances Hodgson Burnett's fictional children's classic; the other two films were inspired by fascinating real-life stories. Of the three, *Olivier Olivier* is the least well-known, the story that Ms. Holland felt most free to embellish with her own imagination.
   Although *Olivier Olivier* and *Europa, Europa* both have adolescent male protagonists, the two films are quite dissimilar. *Europa, Europa* is a profound and deeply moving study of a Jewish boy in Nazi Germany who survives by passing himself off as an Aryan and joining Hitler's army. *Olivier Olivier* is the story of a nine-year-old boy from a French provincial family who disappears one day, only to reappear (presumably) six years later as a Parisian prostitute. Despite its flirtation with Freudian psychological implications, the latter film remains a very good mystery rather than a

profound probing of human experience and motivation. Clues abound, encouraging those addicted to solving mysteries to speculate about past events and to draw conclusions. Yet there are no easy answers. The film's resolution is rich with ambiguity, and one might reverse oneself several times before, if ever, settling on a conclusive view of certain elements in the story.

There is a strong thematic relationship between the story of Olivier (Grégoire Colin) and that of Martin Guerre, an actual sixteenth century French peasant who is the subject of *Le retour de martin guerre* (1983; *The Return of Martin Guerre*, 1983), a film in which Gérard Depardieu plays the enigmatic central character. For some reason, 1993 seemed to be a time ripe for variations on the fascinating themes of disappearance and identity that link these films. A musical stage adaptation of *The Return of Martin Guerre* opened at the Hartford Stage, and *Sommersby*, an American adaptation of the French film—with names, time, and location changed—opened to positive critical response and commercial success. *Olivier Olivier*, an unconventional offering not heavily promoted by Sony Pictures Classics, nonetheless did respectably at the box office. The story, perhaps, has fascination for a generation that is apparently unhappy with and uncertain of its identity.

Martin Guerre, Sommersby, and Olivier are all characters who disappear; many years later, individuals claiming to be them return, similar enough to their family's and friends' memories of the missing parties to gain them acceptance, with all the accompanying rewards. In each story, however, there is enough difference to cause uncertainty that the returning person is actually who he claims to be. Eventually each is challenged by doubters. In *Sommersby* and *The Return of Martin Guerre*, the actual identity of the claimants is significant not only because of the rights to property but also because of connubial rights to the wives of the missing (or once-missing) men that accompany their acceptance. In *Olivier Olivier*, the adolescent who claims to be Olivier is physically attracted to his supposed sister; the potential for incest hinges on his actual identity.

With these intriguing circumstances as background, Holland has provided the viewer an array of clues with which to approach the mystery. On the one hand, the adolescent Olivier resembles the sister, Nadine (Marina Golovine); he also has an appendectomy scar that corresponds with the boy's medical history. Moreover, shortly after having had sex with him, Nadine—who doubted his claim to be her brother— watches him through a window as he has a contest with a boy from the neighborhood to see who can urinate the farthest; he is singing the song and playing the game that Olivier, the child (Emmanuel Morozof), once did. It is then that she is convinced for the first time that this boy is her brother and is dismayed by the thought that she has just committed incest.

Yet, there are also clues on which to build an opposite conviction. The boy Olivier had no ear for music; the adolescent plays the piano. The older Olivier seems, at first, not to recognize his father, Dr. Serge Duval (François Cluet), and a neighbor, Marcel (Frédéric Quiring), who was the last person known to see the boy before his disappearance six years earlier. His momentary hesitancy when confronted by them for the first time (or for the first time in six years) can be interpreted as needed space in which to formulate his guess as to who they are and what his responses should be. If one argues that a mother should know her own son, Elisabeth Duval (Brigitte Roüan) has such a strong wish that the fifteen-year-old be her son that her conclusions are not to be trusted.

As played by Colin, the teenage Olivier is charming but almost too nonchalant. Although he makes shows of affection and is polite and determined to please, he is not above discreetly seeing to his own pleasure or accepting lavish gifts from his parents. He becomes aware that Elisabeth especially has an emotional need for his continued presence. After being given a motorbike, he facetiously tells a neighboring girl that the prodigal son has been bribed. It is difficult to know whether he is an impostor or the real Olivier trying, despite a somewhat unrestricted and unsavory life on the streets of Paris, to adjust to the new demands made by his actual identity. How he should reintegrate himself into his family is a question he might be asking himself.

Not the least of the film's virtues is its tracing of the evolving interrelationships of a troubled provincial family before, during, and after its exceptional crisis. Life has already soured for Serge before Olivier's disappearance. His marriage leaves much to be desired; to say that Elisabeth's attentions seem too much focused on her son to the neglect of her husband would be an understatement. Indeed, she fondles Olivier in a way that might raise eyebrows. When the boy is lost, the wife becomes irascible, turning the family into an even more dysfunctional unit than before. Elisabeth blames Nadine for Olivier being missing; the boy had been sent with a basket of food to his grandmother's in place of Nadine, who had not made herself available for the errand. Later, however, Elisabeth asks Nadine's forgiveness and apparently transfers her love for the missing Olivier to her daughter. She also tries to seduce Serge with the intention of bearing a child to replace Olivier, but Serge, who has cultivated the bitter belief that women need someone to crush, separates from Elisabeth. Nadine stays with her troubled mother, takes care of her, and in a short while seems more the adult than Elisabeth.

The arrival of the fifteen-year-old alters relationships once again: Serge returns, Elisabeth has her Olivier to love, and Nadine, upset because her mother is no longer hers alone, becomes the only one of the three who seems intent on pursuing the truth. Eventually, perhaps as a way of striking back, she becomes her mother's rival.

Holland based her screenplay on accounts of actual events reported in French newspapers in 1984. The film is nevertheless a work of the imagination. Holland has modified the original story so that her own experience and sensibilities are reflected in the telling. Also, the actual events in a story such as this can seem implausible, and the artist may have to alter events in order to make them more believable. Holland's purposes are artistic, not journalistic. Her choice to have the boy Olivier wear a red hat as he rides his bicycle toward his grandmother's house is an artist's attempt to mythicize her subject and give it a universal resonance. While she may not have succeeded completely in that ambitious aim, she has successfully provided an idyllic image—a red hat on a boy's head moving in a smooth horizontal line through a field of red poppies, the bicycle and most of the boy concealed by vegetation—to serve as a dramatic contrast and yet a prelude to the horror of the boy's imminent disappearance, with its possibility of violence and bloodshed.

Holland withholds the most significant revelations until the film's climax as a means of heightening suspense, as would most good storytellers. When the climax does occur, it has considerable impact and will surprise many.

Cono Robert Marcazzo

Reviews

Chicago Tribune. April 2, 1993, VII, p. 36.
The Christian Science Monitor. February 3, 1993, p. 14.
Entertainment Weekly. April 2, 1993, p. 34.
Film Comment. November/December, 1992, p. 62.
The Hollywood Reporter. September 25, 1992, p. 19.
Los Angeles Times. March 12, 1993, p. F8.
The New Republic. CCVIII, February 15, 1993, p. 26.
The New York Times. September 26, 1992, p. B1.
Newsweek. March 15, 1993, p. 74.
Time. CXLI, March 8, 1993, p. 72.
Variety. September 11, 1992, p. 12.
The Wall Street Journal. March 4, 1993, p. A12.
The Washington Post. March 19, 1993, p. F7.

ORLANDO

Origin: Great Britain, Russia, France, and The Netherlands
Released: 1993
Released in U.S.: 1993
Production: Christopher Sheppard for Adventure Pictures; released by Sony
    Pictures Classics
Direction: Sally Potter
Screenplay: Sally Potter; based on the novel by Virginia Woolf
Cinematography: Alexei Rodionov
Editing: Herve Schneid
Production design: Ben Van Os and Jan Roelfs
Art direction: Michael Buchanan and Michael Howells
Costume design: Sandy Powell
Music: David Motion and Sally Potter
MPAA rating: PG-13
Running time: 93 minutes

> *Principal characters:*
> Orlando . . . . Tilda Swinton
> Shelmerdine. . . . . Billy Zane
> Khan. . . . . Lothaire Bluteau
> Archduke Harry. . . . . John Wood
> Sasha . . . . Charlotte Valandrey
> Nick Greene/Publisher . . . . Heathcote Williams
> Queen Elizabeth I . . . . Quentin Crisp

Director, screenwriter, and composer Sally Potter's *Orlando* is a unique journey through four hundred years in the life of one character, Orlando (Tilda Swinton). The journey begins in the 1600's, when Queen Elizabeth I (Quentin Crisp) tells the Lord Orlando, "Do not fade, do not wither, do not grow old." Lord Orlando then begins his four-hundred-year quest for love, first as a man, later as a woman.

Orlando's first love is visiting Russian princess Sasha (Charlotte Valandrey). Orlando forgoes propriety, leaving his betrothed to woo the princess. When Orlando is warned of his questionable decision to risk all for the princess, he replies that he does not care for a career, that he is interested only in love. The affair is doomed, however, and Orlando is left alone in the icy rain as the princess sails away.

In the 1700's Orlando travels to Asia as an ambassador. He soon finds himself in battle yet cannot fight. Turning his back on what is manly, he awakens as a woman. Orlando looks at her new female body in the mirror, remarking, "Same person. No difference at all. Just a different sex."

When Orlando returns to England as a woman, she finds that life offers new challenges. As a woman, Orlando cannot own property. She does, however, receive a marriage proposal from Archduke Harry (John Wood), who claims she must accept on the grounds that he adores her. Orlando ironically had uttered the same line even more earnestly to his departing Russian princess; now as a woman, she quickly rejects the archduke's proposal. It is difficult to say which irks Orlando more—losing her land because she is a woman or having to endure the chauvinistic male poets of the time who fancy themselves deep thinkers.

In the nineteenth century, Orlando encounters Shelmerdine (Billy Zane), with whom she falls in love. Yet when Shelmerdine opts to sail to America, Orlando declines to accompany him. Orlando again finds herself in the icy cold of a lonely downpour. As a result of her liaison with Shelmerdine, however, Orlando emerges in the twentieth century with a new daughter and an inner peace. She has found what she needs—love—in her child. The long journey was necessary, and Orlando is content.

One of the themes running throughout Sally Potter's film adaptation of Virginia Woolf's novel is the search for love. Orlando's need of love is revealed to the viewer in a narrated prologue, where it is said of Orlando that he did not seek privilege but company. This search takes Orlando through four hundred years of dissatisfaction and longing. Orlando follows his heart over centuries, to a faraway land, and through a change in gender. In fact, Orlando's failed affair with Sasha sets the pattern for most of Orlando's life. Heartbroken, Orlando first turns to poetry, then to politics, and finally to rearing her daughter.

Another strong theme running through the film is the link between Orlando's emotional turmoil and the forces of nature. When the frozen water strands Sasha, she and Orlando meet. Nature brings these two together just as it later tears them apart. Sasha sails when the ice breaks, and Orlando is left behind. Orlando and Shelmerdine's relationship is similarly controlled by the will of nature. Upon rejecting Archduke Harry's marriage proposal, Orlando flees and throws herself to the ground, begging nature to take her as its bride. What she is given is Shelmerdine, who rides triumphantly up, then falls to meet her face to face. After the two are thrown together in this way, however, the southwest winds pick up and take Shelmerdine away. In both of Orlando's intense love affairs, Orlando is left alone in the mocking chill of nature's cold rain.

Throughout, *Orlando* addresses the different roles of the sexes. Orlando lives first as a man, then as a woman, and thus gains a unique insight into the different roles each gender has played over several centuries. Orlando's life as a man is ultimately unsatisfying. In Asia he ponders the male condition, convincing himself of its merit. He attempts sincerity when he toasts with Khan (Lothaire Bluteau) to the manly virtues—loyalty, courage. That is all Orlando can muster as he fails to convince himself that it is good to be manly. Khan later refers to this manliness when requesting Orlando's assistance in battle. Khan says, "Surely you, Orlando, an Englishman, are not afraid." Orlando's doubts are proven as he witnesses, but does not participate in, war. When Orlando gasps at the sight of a dying human, Orlando is told that the wounded soldier is not a man, only the enemy. As a result, Orlando rejects all that is male and leaves the battle in a daze. When he awakens the next morning, he gently rinses his face in a delicate, glittering basin and is a woman.

Life as a woman is no easier. Orlando's land is taken from her, and she becomes a second-class citizen. She can now see men in a new light, not as brave or noble but as oppressive. The Lady Orlando is excited to attend a formal lunch with some of the great literary men of the time, but her illusions are shattered upon meeting them. They are not brave or noble; they are men with some wit but who are very disrespectful of women. Orlando leaves the lunch angry. Her beliefs that men are not a noble sex have been harshly validated.

Orlando discusses the manly condition later with Shelmerdine. She asks him, "You've fought in battle? Like a man?" to which Shelmerdine replies, "I have fought." She knows the folly of his beliefs and of his sex. Shelmerdine counters by commenting on the womanly condition. He claims that although he would sacrifice his life in battle, he would not care to rear a child. When Orlando realizes that their relationship will not work, she tells Shelmerdine, "I can't just follow you."

The image of Shelmerdine riding off to fight is juxtaposed to that of sad Orlando standing with one arm bent to her hip, mirroring the large teacup shapes of the yard's bush sculptures, one of the many intriguing images to be found in the film. Orlando is allegorized here as a delicate object, fragile and breakable like the teacup. The image is a powerful one, but one that Orlando later disproves. She does not follow Shelmerdine but instead takes charge of her life and finds her happiness in her own, independent way.

On a story level, *Orlando* is an intriguing tale, and the filmmakers have done an excellent job of bringing it to the screen. Notable assets to this production are the sets and costumes (the film was nominated for Academy Awards in both Art Direction and Costume Design). The opulent surroundings and outfits are consistently magnificent yet do not call unnecessary attention to themselves. They invoke the proper periods, helping the audience follow the large jumps in time. The sets also make for a visually rich and engaging film.

The only element that rivals the look of the film is the music, co-composed by both Potter and David Motion, but it is insufficiently exploited. Orlando's introduction into politics is dramatized with marvelous, regal music married with the image of a stately courtyard. The music is also powerfully present as Orlando flees Archduke Harry, unknowingly running off to find Shelmerdine. The music always seems to complement the story and image, pulling the viewer deeper emotionally into the proceedings.

Unfortunately, the cinematography detracts from an otherwise fine film. The camera in *Orlando* does not like to remain still. This generally works well, maintaining a moving, changing feast for the eyes, as well as a chance to exhibit the fantastic sets and locations. Yet the film contains some amateurish oscillating pans and some unnecessary hand-held shots. In these instances, the camera movements pull the viewer out of the story by drawing attention to themselves. They shatter the illusion of an otherwise engaging film.

The key to the film's success lies in the performance of Tilda Swinton in the central role of Orlando. With her androgynous good looks and the elaborate wigs and costumes, she succeeds in portraying Orlando first as an adolescent male and later as a woman. Her comments directed at the camera, sometimes as minimal as the arching of an eyebrow, are very amusing. It is Orlando's ironic wit that wins over the audience.

Sally Potter's *Orlando* is a sweet, big film that most audiences will not uncover at its art-house venues. The film takes the viewer on a journey at once familiar and original—the quest for love, but over four hundred years. To anyone interested in a unique, well-executed, thought-provoking film, *Orlando* should not be missed.

Pete Peterson

Reviews

Chicago Tribune. July 9, 1993, VII, p. 33.
Los Angeles Times. June 25, 1993, p. F8.
The Nation. CCLVII, July 12, 1993, p. 77.
The New Republic. CCVIII, June 28, 1993, p. 26.
New Statesman and Society. March 12, 1993, p. 34.
Newsweek. June 21, 1993, p. 65.
The New Yorker. June 14, 1993, p. 96.
Newsweek. CXXI, June 21, 1993, p. 65.
Variety. CCCXLVIII, September 14, 1992, p. 48.
The Washington Post. June 25, 1993, p. C7.

THE PELICAN BRIEF

Production: Alan J. Pakula and Pieter Jan Brugge; released by Warner Bros.
Direction: Alan J. Pakula
Screenplay: Alan J. Pakula; based on the novel by John Grisham
Cinematography: Stephen Goldblatt
Editing: Tom Rolf and Trudy Ship
Production design: Philip Rosenberg
Art direction: Robert Guerra
Set decoration: Lisa Fischer and Rick Simpson
Casting: Alixe Gordon
Sound: James J. Sabat
Costume design: Albert Wolsky
Music: James Horner
MPAA rating: PG-13
Running time: 141 minutes

Principal characters:
Darby Shaw	Julia Roberts
Gray Grantham	Denzel Washington
Thomas Callahan	Sam Shepard
Gavin Verheek	John Heard
Fletcher Coal	Tony Goldwyn
Denton Voyles	James B. Sikking
Bob Gminski	William Atherton
President	Robert Culp
Khamel	Stanley Tucci
Justice Rosenberg	Hume Cronyn
Smith Keen	John Lithgow

A banner year for author John Grisham, 1993 saw two of his best-selling novels released as hit films. The first, *The Firm*, starring Tom Cruise, was extremely successful, becoming one of the top-grossing films of the year. *The Pelican Brief*, starring Julia Roberts and Denzel Washington, also did well, although it did not receive the rave reviews that the earlier film did. Interestingly, producer-director-screenwriter Alan J. Pakula acquired the film rights to *The Pelican Brief* before the novel was even written.

The film begins with a shadowy figure arriving by boat and driving off to Washington, D.C., in an old pickup truck. The audience later learns that this is the infamous Khamel (Stanley Tucci), an international assassin who will murder two Supreme Court justices in a single night, a mysterious crime around which the rest of the thriller revolves. Enter Darby Shaw (Julia Roberts), a twenty-four-year-old law student at Tulane University in New Orleans. She is having an affair with her professor, Thomas

Callahan (Sam Shepard), who clerked for one of the two dead judges, the elderly and controversial Justice Rosenberg (Hume Cronyn).

Callahan, significantly older than Darby, has a drinking problem and allows himself to become thoroughly soused upon the death of his hero and mentor Rosenberg. Darby, in turn, buries herself at the library, where she researches possible suspects in the killings. She then types up a brief detailing the reasons for the murders and the man behind them both, a brief that implicates the White House. Although she admits that her theory is far-fetched, she hands it over to Thomas, who in turn passes it on to a friend who works as legal counsel for the Federal Bureau of Investigation (FBI), Gavin Verheek (John Heard).

As they leave a restaurant late at night, Thomas is so drunk that Darby insists on driving. When Thomas refuses to give up his keys, Darby walks away. In a shocking sequence, the car explodes into a fireball, killing Thomas instantly. Darby regains consciousness in a strange car, interrogated by two men who identify themselves as police officers. When a police siren is heard in the distance, the men disappear and Darby—still in a state of shock—is taken to a crowded city hospital, where she slowly comes to realize that she was the intended victim of the bombing. She gets up and walks away, thus beginning the lengthy cat-and-mouse chase that makes up the remainder of the film.

In an interesting casting choice, Denzel Washington plays *Washington Herald* reporter Gray Grantham, with whom Darby teams in order to prove her suspicions. In the novel, Grantham was a middle-aged Caucasian who was interested in Darby for more than just her information regarding the assassinations. In fact, at the end of the book, he joins her in a tropical island retreat. Washington, an African American, assumes only the role of the supreme professional, a good friend but nothing more. There is, nevertheless, an interesting chemistry between Washington and Roberts that renders their characters an extremely likable couple. Washington—nominated for an Academy Award for his starring role in the critically acclaimed *Malcolm X* (1992)— like Grisham, saw two of his efforts released in close succession with the December, 1993, release of *Philadelphia*, in which he stars opposite Tom Hanks.

According to the production notes, Grisham wrote the part of Darby with Julia Roberts in mind. Roberts is perhaps best known for her Academy Award-nominated role as Vivian, the prostitute-cum-Cinderella of *Pretty Woman* (1990). In the book, Darby is described as a long-legged beauty with a head of thick red hair, and Roberts certainly fits the bill. In the novel, however, Darby is forced to cut and dye her hair repeatedly in her frenzied escape from her would-be assassins. Roberts, rather than cutting that beautiful mane, wears wigs or braids as her disguise. Unfortunately, although the story centers on this beautiful female law student, the character of Darby was never fully fleshed out either in the novel or in the film. Moreover, with the casting of Washington as the reporter, the end result may be more symbolic of 1990's America than was originally intended: a black man and a woman being persecuted by middle-aged white men in suits.

The problems of the film are basically the same problems of the novel: complexity and unbelievability. Even at the end of the film, one does not know who all those white men in ties were or exactly how they were involved in the plot. After a while, they all start to look alike. Admittedly, the novel itself was extremely complicated, with a plot that involved environmental groups, a rich and powerful capitalist, oil drilling, the Supreme Court, and the White House. One almost could have used subtitles that identified who each man was and how he was involved. Moreover, Khamel himself is a master of disguise, physically altering his appearance every time he appears on screen.

At the center of this web of intrigue lies the White House and a president (Robert Culp) who is a cross between Ronald Reagan, George Bush, and Richard Nixon. In essence, he has a big white smile, prefers to play golf, and for most of his policy decisions depends on his chief aide, Fletcher Coal (Tony Goldwyn)—a man whose role model must have been former Nixon aide H. R. Haldeman. Coal is misguided at best, even advising the president to ask FBI chief Denton Voyles (James B. Sikking) to "back off" his investigation of the Pelican Brief, merely because such an investigation might make the president look bad. The president becomes such a comic caricature that no one will take him seriously.

In the end, the entire affair is wrapped up so neatly that it all seems like much ado about nothing. Triumphant music plays as reporter Grantham calls up each political pawn in this perplexing puzzle and asks for any comments on his forthcoming tell-all article, upon which they all fume and make empty threats. The two men who did the actual hands-on killings both die. More disappointing, the prime bad guy, Victor Mattiece, never even appears on screen. Darby leaves the country and simply says good-bye to Grantham, with whom she has spent some very intimate moments.

Technical credits were fine, with a soundtrack that becomes ominous at all the appropriate times. Because different parts of the story take place in several major cities, many famous landmarks appear in the background to help the viewers place the events. The federal buildings in Washington, D.C., Central Park in New York City, Bourbon Street in Louisiana, even Mount Vernon—all figure prominently in the film, adding to the story's larger-than-life events. Unfortunately, the filmmakers tend to alternate these scenic shots with murky, nameless building interiors that leave one squinting, trying to distinguish the major players.

Despite its flaws, *The Pelican Brief* is still an entertaining film and corrects a major fault of the novel: In the book, once Darby teams with Grantham, although she claims to see people following her, nothing ever comes of it. In contrast, in the film, Darby and Grantham experience one last climactic chase sequence in a parking garage after they retrieve key evidence from a bank's lockbox. Because the film drags while the two gather proof for Grantham's article, the chase adds the necessary energy to bring the film to its momentous conclusion. Furthermore, Roberts and Washington, in spite of their poorly defined roles, have an on-screen chemistry that transcends the characters' more sexual relationship in the novel. Although *The Pelican Brief* may not fare as well as *The Firm*, it will certainly enjoy its day in court.

Cynthia K. Breckenridge

Reviews
Chicago Tribune. December 17, 1993, VII, p. 25.
Entertainment Weekly. December 24, 1993, p. 38.
The Hollywood Reporter. December 13, 1993, p. 8.
Los Angeles Times. December 17, 1993, p. F1.
The Nation. CCLVIII, January 3, 1994, p. 32.
The New York Times. December 17, 1993, p. B1.
The New Yorker. LXIX, December 27, 1993, p. 150.
Newsweek. CXXII, December 20, 1993, p. 121.
Sight and Sound. IV, March, 1994, p. 44.
Time. CXLII, December 20, 1993, p. 62.
Variety. December 13, 1993, p. 4.
The Washington Post. December 17, 1993, p. C6.

A PERFECT WORLD

Production: Mark Johnson and David Valdes for Malpaso; released by Warner Bros.
Direction: Clint Eastwood
Screenplay: John Lee Hancock
Cinematography: Jack N. Green
Editing: Joel Cox
Editing: Ron Spang
Production design: Henry Bumstead
Art direction: Jack Taylor, Jr.
Set decoration: Alan Hicks
Casting: Phyllis Huffman and Liz Keigley
Sound: Jeff Wexler
Costume design: Erica Edell Phillips
Music: Lennie Niehaus
MPAA rating: PG-13
Running time: 137 minutes

> *Principal characters:*
> Butch Haynes. . . . . Kevin Costner
> Red Garnett . . . . Clint Eastwood
> Sally Gerber. . . . . Laura Dern
> Phillip Perry. . . . . T. J. Lowther
> Terry Pugh . . . . Keith Szarabajka
> Tom Adler . . . . Leo Burmester
> Dick Suttle. . . . . Paul Hewitt
> Bobby Lee . . . . Bradley Whitford
> Bradley. . . . . Ray McKinnon
> Gladys Perry . . . . Jennifer Griffin
> Naomi Perry. . . . . Leslie Flowers
> Ruth Perry . . . . Belinda Flowers
> Mr. Hughes . . . . Darryl Cox
> Mack . . . . Wayne Dehart

Kevin Costner stars as Butch Haynes, an escaped felon who takes a young boy hostage, in this action-drama set in 1963 and directed by Clint Eastwood. Although a violent criminal, Butch is shown to have had a troubled childhood and forms a father-son bond with the fatherless boy as he flees a Texas Ranger played by Eastwood.

As the film begins, seven-year-old Phillip Perry (T. J. Lowther) lives a subdued life with his family of Jehovah's Witnesses. Fatherless, he lives with his mother and two sisters. While outside, children wear costumes and go trick-or-treating on Halloween, Phillip must sit inside his house, watching the fun outside through his window. Then, early one morning come two escaped convicts, the thoroughly psychopathic Terry

Pugh (Keith Szarabajka) and rebel-with-a-cause Butch Haynes (Costner). Although Butch saves Phillip's mother from Terry, it is Butch who decides to take Phillip hostage. So, on the eve of President John F. Kennedy's visit to Dallas, Texas Ranger Red Garnett (Eastwood) commences the hunt for the two escaped criminals. He is assisted by Sally Gerber (Laura Dern), a criminologist for the state prison system, who joins Red in his "headquarters on wheels," an "Airstream" house-trailer that is to be used by the Texas governor for the Kennedy visit. Although Red views Sally as a schoolgirl who has wandered into the boys' locker room, Sally brings an intellectual competence and insight that complements Red's years of practical experience. Together, they take to the back roads of Texas to recapture Butch and Terry and rescue Phillip.

Although Phillip begins as Butch's hostage, the two soon develop a bond. During the adventures that follow, the young boy finds both excitement and a father figure, even if a rather questionable one, and Butch finds himself caring for the boy the way he wishes his own father had cared for him.

As Red closes in on Butch, it is revealed that the two have met before. Born in Amarillo, Butch grew up in New Orleans, where he lived with his mother, a prostitute. When he was eight, he killed a man who was harming her, and when he was twelve, the syphilitic woman hanged herself. Butch then returned to Amarillo to live with his father, who beat anything he "met, screwed, or fathered." When Butch stole a car, Red—who was then the sheriff of Amarillo—saw to it that Butch went to the toughest juvenile facility in Texas rather than be paroled to his abusive father. Red thought he was doing Butch a favor, but in reality, this turn of events probably turned the very smart Butch into a career criminal.

To Phillip, the likable Butch represents not only the father he never knew but also someone who could offer him a life he had been deprived of. Nevertheless, cracks develop in Butch's facade that even the young Phillip can perceive. He becomes frightened by Butch's outbursts of temper and his casual use of violence. By the time the paths of Red and Butch cross, Phillip is torn between what he wants Butch to be and what he knows he really is. It is a tough decision for a seven-year-old boy wearing a stolen Casper the Friendly Ghost costume.

Unfortunately, in *A Perfect World*, little is perfect. Law officers, despite the best intentions, end up making things worse. Smart children—who might have made something of their lives under different circumstances—are trapped by their environment. Criminals with a spark of humanity are forced to subdue it to survive. Little boys who just want to have fun must make terrible sacrifices.

The resulting film is initially captivating—as is Butch's character—but ends up leaving a disturbing afterimage in its wake. Costner's Butch is part likable crook—as was another Butch, Paul Newman's Butch Cassidy in the classic *Butch Cassidy and the Sundance Kid* (1969)—part boyhood hero Shane, and part Charles Manson when he is pushed over the psychological edge. He protects the innocent, pricks the balloon of pretentiousness, grants childhood wishes, and avenges children who are victims. He has a smooth glibness and a relaxed easiness (except when he sees children being abused). Yet he is also someone who should repulse a 1990's audience through his actions and the lessons he teaches the innocent Phillip. He instructs the impressionable boy on how to swear, rob stores, point guns, and steal and drive cars.

A Perfect World was originally given an R rating, but the powerful Clint Eastwood managed to get it changed to the more lucrative PG-13. With youngsters now allowed in the audience unescorted, one has to wonder if these are the kinds of themes they should be exposed to. For years experts and parents have been telling children that no one has the right to see or touch their "private parts," and then along comes Butch who casually asks to see Phillip's with no consequence other than building the young boy's ego. Set in the 1960's, the film feels as if somehow it was even meant for a 1960's audience—not the sophisticated ones of the 1990's who are inundated with headlines about crime and child abuse.

Costner, too, seems caught in a time warp. His portrayal of the engaging criminal with the tormented past is flawless. His smile is charming, but his eyes seem vacant. Costner's role in this film conjures up aspects of two of his previous roles, that of the dreamer of 1989's *Field of Dreams* and the genial bad-boy of 1988's *Bull Durham*. When one considers how antithetical those two characters are, one realizes the inherent problems of this role.

Because Eastwood won two Oscars for 1992's *Unforgiven*, *A Perfect World* was eagerly awaited. The resulting product, in many ways, does not disappoint. It is a film rich in characters (some of whom viewers almost hate themselves for liking) and beautiful to look at (cinematographer Jack Green was also nominated for an Academy Award for his work on *Unforgiven*), but is also a bit slow at times, especially at the end. It is stylistically typical of Eastwood with its incisive and spare direction and its unrelenting look at bitter but sympathetic characters. And the powerful box-office appeal of a Costner-Eastwood collaboration cannot be denied, for it was among Warner's top-grossing films for 1993.

If one did not have to worry about the children, both in the film and in the audience, it would be easier to like the film. Adults who feel any degree of social responsibility, however, may find it difficult to relax and enjoy its contradictory but compelling mix of action, compassion, and melancholy.

Beverley Bare Buehrer

Reviews

Chicago Tribune. November 24, 1993, Section 2, p. 1.
Entertainment Weekly. December 3, 1993, p. 44.
The Hollywood Reporter. November 19, 1993, p. 6.
Los Angeles Times. November 24, 1993, p. F1.
The Nation. CCLVII, December 20, 1993, p. 778.
New Statesman and Society. VI, December 17, 1993, p. 58.
The New York Times. November 24, 1993, p. B1.
The New Yorker. LXIX, December 6, 1993, p. 135.

Newsweek. CXXII, November 29, 1993, p. 72.
Time. November 29, 1993, p. 74.
Variety. November 19, 1993, p. 2.
The Wall Street Journal. December 2, 1993, p. A14.
The Washington Post. November 24, 1993, p. C6.

PHILADELPHIA

Production: Edward Saxon and Jonathan Demme for Clinica Estetico; released by
   TriStar Pictures
Direction: Jonathan Demme
Screenplay: Ron Nyswaner
Cinematography: Tak Fujimoto
Editing: Craig McKay
Production design: Kristi Zea
Art direction: Tim Galvin
Set decoration: Karen O'Hara
Casting: Howard Feuer
Sound: Chris Newman
Costume design: Colleen Atwood
Music: Howard Shore
Song: Bruce Springsteen, "Streets of Philadelphia" (AA)
MPAA rating: PG-13
Running time: 119 minutes

   Principal characters:
   Andrew Beckett......................... Tom Hanks (AA)
   Joe Miller...................... Denzel Washington
   Charles Wheeler .... Jason Robards
   Belinda Conine .... Mary Steenburgen
   Sarah Beckett..................... Joanne Woodward
   Miguel Alvarez .... Antonio Banderas
   Bud Beckett......................... Robert Castle
   Bob Seidman .... Ron Vawter
   Walter Kenton .... Robert Ridgely
   Anthea Buton.................. Anna Deavere Smith
   Judge Garnett....................... Charles Napier
   Lisa Miller....................... Lisa Summerour

   Until *Philadelphia*'s release, no major motion picture had effectively dealt with the
disturbing and complicated issue of AIDS (acquired immune deficiency syndrome) in
any notable fashion—a glaring omission, even to the politically unsophisticated. After
all, AIDS had taken countless numbers of people in the entertainment industry, in
visibly higher proportion to people in other industries. The political issues were well
known: Hollywood's legendary fear of presenting gay people (still the group hardest
hit by AIDS) in a positive light, combined with a national paranoia concerning the
mysterious and frightening disease.
   Perhaps out of a director's need to make amends, perhaps because it was time,
Philadelphia became Hollywood's first big-budget "AIDS film." It follows numerous

films in the gay cinema dealing with this subject, as well as the highly successful, independent film *Longtime Companion* (1990). The director and producer of *Philadelphia* is Jonathan Demme, Academy Award winner for *The Silence of the Lambs* (1991). In that film, the sadistic killer was a homosexual, causing outrage among many viewers of the film that yet again Hollywood was only able to portray gay people in one light: perverted and psychologically damaged. Demme himself came under great scrutiny for the inclusion of that character's homosexuality.

According to some industry observers, it was this experience that caused Demme to try to make it up to the gay community in the form of a long-awaited film addressing head-on the issues of discrimination against gays in American culture. Demme himself attributes the desire to do the film to the death of a friend who succumbed to AIDS. Whatever the reason, the film arrives in a rich and controversial cultural context. Highly successful and receiving numerous honors and critical acclaim, *Philadelphia* is a dignified and handsomely-made film with excellent performances and a solid screenplay, buoyed by the thoughtful direction of Demme.

Andrew Beckett (Tom Hanks) is a brilliant young attorney working in a prestigious firm in Philadelphia, headed by the estimable Charles Wheeler (Jason Robards). Early in the film, Andrew is given charge of a new and important client, representing an important endorsement by the firm's partnership, not to mention a huge promotion. As he is being congratulated by the partners, however, one of them notices a lesion on the top of his forehead, saying (rather ominously), "What's that on your forehead, pal?" It is, in fact, a Kaposi's sarcoma lesion. (Kaposi's sarcoma is one of the opportunistic diseases often caught by AIDS patients.)

The scene shifts ahead several months, and Andrew, now more frail and wearing a hat to cover hair loss from radiation treatments, comes to Joe Miller (Denzel Washington) because he wants to bring a wrongful termination lawsuit against his firm. Joe, a brilliant and savvy personal injury attorney, initially turns down Andrew's case on the basis of his homophobia and his AIDS-phobia. After running into Andrew in a law library, however, Joe becomes hooked on the injustice of Andrew's termination and takes on the case in spite of his personal distaste for Andrew's illness and sexual orientation.

Joe's fears and his personal discoveries mirror those of the general public of the early 1990's: The world of gay people and the world of AIDS are both areas of which Joe has no knowledge, except some sketchy stereotypes and myths. As the film progresses, his prejudices gradually give way to an understanding of Andrew that is tentative at best. His small acceptance of Andrew only appears at the end of the film, when he brings a bottle of expensive champagne to Andrew at the hospital, calls Andrew "counselor," and smiles.

Although desirable, it would have been unrealistic for Joe to have had a complete change of heart. Because of this decision, however, critics and supporters clashed on the film's success as the first "AIDS film." Critics complained that Joe should not be the focal point of the story and that the intelligent and happy family man that Washington portrays only reinforces the notion that it is normal for all good Americans to fear and loathe gay people. There are other examples of the film's heterosexism and homophobia, pointed out by critics of the film.

For example, Andrew and his lover, Miguel (Antonio Banderas), dressed in Navy uniforms, dance together at a costume ball that Andrew throws for himself during the trial. This is seen by some critics as another reinforcement of the stereotype that gay men are obsessed with costumes and uniforms and try to embarrass other people by dancing together in mixed social functions. The inclusion of this scene is gratuitous, even though it is one of the few times that Andrew and Miguel show affection for each other. It is unnecessary for the audience to see them dressed up in costumes, and their dance tends to sensationalize their physical affection for each other. This scene is contrasted with a scene in which Joe goes home and holds his baby daughter and then his sleeping wife (Lisa Summerour), a scene which sentimentalizes rather than sensationalizes Joe's physical affection.

Controversy is not the only element of this film, however. It has a fine script by Ron Nyswaner, who skillfully crafts the story of Andrew's lawsuit as it coincides with his final months. An example of Nyswaner's ability is his choice of making Andrew an attorney; in so doing he levels the playing field between the two main characters. This choice also further underscores the film's theme of justice, particularly when, as a witness, Andrew says he loves the law because "every now and then, you get to be a part of justice being done, and that really is quite a thrill when that happens." Setting the film in Philadelphia, the "cradle of liberty" and the "city of brotherly love," underscores its themes further. The opening sequence sets the thematic tone, as people from every walk of life are depicted in everyday activities all over the city, waving to the camera, living their lives in a complicated urban mosaic. Later in the film, that mosaic is reflected in the diverse faces of the jury members.

Demme directs with characteristic grace and authority. He utilizes a simple, almost documentary style that clearly attempts to avoid the overly emotional style that another director may have chosen. What emerges is similar to a trial: a presentation of the evidence, allowing people to make their own judgments. Demme uses constant close-ups to draw the audience into the action, also forcing viewers to see up close the unpleasant effects of the disease as Andrew's condition worsens. The film is sure to bring many people in the audience closer than they have ever been to the effects of AIDS.

Tom Hanks lost thirty pounds over the course of the film to depict accurately the ravages of the disease, and he gets wonderful assistance from makeup artist Carl Fullerton and hairstylist Alan D'Angerio. Hanks delivers a wonderful performance, full of range and emotion, one that could be construed as dispassionate because of the almost documentary style of the direction. He shines in particular in his restrained physical collapse in the courtroom. Subtle moments like these are what have made Hanks one the finest film actors of his generation. He won the Academy Award for Best Actor for this performance.

Denzel Washington gives another excellent performance as Joe: There are no emotional pyrotechnics, except for one scene. At one point, Joe becomes furious at a man who tries to "pick him up" in a drugstore. Like Hanks, Washington's subtlety is representative of the film's intention not to hit anyone over the head with this subject matter.

There are other notable contributions to the film: Mary Steenburgen as the defense attorney who states, under her breath, "I hate this case," to Jason Robards' snarling Charles Wheeler; Joanne Woodward's stalwart mother; a performance by Ron Vawter, one of the only working actors at the time who was candid about having AIDS; and the contribution of Bruce Springsteen, who won the Academy Award for his song, "The Streets of Philadelphia," his first song written specifically for a film.

Philadelphia attempted to shed light on and bring out into the open the hatred and bigotry against gays in general, and AIDS victims in particular. Thus, the national debate on these issues moved from often esoteric political discussion into the world in which most Americans truly receive and digest cultural information: the movies.

Although the film does at times appear to pander to existing stereotypes and myths, supporters have quoted a line from the film to defend its middle-of-the-road qualities: The judge (Charles Napier) tells Joe, "in this courtroom, justice is blind." Joe replies, "But we don't live in this courtroom, do we?" Unfortunately, Americans do not yet live in a world in which discrimination and homophobia are nonexistent. This well-intentioned film, while far from perfect, will most likely bring a lot of people further along the continuum of understanding and tolerance of gay people and AIDS victims. For a mainstream motion picture, that is a momentous accomplishment.

Kirby Tepper

Reviews

The Christian Century. CXI, March 16, 1994, p. 268.
Commonweal. CXXI, February 25, 1994, p. 16.
Entertainment Weekly. December 24, 1993, p. 34.
The Hollywood Reporter. December 6, 1993, p. 5.
Los Angeles Times. December 22, 1993, p. F1.
National Law Journal. XVI, December 20, 1993, p. 8.
New Statesman and Society. VII, February 25, 1994, p. 33.
The New York Times. December 22, 1993, p. B1.
The New Yorker. LXIX, December 27, 1993, p. 148.
Newsweek. CXXII, December 27, 1993, p. 46.
Variety. December 7, 1993, p. 4.
The Washington Post. January 14, 1994, p. G1.

THE PIANO

Origin: Australia
Released: 1993
Released in U.S.: 1993
Production: Jan Chapman; released by Miramax Films
Direction: Jane Campion
Screenplay: Jane Campion (AA)
Cinematography: Stuart Dryburgh
Editing: Veronika Jenet
Production design: Andrew McAlpine
Casting: Diana Rowan, Susie Figgis, Victoria Thomas, and Alison Barrett
Costume design: Janet Patterson
Music: Michael Nyman
MPAA rating: R
Running time: 121 minutes

> *Principal characters:*
> Ada. . . . . Holly Hunter (AA)
> Baines . . . . Harvey Keitel
> Stewart. . . . . Sam Neill
> Flora. . . . . Anna Paquin (AA)

The Piano is, among other things, a Gothic romance in Victorian clothes about a woman with modern—or at least utterly unconventional—sensibilities. From the opening credits, filmgoers know that they are watching an unconventional film: The initial scene is shot through a hazy curtain of pink formed by ten fingers, as Ada (Holly Hunter) relates in voice-over narration that, for reasons even she cannot comprehend, she has been willfully mute since the age of six. These are the last words one hears her speak until she narrates, again in voice-over, the final scenes of the film.

While the opening of *The Piano* indicates that the film will be concerned with communication—Ada says that because she could play the piano, she never felt inarticulate—it will be some time before the import of this early sign is made manifest. The camera shifts abruptly to a wild shore in New Zealand, where Ada, a nineteenth-century Scotswoman, and her nine-year-old daughter, Flora (Anna Paquin), have come to settle with a stranger, Stewart (Sam Neill), to whom Ada is to be married by arrangement. These scenes, too, are extraordinary. Instead of dwelling on the customary aspects of sea voyages—sea spray, heaving decks—the camera shoots the boat carrying Ada and Flora from underwater, as if to emphasize the foreignness of the world into which they are about to be thrust.

When Ada and her daughter are forsaken on shore by those who brought them, director-screenwriter Jane Campion provides yet another singular image: the vision of Ada's hoop skirt, lit from within, serving as a makeshift tent. Within this self-contained world, mother and daughter converse in a sign language unlike any other, so angular and private that no outsider could decode it. Ada seems almost to be speaking to her mirror image. Flora, as her name might indicate, is a natural child, and her father is never accurately identified. This matters not at all: Ada seems to have given birth to Flora by parthenogenesis, strictly through an exercise of will. In the early scenes of *The Piano*, before Flora begins to interact with the outside world, she serves solely as her mother's mouthpiece, seemingly reading Ada's mind.

When Stewart finally does arrive to fetch his bride, this mundane English settler agrees to move all of Ada's goods into the bush except her piano, abandoned at water's edge, still in its crate. The vision of this token of Western civilization surrounded by antipodean wildness points up at once Ada's isolation and the incongruousness—and precariousness—of the whole Victorian colonial adventure.

In depriving Ada of her sole means of self-expression, Stewart dooms their marriage. Unfortunately, Stewart, a blinkered, rigidly conventional man, cannot begin to anticipate the fate he has set in motion, just as he cannot see that one cannot use buttons to buy a Maori burial ground. A Victorian man of property, he views Ada and her piano as his possessions, and he barters both away to increase his holdings.

Stewart sells the piano to Baines (Harvey Keitel), a lower-class English or Scottish exile whose tattooed face indicates his integration with the Maoris and their element. Able to speak the Maori language, Baines is nevertheless an illiterate recluse nearly as solitary, silent, and self-contained as Ada. It is no accident that when he succumbs to her entreaties to be taken to her beached piano, the pure emotion of the music she plays speaks to him.

Baines formulates a plan: he will rescue the piano, then swap it, first with Stewart for land, then with Ada for lessons, one for each black key, by means of which she can earn it back. Baines, of course, has no intention of learning to play—as he tells Ada, he has things he wants to do while listening to her play—what he wants is access to Ada. Soon he abandons the arrangement because, he says, the process of bartering keys for sexual liberties is making her into a whore and him into an idiot. Ada, however, recognizes a kindred soul, or at least a man capable of passionate expression. Baines is captivated as much by the outpouring of Ada's soul in her music as he is by the sight of her bare arms. Baines restores the piano to her, and after this long-awaited sign of respect, Ada surrenders to him.

The ensuing affair, although passionate and brief, sets in motion a sequence of inevitable and tragic events as first Flora, then Stewart, spies on the lovers. As in any good Gothic tale, the audience is prepared well in advance for the dire consequences of the characters' actions. Indeed, a large part of the genre's appeal is the delicious feeling of dread that accompanies the rush toward foreordained events. Campion does a superior job of providing Gothic elements and atmosphere, with signs and portents than imbue every aspect of Ada and her story with significance.

Early in *The Piano*, Flora gets involved in a school theatrical production of the tale of Bluebeard, presented as a shadow play. When one of the Maoris in the audience interrupts a backlit ax murder, his naïveté is not only amusing but also unnerving, for one senses that this scene is more than whimsy. Similarly, when Flora dons wings to play the part of an angel in the play, she is charming; when she continues to wear them afterward, the gossamer fabric assumes symbolic heft, foreshadowing her future role as an avenging angel.

The New Zealand bush likewise plays an ambiguous role, at once paradisal and claustrophobic. Like the music Michael Nyman has composed for Ada, the bush as filmed in *The Piano* is anachronistic and out of this world, an environment so remote from the strangled sexuality of Victorian society that it paradoxically provides the perfect backdrop for the emotional extremes of Campion's singular heroine. In a scene where Stewart attacks Ada on her way to Baines, the bush assumes a life of its own as a web of branched creeping vines snatches at Ada, tripping her while mimicking the heavy, hoop-skirted garments that impede her progress. Scenes such as this one, fraught with a sort of nightmare logic, point up the unreality of the Victorian experience and go some distance toward explaining why a passionate and original person like Ada would choose not to conform.

As played by Holly Hunter, Ada is an uncompromising individual—and hers is an uncompromising performance. Hunter is on screen almost constantly, and she manages to overpower all else in the film without saying a word—indeed, without making a sound or even allowing her face or physical gestures to betray much emotion. With an utter lack of vanity, she plays her love scenes realistically, naked and with hair which, once freed of its nineteenth century parts and braids, is noticeably greasy. Her face suits the daguerreotype that serves as her introduction to Stewart, but when seen in close-up, the pale facial makeup and dark lipstick she wears gives her an unearthly look. In addition, Hunter is credited with playing solo piano and, according to the production notes, worked with composer Nyman, who tailored Ada's music for Hunter's abilities.

Harvey Keitel exhibits a similar lack of self-consciousness as Baines, and he does a remarkable job of conveying at once the wildness and vulnerability of this outcast. Sam Neill has, in a sense, a more difficult job, in that he must portray a limited individual whose very conventionality compels him to commit monstrous acts. It is a tribute to his acting skill—and to Campion's script—that he emerges as a sympathetic character, one who eventually is able to hear what Ada has to say. Finally, Anna Paquin imbues Flora with the same air of eerie precociousness that marks another memorable juvenile character in a Gothic tale of adultery: Pearl, in Nathaniel Hawthorne's *The Scarlet Letter* (1850).

The Piano has garnered numerous awards. It was nominated for 1993 Academy Awards in the following categories: Best Picture, Film Editing, Cinematography, Costume Design. Jane Campion was nominated as Best Director and her writing for the film was honored with an award for Best Original Screenplay. In addition, Holly Hunter won as Best Actress and Anna Paquin as Best Supporting Actress. *The Piano* shared the 1993 Cannes Film Festival Palme d'or with the Chinese film, *Farewell, My Concubine*. Campion was honored by the New York Film Critics Circle with awards for Best Direction and Best Screenplay. Hunter has won, additionally, the Golden

Globe award as Best Actress and been granted similar honors from the New York Critics Circle, the Los Angeles Film Critics Association, and the Cannes Film Festival. Not surprisingly, *The Piano* also swept the 1993 Australian Film Institute Awards, winning eleven out of the fifteen feature film awards.

Lisa Paddock

Reviews

America. CLXX, January 15, 1994, p. 14.
Chicago Tribune. November 19, 1993, VII, p. 39.
Commonweal. CXXI, January 14, 1994, p. 27.
Entertainment Weekly. November 19, 1993, p. 66.
The Hollywood Reporter. May 18, 1993, p. 11.
Los Angeles Times. November 19, 1993, p. F1.
The Nation. CCLVII, December 6, 1993, p. 704.
The New York Review of Books. XLI, February 3, 1994, p. 29.
The New York Times. October 16, 1993, p. 13.
The New Yorker. November 29, 1993, p. 148.
Newsweek. May 31, 1993, p. 53.
Variety. May 14, 1993, p. 2.
The Washington Post. November 19, 1993, p. D1.

POETIC JUSTICE

Production: Steve Nicolaides and John Singleton; released by Columbia Pictures
Direction: John Singleton
Screenplay: John Singleton
Cinematography: Peter Lyons Collister
Editing: Bruce Cannon
Poetry: Maya Angelou
Production design: Keith Brian Burns
Art direction: Kirk M. Petruccelli
Set decoration: Dan May
Casting: Robi Reed
Sound: Robert D. Eber
Costume design: Darryle Johnson
Music: Stanley Clarke
MPAA rating: R
Running time: 110 minutes

Principal characters:
Justice .... Janet Jackson
Lucky................................. Tupac Shakur
Iesha................................. Regina King
Chicago .... Joe Torry
Jessie .... Tyra Ferrell
Heywood .... Roger Guenveur Smith
Aunt June........................... Maya Angelou
Markell.................................... Q-Tip
J Bone .... Tone Lōc
Maxine............................... Miki Howard
Dexter .... Keith Washington
Uncle Earl .... John Cothran, Jr.

   Poetic Justice, talented writer/director John Singleton's second feature-length film, follows his very successful debut effort, *Boyz 'n the Hood* (1991). The youngest person and the first African American ever nominated for the Best Director Academy Award (for *Boyz 'n the Hood*), Singleton, who was born in 1968, also received a nomination for the script. Made in six weeks on a small, six-million-dollar budget, *Boyz 'n the Hood* was reported to have been the single most profitable new film of 1991. The power of *Boyz 'n the Hood* lies in its humanity and its realism: the humanity of parents from South Central Los Angeles who fear that their boys will become involved in youth gangs, and the realism of the day-to-day violence that threatens the characters. Like *Boyz 'n the Hood*, *Poetic Justice* begins in South Central Los Angeles. Subtitled "A Street Romance," *Poetic Justice* succeeds in its attempts at realism, but it lacks the humanity that gave *Boyz 'n the Hood* much of its emotional depth.

The film opens with Justice (Janet Jackson) at a drive-in with her boyfriend, Markell (Q-Tip). When two gang members recognize Markell as someone with whom they are feuding, they follow him from the concession stand to his car and shoot him, running away as Justice screams for help. Following this violent episode, Justice, who works as a hairdresser at Jessie's Beauty Salon, is comforted by both Jessie (Tyra Ferrell) and Justice's friend Iesha (Regina King), who try to help her overcome the grief of Markell's death. Justice's outlet for coping with life's harshness is writing poetry. When the salon workers must travel to Oakland to take part in a hair show, Justice decides to drive herself rather than ride with the group. At the last minute, however, her car will not start, and she has to travel to Oakland in a mail truck with Iesha, Iesha's boyfriend Chicago (Joe Torry), and Chicago's friend Lucky (Tupac Shakur). Both Chicago and Lucky are postal workers who want some company while they transfer mail on the weekend run from Los Angeles to Oakland. Lucky, an aspiring rap performer, also plans to work on songs with his cousin in Oakland. Singleton uses the road trip to contrast the disintegrating relationship of Iesha and Chicago with the growing attraction between Justice and Lucky.

Singleton provides his couples with stops along the way to Oakland that reveal the characters' personalities and define relationships. A scene at a convenience store cross-cuts between two simultaneous conversations. Inside the store, Iesha tells Justice that she controls Chicago by rationing her affection; at the same time, outside at the gas pump, Chicago brags to Lucky that Iesha cannot get enough of him. The couples later stop at a family reunion and mingle with the crowd in order to enjoy a free meal. A trio of stern-faced aunts (one of them played by Maya Angelou, who also wrote the poetry in the film) talks to Iesha and predicts trouble for her and Chicago. Elsewhere, a tipsy uncle (John Cothran, Jr.) tells Lucky and Justice that they make an attractive couple. As expected, before the sojourn at the reunion concludes, Iesha's drinking and flirting have angered Chicago, and Lucky intervenes to prevent a fight. The travelers stop again at an African market festival, where Lucky and Justice come together through their mutual escape from the city and their appreciation for each other's creativity. By now, Iesha and Chicago have all but decided to end their relationship.

The characters in *Poetic Justice* are more stereotypical and the performances less real than those in *Boyz 'n the Hood*. Although Justice and Lucky have the most facets to their personalities, Janet Jackson's narrow range oversimplifies Justice. Before the road trip, Singleton attempts to show the loneliness and grief of Justice in a montage. The sequence concludes with a series of close-ups of Justice merely looking into a mirror while she arranges her hair and assumes different facial expressions. In contrast, Tupac Shakur makes Lucky more individualized and is believable in every scene of the motion picture. A surprising number of the other characters can be summed up simply by attaching the proper stereotype: Alcoholic Teen (Iesha), Jaded Flirt (Jessie), Gay Hairstylist (Heywood, played by Roger Guenveur Smith), and Macho Stud (Dexter, played by Keith Washington).

Singleton's two films place him in the tradition of American cinematic realists such

as William Wyler, Fred Zinnemann, and Elia Kazan. Singleton favors location shooting because of its authentic look, rather than sound-stage filming with the greater
control that it offers. The most memorable shot in *Poetic Justice* appears at the start
of the road trip when the two couples leave South Central Los Angeles. Singleton had
his director of photography, Peter Lyons Collister, film the mail truck from the charred
interior of a building destroyed during the April, 1992, riots in Los Angeles. As another
reminder of the violent backdrop to the characters' lives, this use of a location setting
illustrates the social pain against which the love of Justice and Lucky struggles.

Like most realists, Singleton also tends to reject displays of cinematic style for their
own sake. For example, he originally planned to begin a scene at the post office sorting
room on a close-up of a photograph of George Bush's face that has been taped to a
dart board. In his screenplay Singleton wrote, "Suddenly, it is hit with many darts.
Maybe a shot on dart P.O.V., as in *Robin Hood*." In the finished film, however, the
audience sees the postal workers talking to each other and tossing darts off-screen.
Not until one of them walks over to retrieve the darts does the camera pan with him
and reveal on the wall the pockmarked picture of George Bush. The playful point-of-
view shot described in the script does not appear at all. Apparently, the director felt
that such a flourish of style did not belong in a story of urban realism. Other changes
from original script to finished film indicate the same urge to maintain an austere,
utilitarian style. When a preview audience responded that the film ran too long,
Singleton trimmed some footage. Most of his changes and deletions—a montage at
the Monterey aquarium, a lyrical scene of Justice playing with zebras that have
wandered away from a zoo—sacrifice touches of style and preserve the linear
development of plot. Singleton sees style as something functional, a tool that serves
his content and not the other way around.

The street slang of both *Boyz 'n the Hood* and *Poetic Justice* exemplifies Singleton's
realism perhaps best of all. In his first film, different types of language sharply
delineate the two worlds of the family and the gangs. In *Poetic Justice*, street slang
invades nearly every scene of the motion picture, and this idiom produces some
unconventional lovers' quarrels and reconciliations. An initial friction between Lucky
and Justice reveals itself suddenly in a profane shouting match while they drive. The
intensity of their words cannot fail to hold interest, but the potency of the language in
this scene and elsewhere begins to overwhelm the more delicate emotions required by
the genre of romance. The arguments in the film seem more convincing than the love
scenes. Singleton has defended the language as simply being the way the real-life
prototypes talk, and though it causes the love scenes to miscarry, the technique does
suggest some interesting insights. The verbal violence implies, whether intentionally
or not, that life in the "'hood" can threaten a person's capacity to reach out to others
and that the pressures of the neighborhood can erupt in a verbal fusillade as easily as
in gunplay.

Justice's sensitivity to language in her poetry fails to provide the needed balance to
the rawness of the film's casual conversation. She tells Lucky at one point, that "You
gotta have something to say. Somethin different, a perspective. . . . A voice." A more

varied cinematic voice strengthens *Boyz 'n the Hood*, and its absence dulls the scenes in *Poetic Justice*, in which Singleton's use of language is less careful and precise than in his first work. In *Poetic Justice*, John Singleton's realism gives the film its authenticity and bite, but it also robs it of any consistent tenderness or warmth. This weakness, paradoxically, does create some interest for the film. Young artists sometimes find tone an elusive element. Singleton's uncertainties and inconsistencies in this area reveal him as a young realist still acquiring artistic finesse. In retrospect, *Poetic Justice* my be regarded by its director as an instructive failure.

Glenn Hopp

Reviews

Chicago Tribune. July 23, 1993, VII, p. 19.
The Christian Science Monitor. July 23, 1993, p. 13.
Entertainment Weekly. July 23, 1993, p. 42.
Essence. XXIV, August, 1993, p. 48.
The Hollywood Reporter. July 19, 1993, p. 5.
Jet. LXXXIV, July 19, 1993, p. 54.
Los Angeles Times. July 23, 1993, p. F1.
The New York Times. July 23, 1993, p. B1.
The New Yorker. August 2, 1993, p. 76.
Rolling Stone. May 27, 1993, p. 18.
Time. July 26, 1993, p. 67.
USA Today. July 23, 1993, p. 8D.
Variety. July 20, 1993, p. 2.
The Washington Post. July 23, 1993, p. C1.

POINT OF NO RETURN

Production: Art Linson; released by Warner Bros.
Direction: John Badham
Screenplay: Robert Getchell and Alexandra Seros; based on the film *La Femme Nikita* (1990), by Luc Besson
Cinematography: Michael Watkins
Editing: Frank Morriss
Production design: Philip Harrison
Art direction: Sydney Z. Litwack
Set decoration: Julia Laughlin
Casting: Bonnie Timmermann
Sound: Willie Do Burton
Costume design: Marlene Stewart
Music: Hans Zimmer
MPAA rating: R
Running time: 110 minutes

Principal characters:
Maggie	Bridget Fonda
Bob	Gabriel Byrne
J. P.	Dermot Mulroney
Kaufman	Miguel Ferrer
Amanda	Anne Bancroft
Angela	Olivia d'Abo
Fahd Bahktiar	Richard Romanus
Victor the Cleaner	Harvey Keitel

When Maggie (Bridget Fonda) is arrested during a violent drugstore robbery in which she kills a police officer in cold blood, she is tried and sentenced to death. When it is time to carry out the sentence, however, Maggie's death is faked, right down to the funeral. Someone has seen potential in the drug-addicted criminal, "killing off" the old Maggie with the intention of creating a new one. That someone is Bob (Gabriel Byrne), and Maggie's new identity will capitalize on her cold-bloodedness: She will be an assassin employed by the covert agency that Bob represents.

First, however, Maggie must be tamed. One of those hired by the agency to civilize Maggie is Amanda (Anne Bancroft), who teaches her which fork to use, how to speak French, what makeup highlights her attractiveness, and which genteel phrase to use while smiling at an insult. At first, the job seems impossible: No one can penetrate Maggie's hard exterior or control her savage emotions. Yet Maggie eventually realizes that it is in her best interest to cooperate. While being trained and domesticated, the wily Maggie actually undergoes a change: one that replaces the wild killer with an intelligent individual. When the time comes to release her into society under the cover name, Maggie finds it increasingly difficult to carry out her callous missions of murder. When she falls in love with her landlord, photographer J. P. (Dermot Mulroney), she discovers a long-lost, vulnerable part of herself. She soon decides to rid herself of the agency's demands, but the agency owns Maggie's life.

This is the premise of *Point of No Return*, an American remake of the successful 1990 French film *La Femme Nikita*. It was France's biggest French-made box office hit of 1990 and the top-grossing foreign-language film in the United States in 1991. In a typical move, Hollywood producers saw a great story filmed in a foreign language and with actors who were relatively unknown (to Americans, that is) and wondered what they could do to Americanize it. Normally, the result is a weak imitation of the original, with the heart cut out and replaced by a pacemaker. Yet, while *La Femme Nikita* was stylishly entertaining, with the help of Bridget Fonda *Point of No Return* does not lose much in the translation.

While the two films are almost the same scene for scene, there are some crucial differences that make each film worth watching. The first thing to compare is Anne Parillaud's Nikita to Bridget Fonda's Maggie. Parillaud, who made her American film debut in *Innocent Blood* (1992), is wild and cool by turns, giving her performance an edge that carries through until the final frame. Fonda, on the other hand, starts out like a caged animal but is transformed by the end of the film, offering a character who is likable and for whom the audience can root. Fonda, born of Hollywood royalty—the granddaughter of Henry, the niece of Jane, and the daughter of Peter—here proves that she is more than capable of carrying a major film. She is more than successful at allowing Maggie's childlike innocence to crack through her hard veneer in a believable way. Even after early scenes in which the character is so malevolent that it would seem impossible for audiences to like her or for her transformation to be convincing, Fonda manages to do the inconceivable.

As originally written by Luc Besson, this character is a great part, and it was said that every actress in Hollywood over seventeen and under thirty tried out for it. Director John Badham, after seeing footage of Fonda in *Single White Female* (1992), decided that she was right for the role. Women's action films are very rare, Sigourney Weaver's *Alien* series being one exception, and it would seem understandable that the industry might shy away from them. Yet any film, if made well, will transcend genre pitfalls. *Point of No Return* shows that there is a market for strong and capable women protagonists.

Point of No Return is also helped by the quietly solid performance of Gabriel Byrne as Bob, who alternately trains and seduces Maggie, although never sexually. He is the one who acts as the catalyst for Maggie's awakening sense of humanity. Perhaps the real Pygmalion to Fonda's Galatea, however, is Anne Bancroft's Amanda, who alternates intimidation and charm to discipline her charge. She becomes Maggie's surrogate mother, just as Bob has become her surrogate boyfriend.

Working with Alexandra Seros, screenwriter Robert Getchell, who won Oscar nominations for *Alice Doesn't Live Here Anymore* (1975) and *Bound for Glory* (1976), provides a faithful adaptation of the original thriller while also affording a stronger understanding of the lead character's psychological foundation.

Frenchman Luc Besson, who not only wrote but also directed the original *La Femme Nikita*, was offered the opportunity to direct this remake, but he (perhaps wisely) rejected the offer. The project was given to John Badham, the director of *Saturday Night Fever* (1977) and *Wargames* (1983), who recognized that most Americans will not see a film with dreaded subtitles. If he retold the story, in English, it would become acceptable to them. And it did, indeed, prove acceptable; it was among Warner's top box-office winners for 1993.

If there is one aspect in which *Point of No Return* does pale in comparison to the original film, it is in the cinematography. *La Femme Nikita* is stylish to the end of the film. *Point of No Return* starts out that way, but by the time that Maggie is in the underground agency, the look has become antiseptic. The photography then turns to the positively sunny when the story reaches Maggie's new life in Venice, California. According to the film's production notes, *Point of No Return* became the first major feature to use Kodak 96 film stock, a film requiring little light, which cinematographer Michael Watkins uses to good effect in the first part of the film. When Maggie emerges from the agency, however, the film seems almost too bright and cheery. While probably meant to depict the emergence of her humanity, this look does not seem to reflect the cloud that still hangs over Maggie's head.

For some viewers, *Point of No Return* will not reflect the style, the edge, or the novelty of the original film. Yet, bolstered by Fonda's concentrated performance, it is a film worth seeing in its own right.

Beverley Bare Buehrer

Reviews

Chicago Tribune. March 19, 1993, VII, p. 31.
The Christian Science Monitor. March 26, 1993, p. 12.
Entertainment Weekly. April 2, 1993, p. 30.
The Hollywood Reporter. March 19, 1993, p. 6.
Los Angeles Times. March 19, 1993, p. F1.
The New Republic. CCVIII, April 19, 1993, p. 28.
The New York Times. March 19, 1993, p. B4.
Newsweek. March 29, 1993, p. 65
Time. March 29, 1993, p. 67.
Variety. March 19, 1993, p. 2.
The Wall Street Journal. April 1, 1993, p. A12.
The Washington Post. March 19, 1993, p. F7.

POSSE

Origin: USA and Great Britain
Released: 1993
Released in U.S.: 1993
Production: Preston Holmes and Jim Steele for PolyGram Filmed Entertainment, in association with Gramercy Pictures and Working Title Films; released by Gramercy Pictures
Direction: Mario Van Peebles
Screenplay: Sy Richardson and Dario Scardapane
Cinematography: Peter Menzies, Jr.
Editing: Mark Conte
Production design: Catherine Hardwicke
Art direction: Kim Hix
Set decoration: Tessa Posnansky
Casting: Pat Golden
Sound: Don Sanders
Costume design: Paul Simmons
Music: Michel Colombier
MPAA rating: R
Running time: 109 minutes

Principal characters:

Jesse Lee	Mario VanPeebles
Little J	Stephen Baldwin
Weezie	Charles Lane
Obobo	Tiny Lister, Jr.
Father Time	Big Daddy Kane
Colonel Graham	Billy Zane
Carver	Blair Underwood
Papa Joe	Melvin Van Peebles
Lana	Salli Richardson
Angel	Tone Lōc
Phoebe	Pam Grier
Cable	Isaac Hayes

Attempting to summarize the essence of Mario Van Peebles' *Posse* in the catchy jargon favored by the entertainment press, reviewers labeled the film a "New Jack Western" or tagged the characters as "New Jack cowboys." The phrase refers to Van Peebles' big-screen directorial debut *New Jack City* (1991), which, like *Posse*, featured a mostly African American cast, a hyperkinetic style, and plenty of attitude. The phrase does succinctly describe for viewers *Posse*'s superficial characteristics, and it also denotes a certain hipness, but, like most labels and catchphrases originated by the popular press, it masks the most intriguing aspects of the film.

More interesting than its overheated visual style are *Posse*'s references and homages to various "histories," which provide a subtext that suggests the significance of historical forces in shaping cultural identity. Van Peebles intended to make a Western that would help correct the erroneous notion that the Wild West was tamed mainly by white pioneers and white cowboys. Pains were taken to include in the dialogue historical facts about the establishment of black communities in the West, details about the number of blacks who helped settle the West, and an interpretation of how minority groups were disenfranchised by the white majority. In addition to African American history, *Posse* pays its respects to the whole of the Western genre through homages to past directors. It also refers to the history of blacks in Hollywood film by featuring prominent black actors from past generations. Though the film was touted as histori- cally accurate, it should not be taken as history. With *Posse*, Van Peebles attempts to honor and emphasize the contributions of African Americans to American history not by faithfully rendering events and details but by reworking the conventions of the Western to fit a black perspective. He is using the genre for his own ends—as did the Western auteurs he acknowledges.

Certain events of the story line are so familiar that even the casual viewer should have no trouble recognizing the similarity to past Westerns. The film opens with a framing device that depicts an old black man (Woody Strode) looking through a pile of sepia-toned photographs from the distant past. The old storyteller begins to weave a tale about the Wild West, beginning with the adventures of a group of black soldiers in Cuba during the Spanish-American War. The soldiers are set up by their racist commanding officer, Colonel Graham (Billy Zane), to be ambushed during a raid. The unofficial leader of the black soldiers, Jesse Lee (Van Peebles), decides they should desert the Army and return to the United States with a cache of gold uncovered in the raid. Casting his lot with the "posse" is a rebellious Southern white named Little J (Stephen Baldwin). Jesse's posse members represent a range of types played mostly by nonactors. Director Charles Lane portrays the tiny, chattering Weezie; rap perform- ers Big Daddy Kane and Tone Lōc play gambler Father Time and the raspy-voiced Angel, respectively; and former wrestler Tiny Lister, Jr., portrays the slow-thinking but good-hearted giant, Obobo. The raucous good times and male bonding that occur among the posse's diverse members recall such lighthearted Westerns from Howard Hawks as *Rio Bravo* (1959) and *El Dorado* (1967).

Pursued by Graham from New Orleans across most of the West, the posse eventually arrives in Freemanville, a black-operated township where hard-edged, soft-spoken Jesse has a score to settle. Jesse seeks revenge against the men responsible for his father's death and has returned to Freemanville to right the wrongs committed in his past, not unlike Clint Eastwood's character in *High Plains Drifter* (1973). The arrival of Jesse and his posse attracts the attention of Sheriff Bates (Richard Jordan), the vicious white sheriff of a nearby town and leader of the local Ku Klux Klan. Bates and the corrupted leaders of both towns have concocted a plan to cheat the black settlers out of their land in order to sell it to the railroad at inflated prices.

After Little J is killed in the streets by Bates's associates, and the citizens of

Freemanville realize that their days are numbered, they ask for help in defending themselves against Bates's cohorts. In a sequence reminiscent of *The Magnificent Seven* (1960), the posse saves the town from the Klan, the crooked leaders, and even Colonel Graham, who participates in the climactic battle in order to vanquish Jesse. The only posse members to survive are Jesse, Weezie, and Obobo.

The final sequence returns to the present to reveal that the old storyteller has been spinning his tale to two black documentary filmmakers (real-life directors Reginald and Warrington Hudlin). It seems that as a young boy, the old man was rescued from the desert and sure death by the posse. Jesse Lee gave the boy a book of poetry that Jesse's father, a minister and educator, had given him. The book contains a poem about a black slave who strives for a better life, and throughout the film, different characters have taken turns reading from this poem. The old man then gives the book to the filmmakers, as if to suggest that it is now their responsibility to pass this heritage to future generations.

Aside from the references in the story line, the film *Posse* alludes to the Western: both to the genre's characterizations and to its visual style. Jesse Lee has obviously been patterned after Clint Eastwood's legendary persona from Sergio Leone's Italian "spaghetti" Westerns. From his Mexican-style poncho to his flat, wide-brimmed hat to his laconic manner, Jesse Lee evokes the Man With No Name. Even the way Jesse is depicted invites comparison: From Eastwood's Westerns, Van Peebles borrows the device of suggesting that the character has mythic overtones. When alone in the frame, Jesse is often shot from below to make him appear larger than life, or he is shot with light streaming from behind him to evoke an otherworldly presence. In the climactic shoot-out between Jesse Lee and his enemies, Jesse appears silently at the doorway of the saloon. A gunman sees him, scrambles for his Colt .45, and turns to shoot him a split second later. Jesse Lee has vanished, like a phantom from another time and place.

Leone's influence is also readily apparent in the visual style—from the early scenes of the black soldiers in Cuba, in which Jesse Lee's determination and grit are indicated by the extreme close-ups of his eyes, to the climactic shoot-out in which Jesse is shown in slow motion, racing toward the camera on horseback with a stick of dynamite in his mouth. Other influences are also evident: At one point in its journey, the posse passes through Monument Valley, clearly an homage to classic Western director John Ford. This reference to Ford becomes significant in reference to the actor who plays the storyteller in *Posse*, Woody Strode. Strode appeared in Ford's *The Man Who Shot Liberty Valance* (1962) and played the title character in *Sergeant Rutledge* (1960). He also appeared in Leone's *Once Upon a Time in the West* (1968), and to honor both Strode and Leone, Van Peebles includes footage from that film under the closing credits. The use of Strode, who is as physically commanding now as he was thirty-five years ago, serves as a connecting point between the classic Westerns of Ford and the revisionist Westerns of Leone. Through Strode, it is suggested that African American performers have contributed to the whole history of the Western genre, even if their contributions have been largely unsung. To underscore that, Van Peebles also includes under the closing credits a few clips from the Westerns of Spencer Williams, a black actor-director from Hollywood's Golden Age who made genre films with all-black casts that were marketed to black audiences.

To emphasize further the contributions of African Americans to American cinema, Van Peebles populates the town of Freemanville with characters played by black actors prominent in the past, including comic actor Nipsey Russell; "blaxploitation" stars Robert Hooks, Pam Grier, and Isaac Hayes; and his father, actor and independent director Melvin Van Peebles (*Sweet Sweetback's Baadasssss Song*, 1971). The use of these actors and the references to the contributions of Strode and Williams suggest a sense of tradition and historical continuity that points to the film's subtext, which involves the importance of history/histories in shaping cultural identity.

On a surface level, *Posse* reminds viewers that the contributions of African Americans have been omitted from mainstream history books. With the references to prominent Western films and directors and the keen use of Strode in such a pivotal role, Van Peebles also suggests that blacks have contributed to the Western genre but have been excluded from its mythology. The characters of Jesse Lee and his posse attempt to atone for that absence by providing mythic figures, or cultural heroes, along the same lines as Eastwood's Man With No Name or the Magnificent Seven. To make those heroes relevant to today's black audience, Van Peebles neatly merges the image of the Western hero with that of the urban "gangster" persona as constructed and circulated through contemporary rap performers, which is underscored by the casting of rappers Tone Lōc and Big Daddy Kane in key roles. Also, it is no accident that Jesse Lee must make choices that foreshadow the tension between two paths: Martin Luther King's philosophy of nonviolence versus Malcolm X's "by any means necessary."

Finally, the film's cleverest attempt to make a traditional Hollywood genre relevant to today's African American audiences is the title, *Posse*. It not only denotes the Old West and a band of cowboys united for the common good but also is contemporary African American slang connoting the camaraderie and bonding of youth.

Susan Doll

Reviews
Chicago Tribune. May 14, 1993, VII, p. C.
Entertainment Weekly. May 21, 1993, p. 30.
Essence. XXIV, June, 1993, p. 46.
The Hollywood Reporter. April 28, 1993, p. 5.
Jet. LXXXIV, May 31, 1993, p. 56.
Los Angeles Times. May 14, 1993, p. F1.
The New Republic. CCVIII, June 14, 1993, p. 30.
The New York Times. May 14, 1993, p. B3.
Rolling Stone. June 10, 1993, p. 73-74.
Variety. April 28, 1993, p. 2.
The Washington Post. May 14, 1993, p. B1.

THE REMAINS OF THE DAY

Origin: Great Britain
Released: 1993
Released in U.S.: 1993
Production: Mike Nichols, John Calley, and Ismail Merchant; released by
    Columbia Pictures
Direction: James Ivory
Screenplay: Ruth Prawer Jhabvala; based on the novel by Kazuo Ishiguro
Cinematography: Tony Pierce-Roberts
Editing: Andrew Marcus
Production design: Luciana Arrighi
Art direction: John Ralph
Set decoration: Ian Whittaker
Casting: Celestia Fox
Sound: David Stephenson
Makeup: Christine Beveridge and Norma Webb
Costume design: Jenny Beavan and John Bright
Music: Richard Robbins
MPAA rating: PG
Running time: 134 minutes

Principal characters:
Mr. Stevens	Anthony Hopkins
Miss Kenton	Emma Thompson
Lord Darlington	James Fox
Lewis	Christopher Reeve
Mr. Stevens senior	Peter Vaughan
Cardinal	Hugh Grant
Dupont D'Ivry	Michael Lonsdale
Benn	Tim Pigott-Smith
Spencer	Patrick Godfrey

Film audiences have come to expect certain ingredients in every Ismail Merchant/ James Ivory production: carefully constructed and often lavish historical settings; the clash of individuals from different social classes and sometimes divergent cultures; an emphasis on characterization and the subtleties of plotting; meticulous attention to art direction, costumes, and the interplay of social mores; and the re-creation of a Victorian sensibility reflected in the characters' inability to deal openly with their emotions. Teamed with Ruth Prawer Jhabvala, who adapted E. M. Forster's novels *A Room with a View* (1986) and *Howard's End* (1992), and Kazuo Ishiguro's novel *The Remains of the Day*, Merchant and Ivory have created a canon of works that have classic appeal to a film audience dissatisfied with standard action/adventure fare. All three of these films garnered Oscar nominations for Best Picture, and *The Remains of the Day* was nominated for an additional seven Academy Awards. In some respects the success of Merchant/Ivory films have made audiences more receptive to and accepting of literate, psychologically complex human dramas.

The action begins in the late 1950's. For more than twenty years, Mr. Stevens (Anthony Hopkins) was the butler and head of a large staff in a great English house owned by Lord Darlington (James Fox). Now Stevens finds himself serving Mr. Lewis (Christopher Reeve), a former American congressman, who has bought the house after Lord Darlington's death. Stevens' recollections of his years at Darlington Hall reveal a life that was limited and incomplete because of his unflagging devotion to his profession, his unquestioning loyalty to Lord Darlington, and his failed relationship with Miss Kenton (Emma Thompson), the former housekeeper at Darlington Hall.

The plot is set in motion when Stevens receives a letter from Miss Kenton in which she indicates that her marriage has ended. She recalls fondly the days when she worked at Darlington Hall. Stevens sets out on a journey to Clevedon, where she is now living, in order to request that she return to Darlington Hall as housekeeper. Behind this overt reason for the journey, however, is a subtler, hidden meaning: Stevens means to bring Miss Kenton back in order to resolve a long-standing emptiness in his personal life as well. The structure of the film moves back and forth between scenes of Stevens on his trip to flashbacks from Stevens' point of view of events at Darlington Hall in the 1930's and 1940's. Scenes in the past focus on international conferences held at Darlington Hall, the routines and obligations of the servants, and Miss Kenton's eventual decision to leave service and marry. When Stevens reaches Clevedon near the end of the film, Miss Kenton and he have a cordial conversation. She tells him that she will not leave her husband after all, and they go their separate ways. Stevens is disappointed. Now he faces the prospect of returning alone to Darlington Hall and serving his American master.

In the 1930's Miss Kenton was one of two people hired because the former housekeeper ran off with a servant, a common occurrence in a large staff. The person Stevens hires to replace the other servant who ran away is his own father, the elder Mr. Stevens (Peter Vaughan), who has been in service for more than fifty years. Stevens views his father with respect and admiration; but their relationship as father and son is reserved and distant. After Stevens hires his father, a conflict arises when the elder Stevens begins to commit errors in his work. Miss Kenton discovers the old man's mistakes, and she delights in pointing them out to Mr. Stevens. He winces at the conflict he faces: How to be a professional when the staff person at fault is one's father? This conflict becomes charged with tension when the old man trips and falls while carrying a large serving tray and has to be reassigned to nonserving duties.

At the same time Lord Darlington has planned an elaborate conference with European representatives to discuss economic and military assistance to Germany. The last night of the conference the elder Stevens suffers a stroke and dies. Although his son finds time to assist his father to his bedroom upstairs, and later to visit him before dinner, for the most part he devotes himself to his responsibilities downstairs.

When Stevens is notified that his father has died, he views this personal crisis as an intrusion upon his responsibilities. He believes he is needed by Lord Darlington and the representatives from other nations. In the next scene Stevens serves after-dinner drinks to the guests, and he seems pale and hunched, and even distracted, as he makes his way around the room. Lord Darlington and another of the guests comment that Stevens appears to be tired. They ask him if he is all right. He can only say he is "a little tired."

Anthony Hopkins delivers the nonverbal information perfectly: Clearly his demeanor and carriage suggest that he is grieving, that he has emotions which cannot always be concealed behind the facade of professionalism and duty. This climactic scene reveals to what extent Stevens has trapped himself in the role of the perfect butler. It is certain that Stevens could have found a replacement for his duties and attended to his father's needs. He chose not to because he felt more comfortable in the well-defined role as butler rather than the more vulnerable and emotionally laden role as son. He became the perfect butler, invisible, ever dutiful, ever present; but he lost touch with the wellsprings of his own emotional life.

Stevens' relationship with Lord Darlington further illustrates the perils of submerging one's identity in one's profession. Stevens always thought of Lord Darlington as a great man, someone to be admired and respected. In all respects Lord Darlington is the consummate gentleman. He believes that all disputes should be settled fairly as two gentlemen would agree to resolve their differences. He believes the Treaty of Versailles unfairly crushed the German economy and military. No gentleman would have treated another gentleman that way. In Lord Darlington's view, Germany should be allowed to rebuild its economy and expand its military strength as befits a fellow nation, an equal among equals. The problem with Lord Darlington's logic becomes clear when Mr. Lewis, an American congressman, arrives at the conference and suspects the Germans of taking advantage of Lord Darlington's simple-minded principles. On the concluding night of the conference, Lewis attacks Lord Darlington as an "amateur," someone who is out of his depth when it comes to combatting subtle political foes. In fact, before the end of the film, Lord Darlington will contribute to the policy of appeasement that led to World War II. The aggression of the Nazis shatters Lord Darlington's ideals, and he dies a humiliated, lonely man.

Stevens is witness to all these events, and yet he cannot bring himself to admit that his loyalty to Lord Darlington was misplaced and even betrayed. On two occasions he denies even having known or worked for Lord Darlington. In an encounter with a doctor in a small town late in the film, Stevens at first denies having known Lord Darlington, but later he admits that he was Lord Darlington's butler. The doctor finds it hard to believe that Stevens does not hate Lord Darlington. How could one serve such a man and not feel betrayed? Stevens can only reply, "I was his butler. I was there to serve him." The film suggests that the perfect butler, like the perfect gentleman, can become an unwitting accomplice to forces of evil when his emotional life is dominated by narrow rules of duty, propriety, and civility.

Stevens views his journey to Miss Kenton as a means of redeeming what he has lost in the past twenty years. From their first meeting it is clear that since they are both members of the same class, with similar values, their close association should invite a romantic relationship. After all, the same actors, Anthony Hopkins and Emma Thompson, played characters who met and fell in love in *Howards End* (1992), another Merchant/Ivory production. In that film Anthony Hopkins played Henry Wilcox, a man of Lord Darlington's stature. Emma Thompson's character, Margaret Schlegel, awakened Hopkins' character to sensitivity, love, and trust. So it is natural to imagine that Miss Kenton will crack Mr. Stevens' cool facade and reveal the warm-blooded and passionate heart that beats within him.

Despite her numerous attempts to engage Stevens on a social and personal level, Stevens remains inaccessible and insular, a mystery even to himself. The film underscores the lost opportunities, failed hopes, and unrealized love in Stevens' relationship with Miss Kenton. The crucial scene in their relationship occurs when one day Miss Kenton comes upon Stevens asleep in his chair, a book folded over his chest. He retreats immediately to the other side of his desk. She advances and begins to tease him about what he has been reading. He retreats farther into the corner of the room. She pursues him and begins to pry his hand away from the book. Stevens scans her face and her hair. For a moment it seems as if he may touch her or say something about his feelings for her. She is surprised to discover that he has been reading a romance novel. The scene rings with the prospect of intimacy and with Stevens' fear of that intimacy. He complains that she is invading his privacy. The moment passes, and their relationship never sustains this level of intimacy again.

In these and other scenes, the acting of Anthony Hopkins and Emma Thompson is extraordinary. Both received Academy Award nominations as Best Actor and Best Actress for their work in this film, and Hopkins received the award for Best Actor from the Los Angles Film Critics. Hopkins plays his role with a typically understated quality. His tone of voice and the nuances in his pronunciations are perfect for a character who has alienated himself from his emotional life. Thompson is perfect as a dedicated housekeeper who is not afraid to challenge her supervisor. Her face is more animated and her character is livelier and more freely expressive than Stevens'. Watching Hopkins and Thompson is the main pleasure of this film-viewing experience. When they are in a scene together, a special chemistry is evident. Their spirited interplay is reminiscent of the sparring of Tracy and Hepburn in their classic films from the 1940's and 1950's.

The emphasis in this film is on a man whose failed hopes and unrealized dreams can be traced to his self-imposed limits on his emotional life. Other films with a similar theme include *The Age of Innocence* (1993; reviewed in this volume), where the character Newland Archer is unable to free himself from the obligations and rules of his upper-class society and seize an opportunity for fulfillment, and two French films, *Life and Nothing But; la vie et rien d'autre* (1990) and *Un coeur en hiver; A Heart in Winter* (1992), whose main characters are constrained by their inability to declare their feelings to women who love them.

Robert Yahnke

Reviews

Entertainment Weekly. November 5, 1993, p. 48.

The Hollywood Reporter. September 24, 1993, p. 6.

Los Angeles Times. November 5, 1993, p. F1.

New York. XXVI, November 8, 1993, p. 74.

The New York Times. November 5, 1993, p. B1.

The New Yorker. LXIX, November 15, 1993, p. 114.

Newsweek. CXXII, November 8, 1993, p. 78.

Sight and Sound. III, December, 1993, p. 51.

Time. CXLII, November 8, 1993, p. 85.

The Times Literary Supplement. November 12, 1993, p. 21.

Variety. September 24, 1993, p. 4.

The Village Voice. XXXVIII, November 9, 1993, p. 60.

RICH IN LOVE

Production: Richard D. Zanuck and Lili Fini Zanuck for the Zanuck Company; released by Metro-Goldwyn-Mayer
Direction: Bruce Beresford
Screenplay: Alfred Uhry; based on the novel by Josephine Humphreys
Cinematography: Peter James
Editing: Mark Warner
Production design: John Stoddart
Set decoration: John Anderson
Casting: Shari Rhodes
Sound: Hank Garfield, Steve Maslow, and Gregg Landaker
Costume design: Colleen Kelsall
Music: Georges Delerue
MPAA rating: PG-13
Running time: 105 minutes

Principal characters:
Warren Odom	Albert Finney
Helen Odom	Jill Clayburgh
Lucille Odom	Kathryn Erbe
Billy McQueen	Kyle MacLachlan
Vera Delmage	Piper Laurie
Wayne Frobiness	Ethan Hawke
Rae Odom	Suzy Amis
Rhody Poole	Alfre Woodard

American cinema is not especially known for presenting realistic family portraits. Either overly romanticized or utterly dysfunctional, most film families share the same problems and come to the same solutions. Such is not the case for *Rich in Love*, a collaboration between producers Richard and Lili Fini Zanuck, writer Alfred Uhry, and director Bruce Beresford, the team that created Best Picture Oscar winner *Driving Miss Daisy* (1989).

Driving Miss Daisy is a masterpiece of subtlety, a study of character, place, and time. It finely mixes relevant social issues with a gentle and careful relationship between two people. What made *Driving Miss Daisy* such a critical and commercial success was its ability to stay true to character without attempting to tell a larger-than-life tale. *Rich in Love* realizes the same vision, the same notion that the best stories are often the ones that come naturally, from well-drawn characters placed in a certain circumstance. In *Driving Miss Daisy*, the story and plot derives from the simple question of what would happen if an elderly Jewish lady were suddenly forced to make a bond with an elderly black man. *Rich in Love* is based on the premise of what would happen to a normal Southern family if, suddenly and without explanation, the mother walked out. The beauty of good filmmaking is allowing the characters to make the story, instead of the other way around. It is this simple plot device that sets the film in motion, and it is the characters who keep it moving.

The Odom family is an otherwise normal Southern family with a beautiful old South Carolina house perched overlooking one of the state's many lakes. Warren Odom (Albert Finney) is recently retired, and daughter Lucille (Kathryn Erbe) is earning straight A's in high school. All seems well until Lucille arrives home from school one day to a note from her mother, Helen (Jill Clayburgh), saying that she is leaving and not coming back. Very little explanation is given, and it is up to Lucille to break the news to her father. She takes it upon herself to protect and care for him in her mother's absence. Warren refuses to accept his wife's sudden and unexplained departure. After all, he had recognized no signs of unhappiness—he was perfectly content with the marriage. Sure that she will soon return, or at least make contact with her abandoned family, Warren and Lucille sit by the phone, day and night, waiting for word. As weeks pass with no call from Helen, however, they both realize that she is not coming back.

Things become even more complicated when the elder Odom sister, Rae (Suzy Amis), pregnant and newly married, arrives home with her husband, Billy (Kyle MacLachlan). While Rae's arrival is ostensibly to help Lucille and Warren cope with Helen's disappearance, Rae and Billy have their own problems from which they are running. Rae's unintentional pregnancy is making her hostile and bitter, especially toward Billy, whom she now perceives as the enemy. Rae had always been a free spirit, and she resents Billy for taking away her freedom. Lucille continues her new position as family matriarch by attempting to bring Rae and Billy closer together. Amid the turmoil within the Odom house, Billy and Lucille find in each other a soul mate, and Billy confides to Lucille that he made Rae pregnant on purpose to force her to marry him and to avoid losing her. Despite his questionable methods, Lucille recognizes Billy's love for Rae and agrees to help her new friend win Rae back.

Lucille is much better at recognizing other people's problems and solutions that she is at realizing her own. Stuck in a near-permanent state of denial, Lucille has not quite faced the fact that her mother is never returning. In an effort to avoid accepting the reality of the situation, Lucille becomes the mother figure to everyone else in the family, denying her own needs to be mothered and protected herself. She even denies herself the simplest pleasure of being adored by a neighborhood boy (Ethan Hawke). When she finally sees her mother (a mutual friend sets up a meeting), however, Lucille breaks down and allows herself to feel the pain and sadness from which she has tried to protect herself and her family. She has shoved her feelings down so deep that she is only able to reconnect with them when she comes face-to-face with her mother and is able to accept her reasons for leaving.

More than anything, *Rich in Love* is about Lucille's coming-of-age—not in the sexual sense, but in every other sense. Always thought of as the smart one in the family, the seventeen-going-on-forty Lucille has somehow lost her youth long before having to step into her absent mother's shoes. Lucille has spent her life looking through rose-colored glasses by idealizing her mother, admiring her father, and idolizing her sister's reckless abandon. When each of these role models breaks down, Lucille is forced to recognize that life is not perfect and is certainly not what she expected.

Lucille's coming-of-age is also about finding the child in herself and recognizing that, despite her willingness to look out for everyone else, she needs to be cared for as well. In all the emotional rescuing that Lucille performs for her family, she fails to pay attention to her own emotional needs, suppressing all the anger and sadness caused by her mother's leaving. When Helen departs, Lucille runs even further from reality than Warren does.

Veteran screen and stage actor Albert Finney turns in yet another fine performance, fresh off his brilliant showing in *The Playboys* (1992). Displaying his versatility, Finney masters an American Southern accent in *Rich in Love*, making the audience nearly forget that Finney is best known for his classically British role in *Tom Jones* (1963). Kyle MacLachlan, propelled to stardom by the television series *Twin Peaks*, continues his string of strong performances in film. Yet despite the powerhouse acting talent that presides over *Rich in Love*, the film is single-handedly in the grasp of young Kathryn Erbe, who steals the screen with her carefully defended vulnerability. Erbe, making a stunning starring debut in *Rich in Love*, is solid as Lucille. She has no difficulty fitting in with her well-known costars, even overshadowing them at times.

In addition to the strength of the acting, *Rich in Love* boasts strong writing and directing. Writer Alfred Uhry, working from the novel by Josephine Humphreys, emphasizes in *Rich in Love* how deceptive first appearances can be. The characters who seem to be the most lost and confused turn out to be the strongest and most resilient. Such is the case with Warren, the seemingly slow-moving, devoted husband who appears to fall apart when his wife leaves. Yet it is Warren who recovers the quickest and the best. He is able to find not only companionship but also love in local hairdresser Vera Delmage (Piper Laurie).

The relationship between Rae and Billy is also deceptive and is one of the most fascinating elements of *Rich in Love*. Director Beresford avoids all the clichés and formulaic pitfalls that could easily have come with a passionate newlywed couple. Rae and Billy are drawn as two complex individual personalities with honest conflicts. Even as the film ends, the audience is not left with a smoothed-over ending in which everyone lives happily ever after. All that is known is that the characters have traveled to a different place from where they were when the film began.

Catherine R. Springer

Reviews

Chicago Tribune. March 5, 1993, VII, p. 28.
The Christian Science Monitor. March 5, 1993, p. 14.
The Hollywood Reporter. September 28, 1992, p. 5.
Los Angeles Times. March 5, 1993, p. F 6.
The New York Times. March 5, 1993, p. B8.
Variety. September 28, 1992, p. 2.
The Washington Post. March 19, 1993, p. F7.

RISING SUN

Production: Peter Kaufman for Walrus and Associates Ltd.; released by Twentieth Century-Fox
Direction: Philip Kaufman
Screenplay: Philip Kaufman, Michael Crichton, and Michael Backes; based on the novel by Crichton
Cinematography: Michael Chapman
Editing: Stephen A. Rotter and William S. Scharf
Production design: Dean Tavoularis
Art direction: Angelo Graham
Set decoration: Gary Fettis
Casting: Donna Isaacson
Sound: Alan Splet
Costume design: Jacqueline West
Music: Toru Takemitsu
MPAA rating: R
Running time: 129 minutes

> *Principal characters:*
> John Connor . . . . Sean Connery
> Web Smith. . . . . Wesley Snipes
> Tom Graham . . . . Harvey Keitel
> Eddie Sakamura . . . . Cary-Hiroyuki Tagawa
> Bob Richmond . . . . Kevin Anderson
> Yoshida-san. . . . . Mako
> Senator John Morton . . . . Ray Wise
> Ishihara . . . . Stan Egi
> Phillips . . . . Stan Shaw
> Jingo Asakuma . . . . Tia Carrere
> Willy "the Weasel" Wilhelm . . . . Steve Buscemi
> Cheryl Lynn Austin. . . . . Tatjana Patitz
> Greg . . . . Peter Crombie
> Rick. . . . . Sam Lloyd
> Julia. . . . . Alexandra Powers

In an interview, it was observed that each of director Philip Kaufman's films features an invasion or incursion. For example, both *The Right Stuff* (1983) and *Henry and June* (1990) tested the characters by placing them in what was for them an untried, unknown setting, while *Invasion of the Body Snatchers* (1978) brought an unknown entity into a setting that the characters knew well. *Rising Sun* can be read allegorically and stylistically to mean a variety of things. It is clearly, however, a story of invasion, even collision: in Kaufman's terms, the collision of cultural and personal codes.

In *Rising Sun*, Los Angeles police officer Web Smith (Wesley Snipes) has been assigned to investigate the murder of a "professional blonde," Cheryl Lynn Austin (Tatjana Patitz), found dead on the boardroom table during a gala reception celebrating the opening of the fifty-three-story Nakamoto Building. Also assigned to the case (under mysterious circumstances) is John Connor (Sean Connery), here a legendary figure for his knowledge of and relationships with the Japanese. Together Smith and Connor represent two different approaches to police work and to life—high-energy physicality (Smith) versus philosophical, studied maneuvering (Connor). Not unlike Watson to Sherlock Holmes, however, Smith defers to Connor's expertise. Forming an American version of the Japanese *senpai* (older, wise leader) and *kohai* (young follower), this unlikely pair must determine who murdered the young beauty.

Perhaps the best place to begin analyzing this complex film is with the story itself. As a mystery, *Rising Sun* falls flat. The killer's identity is relatively obvious long before it is revealed in the film. Furthermore, anyone unsure of the murderer's identity and therefore trying to unravel the clues would quickly become lost in the mountain of minutiae that remains of the much larger Michael Crichton novel on which the film is based. That is not to say, however, that the film is uninteresting. Scattered throughout the film are memorable performances and images—even if they do add up to little in the end.

When the film opens, for example, one of the villains, Eddie Sakamura (Cary-Hiroyuki Tagawa), is singing in a karaoke bar. Before the audience is aware of his presence, however, it is aware of the Western-genre footage playing behind the "give me land, lots of land" refrain that serves as the film's opening song. In a series of interviews given at the time of the film's release, director Kaufman identified these scenes as homages to Japanese director Akira Kurosawa: The footage of the cowboy and the dog recalls *Yojimbo* (1961); a girl on horseback, whom Kaufman has dressed exactly like the woman in the Kurosawa film, recalls *The Hidden Fortress* (1958). While such little-known facts are interesting filmic lore, the scenes and their references have a broader significance. The irony of a Japanese gangster singing "give me land, lots of land" even as he acquires more of this country does not escape Kaufman. Further, the collision of East and West is overt here, as the Japanese gangster sings the Western theme song. Finally, this scene serves as a lesson in illusion and reality, teaching the audience that what it sees may not be what it thinks it sees. For example, the opening Western scenes are startling, not what one expects. Then "reality" is revealed: a film within a film. This tension between what the audience and characters see and what is indeed the truth proves to be one of the key effects of the film.

Another well-crafted scene is one in which Austin and Sakamura dress for the gala opening. As Sakamura menaces in the distance, Austin applies makeup to her neck and gazes at the television screen in the foreground. A hint of a smile crosses her face. On the television, a senator discusses an upcoming vote on the acquisition of a software corporation by the Japanese. This scene is typical of Kaufman; on several occasions, the director has commented on his placing everything relevant to a scene within the frame at any given moment. This scene reveals the motive, the opportunity, and the method of the upcoming murder. Kaufman's work is about control, and this scene is an excellent example of how he builds a scene and a film.

Additionally, Sean Connery's performance in *Rising Sun* is seamless. In fact, Michael Crichton had Connery in mind even as he wrote the character of John Connor, as hinted by the name and confirmed in various interviews given at the time of the film's release. From his rise to stardom in the action genre as James Bond, Connery has evolved slowly into the philosopher-patriarch he plays here. Citing obscure Asian proverbs (such as "If you sit by a river long enough, you'll see the body of your enemy float by") and sporting a tailor-made Armani suit, Connor/Connery serves more as icon than as hero. If *Rising Sun* is indeed the story of a heroic individual confronting an alien social order, then Connor/Connery is not the center of the tale. If the lesson of the film is learning to trust other people beyond the standard cultural perceptions, then truly Connor/Connery becomes spiritual guide, perhaps even healer, to Smith. Yet, in true Connery style, he also is on the Nakamoto payroll, playing golf often with the leader of the Japanese corporation and getting paid for explaining American ways. Once again Kaufman juxtaposes illusion and reality. Connor is neither as good nor as bad as he might appear initially. Throughout, Connery remains cool, stylish, interesting to watch.

On the other hand, Wesley Snipes appears out of place and uncomfortable throughout the film. All of his personal power and presence is restrained in this film, in which he plays a confused follower. As with Connery's character, Snipes's Web Smith is neither all good nor all bad. He has a lovely child and a failed marriage. He is a "good" officer, but he has been accused of wrongdoing on at least one occasion. In fact, Kaufman revised the character of Smith to make him even a larger part of the overall themes. Specifically, in Crichton's novel, the Smith character was white; here Smith is African American. While this change adds complexity to the idea of insider-outsider for each character, it also leads to a scene that has created much controversy. In this scene, Smith enters an African American neighborhood to ask the help of gathered young people in evading their Japanese pursuers. Although audiences and critics believed that this scene trivialized the current tension between the races, Kaufman intended it as an accurate reflection of contemporary Los Angeles. In a larger sense, action hero Snipes is really wasted in a role in which his main attributes are confused, fallen, lost.

Minor characters, however, provide much of the entertainment value of this film. Jingo Asakuma (Tia Carrere) is the media consultant/computer whiz who—with the help of Industrial Light and Magic—unravels the high-tech portion of the mystery. Although she appears in only a few scenes, Carrere unites the tensions in the film: East versus West, surface versus interior, illusion versus reality. In one key (although heavy-handed) scene, Jingo Asakuma (self-described as half-Japanese, half-African American) demonstrates how easily video images can be manipulated. In so doing, she juxtaposes the heads of Connor and Smith within their video images. For Kaufman, the issues are—on at least some levels—just that easy. Very little separates races, ages, cultures, mind-sets.

Perhaps more fun, however, is Eddie Sakamura, played by Tagawa with carefree venom. Sakamura is a perfectly happy, perfectly wicked character, and Tagawa captures that dichotomy exactly. Much of what this character does is clearly reprehensible; yet he is oddly likable. He is dangerous, with a lightning-quick temper and a penchant for abuse. Nevertheless, it is hard not to appreciate his brand of venom. He is honestly evil, honestly corrupt. Perhaps in Sakamura, illusion and reality are one. For example, in a feat of old-style unenlightened hedonism, Sakamura eats sushi off the abdomen of a naked woman. Audience members and critics alike have voiced considerable concern over these images that objectify women. Yet when Sakamura is unjustly accused of more criminal misdeeds, audience members may find themselves forgiving him his nasty predilections. After all, the story offers many more treacherous, less likable villains.

Nevertheless, for all of *Rising Sun*'s emphasis on the art of filmmaking, the reality of race relations, and the nature of reality in general, it is a film that goes nowhere. For all of its aspirations, it is finally rather dull. The Japanese, the film tells viewers, consider Americans stupid and dishonest, and by film's end, *Rising Sun* has shown Americans to be just that. Billed as a high-tech erotic mystery, *Rising Sun* casually blasts Asians, African Americans, Americans, and women. It is a slick, attractive motion picture, filmed by Michael Chapman, who was nominated for an Academy Award for 1980's *Raging Bull*, and designed by Dean Tavoularis, who won an Academy Award for 1974's *The Godfather: Part II*. And by year's end the film had grossed $98 million worldwide. Still, viewers may be more disappointed than entertained or enlightened by *Rising Sun*.

Roberta F. Green

Reviews
Boston Globe. July 30, 1993, p. 25.
Chicago Tribune. July 30, 1993, Tempo Section, p. 4.
The Christian Science Monitor. July 30, 1993, p. 13.
Entertainment Weekly. July 30, 1993, p. 38.
Films in Review. XLIV, September, 1993, p. 340.
The Hollywood Reporter. July 26, 1993, p. 7.
Los Angeles Times. July 30, 1993, p. F1.
The New York Times. July 30, 1993, p. B1.
Newsweek. CXXII, August 2, 1993, p. 54.
Sight and Sound. III, October, 1993, p. 12.
Time. CXLII, August 2, 1993, p. 56.
Variety. August 2, 1993, p. 43.
The Washington Post. July 30, 1993, p. 38.

ROOKIE OF THE YEAR

Production: Robert Harper; released by Twentieth Century-Fox
Direction: Daniel Stern
Screenplay: Sam Harper
Cinematography: Jack N. Green
Editing: Donn Cambern and Raja Gosnell
Production design: Steven Jordan
Art direction: William Arnold
Set decoration: Leslie Bloom
Casting: Linda Lowy
Special effects coordination: Dieter Sturm
Sound: Scott Smith
Costume design: Jay Hurley
Music: Bill Conti
MPAA rating: PG
Running time: 105 minutes

> *Principal characters:*
> Henry Rowengartner .... Thomas Ian Nicholas
> Chet Steadman .... Gary Busey
> Larry Fisher .... Dan Hedaya
> Mary Rowengartner .... Amy Morton
> Jack Bradfield....................... Bruce Altman
> Bob Carson......................... Eddie Bracken
> Clark .... Robert Gorman
> George......................... Patrick LaBrecque
> Martinella .... Albert Hall
> Brickma............................. Daniel Stern

Just short of a home run, *Rookie of the Year* is a pint-sized film about a big-time fantasy. The fertile premise—what happens if a little guy makes it to the big leagues— is the dream of every baseball fan, regardless of age. Even those who are not sports enthusiasts will find this tale of a dream come true to be a fun and exciting experience. The fine mix of humor, character, and plot make this film wholesome, family fun.

Henry Rowengartner (Thomas Ian Nicholas) is a Little League baseball player whose enthusiasm for the game far surpasses his ability. On the field he is a disaster— giving new meaning to the word "klutz." Once, for example, while playing outfield, he accidentally throws the ball over the fence, giving the opposing team a run. At school, he is continually teased and harassed for his on-field mistakes. Nevertheless, his passion endures.

Then a fortuitous accident occurs. Trying to impress a girl, Henry pursues a pop fly in the schoolyard. As he runs toward the ball, however, he slips and is propelled into the air; he lands on his side with a sickening thud, and his pitching arm is broken. Four months later, when the cast is removed, the doctor is intrigued by the strange way Henry's tendons have healed: They are tighter than normal. Further investigation is curtailed when Henry accidentally slaps the doctor in the face. His arm seems to be out of control.

To celebrate the removal of Henry's cast, his ever-supportive single mother, Mary (Amy Morton), gives him and two friends tickets to a Chicago Cubs game. There, a fly ball comes their way, landing nearby. Henry rockets the ball back to the field at unearthly speed, catching the attention of everyone in the stadium. "Who threw that?" echoes through the bleachers. Within no time, the struggling Cubs, who are in dire need of a "miracle," ask Henry to sign on as their star pitcher. "I gotta ask my mom," he replies. Within no time, the contracts are signed and he is a media sensation. He and his beloved Cubs are on the way to the pennant. Of course, things never go so smoothly.

Screenwriter Sam Harper has laced the script with abundant conflict and humor, turning a solid premise into a great story. From the beginning, it is questionable whether Henry can parlay his superhuman arm into proficient pitching—he lacks any kind of control. To solve this problem, aging Cubs pitcher Chet Steadman (Gary Busey), once the team's shining star, is enlisted as Henry's mentor. Although Steadman initially refuses to "play wet nurse" to a kid who might eventually take his job, he is given no choice. Also, his mother's new boyfriend, Jack (Bruce Altman), who has contrived to become Henry's manager, is an ever-present thorn in Henry's side. Henry resents Jack's trying to take his father's place.

Despite the glitz and glamour of being a professional ballplayer, Henry discovers a number of drawbacks. He no longer has time for his friends or schoolwork. He is constantly on the road, always thinking about the game. As the season continues and these conflicts play out, they eventually become intertwined. Steadman discovers his value as a mentor and not only befriends Henry but also develops a romantic interest in his mother. Jealous, Jack schemes with self-serving Chicago Cubs executive Larry "Fish" Fisher (Dan Hedaya) to sell Henry to the New York Yankees and have Steadman released from the team. Luckily, the flighty team owner (Eddie Bracken) foils their plan before the damage is done.

Unfortunately, it has all been too much for Henry. After almost losing his friends for good, Henry takes a day off. As a result, he realizes the advantages of being a kid and decides to retire, announcing that he will play one last game—the one that can send his beloved Cubs to the World Series.

For this important game, the management decides to use the more experienced Steadman as starting pitcher. Steadman gives it all he has, but it is not enough. When he injures his arm yet again, he knows his ball-playing days are over. Henry is called into the game in the top of the ninth. On his way to the mound, Henry once again trips and is propelled into the air. This time his arm does not break, but the fall does loosen his tendons to their natural state—thus the "gift" is gone. While everyone on the team panics, Henry devises a plan. With childlike trickery and a funny pitch his mother taught him, Henry wins the game and becomes a hero. Months later, Henry is once again involved in Little League. He is now a skillful player, however, thanks to Steadman—his new coach and his mother's new boyfriend.

Rookie of the Year is a heartwarming, emotional film much in the vein of *The Karate Kid* (1984). Although the film offers both action and comedy, it is the characters and their relationships that actually drive the story, not the game. Particularly touching is Henry's relationship with his ever-supportive, modern, working mother. Like many single mothers, she believes that her son needs a father. Although Chet Steadman eventually fits the bill, she and Henry discover just how much they actually give each other.

Other relationships, though less important, play a big part in the story's success. Henry effects a change in Steadman, who starts off as bitter and foreboding but eventually learns that there is more to life than being a stellar ballplayer. In turn, Henry learns a similar lesson from his friends. Through them he realizes what he is missing by growing up too soon.

Veteran actor Daniel Stern—perhaps best known for his roles in *City Slickers* (1991) and *Home Alone* (1990)—makes his feature-film directorial debut with *Rookie of the Year*. Judging from their performances, one can see that he chose his cast carefully. Thomas Ian Nicholas is fun-loving and likable in his comic turn as the klutzy Henry. Amy Morton plays Henry's 1990's mom with 1950's warmth and support. Even Stern's few moments before the camera as the Cubs' goofy pitching coach, so inept he rarely finds his way onto the field, are well played. Though his character does sometimes seem out of place, he provides added comic relief.

Highest marks, however, go to the always reliable Gary Busey, who brings particular depth to his role as Chet Steadman, the aging pitcher struggling to remain in the spotlight. His minor facial twitches, the fire in his eyes, and his fading smile convey his inner turmoil.

Stern also did a wonderful job choosing his behind-the-camera talent. Cinematographer Jack Green, with his quick close-ups and low, gliding camera shots, creates a real sense of ballpark wonderment. The viewer experiences how it feels to be a little boy playing on a field with grown-ups. Music master Bill Conti, with his emotional score, draws the audience even closer to the material.

Rookie of the Year boasts a talented cast and crew and an intriguing premise. The action is fast-paced, with little time for diversionary filler. Thus this entertaining story should have broad appeal. It is good, plain fun, with much to recommend it.

Jonathan David

Reviews

Chicago Tribune. July 7, 1993, V, p. 1.
The Hollywood Reporter. June 28, 1993, p. 7.
Los Angeles Times. July 7, 1993, p. F1.
The New York Times. July 7, 1993, p. B3.
Sports Illustrated. LXXIX, July 26, 1993, p. 10.

Time. CXLII, July 19, 1993, p. 64.
USA Today. July 7, 1993, p. D5.
Variety. June 29, 1993, p. 2.
Video Review. XV, Winter, 1994, p. 72.
The Wall Street Journal. July 15, 1993, p. A10.
The Washington Post. July 7, 1993, p. C7.

RUBY IN PARADISE

Production: Sam Gowan and Peter Wentworth for Full Crew/Say Yeah, in
   association with Longstreet Prods.; released by October Films
Direction: Victor Nuñez
Screenplay: Victor Nuñez
Cinematography: Alex Vlacos
Editing: Victor Nuñez
Production design: John Iacovelli
Art Direction: Burton Rencher
Casting: Judy Courtney
Sound design: Pete Winter
Costume design: Marilyn Wall-Asse
Music: Charles Engstrom
MPAA rating: no listing
Running time: 115 minutes

> *Principal characters:*
> Ruby Lee Gissing . . . . Ashley Judd
> Mike McCaslin . . . . Todd Field
> Ricky Chambers . . . . Bentley Mitchum
> Rochelle Bridges . . . . Allison Dean
> Mildred Chambers . . . . Dorothy Lyman
> Debrah Ann . . . . Betsy Dowds
> Persefina . . . . Felicia Hernandez
> Indian Singer . . . . Divya Satia
> Wanda . . . . Bobby Barnes

Ruby in Paradise is a dignified, entertaining, and reflective film, widely praised by
critics and enjoyed by audiences. Both a commentary on contemporary American
society and an unassuming character study of a young woman's inner struggle to find
herself, it is the story of Ruby Lee Gissing (Ashley Judd), who leaves the oppressive
world of the mountains of Tennessee to start a new life in Panama City, Florida, the
"Redneck Riviera." She quickly lands a job in a garish tourist gift shop owned by
Mildred Chambers (Dorothy Lyman) and her oafish son, Ricky (Bentley Mitchum).
As she tries to assert herself for the first time in her life, Ruby struggles between a
long-held pattern of deferring to men and an inner need to make her own way in the
world.

   After initial difficulty the filmmakers experienced in raising money for this film
because it was not considered "hip" enough, the film achieved its success at the famed
Sundance Film Festival in 1993, earning the Festival's Grand Prize. Since then, it has
earned critical raves and a substantial amount of money (compared to its minuscule
budget).

Ruby in Paradise is deserving on all counts. It is a wise and contemplative film, full of rich imagery and symbolism, thoughtful dialogue, and textured performances. It belongs in a small category of films that touch the heart and appeal to the intellect, films characteristic of such filmmakers as Claude Chabrol or François Truffaut. It is uniquely American in tone, however, similar to *Tender Mercies* (1983), *Alice Doesn't Live Here Anymore* (1974), or *Rambling Rose* (1991). *Ruby in Paradise* will inevitably be compared to *Mississippi Masala* (1992), because of its story about real people who do not fit the stereotype of redneck Southerners and because both films share an unpretentious intelligence and an interesting glimpse of East Indian women in America: In *Ruby in Paradise*, the recurring role of an Indian woman who sings as she does her menial chores catches Ruby's imagination.

Furthermore, the film perfectly captures the different ways some men try to seize power without sharing it—a perfect contrast to the way the women in this film share power and a sad commentary on the ultimate weakness of the contemporary American male.

Several situations in the film illustrate how contemporary men feel a sense of entitlement over women. Ricky is physically and sexually abusive, feeling entitled to Ruby simply because he is attractive and is the son of Ruby's employer. Then Ruby meets the gentle Mike McCaslin (Todd Field), who is oppressive in a less threatening but more insidious way. When Mike and Ruby are in a motion-picture theater, he decides that he does not like the film and wants to leave, and he expects her to go without question. When Ruby loses her job and runs out of money, Mike happily says that she can move in with him and let him pay for everything, to which she replies, with a sarcastic weariness, "Every girl's dream." She writes in her journal, "Everybody's fantasy: tender unions, precious ties. It's the woman who pays most for security, for belonging. Lord help us if we don't fit the mold."

Writer/director Victor Nuñez ensures that the audience sees women at varying points along the continuum of personal growth. The inner struggle is represented by Ruby. Mrs. Chambers is a bit farther along on the continuum; she is a mature, savvy divorced woman who owns her own business. At a point earlier on the continuum is Ruby's youthful neighbor, Debrah Ann (Betsy Dowds), who lives a pathetic life with two men who clearly abuse and exploit her. Nuñez clearly intends to have Debrah Ann represent the women Ruby used to be, and Mrs. Chambers represents at least a part of who she hopes to become.

Nuñez is thoughtful and liberal with his use of symbolism. He has clearly learned from some of the great film masters, such as Federico Fellini, to respect the intelligence of his audience and to use symbols as a guide to the emotional core and thematic content of the film. Nuñez chose Panama City because it is, in his words, "the perfect metaphor for America at the end of the century: a culture that seems for better or worse, intentionally or not, to be choosing life without a past." The "life without a past" is represented in the character of Ruby, who has chosen to forsake her oppressive world for a seemingly freer one. At the beginning of the film, which takes place in autumn, and at the end, in spring, a man can be seen combing the beach with a metal detector, searching for buried jewels or items of value. This represents the individual constantly searching for something better. Nuñez' inclusion of this character in the end is a significant comment on the consistency of Ruby's desire to continue searching for a better life, and of a general human need to keep hoping that the answers to life's questions lie just below the surface, waiting to be discovered.

The change in Ruby is underscored by the change from fall to winter to spring. Another subtle reminder of spring is in the character of Persefina (Felicia Hernandez), a woman with whom Ruby works briefly in a laundry after she loses her gift-shop job. Persefina appears to be symbolic of the goddess Persephone, who was abducted by Pluto to be goddess of the underworld, but was allowed to return to Earth once a year in spring. Persephone is known as the personification of spring, and perhaps not coincidentally, Nuñez is offering some hope to Ruby in the character of this strong woman working in the bowels of a laundry. There is an abundance of other symbolic representations, from Mike's ownership of a nursery and his knowledge about plants, which brings to mind the Garden of Eden, to a television evangelist who lectures, "Obey and be loved. Turn away and be damned for all eternity," as Mike and Ruby innocently watch.

Nuñez was reared in Florida and has also situated his other films in his native state. He made the films *Gal Young 'un* (1979) and *A Circle in the Fire* (1977), the first based on a story by Marjorie Kinnan Rawlings, and the latter on a Flannery O'Connor short story. He clearly is a director who knows the value of allowing the characters to guide the story and so lets his camera linger in close-ups that penetrate their inner thoughts. He retains an understated simplicity that is refreshing, even in a brief sex scene which is realistic without being pornographic and looks nothing like the silly, overblown fantasies presented in such films as *Basic Instinct* (1992).

The cast is superb. Dorothy Lyman is Mrs. Chambers, playing a subtle and adult variation on the "tough-but-vulnerable" roles she has played, mostly on television, for years. Lyman is a two-time Emmy winner for television's *All My Children* and is a respected actress and director. Her performance is true and delicate, finding the tenderness in the character of a saleswoman and shopkeeper who has dreadful taste, but a solid heart.

As Mike McCaslin, Ruby's intense boyfriend, Todd Field creates a complex man who simply wants Ruby to love him. Ruby says about him that "Mike is like that blue sweater I had when I was thirteen. I wanted to wear it all the time, even when I was hot." Field is so likable that the description fits the actor as well as the character. Also adding well-crafted performances are Bentley Mitchum as Ricky and Betsy Dowds as Debrah Ann.

The film's star, in all senses, however, is Ashley Judd. Judd, the younger sister of country music star Wynonna Judd, is thoughtful, wise, and beautiful in this role. She retains a vivid inner life as the camera closes in on her, and her gentle Southern drawl perfectly captures the spirit of a young woman determined to rebuild herself from a painful past. The film does not show or describe much of what happened to Ruby to cause her flight into introspective self-determination. The audience, however, does not need to know details, because Judd so clearly wears her character's pain and turmoil: "There's more to life than working in Uncle Jack's store and taking crap from men. I got out of Manning without getting pregnant or beat up. That's something." That is all she needs to say. The rest of the story is etched in her remarkable performance and in this remarkable little film.

Kirby Tepper

Reviews
Artforum. XXXII, October, 1993, p. 62.
Chicago Tribune. November 26, 1993, VII, p. 29.
Cosmopolitan. CCXV, October, 1993, p. 26.
The Hollywood Reporter. February 1, 1993, p. 12.
Interview. XXIII, August, 1993, p. 64.
Los Angeles Times. October 15, 1993, p. F14.
The New York Times. October 6, 1993, The Living Arts, p. B3.
The New Republic. CCIX, November 1, 1993, p. 26.
Sight and Sound. III, December, 1993, p. 52.
Variety. February 2, 1993, p. 2.
The Washington Post. November 6, 1993, p. D2.

THE SAINT OF FORT WASHINGTON

Production: David V. Picker and Nessa Hyams, in association with Carrie
    Productions; released by Warner Bros.
Direction: Tim Hunter
Screenplay: Lyle Kessler
Cinematography: Frederick Elmes
Editing: Howard Smith
Production design: Stuart Wurtzel
Art direction: Steve Saklad
Set decoration: Debra Schutt
Casting: Nessa Hyams
Sound: Bill Daly
Makeup: Diane Hammond
Costume design: Claudia Brown
Music: James Newton Howard
MPAA rating: R
Running time: 108 minutes

        Principal characters:
           Jerry . . . . Danny Glover
           Matthew . . . . Matt Dillon
           Rosario . . . . Rick Aviles
           Tamsen . . . . Nina Siemaszko
           Little Leroy . . . . Ving Rhames
           Spits . . . . Joe Seneca

    Starring Danny Glover and Matt Dillon, this tragic story centers on the plight of the
homeless in 1990's New York City. In almost documentary fashion *The Saint of Fort
Washington* begins by focusing on a run-down New York neighborhood in which a
tenement building is about to be demolished. The first interior shot is of Matthew
(Dillon) in bed listening to his portable cassette player. A man is heard knocking on
the doors of this condemned building, warning people that they have five minutes left
to vacate. Matthew does not hear the announcement, so wrapped up is he in his own
world. The next series of shots shows the building being wrecked, bricks crumbling,
the demolition equipment gouging into walls and digging deep into the heart of the
tenement. For a split second it is not clear whether Matthew is still inside the building.
Then he appears walking out onto the street with several other evicted residents.
    This opening sequence establishes the film's greatest strength: its setting. Striving
for authenticity, the filmmakers shot much of the film on location, including such
diverse sites as the Fort Washington Armory, the Emergency Assistance Unit in
Chinatown, and Potter's Field on Hart Island. Thus, they ground the viewer in the
environment of the homeless, portraying the world as the homeless see it. Better than

the plot, the dialogue, or the acting, this scene not only undergirds the integrity of the film but also emphasizes Matthew's tragedy: Extremely isolated, he finds it difficult to communicate with others. Therefore, he takes refuge in his music.

Matthew is next seen in an unidentified government office, seeking his four-hundred-dollar-check. The clerk tells him that it has been sent to the address of the tenement—which has been demolished. When Matthew explains that the building no longer exists, the clerk replies that without an address another check cannot be issued. She says his landlord must contact her office. He repeats that he has no landlord, the building no longer exists. When she repeats the rules, he gives up, leaving the office frustrated and saying he is owed four hundred dollars.

The only alternative Matthew has is to sleep in the shelter at Fort Washington in the Bronx. Outside the facility Matthew spots Jerry (Danny Glover) rubbing his knee. Matthew takes out his camera and snaps a picture of Jerry, who is angered by what he considers a violation of his privacy. When he tries to grab the camera, Matthew holds on, showing Jerry that the camera has no film. Why take pictures without film? a curious Jerry asks. "I'm a photographer," Matthew announces, without any further explanation. Inside the shelter Matthew and Jerry find themselves side by side preparing for bed. Matthew offers Jerry a cigarette, and Jerry offers Matthew advice about protecting his valuables. The armory is a dangerous place, terrorized by the likes of the hulking Little Leroy (Ving Rhames), who steals anything that is valuable.

Frightened by the shelter, Matthew tries to go home. A neighbor tells him, however, that his mother has left for Florida. Because she changed the locks on the door, he cannot get into her apartment. So he is forced back into the world of the homeless, encountering Jerry again, who has warmed to Matthew's gentleness and generosity. Jerry quickly formulates a plan in which he and Matthew will wash windshields on the streets of Manhattan and pool their proceeds so that in a couple of months they can have enough for a deposit on a cheap apartment. A friend of Jerry's has promised to supply him with produce to sell once he and Matthew have shown they are settled.

It is only at this point that the backgrounds of Matthew and Jerry are revealed. Up to now Matthew and Jerry are intriguing characters—Matthew because of his fragility and warmheartedness; Jerry because of his voluble, upbeat manner. Their personalities rise above their squalid circumstances, but they are not sentimentalized because not much is known about them; they have to be taken as is, for what the film can show about them in their gestures and facial expressions. Both Dillon and Glover are masters at allowing the camera to simply wash over their faces, registering their pain and anxiety, their wonder and delight at forming a new friendship.

The difficulty with *The Saint of Fort Washington* arises at just this point. When Jerry explains that he has lost his family and produce business because of his spendthrift partner, and when Matthew explains that he has been institutionalized for schizophrenia, the film loses most of its energy and interest. It is not that the stories are not credible, but merely banal. They are meant to be representative, no doubt, of the countless similar stories the homeless could tell. What these two have to say, however, is not nearly as interesting as how they behave. Watching them is fascinating; listening to them—especially because the script sentimentalizes them—is tedious. What they say is true but trite: The homeless, too, are human beings.

The rest of the film is all too predictable. The cheerful Jerry has prodded a reluctant Matthew to believe in his dream of salvation. He says the voices Matthew hears do not necessarily mean he is schizophrenic. Saints have always heard voices, Jerry observes, citing both Joan of Arc and Moses. People who have heard voices have changed the world, Jerry exclaims. He buys Matthew film for his camera and later learns that one of Matthew's photographs appeared in a national magazine before his hospitalization. He sews a bag for the dollars they earn washing windows and ties it around Matthew's waist—an obvious sign of trust and affection. Yet this seems a stupid thing to do, since Matthew has shown himself to be gullible and intensely frightened by bullies on the street and at the shelter.

When Jerry defends Matthew from an attack by Little Leroy, breaking Little Leroy's wrist, they have to flee the shelter. Settling in Jerry's old produce van, Jerry discovers that Matthew has wondrous powers in his hands: Jerry has run out of painkillers for his shrapnel wound from Vietnam, and Matthew miraculously massages the pain away. Unfortunately, the van is eventually towed away.

Jerry's friend Rosario (Rick Aviles) takes them in, and Matthew is welcomed by Rosario's girlfriend, Tamsen (Nina Siemaszko), and Spits (Joe Seneca), whose fingers are crippled from arthritis. Soon Matthew is massaging Spits's hands and relieving his pain. By this point, the atmosphere of the film is cloying. It is not helped by melodramatic episodes—such as Tamsen's miscarriage, brought on by her fall down a staircase. In his grief, Rosario tries to continue his work washing windshields, but he is enraged when a driver yells at him not to touch his car and says he should get a job. Rosario bashes the car windows with superhuman strength, not merely cracking them but actually crashing through them—the most embarrassing and improbable scene in the film.

Such scenes suggest that most of the homeless face overwhelming odds and that Jerry's dream of reestablishing himself is just that—a fantasy. The point is made, however, with a series of clichés that rob the film of the authentic quality it established in its opening frames. There can be no happy ending. Caught on the street during a cold wave, Jerry and Matthew are forced by the police into a van sending them to Fort Washington. While Jerry resists and is beaten by an officer, Matthew is hustled into the van. Inevitably, he has a final confrontation with Little Leroy, who stabs him to death. Jerry, who has managed to escape, arrives too late to save his friend. In a coda, Jerry appears at Potter's Field, mourning over Matthew and placing on his wooden casket the developed photographs that Matthew never had a chance to see. Despite the authentic locations and good performances by Glover and Dillon, *The Saint of Fort Washington* was less than successful.

Carl Rollyson

Reviews

Boston Globe. January 7, 1994, p. 71.

Film Quarterly. XLVII, Fall, 1993, p. 8.

The Hollywood Reporter. September 13, 1993, p. 7.

Interview. XXIII, November, 1993, p. 50.

Los Angeles Times. November 17, 1993, p. F1.

The Nation. December 13, 1993, p. 744.

The New York Times. November 17, 1993, p. B1.

San Francisco Chronicle. January 7, 1994, p. D3.

Variety. September 13, 1993, p. 12.

SCHINDLER'S LIST

Production: Steven Spielberg (AA), Gerald R. Molen (AA), and Branko Lustig
   (AA) for Amblin Entertainment; released by Universal Pictures
Direction: Steven Spielberg (AA)
Screenplay: Steven Zaillian (AA); based on the novel by Thomas Keneally
Cinematography: Janusz Kaminski (AA)
Editing: Michael Kahn (AA)
Production design: Allan Starski (AA)
Art direction: Ewa Skoczkowska, Maciej Walczak, Ewa Tarnowska, Ryszard
   Melliwa, and Grzegorz Piatkowski
Set decoration: Ewa Braun (AA)
Casting: Lucky Englander, Fritz Fleischhacker, Magdalena Szwarcbart, Tova
   Cypin, Liat Meiron, and Juliet Taylor
Sound: Ronald Judkins, Andy Nelson, Steve Pederson, and Scott Millan
Makeup: Christina Smith, Matthew Mungle, and Judith A. Cory
Costume design: Anna Biedrzycka-Sheppard
Violin solos: Itzhak Perlman
Music: John Williams (AA)
MPAA rating: R
Running time: 195 minutes

   Principal characters:
   Oskar Schindler .... Liam Neeson
   Itzhak Stern.......................... Ben Kingsley
   Amon Goeth .... Ralph Fiennes
   Emilie Schindler.................... Caroline Goodall
   Poldek Pfefferberg .... Jonathan Sagalle
   Helen Hirsch....................... Embeth Davidtz
   Victoria Klonowska .... Malgoscha Gebel
   Wilek Chilowicz...................... Shmulik Levy
   Marcel Goldberg....................... Mark Ivanir

   Steven Spielberg astonished the film industry twice in 1993, first with the predictable success of *Jurassic Park*, which was setting records by summer's end, and then
with *Schindler's List*, released at year's end, which surprised and disarmed the critics.
Jurassic Park was a typical Spielberg project—*Jaws* with teeth, and, most important
by industry standards, with legs—a monster movie with cute kids and a diluted moral
about human presumption and dangerously experimental science, but mainly a summer toy made interesting by special effects rather than by human potential.
   Schindler's List, on the other hand, was something else again, a meditation upon
the plight of the Jews during the Third Reich, a moral study of the Holocaust and the
courageous behavior of a war-profiteering Nazi industrialist who discovers, in the

process of making money, that he has a heart and a conscience. The screenplay was based upon the book by the Australian writer Thomas Keneally, which won the coveted Booker Prize in Great Britain in 1982. The screenplay was adapted by Steven Zaillian, whose own film, *Searching for Bobby Fischer*, has earned a place on several critics' "Ten Best" lists for 1993.

The audience is first introduced to Oskar Schindler, played with ambiguous perfection by Liam Neeson, as a glad-handing flamboyant businessman in Poland. Schindler courts the influence and cooperation of SS Commandant Amon Goeth—a sadistic, Nazi brute in charge of the Plaszow concentration camp—played by Ralph Fiennes, a gifted British actor generally unknown to American audiences. At first, Schindler appears to be merely an immoral entrepreneur, a supersalesman who takes over a confiscated enamelware factory in Krakow, eager to make quick millions by exploiting unpaid Jewish workers. He deals in blackmarket contraband to procure appropriate bribes to put the local SS staff in his pocket, always ready to bluff by claiming that he has "friends in high places." Although he is a hedonist and a womanizer, Schindler is a moral paradigm compared to Goeth, who kills Jews for sport, picking off women and children from his bedroom balcony.

Schindler understands, however, that he desperately needs an efficient work force, and his factory becomes a safe haven for his Jewish workers. That is their main inducement for cooperating: Schindler gives them his word that they will be protected as skilled workers. Yet from the start Schindler hires workers who are not especially skilled—an old man with one arm, a professor of literature whom the anti-intellectual Nazis would consider "worthless," and a rabbi. His hiring practices are influenced by his accountant and plant manager, Itzhak Stern (Ben Kingsley), who is uncommonly shrewd and brave. While Stern is making money for Schindler, Schindler is making deals with the Nazis. Together, they are an unbeatable combination. When he strikes his initial bargain with Stern, Schindler remarks, "My father used to say you need three things in life: A good doctor, a forgiving priest, and a clever accountant."

In order to protect his workers from the whimsical and random brutality of Goeth and his subordinates, Schindler builds and operates his own subcamp, separate from the Plaszow forced labor camp. This workable arrangement is threatened in 1944, however, when the Nazis order the closing of Plaszow and its subcamps as part of the "Final Solution." Schindler's workers are to be conveyed to various extermination camps, such as Auschwitz.

To answer this challenge, Schindler convinces Goeth that he should be able to move his factory to Brinnlitz, a town on the Polish border with Czechoslovakia, taking with him a list of "essential" Jewish workers. Hence, the "list" of the title, typed up by Itzhak Stern, of 800 men and 300 women and children, 1,100 names in all. At the end of the film a subtitle informs the audience that by the end of the war, only 4,000 Jews were still alive in Poland. By contrast, the descendants of the "Schindlerjuden" (Schindler Jews) now number 6,000.

News reaches Schindler on May 7, 1945, that Germany has surrendered. Schindler knows he must escape before the Soviet army arrives to liberate Brinnlitz. Before he leaves, and after he persuades the remaining German soldiers that it is not their "duty" to exterminate all the Jewish factory workers, the workers fashion a ring from gold extracted from their teeth with the Talmudic inscription, "Whoever saves one life, saves the world entire."

In his earlier films, Steven Spielberg had demonstrated that he was a master of sentimentality. One sees this clearly in *E. T.: The Extra-Terrestrial* (1982). One even finds this sort of Spielberg touch in the "God's trying to tell you something" Shug Avery sequence in *The Color Purple* (1985). In general, although Spielberg manages to hold himself in check for *Schindler's List*, he factors in a last-minute rescue when, after the 800 men have been sent by train to Brinnlitz, the 300 women and children are sent by mistake to the Auschwitz-Birkenau death camp. Once there, they are stripped, shorn and sent to the showers. The audience is led to believe they are then being sent to their death, but that is not the case, and Schindler manages to get them released from Birkenau and transported to Brinnlitz.

The film is splendidly made. Spielberg opted to shoot the film in black and white to create a sense of 1940's documentary realism, since what film footage survives of the death camps is in black and white. Like Alain Resnais' documentary *Night and Fog* (1955), however, *Schindler's List* begins and ends in color. At one point in the middle of the film, Spielberg nevertheless cheats on the color coding to make a point through dominant contrast. Schindler notices a little Jewish girl being herded up in the ghetto, and the audience knows he is watching her because her dress becomes a moving patch of red against a background of black and white. His presumed interest in her fate seems to make a turning point for Schindler's conscience. Later in the film, he sees her body after a particularly awful massacre of Jews, and, again, the dress is red. Yet such touches are forgivable here because they are effective.

Schindler's List was a risky film, even for such a commercially successful director as Spielberg, but it paid off. Spielberg avoided casting major stars for this picture; most of the cast consists of entirely appropriate actors who are not recognizable. The only compromise made the popular audiences is that the dialogue is in English and not subtitled from German, Polish, and Yiddish, which might have enhanced the realism, were it not for the fact that the main actors would have had dubbed lines. The film was made on a budget of only $22 million.

Schindler's List proved to be not only a commercially successful film but an award-winning one as well. The film won the New York Film Critics Circle award in January, marking the first in a long string of acceptance speeches given by Spielberg. He was again honored at the Golden Globe awards ceremony—accepting the film's award for best dramatic picture and receiving the first of his awards as best director (in addition, scriptwriter Steven Zaillian received an award for best screenplay). The Directors Guild of America honored Spielberg as best director, continuing the film's sweep of directorial awards within a strong field, including contenders such as Jane Campion, James Ivory, and Martin Scorsese. Spielberg had won the DGA award previously in 1985 for *The Color Purple*, and industry watchers speculated whether *Schindler's List* would break Spielberg's drought at the Oscars by bringing long awaited recognition for his directorial skills. The film went on to win seven Academy Awards (Best Picture, Director, Adapted Screenplay, Cinematography, Editing, Art Direction and Set Decoration, and Score) and nominations for Actor (Liam Neeson), Supporting Actor (Ralph Fiennes), Sound, Makeup, and Costumes.

From the text of his remarks in accepting his many awards, it became clear that Steven Spielberg was compelled by something more than the desire to make a prestigious film. Inspired by his sense of duty "as a filmmaker and a Jew," Spielberg became convinced that *Schindler's List* contained the seeds of a story that needed to be told "because the generations forget and every new generation needs to face their past all over again." In making the film, Spielberg strove not only to remind the world of the horrors committed during the height of the Third Reich but also to celebrate the courage of an initially self-interested observer whose compassion for the plight of his employees inspired him to take great risks to make a difference in their lives.

James M. Welsh

Reviews
America. CLXX, February 12, 1994, p. 20.
Baltimore Sun. December 26, 1993, p. H7.
Chicago Tribune. December 15, 1993, V, p. 1.
The Christian Century. CXI, February 16, 1994, p. 172.
Commonweal. CXXI, February 11, 1994, p. 16.
Entertainment Weekly. December 17, 1993, p. 44.
The Hollywood Reporter. December 6, 1993, p. 6.
Los Angeles Times. December 15, 1993, p. F1.
Newsweek. December 20, 1993, p. 112.
The New Yorker. December 29, 1993, p. 129.
The New York Times. December 15, 1993, p. C19.
Premiere, VII, January, 1994, p. 66.
Time. CXLII, December 13, 1993, p. 74.
Variety. December 6, 1993, p. 2.
The Wall Street Journal. December 16, 1993, p. A16.
The Washington Post. December 15, 1993, p. B1.

SEARCHING FOR BOBBY FISCHER

Production: Scott Rudin and William Horberg for Mirage; released by Paramount
    Pictures
Direction: Steven Zaillian
Screenplay: Steven Zaillian; based on the book by Fred Waitzkin
Cinematography: Conrad L. Hall
Editing: Wayne Wahrman
Production design: David Gropman
Costume design: Julie Weiss
Music: James Horner
MPAA rating: PG
Running time: 110 minutes

    Principal characters:
        Josh Waitzkin . . . . Max Pomeranc
        Fred Waitzkin . . . . Joe Mantegna
        Bonnie Waitzkin . . . . Joan Allen
        Bruce Pandolfini . . . . Ben Kingsley
        Vinnie . . . . Laurence Fishburne
        Jonathan Poe . . . . Michael Nirenberg

    Based on a true story, *Searching for Bobby Fischer* is a heartfelt and inspirational drama that centers on a young chess prodigy, Josh Waitzkin (Max Pomeranc), and his mastery not only of the game but also his integrity.

    As the film opens, Josh, a seven-year-old boy interested in sports and the usual assortment of toys that appeal to his age group, becomes fascinated with the chess players in New York City's Washington Square Park. As his mother, Bonnie (Joan Allen), escorts him through the park, his dark, wondering eyes study the chessboards. One day he persuades her to pay an older player five dollars to play a game with him. Although Josh loses, it is clear that he has a precocious understanding of the game, and he catches the attention of one of the park's regular players, Vinnie (Laurence Fishburne), an African American man renowned for his aggressive chess style.

    Bonnie also senses that her son has enormous potential and tells her husband, Fred (Joe Mantegna), of Josh's new interest. Intrigued, Fred challenges Josh to a game with him. Josh is reluctant but finally agrees. When his father wins, Bonnie suggests that perhaps Josh simply did not want to embarrass his father. As a result, Fred proposes another game to an even more diffident Josh, who agrees to play only after his mother emphasizes that Josh will not hurt his father's feelings by winning the game, which he then proceeds to do. Josh's sensitivity toward his father had caused him to lose rather than humiliate him, a character trait that will continue to surface throughout the story.

    Fred takes charge of his prodigy, finding him a world-class teacher, Bruce Pandolfini (Ben Kingsley), who informs Fred that Josh has the potential to become another Bobby Fischer, America's first world chess champion. Fischer, however, was a legendary recluse, a ruthless player, and, as the documentary sequence at the beginning of the film makes clear, also something of a monster, with incredible contempt for his rivals and a concentration on chess that excluded all other activities, including his schooling.

Josh wins tournaments, worships his teacher, and strives to please his father, who has become obsessed with Josh's potential. Fred even goes so far as to reject brutally a schoolteacher's concern that Josh is losing friends and falling behind in class work. Bonnie, on the other hand, sees the teacher's point. When she finds Pandolfini grooming Josh to be as merciless and focused as Bobby Fischer, she throws Pandolfini out of her home. Unfortunately, it is already clear that Josh's decency has been outraged and abused by his teacher's and his father's obsession with winning. Josh, feeling the pressure of being number one in his age group, loses an early round in a tournament and is chastised by his father. Nevertheless, Fred, realizing that he has been pushing his son too hard, offers Josh the possibility of quitting chess altogether.

Josh, however, wants to win—but to win by his standards. He has already told his teacher that he is not another Bobby Fischer, yet he grudgingly obeys Pandolfini's order to stop playing with the chess players in Washington Square. Pandolfini justifies this request by telling Josh that they are losers and will corrupt his style of play with their brand of speed chess—a rapid game that encourages players to be reckless gamblers rather than artists and strategists. In the end, however, with his father's blessing, Josh returns to Washington Square and to Vinnie, who becomes his mentor and encourages a risk-taking approach.

When Josh returns to tournament play, he looks refreshed. As he confides to one of his chess-competing friends, he has just come from two weeks of fishing, with no studying of chess lessons. Yet Josh worries that he cannot beat the tournament's top-ranked player, a dour boy, Jonathan Poe (Michael Nirenberg), programmed to perform flawlessly and fiercely in the style of Bobby Fischer. Josh is heartened by the return of Pandolfini, who attends the tournament and tells Josh that he is proud of him. Surprisingly, Pandolfini seconds Josh's fear that he might not be able to beat Poe, even while saying he probably should not admit as much to Josh, for he is violating his own advice of having contempt for one's opponent.

In the final matchup, Josh employs what he learns from both Pandolfini and Vinnie; that is, he has a strategy, but he pursues it much more boldly than Pandolfini would recommend. His seeming recklessness startles Poe, who appears to have the game firmly in hand. Nevertheless, Poe makes a mistake, which Josh seizes on—but not before offering Poe his hand, signaling that he will accept a draw so that they can share the first-place prize. Poe reacts contemptuously, and Josh annihilates him. Josh has, indeed, found his own way to win without forsaking his decency.

It is a tribute to this engrossing film that its obvious message about winning and losing with dignity does not seem trite. The film succeeds largely because of Max Pomeranc. His quiet, understated personality and wide-eyed innocence are captivating, especially when he reveals a core of character that cannot be corrupted by the adults who try to engineer his career. Director/screenwriter Steven Zaillian wisely trains the camera on Josh most of the time. It is Pomeranc's open, impressionable, and concentrated face that dominates the film, and the other actors—especially Joe Mantegna, Joan Allen, and Ben Kingsley—are shown mainly in reaction shots, as the adults who have to struggle to interpret Josh's often unstated emotions and laconic dialogue.

Pomeranc ranks in the top one hundred chess players in his age group in the United States, and although this is his first acting role, his experience as a chess player subtly enhances his performance. Clearly, he does not have to be told how to concentrate on the game. He was also aided by the presence of the real-life Josh Waitzkin (who, now sixteen, has become one of the top young players in the United States) and Waitzkin's coach, Bruce Pandolfini. Consequently, he was able to rehearse every move with them and yet infuse the games with his own style, handling the chess pieces with authority.

The camera work is unobtrusive. When Josh is not the focus, the rapidly moving chess pieces are tracked across the board. The action is as dynamic and taut as in any sports or action film. The crosscutting of shots between Josh and the board involves the viewer in the action without any knowledge of chess being necessary.

Not surprisingly, chess is discussed at great length in the film. Is it just a game? Is it a science? Is it an art? These are just some of the questions discussed throughout the film. In *Searching for Bobby Fischer*, chess also becomes a metaphor for life, for how the game of life is played. When Josh cannot bring himself to hate his opponents and says he is no Bobby Fischer, Pandolfini snidely replies he sure isn't, meaning that Josh does not have the killer instinct required of a world champion. Yet it is Josh's respect of his ultimate opponent, Jonathan Poe, that helps him prevail. Poe, on the other hand, dismisses Josh's offer of a draw because he has contempt for him and cannot conceive of losing.

Josh's quiet, intuitive mother has seen the truth all along. As she tells her husband, Fred, Josh is not weak. Yet he will not play if he is forced to inflict humiliation on others, whether it is his father or a competitor in a tournament. On the other hand, the cost of losing one's decency is clearly written on the face of Jonathan Poe. Throughout the film he has been photographed looking sullen and arrogant. Just before Josh joins him for their showdown match, however, Poe is clearly shown looking away from the board, his face falling into a sad, wistful pose, revealing a hollowness within.

The film's title comes to have an ironic meaning: The search for another Bobby Fischer is futile, for the next champion will have to put together his or her own style—inspired perhaps by Fischer's total dedication to the game and awesome courage—but in the final analysis a player all his or her own. This is perhaps why Josh enjoyed those Washington Square players so much. They were not afraid to be themselves and to commit everything they had to the game, using it as an expression of a whole personality and not merely that of an efficiently tuned chess machine.

Carl Rollyson

Reviews

American Cinematographer. LXXV, February, 1994, p. 50.
Chicago Tribune. August 11, 1993, V, p. 1.
The Christian Science Monitor. August 11, 1993, p. 13.
Entertainment Weekly. August 20, 1993, p. 40.
The Hollywood Reporter. August 2, 1993, p. 8.
Los Angeles Times. August 11, 1993, p. F1.
The New Republic. CCIX, September 20, 1993, p. 36.
The New York Times. August 11, 1993, p. B1.
Newsweek. CXXII, August 30, 1993, p. 52.
Time. CXLII, August 9, 1993, p. 63.
Variety. August 2, 1993, p. 2.
The Washington Post. August 11, 1993, p. D1.

THE SECRET GARDEN

Production: Fred Fuchs, Fred Roos, and Tom Luddy for Francis Ford Coppola and American Zoetrope; released by Warner Bros.
Direction: Agnieszka Holland
Screenplay: Caroline Thompson; based on the book by Frances Hodgson Burnett
Cinematography: Roger Deakins
Editing: Isabelle Lorente
Production design: Stuart Craig
Art direction: John King and Peter Russell
Set decoration: Stephenie McMillan
Casting: Karen Lindsay-Stewart
Sound: Drew Kunin
Costume design: Marit Allen
Music: Zbigniew Preisner
MPAA rating: G
Running time: 101 minutes

> *Principal characters:*
> Mary Lennox . . . . Kate Maberly
> Colin Craven. . . . . Heydon Prowse
> Dickon. . . . . Andrew Knott
> Mrs. Medlock . . . . Maggie Smith
> Martha. . . . . Laura Crossley
> Lord Craven . . . . John Lynch
> Ben Weatherstaff. . . . . Walter Sparrow

Director Agnieszka Holland's beautifully photographed interpretation of the classic children's story *The Secret Garden* (1911), by Frances Hodgson Burnett, will prove to be a delight to adults and children alike. Although occasionally slow-moving and deviating at times from the original story, overall the motion picture is excellent family fare, with strong performances by its leads and high production values.

Neglected and spoiled, ten-year-old Mary Lennox (Kate Maberly) lives in late nineteenth century India with her military father and beautiful mother. A catastrophic earthquake leaves Mary an orphan, and she is sent to England by boat to live with an uncle whom she has never met. Teased by the other children on board because she is so contrary, Mary appears to have been forgotten upon arrival, as all the other children are claimed but her. Arriving late, Mrs. Medlock (Maggie Smith), housekeeper of Misselthwaite Manor, belittles Mary's appearance and demeanor from the moment she sets eyes on her. Haughty Mary simply ignores her.

The two then make the long voyage to Misselthwaite, seemingly at the ends of the earth. The enormous and remote mansion lies out in the middle of the vast, barren Yorkshire moor—a forbidding setting for a young girl's new home. At Misselthwaite,

Mrs. Medlock proves to be as stern and forbidding as the house itself. Mary is assigned to her quarters and told in no uncertain terms that she is not to roam and not to bother anyone.

From this inauspicious beginning, Mary befriends a local boy, Dickon (Andrew Knott), and inadvertently comes to know her ten-year-old cousin, Colin Craven (Heydon Prowse), an invalid who has been hidden away in a corner of the large house. Colin makes a perfect match for Mary, as he is as spoiled and sullen as she is. Sickly since birth, Colin speaks of his "imminent" death as matter-of-factly as others speak of the weather. Surprisingly, the two contrary cousins become fast friends, if only to spite Mrs. Medlock, who has ordered that Colin's existence be kept a secret from Mary. When she discovers that Mary has been visiting Colin in secret, the vexed Mrs. Medlock lashes out at innocent servant girl Martha (Laura Crossley), Dickon's sister, who has been caring for Mary.

As Mary roams the grounds, she discovers among the vast gardens a "secret" garden—one surrounded by a high wall, whose only entrance is through a door that has been locked for ten years. Mary learns that Lord Craven's beautiful wife, her mother's identical twin sister, died in an accident in the garden, and Lord Craven, in his grief, had it shut up just as he shut away his infant son. Unable to bear these memories, Lord Craven is rarely in residence. Mary, who has discovered the key, develops the idea of restoring this garden to life, with the aid of Dickon. As the garden grows to idyllic splendor, Mary and Dickon contrive to coax Colin out of doors, to their secret place away from the prying eyes of the adults.

The secret garden's restorative powers—which have worked their magic on Mary, who since tending the garden has become less listless and mean, and more solicitous and outgoing—work a similar miracle on Colin, who gradually grows stronger with each outing and eventually is able to walk. Overjoyed, the three children, in the company of the elderly gardener, Ben Weatherstaff (Walter Sparrow), who has discovered their secret, work magic themselves one dark night around a bonfire in the garden in order to bring Lord Craven home to his son for good. When Lord Craven answers the supernatural call and returns to Misselthwaite, he is dismayed when Colin is not in his room. The requisite happy ending is achieved when he finds his way into the secret garden and happens upon Colin playing blindman's bluff with Mary and Dickon.

This classic story has been brought to life by director Holland much as Mary Lennox brought to life her secret garden. Holland, whose previous films include the internationally acclaimed *Europa, Europa* (1990) and *Olivier Olivier* (1993; reviewed in this volume), both of which center on youths, claims that *The Secret Garden* was a childhood favorite of hers when she was growing up in Poland. In her on-screen realization of that book, Holland has succeeded in maintaining its literary quality with her excellent cast and production values.

Kate Maberly as Mary has the appearance of a late nineteenth century porcelain doll, complete with period costumes and luxurious, long brown hair. She gives an unaffected, earnest portrayal of this privileged little girl who has never known what it is to be hungry or, by the same token, to be loved. Her friendship with the two boys is realistic, given just a hint of sexual awakening by director Holland. Cousin Colin is played by Heydon Prowse, who makes his acting debut with this film. Thin and pale-skinned with sunken, saucer-shaped eyes, Prowse is believable as a young boy who has spent his entire life indoors and in bed. Andrew Knott as Dickon is as healthy and happy as Colin is sickly and perverse. Perpetually good-natured, with plump, pink cheeks, he is proof positive of the effects of the fresh, clean Yorkshire air. Maggie Smith is a grim, determined Mrs. Medlock, a woman who is only trying to do her duty. Although stiff and unemotional throughout most of the film, Medlock gains the audience's sympathy at the end when, distraught and crying on Martha's shoulder, she feels dazed, hurt, and confused by the events that have transpired.

The realization of the secret garden, in and around which all the drama occurs, is breathtaking and supports the premise that it is an enchanted place. The garden is filled not only with flowers but also with animals, such as lambs, squirrels, ducks, and rabbits. Time-lapse photography was used to show the garden coming magnificently into bloom, as in a fairy tale. Ironically, the scenes in the garden when it is in full bloom were filmed first, and then four months elapsed before the winter sequences were shot in order for the garden to appear dead, the way Mary would have found it—just the opposite of the order of events in the story. The garden represents the healing power of nature, which is amply demonstrated in Mary's, Colin's, and Lord Craven's changes for the better by the end of the film.

It is a mystery, however, why Holland has chosen to alter certain details. For example, in the original story, Mary's mother and Lord Craven's wife were not identical twin sisters. In fact, Mary is related to Lord Craven through her father, who was Lord Craven's wife's brother. Also, in the original story, Mary's parents died of cholera, not in an earthquake. With respect to the key to the secret garden, in the film Mary finds it in a drawer in the room that belonged to Lord Craven's wife; in the book, she finds it buried outside. Furthermore, the Mrs. Medlock of the original story was not as vicious as Maggie Smith's portrayal of the character in the film. Medlock was rather a well-meaning woman who was merely following the doctor's orders to the best of her ability. In the film, the doctor never appears; yet in the book, he was a poor cousin of Lord Craven who stood to inherit Misselthwaite should Colin die.

Aside from these details, a major theme of the book is lacking—the difference between the classes. Throughout the original story, the broad Yorkshire accent and dialect are emphasized; Mrs. Medlock tells Martha that she must speak carefully or Mary will not be able to understand her. Further, Martha confesses that, had there been a mistress of Misselthwaite, Martha would never have been more than a scullery maid because of her broad accent. In the book, Martha and Martha's family play a larger role. Mary, who has never known want, is fascinated by Martha's family—twelve people in a small moorland cottage who rarely get enough to eat. In fact, in the book, Dickon maintains a vegetable garden to help feed his large family—quite a contrast to the beautiful flower garden on which Mary and Colin are able to lavish their attention. Ironically, it is the wise and kindly Mrs. Sowerby, Martha's mother, who thinks to send Mary and Colin a pail of fresh milk and some currant buns to take the edge off the children's increasing appetites so that the servants will not notice how much Colin is improving—despite the hungry mouths she must feed in her own home. The healthy minds and bodies of this simple Yorkshire family, represented by Martha, Dickon, and their mother, are contrasted with the tragedy-ridden lives and sickly nature of the wealthy Mary, Colin, and Lord Craven, a theme that could have been more thoroughly examined in the film.

Despite these objections, *The Secret Garden* captures the essence of the novel—the lush, enchanted paradise that has been reclaimed by three children. The garden takes on a life of its own, as it was meant to in Burnett's story. The production design, costuming, and cinematography complement one another beautifully, and the three child actors carry the story to its enchanting conclusion. It is an entertaining interpretation of a classic story.

Cynthia K. Breckenridge

Reviews
Chicago Tribune. August 13, 1993, VII, p. 27.
The Christian Science Monitor. August 13, 1993, p. 13.
Entertainment Weekly. August 13, 1993, p. 54.
Films in Review. XLIV, September, 1993, p. 332.
The Hollywood Reporter. August 6, 1993, p. 6.
Los Angeles Times. August 13, 1993, p. F1.
The New York Times. August 13, 1993, p. B1.
Newsweek. CXXII, August 23, 1993, p. 53.
Sight and Sound. III, November, 1993, p. 52.
Time. CXLII, August 16, 1993, p. 58.
Variety. August 6, 1993, p. 4.
The Washington Post. August 13, 1993, p. D1.

SHADOWLANDS

Origin: Great Britain and USA
Released: 1993
Released in U.S.: 1993
Production: Richard Attenborough and Brian Eastman for Price Entertainment, in association with Spelling Films International; released by Savoy Pictures
Direction: Richard Attenborough
Screenplay: William Nicholson; based on his play
Cinematography: Roger Pratt
Editing: Lesley Walker
Production design: Stuart Craig
Art direction: Michael Lamont
Set decoration: Stephenie McMillan
Casting: Lucy Boulting
Sound: Simon Kaye, Jonathan Bates, and Gerry Humphreys
Costume design: Penny Rose
Music: George Fenton
MPAA rating: PG
Running time: 130 minutes

> *Principal characters:*
> C. S. "Jack" Lewis .... Anthony Hopkins
> Joy Gresham .... Debra Winger
> Warnie Lewis .... Edward Hardwicke
> "Harry" Harrington................. Michael Denison
> Christopher Riley .... John Wood
> Douglas Gresham .... Joseph Mazzello

Said *Shadowlands* playwright and screenwriter William Nicholson according to the film's production notes, "*Shadowlands* is based on events that occurred in the lives of two real people—C. S. Lewis and Joy Gresham—but it is not a documentary drama. I have used parts of their story, not used other parts, and imagined the rest. The love affair was real enough, but they were both intensely private about it. No one knows exactly how and why they fell in love. It is in this uncharted region that I have created a story."

The story begins with fact. C. S. "Jack" Lewis (Anthony Hopkins) lived a privileged and protected life in 1950's Oxford. His career as a classicist, Anglican theologian and author was firmly established, and his private life with his alcoholic retired-soldier brother, Warnie (Edward Hardwicke), was peaceful and orderly. Abandoned by a mother who died in their childhood, Jack and Warnie live life like well-mannered but motherless children. Entertained by his fame, Jack personally answers each of the fan letters he receives from readers. In the process, he strikes up a correspondence with American poet Joy Gresham (Debra Winger). Over the course of their seven-year relationship, they begin as correspondents and progress through friendship and marriage to Joy's death from cancer.

No doubt the strengths of *Shadowlands* are the performances. While Hopkins, Winger, and Hardwicke are exceptionally fine, not a single performance, not a single major or minor character, rings untrue. The finest performance, however, is given by Anthony Hopkins. As the film begins, Hopkins creates a magnificently secure Lewis. His lectures and tutorials are canned, delivered as a piece. As one of his students notes, he never asks questions unless he is sure of the answer. Also pat are Warnie's and Jack's lives; the working, dining, retiring is enough for them. Into this simple, uncomplicated existence comes the complex, difficult Joy Gresham. What Jack's relationship with Joy brings him is doubt and humanity; in other words, she brings him life. Hopkins is able to portray the confidence, the lack of confidence, and the acceptance of humanity and humility that is Lewis' later life. Charming, witty in his fame, humble and engaging in his doubt, Hopkins holds center stage.

Hopkins made a career in the early 1990's of playing characters without emotion, as in *The Silence of the Lambs* (1991), *Howards End* (1992), and *The Remains of the Day* (1993; reviewed in this volume). Specifically, in *The Remains of the Day*, Hopkins plays the central character, a butler who realizes too late that he has wasted his life serving others, living within the periphcry of others' lives. What is key about his performance in *Shadowlands*, then, is that while Hopkins' Lewis initially appears shut out of emotion, risk, even life itself, the film chronicles his late-in-life reversal. That is, in *Shadowlands* Hopkins perfects a character whose life is marked by the late acceptance of humanity, including the uncertainty and the emotion. Particularly fine are scenes in which Lewis rails against a God he sees as giving happiness even as He takes it away, and a scene in which Lewis and Joy Gresham's son Douglas (Joseph Mazello) mourn Joy. The Los Angeles Film Critics Association awarded Hopkins the best actor award for both *Shadowlands* and *Remains of the Day*.

Also fine is Debra Winger, who has made a career for herself playing unconventional women—in both appearance and behavior. Perhaps the best feature Winger brings Gresham—a brash, Jewish, divorced woman traveling abroad without her husband in the 1950's—is believability. While Winger delivers her lines with assurance, she avoids playing so broadly as to make Gresham an embarrassment. For example, in the oft-quoted scene in which Gresham silences an Oxford don by inquiring whether he is trying to be offensive or just stupid, Winger is able to control the delivery—a verbal slap, rather than an all-out assault. It plays quite well.

While Winger has played a wide variety of characters—working-class heroine in *Urban Cowboy* (1980) and *An Officer and a Gentleman* (1982); beleaguered wife and daughter in *Terms of Endearment* (1983); bored wife and lover in *The Sheltering Sky* (1990); principled professional in *Legal Eagles* (1986); unprincipled "professional" in *Leap of Faith* (1992); and psychotic misfit in *A Dangerous Woman* (1993)—she is able to shed the residue of these roles and create Joy Gresham out of whole cloth. While a film chronicling a middle-age love affair could be embarrassing or boring, Winger is able to bring such life and love to her lines as to make the lovers sympathetic and realistic. For example, when the lovers journey to find the actual place depicted in Jack's favorite painting, they are caught in the rain and must seek shelter in an abandoned barn. There Jack laments finding love so late only to lose it again so soon. Winger's Gresham responds by explaining that the current love is sweet only or especially in light of its impending end. It is a memorable love scene for its emotion and its language. While many reviewers focused on Gresham as Lewis' one experience with physical love, scenes such as this one have much more impact than most—if not all—of the more physically graphic love scenes available in other films of the same period.

The experience of the filmmakers with the genre and the materials also helps explain the success of *Shadowlands*. Director-producer Richard Attenborough has finely tuned his craft with biographical films, "stories about real people, who, in some way, change the world around them." He won two Academy Awards for *Gandhi* (1982), for Best Picture and Best Direction, and has made several other biographical films, including *Young Winston* (1972) and *Chaplin* (1992). This is Attenborough's fifth film with Hopkins. Screenwriter Nicholson was drawn to the Lewis-Gresham relationship because of "the dramatic effect Joy had on Lewis' well-ordered life." *Shadowlands* began as a BBC telefilm; then Nicholson's stage adaptation opened in London in 1989 and on Broadway in 1990.

Shadowlands is both a quiet little film and the story of a love of epic proportions. Set against the history and majesty of Oxford, limited by the hospital rooms and sick beds that are inescapably a part of the story, the film and the lives of its characters nevertheless manage to dwarf the institutions that otherwise might engulf them. The film also garnered two Academy Award nominations—for Best Actress (Debra Winger) and Adapted Screenplay (William Nicholson). Thoughtful filmgoers everywhere will want to make a point of seeing *Shadowlands*.

Roberta F. Green

Reviews

Chicago Tribune. January 7, 1994, Friday Section, p. C.
The Christian Century. CXI, February 23, 1994, p. 200.
The Christian Science Monitor. December 31, 1993, p. 12.
Commonweal. CXXI, January 28, 1994, p. 22.
Christianity Today. XXXVIII, February 7, 1994, p. 50.
Entertainment Weekly. January 28, 1994, p. 34.
The Hollywood Reporter. December 6, 1993, p. 8.
Los Angeles Times. December 29, 1993, p. F1.
The New Republic. CCX, February 7, 1994, p. 26.
The New York Times. December 29, 1993, p. B2.
Variety. December 3, 1993, p. 4.
The Washington Post. January 7, 1994, Weekend, p. 34.

SHORT CUTS

Production: Cary Brokaw, in association with Spelling Films International and
  Avenue Pictures; released by Fine Line Features
Direction: Robert Altman
Screenplay: Robert Altman and Frank Barhydt; based on the writings of Raymond
  Carver
Cinematography: Walt Lloyd
Editing: Geraldine Peroni
Production design: Stephen Altman
Art direction: Jerry Fleming
Set decoration: Susan J. Emshwiller
Sound: John Pritchett
Costume design: John Hay
Music: Mark Isham
MPAA rating: R
Running time: 189 minutes

Principal characters:

Ann Finnigan	Andie MacDowell
Howard Finnigan	Bruce Davison
Marian Wyman	Julianne Moore
Dr. Ralph Wyman	Matthew Modine
Claire Kane	Anne Archer
Stuart Kane	Fred Ward
Lois Kaiser	Jennifer Jason Leigh
Jerry Kaiser	Chris Penn
Honey Bush	Lili Taylor
Bill Bush	Robert Downey, Jr.
Sherri Shepard	Madeleine Stowe
Gene Shepard	Tim Robbins
Doreen Piggot	Lily Tomlin
Earl Piggot	Tom Waits
Betty Weathers	Frances McDormand
Stormy Weathers	Peter Gallagher
Tess Trainer	Annie Ross
Zoe Trainer	Lori Singer
Paul Finnigan	Jack Lemmon
Andy Bitkower	Lyle Lovett
Gordon Johnson	Buck Henry
Vern Miller	Huey Lewis
Chad Weathers	Jarrett Lennon
Casey Finnigan	Zane Cassidy

After a series of commercial and critical disasters, culminating in the frigid reception of the highly stylized, live-action staging of the cartoon characters of *Popeye* (1980), director Robert Altman was banished from Hollywood filmmaking for more than a decade. He was, in industry vernacular, "box-office poison." Following the critical success of 1992's *The Player*, film aficionados now have hailed the 1990's as the Second Coming of director Robert Altman. Like fellow one-time critical outcast Clint Eastwood, Altman further proves that yesterday's laughingstock may well be embraced as tomorrow's creative genius.

With a running time of more than three hours, Altman's *Short Cuts* crisscrosses the lives of twenty-two "significant" characters. The film attempts to interweave nine disparate Raymond Carver stories, relocating them from the Pacific Northwest to the environs of Los Angeles—which serves to diffuse some of the biting social commentary by placing the characters in a setting easily satirized and dismissed as removed from reality—and expanding class lines from working class to white collar and affluent. While Carver's work dealt with the common person's ability to handle sudden upheaval, Altman has shifted the emphasis to the element of chance and randomness. If there is one unifying theme in Altman's interpretation of these nine stories, it appears to be one of alienation. Men are little more than sadistic, egocentric louts and women insufferable masochists.

Short Cuts opens with the apocalyptic drone of helicopters, showering Los Angeles residents with the pesticide malathion—a metaphor for postmodern society if ever there was one—and follows an ensemble cast of characters as their lives converge and diverge over the course of several days. Television commentator Howard Finnigan (Bruce Davison) and his wife, Ann (Andie MacDowell), find their relationship tested when their only son, Casey (Zane Cassidy), is struck by a car driven by waitress Doreen Piggot (Lily Tomlin). On her way home to the trailer park after work, Doreen is distracted by yet another encounter with her alcoholic husband, Earl (Tom Waits), a limo driver who may have molested Doreen's daughter, Honey Bush (Lili Taylor). When Ann forgets about the birthday cake she had ordered for Casey, she soon finds herself on the receiving end of harassing phone calls from the disappointed baker, Andy Bitkower (Lyle Lovett). Meanwhile, Howard copes with the unexpected arrival of his long-absent father (Jack Lemmon) and his confessions of a dark secret that destroyed their family years before.

Honey is married to Bill Bush (Robert Downey, Jr.), a misogynistic makeup artist with a penchant for painting bruises on his young wife's face. The couple are friends with Jerry Kaiser (Chris Penn), a pool serviceman whose clients include the Finnigans, and his wife, Lois (Jennifer Jason Leigh), who earns extra money by selling phone sex while she diapers her baby. Lois remains oblivious to her husband's obvious discomfort, and despite her torrid talk there is a chill that emanates from Lois that eventually triggers Jerry to vent his anger and pain on a complete stranger.

The Carver story "Will You Please Be Quiet, Please?" provides the inspiration for the tale of repression, jealousy, and marital infidelity between Marian (Julianne Moore), an artist who insists her paintings of nude bodies are all about "seeing and the responsibility that comes with it," and her jealous husband, Dr. Ralph Wyman (Matthew Modine), Casey's physician. The couple's row and Marian's coerced confession precede the arrival of dinner guests, a couple the Wymans recently met at a classical quartet concert. Claire (Anne Archer) works as a children's party clown, while her out-of-work salesman husband, Stuart Kane (Fred Ward), goes off on a fishing expedition with pals Gordon Johnson (Buck Henry) and Vern Miller (Huey Lewis). Unbeknownst to the Wymans, the Kanes are also covering up their own marital rift, precipitated by Stuart's casual reaction to the discovery of a dead woman's body in the fertile trout waters.

Malathion helicopter pilot Stormy Weathers (Peter Gallagher) repeatedly tries to reconcile with his spiteful, estranged wife, Betty (Frances McDormand), but she is caught up in the throes of an extramarital affair with philandering L.A.P.D. motorcycle cop Gene Shepard (Tim Robbins), whose wife, Sherri (Madeleine Stowe in her most compelling work to date), poses nude for her sister, Marian. With cocky swagger and fascistic glare, Robbins, so powerful as studio head Griffin Mill in Altman's *The Player*, perfectly captures every blue-collar nuance and manipulative maneuvering of a man capable of dumping the family dog. Finally, in the least compelling of all the vignettes, there are the Trainers: mother Tess (Annie Ross), a washed-up jazz singer who reminisces incessantly about her dead junkie husband, and her daughter, Zoe (Lori Singer), an icy concert cellist with a melodramatic flair for trying to gain her mother's attention. Altman primarily uses the Trainers to provide the film's musical sound track.

During the early 1970's, Robert Altman's visionary style broke filmic conventions, with its use of overlapping, chaotic dialogue and story lines, richly inhabited background action and a self-acknowledged reflexivity. In *M*A*S*H* (1970), the director's renegade breakthrough film, Altman forced audiences to confront graphically the horrors of war in a way that had never been done before, by delicately balancing near-insanity with moments of compassion and humor. Throughout, it was politics that drove Altman's earlier, more poignant work. His film form mirrored the content: a revolutionary new style infused with political commentary. While Altman attempts to recapture his previous style, the content now is weak. What easier targets to satirize than the superficial, self-involved film industry and the residents of Los Angeles, a town so unlike anywhere else in the world that it is nicknamed "La-La Land."

Robert Altman displays a masterful control of pace and rhythm in *Short Cuts*, yet he maintains so much emotional distance by way of his fragmented structure, his extensive character ensemble, and his own innate cynicism (not to mention an unabashed predilection for female nudity that borders precariously on exploitation, but which has been dismissed by many critics as central to the "art") that it is difficult to feel compassion for any of the characters. It is easy to laugh at their foibles, but viewers may be hard pressed to identify with or understand any of their predicaments. In many ways, Altman's style of quick cutting between stories seems inadvertently to reinforce one of the very things that the director is intent on satirizing, both in this film as well as in *The Player*: Americans' cultural and moral bankruptcy. Altman himself confessed that fragmentation was required "because we don't have enough attention span to stay on one subject too long." As film critic Georgia Brown put it so succinctly, *Short Cuts* is "a channel-surfer's dream."

In real life, people seldom if ever achieve any kind of resolution. People remain trapped interminably in their quiet suffering, seldom knowing what is wrong or how to move on to a better understanding of their own misery. Perhaps it is the documentarist in Robert Altman that compels him to capture so much suffering on film; but film is not reality. It is intended as escapism, a momentary refuge from the cold, cruel world; thus it is disheartening to be bludgeoned by such relentless bleakness as Altman presents in *Short Cuts*. The director remains aloof, barely connecting with his characters, preferring instead to cruelly ridicule them.

There is nothing new and certainly nothing shocking about Altman's form; it was a style that he had long since perfected in *Nashville* (1975), a scathing indictment of the country music scene. Altman's form now feels more debasing in an already alienated society in which people have become so desensitized to violence and human suffering, due perhaps in part to the proliferation of "reality-based" television programs and "shock-jock" radio shows. In many ways, viewers have already seen it all, and in postmodern society Robert Altman seems lost. Perhaps that is the very reason Hollywood can now embrace its prodigal son.

Critics were decidedly split in their reception of *Short Cuts*, with three of the prominent New York critics voicing their disdain over Altman's prevailing tone of disgust and mysterious rage, as well as his emotional distance from his characters. Altman, however, did receive an Academy Award nomination for Best Director (but the film itself was bypassed in the nominations). *Short Cuts* shared the top prize at the Venice film festival with Polish Director Krzystof Kieslowski's far more deserving film, *Trois Coleurs: Bleu*.

Patricia Kowal

Reviews

Chicago Tribune. October 7, 1993, V, p. 5.
Entertainment Weekly. October 1, 1993, p. 36.
Film Comment. XXIX, September, 1993, p. 34.
Films in Review. XLIV, November, 1993, p. 410.
The Hollywood Reporter. September 7, 1993, p. 6.
Los Angeles Times. October 8, 1993, p. F1.
The New York Times. October 1, 1993, p. B1.
The New Yorker. LXIX, September 27, 1993, p. 98.
Newsweek. April 26, 1993, p. 62.
Rolling Stone. October 14, 1993, p. 125.
Time. CXLII, October 4, 1993, p. 80.
Variety. September 7, 1993, p. 2.
The Village Voice. XXXVII, October 5, 1993, p. 54.
The Washington Post. October 22, 1993, p. C1.

SISTER ACT II
Back in The Habit

Production: Dawn Steel and Scott Rudin for Touchstone Pictures; released by
    Buena Vista Pictures
Direction: Bill Duke
Screenplay: James Orr, Jim Cruickshank, and Judi Ann Mason; based on characters
    created by Joseph Howard
Cinematography: Oliver Wood
Editing: John Carter, Pembroke Herring, and Stuart Pappé
Production design: John DeCuir, Jr.
Art direction: Louis M. Mann
Set decoration: Bruce Gibeson
Casting: Aleta Chapelle
Sound: Jim Webb
Costume design: Francine Jamison-Tanchuck
Choreography: Michael Peters
Music supervision: Marc Shaiman
Music: Miles Goodman and Mervyn Warren
MPAA rating: PG
Running time: 100 minutes

> *Principal characters:*
>
> Deloris . . . . Whoopi Goldberg
> Sister Mary Patrick . . . . Kathy Najimy
> Father Maurice . . . . Barnard Hughes
> Sister Mary Lazarus. . . . . Mary Wickes
> Mr. Crisp . . . . James Coburn
> Father Ignatius. . . . . Michael Jeter
> Sister Mary Robert . . . . Wendy Makkena
> Florence Watson . . . . Sheryl Lee Ralph
> Joey Bustamente . . . . Robert Pastorelli
> Father Wolfgang . . . . Thomas Gottschalk
> Mother Superior . . . . Maggie Smith
> Rita Watson . . . . Lauryn Hill
> Father Thomas. . . . . Brad Sullivan
> Maria . . . . Alanna Ubach
> Ahmal . . . . Ryan Toby
> Sketch . . . . Ron Johnson

   Whoopi Goldberg returns as a Las Vegas lounge act impersonating a nun in *Sister
Act II: Back in the Habit*, a lackluster sequel to the 1992 box-office smash *Sister Act*.
Goldberg reprises her role as Deloris Van Cartier, a successful headliner at the Desert

Inn in Las Vegas, who is talked into helping her former nun pals by teaching a rogue band of students in a music class.

The film opens promisingly with Goldberg performing a mind-boggling medley of songs that basically recaps the story of the first film. Music supervisor Marc Shaiman, best known for his award-winning work with Bette Midler and Billy Crystal, managed to incorporate songs as diverse as "Devil with the Blue Dress" and "Le Freak" with "The Hallelujah Chorus" and virtually everything in between. The result is a hilarious spoof of every bad Las Vegas show ever done, and Goldberg pulls it off with great style. Too bad, however, that this is the high point of the film until the very end, with nearly one hundred minutes of uninteresting and unimaginative filler in between.

Deloris is visited after her show by three of the nuns who helped her evade the mob in the first film. Reprising their roles from that motion picture are Kathy Najimy as Sister Mary Patrick, Mary Wickes as Sister Mary Lazarus, and Wendy Makkena as Sister Mary Robert. These three talented actors, who helped make the original so enjoyable, are greatly underutilized here. The Sisters convince Deloris that her help is needed at the St. Francis school in San Francisco, and after a brief, guilt-filled conversation with the Mother Superior, played by Maggie Smith, Deloris is once again back in her nun's habit as Sister Mary Clarence.

The Sisters give her the job of teaching an unruly music class, although it is never made clear as to why this is so important to the school's survival. This kicks off a standard and tired plot line of misfit underdogs turned into victorious winners, as Deloris shapes the class into a world-class gospel choir. Along the way, of course, she single-handedly manages to save the school from closing, enlists broad-based community support from an uninterested neighborhood, and saves more than one child from a dead-end life. She also redecorates part of the school in her spare time.

Goldberg appears to be coasting through her role as Deloris, for which she was paid a reported $7 million. Although she occasionally shows sparks of enthusiasm during the musical numbers, her acting performance throughout the film is sedate at best. No insight is given as to why Deloris would want to give up her Las Vegas life-style for a convent job again. It is never made clear why she puts up with the abuse heaped upon her by the students or the school. Some of the blame for this must be placed on the formulaic script, but Goldberg has done many films in which she made the characters more than the words on the page through her immense talent. In *Sister Act II* she seems to be uninterested in doing that.

The supporting cast is, for the most part, enjoyable but most often in roles too small to be of any note. Najimy, Wickes, Makkena, and Smith as the "wacky" nuns are playing true to their characters from the first film, but this sequel hardly acknowledges their presence. Likewise for the equally "wacky" priests, played by Barnard Hughes, Michael Jeter, Thomas Gottschalk, and Brad Sullivan. These four men are supremely talented performers, yet their screen time limits their parts to little more than cameos. Granted, this story is not about these characters or their concerns, but perhaps if it had been, the film would have been funnier.

Three other impressive talents wander on and off screen briefly. Film legend James

Coburn is cast as Mr. Crisp, the supposed "bad guy" of *Sister Act II*. The only problem is that he really is not much of a bad guy, and Coburn seems almost confused as to what to do with such an underwritten part. Robert Pastorelli, best known as Eldin on television's *Murphy Brown*, plays Deloris' manager in the first five minutes of the film and is never seen again. Florence Watson, the mother of one of Deloris' students, is played by Sheryl Lee Ralph, whose performance in the Broadway hit musical *Dream Girls* was nominated for a Tony Award. Ralph is one of few actors in this film who took a small part and made it into something powerful. Her affecting performance as the protective mother leaves a lasting impression.

The real heroes of this film, however, are none of the established stars mentioned above. The true talent that provides the film's most interesting moments lies in the young group of relative newcomers cast as the choir that Deloris is assigned. Leading the pack is Lauryn Hill, who plays classroom malcontent Rita Watson with such intensity and force that it is hard to believe this eighteen-year-old had only one other film under her belt. Rita is a young girl whose passion for music upsets her overprotective mother. Hill shows all of her pain, anger, and frustration in a heartfelt and heartbreaking performance that is overshadowed only by her even more incredible singing voice.

Other classroom-kid standouts are Devin Kamin as the wisecracking rapper Frankie; Ron Johnson as rapper/graffiti artist Sketch; and Ryan Toby as the culturally obsessed Ahmal. These young performers, along with twenty or so others in smaller parts, are a constant joy to watch, throughout. Their ensemble performance near the end of the film at a state choir competition is dramatic and uplifting. All involved seem to have promising careers ahead.

Critically acclaimed director Bill Duke, whose film *Deep Cover* (1992) was considered by most to be nothing short of brilliant, seems to be working with material far beneath him here. Perhaps he believed this as well, which is why he did not bother to elicit interesting performances from most of the ensemble. Duke obviously enjoyed the kids in the film, however, and their musical numbers are staged and shot beautifully.

As mentioned before, the script by James Orr, Jim Cruickshank, and Judi Ann Mason is bland and unoriginal. There is no real impetus for what passes as a story in the film nor is there any attempt to make interesting characterizations. Instead, the trio has served up a series of cardboard cutouts programmed to elicit laughs or tears depending on the circumstance. Most of the talent in this film was wasted on the one-note nuns and priests, who may as well have not been here in the first place since they are not even all that funny.

The lone standouts on the technical side are music supervisor March Shaiman and musical arranger/producer Mervyn Warren. Their contribution to this film is immeasurable, since they have provided most of the funny and moving moments. The previously mentioned opening medley with Whoopi Goldberg and the choir performance of "Joyful, Joyful" at the end are brilliant. Other musical highlights include Deloris and the nuns performing "Get Up Offa That Thing" at a community fundraiser, with Goldberg doing a riotous James Brown impersonation; "Oh, Happy Day," performed by Ryan Toby and the choir; and a beautiful and moving rendition of the gospel classic "His Eye Is on the Sparrow," sung by Tanya Blount and Lauryn Hill.

Overall, *Sister Act II: Back in the Habit* is disappointing, not because of high hopes created by the original, since artistically and creatively speaking it was not one of 1992's greatest films. The true letdown of this film comes from the expectations generated from the opening credits of a cast that includes more Oscar, Emmy, Tony, Grammy, and American Comedy Award winners than can fit in a moving van. More should have been expected of this talented cast and more should have been given them to work with. Perhaps then they would not have been outshone by a group of kids whose only awards have been limited to drama recognition night at their local high schools.

Rick Garman

Reviews

Afro-American. December 11, 1993, p. B6.
Boston Globe. December 10, 1993, p. 53.
Chicago Tribune. December 10, 1993, VII, p. 37.
Entertainment Weekly. December 17, 1993, p. 46.
The Hollywood Reporter. December 10-12, 1993, p. 10.
Houston Post. December 10, 1993, sec. E, p. 1.
Los Angeles Times. December 10, 1993, p. F1.
The New York Times. December 10, 1993, p. B7.
Time. CXLII, December 20, 1993, p. 63.
Variety. December 10, 1993, p. 14.
The Washington Post. December 10, 1993, p. B1.

SIX DEGREES OF SEPARATION

Production: Fred Schepisi and Arnon Milchan for Maiden Movies/New Regency;
   released by Metro-Goldwyn-Mayer
Direction: Fred Schepisi
Screenplay: John Guare; based on his play
Cinematography: Ian Baker
Editing: Peter Honess
Production design: Patrizia von Brandenstein
Art direction: Dennis Bradford
Set decoration: Gretchen Rau
Casting: Ellen Chenoweth
Sound: Bill Daly
Costume design: Judianna Makovsky
Music: Jerry Goldsmith
MPAA rating: R
Running time: 111 minutes

> *Principal characters:*
> Ouisa Kittredge . . . . Stockard Channing
> Paul . . . . Will Smith
> Flan Kittredge . . . . Donald Sutherland
> Geoffrey. . . . . Ian McKellen
> Kitty. . . . . Mary Beth Hurt
> Larkin. . . . . Bruce Davison
> Dr. Fine . . . . Richard Masur
> Trent Conway . . . . Anthony Michael Hall
> Elizabeth . . . . Heather Graham
> Rick . . . . Eric Thal
> Ben. . . . . Anthony Rapp
> Woody Kittredge . . . . Osgood Perkins
> Tess Kittredge . . . . Catherine Kellner
> Mrs. Bannister . . . . Kitty Carlisle Hart

The tag line in advertisements for the film version of *Six Degrees of Separation*—
some of which prominently feature the Manhattan skyline—reads, "Everyone wants
to be connected." These advertisements are in fact an excellent shorthand for the
import of playwright John Guare's film adaptation of his award-winning play—and
for its puzzling title. In this overcrowded, vertical world that has come to symbolize,
for many, the modern home of alienation, Guare's main character, Ouisa Kittredge
(Stockard Channing, who was nominated for the 1993 Best Actress Oscar for her
work), delivers the speech explaining the film's title—that each of us is separated from
everyone else in the world by only six other people.

Ouisa is a New York society matron married to a wealthy art dealer, Flan Kittredge (Donald Sutherland), who works out of their well-appointed Fifth Avenue apartment overlooking Central Park. One night, as they are entertaining a friend, Geoffrey (Ian McKellen)—a South African gold magnate they hope will offer financial backing for Flan's next deal—they are interrupted by a well-dressed, seemingly affluent young African American man, who claims to have been mugged nearby in Central Park. As he clutches his bleeding side (he says he was stabbed), Paul (Will Smith) explains that he came to Ouisa and Flan for help because he is a friend of their children, who are both away at college.

Ouisa and Flan, who plainly think of themselves as liberals, take pity on the young man. After bandaging his wound and offering him a clean shirt, they succumb to his charms. Paul gradually reveals not only that he knows much about them and their lives but that he is the son of Sidney Poitier, who is supposedly coming to New York the next day to begin work on a film version of the Broadway musical *Cats*. As implausible as this whole scenario is, Ouisa and Flan gradually buy into it, as Paul first cooks a magical meal for them, then mesmerizes them with an eloquent oration on the imagination. Geoffrey also buys into Paul's story, literally, offering the financial backing the Kittredges had been seeking. Paul's help in securing Flan's next big sale does not go unrewarded: The Kittredges offer him money and shelter for the night.

Early the next morning, Ouisa, hearing strange noises emanating from Paul's room, goes to investigate. When she discovers that Paul has used the fifty dollars the Kittredges gave him to pick up a male hustler on the street, Flan and Ouisa throw both men out of the apartment. Their initial reaction to the discovery that they have been deceived is to scurry around their apartment, checking to make sure all their possessions remain undisturbed.

Ouisa and Flan have been more thoroughly duped, however, than they at first realize. Discussing their adventure over brunch with friends, Flan and Ouisa discover that they are not the only people Paul has deceived. Further investigations reveal that Paul has successfully posed as Sidney Poitier's son on at least one other occasion and, ironically, that Sidney Poitier has no son.

Ouisa and Flan, thinking that they have lost fifty dollars but acquired a sparkling party anecdote, go to Rome, where they visit, among other things, the Sistine Chapel. Upon their return, however, they discover that Paul's grip on their lives has not loosened. Far from it: when they arrive back home, their own doorman, convinced that Paul is Flan's spurned and illegitimate black son, spits on Flan as he attempts to enter his building. It seems that Paul, once again exhibiting great credibility, has been able to play on the sympathies of another couple, this time a couple of poor young immigrants from Utah. Paul seduces them figuratively with his pose as Flan's outcast bastard son, then literally, as he seduces the young man, depriving him of his money and, finally, his life. What had been a diverting adventure for New York's elite proves a deadly game for those who lack their wealthier counterparts' financial insulation.

Yet as Donald Sutherland has remarked, the Kittredges themselves merely "live hand-to-mouth on a higher level." One character, Ouisa, recognizes how much she and the others have in common with Paul. It is she who muses over her "six degrees of separation" from him and she who listens to his final call for help. He tells her—truthfully or not—that of all the people he has met in New York, only she seems to have some sympathy for him. Recognizing both his gifts and his neediness, Ouisa promises to help Paul turn himself in to the police, but she and Flan arrive at the scene of Paul's arrest too late. Because they do not know his name and are not related, they lose Paul forever to the anonymity of the New York penal system.

Paul's upper-class victims are able to piece together the means by which he inveigled his way into their lives: in exchange for sexual favors, a prep-school friend of their children schooled Paul, a street hustler, in refinement and fed him details of his classmates' lives. Only Ouisa, however, understands that a deeper, truer connection exists between Paul and those he has conned. Their lives, like the two-sided Kandinsky painting that acts as a leitmotif in the film, featuring chaos on one side, order on the other, are merely the obverse of his. Superficially, Paul is everything they are not and which their society rejects: poor, African American, homosexual, and homeless. Yet he has demonstrated to them all too vividly what an illusion their remove from him is; with the right clothes, the right accent, the right manners, the right pedigree, and a little imagination, this clever young man was able to convince them—if only for a little while—that he was one of them.

For most of them, when the fantasy of appearing as extras in *Cats* disappears, so does their connection with Paul. For Ouisa, however, who has gaily touched the hand of God in Michelangelo's Sistine Chapel ceiling, the sense of connectedness remains, as does her sense of obligation. As she says, Paul has done more for them than their own children ever have (a point Guare drives home by making the Kittredge children and their fellows the whiniest, most obnoxious offspring imaginable). In view of the depth of Paul's commitment to his own singular vision of getting ahead, of becoming like his upper-class hosts—he even goes so far as to knife himself in the torso— everyone else in Ouisa's charmed circle seems to her superficial, her relationship to them hollow. Explaining why he hired a hustler during the night he spent at the Kittredges', Paul tells Ouisa he was so happy that he wanted to add sex to the experience to make it complete. When he assumes that Ouisa does the same, and Ouisa answers that she does not, the audience and Ouisa begin to understand that even her marriage is a sham.

In the theater version of *Six Degrees of Separation*, the characters speak directly to the audience, delivering their lines at breakneck speed to conjure up the quick pace and ambiance of modern life in Manhattan. The film version of Guare's play can, because of its very nature, make the city of New York an even more integral part of his story, to the point that it almost becomes a character itself. Director Fred Schepisi devotes a considerable amount of footage to the city, playing up the importance of the locations that form the backdrop for the lives of the Kittredges and their privileged fellows—Lincoln Center, the Rainbow Room—and the contrast they make with the stark landscape Paul inhabits in the same metropolis. *Six Degrees of Separation* is rooted in reality, based on a real individual who managed to pass himself off as Sidney

Poitier's son in New York high society. Guare saw in this story the makings of a modern parable, one which—as the film version of his play makes clear—could only happen in this city of stark contrasts, where opposites rub elbows and fact and fiction coexist, separated only by degree.

Lisa Paddock

Reviews

American Cinematographer. LXXV, March, 1994, p. 50.
Chicago Tribune. December 22, 1993, V, p. 1.
Entertainment Weekly. December 10, 1993, p. 50.
The Hollywood Reporter. December 1, 1993, p. 9.
Los Angeles Times. December 10, 1993, p. F4.
The Nation. CCLVIII, January 3, 1994, p. 32.
The New Republic. CCIX, December 27, 1993, p. 24.
The New York Times. December 8, 1993, p. C17.
Newsweek. CXXII, December 20, 1993, p. 121.
Time. CXLII, December 13, 1993, p. 80.
Variety. December 1, 19193, p. 4.
The Washington Post. December 22, 1993, p. F1.

SLEEPLESS IN SEATTLE

Production: Gary Foster; released by TriStar Pictures
Direction: Nora Ephron
Screenplay: Nora Ephron, David S. Ward, and Jeff Arch; based on a story by Arch
Cinematography: Sven Nykvist
Editing: Robert Reitano
Production design: Jeffrey Townsend
Art direction: Gershon Ginsburg and Charley Beal
Set decoration: Clay Griffith
Casting: Juliet Taylor
Sound: Kirk Francis
Costume design: Judy Ruskin
Music: Marc Shaiman
MPAA rating: PG
Running time: 100 minutes

Principal characters:

Sam Baldwin	Tom Hanks
Annie Reed	Meg Ryan
Jonah Baldwin	Ross Malinger
Suzy	Rita Wilson
Walter Jackson	Bill Pullman
Dr. Marcia Fieldstone	Caroline Aaron
Becky	Rosie O'Donnell
Jessica	Gaby Hoffmann
Greg	Victor Garber
Victoria	Barbara Garrick
Maggie Baldwin	Carey Lowell
Jay	Rob Reiner
Claire	Dana Ivey
Barbara Reed	Le Clanché du Rand
Cliff Reed	Kevin O'Morrison
Dennis Reed	David Hyde Pierce
Betsy Reed	Valerie Wright
Rob	Tom Riis Farrell

Regarding *Sleepless in Seattle*, director Nora Ephron has said that it is not a film about love but rather a film about love in films, a key distinction, as it turns out. To emphasize this, interspersed throughout the film are clips from *An Affair to Remember* (1957), a bittersweet romance starring Cary Grant and Deborah Kerr. Although it, too, is a film that centers on the phenomenon of falling in love, its use here is to point up how contemporary society's concept of romance has been influenced by motion pictures.

Sleepless in Seattle begins in Chicago at the funeral of beloved Maggie Baldwin (Carey Lowell), wife of Sam (Tom Hanks) and mother of Jonah (Ross Malinger). In an effort to begin again, father and son move to a houseboat in Seattle, a perfect home for a family set adrift by the death of a loved one. The narrative then leaps across the continent to Baltimore, where Annie Reed (Meg Ryan) and Walter Jackson (Bill Pullman) are announcing their engagement at the Reed family's Christmas Eve gathering. Walter, despite his preoccupation with multiple allergies, is in many respects Annie's ideal mate: sensible, successful, and caring—yet it is clear that Annie is not in love with him. After dinner, Annie and Walter leave in separate cars for Washington to spend Christmas with Walter's parents. As Annie drives along, she randomly flips through radio channels—singing carols, pausing momentarily to hear a program on "You and Your Spleen," and stopping at a radio call-in show with Dr. Marcia Fieldstone (Caroline Aaron). As luck would have it, Sam is on the air, reluctantly discussing his lingering sadness over the loss of his wife. He speaks of their life together and the "magic" of their love for each other—a magic that Annie both desires and misses in her relationship with her fiancé. Thousands of women from coast to coast listen, responding the next day by offering to take Maggie's place. The remainder of the film tracks Annie and Sam's developing relationship as each treks back and forth across the country, never meeting. Although the film teases the viewer with a series of near misses, the two do indeed get together before the close of the film.

Nora Ephron came to prominence in Hollywood as a screenwriter, gaining critical attention for her screenplay for *When Harry Met Sally . . .* (1989), another very successful romantic comedy. Both *Sleepless in Seattle* and *When Harry Met Sally . . .* emphasize the language and the look of love rather than its physical manifestations. Early in *Sleepless in Seattle*, Annie's mother, Barbara Reed (Le Clanche du Rand), tells the story of how she met Annie's father, Cliff (Kevin O'Morrison). A story filled with fateful meetings and moonlit handholding, it reinforces the grounding of this film in romance, the genealogy of romance, and the continuing epic of everyday romance. On the other hand, the film also presents women bodybuilders who request sexual pleasures by name and the potentially dangerous situations, as in 1987's *Fatal Attraction*, that await those who pursue love with strangers. Thus the choice between romance and "dating" becomes easy. The audience members, whether initiates to or veterans of romance, root for the magic that stirs and motivates Sam and Annie throughout the film. The overwhelming mood of the film is contagious.

Tom Hanks and Meg Ryan make a perfect couple, better here than in their previous pairing in *Joe Versus the Volcano* (1990). Hardly the traditional leading man, Hanks brings life to Sam, who is desirable because he is unafraid to feel and to discuss those feelings. Sam is a great friend, a great dad, a great husband. Meg Ryan's Annie is similar in many respects to her character in *When Harry Met Sally. . . .* Both women are strong, smart, and resourceful. Ryan is enjoyable to watch as her character wrestles with the competing allures of common sense (embodied in Walter) and romance (recognized in Sam). The chemistry between Hanks and Ryan transcends the distances imposed by the narrative and makes for enjoyable viewing.

A series of minor characters add depth and even wisdom to the story. For example, the loyalty and support of Annie's best friend, Becky (Rosie O'Donnell), enhance several scenes. While O'Donnell has some overtly comic scenes (such as a discussion of sentimental television ads), her character is more artfully drawn in smaller scenes. One particularly fine O'Donnell vignette occurs when her character converses by telephone with Annie, who has gone to Seattle to catch a glimpse of Sam and son. Becky's gentle encouragement and support calm Annie even as Becky urges her to go for what she wants rather than settling for what she has. Thus O'Donnell's Becky wins the audience's approval. Her performance is the epitome of fine timing.

Bill Pullman—not unlike Ralph Bellamy—seems to play a succession of characters who lose the love of a woman to the male lead, as he did in *Singles* (1992). In *Sleepless in Seattle*, his character is likable if dull. Walter is allergic to everything, sneezing through scenes with runny eyes and plenty of tissue. He is the nerd, a nicknameless Walter to their Annie, Sam, and Maggie. Nevertheless, he is no fool. He tells Annie that he does not want someone merely to settle for him; he wants to be someone's first choice. In giving Walter such strong, sensible lines, the writers elevate his character from merely comic or pathetic to simply the wrong match for Annie, a distinction that rings true.

Ross Malinger, eight years old at the time of filming, is a veteran of both films— *Kindergarten Cop* (1990), *Eve of Destruction* (1991), and *Late for Dinner* (1991)— and television—*Good Advice*, *Beverly Hills 90210*, *Who's the Boss?*, and *Roseanne*. While the role of Jonah is not a minor one, his main contribution is as a catalyst for Annie and Sam's romance. Malinger is charming, and the father-son relationship played by Hanks and Malinger works well. For example, when the two exchange glances while sitting side by side talking to Dr. Marcia Fieldstone, the love, concern, and frustration that their characters are experiencing is made manifest. Malinger's performance is believable with adults and with his friend, Jessica (Gaby Hoffmann), perhaps the world's youngest travel agent. While many critics have focused on Malinger's ability to keep pace in his comic dialogues with Hanks, perhaps a finer indication of his abilities is a scene in which Jonah wakes from a nightmare and is comforted by Sam. As father and son discuss Maggie, the expressions of their grief and love are somehow less rehearsed and more authentic.

Two other fine performances are given by Rob Reiner as Jay, who explains the 1990's dating ritual to Sam, and Rita Wilson as Suzy, who has one great scene in which she retells the plot of *An Affair to Remember*, complete with voices and tears. Finally, no one does New York better than Nora Ephron, except perhaps Woody Allen. Therefore, it is no surprise that some of the best lines and big laughs in the film come from gruff New Yorkers who actually have hearts of gold, such as cabdrivers and the employees at the Empire State Building.

In addition to trying to re-create the romance of the Golden Age of Cinema, Ephron wanted to avoid grounding the film in a particular era. For that reason, she instructed all the designers on the film to avoid anything trendy, anything that would place the film in a certain time period. What viewers will remember after the film are not the houses or costumes or cars but rather the very likable people and the larger-than-life love in which they believed.

Sleepless in Seattle ended the year with the eighth-highest box office (over $188 million worldwide). Further, it received two Academy Award nominations, one for its original screenply and one for the song "A Wink and a Smile."

The reviews of *Sleepless in Seattle* indicated the power of romance and the difficulty late twentieth century audiences had dealing with it. While almost every review was positive, each raised the issue of how embarrassing it is to allow oneself to get caught up in the joy and heartache of romance. *Sleepless in Seattle*, proclaimed by some critics to be "shamelessly romantic," captured filmgoers' hearts during a summer season that was otherwise dedicated to dinosaurs and action/adventure fare.

Roberta F. Green

Reviews

Boston Globe. June 25, 1993, p. 43.
Chicago Tribune. June 25, 1993, Tempo, p. 4.
Entertainment Weekly. Summer Double Issue, 1993, p. 84.
Films in Review. XLIV, September, 1993, p. 333.
The Hollywood Reporter. June 8, 1993, p. 10.
Los Angeles Times. June 25, 1993, p. F1.
The New Yorker. July 19, 1993, p. 79.
Newsweek. CXXI, June 28, 1993, p. 65.
Sight and Sound. III, October, 1993, p. 52.
Time. CXLII, July 5, 1993, p. 58.
Variety. June 8, 1993, p. 2.
The Washington Post. June 25, 1993, Weekend Section, p. 42.

SLIVER

Production: Robert Evans; released by Paramount Pictures
Direction: Phillip Noyce
Screenplay: Joe Eszterhas; based on the novel by Ira Levin
Cinematography: Vilmos Zsigmond
Editing: Richard Francis-Bruce and William Hoy
Production design: Paul Sylbert
Art direction: Peter Lansdown Smith
Set decoration: Lisa Fischer
Casting: Amanda Mackey and Cathy Sandrich
Sound: Tom Nelson
Costume design: Deborah L. Scott
Music: Howard Shore
MPAA rating: R
Running time: 106 minutes

Principal characters:
Carly Norris .... Sharon Stone
Zeke Hawkins .... William Baldwin
Jack Landsford .... Tom Berenger
Vida Jordan .... Polly Walker
Judy .... Colleen Camp
Alex Parsons .... Martin Landau
Lieutenant Victoria Hendrix .... CCH Pounder
Mrs. McEvoy .... Nina Foch
Gus Hale .... Keene Curtis

Named for the building in which it is set, this erotic thriller takes place in a tall, slender apartment building in New York City known as a "sliver" because of its odd shape: It is built straight up on a very small parcel of land. What distinguishes this building from others, besides its shape, is that each room is secretly equipped with high-tech video and audio surveillance equipment that has been installed by the wealthy and eccentric owner, Zeke Hawkins (William Baldwin). Zeke spends his days and nights behind an automated control center that faces a huge bank of video monitors, watching the most fascinating soap opera of all, real life. It is this voyeur's paradise that the unsuspecting Carly Norris (Sharon Stone) enters when she leases a vacant apartment in the building, succeeding the previous occupant, whose murder was disguised as a suicide.

Recently divorced, Carly is looking for a change in her life. She is shocked, however, to learn not only of the previous tenant's death but also of her own uncanny resemblance to the deceased. Further, Carly soon finds herself romantically pursued by Zeke, as well as another of the building's occupants, best-selling true-crime author

Jack Landsford (Tom Berenger). As a book editor for a New York publishing house, Carly would seem to have more in common with Jack, but she is attracted instead to Zeke, who is several years her junior. Carly is both vulnerable because of her recent marital breakup and naïve concerning dating etiquette. Hence, she allows Zeke to humiliate her in public: He persuades her to remove her underwear in a crowded restaurant. This idiotic scene not only fails to titillate but also succeeds in extinguishing any sympathetic feelings that the audience may have had for Carly.

Director Phillip Noyce and screenwriter Joe Eszterhas make many such miscalculations along the way. For example, early in the film, Carly masturbates in her bathtub, unwittingly observed by Zeke, who is watching on his television monitors. Noyce and Eszterhas shy away from making this act a mutual one, however, in which both parties would participate from their separate apartments, as they did in Ira Levin's novel, on which the film is based. By rendering Zeke a passive rather than a participatory observer, this crucial scene loses its power and becomes merely gratuitous. Zeke is, after all, the one who installed this six-million-dollar toy in his building. It only makes sense at least to imply that this is what he uses it for.

As is common with Hollywood adaptations of popular novels, Eszterhas has made a number of changes to Levin's original story, the most significant being the identity of the killer. Aside from this important alteration, other changes were warranted, especially considering the book's silly ending, in which a cat claws the killer's eyes out. Unfortunately, Eszterhas conceives an ending every bit as ridiculous, with one of the characters uttering the remark, "Get a life." Neither witty nor ironic, this line is merely moronic. Eszterhas has had problems before in devising suitable endings for his screenplays. *Basic Instinct* (1992), an otherwise fair film, was effectively ruined by its implausible ending. Furthermore, Eszterhas' *Flashdance* (1983) did not simply falter at the end; its characters and situations were implausible from the beginning of the film. In the case of *Sliver*, Eszterhas, like Levin, took a fascinating idea but went absolutely nowhere with it.

Although more tenants are murdered, voyeurism remains the film's focus. Soon after Carly moves in, she receives from a secret admirer a telescope, which, during a party in her apartment, she and her guests use to spy on a couple making love in an apartment across the street. The guests anxiously stand in line behind the telescope, waiting for their turn to get a peep at the unsuspecting couple. Carly later looks through the telescope, hoping to watch the same couple again, only to discover that they are looking back at her through their own telescope. Even the health club that Zeke and Carly attend is lined with mirrors, with everyone there watching everyone else. Voyeurism is an obsession to which Carly quickly becomes addicted. Despite her initial anger concerning Zeke's elaborate surveillance system, Carly relents when Zeke points out the telescope in her apartment. Zeke informs her that she too is a voyeur; the only difference between them is that he has better technology.

Voyeurism is nothing new in film. Such classic films as *Rear Window* (1954) and *Peeping Tom* (1960) made excellent use of the technique. While *Sliver* comes nowhere close to duplicating the success of these previous films, its technology is far more advanced. Editor William Hoy is credited with editing together the footage of the various tenants as they appear on the television monitors. A separate film unit spent six weeks shooting this footage. As a result, the audience becomes just as engrossed observing the tenants' private lives as Zeke and Carly do, a circumstance that lends validity to the characters' motivations and obsessive behavior. It is also important to note that not all the activities shown are of a sexual nature: Many scenes in the various apartments consist of such prosaic activities as brushing one's teeth. Although billed as an erotic thriller, *Sliver* is neither particularly erotic nor much of a thriller. The film's pacing is excruciatingly slow and the love scenes are surprisingly dull, perhaps because of the film's last-minute reediting, reportedly done to tone down the steamy love scenes. Any eroticism that may have been in these scenes before is certainly not evident now.

Director of photography Vilmos Zsigmond, who won an Academy Award for his cinematography in *Close Encounters of the Third Kind* (1977), does an excellent job, as usual. Despite the fact that Zsigmond and production designer Paul Sylbert collaborate to give the film a very polished look, their contributions were wasted on this film. Hoy's editing brings Zeke's surveillance system to life (although it does seem odd that a six-million-dollar, state-of-the-art surveillance system does not have color capability). The film itself reflects its own voyeuristic theme: It is wonderful to look at, but ultimately it contains nothing of substance.

Sharon Stone is far more appealing as Carly than she was in the flashier role of Catherine Tramell in *Basic Instinct*, the film that made her a star. Her performance as Carly is much more subdued and, at the beginning of the film, downright dowdy. Carly Norris is not a star-making role, but Stone shows that she is capable of turning in a credible performance.

William Baldwin, fresh from his portrayal of a low-rent male prostitute in the disastrously bad *Three of Hearts* (1993; reviewed in this volume), rebounds somewhat in this film. Baldwin is convincingly creepy as the rich kid playing God in his own world, encased within a high-rise building. Despite the fact that his leading-man good looks make it plausible that Carly would be attracted to him, the much ballyhooed difference in their ages is undetectable on screen.

Unfortunately for Tom Berenger, he more closely resembles the scarred Sergeant Barnes whom he portrayed in *Platoon* (1986). As Jack Landsford, his romantic pursuit of Carly is ludicrous. Berenger, a fine actor who is equally capable of playing both dramatic and comedic roles effectively, is miscast in this role, his talents wasted.

On the other hand, Polly Walker as Vida Jordan, the high-priced call girl who lives next door to Carly, makes the most of her small role, exuding charm and screen presence. She is a bright spot in a mostly dreary film.

Sliver, on the surface, seemed to have a lot going for it: a fascinating premise, excellent technical work, and two popular and talented leads—Stone and Baldwin. Nevertheless, the film as a whole will leave audiences frustrated.

George Delalis

Reviews

Chicago Tribune. May 21, 1993, I, p. 20.
Entertainment Weekly. June 4, 1993, p. 34.
The Hollywood Reporter. May 24, 1993, p. 5.
Los Angeles Times. May 22, 1993, p. F1.
National Review. XLV, June 21, 1993, p. 76.
New Statesman and Society. VI, August 20, 1993, p. 35.
The New York Times. May 22, 1993, p. 12.
Newsweek. May 31, 1993, p. 54.
Time. CXLI, May 31, 1993, p. 65.
Variety. May 24, 1993, p. 2.
The Washington Post. May 21, 1993, p. B1.

THE SNAPPER

Origin: Ireland
Released: 1993
Released in U.S.: 1993
Production: Lynda Myles for BBC Films and Screen 2; released by Miramax Films
Direction: Stephen Frears
Screenplay: Roddy Doyle; based on his novel
Cinematography: Oliver Stapleton
Editing: Mick Audsley
Production design: Mark Geraghty
Casting: Leo Davis
Sound: Kieran Horgan
Costume design: Consolata Boyle
MPAA rating: R
Running time: 90 minutes

Principal characters:
Dessie Curley	Colm Meaney
Sharon Curley	Tina Kellegher
Kay Curley	Ruth McCabe
Craig Curley	Eanna MacLiam
George Burgess	Pat Laffan
Yvonne Burgess	Karen Woodley
Doris Burgess	Virginia Cole
Jackie	Fionnula Murphy
Mary	Deirdre O'Brien
Lester	Brendan Gleeson
Bertie	Stuart Duine
Paddy	Ronan Wilmot

Unlike most recent Irish films, which have emphasized economic, social, and political conditions in Ireland and Northern Ireland, *The Snapper* is a throwback to the warmhearted Irish domestic comedy/dramas Hollywood occasionally produced during its golden age. The main difference between the earlier type of film and *The Snapper* is the latter's lack of overt sentimentality and its openness about sex. Adapted by Roddy Doyle from his novel, *The Snapper* deals with characters from an earlier Doyle novel, *The Commitments*, made into a film in 1991. Because the producers of the earlier film own the rights to the characters' names, however, the Rabbitte family has become the Curleys. Along with *The Van* (1992), Doyle's novels form a comic trilogy about working-class life in contemporary Dublin. While *The Commitments* presented a rock band united to create unexpectedly moving soul music only to allow petty bickering to break it up, *The Snapper* focuses on a family's unity despite disruptive forces.

Dessie Curley (Colm Meaney), a painting contractor, lives comfortably in the Barrytown section of Dublin with his wife, Kay (Ruth McCabe), and their six children. Their placidly ordinary existence begins to unravel when twenty-year-old Sharon (Tina Kellegher), a grocery clerk, announces she is pregnant. (The film's title is a local term for "baby," shortened from "whippersnapper.") Impregnated during a drunken encounter she barely remembers with a middle-aged neighbor, George Burgess (Pat Laffan), Sharon at first refuses to identify the father. When rumors about Burgess begin circulating, however, she makes up a story about a night in a hotel with a Spanish sailor.

Ironically, Sharon's pregnancy out of wedlock is less a cause for embarrassment for the Curleys than the true identity of the father. George Burgess, coach of a boys' football team, is an overweight, hapless husband and parent, the type of nonentity others make fun of behind his back. Dessie is so upset by the idea of Burgess impregnating Sharon that he stays away from his beloved pub to avoid the ridicule. No one believes the story about the Spanish sailor, even though all the Curleys and their friends insist otherwise.

The Snapper divides itself almost equally between the efforts of Sharon and of her father to deal with this situation. Except for having to go to the bathroom constantly, Sharon does not mind being pregnant and jokes about it with her friends, who include Burgess' daughter Yvonne (Karen Woodley). Once the father is known, however, friends and neighbors choose sides, with Yvonne, who dates Sharon's brother Craig (Eanna Macliam), turning against her friend. The ensuing warfare includes Craig's tossing a trash can through the Burgesses' window and Kay bloodying the nose of George's wife, Doris (Virginia Cole).

Although the easygoing but proud Dessie loves his daughter and defends her, he has never bothered to try to get to know her before. Father and daughter gradually, unmawkishly, grow closer as her pregnancy advances. Dessie even reads a book about women's sexuality to understand better what Sharon is going through and is delighted to learn about oral sex, which he introduces to Kay after twenty-five years of marriage.

The Snapper succeeds as a comedy by delicately skirting its potential for sentimentality and melodrama, except for a jarring scene in which Sharon runs in fear from Yvonne. The film's life-embracing attitude is exemplified by the decision to name the baby Georgina. Neither Doyle, director Stephen Frears, nor the actors condescend to the characters. Only occasionally do Frears and Doyle exaggerate the comic aspects, as when the film cuts from Sharon's painful delivery to Dessie's inability to get snacks out of a hospital vending machine.

As with *The Commitments*, Doyle loads his screenplay with popular-culture references, since the characters' personalities and values have been formed in part by films, television, and popular music. Early in her pregnancy, Sharon entertains her friends in a pub by singing Madonna's "Papa Don't Preach," which deals with another unwed mother-to-be. When Sharon makes up the Spanish-sailor story, her friend Jackie (Fionnula Murphy) compares the situation to that in *Letter to Brezhnev* (1985), in which two young women in Liverpool have affairs with Soviet sailors. Dessie sends his younger children out to buy "that stuff Tina Turner drinks." Hurriedly driving Sharon to the hospital in his truck, he hums the theme to the television series *Rawhide*.

Frears, whose films include *Dangerous Liaisons* (1988) and *The Grifters* (1990), has examined the British working-class milieu in several films, including *Gumshoe* (1972), *My Beautiful Laundrette* (1985), and *Prick Up Your Ears* (1987). Frears, who has made several low-budget films for British television since the late 1960's, made *The Snapper* for the BBC (thus the overuse of close-ups), with Miramax picking up its American theatrical rights in hopes of duplicating the 1992 success of *Enchanted April*. Frears, who may have wanted to make a small-scale film after the big-budget disaster of *Hero* (1992), handles intimate subjects with great expertise. The director makes the Curleys' neighborhood a microcosm of working-class Dublin by showing little awareness of the world outside except that communicated by the media. Frears and Doyle could be faulted for failing to give any indications of the economic hardships facing the Curley children and grandchild, but such concerns would unnecessarily intrude on the fragile comedy.

With a simple story and a no-frills production, a film such as *The Snapper* works only if it is cast properly. All the actors are convincing as the colorful inhabitants of Barrytown, with the three leads standing out. McCabe, best known as Christy Brown's nurse in *My Left Foot* (1989), plays the mother as someone completely open to life's surprises. Except for striking Doris, McCabe's Kay is amused by and accepting of all that transpires. Kellegher expertly conveys both Sharon's desperate need to have a good time and her acceptance of her fate. (Some viewers may be upset by Sharon's drinking alcoholic beverages throughout her pregnancy.) As portrayed by Kellegher, Sharon possesses an intelligence and enthusiasm for life for which she can find few outlets.

Meaney played the father in *The Commitments* as a rather thick-witted man who cared passionately about little but Elvis Presley. Having dropped the sideburns and more than a few pounds since the earlier film, Meaney portrays Dessie as an earthy man with simple tastes and, like his wife, a healthy optimism toward the unexpected. Dessie could easily have come across as a buffoon, but Meaney and Doyle invest him with equal measures of crassness and compassion. Meaney was named best actor at the 1993 Chicago International Film Festival for this performance and was nominated for a Golden Globe as best actor in a comedy or musical. The film was ineligible for Academy Award consideration because of a new rule excluding feature films made for television.

The Snapper succeeds because of its verisimilitude, its loving attention to detail. The Curley home looks lived in without calling unnecessary attention to the cleverness of Mark Geraghty's production design. *The Snapper*, named best film at the 1993 Toronto International Film Festival, is the kind of minor film that cannot fulfill high expectations but remains a small treasure for what it does achieve.

Michael Adams

Reviews

Boston Globe. September 18, 1993, p. 29.
Chicago Tribune. December 17, 1993, VII, p. 26.
Commonweal. CXXI, March 25, 1994, p. 16.
Entertainment Weekly. January 28, 1994, p. 34.
The Hollywood Reporter. May 17, 1993, p. 5.
Los Angeles Times. December 3, 1993, p. F1.
The New York Times. October 9, 1993, p. 12.
Newsweek. CXXII, December 27, 1993, p. 48.
Rolling Stone. December 9, 1993, p. 78.
Time. CXLII, December 6, 1993, p. 87.
Variety. April 19, 1993, p. 46.
The Washington Post. December 17, 1993, p. C1.

SOMMERSBY

Production: Arnon Milchan and Steven Reuther for Le Studio Canal Plus, Regency Enterprises, and Alcor Films; released by Warner Bros.

Direction: Jon Amiel

Screenplay: Nicholas Meyer and Sarah Kernochan; based on a story by Meyer and Anthony Shaffer and on the film *Le Retour de Martin Guerre*, written by Daniel Vigne and Jean-Claude Carriére

Cinematography: Philippe Rousselot

Editing: Peter Boyle

Production design: Bruno Rubeo

Art direction: Michael Johnston

Set decoration: Michael Seirton

Casting: Billy Hopkins and Suzanne Smith

Sound: Chris Newman

Costume design: Marilyn Vance-Straker

Music: Danny Elfman

MPAA rating: PG-13

Running time: 157 minutes

Principal characters:

Jack Sommersby	Richard Gere
Laurel Sommersby	Jodie Foster
Orin Meecham	Bill Pullman
Judge Isaacs	James Earl Jones
Reverend Powell	William Windom
Little Rob	Brett Kelley
Esther	Clarice Taylor
Joseph	Frankie Faison
Dick Mead	Ronald Lee Ermey
Doc Evans	Richard Hamilton
Mrs. Evans	Karen Kirschenbauer
Storekeeper Wilson	Carter McNeese
Tom Clemmons	Dean Whitworth
John Green	Stan Kelly

In 1983, a French film made its way to American shores and turned a tidy profit on the art-house circuit. Starring Gérard Depardieu and Nathalie Baye, *Le Retour de Martin Guerre* (*The Return of Martin Guerre*) recounts the factual tale of a sixteenth century French peasant who returns to his wife and family after disappearing for eight years. Although the man who reappears seems to be the same man, there are differences: The local shoemaker finds that his feet are smaller now, for example. When passing beggars indicate that he is not Martin but a man named Arnaud, suspicions begin and are fanned by Martin's uncle, from whom an accounting of the land's profits has been demanded by his supposed nephew. *The Return of Martin Guerre* offered not groundbreaking filmmaking but a satisfying romance backed up by solid acting, as well as an interesting history lesson.

The old and original story that formed the plot of that French film has also inspired a play, an operetta, two novels, several nonfiction studies, and a musical. It was of no surprise, then, that Hollywood, too, would want to capitalize on what appears to be a sure thing.

To its credit, *Sommersby*, the Hollywood remake of *The Return of Martin Guerre* set in the Reconstruction South, offers all the things that its predecessor did: a believable romance, strong acting, and a dash of history.

In Tennessee, in the years following the Civil War, Jack Sommersby (Richard Gere) returns to his wife and son to retake control of his estate. He has been gone for seven years, and at first the local townspeople of Vine Hill are not sure who he is. As Jack reveals small details of their lives, however, they eagerly accept him. At first, Jack's wife, Laurel (Jodie Foster), is also a bit reluctant to renew old feelings. Even Jack's old dog snarls at him. Laurel had assumed that her husband was dead and had let her affections drift slightly toward Orin Meecham (Bill Pullman), who has tried to help her and the Sommersby estate survive the war.

Yet there is something more lurking under Laurel's initial rejection. It is soon learned that the Jack Sommersby who left her to fight for the Confederate cause was not quite a homebody. At best indifferent to his wife, it appears he more often abused her. The Jack who has returned from the war, however, is kind, amusing, and generous. Soon Laurel accepts Jack and even becomes pregnant by him, but she is still unsure if he is a changed man or an impostor. Because he offers her the love that she wants in life, perhaps she does not want the question answered.

Jack, who had once gambled and cared for no one but himself, now inspires a venture which could be Vine Hill's economic deliverance. He proposes that the town stop planting cotton and change to tobacco. He also proposes the uncharacteristic idea that they use the Sommersby lands as a communal farm—even the former slaves. Everyone will contribute what they can to buy the precious and expensive seed, and everyone will profit from the crop.

In the meantime, the displaced and jealous Orin plots ways to oust his rival. Because the new Jack treats his former slaves as humans, not as property, Orin encourages the emerging Ku Klux Klan to threaten Jack. Jack is then arrested for the murder of a Mississippi man following a card game. With the people of Vine Hill behind him, Jack heads for trial in the Nashville court of the African American Judge Isaacs (James Earl Jones). For Jack's offense, to be found guilty is to be hanged.

Because there is no question that the real Jack Sommersby is guilty of the crime, the plot instead hinges on the accused man's decision: Does he find refuge in agreeing that he is an impostor, therefore going free but losing everything that he has gained, or does he continue to insist that he is Jack and pay the price of his identity with his life? He must choose between love and honor and his desire for life.

Jon Amiel, the director of *Queen of Hearts* (1989) and *Tune in Tomorrow . . .* (1990), addresses this dilemma in a most entertaining way, but the result is what at one time would have been called a "woman's film." More cynical viewers might not appreciate the sentimental approach, but many others will be reaching for their handkerchiefs. This is one of the most convincingly romantic films to reach the screen in quite a while, and audiences love it. *Sommersby* was among Warner's top ten grossing films for 1993.

Jodie Foster is photographed by Philippe Rousselot, the cinematographer for *A River Runs Through It* (1992), in such a soft way that her beauty is noticeable for the first time over her powerful acting. She more than holds her own against the sexy Richard Gere while imbuing her character with intelligence, determination, and resilience. Gere, on the other hand, has set aside the often sleazy sexiness that he expressed in characters such as Julian Kay in *American Gigolo* (1980), as well as the hard edge that he imparted to the romance in *An Officer and a Gentleman* (1982). Instead he has built on the assets that revived his career in *Pretty Woman* (1990). Throughout *Sommersby* he uses a winning charm and a contagious humor to make his character very appealing to those who are inclined to indulge in romantic fantasy.

The chemistry displayed between Gere and Foster, set within a seductive and insightful story line, makes *Sommersby* an attractive film. Following the precedent set by the romantic, epic 1992 remake of *The Last of the Mohicans*, *Sommersby* proved the appeal of period pieces and showed that there was room for more heartfelt romances in Hollywood. Although the historical romance *Far and Away* (1992), starring Tom Cruise, did not fare well, many critics and viewers hoped that the success of *The Last of the Mohicans* and *Sommersby* would inspire more films relying on intelligence and passion, instead of mere sex, for their romance. It was also hoped that they will be as perceptive and entertaining as *Sommersby*.

Beverley Bare Buehrer

Reviews

Chicago Tribune. February 5, 1993, VII, p. 34.
The Christian Science Monitor. February 8, 1993, p. 14.
Entertainment Weekly. February 19, 1993, p. 43.
Films in Review. XLIV, May, 1993, p. 189.
The Hollywood Reporter. January 29, 1993, p. 8.
Los Angeles Times. February 5, 1993, p. F1.
The Nation. CCLVI, March 8, 1993, p. 316.
The New York Times. February 5, 1993, p. B1.
Rolling Stone. February 18, 1993, p. 65.
Time. February 22, 1993, p. 69.
Variety. January 29, 1993, p. 4.
The Washington Post. February 5, 1993, p. B1.

THE STORY OF QIU JU
(QIU JU DA GUANSI)

Origin: China and Hong Kong
Released: 1992
Released in U.S.: 1993
Production: Ma Fung Kwok for Sil-Metropole Organisation (Hong Kong) and
 Beijing Film Academy-Youth Film Studio (China); released by Sony Pictures
 Classics
Direction: Zhang Yimou
Screenplay: Liu Heng; based on the novel *The Wan Family's Lawsuit*, by Chen
 Yuan Bin
Cinematography: Chi Xiao Ling and Yu Xiao Qun
Editing: Du Yuan
Art direction: Cao Jioping
Sound: Li Lan Hua
Music: Zhao Jiping
MPAA rating: PG
Running time: 100 minutes

Principal characters:
Qiu Ju	Gong Li
Village Head	Lei Lao Sheng
Husband of Qiu Ju	Liu Pei Qi
Sister-in-law	Yang Liu Chun
Officer Li	Ge Zhi Jun
Unnamed character	Zhu Qanqing
Unnamed character	Cui Luowne
Unnamed character	Yang Huiqin
Unnamed character	Wang Jianfa
Unnamed character	Lin Zi
Unnamed character	Ye Jun

Based on Chen Yuan Bin's novella *The Wan Family's Lawsuit*, this film takes a comic look at obsession, justice, stubbornness, bureaucracy, and the mystifying concept of saving face—a factor of great importance among many cultures. Director Zhang Yimou, who was responsible for such intense masterpieces as *Ju Dou* (1990) and *Raise the Red Lantern* (1991), has taken a more lighthearted approach in the making of *The Story of Qiu Ju.*

The film opens with a pregnant Qiu Ju (Gong Li) and her sister-in-law (Yang Liu Chun) carting an injured man through a dense crowd. The man, Qiu Ju's husband (Liu Pei Qi), is being taken to the doctor following a kick to the groin administered by the Village Head (Lei Lao Sheng).

Despite the fact that Qiu Ju's husband will recover after some bed rest, Qiu Ju visits the home of the Village Head seeking restitution. The Village Head, however, is unremorseful and only offers the opportunity for the husband to kick him in the groin. A dissatisfied Qiu Ju then goes to the village seeking justice. This is the beginning of a tortuous journey through the bureaucracy of the Chinese government, as Qiu Ju persists in taking her case slowly, step by step, up the chain of command.

It is important to realize that Qiu Ju is not after money. The initial ruling of Officer Li (Ge Zhi Jun), the local Public Security Bureau chief, would have provided Qiu Ju and her husband money for medical expenses and lost wages. What Qiu Ju wants is an apology and an explanation. She wants to know why a man in a position of power, such as that held by the Village Head, feels justified in committing such an abusive act. She becomes obsessed with obtaining justice, particularly after the Village Head refuses to apologize and attempts to humiliate Qiu Ju. Despite being pregnant, Qiu Ju travels considerable distances, on foot, bicycle, cart, pedicab, and bus, in her quest. A very determined woman, she is stubborn in her belief of right over wrong. Unfortunately, the Village Head is just as stubborn as she is.

Qiu Ju's obstinacy soon becomes a running joke among the locals, and her husband becomes an object of ridicule. Her husband is seen as weak because he allows his wife to fight his battles for him. Pressure begins to mount from all sides to settle this conflict. Qiu Ju's husband wants her to stop appealing the rulings of the Public Security Bureau. The Village Head in turn is pressured by his political superiors to end this increasingly embarrassing incident. Although the Village Head is willing to pay a second, slightly higher amount as a settlement, he still refuses to apologize. Without an apology, Qiu Ju will not allow the matter to be settled.

The reason for the Village Head's refusal to apologize is that he fears losing face, which was the reason for the initial attack in the first place: Qiu Ju's husband had insulted the Village Head during an argument, by ridiculing him for having sired only girls and thus being incapable of producing an heir. In this rural culture, that comment was considered the ultimate insult. The Village Head saved face by kicking Qiu Ju's husband in the groin. In the Village Head's eyes, apologizing would legitimize the initial insult, causing him to lose face.

Losing or saving face is a huge concern for many characters in this film besides the Village Head. In one scene, Officer Li urges Qiu Ju to drop the matter in order for the Village Head to save face. In another scene, Qiu Ju employs an educated man to draft a legal letter clarifying the situation. The man asks Qiu Ju if she prefers a mild letter or a merciless letter, explaining that a mild letter will allow the Village Head to save face. Recognizing the importance of saving face, Qiu Ju insists on a mild letter. After all, she does not want to destroy the Village Head; she wants to leave him a graceful way out. Nevertheless, she will not withdraw completely either.

In *Ju Dou* and *Raise the Red Lantern*, Director Zhang Yimou portrayed the ways and attitudes of the Chinese before the Cultural Revolution. He provided a fascinating look inside a culture as could only be shown by someone intimate with the culture, many aspects of which appeared strange to Western viewers. With *The Story of Qiu*

Ju, Zhang shows that life in postrevolution China can be just as odd.

Zhang has experienced the strange ways of the Chinese, especially those of the government, firsthand: *Ju Dou* was the first Chinese film to be nominated for an Academy Award for Best Foreign-Language Film. Shortly before the actual award ceremonies were held, however, the Chinese government attempted to pull the film from competition, even though the government itself had submitted it, as required by Academy regulations. The Academy refused to withdraw the film.

The next year, *Raise the Red Lantern* was also nominated by the Academy for Best Foreign-Language Film. This time the film was submitted by Hong Kong. Yet both of these films were initially banned in China. The Chinese government was eventually forced to relent, however, in order to save face. Like Qiu Ju, Zhang never received an explanation for the government's ban. Zhang has stated in interviews that he felt much as Qiu Ju did in her story—lost in a world of bureaucracy, not knowing to whom to turn.

Zhang is among the world's most talented and consistently interesting directors. Yet fans of his earlier work may be surprised by this film. While not a complete departure from his earlier films, *The Story of Qiu Ju* is sufficiently different. Although this film is not as serious as his previous ones, the actions of the characters do have serious repercussions. Zhang has specialized in documenting rural life, a tradition that he continues here. Yet he also includes several big-city scenes and comments on big-city life. When Qiu Ju and her sister-in-law go to the city, they look so out of place that they appear to be Chinese versions of the Beverly Hillbillies. Ironically, they add to their inappropriate appearance by purchasing what they think are hip city clothes.

The biggest difference between this film and Zhang's previous films is in the actual look of the film. *Ju Dou* and *Raise the Red Lantern* were beautiful, color-saturated films that looked like paintings come to life, much like the films of Peter Greenaway. Yet in this film Zhang seems to have made a conscious decision to show modern China as a far more dreary, colorless landscape. Zhang's only concession to the use of vibrant colors is in the beautifully rich, red chili peppers hanging to dry in front of Qiu Ju's house, reminiscent of the flowing dyed garments in *Ju Dou.*

Furthermore, Zhang showcases the fascinating rural market culture built around the chili peppers. Generations of families buy and sell the peppers, processing them on the spot: grinding them into powder form or turning them into a paste. To Qiu Ju, the peppers are money, and whenever she needs more money in her pursuit of justice, she brings more of them to the marketplace, where she haggles over price with the vendors. The rate of exchange depicted likens this rural market to an international monetary exchange where dollars are converted to drachmas or yen.

The market in the District, a large town, forms quite a contrast with the rural village market. The District market is far more commercial, dealing more in consumer goods. It is plastered with posters of people mimicking rock stars and models. The emphasis is on entertainment and pleasure rather than on food and survival. Zhang uses the marketplaces to show Qiu Ju's increasing sense of alienation as she furthers her pursuit.

The numerous crowd scenes are expertly done and contribute to the success of the film. Striving for authenticity, Zhang filmed the crowd scenes using two hidden cameras to avoid the tendency of nonprofessional actors to look directly into the camera. His crew planted the cameras the night before, then released the actors into the day's crowds. Almost half of the film was shot with hidden cameras.

In fact, Zhang Yimou utilized only four professional actors for this film. Heading the professional cast, in the role of Qiu Ju, is Gong Li, who also starred in all four of Zhang's previous films. Gong Li, among the world's premiere actresses, has convincingly portrayed a wide variety of roles. For this role, she learned the Shaanxi dialect in only one month. Her performance as Qiu Ju won for her the Best Actress Award at the Venice Film Festival, and the film itself was awarded the Golden Lion Award at the Venice Film Festival.

It is not surprising that Zhang works well with actors. He himself is an award-winning actor, winning the Best Actor Award at the Tokyo Film Festival for his role in Wu Tianming's *Old Well* (1987). Zhang was also an award-winning cinematographer before he started directing his own films.

Between his debut with *Red Sorghum* (1988) and *The Story of Qiu Ju*, Zhang Yimou averaged a film each year. It is rather unusual for a director so well respected, whose work is consistently of such high quality, to be so prolific. *The Story of Qiu Ju* is yet another one of the director's masterpieces. Not only has Zhang put China on the international film map, but he has also given hope and provided joy for serious cinema fans throughout the world.

George Delalis

Reviews
American Historical Review. XCVIII, October, 1993, p. 1158.
Chicago Tribune. May 28, 1993, VII, p. 28.
Films in Review. XLIV, July, 1993, p. 272.
Los Angeles Times. May 7, 1993, p. F12.
The New York Times. October 2, 1992, p. B9.
The New Yorker. April 26, 1993, p. 110.
Rolling Stone. April 15, 1993, p. 72.
San Francisco Chronicle. April 29, 1993, p. E1.
Sight and Sound. III, May, 1993, p. 55.
Time. April 26, 1993, p. 68.
Variety. September 11, 1992, p. 12.
The Wall Street Journal. April 22, 1993, p. A12.
The Washington Post. May 14, 1993, p. 46.

STRICTLY BALLROOM

Origin: Australia
Released: 1992
Released in U.S.: 1993
Production: Tristram Miall and Ted Albert for M & A Film Corporation; released
    by Miramax Films
Direction: Baz Luhrmann
Screenplay: Baz Luhrmann and Andrew Bovell; based on the play by Luhrmann
    and Craig Pearce
Cinematography: Steve Mason
Editing: Jill Bilcock
Production design: Catherine Martin
Casting: Faith Martin
Sound: Ben Osmo
Costume design: Angus Strathie
Choreography: John "Cha Cha" O'Connell
Music: David Hirschfelder
MPAA rating: PG
Running time: 94 minutes

Principal characters:
Scott Hastings . . . . Paul Mercurio
Fran . . . . Tara Morice
Barry Fife . . . . Bill Hunter
Shirley Hastings . . . . Pat Thomson
Liz Holt . . . . Gia Carides
Les Kendall . . . . Peter Whitford
Doug Hastings . . . . Barry Otto
Ken Railings . . . . John Hannan
Tina Sparkle . . . . Sonia Kruger-Tayler

Feature films have always been the United States' most well known and profitable export, but seldom are foreign films able to break into the crowded and competitive American market. In 1993, however, one such import, a low-budget film from Australia called *Strictly Ballroom*, had American audiences sitting up and taking notice.

Strictly Ballroom tells the story of a man and a woman and of a passion they share for the infectious but relatively unknown endeavor known as ballroom dancing. Ballroom dancing is popular and well-loved around the world, where it is regarded as a legitimate competitive sport. The competitions, something comparatively nonexistent in the United States, are often televised on a regular basis. In the United States, ballroom dancing is no more than a hobby for a rare few.

For American audiences, *Strictly Ballroom* may seem to be a cross between *Saturday Night Fever* (1977) and *Dirty Dancing* (1987). Just as these popular American films inspired renewed interest in dancing, *Strictly Ballroom* may begin an American fascination with ballroom, a style of dance that is already popular worldwide. Starring real-life Australian dance sensation Paul Mercurio and newcomer Tara Morice, the film is a labor of love for its first-time director, Baz Luhrmann. He first launched his idea as a student workshop, where it grew into a stage production and, finally, into an internationally acclaimed motion picture, distributed by Miramax Films.

Miramax itself has had much to do with the success of *Strictly Ballroom*. This small, independent film company had a stellar year in 1992, spawning some of the year's most critically acclaimed and awarded films, such as *Passion Fish*, *Enchanted April*, and the sleeper hit of the year, *The Crying Game*. *Strictly Ballroom* found solid audiences in the United States in the wake of these Miramax successes. This is not to say, however, that *Strictly Ballroom* does not stand on its own. Unlike these Miramax releases of 1992, it is not a drama. In fact, it plays more as a comic farce than anything else. Featuring quick edits, a fast-paced narrative, a handsome leading actor, dancing, and romance, this Australian import soon became an audience favorite. It has won its share of awards, taking the prestigious Prix de la jeunesse award at the 1992 Cannes Film Festival as well as audience awards at the Toronto and Palm Springs film festivals. The motion picture was nominated for thirteen Australian Film Institute Awards, Australia's equivalent to the Oscars, including a nomination for Best Picture.

Paul Mercurio plays Scott Hastings, a champion male ballroom dancer. Talented and handsome, he is the bright hope of his parents, his partner Liz (Gia Carides), and his fans. When Scott decides to break from the traditional steps of ballroom dancing during one regional competition, however, he immediately feels the heat from everyone, especially his partner, who leaves in search of a less selfish and more conventional teammate. Scott, for his part, is bored with the same old routines and longs for the chance to show off his original moves. Although the audiences prefer the new moves, both his manager (Peter Whitford) and his mother (Pat Thomson) come down firmly on the side of tradition. They order him to comply with the rigid ballroom codes, which restrict original steps. Scott's manager and mother are fully supported by the president of the Australian Dance Federation (Bill Hunter), a man determined to maintain his own tight grip on the standards and traditions of ballroom dancing in Australia.

Scott seems to have only one ally in his quest to dance his way: a dance student named Fran (Tara Morice). She offers to be his new partner in spite of her beginner status. Once she persuades Scott that she is as excited as he is about bringing new moves and passion into ballroom dancing, Scott takes her under his wing and teaches her the steps required for competition. Along the way, they experiment with new moves and find themselves slowly falling in love.

Despite appearances, however, *Strictly Ballroom* is far from pure romance. Although Scott and Fran are the central characters in the film, it is the environment surrounding them that provides the real essence and temper of the film. Because

Luhrmann films *Strictly Ballroom* in a partially documentary style, he is able to present caricatures, such as the domineering mother, the mousy father, the self-consumed dancers, and the bombastic federation president. These caricatures, along with the quick-paced editing that begins the film, create a comic and thoroughly enjoyable mood which is carried throughout the film.

Luhrmann provides an atmosphere where nothing is taken at all seriously, except the dancing—the dancing is always center stage. As in *Saturday Night Fever*, the working-class heroes find glamour and glory only on the dance floor. Scott's family owns and operates a dance studio, and Fran's father and grandmother own a corner market. Both characters are from humble circumstances, yet Scott's parents are themselves former champions. What gives *Strictly Ballroom* its unique and original look, however, is the film's inattention to glamour in other aspects of the characters' lives. The world Scott and Fran live in is a modest and simple one. They have one single dream: to dance. They have nothing to prove, except to themselves, and it is refreshing that there is no talk of fame or fortune. Instead, the characters speak of feeling and expressing the passion brought out by the dance.

Mercurio and Morice work well together as Scott helps ugly duckling Fran blossom into a swan just in time for the big competition. American audiences will find a natural comparison between *Strictly Ballroom* and the American sleeper hit *Dirty Dancing*. Each film features a talented and good-looking male dancer who teaches an awkward girl about dancing and about life. While Luhrmann does well to distance himself from being overly predictable, a happy ending is par for the course.

What makes *Strictly Ballroom* an original pleasure is its fast-paced but innocent style, using sight gags and caricatures within a serious narrative structure. Although there are times when the film seems to be a documentary, there are other times when it almost resembles an absurdist fantasy. This fantasy is what makes *Strictly Ballroom* such a treasure.

Catherine R. Springer

Reviews

Chicago Tribune. February 26, 1993, VII, p. 18.
Dance Magazine. LXVI, October, 1992, p. 60.
The Hollywood Reporter. May 18, 1992, p. 5.
Los Angeles Times. February 12, 1993, p. F10.
The New York Times. September 26, 1992, p. 12.
The New Yorker. LXVIII, February 15, 1993, p. 95.
Time. CXLI, February 15, 1993, p. 67.
Variety. May 14, 1992, p. 18.
The Wall Street Journal. February 11, 1993, p. A12.
The Washington Post. February 26, 1993, p. C7.

THE SUMMER HOUSE

Origin: Great Britain
Released: 1993
Released in U.S.: 1993
Production: Norma Heyman for BBC Films; released by the Samuel Goldwyn Company
Direction: Waris Hussein
Screenplay: Martin Sherman; based on the novel *The Clothes in the Wardrobe*, by Alice Thomas Ellis
Cinematography: Rex Maidment
Editing: Ken Pearce
Production design: Stuart Walker
Casting: Susie Figgis
Sound: John Pritchard
Costume design: Odile Dicks-Mireaux and Leah Archer
Music: Stanley Myers
MPAA rating: no listing
Running time: 82 minutes

Principal characters:
Lili . . . . Jeanne Moreau
Mrs. Monro . . . . Joan Plowright
Margaret. . . . . Lena Headey
Monica. . . . . Julie Walters
Syl . . . . David Threlfall
Nour. . . . . Padraig Casey
Mother Joseph . . . . Britta Smith
Mrs. Raffald. . . . . Maggie Steed
Robert . . . . John Wood
Cynthia. . . . . Gwyneth Strong
Derek . . . . Roger Lloyd Pack
Marie-Clair . . . . Catherine Schell

The Summer House is set in the London suburb of Croydon in 1959. It is a plain, unexceptional community, and the center of a celebrated, yet ordinary event: an impending wedding. Young Margaret (Lena Headey) has accepted the proposal of Syl (David Threlfall). Family and friends gradually arrive to mark the occasion and to reminisce.

Margaret, however, is a most reluctant bride. In fact, she finds Syl repugnant. He is a forty-year-old, self-important bore who still lives with his mother, Mrs. Monro (Joan Plowright). He senses but largely ignores Margaret's lack of interest in him, taking her passivity as a sign of willingness to be wooed. Margaret dreams of much more exotic terrain, of the Egypt she has recently visited, where she had an intense love affair with a reckless, perhaps even dangerous, young man (Padraig Casey). Croydon—and most especially Syl—seem depressingly dull to Margaret.

Yet *The Summer House* is not a dreary study of suburban banality, a coming-of-age film, or an exposé of conformism in the 1950's. Both the screenplay and the acting have a freshness and exhilaration that shatters conventional treatments of such subjects. For one thing, although Margaret longs for Egypt, it is not really because of her lover—as stirring as that episode was. She yearns, surprisingly, to be a nun and has succumbed to Syl only to please her anxious mother, Monica (Julie Walters). By herself, Margaret is not strong enough to escape her suburban trap.

Again, *The Summer House* surprises by sprucing up its theme with vivid characterization. Monica, for example, is a wonderful creation. Her values are thoroughly conventional, but she throws herself with such relish into preparations for the wedding that it is hard for the reticent Margaret to convey how she feels to her spirited, buxom mother. Why should Margaret not be happy, wonders Monica, who treats her daughter's jitters as typical prenuptial behavior.

Next door, Syl waits on his mother and patiently explains to her that life will not change that much after he has married Margaret. After all, his mother has known Margaret all her life. One's first impression is that Mrs. Monro must be domineering, and Syl, a mama's boy. Yet this is not the case at all. Mrs. Monro has grave reservations about her son (expressed very subtly by Joan Plowright's severe reserve), and she soon realizes that Margaret has no affection for Syl, who is a chip off the old block—that is, he is a womanizer just like his father. Mrs. Monro does not feel the least bit sentimental about this wedding or confident about her son's faithfulness to Margaret.

It would seem everything is headed for disaster, with Syl smugly pursuing Margaret, Monica gaily fitting her daughter for her wedding gown, and Mrs. Monro sulkily resigning herself to the not-so-blessed event. Then Lili, a family friend, (Jeanne Moreau), arrives with a flourish. As this great French actress has said of herself and her role: "I have fought and shunned convention and routine all my life. Anything that progresses and moves on, breaking the rules, fascinates me. I feel my energy should be spent on the unconventional. Lili was therefore inevitable."

Moreau plays Lili as a great actress, a charming, vibrant eccentric. The actress and her role fuse inextricably. Lili soon sizes up the situation, correctly identifying Margaret's sense of doom, Monica's ebullient obliviousness to her daughter's suffering, and Syl's insufferable, leering confidence. How to prevent the wedding without hurting Monica or compromising Margaret is what Lili must puzzle out as she shares the confidences of mother and daughter. She even manages to befriend the aloof Mrs. Monro—an especially hard case, since many years before Lili had had an assignation with Mrs. Monro's husband in the summer house.

Lili makes her first decisive move by paying a social call on Mrs. Monro in the company of Margaret. Mrs. Monro is frigid but correct, and the visit—a sedate tea—occurs without incident. Lili maintains her initiative by immediately returning to Mrs. Monro, who is prepared to treat Lili as a nuisance. She is startled and won over, however, when Lili suddenly produces from her coat a pint of whiskey. In the kitchen, the two women drink and confide in each other, losing all their inhibitions and frankly admitting that a marriage between Syl and Margaret would be a calamity.

Although revealing the end of the film would take little away from its wonderful sense of fun and the superb acting that supports it, perhaps it is still best to reserve a few surprises. Nevertheless, as the film's title indicates, the denouement occurs in the summer house, a place where inhibitions disappear and the raw desires that subsist in suburban lives are realized.

The Summer House shrewdly delays its denouement by heightening the comedy of the occasion. For example, at a party in Monica's house the night before the wedding, Mrs. Monro is badgered by a well-meaning but oafish male. She exacts her revenge by deftly spilling her drink on him, effectively dousing his attentions. Joan Plowright executes this move so quickly, masking her character's venom with a startled look, followed for a split second by an expression of satisfaction, that the viewer virtually shares her pleasure—both the actress's and the character's pleasure in the incident. It is a delicious moment in which professional and social acting coincide—so real and yet so obviously rehearsed in its exquisite timing. Like the film itself, Plowright's acting is never labored, never explicit. She is always on, so that there are no dead spots.

All the performances in *The Summer House* are strong. David Threlfall plays the smirking male to the hilt, with just a hint, perhaps, of self-doubt that he silences by pretending that Margaret's increasing objections to him are merely silly. He has just enough humanity to mask his concern. Yet he does not play the part so broadly as to make it a cartoon. Each character, indeed, is given not only quirks but an interesting point of view, so that each one stands out as an individual—tied to the plot yet more than a collection of mannerisms.

The strength of the cast and the story makes Jeanne Moreau's performance even more impressive. For she has to be not only flamboyant but a bit of a detective, searching out the best way of maneuvering things so that Margaret will not have to commit herself to this unfortunate marriage. As Lili, Moreau has to make things look easy while admitting to Mrs. Monro (who becomes Lili's only confidant) that she is really stumped as to what to do. In the end, Lili must act on her own—playing the part of the renegade, the scandalous neighbor, even as she maintains her humanity and endears herself to everyone. Seldom have the problems of acting (how to convey all these different shades of character) and of plot (how to extricate Margaret from her fate) corresponded so exquisitely.

Carl Rollyson

Reviews
Chicago Tribune. December 24, 1993, VII, p. 32.
The Christian Science Monitor. March 11, 1994, p. 14.
The Hollywood Reporter. December 21, 1993, p. 10.

Los Angeles Times. December 21, 1993, p. F10.
The New Republic. CCX, January 10 and 17, 1994, p. 31.
The New York Times. December 21, 1993, p. B1.
San Francisco Chronicle. December 24, 1993, p. D3.
Time. CXLIII, January 31, 1994, p. 108.
Variety. October 23, 1993, p. 6.
The Washington Post. December 24, 1993, p. C1.

THIS BOY'S LIFE

Production: Art Linson; released by Warner Bros.
Direction: Michael Caton-Jones
Screenplay: Robert Getchell; based on the book by Tobias Wolff
Cinematography: David Watkin
Editing: Jim Clark
Production design: Stephen J. Lineweaver
Art direction: Sandy Cochrane
Set decoration: Jim Erickson
Casting: Owens Hill and Rachel Abroms
Sound: Rob Young
Costume design: Richard Hornung
Music: Carter Burwell
MPAA rating: R
Running time: 115 minutes

Principal characters:

Dwight Hansen	Robert DeNiro
Caroline Wolff	Ellen Barkin
Toby Wolff	Leonardo DiCaprio
Arthur Gayle	Jonah Blechman
Pearl	Eliza Dushku
Roy	Chris Cooper
Norma	Carla Gugino
Skipper	Zack Ansley
Kathy	Tracey Ellis
Marian	Kathy Kinney

Based on Tobias Wolff's 1989 memoir of his youth and set in the late 1950's, *This Boy's Life* tells the story of an adolescent trying to cope with an abusive stepfather and an immature mother who continuously shows poor judgment in trying to rear the boy. The mother, Caroline (Ellen Barkin), and her son, Toby Wolff (Leonardo DiCaprio), are running away as the film opens. It soon becomes apparent that this is not the first time but rather fits an established pattern. They are on their way to Salt Lake City, Utah, because Caroline has an absurd notion of getting rich there through uranium. Most important, however, they are running from Roy (Chris Cooper), who was Caroline's loutish boyfriend in Florida. Fully aware of the situation, the teenage Toby comments on his mother's poor taste in men. Once they reach Salt Lake City, Caroline abandons the car when it breaks down. This is the way she handles all of her problems. Not long after they have settled in, Roy catches up with them. Although Roy makes an effort at reconciliation, he is soon forcing himself on Caroline. Toby listens from the other room as Roy rapes her. The next day Toby and Caroline are on the run again.

Toby and Caroline next choose Seattle, mainly because a bus is leaving shortly for that destination. Six months later, still in Seattle, Caroline once again becomes involved in a relationship that inevitably leads to disaster. The moment she brings Dwight Hansen (Robert De Niro) home, Toby immediately takes a dislike to him. Toby can see right through Dwight's false sincerity, his phony manners, and his corny jokes. Dwight is a strange person, but characteristically Caroline is blind to these signals of his true personality. Dwight manages to hide his abusive nature until after he has persuaded Caroline to marry him. Caroline, for her part, does not marry Dwight out of love but out of some bizarre notion that Toby requires a strict male role model to check his rebellious behavior. Poor Caroline is a born victim. She discovers during her wedding night what a mistake she has made when Dwight turns into an abusive, domineering beast. She compounds her mistake by deciding to endure the situation, explaining that she is tired of running. Yet if there were ever a time for her to run away, this is it.

Although Dwight is a brute, he is not solely responsible for the situation in which Caroline and Toby find themselves. Caroline must share the blame, not only for putting Toby and herself in this hellish situation but also for refusing to extricate them from it. Caroline was, after all, exposed to Dwight's true nature before their marriage when she won the local Thanksgiving Day turkey shoot in Dwight's hometown of Concrete, Washington. As a result of her success, Dwight became incensed and brooded. Even Toby is not blameless. He lived with Dwight for a few months before the marriage—in a misguided effort on his mother's part to straighten out her son after some trouble at school. Instead of warning his mother about Dwight's idiosyncrasies, Toby simply resigned himself to the situation.

Now that Caroline, Toby, Dwight, and Dwight's own three children have formed a household, matters go from bad to worse. Dwight does not treat his own three children as harshly as he does Toby. Dwight is verbally and mentally abusive of his own children (who anticipate escaping Dwight's oppression as soon as they are graduated from high school), but he saves the physical abuse for Toby. For two years this nightmare continues, until Toby finally finds a means of escape through a scholarship to a preparatory school back East. An enraged Dwight then goes so far as to attempt to strangle Toby on the kitchen floor, until Caroline hits Dwight over the head with a baseball bat in her first challenge to Dwight's abuse of Toby. The episode has finally forced Caroline to wake up, and she and Toby once again run away.

This ending bears little resemblance to the ending of Wolff's book. Screenwriter Robert Getchell has constructed a far less complicated ending, but one more appropriate to the needs of the film. Although Getchell also uses a bit of creative license in exaggerating Dwight's abusiveness, he otherwise stays true to Wolff's book in both spirit and circumstance. The result is a powerful script that translates into an engrossing film.

Director Michael Caton-Jones here delivers on the promise shown in his directorial debut, *Scandal* (1989), after the subsequent disappointments of *Memphis Belle* (1990) and *Doc Hollywood* (1991). For this film, Caton-Jones has surrounded himself with impressive artists, expertly merging their respective talents to produce a successful film.

Robert Getchell, nominated for Academy Awards for Best Screenplay for *Alice Doesn't Live Here Anymore* (1974) and *Bound for Glory* (1976), no doubt felt comfortable in the writing of this screenplay, since it is in many ways similar to that of *Alice Doesn't Live Here Anymore*. Both films featured a mother taking her young son on the road in search of a better life.

In addition, this film boasts the talents of David Watkin, who was responsible for the Academy Award-winning cinematography of *Out of Africa* (1985); Jim Clark, who won an Academy Award for editing *The Killing Fields* (1984); and costume designer Richard Hornung, who was nominated for an Oscar for his work in *Barton Fink* (1991). These individuals form an impressive team, and they are all in top form for *This Boy's Life*. Watkin's photography is stunningly beautiful, contrasting the lush surroundings of Utah and the Pacific Northwest with the starkness of the doomed family. Hornung and production designer Stephen J. Lineweaver do an amazing job of re-creating the period, paying attention to the minutest of details.

While *This Boy's Life* is a strong film technically, it is ultimately the acting that makes it remarkable. Known primarily through his work in television, eighteen-year-old Leonardo DiCaprio is astounding as Toby, deftly defining the boy not only as a victim but also as a character about whom the audience truly comes to care. DiCaprio not only manages to keep up with acting veterans De Niro and Barkin but also delivers the film's most exemplary performance. He shows both confidence and range as an actor, investing his character with humor, sensitivity, rage, and vulnerability. When the film skips forward two years, DiCaprio effortlessly bridges the gap, appearing older and even taller through his use of body language and posture. DiCaprio also possesses expressive eyes capable of conveying far more than dialogue can.

De Niro, unquestionably one of the greatest actors in the history of film, turns in another excellent performance as the maniacal Dwight. Instead of portraying Dwight as pure evil, in essence recycling his performance as Max Cady in *Cape Fear* (1991), De Niro decides instead to bring a certain goofiness to the characterization of Dwight. At times, Dwight seems closer in spirit to another De Niro character, the imbecile Rupert Pupkin of *The King of Comedy* (1983), especially when Dwight tries to be comical or goes through his elaborate cigarette-lighting ritual. This disparity adds complexity to Dwight's character.

Ellen Barkin also does a good job as Caroline, although she has less to work with than De Niro and DiCaprio. It is difficult to feel much sympathy for Caroline. When she finally does stand up to Dwight for the first time, she does so not for Toby but for herself, when she wants to work on the Kennedy presidential campaign. Furthermore, when Toby moves in with Dwight on a trial basis and her character disappears for a portion of the film, the audience does not even miss her. Just as Toby would be better off without Dwight, he is also better off without his mother. Nevertheless, Barkin manages to make Caroline an interesting and believable character.

Another interesting character is Toby's effeminate best friend, Arthur Gayle (Jonah

Blechman). Blechman effectively communicates the pain of dealing with his sexuality, as well as the fear of a life trapped in Concrete, Washington.

This Boy's Life could have been turned into a far more sensational film, but luckily it was not. In one scene, the whole family is watching television news coverage of the murder trial of Lana Turner's daughter, Cheryl Crane, who was accused of murdering her mother's abusive lover, Johnny Stompanato. As Toby and Caroline exchange meaningful glances, the scene drives home the direction the story could have taken, and almost did. The film closes with an epilogue which reveals that all the characters successfully escaped their respective confinements except for Dwight, who lives out the remainder of his life alone in concrete. It is a fitting ending for such a well-made film, rejoicing in the victory, instead of dwelling on the agony.

George Delalis

Reviews

Chicago Tribune. April 23, 1993, VII, p. 23.
Entertainment Weekly. April 9, 1993, p. 35.
Films in Review. XLIV, July, 1993, p. 263.
The Hollywood Reporter. March 18, 1993, p. 6.
Los Angeles Times. April 9, 1993, p. F1.
The New York Times. April 9, 1993, p. B4.
Newsweek. April 5, 1993, p. 56.
Rolling Stone. April 15, 1993, p. 67.
Time. CXLI, April 19, 1993, p. 63.
Variety. March 18, 1993, p. 2.
The Washington Post. April 23, 1993, p. D1.

THE THREE MUSKETEERS

Production: Joe Roth and Roger Birnbaum for Caravan Pictures; released by Walt
   Disney Pictures
Direction: Stephen Herek
Screenplay: David Loughery; based on the novel by Alexandre Dumas
Cinematography: Dean Semler
Editing: John F. Link
Production design: Wolf Kroeger
Art direction: Herta Hareiter-Pischinger and Neil Lamont
Set decoration: Bruno Cesari
Casting: Jeremy Zimmermann, Davis & Zimmermann, Lucky Englander, and Fritz
   Fleischhacker
Sound: Colin Charles
Costume design: John Mollo
Music: Michael Kamen
Songs: Bryan Adams (music and lyrics), Robert John "Mutt" Lange (music and
   lyrics), Michael Kamen (music and lyrics), Bryan Adams (performer), Rod
   Stewart (performer), Sting (performer), "All For Love"
MPAA rating: PG
Running time: 105 minutes

Principal characters:
Aramis	Charlie Sheen
Athos	Kiefer Sutherland
D'Artagnan	Chris O'Donnell
Porthos	Oliver Platt
Cardinal Richelieu	Tim Curry
Milady	Rebecca De Mornay
Queen Anne	Gabrielle Anwar
Rochefort	Michael Wincott
King Louis	Hugh O'Conor

Disney's version of the classic tale of *The Three Musketeers* is more a mixed bag
of tricks than a well-told story. It combines the best elements of some of the most
successful films of the past decade or so, including *Star Wars* (1977), *Top Gun* (1986),
The Princess Bride (1987), and *Robin Hood: Prince of Thieves* (1991). If there is one
thing Hollywood is known for, it is for repeating its successes. *The Three Musketeers*
was successful at the box office because it utilizes every Hollywood formula. In other
words, *The Three Musketeers* knows what the audience wants and delivers it in spades.
   In the true Hollywood reality, the classic tale, based on Alexandre Dumas' time-
tested novel of the same name, which was written in 1844, *The Three Musketeers* could
not fail. Prior to this film, there were five versions of the swashbuckling tale, in 1921

with Douglas Fairbanks; in 1935 with Walter Abel; in 1939 with Don Ameche; in 1948 with Gene Kelly, Lana Turner, June Allyson, and Van Heflin; and in 1974 with Oliver Reed, Michael York, Richard Chamberlain, and Raquel Welch. The stars this time around are Hollywood hotshots, led by Charlie Sheen, who plays the somber Aramis. The other Musketeers are Kiefer Sutherland as Athos and Oliver Platt as Porthos, and the film's protagonist, D'Artagnan, is played by Chris O'Donnell, fresh off an Oscar nomination for *Scent of a Woman* (1992). After witnessing the staggering success of 1991's adaptation of the classic tale of Robin Hood with Kevin Costner in *Robin Hood: Prince of Thieves*, the producers of *The Three Musketeers* must have known that the time was ripe for a remake of this classic swashbuckling adventure.

The setting is seventeenth century France, although the film was shot on location in Austria, and the evil Cardinal Richelieu (Tim Curry) is seeking to overthrow the innocent and young King Louis (Hugh O'Conor). With the help of his henchman, Rochefort (Michael Wincott), and the beautiful spy Milady De Winter (Rebecca De Mornay), Richelieu nearly succeeds in embroiling France in a war with Europe, which would certainly dethrone the young Louis and propel Richelieu to the seat of power in France.

Richelieu knows that in order to betray the king he must have the king's loyal band of guards, the Musketeers, disbanded. There are three renegade Musketeers, however, who refuse to turn in their swords and are determined to protect the king from Richelieu's treacherous ways. These loyal servants are three of the bravest men in France, despite their eccentricities. Aramis is a master of theology who "takes death very seriously" and takes his women just as seriously. Athos is a brooding loner who is reluctant to discuss his heartbreaking past and prefers to drown his sorrows in wine. Porthos, portly and full of life, is a wise-cracking adventurer who loves a good fight as much as he loves a good meal. Together, these three friends live to protect their king, under the motto of "one for all and all for one."

The Musketeers have had a long tradition in France and those traditions were often passed down from father to son. Young D'Artagnan dreams of one day becoming a Musketeer, just like his father. Bold and headstrong, D'Artagnan makes his way to Paris to join the ranks of the legendary protectors, only to find Musketeer headquarters deserted and the ranks abandoned. When D'Artagnan learns of the three renegade Musketeers who carry on the traditions, D'Artagnan joins them, and the four coura-geous soldiers join forces to topple Richelieu's evil scheme and restore dignity and pride to King Louis and to France.

Many strains within *The Three Musketeers'* will strike a familiar chord with American audiences. Elements of some of the best adventure films stand out, such as the father-son traditions of *Top Gun*, the good-versus-evil theme of *Star Wars*, the friends helping one another from *Robin Hood: Prince of Thieves*, and the vengeance and tragic romance of *The Princess Bride*. Of all these films, *Robin Hood: Prince of Thieves* comes most to mind when discussing *The Three Musketeers* because it seems to be the one film that was the most influential in director Stephen Herek's adaptation of this classic tale.

Robin Hood: Prince of Thieves was a great success because it placed a Hollywood icon, Kevin Costner, in a classic tale of adventure and romance. It had all the elements that make any good adventure work: a recognizable star, a classic villain, love, friendship, and adventure. Not surprisingly, these same elements can be found in *The Three Musketeers*. The film was shot entirely on location in Europe, with authentic castles and landmarks used to help re-create the time period. The four swashbuckling heroes are endearing and courageous, as any good hero should be. *The Three Musketeers* has humor, action and villainy, not to mention a hit score by composer Michael Kamen, who also composed the score for *Robin Hood: Prince of Thieves*.

Perhaps *The Three Musketeers* succeeds because it does, in fact, provide all the elements, including high-quality production values. Dean Semler, who won an Academy Award for his work on *Dances with Wolves* (1990), serves as the director of photography, and the costumes were designed by Academy Award winner John Mollo, whose credits include *Star Wars* and *Gandhi* (1982).

Hollywood does have a way of producing clones of its own successes, and as long as these films continue to draw crowds, nothing will change. The makers of *The Three Musketeers* are probably not concerned with critical acclaim or numerous awards from their peers. Films such as *The Three Musketeers* are made and will continue to be made because of the overwhelming public demand for adventure and classic stories. *The Three Musketeers* performed well at the box office and will continue to please audiences for a long time to come on video. Hollywood is an industry like any other; it will continue to produce whatever sells.

Catherine R. Springer

Reviews
Chicago Tribune. November 12, 1993, VII, p. 21.
Film Review. March, 1994, p. 24.
The Hollywood Reporter. November 12, 1993, p. 6.
Los Angeles Times. November 12, 1993, p. F1.
The New York Times. November 12, 1993, p. B10.
Rolling Stone. November 25, 1993, p. 124.
San Francisco Chronicle. November 12, 1993, p. C1.
Sight and Sound. IV, March, 1994, p. 51.
USA Today. November 12, 1993, p. D4.
Variety. November 12, 1993, p. 4.
The Washington Post. November 12, 1993, p. C6.

THREE OF HEARTS

Production: Joel B. Michaels and Matthew Irmas; released by New Line Cinema
Direction: Yurek Bogayevicz
Screenplay: Adam Greenman and Mitch Glazer; based on a story by Greenman
Cinematography: Andrzej Sekula
Editing: Dennis M. Hill
Production design: Nelson Coates
Art direction: Douglas Hall
Set decoration: Linda Lee Sutton
Casting: Penny Perry and Annette Benson
Sound: Peter Halbert
Costume design: Barbara Tfank
Music: Joe Jackson
MPAA rating: R
Running time: 103 minutes

    Principal characters:

Joe	William Baldwin
Connie	Kelly Lynch
Ellen	Sherilyn Fenn
Mickey	Joe Pantoliano
Yvonne	Gail Strickland
Allison	Cec Verrell
Isabella	Claire Callaway
Gail	Marek Johnson

Fueled by a charismatic cast and a witty screenplay, *Three of Hearts*, directed by Yurek Bogayevicz, is a twist on the typical love-triangle formula: A lesbian woman hires a male prostitute to woo her former love in an absurd attempt win her back.

Connie (Kelly Lynch) is an offbeat nurse who wears a motorcycle jacket and boots when she is not wearing her nurse's white uniform. With her long, straight hair and her unusual outfits, she looks like an androgynous rock star. In fact, she is aptly described in the film as resembling the lead singer of Guns 'n Roses. Connie has been living with her bisexual lover, an English literature teacher named Ellen (Sherilyn Fenn): As the film opens, however, Ellen is in the process of leaving Connie because she needs time by herself. Because Connie intended to announce the lesbian relationship at her sister's wedding the following day, the breakup is especially upsetting. Without her lover, and without a date for the wedding, Connie takes a friend's advice and hires a male escort, Joe (William Baldwin).

Because Joe is so winning and handsome, Connie then hires him to seduce Ellen and then break her heart. By Connie's absurd logic, Ellen's broken heart will send her running back to Connie. Unfortunately, something goes wrong, and Joe falls in love with Ellen. It is an age-old story, updated for the 1990's.

The film was generally well received, due to the filmmakers' success in presenting the lesbian relationship without apologizing for it or making a self-righteous statement. The advertisements described the film quite succinctly: "Just your average girl meets girl. Girl loses girl. Girl hires boy to get girl back story. With a twist."

Furthermore, *Three of Hearts* provides another unusual perspective besides the issue of sexual orientation: male prostitution. Joe is a heterosexual "escort" who is at a crisis in his "career." He is the most popular of a stable of escorts run by a seedy character named Mickey (Joe Pantoliano). Joe, like Julia Roberts' character in *Pretty Woman* (1990), reexamines his life and his priorities once he falls in love. *Three of Hearts*, however, depicts this character's progression with more substance than did *Pretty Woman*. Baldwin's character earns his self-knowledge; his character develops from charming street kid to weary hustler to hopeful romantic. Perfectly cast as the sex object with a heart of gold; Baldwin is streetwise and sexy, and plays his character with an intelligent smirk and a warmhearted earthiness. This film will most likely be remembered in part because it was released only months prior to the highly publicized *Sliver*, in which Baldwin starred with Sharon Stone.

The filmmakers wisely maintain a balance between comedy and reality in depicting Joe's profession. Thus, Joe's "work" is humorous enough to gain the audience's sympathy but real enough to help the audience understand why Joe would welcome an opportunity to leave this seedy life-style. The scenes of Joe at work with a regular customer, Yvonne (Gail Strickland), manage to be humorous and degrading at the same time. Strickland is hilarious as a wealthy woman who relishes her afternoon trysts with Joe. Similarly excellent are the scenes inside the offices of the escort service. The images of several women "at work" on phone-sex calls are humorous and further illustrate the situation from which the audience hopes Joe will escape.

Kelly Lynch is funny, pathetic, and fascinating as Connie. Lynch is a beautiful woman who started her career as a model. Here, she is the quintessential bohemian: attractive but too iconoclastic in her clothing and behavior to be beautiful. Lynch pounces on this material with apparent glee; she manages to maintain believability and likability even though her character spends most of the time cruelly plotting to manipulate her former lover back into her arms. Although Connie is required to spend considerable time crying or whining about how sad and lonely she is, Lynch is thoroughly entertaining in her portrayal, finding the logic within her character. Her throaty voice and lush strawberry blond hair render her a unique screen presence.

Sherilyn Fenn is lovely in a role that although crucial is not as much fun as the other leads. Fenn, who has developed a fine body of work since her breakthrough role in television's *Twin Peaks*, is beautiful and gentle as Ellen—the love interest of both Connie and Joe.

Director Yurek Bogayevicz has proven again his expertise in directing small, offbeat "relationship" films. Bogayevicz directed Sally Kirkland in her Oscar-nominated performance in *Anna* (1987). He is very comfortable with small scenes, using the camera in a straightforward fashion that emphasizes relationships and conflicts. Whenever he can, he creates a unique atmosphere that enhances the quality of the scene. For example, in the beginning of the film, Connie conceives the idea to hire Joe to woo Ellen in the back seat of a cab. Thus, the cabdriver overhears this lesbian woman ask a male escort to woo her former girlfriend and then break her heart. Playing the scene in front of the driver accomplishes two things: The scene perfectly depicts Connie's free-spirited nature, and it allows the audience to see a third party react to Connie's ridiculous plan. As absurd as the plan is, it is made palatable in part because the audience has been visually informed that the filmmakers know the plan is absurd. Bogayevicz continually uses simple but clever images to underscore the action.

The luxurious cinematography of Andrezj Sekula makes New York look forbidding without being mean, hip without being trendy. The eclectic score, featuring a wonderful song by Sting from his *Ten Summoner's Tales* album (1993), is never intrusive and always interesting. The set design and decoration effectively evoke New York, from seedy office to upper-class penthouse. There are numerous subtle, clever touches. When Connie confronts Joe about his love for Ellen, for example, a framed piece of sheet music entitled "Nobody's Sweetheart" hangs on a background wall.

The screenplay is equally witty and textured. In one comic scene, a prospective employee of the phone-sex service is asked to count to ten as if she were having sex. Not only do the writers create humor, they make excellent use of dramatic techniques as well. When Ellen discovers that Joe is not a real student but was hired by Connie, rather than confront him, she asks him to sit down and write about his fears while she watches. This sophisticated device builds tension and prevents the scene from becoming a simple soap opera-style confrontation.

Unfortunately, this otherwise charming film missteps in its closing moments; the story line succumbs to convention just in time for the credits to roll. *Three of Hearts'* fine performances and crisp dialogue, however, should more than compensate for its weak ending.

Kirby Tepper

Reviews

Chicago Tribune. April 30, 1993, VII, p. 29.
Entertainment Weekly. May 7, 1993, p. 41.
Films in Review. XLIV, July, 1993, p. 264.
The Hollywood Reporter. February 1, 1993, p. 23.
Los Angeles Times. April 30, 1993, p. F1.
The New York Times. April 30, 1993, p. B2.
Rolling Stone. May 27, 1993, p. 58.
Variety. February 5, 1993, p. 14.
The Village Voice. May 4, 1993.
The Wall Street Journal. April 28, 1993.
The Washington Post. April 30, 1993, p. B7.

TOMBSTONE

Production: James Jacks, Sean Daniel, and Bob Misiorowski for Hollywood
  Pictures; released by Buena Vista Pictures
Direction: George P. Cosmatos
Screenplay: Kevin Jarre
Cinematography: William A. Fraker
Editing: Frank J. Urioste, Roberto Silvi, and Harvey Rosenstock
Production design: Catherine Hardwicke
Art direction: Chris Gorak, Kim Hix, and Mark Worthington
Set decoration: Gene Serdena
Casting: Lora Kennedy
Sound: Walt Martin
Costume design: Joseph Porro
Music: Bruce Broughton
MPAA rating: R
Running time: 128 minutes

Principal characters:

Wyatt Earp	Kurt Russell
Doc Holliday	Val Kilmer
Johnny Ringo	Michael Biehn
Curly Bill	Powers Boothe
Frank McLaury	Robert Burke
Josephine	Dana Delany
Virgil Earp	Sam Elliott
Kate	Joanna Pacula
Mattie	Dana Wheeler-Nicholson
Morgan Earp	Bill Paxton
Billy Breckenridge	Jason Priestley
Henry Hooker	Charlton Heston
Billy Claiborne	Wyatt Earp
Narrator	Robert Mitchum
Marshall Fred White	Harry Carey, Jr.

Perhaps it is because the 1990's is a post-cold-war era that Hollywood is once again looking to Westerns. From reluctant Westerns such as *City Slickers* (1991), to designer Westerns such as *Posse* (1993; reviewed in this volume), to revisionist Westerns such as *Unforgiven* (1992), to politically correct Westerns such as *Geronimo: An American Legend* (1993; reviewed in this volume), Hollywood has rekindled its romance with the genre. *Tombstone*, although a flawed attempt, nevertheless offers some real viewing pleasure.

As the film begins, the Cowboys, a group of bad-to-the-bone misfits, are shooting up a wedding party. Once the dust settles, a tired and discouraged Wyatt Earp (Kurt Russell) arrives across town in Tombstone by train to meet the other two Earp brothers, Virgil (Sam Elliott) and Morgan (Bill Paxton). The Earp brothers have decided to settle in Tombstone to make their fortunes. Wyatt, fresh from Dodge City, is looking for rest and solace, a place to retire from being a law man, from fighting other people's fights. Unfortunately, peace and quiet are not that easy for the Earps to find, particularly with Tombstone in the grip of the murderous Cowboys, who are readily identifiable by the bright red sashes they wear. What develops should come as no surprise: the gunfight at the O.K. Corral.

In many ways, *Tombstone* is a hybrid Western, revising history only slightly in order to be politically correct in the 1990's concerning such topics as racism, drug addiction, gender equity, and violence. Clint Eastwood's critically acclaimed *Unforgiven* is almost certainly responsible for this new breed of Western. Therefore, while the traditional Western icons are firmly in place here—moustaches, guns, boots, spurs, horses—there is also a new breed of "bad guys": people who beat horses, people who discriminate against the Chinese, and "gangsters" who shoot innocent persons. Although the sentiments are not misplaced, they are rather burdensome for a Western—arguably one of the simplest of film genres.

Unfortunately, *Tombstone* fumbles a bit under the weight of all this baggage. For example, several times in the film suffragettes are shown advocating women's rights amid the violence and veneer of civilization that is Tombstone. At one point, a woman marches through the frame carrying a placard asking for the vote for women. Later, a literal wagon-load of women crosses the screen, all the women carrying placards such as "Equal pay for equal work." Another issue is addressed when Wyatt Earp's horse is unloaded from the train. When the horse shies away from its new surroundings, rears up and whinnies, the groom strikes the horse. Wyatt sees the trouble, rushes over, and strikes the groom in the same fashion so he will understand how much it hurts. While the filmmakers are trying to touch on key issues and make a wiser, more thoughtful Western, these efforts not only muddy the waters but also run counter to all the strengths of the Western genre. That is, if a filmmaker wants to say something about late nineteenth century attempts by women to "get the vote," then many other more appropriate vehicles exist than an otherwise shoot-'em-up Western. While Eastwood's Academy Award-winning *Unforgiven* did change the form by questioning the values espoused by Westerns, the form is best when it is neat: good and evil battling it out on a vanishing frontier. *Tombstone* allows itself to get muddled with a good number of ancillary issues, which also helps account for the more-than-two-hour running time.

In addition to the suffragettes who appear sporadically throughout the film are the female characters who decorate the lives of the Earp brothers and their friend Doc Holliday (Val Kilmer). Because *Tombstone* is really the story of men, horses, guns, and friendship (not necessarily in that order), the fact that each Earp brother comes to town with a blonde and forgettable wife seems a needless historical accuracy. The Earp wives do little but implore and grieve—except, of course, Mattie (Dana Wheeler-Nicholson), who is addicted to laudanum, and so gets to moan and fidget alternately.

Even Joanna Pacula's amoral, exotic Kate, paramour of Doc Holliday, is merely a cipher, as is the female lead, Dana Delany, who plays Josephine, the performer who steals Wyatt's heart. The best Western is a Western that sticks to what Westerns do well. *Tombstone* tries to deliver what it cannot, and that contributes to its overall failure.

Parts of *Tombstone*, however, work quite well. For example Val Kilmer's portrayal of Doc Holliday is sheer genius. Byronesque in his world-weary debauchery, Kilmer's Holliday is a poet; handsome and terminally ill, he is, in the words of one critic, "droll, sly, honorable, weary and even poignant." Whether he is cheating at cards, trading Latin barbs with an educated thug, or employing the fast-draw that made him famous, Holliday is tragic in epic scale. While Kilmer received rave reviews for playing another tragic, ill-fated poet—Jim Morrison in Oliver Stone's *The Doors* (1991)—his portrayal of Doc Holliday is gentler, more carefully crafted, underplayed. It soon becomes clear in the film (and was clear to most reviewers) that the true love story is between Doc Holliday and Wyatt Earp. This is much truer to the Western genre, a notion supported by Robert Mitchum's voice-over conclusion that tells the viewers that Tom Mix wept at Wyatt Earp's funeral. That is, women are women, but a good friend, a good horse, and a true hero are few and far between. That is the world of the Western, and Kilmer's Holliday fits right in. Even audience members who dislike Westerns will appreciate the craft with which Kilmer has created his character.

Sam Elliott also gives a good—although now trademark—performance as Virgil Earp. Stony-faced and sporting the best and biggest moustache in the film, Elliott brings a quiet reserve to the raucous town and film of *Tombstone*. It is Virgil who first recognizes the effects of the boomtown life on the citizens of Tombstone. Elliott's portrayal of Virgil surveying the town is believable and engaging. While it may seem a small point, it is key. The audience has to believe that something must be done and done by the Earp group. Otherwise, the lines between good and evil become too obscure for the genre. While Elliott has created the heroes of various Louis L'Amour Westerns, such as cable television's *Conagher* (1991), he brought the same quiet thoughtfulness to his earlier non-Western performances, such as *Lifeguard* (1976).

Also well-crafted are the "bad guys," the Cowboys. Led by the opium-smoking Curly Bill (Powers Boothe) and the Latin-spouting Johnny Ringo (Michael Biehn), they are bad—they shoot a wedding party and then eat the wedding feast. They attend a theater performance and shoot at the performers. They are happily uncivilized in an area determined to become civilized. Kevin Jarre's screenplay also attempts to give various members of the group intriguing personalities—such as Billy Breckenridge, played by Jason Priestley, who is gentle and learned. Yet what the Cowboys do best is be bad, and at that they have succeeded.

In addition to writing the screenplay, Jarre also began as director of the film. He was replaced by George P. Cosmatos, who also directed *Rambo: First Blood Part II* (1985). Cosmatos certainly seems to understand filmic violence. While reviews of the film commented on some of the clichéd shots—such as low-angle shots of the good guys in frock coats, silhouetted against the big sky—the film has the right look: dust, close-ups of guns, close-ups of horses, close-ups of squinting men. After all, it is a Western.

Audiences will also enjoy some of the surprise appearances in *Tombstone*. As mentioned previously, Robert Mitchum narrates, adding his gravelly voice to an already dusty film. Also in attendance are Charlton Heston as Henry Hooker, an Arizona rancher, and veteran actor Harry Carey, Jr., as Marshall Fred White. Audiences may also be surprised to see the name Wyatt Earp appear in the credits—a descendant of the actual Wyatt Earp. With more than eighty-five speaking parts, *Tombstone* offers a wide variety of performances and characters.

Much effort was also given to making the film as authentic as possible. The production notes report that costume designer Joseph Porro found "a cache of calicos and linen dresses that had been purchased . . . from the time period of the film. They had never been worn, and were sitting in a warehouse for 120 years." The film's location is actually Mescal, a town forty miles south of Tucson, Arizona. The art department refurbished buildings to try to create an image of the "Las Vegas of the Old West," which they believed was in keeping with Tombstone's boomtown image. Using archival photographs, the filmmakers re-created specific spots in Tombstone, including the Bird Cage Theatre, the Tombstone Engine Company, and the Tombstone Epitaph, because, as newspaper editor John Clum declared, "Every tombstone must have an epitaph." According to the production notes, at the time, the Bird Cage Theatre "was the most renowned honky-tonk in America, referred to by *The New York Times* as 'the wildest, wickedest night spot between Basin Street and the Barbary Coast.'" Despite its shortcomings, *Tombstone* certainly has the right look.

Finally, as Westerns go, *Tombstone* is rather the good, the bad, and the ugly. Nevertheless, if for no other reason, film buffs will want to watch this one to see Val Kilmer's Doc Holliday. It is the performance of a lifetime.

Roberta F. Green

Reviews
Chicago Tribune. December 24, 1993, p. 7C.
Entertainment Weekly. January 14, 1994, p. 36.
Film Review. March, 1994, p. 29.
The Hollywood Reporter. December 23, 1993, p. 8.
Los Angeles Times. December 25, 1993, p. F12.
The New Republic. CCX, February 14, 1994, p. 30.
The New York Times. December 24, 1993, p. C6.
San Francisco Chronicle. December 25, 1993, p. E1.
Sight and Sound. IV, March, 1994, p. 53.
Variety. December 23, 1993, p. 2.
The Washington Post. December 24, 1993, p. 39.

TRUE ROMANCE

Production: Bill Unger, Steve Perry, and Samuel Hadida for Morgan Creek, in association with Davis Film; released by Warner Bros.
Direction: Tony Scott
Screenplay: Quentin Tarantino
Cinematography: Jeffrey L. Kimball
Editing: Michael Tronick and Christian Wagner
Production design: Benjamin Fernandez
Art direction: James J. Murakami
Set decoration: Thomas L. Roysden
Casting: Risa Bramon Garcia and Billy Hopkins
Sound: William B. Kaplan
Costume design: Susan Becker
Music: Hans Zimmer
MPAA rating: R
Running time: 116 minutes

Principal characters:

Clarence Worley	Christian Slater
Alabama Whitman Worley	Patricia Arquette
Clifford Worley	Dennis Hopper
Mentor	Val Kilmer
Drexl Spivey	Gary Oldman
Floyd	Brad Pitt
Vincenzo Coccotti	Christopher Walken
Elliot Blitzer	Bronson Pinchot
Big Don	Samuel L. Jackson
Dick Ritchie	Michael Rapaport
Lee Donowitz	Saul Rubinek
Mary Louise Ravencroft	Conchata Ferrell
Virgil	James Gandolfini
Lucy	Anna Thomson
Lenny	Victor Argo
Marty	Paul Bates
Nicky Dimes	Chris Penn
Cody Nicholson	Tom Sizemore

In this violent, romantic thriller, Christian Slater and Patricia Arquette play two unlikely lovers, Clarence Worley and Alabama Whitman, who double-cross the Detroit mob by stealing a load of contraband and fleeing to Hollywood. Once in Hollywood, they plan to sell the loot and begin a new life. Unlike other young-lovers-on-the-run films such as *Bonnie and Clyde* (1967) and *You Only Live Once* (1937), the film does not end in tragedy. Instead, *True Romance* allows the lovers—and their infant son, Elvis—to live happily ever after in Mexico. In fact, *True Romance* is full of surprises. Here is a rare Hollywood film with an explosive mix of wit and whimsy, passion and gruesome violence. Borrowing elements from dozens of classic Hollywood crime thrillers, *True Romance* attempts to rise above its genre conventions and presents a 1990's version of *Bonnie and Clyde* along the lines of *Sid and Nancy* (1986).

Clarence and Alabama are gun-crazy, lustful, immature adults, doing the best they can in a world of terror, on the run amid a never-ending stream of pop-culture images: kung fu films, Spiderman comics, purple Cadillacs, and fake leopard-skin covers.

Clarence, who works in a Detroit comic-book store and idolizes Elvis Presley, and Alabama, a prostitute hired as a birthday present for Clarence, meet in a motion-picture theater when she spills her popcorn on him during a triple bill of Sonny Chiba kung fu flicks. It is love at first sight and they are soon married. Then, in a chat with an imaginary Elvis (played by Val Kilmer), Clarence decides to kill Alabama's evil pimp, and he snags a drug-filled suitcase by mistake. The chase is on, with the young pair pursued by both the police and the mob from whom they stole the uncut cocaine. Because Clarence is foolish enough to think this is his only chance for happiness, he and Alabama skip town to go to Hollywood to sell the stash—in a purple Cadillac convertible.

Like many a crime thriller with a predictable plot, *True Romance* is most interesting because of its rogues' gallery of secondary characters. In particular, Hollywood producer Lee Donowitz (Saul Rubinek) displays an ego the size of Texas, yet he is the lone realist in a film of crazies. Clarence's estranged dad, a retired cop, is wonderfully played by Dennis Hopper. Christopher Walken, as the mob don, interrogates Hopper, and the sparks fly as two of Hollywood's celebrated ham actors confront each other in a scene of utter terror.

True Romance is a *film noir* of the 1990's, owing much to Joseph Lewis' *Gun Crazy* (1949) and Nicholas Ray's *They Live by Night* (1949). As such, its cinematography is stunning and logical. The film begins as grimly as possible in an overcast Detroit. Hollywood is better, but still dark. Only when the couple make their way to Mexico and a new life does one finally gaze on the sun directly at film's end.

For such a complex work, *True Romance* did surprisingly well in its opening weeks of release. The major reviews varied across the spectrum of opinion. On one hand *The Wall Street Journal* found *True Romance* "a vile, soulless fairy tale," directed by "a slick hack." On the other hand, in a special Sunday feature, the analysis of Caryn James of *The New York Times* was aptly summarized by her article's headline, "As a B Movie, 'True Romance' Is Grade A."

Yet no one found the film uninteresting. Generally the reviews, whether favorable or not, tantalized film buffs. *True Romance* ought to be seen as a serious film about hip postmodern pop culture of the 1990's. It succeeds as an oblique, frequently amusing look at the pursuit of the American Dream, directed in a complex, visually interesting style by Tony Scott of *Top Gun* (1986) and *Days of Thunder* (1990) fame. Like author Quentin Tarantino's *Reservoir Dogs* (1992), *True Romance* fashions a world of cross fires, tough cops, tougher mobsters, and mere survival by those caught in-between.

True Romance is surely a violent film, with the body count at the climax approaching several dozen as the police shoot it out with the mobsters and a Hollywood producer's bodyguards. Nevertheless, *True Romance* is more than simply violence for violence's sake. Despite the violence, *True Romance* is, at its heart, a sweet romantic comedy, with a stunning performance by Patricia Arquette as Alabama. *True Romance* is also a film that captures the 1990's: an age of violence, of pop culture, of postmodern society. The formulaic unreality in this road film so distances the viewer that the violence is far more interesting and complex than Hollywood's usual shoot-'em-up action/adventure fare.

It is the obsession with popular culture, however, that makes this film special. Clarence raises "Elvis" from icon to a God-like figure. This is a world twisted in macabre yet comic ways. The very title, *True Romance*, comes to suggest a new version of the reality of love, Hollywood-style. *True Romance* is a dark comedy with a number of amusing lines, revealing the violent and darkly comic sides of us all. It is visually stylish and thematically complex in its commentary on 1990's pop culture.

True Romance combines magical music and uniformly wonderful performances and pushes the elements of a familiar genre to the limit of a studio-produced product. Some loathe a film that grapples with the dark side of the American character. Yet many of the best films ever made in the studio system, from *Citizen Kane* (1941) to *The Searchers* (1956) to *The Godfather* (1972), have done precisely that. *True Romance* succeeds on many levels.

Douglas Gomery

Reviews

Chicago Tribune. September 10, 1993, Take 2, p. 4.
Commonweal. CXX, October 22, 1993, p. 22.
Films in Review. XLIV, November, 1993, p. 416.
Entertainment Weekly. September 10, 1993, p. 48.
The Hollywood Reporter. August 30, 1993, 1993, p. 5.
Los Angeles Times. September 10, 1993, p. F1.
New Statesman and Society. VI, October 22, 1993, p. 33.
The New York Times. September 10, 1993, p. B7.
Time. CXLII, September 13, 1993, p. 78.
Variety. August 27, 1993, p. 2.
The Wall Street Journal. September 21, 1993, p. A14.
The Washington Post. September 10, 1993, p. D1.

UNTAMED HEART

Production: Tony Bill and Helen Buck Bartlett; released by Metro-Goldwyn-Mayer
Direction: Tony Bill
Screenplay: Tom Sierchio
Cinematography: Jost Vacano
Editing: Mia Goldman
Production design: Steven Jordan
Art direction: Jack D. L. Ballance
Set decoration: Cliff Cunningham
Casting: Marci Liroff
Sound: Matthew Quast
Costume design: Lynn Bernay
Music: Cliff Eidelman
MPAA rating: PG-13
Running time: 102 minutes

Principal characters:
Adam............................. Christian Slater
Caroline............................ Marisa Tomei
Cindy................................. Rosie Perez
Howard .... Kyle Secor
Patsy .... Willie Garson
Mother Camilla..................... Claudia Wilkens

Caroline (Marisa Tomei) works as a waitress at a Minneapolis diner. She is twenty-five years old. Having recently broken up with her boyfriend, ending the latest in a string of unsuccessful relationships, she is at a low ebb and greatly disheartened. It is not typical for her to feel this way, because by nature she is a friendly and outgoing person. Her life takes a dramatic turn one night when Adam (Christian Slater), the reclusive busboy from the same diner, saves her from being raped by two men. Fearing the humiliation, she does not mention this incident to anyone, not even to her closest friend, Cindy (Rosie Perez). As a result of this secrecy, a close bond develops between her and Adam.

Caroline's growing attachment to Adam is fueled not only by her gratitude but by a curiosity about his odd ways as well. After all, at one point Cindy had said to her in confidence, "The story goes that he has some sort of ape parts in him." There is some truth to that observation, as Caroline soon discovers, and in the process she finds herself in an unfamiliar world of make-believe, heroism, and ultimately sadness.

The opening scenes of the film, photographed in a sepia tone, provide a brief glimpse into Adam's childhood in an orphanage, where he was brought up by Mother Camilla (Claudia Wilkens). As a child, Adam was sick with a diseased heart and found comfort in the magical story that Mother Camilla invented for him. In the story, Adam's father, an adventurer who lived in the jungle, was killed in a duel with the Great King of the Silver Baboons. Overcome with grief and guilt, the King sacrificed his own heart and offered it to the ailing child, Adam. Even as an adult, Adam continues to believe that this really happened. In that sense, he is living a delusion, so strongly imbedded in his mind that he cannot relate to people around him. The film derives much of its charm and appeal in the way that Caroline reacts to the story when Adam confides in her. She does not scoff at it, but neither does she try to perpetuate the fantasy. Instead, she develops a sympathetic understanding about his disposition, allowing him his own space to dream and to be himself. Marisa Tomei, an actress with extensive stage experience in New York and Los Angeles who won an Academy Award for Best Supporting Actress for her work in *My Cousin Vinny* (1992), brings a wonderful authenticity to her role, playing every little nuance with tenderness while conveying the fragile nature of human emotions. When Caroline invites Adam to a Christmas dinner and finds out that he had been sitting outside on the porch for two hours, she tenderly says to him, "You'd rather be out here in the cold, playing with a cat than in a room full of strangers." It is an indication of Tomei's talents that she can deliver this dialogue in a manner that is consistent with her character. It is therefore fitting that Caroline would find solace in a relationship with Adam. She will not cause him any harm, just as she knows that he is incapable of cynicism. Adam's solitary existence is matched by Caroline's own isolation from her family, about whom she speaks in apathetic tones. Her family, and the part it plays in her life, is as much a myth as is Adam's. In fact, there are no scenes between Caroline and her family. By reducing her mother and stepfather to mere shadows, the film creates a closed world for Adam and Caroline, one that only they can inhabit.

Over the years, the subject of alienated youth and loneliness has been vividly presented in American films such as *Marty* (1955), *East of Eden* (1955), *Splendor in the Grass* (1961), and *Hud* (1963). Tony Bill, the director of *Untamed Heart*, created a tough, uncompromising portrait of disturbed blue-collar youth in *Five Corners* (1987). In all these films, the principal characters acted out their frustrations in a language that came to represent a form of rebellion. Society and the family structure places a pressure on the younger generation to conform to established norms of behavior. This status quo is nearly always instrumental in creating the conflict that makes these films memorable. When the characters are functioning in a particular socioeconomic context, the film widens in scope. In *Untamed Heart*, Adam and Caroline appear to bring all the appropriate baggage that makes them outcasts. Yet once their relationship unfolds, the film, in spite of its honesty, instead narrows down its range and scope with every scene. At one point, late in their relationship, Adam confesses to Caroline that he has been following her home every night, sneaking into her bedroom and watching her sleep. He goes on to tell her that it gives him a sense of tranquillity. When Caroline takes the disturbing explanation in her stride, and reads it as another sign of his devotion to her, the film more than likely makes itself inaccessible to the same audiences who had been following it closely until then.

Nothing threatens Caroline and Adam's life together except their own fragility. The only counterpoint comes in the form of mild skepticism expressed by Cindy. Her concern is whether Caroline is capable of seeing any kind of relationship through to its conclusion. She reminds Caroline of her short-lived stints at the beauty academy and as a magician's assistant. Caroline herself is conscious of the many endeavors that she began but did not finish. This pattern does not prevent her, however, from falling in love with Adam. In fact, it is quite apparent that she is setting herself up for another disappointment.

Their need for each other is expressed in simple terms. Caroline treats Adam with gentleness. He, in turn, showers her with gifts and surprises that leave her completely overwhelmed. He points out the stars in the sky, gives her all his precious records, and even presents her with a Christmas tree that he manages to place in her bedroom for an early morning surprise. On the night that Adam rescues her from her attackers, he carries her home, rests her on the porch, and stays up all night in the cold, watching her closely right until the morning, when she finally regains consciousness. Seeing Adam seated across her, Caroline is naturally startled. She notices that Adam's jacket had kept her warm all night, but her clothes are dishevelled. She then looks at Adam in confusion. Gradually, a realization comes to her, and she knows exactly what happened the night before. Adam takes a cue from her look, steps out on the road, huddled up in cold, and makes his way back home. No words are exchanged in this scene, but much is said. Christian Slater's portrayal of Adam, bears, in its physicality, a slight resemblance to that of Johnny Weissmuller as Tarzan of the Apes. He speaks very little, is nearly paralyzed when in the presence of the opposite sex, moves with uncertainty, shuffles his feet, and shoots sharp glances back and forth, not quite comprehending what he sees.

The crucial moment in the film arrives when Howard (Kyle Secor) and Patsy (Willie Garson), the two men who attacked Caroline, return to take revenge on Adam. They assault him with a knife in the alley behind the diner. Adam is rushed to the hospital, where the doctor pronounces that the danger to Adam's life is caused not by the stab wound but by his weak heart, a congenital defect, and that a transplant should be considered. This is when Caroline realizes the seriousness of his condition and what it means to him. Adam is resistant to the notion of a heart transplant. He tells Caroline that he fears that, if his heart is taken away from him, it will change the way he feels about her. To this she replies, "It's only a story. We love with our minds and souls, not with our hearts."

Adam's death at the end of the film draws it to a natural but not a foregone conclusion. For Caroline, it is the beginning of a new phase in her life. She says to Cindy, "Adam was something I was good at. It was the one thing I followed through till the end. From now on, things are going to be different." Perhaps Caroline has found the way to reconcile her feelings to the tragedy, which has changed her. Unfortunately, it is not entirely convincing that no other suitable way could be found to bring about her transformation.

Nalin Bakhle

Reviews

Chicago Tribune. February 12, 1993, VII, p. 22.
The Christian Science Monitor. February 26, 1993, p. 14.
Film Review. June, 1993, p. 36.
The Hollywood Reporter. January 26, 1993, p. 10.
Los Angeles Times. February 12, 1993, p. F15.
The New York Times. February 12, 1993, p. C14.
The New Yorker. February 15, 1993, p. 95.
Sight and Sound. III, May, 1993, p. 58.
Variety. January 26, 1993, p. 4.
The Wall Street Journal. February 18, 1993, p. A16.
The Washington Post. February 12, 1993, p. C7.

THE WEDDING BANQUET
(HSI YEN)

Origin: Taiwan
Released: 1993
Released in U.S.: 1993
Production: Ted Hope, James Schamus, and Ang Lee for Central Motion Picture Corp., in association with Good Machine; released by The Samuel Goldwyn Company
Direction: Ang Lee
Screenplay: Ang Lee, Neil Peng, and James Schamus
Cinematography: Jong Lin
Editing: Tim Squyres
Production design: Steve Rosenzweig
Art direction: Rachael Weinzimer
Casting: Wendy Ettinger
Sound: Tom Paul
Costume design: Michael Clancy
Music: Mader
MPAA rating: R
Running time: 107 minutes

Principal characters:
Wai-tung .... Winston Chao
Wei-wei................................. May Chin
Simon .... Mitchell Lichtenstein
Mr. Gao............................... Sihung Lung
Mrs. Gao.............................. Ah-Leh Gua
Old Chen................................ Tien Pien

The Wedding Banquet is one of the few Taiwanese films to have received wide distribution in the West, where it has also garnered its share of critical acclaim. The film won the Golden Bear at the 1993 Berlin Film Festival and the best film and best director awards at the 1993 Seattle International Film Festival. It was nominated as Best Foreign Film of 1993 by the Academy of Motion Picture Arts and Sciences. Indeed, there is much about this classical sex farce, directed by Ang Lee, who attended New York University's film school, that appeals to Occidental sensibilities. While the situations presented in *The Wedding Banquet* may be familiar, however, their execution is not. Lee brings a fresh perspective to this delicately balanced comedy.

The central character, Wai-tung (Winston Chao), is a successful young businessman working in New York City, where he has for five years shared a home with his male lover, Simon (Mitchell Lichtenstein). Wai-tung's parents (Sihung Lung and Ah-Leh Gua), who still live in Taiwan, are unaware of his sexual orientation but they are acutely aware that they lack the grandchild it is Wai-tung's duty to supply. Because their only son gives no indication that he is searching for a wife, his mother acts as a matchmaker, even sending him a Taiwanese prospect who meets Wai-tung's ludicrous, trumped-up requirements: she has two Ph.D.s and is an opera singer.

Wai-tung is, among other things, a New York slumlord. One of his tenants, a beautiful Chinese woman named Wei-wei (May Chin), is a starving artist who is unable to pay her rent, in part because she has no green card. Simon suggests that Wai-tung can solve both his and Wei-wei's problems by undergoing a pro forma marriage ceremony with her at city hall.

What none of the three young people anticipates is the tenacity with which Wai-tung's parents cling to their dream. Quite unexpectedly, they decide to attend the wedding, which was originally to have been a modest affair. Because Wai-tung's father, a retired military commander, is recognized by a former retainer, now the proprietor of one of New York's finest Chinese restaurants, the couple soon find themselves enmeshed in an elaborate—and highly traditional—wedding celebration. The wedding banquet ends with a series of apparently customary Taiwanese wedding party games, one of which results in Wei-wei and Wai-tung's conceiving a child.

Lee's theme, the role tradition plays in the lives of these supremely contemporary young immigrants, is reinforced when, after the celebrations, Wai-tung's father suffers a mild stroke that makes it impossible for him to travel. What began as a short-term visit to Simon and Wai-tung's home turns into a reshuffling of domestic arrangements in order to maintain the charade. The long-suffering Simon, now Wai-tung's "land-lord," does all the cooking, while Wei-wei pretends to cook, playing her assigned role as dutiful daughter-in-law. The parents' desire for a future, for a sense of continuity, is symbolized by Wei-wei's pregnancy, which must be nurtured by their presence. The counterfeit marriage, born of the younger generation's desire to get on with their disparate lives, leads instead to a recognition of the inescapable power and significance of those customs and conventions that promote posterity.

Lee has not, however, created a story that exalts convention at the expense of change and social evolution. Simon and Wai-tung's love for each other is never belittled; indeed, one of the film's tenderest moments occurs when Wai-tung, exiled from his and Simon's bedroom because of his parents' presence, gets up in the middle of the night simply to talk with Simon for a few unguarded moments via cellular telephone from a bathroom in their house. Even Wai-tung's father eventually acknowledges Simon's importance in the life of his son and grandson-to-be: in giving Simon, as well as Wei-wei, a financial wedding present, he implicitly acknowledges that Simon will be, as Wei-wei has requested, a second father to the baby.

By making the white American Simon Wai-tung's true love and Wei-wei the mother of Wai-tung's child, Ang Lee has devised a series of culturally and sexually ambiguous situations that put a novel gloss on the conventions of the genres he has appropriated. *The Wedding Banquet* may, as one critic has suggested, owe something to the studies of sexual mores executed by such directors as Pietro Germi—in, for example, *Divorce—Italian Style* (1962)—in the 1960's. Nevertheless, such aspects of Lee's film as the obeisance shown Wai-tung's parents—a crucial source of the *The Wedding*

Banquet's comedy, as well as its lingering depth—would be neither as believable nor as touching in a film featuring only Occidental characters. While Wayne Wang has, in such films as *Dim Sum: A Little Bit of Heart* (1985), found much gentle humor in the lives of Chinese Americans, Lee intensifies his main character's cultural dilemma by adding Wai-tung's homosexuality to the mix.

Winston Chao, who previously worked as a model, has had little acting experience, and he lacks the cinematic fluency and self-possession displayed by more practiced actors. Yet he and the director use this feature of his persona to advantage. As Wai-tung, Chao projects a degree of self-consciousness and self-seriousness that seems true to the character—a man who has made a success of himself in a foreign land, yet who is not entirely at ease there, owing to his youth and his status as an outsider. The fact that his delivery of English lines is often stiff (most of the film is in Chinese with English subtitles) furthers this impression.

If Wai-tung's English is stiff, Wei-wei's is almost nonexistent. Lee often uses Wei-wei's unfamiliarity with, or disregard for (one is never sure which), the intricacies of the English language to great comic effect. For example, in one scene she mangles the traditional wedding vows during the city hall ceremony, and in another she monosyllabically translates Simon's complex answers to questions posed by Wai-tung's mother. May Chin does a wonderful job of conveying the powerful emotions at war in Wei-wei, a contemporary, self-reliant woman who must play the role of a blushing, traditional bride, a part she approaches with utter ambivalence.

Wai-tung's parents, played by Sihung Lung (Mr. Gao) and Ah-Leh Gua (Mrs. Gao), also display more depth than one might expect. Standard-bearers of tradition and morality, they are overbearing and demanding, and certainly they outstay their welcome. Nevertheless, just as Mr. Gao belatedly reveals that he does, in fact, speak some English, one comes to see that the elderly couple understand far more than they initially let on. Without them, there would be no wedding banquet, no pregnancy, no grandchild. Once their mission is accomplished, they board a plane for Taiwan, in the process providing the film with a wonderful parting gesture. As Wai-tung's father, now frail but still carrying himself with the commanding posture of former general, raises his arms so that he can be searched with a manual metal detector, his broad display conveys both his blessing and his farewell.

Lisa Paddock

Reviews
Chicago Tribune. August 27, 1993, VII, p. 21.
The Christian Science Monitor. August 6, 1993, p. 12.
Entertainment Weekly. September 10, 1993, p. 50.
Films in Review. XLV, January, 1994, p. 50.
The Hollywood Reporter. August 4, 1993, p. 5.
Los Angeles Times. August 4, 1993, p. F1.
The New Republic. CCIX, August 16, 1993, p. 25.

New York. XXVI, August 20, 1993, p. 136.
The New York Times. August 4, 1993, p. B3.
Newsweek. CXXII, August 16, 1993, p. 61.
Variety. February 26, 1993, p. 68.
The Wall Street Journal. September 9, 1993, p. A20.
The Washington Post. August 27, 1993, p. C8.

WHAT'S EATING GILBERT GRAPE

Production: Meir Teper, Bertil Ohlsson, and David Matalon; released by
  Paramount Pictures
Direction: Lasse Hallström
Screenplay: Peter Hedges; based on his novel
Cinematography: Sven Nykvist
Editing: Andrew Mondshein
Production design: Bernt Capra
Art direction: John Myhre
Set decoration: Gretchen Rau
Casting: Gail Levin
Sound: David Brownlow
Costume design: Renee Ehrlich Kalfus
Music: Alan Parker and Björn Isfält
MPAA rating: PG-13
Running time: 118 minutes

Principal characters:
Gilbert Grape . . . . Johnny Depp
Becky . . . . Juliette Lewis
Betty Carver . . . . Mary Steenburgen
Arnie Grape . . . . Leonardo DiCaprio
Momma. . . . . Darlene Cates
Amy Grape . . . . Laura Harrington
Ellen Grape. . . . . Mary Kate Schellhardt
Mr. Carver. . . . . Kevin Tighe
Tucker Van Dyke . . . . John C. Reilly
Bobby McBurney . . . . Crispin Glover
Becky's grandma . . . . Penelope Branning

Johnny Depp has built a career out of highly idiosyncratic characters in unusual
films, such as *Edward Scissorhands* (1990) and *Benny and Joon* (1993; reviewed in
this volume). In *What's Eating Gilbert Grape*, he brings his understated quirkiness to
the role of Gilbert, the oldest son in an unusual family stuck in a small town. It is a
film about longing, about comings and goings, and about a young man's attempts to
make sense out of his own life. It gracefully captures the humanity in a number of
characters in a small town in Iowa, reflecting in them the truth that most people have
something they wish for and something that holds them back.

Director Lasse Hallstrom and author Peter Hedges have, with the help of brilliant
performances, beautiful cinematography (by Sven Nykvist), and wonderful music (by
Alan Parker and Björn Isfält), created a film of lasting beauty and terrific emotional
power that has received broad critical praise. Although *What's Eating Gilbert Grape*

is not a blockbuster, its grace and artistry put it in the category of such classic American films as *Driving Miss Daisy* (1989) or *Fried Green Tomatoes* (1991).

Gilbert lives in Endora, Iowa, population 1,091, with his unusual family: his five-hundred-pound Momma (Darlene Cates), who has not left the house in years; his older sister Amy (Laura Harrington), who cooks and cleans all day; his teenage sister Ellen (Mary Kate Schellhardt), who is angry with everyone; and his seventeen-year-old brother, Arnie (Leonardo DiCaprio), who is severely mentally handicapped. Gilbert is a clerk at a small grocery store in Endora, which is being slowly put out of business by a large supermarket in a nearby town. Among the town residents are Betty Carver (Mary Steenburgen), an older woman with whom he is having an affair; Bobby (Crispin Glover), the undertaker's son, who is constantly searching for new business; and Tucker (John C. Reilly), who is highly excited that a Burger Barn is going to open in town. Into this mix comes Becky (Juliette Lewis), who is stranded briefly in Endora with her grandmother (Penelope Branning), awaiting an auto part in order to continue their recreational-vehicle vacation.

One of the themes of this film is that everyone is handicapped in some way and that one must struggle to understand and accept one's handicap, whatever form it takes. Each character in the film is handicapped in some manner: Becky's vehicle has broken down; Momma's weight incapacitates her; Arnie's mental state makes him dependent on the doting Gilbert; and Gilbert feels obligated to his family. Betty feels restrained by her children and middle-class life-style, for which she tries to compensate with her affair with Gilbert. Steenburgen is simultaneously hilarious and pathetic as Betty, telling her children to "go outside" as she forces herself hungrily on Gilbert over her kitchen table.

This image of Betty "devouring" Gilbert over the kitchen table is no accident. This is a story full of people who ache and hunger for something else, symbolically embodied by Momma's obesity, but apparent in other ways. Becky tells Gilbert the story of the insect that eats her mate. Gilbert works in a grocery store, but it is a store that is hungry for business. His friend Tucker eagerly anticipates the opening of the Burger Barn because it will bring jobs to the town, not to mention good burgers. It appears to be an intended irony that Momma is, spiritually speaking, always hungry and yet is obese, while Becky is spiritually sated and is rail-thin. Their meeting is one of the most important moments in the film: "I haven't always been like this," says Momma, and Becky replies, gently, "I haven't always been like this," emphasis on "this."

Thematically, the character of Gilbert is reminiscent of George Bailey in *It's a Wonderful Life* (1946), trapped in a small town with his family because of their problems. Depp is stoic and restrained, as if he cannot show too much emotion or he will burst. His character stays very even until a climactic scene, when his emotion becomes alarming, as if he is afraid that now that he has uncorked it, he will not be able to go back to being who he was. One of those performances that is exquisite in its restraint, it is the linchpin of the film.

Yet the unstoppable performance of Leonardo DiCaprio as Arnie steals the show.

DiCaprio, who previously had co-starred in the highly dramatic *This Boy's Life* (1993; reviewed in this volume) with Robert De Niro, has won vast critical acclaim and numerous honors for this role. He did extensive research on the physical mannerisms of a mentally disabled youth, and his preproduction research pays off handsomely for him as he perfectly captures the physical as well as emotional traits of Arnie. DiCaprio imbues Arnie with a childish innocence that is sometimes funny, as when he is playing hide-and-seek with Gilbert, and sometimes frightening, as when he is climbing up the forbidden ladder of a huge water tower, getting his foot stuck in the ladder and yelling, "I did it!"

DiCaprio throws himself into the role so completely that many viewers thought he was actually mentally disabled. The scenes with Gilbert, particularly a struggle about whether Gilbert is going to bathe him, might have lapsed into mawkishness in the hands of a lesser actor. DiCaprio's Arnie is so fully realized that the differences between the character and the actor are never apparent, and so he is never over-the-top or bathetic. This is an extraordinary high point in DiCaprio's nascent career.

Unlike DiCaprio, Cates did not have to research her role or alter her physical appearance. She weighs five hundred pounds and, like the character she plays, had not ventured out of her house for several years (prior to being discovered by Hallstrom during a television appearance on the *Sally Jessy Raphael* show). In interviews, Cates has described some of the same feelings expressed and experienced by Momma in the film. Most notably, Cates, like her character, has essentially lost the use of her legs because of her weight: A crucial scene where she walks out of the jailhouse after demanding Arnie's release—he was imprisoned for climbing the water tower—was, by her account, excruciatingly painful for her, which only makes more horrific the pain that is apparent on-screen.

Rarely has a person with a severe handicap played on-screen a character who is limited by that handicap: Harold Russell, who lost both hands in World War II, and Marlee Matlin, who is hearing impaired, both won Academy Awards portraying characters challenged by the same handicaps by which they were challenged in, respectively, *The Best Years of Our Lives* in 1946, and *Children of a Lesser God* in 1986. Their own experiences resonated throughout their performances in the same extraordinary way that Cates's experience does.

Cates has also said that it was psychologically painful to film the aforementioned scene. Since it required Momma to be stared at in revulsion and fascination by townspeople as she emerges from the jailhouse, it revived Cates's own personal fears and feelings about other people's reaction to her enormous size. All of this lends believability and humanity to Momma's plight: She is very realistic.

Juliette Lewis is superb as the free-spirited Becky. Lewis has a quirky earthiness that makes everything she does interesting: She makes Becky an inquisitive and comfortable person who looks with a penetrating gaze at everyone, as if to understand them better. Lewis made her initial mark in *Cape Fear* (1991) as the daughter of the characters played by Jessica Lange and Nick Nolte. Hers was a critically acclaimed performance that was striking in its realism and sexuality. She brings the same realism to *What's Eating Gilbert Grape*, now accompanied by a serenity and warmth essential to the character of a woman who enters Gilbert's life, opening him up to new possibilities for happiness. When Gilbert reveals to her the things that he wants out of life, they are all for other people in his family. Becky asks, "But what do you want for you?" She understands that this is the first time someone has asked this question of Gilbert, and her empathy is pivotal to the story.

Hallstrom shows that he has great empathy as well, for the characters of this story and for the people of traditional America. He and Sven Nykvist create beautiful images out of the simplest things: a meadow by a lake, as Becky and Gilbert look at the stars; the grand opening of the Burger Barn, complete with band; the venerable home where Gilbert and his family live; or the shiny line of trailers lumbering down the highway. They have created a world where nothing is possible because nothing really happens, and yet where everything is possible because people have aspirations. These people care about what happens to them, even if it is as small a detail as climbing a tree and playing hide-and-seek. Viewers will see many different things in this richly textured film, but most of all, they will see themselves.

Kirby Tepper

Reviews
Entertainment Weekly. January 14, 1994, p. 34.
The Hollywood Reporter. December 6, 1993, p. 8.
Los Angeles Times. December 17, 1993, p. F1.
New York. XXVII, January 17, 1994, p. 55.
Newsweek. CXXII, December 27, 1993, p. 48.
San Francisco Chronicle. January 21, 1994, p. C3.
Time. CXLIII, January 10, 1994, p. 58.
USA Today. December 17, 1993, p. D7.
Variety. December 6, 1993, p. 4.
The Wall Street Journal. December 23, 1993, p. A9.
The Washington Post. March 5, 1994, p. G3.

WHAT'S LOVE GOT TO DO WITH IT

Production: Doug Chapin and Barry Krost for Touchstone Pictures; released by
    Buena Vista
Direction: Brian Gibson
Screenplay: Kate Lanier; based on the book *I, Tina,* by Tina Turner and Kurt Loder
Cinematography: Jamie Anderson
Editing: Stuart Pappé
Production design: Stephen Altman
Art direction: Richard Johnson
Set decoration: Rick Simpson
Casting: Reuben Cannon and Associates
Sound: Arthur Rochester
Costume design: Ruth Carter
Choreography: Michael Peters
Music supervision: Daniel Allan Carlin
Music: Stanley Clarke
MPAA rating: R
Running time: 119 minutes

Principal characters:
Tina Turner . . . . Angela Bassett
Ike Turner . . . . Laurence Fishburne
Jackie . . . . Vanessa Bell Calloway
Zelma Bullock . . . . Jenifer Lewis
Alline Bullock. . . . . Phyllis Yvonne Stickney
Darlene . . . . Khandi Alexander
Leanne. . . . . Pamala Tyson
Lorraine. . . . . Penny Johnson
Anna Mae (as a young girl) . . . . Rae'ven Kelly
Fross . . . . Chi
Phil Spector. . . . . Rob LaBelle
Roger Davies . . . . James Reyne

Based on Tina Turner's autobiography, *I, Tina* (1986), cowritten with Kurt Loder,
What's Love Got to Do with It portrays the world-renowned singer's turbulent life and
rise to superstardom. In addition to being one of the most dynamic, internationally
acclaimed singer/performers of the rock/rhythm-and-blues era, Tina Turner is an
internationally recognized symbol of strength, independence, and sexual allure. With
her boundless energy, aggressive singing style, wild hair, revealing costumes, and
fondness for strutting uninhibitedly in high heels across the stage, Tina has been
startling and delighting audiences worldwide ever since she first began performing in
the late 1950's.

Because of her unmistakably unique show-business persona, one that celebrates the unbridled, untamed joy of being fully and vibrantly alive, any film about Tina's life must somehow capture this incredibly dynamic and unique aspect of her character. Unfortunately, the filmmakers have diluted Tina's allure by concentrating on an aspect of her character that is diametrically opposed to her most appealing and dynamic attributes.

The film begins with Tina as young Anna Mae Bullock (Rae'ven Kelly) living in rural Tennessee, who is dismissed from the local church choir for singing too spiritedly. When Anna Mae returns home, she arrives just as her mother, Zelma (Jenifer Lewis), is leaving, abandoning Anna Mae after being physically abused once too often by Anna Mae's roving, violent father.

After living with her grandmother for several years, Anna Mae, now a teenager (Angela Bassett), travels to St. Louis, where she is reunited with her mother and sister, Alline (Phyllis Yvonne Stickney). Alline, a waitress at a music club, invites Anna Mae to accompany her to work. Anna Mae is dazzled by the verve and excitement of the club, which features a rhythm-and-blues band, the Kings of Rhythm, headed by guitarist/songwriter Ike Turner (Laurence Fishburne).

As part of the act, Ike invites young women on stage to sing lead vocals. Although Alline warns her that Ike is notorious as a ladies' man, Anna Mae is determined to get her chance on stage with him. When she returns to the club, dressed in a flashy new dress, Anna Mae dominates the act, belting out one of Ike's songs while strutting commandingly across the stage. Impressed, Ike invites her to dinner and then asks if she would like to become a permanent member of his band, a proposal to which she responds enthusiastically. After Ike persuades Mrs. Bullock to agree to the venture (in part by surreptitiously giving her several hundred dollars), Anna Mae begins rehearsing with the band in preparation for a multicity tour.

While rehearsing the song "I Wanna Be Made Over," Anna Mae realizes that Ike, although an extremely talented musician, is also a demanding perfectionist who takes an almost sadistic pleasure in manipulating and dominating his band members, especially Anna Mae and the three female backup singers. Anna Mae also discovers that Ike has a girlfriend, Lorraine (Penny Johnson), with whom he has had two boys.

One evening, while Anna Mae is staying overnight in Ike's home with other band members, Lorraine threatens her at gunpoint, telling her to keep her distance from Ike. A severely depressed Lorraine then goes into her bedroom and shoots herself. After the ambulance arrives and rushes her to the hospital, Ike feigns remorse, crying in Anna Mae's arms while telling her that she is the only person who really understands him. His pleas for sympathy work, and Anna Mae soon replaces Lorraine as Ike's girlfriend.

When the tour begins, Ike's zeal to transform Anna Mae into his image of the perfect lead vocalist results in her assuming a startling new personality on stage: that of a sexy, strutting dynamo, who looks and sings like a sleek, shrieking wildcat. Following a disastrous visit to the beauty parlor, during which Anna Mae's hair falls out after being treated with harsh dyes, she and the backup singers—called the Ikettes—don matching wigs for the first show. This flamboyant touch becomes a permanent part of their stage personas. The act is a success, leading to a recording contract. Ike then makes another change in Anna Mae's total makeover: She is now called "Tina."

With one of their first hit singles playing on the radio, "A Fool in Love," Tina discovers that she is pregnant. When she gives birth to a baby boy, Ike films the event with a home movie camera. Later, to the tune of "It's Gonna Work Out Fine," the band journeys to Mexico, where she and Ike are married.

In 1964, after another baby and several more years of touring, Ike and Tina buy a house in Hollywood, in which Ike establishes a recording studio. As Tina frolics with the children—including the two boys from Ike's previous relationship—he writes songs while sniffing cocaine. When Ike later asks Tina to rehearse a song and she comments on its similarity to many of his others, he explodes into a fury of violence, beating her severely and humiliating her in front of the others, including the children.

Ike's erratic and violent behavior continues to escalate over the years as he fails to adapt to the changing music trends influenced by the Beatles and other British bands of the mid-1960's. During this period, Tina tries repeatedly to leave Ike, but he always manages to locate her and intimidate her into returning home. Several years later, feeling frustrated and trapped, Tina takes an overdose of pills and is hospitalized. Afterward, she visits Jackie (Vanessa Bell Calloway), a former Ikette, who quit after Ike attacked her. In spite of the fact that Jackie encourages Tina to leave Ike, Tina confesses that she cannot stand the thought of abandoning anyone, even Ike, after having been abandoned by her own mother when she was a child. Jackie then introduces Tina to Buddhism, telling her that it will help her see life more clearly. "When you see yourself clearly," she says, "you can change anything."

Once Tina embraces Buddhism, she finds the strength to oppose the abusive Ike. En route to a performance one evening, when Ike begins slapping her in the back of their chauffeured limousine, Tine responds by scratching and kicking him fiercely, then fleeing, never to return. A messy divorce follows, which leaves Tina nearly bankrupt. She then performs a solo act in less-than-prestigious venues in order to survive. She is still a dynamic performer, however, and one night catches the eye of an influential record producer. The result is a new album of all-new, rock-influenced material, which proves to be a smash success.

At age forty-four, Tina begins a triumphant international tour. As she dons her legendary wild-woman wig, black leather miniskirt, and red high heels in preparation for her opening-night concert, Ike appears in her dressing room and begs her to return to him. When she refuses, he draws a gun. Defying him to shoot, Tina takes the stage and launches into the song "What's Love Got to Do with It," at which point the real Tina Turner appears on stage, singing and wowing the audience until the final fade-out.

What Love Got to Do With It covers four decades and re-creates each one with incredible flair. The set designs, the costumes, and the hair styles—especially for the 1950's and 1960's—all capture the look and feel of each era with a playful, energetic zeal, perfectly complementing the aggressively flamboyant characters. The music, a crucial ingredient, is exceptionally well integrated into the action, sometimes acting as a musical Greek chorus, illustrating key moments in Tina's life with its raw energy and timely lyrics. Only in a few instances is the music overbearing; for example, when Tina returns home from the hospital and finds Ike fondling an Ikette while in a drugged stupor, Edgar Winter's "Frankenstein" is heard blaring on the home stereo, a much-too-obvious choice. Overall, however, the music, like the sets and costumes, helps define the eras depicted. At the same time, it links the film's dramatic developments together.

The concert re-creations, also a major element, are all extremely well staged, choreographed, and edited for maximum excitement and energy. It is during these moments that the public Tina, the internationally acclaimed wild woman of rock and soul, is captured on film. One standout musical segment is the "Proud Mary" sequence, a key song that became an integral part of her act. In the film, Tina begins singing the song on a London stage in the early 1970's and, after an expertly edited montage of dramatic events, finishes the song five years later in Los Angeles.

Angela Bassett who received a Best Actress Academy Award nomination for her portrayal of Tina, plays the legendary entertainer with boundless, joyful verve, the key ingredient of Tina's character. Her movements, mannerisms, dancing, and singing (actually lip-synching; the real Tina provides the vocals) are near-perfect re-creations of Tina herself. Even Bassett's lithe, muscular body resembles Tina's. Bassett's performance is hampered somewhat by the fact that she must play Tina for much of the film as a complacent, naïve innocent, the antithesis of Tina's stage persona. Although Bassett is always boundlessly energetic, even when she is being abused, the film would have been more successful if Bassett had been given the opportunity to express other aspects of Tina's character.

Best Actor Oscar nominee Laurence Fishburne has a harder time bringing Ike to life. The earlier scenes are best, when he portrays Ike as a cool, smooth-talking, sexy artist/musician. It is easy in these early scenes to see why Tina—and hordes of other women—were attracted to Ike; Fishburne, with his sleek, sleepy-eyed good looks and in-control aura, exudes a charismatic confidence as Ike that is very appealing. After Ike takes his first sniff of cocaine, however, his character ceases to grow, and Fishburne is given the thankless task of playing a one-dimensional maniac for the rest of the film. Although he plays it well, his later scenes as an abusive drug addict become repetitious and predictable.

The film's major flaw is its story line, which resembles that of countless other film biographies, specifically *What Price Hollywood?* (1932), which was later remade three times as *A Star is Born* (1937, 1954, 1976). Each one centers on a young, innocent, and talented nobody discovered by a gifted artist who then molds her into a fantastic performer, gradually losing his own artistic talents along the way as his creation goes on to achieve legendary greatness. Because this plot is so familiar, it diminishes the film's overall impact.

Furthermore, far too much time is spent detailing Ike's violent attacks against Tina, so much in fact that the repetitive action fails to give the principal actors enough varied material to bring their characters fully to life. Screenwriter Kate Lanier relies on stereotypical situations and characterizations, portraying Tina as a naïve, eternally suffering martyr and Ike as an out-of-control cretin. So much time is devoted to staging violent confrontations that when Tina finally embraces Buddhism and begins to show some assertiveness, her transformation comes so quickly that it fails to be convincing.

Despite its shortcomings, *What's Love Got to Do with It* has enough verve and flamboyant energy to emerge as an excellent and entertaining film biography. Because the filmmakers understand the essence of Tina's character—even though they spend too much time on scenes that undermine it—the film does justice to its talented, exciting, and beloved subject.

Jim Kline

Reviews

Chicago Tribune. June 11, 1993, VII, p. 35.
Ebony. XLVIII, July, 1993, p. 110.
Entertainment Weekly. Summer Double Issue, 1993, p. 82.
The Hollywood Reporter. June 7, 1993, p. 8.
Los Angeles Times. June 9, 1993, p. F1.
The New York Times. June 9, 1993, p. C15.
The New Yorker. June 28, 1993, p. 98.
Newsweek. June 21, 1993, p. 66.
Rolling Stone. June 24, 1993, p. 89.
Sight and Sound. III, October, 1993, p. 14.
Variety. June 7, 1993, p. 4.
The Washington Post. June 11, 1993, p. G1.

WIDE SARGASSO SEA

Origin: Australia
Released: 1993
Released in U.S.: 1993
Production: Jan Sharp for Laughing Kookaburra; released by Fine Line Features
Direction: John Duigan
Screenplay: Jan Sharp, Carole Angier, and John Duigan; based on the novel by Jean Rhys
Cinematography: Geoff Burton
Editing: Anne Goursaud and Jimmy Sandoval
Production design: Franckie D.
Art direction: Susan Bolles
Set decoration: Ron von Blombert
Sound: Harry Cohen
Costume design: Norma Moriceau
Music: Stewart Copeland
MPAA rating: NC-17
Running time: 100 minutes

> *Principal characters:*
> Antoinette Cosway . . . . Karina Lombard
> Edward Rochester . . . . Nathaniel Parker
> Annette Cosway . . . . Rachel Ward
> Paul Mason . . . . Michael York
> Christophène . . . . Claudia Robinson
> Aunt Cora . . . . Martine Beswicke
> Amélie . . . . Rowena King
> Daniel Cosway . . . . Ben Thomas

Based on Jean Rhys's best-selling 1966 novel, *Wide Sargasso Sea* is a story of eroticism, madness, and colonialism set in 1840's Jamaica. Basing the protagonist of her novel on the character of the insane first Mrs. Rochester from the Charlotte Brontë novel *Jane Eyre*, Rhys has created a fascinating story that is completely independent of that of Brontë. Using the character as a starting point, Rhys invents the circumstances that lead to the first Mrs. Rochester's madness. For the film, director/cowriter John Duigan, producer/cowriter Jan Sharp, and cowriter Carole Angier do an admirable job with the difficult task of bringing Rhys's story to the screen.

Set shortly after the emancipation of the slaves in Jamaica, the story unfolds through the voice-over narration of Antoinette Cosway (Karina Lombard), a young, white, West Indian girl who lives on the Coulibri plantation, which has fallen into a state of neglect since the end of slavery. Antoinette's mother, Annette Cosway (Rachel Ward), who owns the plantation, is virtually destitute, and, in an act of desperation, marries a wealthy Englishman, Paul Mason (Michael York).

Paul embodies all the abhorrent attitudes inherent in British colonialism. He is racist, condescending, and arrogant beyond belief. He considers all natives to be lazy and speaks in front of the servants as if they are not human and are incapable of understanding what is being said about them. When Annette warns him to be careful when talking in front of the servants, Paul scoffs at her, incapable of believing that the poverty-stricken natives would dare revolt against the rich white people.

The natives do in fact revolt, burning the house down. Annette subsequently goes insane, grieving over the death of her young son who died from injuries sustained in the fire. Paul flees to England, abandoning Annette to the care of a servant and Antoinette to a convent. Several years later, Antoinette inherits Paul's Jamaican properties, on the condition that she marry a proper husband. A marriage is soon arranged, and Antoinette weds Edward Rochester (Nathaniel Parker), an Englishman of good family but no property.

Initially, Rochester and Antoinette's relationship is fueled by erotic desire. Eventually, however, Rochester's attitudes, similar to those of Paul, strain the relationship. He loathes the island, the heat, and the carefree ways of the natives. He fears the magic that some are said to possess, especially that of Christophène (Claudia Robinson), who has cared for Antoinette since childhood. Rochester longs for England, while Antoinette loves her home passionately. Rochester's British elitism extends beyond his attitude toward the natives, encompassing how he feels about Antoinette as well, whom he considers coarse and uncivilized. Theirs is a doomed relationship, foreshadowed by the disastrous coupling of Paul and Annette.

The cultural differences assume greater meaning as the relationship between Rochester and Antoinette comes to represent colonialism itself: Antoinette represents Jamaica, while Rochester represents England. Thus their attitudes and actions mirror those of their respective countries.

Gender also plays an important role. Under English law, all Antoinette's property becomes Rochester's upon their marriage, solely because he is a man. Therefore, Rochester's perceived superiority is not only cultural but also gender-specific. In addition, Rochester's dominance is expressed through the voice-over narration: Although Antoinette narrates the story in the beginning of the film, Rochester takes over the moment he enters the story. *Wide Sargasso Sea* takes a dim view of both males and the English in general.

Sexual obsession is the most important aspect of the story. Upon exiting the convent, Antoinette experiences a sexual awakening when she marries Rochester. There is also the unspoken sexual desire between the natives and the white landowners, the passion of the forbidden fruit that for a brief moment pushes all the prevalent views and attitudes between the classes out of mind. The island culture itself is very sexual. The wild, erotic dancing done by the natives is in sharp contrast to the formal, regimented dancing favored by the English. Even the music—the pounding percussive beats used throughout the film, but especially during the dance sequences—evokes a powerful eroticism. As if the symbolism of the music and dancing were not obvious enough,

Duigan drives home the point when he intercuts a scene in which Antoinette and Rochester make love, with native dancing and drumming. This heavy-handedness insults the audience's intelligence.

Magic also plays a role in the sexual politics of the film. When Antoinette fears that she has lost Rochester, she goes to Christophène for help. Christophène reluctantly supplies a potion, which has the opposite effect of further distancing the doomed lovers. This crucial scene is once again given heavy-handed treatment by Duigan, who employs one of the ultimate cinematic clichés to show disorientation: the spinning camera move. This type of camera movement is more at home in a bad 1960's drug film than in a 1990's art film.

Aside from these occasional lapses in judgment, Duigan does a creditable job directing. He takes advantage of the spectacular locations, and he elicits convincing performances from his actors. As a male director bringing a very female-oriented story to the screen, he must be well prepared and aware of his material. He was no doubt assisted along the way by his two female coscreenwriters, Sharp and Angier. Angier's input must have been especially valuable, in that she is also the author of a Rhys biography.

Duigan shows good judgment in casting the film. Newcomer Karina Lombard is impressive in the role of Antoinette. She has a charming innocence yet at the same time capably conveys the confidence of a competitor with the home-field advantage. She is breathtakingly beautiful yet does not rely on her beauty as a substitute for acting, as many other former models do. She is a skillful and intelligent actress who bears watching in the future. Claudia Robinson, who until this film worked primarily on the stage, is amazing as Christophène. Her expressive, weathered face exudes the mystical qualities inherent in her character. Although Nathaniel Parker also performs well as Rochester, it is Lombard and Robinson who carry the film.

Perhaps Duigan's shrewdest move was in his actively seeking out the NC-17 rating for this film. The production notes state that the film is being released with this rating in an effort to remove the stigma associated with the rating. While this is admirable, the rating also places this film in a league with other adult-oriented art films, such as *The Cook, the Thief, His Wife, and Her Lover* (1989) and *Henry and June* (1990). While Duigan should be commended for contributing to the destigmatization of the NC-17 rating, he cannot be faulted for using the rating to his advantage. Nevertheless, not until mainstream films such as *Basic Instinct* (1992) and *Sliver* (1993; reviewed in this volume)—both recut to achieve R ratings—embrace the NC-17 rating will the battle be won.

Wide Sargasso Sea is an adult-oriented film in the sense that it would hold little interest for anyone under seventeen years of age. It deals with adult themes, and while it contains several scenes of nudity, it never lapses into anything gratuitous or pornographic. It is a film that has its faults but ultimately overcomes them.

George Delalis

Reviews

Chicago Tribune. May 7, 1993, VII, p. 27.
Entertainment Weekly. May 21, 1993, p. 32.
The Hollywood Reporter. April 21, 1993, p. 5.
Los Angeles Times. April 23, 1993, p. F4.
The New York Times. April 16, 1993, p. B3.
The New Yorker. April 19, 1993, p. 110.
Rolling Stone. May 13, 1993, p. 116.
San Francisco Chronicle. May 14, 1993, p. C11.
Sight and Sound. III, July, 1993, p. 56.
The Times Literary Supplement. June 25, 1993, p. 20.
Variety. April 14, 1993, p. 2.
The Washington Post. May 8, 1993, p. B3.

MORE FILMS OF 1993

Abbreviations: *Pro.* = Production *Dir.* = Direction *Scr.* = Screenplay *Cine.* = Cinematography *Ed.* = Editing *Mu.* = Music *P.d.* = Production design *A.d.* = Art direction *S.d.* = Set decoration *R.t.* = Running time *MPAA* = MPAA rating

---

THE ADVENTURES OF HUCK FINN
Pro. Laurence Mark for Walt Disney Pictures, in association with Steve White Productions; Buena Vista Pictures *Dir.* Stephen Sommers *Scr.* Stephen Sommers; based on the novel *The Adventures of Huckleberry Finn*, by Mark Twain *Cine.* Janusz Kaminski *Ed.* Bob Ducsay *P.d.* Richard Sherman *A.d.* Randy Moore *S.d.* Keith Neely and Michael Warga *Mu.* Bill Conti *MPAA* PG *R.t.* 108 min. *Cast:* Elijah Wood, Courtney B. Vance, Robbie Coltrane, Jason Robards, Ron Perlman, Dana Ivey, Anne Heche, James Gammon, Paxton Whitehead, Tom Aldredge, Laura Bundy, Garette Ratliff Henson, Renee O'Connor.

In this Disney production of Mark Twain's classic tale, Elijah Wood stars as Huck and Courtney B. Vance as Huck's friend and traveling companion, Jim. Jason Robards and Robbie Coltrane also star as the rascally pair of connivers, the King and the Duke.

AIRBORNE
Pro. Bruce Davey and Stephen McEveety for I; Warner Bros. *Dir.* Rob Bowman *Scr.* Bill Apablasa; based on a story by Apablasa and Stephen McEveety *Cine.* Daryn Okada *Ed.* Harry B. Miller III *P.d.* John Myhre *Mu.* Stewart Copeland *MPAA* PG *R.t.* 89 min. *Cast:* Shane McDermott, Seth Green, Brittney Powell, Chris Conrad, Edie McClurg, Patrick O'Brien.

When a carefree California teenager, Mitchell Goosen (Shane McDermott), is sent to live with relatives in Cincinnati while his parents go to Australia, he has difficulty fitting in to the Midwestern life-style and incurs the wrath of members of his new school's hockey team. He is eventually able to win over his adversaries when he proves his worth on a pair of Rollerblades.

ALIVE
Pro. Robert Watts and Kathleen Kennedy for Touchstone Pictures, Paramount Pictures, and Kennedy/Marshall; Buena Vista Pictures *Dir.* Frank Marshall *Scr.* John Patrick Shanley; based on the book by Piers Paul Read *Cine.* Peter James *Ed.* Michael Kahn and William Goldenberg *P.d.* Norman Reynolds *A.d.* Frederick Hole *S.d.* Tedd Kuchera *Mu.* James Newton Howard *MPAA* R *R.t.* 123 min. *Cast:* Ethan Hawke, Vincent Spano, Josh Hamilton, Bruce Ramsay, John Haymes Newton, David Kriegel, Kevin Breznahan, Sam Behrens, Illeana Douglas, Jack Noseworthy, Christian Meoli, Jake Carpenter, Michael De Lorenzo, Jose Zuniga.

As members of a Uruguayan rugby team fly to a match in Chile, their lives are forever changed when their plane crashes high in the Andes mountains. Forced to find hope where they can, and leaders who will provide it, the survivors must do whatever it takes to live and be rescued, even if it means consuming their dead companions.

AMERICAN FRIENDS
Pro. Patrick Cassavetti and Steve Abbott; Castle Hill Productions *Dir.* Tristram Powell *Scr.* Michael Palin and Tristram Powell *Cine.* Philip Bonham-Carter *Ed.* George Akers *P.d.* Andrew McAlpine *A.d.* Chris Townsend *Mu.* Georges Delerue *MPAA* PG *R.t.* 95 min. *Cast:*

Michael Palin, Connie Booth, Trini Alvarado, Alfred Molina.

In this comedy inspired by the diaries of Michael Palin's great grandfather, Palin, a Monty Python alumnus, stars as Reverend Francis Ashby, a senior tutor at an Oxford college, who hopes to succeed the college's senile president. The happily celibate Ashby, however, falls in love while on vacation in Switzerland and ends up competing with a younger don not only for the college's presidency but also for his love.

AMERICAN HEART

Pro. Rosilyn Heller and Jeff Bridges for Avenue Pictures, in association with Live Entertainment, Island World, and World Films; Triton Pictures *Dir.* Martin Bell *Scr.* Peter Silverman; based on the story by Martin Bell, Mary Ellen Mark, and Silverman *Cine.* James R. Bagdonas *Ed.* Nancy Baker *P.d.* Joel Schiller *Mu.* James Newton Howard *MPAA* R *R.t.* 113 min. *Cast:* Jeff Bridges, Edward Furlong, Lucinda Jenney, Tracey Kapisky, Don Harvey, Maggie Welsh.

Set in Seattle, this drama depicts the plight of an ex-con, irresponsible father named Jack Kelson (Jeff Bridges) and his fourteen-year-old son Nick (Edward Furlong), a lonely boy who struggles to win his father's love. When Jack loses his job as a window washer and starts abusing Nick, the youngster finds himself drawn to a young girl for whom he commits petty crime.

AMONGST FRIENDS

Pro. Matt Blumberg for Islet and Last Outlaw Films; Fine Line Features *Dir.* Rob Weiss *Scr.* Rob Weiss *Cine.* Michael Bonvillain *Ed.* Leo Trombetta *P.d.* Terrence Foster *Mu.* Mick Jones *MPAA* R *R.t.* 86 min. *Cast:* Steve Parlavecchio, Joseph Lindsey, Patrick McGaw, Mira Sorvino, Brett Lambson, Michael Artura, Frank Medrano, Louis Lombardi, David Stepkin.

Andy (Steve Parlavecchio), Billy (Joseph Lindsey), and Trevor (Patrick McGaw), friends from wealthy Long Island families, reject their upper-middle-class upbringing and instead adopt the more glamorous life-style of gangsters. Unfortunately for these three, crime does not pay and their friendship dissolves when they get in over their heads.

AMOS AND ANDREW

Pro. Gary Goetzman for Castle Rock Entertainment, in association with New Line Cinema; Columbia Pictures *Dir.* E. Max Frye *Scr.* E. Max Frye *Cine.* Walt Lloyd *Ed.* Jane Kurson *P.d.* Patricia Norris *S.d.* Leslie Morales *Mu.* Richard Gibbs *MPAA* PG-13 *R.t.* 94 min. *Cast:* Nicolas Cage, Samuel L. Jackson, Dabney Coleman, Michael Lerner, Margaret Colin, Brad Dourif, Giancarlo Esposito, Bob Balaban, I. M. Hobson, Chelcie Ross, Jodi Long, Tracey Walter, Aimee Graham.

When black Pulitzer Prize-winning playwright Andrew Sterling (Samuel L. Jackson) moves into a vacation home on an exclusive New England resort island, the bigoted residents think he is a burglar and call the police, who promptly lay siege to his house. Police chief Tolliver (Dabney Coleman) learns of his error and attempts to turn things around by convincing a white prisoner, Amos (Nicholas Cage), to take Sterling hostage so that the police can "rescue" Sterling.

ANOTHER STAKEOUT: STAKEOUT II

Pro. Jim Kouf, Cathleen Summers, and Lynn Bigelow for Touchstone Pictures; Buena Vista *Dir.* John Badham *Scr.* Jim Kouf *Cine.* Roy H. Wagner *Ed.* Frank Morriss *P.d.* Lawrence G. Paull *A.d.* Richard Hudolin *S.d.* Richard Harrison and Rose Marie McSherry *Mu.* Arthur B. Rubinstein *MPAA* PG-13 *R.t.* 109 min. *Cast:* Richard Dreyfuss, Emilio Estevez, Rosie O'Donnell, Dennis Farina, Marcia Strassman, Cathy Moriarty, John Rubinstein, Miguel Ferrer, Sharon Maughan, Madeleine Stowe.

Richard Dreyfuss and Emilio Estevez reprise their roles from *Stakeout* (1987) in this sequel as police detectives Chris Lecce and Bill Reimers, respectively, who are joined on a case by Assistant District Attorney Gina Garrett (Rosie O'Donnell) and her very large dog. Assigned to locate a key witness for an upcoming trial, the three set up shop in a Seattle neighborhood, where Lecce and Garrett pose as husband and wife and Reimers as their son.

ARMY OF DARKNESS

Pro. Robert Tapert for Dino De Laurentiis Communications and Renaissance Pictures; Universal Pictures *Dir.* Sam Raimi *Scr.* Sam Raimi and Ivan Raimi *Cine.* Bill Pope *Ed.* Bob Murawski and R. O. C. Sandstorm *P.d.* Tony Tremblay *A.d.* Aram Allan *S.d.* Michele Poulik *Mu.* Joseph LoDuca *MPAA* R *R.t.* 83 min. *Cast:* Bruce Campbell, Embeth Davidtz, Bridget Fonda, Marcus Gilbert, Ian Abercrombie, Richard Grove.

In this fantasy-horror adventure, a twentieth century store clerk named Ash (Bruce Campbell) accidentally travels back in time to medieval England, where he is forced to live by his wits and his handy chain saw while he works to return to his own time. Having proven himself against knights and "deadites" (zombie monsters), Ash finds himself in a climactic battle with an army of skeletons.

ASPEN EXTREME

Pro. Leonard Goldberg for Hollywood Pictures, in association with Touchwood Pacific Partners I; Buena Vista *Dir.* Patrick Hasburgh *Scr.* Patrick Hasburgh *Cine.* Steven Fierberg and Robert Primes *Ed.* Steven Kemper *P.d.* Roger Cain *A.d.* Dan Self *S.d.* Nina Bradford *Mu.* Michael Convertino *MPAA* PG-13 *R.t.* 117 min. *Cast:* Paul Gross, Peter Berg, Finola Hughes, Teri Polo, William Russ, Trevor Eve, Martin Kemp, Stewart Finley-McLennan, William McNamara, Nicolette Scorsese.

Two Detroit autoworkers, T. J. (Paul Gross) and Dexter (Peter Berg), go to Aspen, Colorado, to become ski instructors, in this weak action/romance. T. J., with his good looks and excellent skiing skills, is an instant hit on the slopes, and soon garners the attentions of a wealthy socialite (Finola Hughes), although his heart belongs to another, Robin (Teri Polo).

BAD BEHAVIOUR (Great Britain, 1993)

Pro. Sarah Curtis for Film Four International, with the participation of British Screen and Parallax Pictures; October Films *Dir.* Les Blair *Scr.* Les Blair *Cine.* Witold Stok *Ed.* Martin Walsh *P.d.* Jim Grant *A.d.* Rebecca M. Harvey *Mu.* John Altman *MPAA* R *R.t.* 103 min. *Cast:* Stephen Rea, Sinead Cusack, Philip Jackson, Clare Higgins, Phil Daniels, Saira Todd, Mary Jo Randle, Amanda Boxer.

Set in a middle-class London neighborhood, this British comedy of manners centers on Gerry (Stephen Rea) and Ellie (Sinead Cusack) McAllister, a happily married couple with two children, who are undergoing a midlife crisis. Comic mishaps abound when Ellie's former husband, Howard Spink (Philip Jackson), a real-estate scam artist, convinces the McAllisters to renovate their bathroom.

BARAKA

Pro. Mark Magidson for Magidson Films; the Samuel Goldwyn Company *Dir.* Ron Fricke *Scr.* Ron Fricke, Mark Magidson, and Bob Green *Cine.* Ron Fricke *Ed.* Ron Fricke, Mark Magidson, and David E. Aubrey *Mu.* Michael Stearns *R.t.* 96 min.

Filmed in twenty-four countries over fourteen months, this breathtaking film highlights the wonder and diversity of the planet Earth by showing diverse images from all over the world. Lacking actors, plot, and dialogue, *Baraka* is not a conventional motion picture but rather a unique visual experience.

BARJO (France, 1993)

Pro. Patrick Godeau in association with PCC Productions-Alecleo-FR3 Films; Myriad Pictures *Dir.* Jerome Boivin *Scr.* Jacques Audiard and Jerome Boivin; based on *Confessions of a Crap Artist*, by Philip K. Dick *Cine.* Jean-Claude Pierrard *Ed.* Anne Lafarge *P.d.* Dominique Maleret *Mu.* Hughes Le Bars *R.t.* 98 min. *Cast:* Anne Brochet, Richard Bohringer, Hippolyte Girardot, Consuelo de Haviland, Renaud Danner, Nathalie Boutefeu, Jac Berrocal.

This weird drama centers on a willful young married woman, Fanfan (Anne Brochet), who becomes involved in an adulterous affair with tragic results, and her extremely odd brother, Barjo (Hippolyte Girardot).

BATMAN: MASK OF THE PHANTASM
Pro. Benjamin Melniker, Michael Uslan, Tom Ruegger (executive producer), Alan Burnett (coproducer), Eric Radomski (coproducer), Bruce W. Timm (coproducer); Warner Bros. *Dir.* Eric Radomski and Bruce W. Timm *Scr.* Alan Burnett, Paul Dini, Martin Pasko, and Michael Reaves; based on a story by Burnett and characters created for DC Comics by Bob Kane *Ed.* Al Breitenbach *Mu.* Shirley Walker *MPAA* PG *R.t.* 76 min. *Voices:* Kevin Conroy, Dana Delany, Hart Bochner, Mark Hamill, Stacy Keach, Jr., Efrem Zimbalist, Jr., Abe Vigoda, Dick Miller, John P. Ryan, Bob Hastings.

The plot of this dark, animated feature film involves a case of mistaken identity, in which Batman (voice of Kevin Conroy) is thought to be a mysterious caped murderer: the Phantasm. Another plotline follows the sudden reappearance of Andrea (voice of Dana Delany), a long-lost flame of Bruce Wayne. The film is a not altogether successful translation of the popular Fox Broadcasting television show to the big screen.

BEING AT HOME WITH CLAUDE (Canada, 1993)
Pro. Louise Gendron for Les Productions du Cerf, in association with the National Film Board of Canada; Strand Releasing *Dir.* Jean Beaudin *Scr.* Jean Beaudin; based on the play by Rene-Daniel Dubois *Cine.* Thomas Vamos *Ed.* Andre Corriveau *A.d.* François Seguin *S.d.* Peter Stratford and Frances Calder *Mu.* Richard Gregoire *R.t.* 84 min. *Cast:* Roy Dupuis, Jacques Godin, Jean-Francois Pichette, Gaston Lepage, Hugo Dube.

Not the usual murder mystery, this drama examines the motives behind a murderer's crime. When a male prostitute, Yves (Roy Dupuis), turns himself in for the murder of his lover, Claude (Jean-Francois Pichette), he undergoes a grueling interrogation by a police inspector (Jacques Godin) who wants to know not only the method but also the reason behind the murder.

BENEFIT OF THE DOUBT
Pro. Michael Spielberg and Brad M. Gilbert for Monument Pictures, in association with CineVox Entertainment; Miramax Films *Dir.* Jonathan Heap *Scr.* Jeffrey Polman and Christopher Keyser; based on a story by Michael Lieber *Cine.* Johnny E. Jensen *Ed.* Sharyn L. Ross *P.d.* Marina Kieser *A.d.* David Seth Lazan *S.d.* Larry Dias *Mu.* Hummie Mann *MPAA* R *R.t.* 90 min. *Cast:* Donald Sutherland, Amy Irving, Rider Strong, Christopher McDonald, Graham Greene, Theodore Bikel, Gisele Kovach, Ferdinand Mayne.

A single mother (Amy Irving) living in a small town in Arizona dreads the return of her father (Donald Sutherland), who has just been released from prison, because it was her testimony as a child some twenty years previous that won his conviction for the murder of her mother.

BEST OF THE BEST II
Pro. Peter E. Strauss and Phillip Rhee for the Movie Group; Twentieth Century-Fox *Dir.* Robert Radler *Scr.* Max Strom and John Allen Nelson; based on characters created by Paul Levine *Cine.* Fred Tammes *Ed.* Bert Lovitt *P.d.* Gary Frutkoff *A.d.* Shari Hangar *S.d.* Bill Rea and Anna Rita Raineri *Mu.* David Michael Frank *MPAA* R *R.t.* 100 min. *Cast:* Eric

Roberts, Phillip Rhee, Christopher Penn, Edan Gross, Ralph Moeller, Meg Foster, Sonny Landham, Wayne Newton, Betty Carvalho, Simon Rhee, Claire Stansfield.

In this sequel to the 1989 action/adventure, two martial arts experts (Phillip Rhee and Eric Roberts) seek revenge against bad guy Brakus (Ralph Moeller), owner of and principal contender at an illegal Las Vegas gladiator arena, who killed their friend (Christopher Penn) in a no-holds-barred fight.

BETTY (France and Great Britain, 1993)
Pro. Marin Karmitz for MK2 Productions U.S.A., C.E.D. Productions, and FR3 Films, with the participation of Canal Plus; MK2 Productions *Dir.* Claude Chabrol *Scr.* Claude Chabrol; based on the novel by Georges Simenon *Cine.* Bernard Zitzermann *Ed.* Monique Fardoulis *P.d.* Françoise Benoit-Fresco *A.d.* Jean-Pierre Lemoine and Pierre Gaillard *Mu.* Matthieu Chabrol *R.t.* 103 min. *Cast:* Marie Trintignant, Stephane Audran, Jean-François Garreau, Yves Lambrecht, Christiane Minazzoli, Pierre Vernier, Pierre Martot, Nathalie Kousnetzoff, Thomas Chabrol.

A profligate young woman, Betty (Marie Trintignant), is befriended in a bar by an older widow, Laure (Stephane Audran), who provides her with a hotel room and to whom she pours out her life story.

BLACK CAT (*Hak Mau.* Hong Kong, 1992)
Pro. Stephen Shin for D & B Films Co.; Headliner *Dir.* Stephen Shin *Scr.* Lam Wai-iun, Chan Bo-shun, and Lam Tan-ping *Cine.* Lee Kin-keung *Ed.* Wong Wing-ming, Kwok Ting-hung, and Wong Chau-on *A.d.* Fu Tsi-tsung *Mu.* Danny Chung *R.t.* 91 min. *Cast:* Jade Leung, Simon Yam, Thomas Lam.

Like the French hit *La Femme Nikita* (1990), this Hong Kong action film centers on a murderous young woman (Jade Leung) who is forced by the government to become a political assassin and who hides her identity from her would-be suitor (Thomas Lam).

BODIES, REST, AND MOTION
Pro. Allan Mindel, Denise Shaw, and Eric Stoltz for Fine Line Features and August Entertainment; Fine Line Features *Dir.* Michael Steinberg *Scr.* Roger Hedden; based on his play *Cine.* Bernd Heinl *Ed.* Jay Cassidy *P.d.* Stephen McCabe *A.d.* Daniel Talpers *S.d.* Helen Britten *Mu.* Michael Convertino *MPAA* R *R.t.* 95 min. *Cast:* Phoebe Cates, Bridget Fonda, Tim Roth, Eric Stoltz, Scott Johnson, Scott Frederick, Alicia Witt, Peter Fonda, Sandra Lafferty.

Four twenty-something adults undergo a major upheaval in their stale lives during a single, eventful weekend. Volatile Nick (Tim Roth) suddenly abandons his girlfriend, Beth (Bridget Fonda), and leaves town; Beth begins a romance with Sid (Eric Stoltz), their house painter; and Nick's former girlfriend, Carol (Phoebe Cates), who is also Beth's best friend, takes a serious look at her own existence.

BODY OF EVIDENCE
Pro. Dino De Laurentiis; Metro-Goldwyn-Mayer/United Artists *Dir.* Uli Edel *Scr.* Brad Mirman *Cine.* Doug Milsome *Ed.* Thom Noble *P.d.* Victoria Paul *A.d.* Michael Rizzo *S.d.* Jerie Kelter *Mu.* Graeme Revell *MPAA* R *R.t.* 99 min. *Cast:* Madonna, Willem Dafoe, Julianne Moore, Joe Mantegna, Anne Archer, Michael Forest, Frank Langella, Jurgen Prochnow.

The passion of Rebecca Carlson (Madonna) for rough sex brings her to the attention of law enforcement authorities when her older lover dies of a heart attack, leaving her $8 million in his will. Her attorney, Frank Dulaney (Willem Dafoe), works to save her, even as he falls under her spell.

BOILING POINT
Pro. Marc Frydman and Leonardo de la Fuente for Hexagon Films; Warner Bros. *Dir.* James

B. Harris *Scr.* James B. Harris; based on the novel *Money Men*, by Gerald Petievich *Cine.* King Baggot *Ed.* Jerry Brady *P.d.* Ron Foreman *A.d.* Russ Smith *S.d.* Rick Caprarelli *Mu.* Cory Lerios and John D'Andrea *MPAA* R *R.t.* 90 min. *Cast:* Wesley Snipes, Dennis Hopper, Lolita Davidovich, Viggo Mortensen, Dan Hedaya, Seymour Cassel, Jonathan Banks, Christine Elise, Tony Lo Bianco, Valerie Perrine, James Tolkan, Paul Gleason, Lorraine Evanoff.

Based on Gerald Petievich's novel *Money Men* (1981), this drama features Wesley Snipes as Jimmy Mercer, a federal agent, and Dennis Hopper as Red Diamond, a con man released from prison. Jimmy is given seven days by his superiors to catch those who have killed his partner, which includes Red, who in turn has seven days to produce the money he owes a mafioso.

BOPHA!

Pro. Lawrence Taubman for Arsenio Hall Communications, in association with Taubman Entertainment Group; Paramount Pictures *Dir.* Morgan Freeman *Scr.* Brian Bird and John Wierick; based on the play by Percy Mtwa *Cine.* David Watkin *Ed.* Neil Travis *P.d.* Michael Philips *A.d.* Tracey Moxham *S.d.* Dankert Guillaume *Mu.* James Horner *MPAA* PG-13 *R.t.* 120 min. *Cast:* Danny Glover, Malcolm McDowell, Alfre Woodard, Marius Weyers, Maynard Eziashi, Malick Bowens, Michael Chinyamurindi, Christopher John Hall, Grace Mahlaba.

Set in 1980's South Africa, this drama centers on a father-son conflict, with tragic results. Danny Glover portrays Micah Mangena, a family man and South African police officer whose devotion to his career conflicts with the radical political stance of his son, Zweli (Maynard Eziashi), who protests the system of apartheid that his father has worked so long to uphold.

BORN YESTERDAY

Pro. D. Constantine Conte for Hollywood Pictures, in association with Touchwood Pacific Partners I; Buena Vista Pictures *Dir.* Luis Mandoki *Scr.* Douglas McGrath; based on the play by Garson Kanin *Cine.* Lajos Koltai *Ed.* Lesley Walker *P.d.* Lawrence G. Paull *A.d.* Bruce Crone *S.d.* Nancy Patton, Philip Toolin, and Rick Simpson *Mu.* George Fenton *MPAA* PG *R.t.* 101 min. *Cast:* Melanie Griffith, John Goodman, Don Johnson, Edward Herrmann, Max Perlich, Fred Dalton Thompson, Nora Dunn, Michael Ensign, Benjamin C. Bradlee, Sally Quinn, William Frankfather, Celeste Yarnall, Meg Wittner, William Forward, Mary Gordon Murray.

This screwball comedy tells how real estate tycoon Harry Brock (John Goodman) and his girlfriend Billie Dawn (Melanie Griffith) come to Washington, D.C., to persuade legislators and government officials to help his shopping center. When Billie proves a social embarrassment, Brock hires a newspaper reporter (Don Johnson) to educate her.

BOUND AND GAGGED: A LOVE STORY

Pro. Dennis J. Mahoney for G.E.L. and Cinescope; Northern Arts Entertainment *Dir.* Daniel Appleby *Scr.* Daniel Appleby *Cine.* Dean Lent *Ed.* Kaye Davis *P.d.* Dane Pizzuti Krogman *Mu.* William Murphy *R.t.* 95 min. *Cast:* Christopher Denton, Elizabeth Saltarrelli, Ginger Lynn Allen, Karen Black, Chris Mulkey, Mary Ella Ross.

A young woman, Leslie (Ginger Lynn Allen), trapped in an abusive marriage with husband Steve (Chris Mulkey), is kidnapped by her lesbian lover, Elizabeth (Elizabeth Saltarrelli), who takes her on a road trip to a professional deprogrammer (Karen Black) in an attempt to persuade her to leave him. The two women are joined by Cliff (Chris Denton), a young man who, depressed following the breakup of his marriage, attempts numerous suicides, in this black comedy.

BOXING HELENA

Pro. Carl Mazzocone and Philippe Caland for Main Line Pictures; Orion Classics *Dir.* Jennifer Chambers Lynch *Scr.* Jennifer Chambers Lynch; based on a story by Philippe Caland *Cine.* Frank Byers *Ed.* David Finfer *A.d.* Paul Huggins *S.d.* Sharon Braunstein *Mu.* Graeme Revell *MPAA* R *R.t.* 107 min. *Cast:* Julian Sands, Sherilyn Fenn, Bill Paxton, Kurtwood Smith, Betsy Clark, Nicolette Scorsese, Art Garfunkel.

In this eerie erotic drama, Julian Sands stars as a surgeon, Dr. Nick Cavanaugh, who is obsessed by a beautiful but cruel neighbor, Helena (Sherilyn Fenn). Injured in a car accident, Helena is taken prisoner by the disturbed Nick, who amputates her limbs in a perverted attempt to win Helena's affections.

A BREATH OF LIFE (*The Plague Sower*. Italy, 1993)

Pro. Massimo Vigliar and Franco Nero for Movie Machine, in collaboration with Rai 1; Surf Film *Dir.* Beppe Cino *Scr.* Beppe Cino and Gesualdo Bufalino; based on the book *Diceria Dell'untore*, by Bufalino *Cine.* Franco Delli Colli *Ed.* Emanuele Foglietti *A.d.* Maurizio Leonardi *Mu.* Carlo Siliotto *R.t.* 90 min. *Cast:* Franco Nero, Lucrezia Lante Della Rovere, Fernando Rey, Vanessa Redgrave.

Set in Italy in 1946, this romantic drama centers on a reserved academic, Angelo (Franco Nero), and a ballerina, Marta (Lucrezia Lante Della Rovere), who meet and fall in love in a Palermo tuberculosis clinic.

BROTHER'S KEEPER

Pro. Joe Berlinger and Bruce Sinofsky for Hand-to-Mouth; American Playhouse Theatrical Films, in association with Creative Thinking International *Dir.* Joe Berlinger and Bruce Sinofsky *Cine.* Douglas Cooper *Ed.* Joe Berlinger and Bruce Sinofsky *Mu.* Jay Ungar and Molly Mason *R.t.* 104 min. *Cast:* Delbert Ward, Roscoe Ward, Lyman Ward, Ralph A. Cognetti, Connie Chung, Harry Thurston.

This critically acclaimed documentary centers on an illiterate, elderly upstate New York farmer who was accused of murdering his brother in 1990. The filmmakers interview Delbert Ward and his two surviving brothers—all of whom live together in a filthy two-room cabin—as well as neighbors, relatives, police, and lawyers in order to present as complete a picture as possible of the circumstances involved in this most unusual case.

BUM RAP

Pro. Daniel Irom; Millennium Productions, Inc. *Dir.* Daniel Irom *Scr.* Daniel Irom *Cine.* Kevin A. Lombard *Ed.* Michael Berenbaum *A.d.* Lyn Pinezich *Mu.* Robert Kessler, Ethan Neuberg, and Robin Monroe *R.t.* 110 min. *Cast:* Craig Wasson, Blanche Baker, Al Lewis, Anita Gillette, Frances Fisher.

When a thirty-year-old New York actor/cabdriver, Paul Colson (Craig Wasson), is diagnosed with a fatal disease, he has three days to come to terms with his life—such as it is. Along the way, he finds solace with a kindhearted prostitute, Lisa DuSoir (Blanche Baker).

BY THE SWORD (Canada, 1991)

Pro. Peter E. Strauss and Marlon Staggs for the Movie Group, in association with SVS Pictures and Foil/Film Horizon; Hansen Entertainment *Dir.* Jeremy Kagan *Scr.* John McDonald and James Donadio *Cine.* Arthur Albert *Ed.* David Holden *P.d.* Gary Frutkoff *A.d.* Kim Rees *S.d.* K. C. Fox *Mu.* Bill Conti *MPAA* R *R.t.* 91 min. *Cast:* F. Murray Abraham, Eric Roberts, Mia Sara, Chris Rydell, Elaine Kagan, Brett Cullen, Doug Wert.

A former champion fencer, Suba (F. Murray Abraham), recently released from a twenty-year prison sentence for killing his trainer, returns to the fencing academy, which is now run by his former teacher's arrogant son, Alexander Villard (Eric Roberts). Working his way up from janitor, Suba slowly gets back into shape and recovers his former skills in order to be able to teach fencing to others and atone for his previous mistakes—and fight the inevitable battle with Villard.

CALENDAR GIRL

Pro. Debbie Robins and Gary Marsh for Parkway; Columbia Pictures *Dir.* John Whitesell *Scr.* Paul W. Shapiro *Cine.* Tom Priestley *Ed.* Wendy Greene Bricmont *P.d.* Bill Groom *A.d.* Sarah Knowles *S.d.* Lynn Wolverton-Parker *Mu.* Hans Zimmer *MPAA* PG-13 *R.t.* 90 min. *Cast:* Jason Priestley, Gabriel Olds, Jerry O'Connell, Joe Pantoliano, Steve Railsback, Kurt Fuller, Stephen Tobolowsky, Emily Warfield, Stephanie Anderson, Cortney Page (voice), Chubby Checker.

Three teenage friends (Jason Priestley, Gabriel Olds, and Jerry O'Connell) leave small-town Nevada for Hollywood in 1962 to pursue their idol—Marilyn Monroe (Stephanie Anderson), in this comedy/adventure.

CB4

Pro. Nelson George for Brian Grazer and Sean Daniel; Universal Pictures *Dir.* Tamra Davis *Scr.* Chris Rock, Nelson George, and Robert LoCash; based on a story by Rock and George *Cine.* Karl Walter Lindenlaub *Ed.* Earl Watson *P.d.* Nelson Coates *A.d.* Martin Charles *S.d.* Karen Steward and Susan Benjamin *Mu.* John Barnes *MPAA* R *R.t.* 86 min. *Cast:* Chris Rock, Allen Payne, Deezer D, Chris Elliott, Phil Hartman, Charlie Murphy, Khandi Alexander, Arthur Evans, Theresa Randle, Willard E. Pugh.

In this mediocre comedy, three middle-class teens (Chris Rock, Allen Payne, and Deezer D) start a rap group named CB4 (cell block 4), assuming the personas of tough gang members in order to lend the group authenticity.

CHAIN OF DESIRE

Pro. Brian Cox for Anant Singh and Distant Horizon; Mad Dog Pictures *Dir.* Temistocles Lopez *Scr.* Temistocles Lopez *Cine.* Nancy Schreiber *Ed.* Suzanne Fenn *P.d.* Scott Chambliss *A.d.* Michael Shaw *S.d.* Judy Becker *Mu.* Nathan Birnbaum *R.t.* 107 min. *Cast:* Linda Fiorentino, Elias Koteas, Malcolm McDowell, Grace Zabriskie, Tim Guinee, Assumpta Serna, Patrick Bauchau, Seymour Cassel, Angel Aviles, Jamie Harrold, Dewey Weber, Holly Marie Combs, Kevin Conroy, Suzzanne Douglas.

Set in New York City, this tale of eroticism and desire follows a chain of sexual encounters that comes full circle a la 1950's *La Ronde*, but in a 1990's-society threatened by AIDS (acquired immune deficiency syndrome).

CHEATIN' HEARTS

Pro. Catherine Wanek for King/Moonstone; Trimark Pictures *Dir.* Rod McCall *Scr.* Rod McCall *Cine.* Barry Markowitz *Ed.* Curtis Edge *P.d.* Susan Brand *A.d.* Stuart Blatt *Mu.* George S. Clinton *MPAA* R *R.t.* 106 min. *Cast:* James Brolin, Sally Kirkland, Pamela Gidley, Kris Kristofferson, Laura Johnson, Renee Estevez.

When the estranged husband (James Brolin) of Jenny (Sally Kirkland) returns to attend the wedding of their youngest daughter (Renee Estevez), neither Jenny nor oldest daughter Samantha (Pamela Gidley) welcomes his presence. Kris Kristofferson costars as a sympathetic friend in whom Jenny confides.

CHILDREN OF THE CORN II: THE FINAL SACRIFICE

Pro. Scott A. Stone and David G. Stanley for Fifth Avenue Entertainment; Dimension *Dir.* David F. Price *Scr.* A. L. Katz and Gilbert Adler; based on the short story by Stephen King *Cine.* Levie Isaacks *Ed.* Barry Zetlin *P.d.* Greg Melton *A.d.* Tim Eckei *S.d.* Natali K. Pope *Mu.* Daniel Licht *MPAA* R *R.t.* 92 min. *Cast:* Terence Knox, Paul Scherrer, Ryan Bollman,

Christie Clark, Rosalind Allen, Ned Romero, Marty Terry, Joe Inscoe, Ed Grady, Wallace Merck, Ted Travelstead.

In this extremely poor sequel to the 1984 original based on a Stephen King short story, the Children of the Corn continue to wreak havoc on the adults of a small Nebraska town. In addition, a tabloid journalist (Terence Knox) arrives in town to cover the sensational events, bringing in tow his estranged son (Paul Scherrer).

CLAIRE OF THE MOON

Pro. Pamela S. Kuri; Demi-Monde Productions *Dir.* Nicole Conn *Scr.* Nicole Conn *Cine.* Randolph Sellars *Ed.* Michael Solinger *P.d.* Kristin Burkland *Mu.* Michael Allen Harrison *R.t.* 102 min. *Cast:* Trisha Todd, Karen Trumbo, Faith McDevitt, Caren Graham.

Two very different professional women, one a free-spirited novelist (Trisha Todd) and the other a reserved therapist and writer (Karen Trumbo), meet at an Oregon writers' conference and fall in love.

UN COEUR EN HIVER (*A Heart in Winter*. France, 1992)

Pro. Jean-Louis Livi and Philippe Carcassonne; October Films *Dir.* Claude Sautet *Scr.* Yves Ulmann, Jacques Fieschi, and Jerome Tonnerrec *Cine.* Yves Angelo *Ed.* Jacqueline Thiedot *P.d.* Christian Marti *Mu.* Philippe Sard *R.t.* 105 min. *Cast:* Daniel Auteuil, Emmanuelle Beart, Andre Dussollier, Elisabeth Bourgine, Brigitte Catillon, Stanislas Carre de Malberg, Maurice Garrel, Myriam Boyer, Jean-Luc Bideau.

Daniel Auteuil, Emmanuelle Beart, and Andre Dussollier star in this award-winning film about a complex love triangle between two men who run a violin repair shop and the beautiful violinist with whom they both fall in love.

CONEHEADS

Pro. Lorne Michaels; Paramount Pictures *Dir.* Steve Barron *Scr.* Tom Davis, Dan Aykroyd, Bonnie Turner, and Terry Turner *Cine.* Francis Kenny *Ed.* Paul Trejo *P.d.* Gregg Fonseca *A.d.* Bruce Miller *S.d.* Jay Hart *Mu.* David Newman *MPAA* PG *R.t.* 86 min. *Cast:* Dan Aykroyd, Jane Curtin, Michelle Burke, Michael McKean, Jason Alexander, Lisa Jane Persky, Chris Farley, David Spade, Dave Thomas, Sinbad, Jan Hooks, Laraine Newman, Phil Hartman, Shishir Kurup.

In this comedy based on a *Saturday Night Live* television sketch, Dan Aykroyd and Jane Curtin star as two aliens who settle in American suburbia with their teenage daughter, Connie (Michelle Burke), while awaiting the arrival of a rescue ship from their home planet.

COP AND A HALF

Pro. Paul Maslansky for Imagine Films Entertainment; Universal Studios *Dir.* Henry Winkler *Scr.* Arne Olsen *Cine.* Bill Butler *Ed.* Daniel Hanley and Roger Tweten *MPAA* PG *R.t.* 91 min. *Cast:* Burt Reynolds, Norman D. Golden II, Ruby Dee, Holland Taylor, Ray Sharkey.

Eight-year-old Devon Butler (Norman D. Golden II) trades information he has on a drug ring with the police for the chance to be the partner of Detective Nick McKenna (Burt Reynolds) for a day. The two grow close through the adventures they share.

CRUSH (New Zealand, 1993)

Pro. Bridget Ikin for Hibiscus Films; Strand Releasing *Dir.* Alison Maclean *Scr.* Alison Maclean and Anne Kennedy *Cine.* Dion Beebe *Ed.* John Gilbert *P.d.* Meryl Cronin *A.d.* Brett Schweiters and David Turner *Mu.* JPS Experience and Antony Partos *R.t.* 97 min. *Cast:* Marcia Gay Harden, Donogh Rees, Caitlin Bossley, William Zappa.

When a literary critic, Christina (Donogh Rees), is nearly killed in a car crash, her friend and the driver of the car, Lane (Marcia Gay Harden), walks away from the accident. Lane then proceeds to manipulate her way into the lives of a reclusive novelist (William Zappa), whom

Christina was en route to interview, and his impressionable teenage daughter, Angela (Caitlin Bossley).

THE CRUSH

Pro. James G. Robinson for Morgan Creek; Warner Bros. *Dir.* Alan Shapiro *Scr.* Alan Shapiro *Cine.* Bruce Surtees *Ed.* Ian Crafford *P.d.* Michael Bolton *A.d.* Eric Fraser *S.d.* Paul Joyal *Mu.* Graeme Revell *MPAA* R *R.t.* 89 min. *Cast:* Cary Elwes, Alicia Silverstone, Jennifer Rubin, Amber Benson, Kurtwood Smith, Gwynyth Walsh, Matthew Walker.

An aspiring writer, Nick Eliot (Cary Elwes), gets more than he bargained for when he rents a guest cottage: He finds himself prey to the ominous affections of his landlords' teenage daughter (Alicia Silverstone).

A DANGEROUS WOMAN

Pro. Naomi Foner for Amblin Entertainment, in association with Island World and Rollercoaster; Gramercy Pictures *Dir.* Stephen Gyllenhaal *Scr.* Naomi Foner; based on the novel by Mary McGarry Morris *Cine.* Robert Elswit *Ed.* Harvey Rosenstock *P.d.* David Brisbin *S.d.* Mary Finn, Renato Franceschelli, and Margaret Goldsmith *Mu.* Carter Burwell *MPAA* R *R.t.* 101 min. *Cast:* Debra Winger, Barbara Hershey, Gabriel Byrne, David Strathairn, Chloe Webb, Jan Hooks, Laurie Metcalf, John Terry, Paul Dooley, Viveka Davis, Richard Riehle.

Debra Winger gives a stellar performance as Martha Horgan, a social misfit who lives next to her Aunt Frances (Barbara Hershey) in a small California town. When an alcoholic handyman (Gabriel Byrne) drifts into their lives, Martha experiences a sexual awakening. Director Stephen Gyllenhaal and scriptwriter Naomi Foner have fashioned a small-scale character study about an eccentric character who is hurt by others' misperceptions of her.

THE DARK HALF

Pro. Declan Baldwin for Dark Half Productions; Orion Pictures *Dir.* George A. Romero *Scr.* George A. Romero; based on the novel by Stephen King *Cine.* Tony Pierce-Roberts *Ed.* Pasquale Buba *P.d.* Cletus Anderson *A.d.* Jim Feng *S.d.* Brian Stonestreet *Mu.* Christopher Young *MPAA* R *R.t.* 124 min. *Cast:* Timothy Hutton, Amy Madigan, Michael Rooker, Julie Harris, Timothy Hutton, Robert Joy, Kent Broadhurst, Beth Grant, Rutanya Alda, Tom Mardirosian, Patrick Brannan, Glenn Colerider, Chelsea Field, Royal Dano.

In this thriller based on the novel by Stephen King, Timothy Hutton stars both as respected novelist Thad Beaumont and as George Stark, the secret pseudonym Beaumont uses to write money-making, bloody novels. When, after being blackmailed, Beaumont decides to get rid of his alter ego, he finds that Stark is real and extremely dangerous.

DEAD ALIVE (New Zealand, 1993)

Pro. Jim Booth; Trimark Pictures *Dir.* Peter Jackson *Scr.* Peter Jackson, Stephen Sinclair, and Frances Walsh *Cine.* Murray Milne *Ed.* Jamie Selkirk *P.d.* Kevin Leonard-Jones *A.d.* Ed Mulholland *Mu.* Peter Dasent *R.t.* 97 min. *Cast:* Timothy Balme, Diana Penalver, Elizabeth Moody, Ian Watkin, Brenda Kendall, Stuart Devenie.

In this spoof of the horror genre, a young man's mother becomes a zombie as the result of a bite from a Sumatran rat monkey, leading to more zombies and lots of blood and gore.

DECEPTION

Pro. Lloyd Phillips for Majestic Films International; Miramax Films *Dir.* Graeme Clifford *Scr.* Robert Dillon and Michael Thomas; based on a story by Dillon *Cine.* Laszlo Kovacs *Ed.* Caroline Biggerstaff *P.d.* Richard Sylbert *A.d.* Peter Smith *S.d.* Jim Erickson and Lisa Fischer *Mu.* John Barry *MPAA* PG-13 *R.t.* 90 min. *Cast:* Andie MacDowell, Liam Neeson, Viggo Mortensen, Jack Thompson.

Andie MacDowell stars as the recently widowed Bessie Faro, whose blue-collar husband

(Viggo Mortensen), head of an aircraft salvage business and a pilot, is killed outside Veracruz, Mexico, in a plane accident. Her discovery of a pack of baseball cards among his belongings leads her on a globe-trotting adventure during which she learns of her husband's illicit dealings and recovers large sums of cash from bank accounts all over the world.

DOUBLE THREAT

Pro. Kimberley Casey for David Winters, in association with Sovereign Investment Corp.; Pyramid Distribution, Inc. *Dir.* David A. Prior *Scr.* David A. Prior *Cine.* Gerald B. Wolfe *Ed.* Tony Malanowski *A.d.* Linda Lewis *Mu.* Christopher Farrell *MPAA* R *R.t.* 96 min. *Cast:* Sally Kirkland, Andrew Stevens, Sherrie Rose, Chick Vennera, Gary Swanson, Richard Lynch, Anthony Franciosa, Monique Detraz, Ted Prior.

An aging film star making a comeback, Monica Martel (Sally Kirkland), becomes jealous when her younger leading man and lover (Andrew Stevens) becomes involved with Monica's body double (Sherrie Rose), in this weak erotic thriller.

DRAGON: THE BRUCE LEE STORY

Pro. Raffaella De Laurentiis; Universal Pictures *Dir.* Rob Cohen *Scr.* Edward Khmara, John Raffo, and Rob Cohen; based on the book *Bruce Lee: The Man Only I Knew*, by Linda Lee Cadwell *Cine.* David Eggby *Ed.* Peter Amundson *P.d.* Robert Ziembicki *A.d.* Ted Berner *S.d.* Dayna Lee *Mu.* Randy Edelman *MPAA* PG-13 *R.t.* 121 min. *Cast:* Jason Scott Lee, Lauren Holly, Robert Wagner, Michael Learned, Nancy Kwan, Kay Tong Lim, Sterling Macer, Ric Young, Luoyong Wang, Sven-Ole Thorsen, Alicia Tao.

This engaging biography recounts the brief and tragic life of Bruce Lee (Jason Scott Lee), the legendary Chinese American martial artist who died in his early thirties. The film is based on the book by Lee's widow.

THE EBRO RUNS DRY (Sweden, 1993)

Dir. Saeed Assadi *Scr.* Saeed Assadi and Mats Brigersson *Cast:* Per Allan Lofberg, Maite Brik, Fernando Chinarro.

When a Swedish man, Mikel (Per Allan Lofberg), learns of his estranged father's death in Spain, where his father fought as a member of the International Brigade in the Spanish Civil War, Mikel travels to Spain to claim his inheritance. While there, he not only learns of his father's great heroism but also finds that his own life is in grave danger.

ED AND HIS DEAD MOTHER

Pro. William Christopher Gorog for ITC Entertainment Group; I.R.S. Releasing *Dir.* Jonathan Wacks *Scr.* Chuck Hughes *Cine.* Francis Kenny *P.d.* Eve Cauley *Mu.* Mason Daring *MPAA* PG-13 *R.t.* 90 min. *Cast:* Steve Buscemi, Ned Beatty, Miriam Margolyes, John Glover, Sam Jenkins.

In this weak black comedy, a young man, Ed (Steve Buscemi), strikes a deal with a conniving salesman (John Glover) to have his dead mother (Miriam Margolyes) brought back to life, with darkly comic results.

EQUINOX

Pro. David Blocker for SC Entertainment International; I.R.S. Releasing *Dir.* Alan Rudolph *Scr.* Alan Rudolph *Cine.* Elliot Davis *Ed.* Michael Ruscio *P.d.* Steven Legler *A.d.* Randye Ericksen *R.t.* 108 min. *Cast:* Matthew Modine, Lara Flynn Boyle, Fred Ward, Marisa Tomei, Tyra Ferrell, Lori Singer, Kevin J. O'Connor, M. Emmet Walsh, Tate Donovan, Gailard Sartain.

Matthew Modine stars in a dual role as identical twin brothers Henry Petosa and Freddy Ace, who were separated at birth, each unaware of the other's existence. One good, one bad, they lead parallel lives in the big city until their paths inevitably cross.

ERNEST RIDES AGAIN

Pro. Stacy Williams; Emshell Producers Group, Inc. *Dir.* John R. Cherry III *Scr.* John R. Cherry III and William M. Akers *Cine.* David Geddes *Ed.* Craig Bassett *P.d.* Chris August *A.d.* Helen-Veronica Jarvis *S.d.* Mary Lou Storey *Mu.* Bruce Arntson and Kirby Shelstad *MPAA* PG *R.t.* 92 min. *Cast:* Jim Varney, Ron K. James, Linda Kash, Tom Butler, Duke Ernsberger, Jeffrey Pillars.

Ernest P. Worrell (Jim Varney) stars as a college janitor who, upon discovering the British crown jewels in a Revolutionary War cannon, is pursued by several oddball characters.

ESPECIALLY ON SUNDAY (Italy, 1993)

Pro. Amedeo Pagani, Giovanna Romagnoli, and Mario Orfini for Basic Cinemagrafica, Titanus Distribuzione, Paradis Film, Intermedias, Dusk, and Eurimages; Miramax Films *Dir.* Giuseppe Tornatore, Giuseppe Bertolucci, and Marco Tullio Giordana *Scr.* Tonino Guerra *Cine.* Tonino Delli Colli, Fabio Cianchetti, and Franco Lecca *A.d.* Francesco Bronzi, Nello Giorgetti, and Gianni Silvestri *Mu.* Ennio Morricone *MPAA* R *R.t.* 86 min. *Cast:* Philippe Noiret, Ornella Muti, Bruno Ganz, Andrea Prodan, Maria Maddalena Fellini, Chiara Caselli, Bruno Berdoni, Jean-Hugues Anglade, Nicoletta Braschi, Ivano Marescotti.

Especially on Sunday comprises three stories by acclaimed screenwriter Tonino Guerra, each by a different director. *The Blue Dog* centers on a shoemaker who is hounded by a dog with a blue spot on its forehead; the title story revolves around a menage a trois; and *Snow on Fire* depicts the voyeurism of an elderly woman who spies on her son and daughter-in-law making love.

FAMILY PRAYERS

Pro. Mark Levinson and Bonnie Sugar; Arrow Entertainment *Dir.* Scott Rosenfelt *Scr.* Steven Ginsberg *Cine.* Jeff Jur *Ed.* Susan R. Crutcher *P.d.* Chester Kaczenski *A.d.* Marc Dabe *S.d.* Judi Sandin *Mu.* Steve Tyrell *MPAA* PG *R.t.* 105 min. *Cast:* Joe Mantegna, Anne Archer, Tzvi Ratner-Stauber, Patti LuPone, Allen Garfield, Paul Reiser, Conchata Ferrell, Shiri Appleby, Julianne Michelle.

A young Jewish boy (Tzvi Ratner-Stauber) tries unsuccessfully to help his gambling-addicted father (Joe Mantegna) and his parents' troubled marriage as he studies for his bar mitzvah.

A FAR OFF PLACE

Pro. Eva Monley and Elaine Sperber for Walt Disney Pictures and Amblin Entertainment, in association with Touchwood Pacific Partners I; Buena Vista Pictures *Dir.* Mikael Saloman *Scr.* Robert Caswell, Jonathan Hensleigh, and Sally Robinson; based on the books *A Story Like the Wind* and *A Far Off Place*, by Laurens van der Post *Cine.* Juan Ruiz-Anchia *Ed.* Ray Lovejoy *P.d.* Gemma Jackson *A.d.* Carine Tredgold and Jonathan McKinstry *S.d.* Ian White *Mu.* James Horner *MPAA* PG *R.t.* 105 min. *Cast:* Reese Witherspoon, Ethan Randall, Jack Thompson, Sarel Bok, Maximilian Schell, Robert Burke, Patricia Kalember, Daniel Gerroll.

Set in Africa, this family adventure centers on two young teenage friends—unpretentious Nonnie (Reese Witherspoon) and snotty Harry (Ethan Randall)—who set out across the Kalahari Desert accompanied only by a native Bushman (Sarel Bok) in order to escape the elephant poachers who murdered their parents.

FATAL INSTINCT

Pro. Katie Jacobs and Pierce Gardner; Metro-Goldwyn-Mayer *Dir.* Carl Reiner *Scr.* David O'Malley *Cine.* Gabriel Beristain *Ed.* Bud Molin and Stephen Myers *P.d.* Sandy Veneziano *A.d.* Daniel Maltese *S.d.* Chris A. Butler *Mu.* Richard Gibbs *MPAA* PG-13 *R.t.* 89 min. *Cast:* Armand Assante, Sherilyn Fenn, Kate Nelligan, Sean Young, Christopher McDonald,

James Remar, Tony Randall, Clarence Clemons, Michael Cumpsty, Carl Reiner, Eartha Kitt, Bob Uecker, Doc Severinsen.

Carl Reiner spoofs classic films noirs and contemporary erotic thrillers in this genre parody. Though clearly patterned after *The Naked Gun* and *Hot Shots!* series, the film extends Reiner's previous efforts at spoofing Hollywood genres, as in *The Man with Two Brains* (1983) and *Dead Men Don't Wear Plaid* (1982). The big-name cast includes Armand Assante as thick-headed detective-lawyer Ned Ravine, Sean Young as the dangerous femme fatale, Kate Nelligan as Ned's beautiful but adulterous wife, and Sherilyn Fenn as his devoted secretary.

FATHER HOOD

Pro. Nicholas Pileggi, Anant Singh, and Gillian Gorfil for Hollywood Pictures; Buena Vista *Dir.* Darrell James Roodt *Scr.* Scott Spencer *Cine.* Mark Vicente *Ed.* David Heitner *P.d.* David Barkham *A.d.* Dins Danielsen *S.d.* Suzette Sheets *Mu.* Patrick O'Hearn *MPAA* PG-13 *R.t.* 94 min. *Cast:* Patrick Swayze, Halle Berry, Sabrina Lloyd, Brian Bonsall, Michael Ironside, Diane Ladd, Bob Gunton.

A small-time crook, Jack Charles (Patrick Swayze), finds himself saddled with his two children (Sabrina Lloyd and Brian Bonsall), who have been living in foster-care homes, on a cross-country trek to his latest heist.

FIFTY-FIFTY

Pro. Maurice Singer and Raymond Wagner; Cannon Pictures *Dir.* Charles Martin Smith *Scr.* Dennis Shryack and Michael Butler *Cine.* David Connell *Ed.* James Mitchell and Christian A. Wagner *P.d.* Errol Kelly *A.d.* Sunil Wijeratne *S.d.* Lal Harindranath *Mu.* Peter Bernstein *MPAA* R *R.t.* 100 min. *Cast:* Peter Weller, Robert Hays, Charles Martin Smith, Ramona Rahman, Kay Tong Lim, Dom Magwili, Azmil Mustapha, Ursala Martin.

In this mediocre action-buddy film, two American mercenaries (Peter Weller and Robert Hays) are hired by a CIA operative (Charles Martin Smith) to overthrow a despotic island dictatorship in Malaysia—only to find themselves ultimately caught up with the freedom fighters' cause.

FIRE IN THE SKY

Pro. Joe Wizan and Todd Black; Paramount Pictures *Dir.* Robert Lieberman *Scr.* Tracy Tormé; based on the book *The Walton Experience*, by Travis Walton *Cine.* Bill Pope *Ed.* Steve Mirkovich *P.d.* Laurence Bennett *A.d.* Mark W. Mansbridge *S.d.* Daniel L. May *Mu.* Mark Isham *MPAA* PG-13 *R.t.* 107 min. *Cast:* D. B. Sweeney, Robert Patrick, Craig Sheffer, Peter Berg, James Garner, Henry Thomas, Bradley Gregg, Noble Willingham, Kathleen Wilhoite, Georgia Emelin, Scott MacDonald, Wayne Grace.

Based on a real-life story, this drama depicts the alleged alien abduction of an Arizona logger, Travis Walton (D. B. Sweeney), who later wrote a book about it.

FLESH AND BONE

Pro. Mark Rosenberg and Paula Weinstein for Mirage/Spring Creek; Paramount Pictures *Dir.* Steve Kloves *Scr.* Steve Kloves *Cine.* Philippe Rousselot *Ed.* Mia Goldman *P.d.* Jon Hutman *A.d.* Charles Breen *S.d.* Samara Schaffer *Mu.* Thomas Newman *MPAA* R *R.t.* 127 min. *Cast:* Dennis Quaid, Meg Ryan, James Caan, Gwyneth Paltrow, Scott Wilson, Christopher Rydell, Ron Kuhlman.

Dennis Quaid stars as Texas loner Arlis Sweeney, whose past catches up with him when he becomes involved with Kay Davies (Meg Ryan), a pretty young woman fleeing a bad marriage. Years ago her family was murdered by Arlis' sinister father, Roy (James Caan), who now returns to tie up loose ends.

FLIGHT OF THE INNOCENT (Italy and France, 1993)
Pro. Franco Cristaldi and Domenico Procacci, in association with Rocket Pictures; Metro-Goldwyn-Mayer *Dir.* Carlo Carlei *Scr.* Carlo Carlei and Gualtiero Rosella; based on a story by Carlei *Cine.* Raffaele Mertes *Ed.* Carlo Fontana and Claudio Di Mauro *P.d.* Franco Ceraolo *Mu.* Carlo Siliotto *MPAA* R *R.t.* 105 min. *Cast:* Manuel Colao, Francesca Neri, Jacques Perrin, Federico Pacifici, Sal Borgese, Lucio Zagria, Giusi Cataldo.

A ten-year-old boy, Vito (Manuel Colao), flees for his life when his entire family is gunned down in cold blood. Set in Italy, this thriller follows Vito's flight from a sadistic killer, Scarface (Federico Pacifici), and his attempt to reach an adult cousin in Rome.

FOR A LOST SOLDIER (The Netherlands, 1993)
Pro. Matthijs van Heijningen for Sigma Film and AVRO-TV Holland; Strand *Dir.* Roeland Kerbosch *Scr.* Roeland Kerbosch; based on the novel by Rudi van Dantzig, adapted by Don Bloch *Cine.* Nils Post *Ed.* August Verschueren *A.d.* Vincent de Pater *Mu.* Joop Stokkermans *R.t.* 92 min. *Cast:* Maarten Smit, Andrew Kelley, Jeroen Krabbe, Feark Smink, Elsje de Wijn.

Based on the autobiographical novel by choreographer Rudi van Dantzig, this drama centers on twelve-year-old Jeroen (Maarten Smit), who, during World War II, is sent by his parents from Amsterdam to the countryside, where he enters into a homosexual relationship with a Canadian soldier, Walt (Andrew Kelley).

FOR LOVE OR MONEY
Pro. Brian Grazer for Imagine Films Entertainment; Universal Pictures *Dir.* Barry Sonnenfeld *Scr.* Mark Rosenthal and Lawrence Konner *Cine.* Oliver Wood *Ed.* Jim Miller *P.d.* Peter Larkin *A.d.* Charley Beal *S.d.* Leslie E. Rollins *Mu.* Bruce Broughton *MPAA* PG *R.t.* 94 min. *Cast:* Michael J. Fox, Gabrielle Anwar, Anthony Higgins, Michael Tucker, Bob Balaban, Udo Kier, Dan Hedaya, Fyvush Finkel, Paula Laurence, Isaac Mizrahi, Patrick Breen, Bobby Short.

Michael J. Fox stars as an ambitious but good-hearted hotel concierge in Manhattan who dreams of opening his own place. Unfortunately, when he meets a wealthy entrepreneur (Anthony Higgins) who can make his dreams come true, he falls in love with the entrepreneur's girlfriend (Gabrielle Anwar).

FORTRESS
Pro. John Davis and John Flock for Davis Entertainment Company and Village Roadshow Pictures; Dimension *Dir.* Stuart Gordon *Scr.* Steven Feinberg, Troy Neighbors, David Venable, and Terry Curtis Fox *Cine.* David Eggby *Ed.* Timothy Wellburn *P.d.* David Copping *Mu.* Frederic Talgorn *MPAA* R *R.t.* 91 min. *Cast:* Christopher Lambert, Kurtwood Smith, Loryn Locklin, Lincoln Kilpatrick.

In this grimly violent futuristic tale, John Brennick (Christopher Lambert) and his wife Karen (Loryn Locklin) are imprisoned in the Fortress for the crime of conceiving a second child when only one is allowed. Run by the sadistic Poe (Kurtwood Smith) and an evil computer, the Fortress is a seemingly impregnable chamber of horrors from which the couple attempts to escape.

FREAKED
Pro. Harry J. Ufland and Mary Jane Ufland for Tommy; Twentieth Century-Fox *Dir.* Tom Stern and Alex Winter *Scr.* Tim Burns, Tom Stern, and Alex Winter *Cine.* Jamie Thompson *Ed.* Malcolm Campbell *P.d.* Catherine Hardwicke *A.d.* Kim Hix *Mu.* Kevin Kiner *MPAA* PG-13 *R.t.* 79 min. *Cast:* Alex Winter, Megan Ward, Michael Stoyanov, Randy Quaid, William Sadler, Mr. T, Brooke Shields, Alex Zuckerman, Derek McGrath.

An egocentric young man, Ricky (Alex Winter), travels to South America as an unsuspecting spokesperson for an evil corporation and, along with two friends (Megan Ward and Michael Stoyanov), is turned into a circus sideshow freak by the maniacal Elijah C. Skuggs (Randy Quaid).

GEORGE BALANCHINE'S THE NUTCRACKER (also known as *The Nutcracker*)
Pro. Robert A. Krasnow and Robert Hurwitz for Elektra Entertainment/Regency Enterprises; Warner Bros. *Dir.* Emile Ardolino *Scr.* Adapted from the New York City Ballet production by Peter Martins, with narration written by Susan Cooper; based on the story by E. T. A. Hoffmann *Cine.* Ralf Bode *Ed.* Girish Bhargava *P.d.* Rouben Ter-Arutunian *Mu.* Peter Ilyitch Tchaikovsky *MPAA* G *R.t.* 92 min. *Cast:* Macaulay Culkin, Jessica Lynn Cohen, Darci Kistler, Damian Woetzel, Kyra Nichols, Bart Robinson Cook, Wendy Whelan, Margaret Tracey, Gen Horiuchi, Tom Gold, Lourdes Lopez, Nilas Martins, William Otto, Kevin Kline.

Macaulay Culkin plays the Nutcracker Prince in George Balanchine's New York City Ballet production of this holiday classic.

GERMINAL (France, 1993)
Pro. Claude Berri for Renn Productions; Sony Pictures Classics *Dir.* Claude Berri *Scr.* Arlette Langmann and Claude Berri; based on the novel by Emile Zola *Cine.* Yves Angelo *Ed.* Herve De Luze *P.d.* Thanh At Hoang and Christian Marti *Mu.* Jean-Louis Roques *R.t.* 158 min. *Cast:* Renaud, Gerard Depardieu, Miou-Miou, Jean Carmet, Judith Henry, Jean-Roger Milo, Laurent Terzieff.

This epic drama—the most expensive French film ever made at the time of its release—is based on Emile Zola's novel of the same name. Set in the nineteenth century, this ambitious film centers on a tragic strike instigated by an outsider, Etienne Lantier (Renaud), in a poverty-stricken French mining community, and on the family that befriended him, headed by Maheu (Gerard Depardieu).

GOD IS MY WITNESS (*Khuda Gawah*. India, 1993)
Pro. Manoj Desai and Nazir Ahmed for Dale Gasteiger and Gregory Hatanaka, in association with Lal Dadlaney and Glamour Films; Headliner Productions, Inc. *Dir.* Mukul S. Anand *Scr.* Santosh Saroj *Cine.* W. B. Rao *Ed.* R. Rajendran *A.d.* Suresh Sawant *Mu.* Laxmikant Pyarelal *R.t.* 180 min. *Cast:* Amitabh Bachchan, Sridevi, Nagarjuna, Shilpa Shirodkar, Kiran Kumar.

In this romantic epic set in Afghanistan, young Badshah Khan (Amitabh Bachchan) falls in love with beautiful Benazir (Sridevi), his opponent in a contest between two opposing clans. In order to marry her, however, he must travel to India and seek revenge against the man who murdered her father.

THE GOOD SON
Pro. Mary Anne Page and Joseph Ruben; Twentieth Century-Fox *Dir.* Joseph Ruben *Scr.* Ian McEwan *Cine.* John Lindley *Ed.* George Bowers *P.d.* Bill Groom *A.d.* Rusty Smith *S.d.* George DeTitta, Jr. *Mu.* Elmer Bernstein *MPAA* R *R.t.* 87 min. *Cast:* Macaulay Culkin, Elijah Wood, Wendy Crewson, David Morse, Daniel Hugh Kelly, Jacqueline Brookes, Quinn Culkin, Ashley Crow, Guy Strauss, Keith Brava, Jerem Goodwin, Andria Hall, Bobby Huber, Mark Stefanich.

When twelve-year-old Mark (Elijah Wood) is sent to stay with the family of his cousin Henry (Macaulay Culkin) after his mother's death, he soon discovers that Henry's charming exterior hides a malicious and evil heart. Unfortunately for Mark, no one will believe him.

THE GREAT PUMPKIN (*Il Grande Cocomero*. Italy, 1993)
Pro. Leo Pescarolo and Fulvio Lucisano for Ellepi Film, Italian International Film, and Chrysalide Films, with the participation of Moonlight Films; RAI Corp. *Dir.* Francesca Ar-

chibugi *Scr.* Francesca Archibugi *Cine.* Paolo Camera *Ed.* Roberto Missiroli *P.d.* Livia Borgognoni *Mu.* Battista Lena and Roberto Gatto *R.t.* 103 min. *Cast:* Sergio Castellitto, Alessia Fugardi, Anna Galiena, Laura Betti.

A dedicated physician (Sergio Castellitto) forms a strong father-daughter bond with a twelve-year-old patient (Alessia Fugardi) who suffers mysterious seizures.

GUILTY AS SIN

Pro. Martin Ransohoff for Hollywood Pictures; Buena Vista Pictures *Dir.* Sidney Lumet *Scr.* Larry Cohen *Cine.* Andrzej Bartkowiak *Ed.* Evan Lottman *P.d.* Philip Rosenberg *S.d.* Enrico Campana *Mu.* Howard Shore *MPAA* R *R.t.* 107 min. *Cast:* Rebecca De Mornay, Don Johnson, Stephen Lang, Jack Warden, Dana Ivey, Ron White, Norma Dell'Agnese, Sean McCann, Luis Guzman, Robert Kennedy, James Blendick, Tom Butler, Christina Baren, Lynne Cormack, Barbara Eve Harris, Simon Sinn, John Kapelos.

Successful attorney Jennifer Haines (Rebecca De Mornay) takes on the challenge of defending handsome and charming David Greenhill (Don Johnson), who has been accused of murdering his wife. Jennifer soon finds herself in danger, when she becomes convinced that Greenhill is indeed guilty and that she may be his next victim.

GUNCRAZY

Pro. Zane W. Levitt and Diane Firestone for Zeta Entertainment, in association with First Look Pictures; Man Ray Associates *Dir.* Tamra Davis *Scr.* Matthew Bright *Cine.* Lisa Rinzler *Ed.* Kevin Tent *P.d.* Abbie Lee Warren *A.d.* Kevin Constant *S.d.* Rafael S. Tapia *Mu.* Ed Tomney *MPAA* R *R.t.* 97 min. *Cast:* Drew Barrymore, James LeGros, Joe Dallesandro, Ione Skye, Billy Drago, Michael Ironside, Rodney Harvey.

Drew Barrymore and James LeGros star in this tragic story of doomed love. Anita (Barrymore) finds a pen pal, learns to shoot a gun, then quickly finds herself on a collision course with destiny.

HAPPILY EVER AFTER

Pro. Lou Scheimer for Filmation; First National Film *Dir.* John Howley *Scr.* Martha Moran and Robby London *Cine.* Fred Ziegler *Ed.* Jeffrey C. Patch and Joe Gall *A.d.* John Grusd *Mu.* Frank W. Becker *MPAA* G *R.t.* 74 min. *Voices:* Edward Asner, Irene Cara, Carol Channing, Dom DeLuise, Phyllis Diller, Zsa Zsa Gabor, Sally Kellerman, Malcolm McDowell, Tracey Ullman.

In this follow-up to the 1937 Disney animated classic *Snow White and the Seven Dwarfs*, the heroine and her prince find themselves pursued by the Wicked Queen's evil and revengeful brother Lord Malis.

HARD TARGET

Pro. James Jacks and Sean Daniel for Alphaville/Renaissance; Universal Pictures *Dir.* John Woo *Scr.* Chuck Pfarrer *Cine.* Russell Carpenter *Ed.* Bob Murawski *P.d.* Phil Dagort *A.d.* Philip Messina *S.d.* Michele Poulik *Mu.* Graeme Revell *MPAA* R *R.t.* 92 min. *Cast:* Jean-Claude Van Damme, Lance Henriksen, Arnold Vosloo, Yancy Butler, Kasi Lemmons, Wilford Brimley, Bob Apisa, Chuck Pfarrer, Douglas Forsythe Rye, Michael D. Leinert, Willie Carpenter, Lenore Banks.

When Chance Boudreaux (Jean-Claude Van Damme) is hired by the beautiful Natasha Binder (Yancy Butler) to find her father, he uncovers a sinister game led by the evil Emil Fouchon (Lance Henriksen), whereby wealthy men pay to hunt and kill homeless war veterans.

HEAR NO EVIL

Pro. David Matalon; Twentieth Century-Fox *Dir.* Robert Greenwald *Scr.* R. M. Badat and

Kathleen Rowell; based on a story by Badat and Danny Rubin *Cine.* Steven Shaw *Ed.* Eva Gardos *P.d.* Bernt Capra *A.d.* John Myhre *S.d.* Susan Mina Eschelbach *Mu.* Graeme Revell *MPAA* R *R.t.* 97 min. *Cast:* Marlee Matlin, D. B. Sweeney, Martin Sheen, John C. McGinley, Christina Carlisi, Greg Elam, Charley Lang, Marge Redmond, Billie Worley.

In this suspenseful thriller, Marlee Matlin stars as Jillian Shananhan, a deaf woman who is stalked by a killer when, unbeknownst to her, a rare coin comes into her possession. Aided by her boyfriend, Ben (D. B. Sweeney), Jillian must determine whether police lieutenant Philip Brock (Martin Sheen) is behind the plot.

HEART AND SOULS

Pro. Nancy Roberts and Sean Daniel for Alphaville/Stampede Entertainment; Universal Pictures *Dir.* Ron Underwood *Scr.* Brent Maddock, S. S. Wilson, Gregory Hansen, and Erik Hansen *Cine.* Michael Watkins *Ed.* O. Nicholas Brown *P.d.* John Muto *A.d.* Dan Webster *S.d.* Anne Ahrens *Mu.* Marc Shaiman *MPAA* PG-13 *R.t.* 104 min. *Cast:* Robert Downey, Jr., Charles Grodin, Alfre Woodard, Kyra Sedgwick, Tom Sizemore, David Paymer, Elisabeth Shue, Eric Lloyd, Bill Calvert, Lisa Lucas, Richard Portnow.

In San Francisco in 1959, a bus swerves to miss an automobile, which is driven by a couple en route to the hospital for the birth of their first child. Although, the bus driver and four passengers are killed, they become angels, who, thirty-four years later, resolve their own past problems and reform the now-grown-up child (Robert Downey, Jr.).

HEXED

Pro. Marc S. Fischer and Louis G. Friedman for Price Entertainment/ Brillstein-Grey; Columbia Pictures *Dir.* Alan Spencer *Scr.* Alan Spencer *Cine.* James Chressanthis *Ed.* Debra McDermott *P.d.* Brenton Swift *A.d.* Albert Locatelli *S.d.* Mary Finn and Sara E. Andrews *Mu.* Lance Rubin *MPAA* R *R.t.* 90 min. *Cast:* Arye Gross, Claudia Christian, Adrienne Shelly, Ray Baker, R. Lee Ermey, Michael Knight, Robin Curtis, Brandis Kemp, Norman Fell, Pamela Roylance, Billy Jones.

In this comedy, a lowly hotel clerk, Matthew Welsh (Arye Gross), with delusions of grandeur, contrives a date with a beautiful model, Hexina (Claudia Christian), who is staying at the hotel. Unfortunately, she is a psychotic killer who mistakes Matthew for a man who has been blackmailing her, and Matthew becomes the unwitting accomplice in murder.

HOCUS POCUS

Pro. David Kirschner and Steven Haft for Walt Disney Pictures; Buena Vista Pictures *Dir.* Kenny Ortega *Scr.* Mick Garris and Neil Cuthbert; based on a story by David Kirschner and Garris *Cine.* Hiro Narita *Ed.* Peter E. Berger *P.d.* William Sandell *A.d.* Nancy Patton *S.d.* Rosemary Brandenburg *Mu.* John Debney *MPAA* PG *R.t.* 96 min. *Cast:* Bette Midler, Sarah Jessica Parker, Kathy Najimy, Omri Katz, Thora Birch, Vinessa Shaw, Amanda Shepherd, Larry Bagby III, Tobias Jelinek, Stephanie Faracy, Charlie Rocket, Doug Jones, Karyn Malchus, Sean Murray, Steve Voboril, Norbert Weisser.

When the three Sanderson sisters (Bette Midler, Sarah Jessica Parker, and Kathy Najimy), witches hanged in Salem, Massachusetts, in 1693, are inadvertently resurrected by young Max (Omri Katz), it falls to him, his sister (Thora Birch), and new girlfriend (Vinessa Shaw) to save the children of the town from the sisters' voracious appetite for youth.

HOLD ME, THRILL ME, KISS ME

Pro. Travis Swords; Mad Dog Pictures *Dir.* Joel Hershman *Scr.* Joel Hershman *Cine.* Kent Wakeford *Ed.* Kathryn Himoff *P.d.* Dominic Wymark *Mu.* Gerald Gouriet *R.t.* 92 min. *Cast:* Adrienne Shelly, Max Parrish, Andrea Naschak, Sean Young, Diane Ladd, Bela Lehoczky, Ania Suli, Timothy Leary.

A young man on the run, Cli (Max Parrish), hides at a trailer park, where he becomes involved with two sisters—sexy, kinky Sabra (Andrea Naschak) and nice, animal-loving Dannie (Adriene Shelly)—in this campy comedy.

THE ICE RUNNER

Pro. Jeffrey M. Sneller for Gold Leaf International, Johan Schotte, and Monarch; Borde Film Releasing *Dir.* Barry Samson *Scr.* Joyce Warren, Clifford Coleman, and Joshua Stallings *Cine.* Brian Capener *Ed.* Joshua Stallings *P.d.* Victor Zenkov and Eric Davies *A.d.* Alexei Speransky *S.d.* Svyatoslav Gavrilov *Mu.* Emilio Kauderer *MPAA* R *R.t.* 116 min. *Cast:* Edward Albert, Victor Wong, Olga Kabo, Eugene Lazarev, Alexander Kuznitsov, Basil Hoffman, Bill Bordy, Sergei Ruban.

Set in Russia in the 1980's, this political action/adventure centers on an American spy, Jeffrey West (Edward Albert), who is betrayed and packed off to a Siberian labor camp. When his train is wrecked en route, he assumes the identity of a deceased fellow prisoner and prepares himself physically for his planned escape across the ice.

INDIAN SUMMER

Pro. Jeffrey Silver and Robert Newmyer for Touchstone Pictures and Outlaw; Buena Vista Pictures *Dir.* Mike Binder *Scr.* Mike Binder *Cine.* Tom Sigel *Ed.* Adam Weiss *P.d.* Craig Stearns *A.d.* Rocco Matteo *S.d.* Diane Bald and Jane Manchee *Mu.* Miles Goodman *MPAA* PG-13 *R.t.* 97 min. *Cast:* Alan Arkin, Matt Craven, Diane Lane, Bill Paxton, Elizabeth Perkins, Kevin Pollak, Sam Raimi, Vincent Spano, Julie Warner, Kimberly Williams.

In this comedy/drama, a group of four men and three women, all childhood friends, reunite twenty years later at Camp Tamakwa, their childhood summer camp. During their reunion, they reveal their nostalgia for bygone days, unleash their frustrations, and share their hopes for a better future.

INSIDE MONKEY ZETTERLAND

Pro. Chuck Grieve and Tani Cohen for Coast Entertainment; IRS Releasing *Dir.* Jefery Levy *Scr.* Steven Antin *Cine.* Christopher Taylor *Ed.* Lauren Zuckerman *P.d.* Jane Stewart *S.d.* Wendy Weaver *Mu.* Rick Cox and Jeff Elmassian *MPAA* R *R.t.* 92 min. *Cast:* Steven Antin, Katherine Helmond, Patricia Arquette, Tate Donovan, Bo Hopkins, Sandra Bernhard, Martha Plimpton, Rupert Everett, Sofia Coppola, Ricki Lake, Debi Mazar, Lance Loud, Francis Bay, Luca Bercovici.

Monkey Zetterland (Steven Antin) is a young, aspiring writer who is constantly interrupted by his quirky family and friends, in this romantic comedy.

INTERVISTA (Italy, 1987)

Pro. Ibrahim Moussa and Michel Vieyte for Aljusha Productions, in association with RAI Channel 1 and Cinecitta; Castle Hill Productions *Dir.* Federico Fellini *Scr.* Federico Fellini *Cine.* Tonino Delli Colli *Ed.* Nino Baragli *P.d.* Danilo Donati *Mu.* Nicola Piovani and Nino Rota *R.t.* 108 min. *Cast:* Sergio Rubini, Maurizio Mein, Paola Liguori, Nadia Ottaviani, Lara Wendel, Antella Ponziani, Federico Fellini, Anita Ekberg, Marcello Mastroianni.

Celebrated filmmaker Federico Fellini creates a mock documentary of his career in this critically acclaimed drama. Fellini, playing himself, is directing a fictional film when a Japanese film crew arrives to produce a documentary about him.

IT'S ALL TRUE (USA and France, 1993)

Pro. Regine Konckier, Richard Wilson, Bill Krohn, Myron Meisel, and Jean-Luc Ormieres for Les Films Balenciaga, in association with the French Ministry of Education and Culture, the French National Center for Cinematography, Canal Plus, R. Films, and La Fondation GAN pour le Cinema; Paramount Pictures *Dir.* Richard Wilson, Myron Meisel, and Bill Krohn *Scr.*

Bill Krohn, Richard Wilson, and Myron Meisel; based on an unfinished film by Orson Welles *Cine.* Gary Graver *Ed.* Ed Marx *Mu.* Jorge Arriagada *MPAA* G *R.t.* 89 min. *Cast:* Miguel Ferrer.

This intriguing documentary centers on a never-completed multipart film of the same name by Orson Welles. Using remaining footage of the original three parts, archival footage of Welles, and interviews with numerous collaborators and cast members, this film documents the difficulties and obstacles that prevented the completion of this supposedly cursed production.

JACK AND HIS FRIENDS

Pro. Benjamin Gruberg and Karen Jaehne; Arrow Entertainment *Dir.* Bruce Ornstein *Scr.* Bruce Ornstein *Cine.* Dan Stoloff *Ed.* Barbara Tulliver *P.d.* Ellen Caldwell *A.d.* Roald Scott Lawson *S.d.* Christine McDowell *R.t.* 96 min. *Cast:* Allen Garfield, Sam Rockwell, Judy Reyes.

When a successful but ineffectual businessman, Jack (Allen Garfield), is kidnapped by a young couple, Rosie (Judy Reyes) and Louie (Sam Rockwell), who are evading the police, he is forced to take them to his summer place, where they can hide over the weekend.

JACK THE BEAR

Pro. Bruce Gilbert for American Filmworks and Lucky Dog; Twentieth Century-Fox *Dir.* Marshall Herskovitz *Scr.* Steven Zaillian; based on the novel by Dan McCall *Cine.* Fred Murphy *Ed.* Steven Rosenblum *P.d.* Lilly Kilvert *A.d.* John Warnke *S.d.* James Truesdale and Cricket Rowland *Mu.* James Horner *MPAA* PG-13 *R.t.* 98 min. *Cast:* Danny DeVito, Robert J. Steinmiller, Jr., Miko Hughes, Gary Sinise, Julia Louis-Dreyfus, Reese Witherspoon, Andrea Marcovicci, Stefan Gierasch, Erica Yohn, Art LaFleur, Bert Remsen.

Set in 1972, this drama centers on a widowed father, John Leary (Danny DeVito), who is trying to rear his two young sons, Jack (Robert J. Steinmiller, Jr.) and Dylan (Miko Hughes). Although well-intentioned, John neglects his sons, who also find themselves threatened by an odd neighbor, Norman Strick (Gary Sinise).

JACQUOT OF NANTES (France, 1992)

Pro. Agnes Varda and Perrine Bauduin for Cine-Tamaris, with the participation of Canal Plus, La Sept, La Sofiarp International, and Les Films du Volcan; Sony Pictures Classics *Dir.* Agnes Varda *Scr.* Agnes Varda; based on the memoirs of Jacques Demy *Cine.* Patrick Blossier, Agnes Godard, and Georges Strouve *Ed.* Marie-Jo Audiard *P.d.* Robert Nardone and Olivier Radot *Mu.* Joanna Bruzdowicz *MPAA* PG *R.t.* 118 min. *Cast:* Philippe Maron, Edouard Joubeaud, Laurent Monnier, Brigitte de Villepoix, Daniel Dublet, Guillaume Navaud, Fanny Lebreton, Marie-Anne Emeriau, Edwige Dalaunay, Jean-Francois Lapipe, Chantal Bezias, Jacques Bourget, Jacques Demy.

Combining dramatizations with actual footage of French director Jacques Demy, this biographical drama pays homage to the late filmmaker. Writer-director Agnes Varda, Demy's widow, assembled this life story, depicting Demy's childhood during World War II and its later influence in his films.

JAMON, JAMON (Spain, 1993)

Pro. Andres Vicente Gomez for Lolafilms and Ovideo TV; Academy Films *Dir.* Bigas Luna *Scr.* Cuca Canals and Bigas Luna *Cine.* Jose Luis Alcaine *Ed.* Teresa Font *P.d.* Chu Uroz *A.d.* Julio Esteban *S.d.* Pep Olive and Gloria M. Palanques *Mu.* Nicola Piovani *R.t.* 94 min. *Cast:* Penelope Cruz, Anna Galiena, Javier Bardem, Stefania Sandrelli, Jordi Molla.

This dark sex comedy centers on a pair of young lovers (Jordi Molla and Penelope Cruz) and the attempts of the man's mother (Stefania Sandrelli) to break them up.

JASON GOES TO HELL: THE FINAL FRIDAY

Pro. Sean S. Cunningham; New Line Cinema *Dir.* Adam Marcus *Scr.* Dean Lorey and Jay Huguely; based on a story by Adam Marcus and Huguely *Cine.* William Dill *Ed.* David Handman *P.d.* W. Brooke Wheeler *S.d.* Natali K. Pope *Mu.* Harry Manfredini *MPAA* R *R.t.* 88 min. *Cast:* John D. LeMay, Kari Keegan, Kane Hodder, Steven Williams, Steven Culp, Erin Gray, Rusty Schwimmer, Richard Gant, Leslie Jordan, Billy Green Bush.

Hockey-masked Jason (Kane Hodder) is back, and only a sadistic bounty hunter, Creighton Duke (Steven Williams), knows the way to rid the world of him forever.

JOSH AND S.A.M.

Pro. Martin Brest for Castle Rock Entertainment, in association with New Line Cinema and City Light Films; Columbia Pictures *Dir.* Billy Weber *Scr.* Frank Deese *Cine.* Don Burgess *Ed.* Chris Lebenzon *P.d.* Marcia Hinds-Johnson *A.d.* Bo Johnson *S.d.* Jan Bergstrom *Mu.* Thomas Newman *MPAA* PG-13 *R.t.* 97 min. *Cast:* Jacob Tierney, Noah Fleiss, Martha Plimpton, Stephen Tobolowsky, Joan Allen, Chris Penn, Maury Chaykin, Ronald Guttman, Udo Kier, Sean Baca, Jake Gyllenhaal, Anne Lange.

Twelve-year-old Josh (Jacob Tierney) and eight-year-old Sam (Noah Fleiss), two brothers living with their divorced mom (Joan Allen), hit the road in a stolen car in a flight of fantasy: Josh has convinced his younger brother that the letters of Sam's name stand for "Strategically Altered Mutant" and that their parents have sold him to the U.S. government as a boy war machine.

JUDGMENT NIGHT

Pro. Gene Levy for Largo Entertainment, in association with JVC Entertainment; Universal Pictures *Dir.* Stephen Hopkins *Scr.* Lewis Colick; based on a story by Colick and Jere Cunningham *Cine.* Peter Levy *Ed.* Timothy Wellburn *P.d.* Joseph Nemec III *A.d.* Dan Olexiewicz *S.d.* Duncan Kennedy, William J. Law III, and John Dwyer *Mu.* Alan Silvestri *MPAA* R *R.t.* 109 min. *Cast:* Emilio Estevez, Cuba Gooding, Jr., Denis Leary, Stephen Dorff, Jeremy Piven, Peter Greene, Erik Schrody, Michael Wiseman.

When four friends (Emilio Estevez, Cuba Gooding, Jr., Stephen Dorff, and Jeremy Piven) head to downtown Chicago for a boxing match, they take a wrong turn and end up in a bad urban neighborhood where they witness a murder and thus become targets themselves.

KALIFORNIA

Pro. Steve Golin, Aristides McGarry, and Sigurjon Sighvatsson for Polygram Filmed Entertainment, in association with Viacom Pictures and Propaganda Films; Gramercy Pictures *Dir.* Dominic Sena *Scr.* Tim Metcalfe; based on a story by Stephen Levy and Metcalfe *Cine.* Bojan Bazelli *Ed.* Martin Hunter *P.d.* Michael White *A.d.* Jeff Mann *S.d.* Kate Sullivan *Mu.* Carter Burwell *MPAA* R *R.t.* 117 min. *Cast:* Brad Pitt, Juliette Lewis, David Duchovny, Michelle Forbes, Sierra Pecheur, Gregory Mars Martin, Judson Vaughn, David Rose.

A writer, Brian Kessler (David Duchovny), and his photographer/girlfriend (Michelle Forbes) embark on a cross-country road trip with an odd couple—bad-tempered Early Grayce (Brad Pitt) and his simple-minded girlfriend Adele (Juliette Lewis)—to share expenses. Although Kessler sets out to tour murder sites for a new book he is writing, he ignores the danger lurking in the back seat.

IL LADRO DI BAMBINI (Italy, 1993)

Pro. Angelo Rizzoli for Erre Produzioni Alia Film, Raidue, Arena Films Paris, and Vega Film Zurich; Samuel Goldwyn Company *Dir.* Gianni Amelio *Scr.* Gianni Amelio, Sandro Petraglia, and Stefano Rulli *Cine.* Tonino Nardi and Renato Tafuri *Ed.* Simona Paggi *A.d.* Andrea Crisanti and Giuseppe M. Gaudino *Mu.* Franco Piersanti *R.t.* 108 min. *Cast:* Enrico

Lo Verso, Valentina Scalici, Giuseppe Ieracitano, Florence Darel, Marina Golovine, Fabio Allessandrini.

This award-winning Italian drama centers on a police officer, Antonio (Enrico Lo Verso), and the two abused children (Valentina Scalici and Giuseppe Ieracitano) who he is taking cross-country by train to a children's home. Hardened by bitter experience, the children are initially wary of their official escort. Before their journey is over, however, they grow to trust Antonio and learn that human caring does exist.

LAST CALL AT MAUD'S

Pro. Paris Poirier and Karen Kiss; Maud's Project *Dir.* Paris Poirier *Cine.* Cheryl Rosenthal and Gary Sanders *Ed.* Paris Poirier and Elaine Trotter *Mu.* Tim Horrigan *R.t.* 74 min. *Cast:* Rikki Streicher, Phyllis Lyon, Del Martin, Gwenn Craig, Jo Daly, Sally Gearhart, Judy Grahn, Joann Shirley.

This well-researched documentary uses photos, archival footage, and interviews in order to provide an entertaining retrospective of a now-defunct lesbian bar, Maud's. From its inception in 1966 in San Francisco to its closing in 1989, Maud's was a rare gathering place for homosexual women, at one time the hub of the West Coast lesbian scene.

THE LAST PARTY

Pro. Eric Cahan, Donovan Leitch, and Josh Richman for Campaign Films, Inc., Athena Film Group, Inc., and Live Entertainment; Triton Pictures *Dir.* Mark Benjamin and Marc Levin *Scr.* Robert Downey, Jr., Donovan Leitch, Marc Levin, and Josh Richman *Cine.* Mark Benjamin *Ed.* Wendey Stanzler *R.t.* 95 min. *Cast:* Robert Downey, Jr., Sean Penn, Bill Clinton, Patti Davis, Spike Lee, Jerry Brown, Oliver Stone, G. Gordon Liddy, Senator John Kerry, Robert Downey, Sr.

Actor Robert Downey, Jr., narrates this documentary that centers on the 1992 presidential campaign. Featuring multiple celebrities such as Oliver Stone, Sean Penn, and Patti Davis, it provides a provocative look at the 1990's political and social climate.

LEPRECHAUN

Pro. Jeffrey B. Mallian; Trimark Pictures *Dir.* Mark Jones *Scr.* Mark Jones *Cine.* Levie Isaacks *Ed.* Christopher Roth *P.d.* Naomi Slodki *Mu.* Kevin Kiner *MPAA* R *R.t.* 92 min. *Cast:* Warwick Davis, Jennifer Aniston, Ken Olandt, Mark Holton, Robert Gorman, John Sanderford, Shay Duffin, John Volstad, Pamela Mant, William Newman, David Permenter, Raymond Turner.

A nasty leprechaun (Warwick Davis) wreaks havoc in rural North Dakota trying to retrieve his pot of gold, stolen by a tourist, in this lame horror film.

LIFE WITH MIKEY

Pro. Teri Schwartz and Scott Rudin for Touchstone Pictures; Buena Vista Pictures *Dir.* James Lapine *Scr.* Marc Lawrence *Cine.* Rob Hahn *Ed.* Robert Leighton *P.d.* Adrianne Lobel *A.d.* Dennis Davenport *S.d.* Gordon Sim *Mu.* Alan Menken *MPAA* PG *R.t.* 90 min. *Cast:* Michael J. Fox, Christina Vidal, Nathan Lane, Cyndi Lauper, David Krumholtz, David Huddleston.

Once a successful television personality, former star Michael Chapman (Michael J. Fox) now works in a third-rate children's talent agency with his brother, Ed (Nathan Lane). When a street urchin, Angie Vega (Christina Vidal), pickpockets Michael's wallet and talks her way out of trouble, Michael becomes convinced that this is another child prodigy.

THE LONG DAY CLOSES (Great Britain, 1993)

Pro. Olivia Stewart for British Film Institute and Film Four International; Sony Pictures Classics *Dir.* Terence Davies *Scr.* Terence Davies *Cine.* Michael Coulter *Ed.* William Diver *P.d.*

Christopher Hobbs *A.d.* Kave Naylor *MPAA* PG *R.t.* 82 min. *Cast:* Leigh McCormack, Marjorie Yates, Anthony Watson, Nicholas Lamont, Ayse Owens, Robin Polley.

Set in 1950's Liverpool, this drama centers on an eleven-year-old boy, Bud (Leigh McCormack), who escapes the harsh and violent reality of post-World War II England and a strict parochial school by going to the cinema.

LOOK WHO'S TALKING NOW

Pro. Jonathan D. Krane; TriStar Pictures *Dir.* Tom Ropelewski *Scr.* Tom Ropelewski and Leslie Dixon *Cine.* Oliver Stapleton *Ed.* Michael A. Stevenson and Harry Hitner *P.d.* Michael Bolton *A.d.* Alexander Cochrane *S.d.* Jim Erickson *Mu.* William Ross *MPAA* PG-13 *R.t.* 97 min. *Cast:* John Travolta, Kirstie Alley, Olympia Dukakis, Lysette Anthony, David Gallagher, Tabitha Lupien, Danny DeVito (voice), Diane Keaton (voice).

John Travolta and Kirstie Alley return in this sequel as James and Mollie, parents of two adorable children, Mikey (David Gallagher) and Julie (Tabitha Lupien). Right before Christmas, the family suddenly takes on two dogs—mutt Rocks (voice of Danny DeVito) and spoiled poodle Daphne (voice of Diane Keaton)—that bicker incessantly.

M. BUTTERFLY

Pro. Gabriella Martinelli for Geffen Pictures; Warner Bros. *Dir.* David Cronenberg *Scr.* David Henry Hwang; based on his play *Cine.* Peter Suschitzky *Ed.* Ronald Sanders *P.d.* Carol Spier *A.d.* James McAteer *S.d.* Elinor Rose Galbraith *Mu.* Howard Shore *MPAA* R *R.t.* 100 min. *Cast:* Jeremy Irons, John Lone, Barbara Sukowa, Ian Richardson, Annabel Leventon, Shizuko Hoshi, Richard McMillan, Vernon Dobtcheff, Margaret Ma.

Based on a true story, this bizarre tale centers on a French diplomat, René Gallimard (Jeremy Irons), who maintained an almost twenty-year-long affair with a Chinese man who he believed was a woman, an opera singer by the name of Song Liling (John Lone).

MALICE

Pro. Rachel Pfeffer, Charles Mulvehill, and Harold Becker for Castle Rock Entertainment, in association with New Line Cinema; Columbia Pictures *Dir.* Harold Becker *Scr.* Aaron Sorkin and Scott Frank; based on a story by Sorkin and Jonas McCord *Cine.* Gordon Willis *Ed.* David Bretherton *P.d.* Philip Harrison *A.d.* Dianne Wager *S.d.* Sydney Litwack, Alan Manzer, Hugo Santiago, Harold Fuhrman, Garrett Lewis, and Tracey Doyle *Mu.* Jerry Goldsmith *MPAA* R *R.t.* 107 min. *Cast:* Alec Baldwin, Nicole Kidman, Bill Pullman, Bebe Neuwirth, George C. Scott, Anne Bancroft, Peter Gallagher, Josef Sommer.

A series of violent rapes coincides with the arrival of a talented but sinister surgeon, Jed (Alec Baldwin), to a New England college town. Jed moves in with an old schoolmate, Andy (Bill Pullman), dean of the college where the rapes are occurring, and Andy's wife, Tracy (Nicole Kidman). When Tracy falls ill, Jed performs emergency surgery, but complications during the operation change forever the characters' futures.

MAN BITES DOG (Belgium, 1993)

Pro. Remy Belvaux, Andre Bonzel, and Benoit Poelvoorde for Les Artistes Anonymes; Roxie Releasing *Dir.* Remy Belvaux *Scr.* Andre Bonzel, Benoit Poelvoorde, Remy Belvaux, and Vincent Tavier *Cine.* Andre Bonzel *Ed.* Remy Belvaux and Eric Dardill *Mu.* Jean-Marc Chenut and Laurence Dufrene *MPAA* NC-17 *R.t.* 92 min. *Cast:* Benoit Poelvoorde, Remy Belvaux, Andre Bonzel.

Created on a shoestring budget, this critically acclaimed drama stars the actual film director, Remy Belvaux, and cinematographer, Andre Bonzel, as fictional documentary filmmakers who track the activities of a ruthless murderer (Benoit Poelvoorde). All three men also served as the film's producers and screenwriters.

MAN'S BEST FRIEND
Pro. Bob Engelman for Roven-Cavallo Entertainment; New Line Cinema *Dir.* John Lafia
Scr. John Lafia *Cine.* Mark Irwin *Ed.* Michael N. Knue *P.d.* Jaymes Hinkle *A.d.* Erik Olson
S.d. Sharon E. Alshams and Ellen Totlebren *Mu.* Joel Goldsmith *MPAA* R *R.t.* 87 min. *Cast:*
Ally Sheedy, Lance Henriksen, Robert Constanzo, Fredric Lehne, John Cassini, J. D. Daniels,
William Sanderson, Trula M. Marcus.

A television journalist (Ally Sheedy) frees a dog from an animal experimentation labora-
tory only to discover what a horror she has unleashed.

MAP OF THE HUMAN HEART (Great Britain, Australia, France, and Canada, 1993)
Pro. Tim Bevan for Polygram, Working Title Productions, Vincent Ward Productions, Les
Films Ariane, and Sunrise Films, in association with Australian Film Finance Corporation,
Nippon Herald, Channel 4, and Telefilm Canada; Miramax Films *Dir.* Vincent Ward *Scr.*
Louis Nowra; based on a story by Vincent Ward *Cine.* Eduardo Serra *Ed.* John Scott *P.d.*
John Beard *S.d.* Michelle Forst and Diane Gauthier *Mu.* Gabriel Yared *MPAA* R *R.t.* 126
min. *Cast:* Jason Scott Lee, Robert Joamie, Anne Parillaud, Annie Galipeau, Patrick Bergin,
John Cusack, Jeanne Moreau, Ben Mendelson, Clotilde Courau, Jerry Snell, Jayko Pitseolak.

As a youth, Avik (Jason Scott Lee), a young Eskimo, falls in love with Albertine (Anne
Parillaud), a mixed-race woman he meets at a Montreal hospital. When the two meet again
years later during World War II, Albertine has metamorphosed into an elegant woman, and the
two resume their romance amid bombing raids and aerial photography.

MARRIED TO IT
Pro. Thomas Baer; Orion Pictures *Dir.* Arthur Hiller *Scr.* Janet Kovalcik *Cine.* Victor J.
Kemper *Ed.* Robert C. Jones *P.d.* Robert Gundlach *A.d.* Jeffrey Ginn and Ann Cudworth
S.d. Gordon Sim and George DeTitta, Jr. *Mu.* Henry Mancini *MPAA* R *R.t.* 110 min. *Cast:*
Beau Bridges, Stockard Channing, Robert Sean Leonard, Mary Stuart Masterson, Cybill
Shepherd, Ron Silver, Donna Vivino.

Three very different couples (Beau Bridges and Stockard Channing, Robert Sean Leonard
and Mary Stuart Masterson, and Ron Silver and Cybill Shepherd) become fast friends while
they work together planning a children's school pageant with a 1960's theme.

MASALA (Canada, 1993)
Pro. Srinivas Krishna and Camelia Frieberg for Divani Films; Strand *Dir.* Srinivas Krishna
Scr. Srinivas Krishna *Cine.* Paul Sarossy *Ed.* Michael Munn *P.d.* Tamara Deverell *A.d.*
Valerie Kaelin *S.d.* Alexa Anthony *Mu.* Leslie Winston *R.t.* 105 min. *Cast:* Saeed Jaffrey,
Zohra Segal, Srinivas Krishna, Sakina Jaffrey, Herjit Singh Johal, Madhuri Bhatia, Ishwarlal
Mooljee, Ronica Sajnani, Les Porter, Raju Ahsan, Jennifer Armstrong, Wayne Bowman, Tova
Gallimore.

Set in Toronto's Indian subculture, this multicultural comedy deals with Indian immigrants' attempts to adapt to life in Canada and centers on Krishna (Srinivas Krishna), a
handsome rebel whose parents and brother died in an airliner explosion five years before.
Krishna feels guilty for having refused to return to India with his family and turns into a drug
addict.

ME AND THE KID
Pro. Lynn Loring and Dan Curtis; Orion Pictures *Dir.* Dan Curtis *Scr.* Richard Tannenbaum;
based on the novel *Taking Gary Feldman*, by Stanley Cohen *Cine.* Dietrich Lohmann *Ed.* Bill
Blunden *P.d.* Veronica Hadfield *A.d.* Roger King *S.d.* Penelope Rene Stames *Mu.* Bob
Cobert *MPAA* PG *R.t.* 94 min. *Cast:* Danny Aiello, Alex Zuckerman, Joe Pantoliano, Cathy
Moriarty, David Dukes, Anita Morris.

When two crooks, Harry (Danny Aiello) and Roy (Joe Pantoliano), break into an upscale New York suburban home to rob its safe, they end up kidnapping the poor little rich boy, Gary (Alex Zuckerman), who lives there. Neglected and lonely, Gary discovers the fun to be had while on the run with the basically good-hearted Harry.

THE METEOR MAN

Pro. Loretha C. Jones for Tinsel Townsend; Metro-Goldwyn-Mayer *Dir.* Robert Townsend *Scr.* Robert Townsend *Cine.* John A. Alonzo *Ed.* Adam Bernardi, Richard Candib, Andrew London, and Pam Wise *P.d.* Toby Corbett *A.d.* Greg Papalia *S.d.* William J. Newmon II, Stephanie J. Gordon, and Kathryn Peters *Mu.* Cliff Eidelman *MPAA* PG *R.t.* 99 min. *Cast:* Robert Townsend, Marla Gibbs, Eddie Griffin, Robert Guillaume, James Earl Jones, Roy Fegan, Cynthia Belgrave, Marilyn Coleman, Don Cheadle, Bobby McGee, Bill Cosby, Big Daddy Kane, Frank Gorshin, Sinbad, Nancy Wilson, Luther Vandross, Another Bad Creation, Tiny Lister, Jenifer Lewis, Stephanie Williams, Beverly Johnson, LaWanda Page, Wallace Shawn.

When an unassuming schoolteacher, Jefferson Reed (Robert Townsend), is struck by a meteor, he gains superhuman powers and becomes a reluctant hero out to do battle against big-city crime.

MR. JONES

Pro. Alan Greisman and Debra Greenfield for Rastar; TriStar Pictures *Dir.* Mike Figgis *Scr.* Eric Roth and Michael Cristofer; based on a story by Roth *Cine.* Juan Ruiz Anchia *Ed.* Tom Rolf *P.d.* Waldemar Kalinowski *A.d.* Larry Fulton *S.d.* Gae Buckley and Florence Fellman *Mu.* Maurice Jarre *MPAA* R *R.t.* 112 min. *Cast:* Richard Gere, Lena Olin, Anne Bancroft, Tom Irwin, Delroy Lindo, Bruce Altman, Lauren Tom, Lisa Malkiewicz, Thomas Kopache.

Richard Gere plays a manic-depressive and Lena Olin is the psychiatrist who loves him, in this drama.

MR. NANNY

Pro. Bob Engelman; New Line Cinema *Dir.* Michael Gottlieb *Scr.* Edward Rugoff and Michael Gottlieb *Cine.* Peter Stein *Ed.* Earl Ghaffari and Michael Ripps *P.d.* Don De Fina *A.d.* Jose Duarte *S.d.* Ed Castiniera and Barbara Peterson *Mu.* David Johansen and Brian Koonin *MPAA* PG *R.t.* 84 min. *Cast:* Terry (Hulk) Hogan, Sherman Hemsley, Austin Pendleton, Robert Gorman, Madeline Zima, Mother Love, David Johansen.

Professional wrestler Hulk Hogan stars as Sean Armstrong, a former wrestler who is persuaded by his old trainer (Sherman Hemsley) to take a job as bodyguard for a computer genius, Alex Mason (Austin Pendleton). Unfortunately, Armstrong finds he has been tricked into playing nanny to the man's two kids (Robert Gorman and Madeline Zima).

MR. WONDERFUL

Pro. Marianne Moloney for the Samuel Goldwyn Company; Warner Bros. *Dir.* Anthony Minghella *Scr.* Amy Schor and Vicki Polon *Cine.* Geoffrey Simpson *Ed.* John Tintori *P.d.* Doug Kraner *A.d.* Steve Saklad *S.d.* Alyssa Winter *Mu.* Michael Gore *MPAA* PG-13 *R.t.* 98 min. *Cast:* Matt Dillon, Annabella Sciorra, Mary-Louise Parker, William Hurt, Vincent D'Onofrio, David Barry Gray, Bruce Kirby, Dan Hedaya, Luis Guzman.

A divorced man, Gus (Matt Dillon), plays matchmaker for his former wife, Lee (Annabella Sciorra), in the hopes that she will remarry so that he can stop making alimony payments and be able to afford to buy a bowling alley with his buddies. In the process, however, he also discovers that he still loves her.

MONEY FOR NOTHING

Pro. Tom Musca for Hollywood Pictures; Buena Vista Pictures *Dir.* Ramon Menendez *Scr.*

Ramon Menendez, Tom Musca, and Carol Sobieski *Cine.* Tom Sigel *Ed.* Nancy Richardson *P.d.* Michelle Minch *A.d.* Beth Kuhn *S.d.* Susan Raney *Mu.* Craig Safan *MPAA* R *R.t.* 100 min. *Cast:* John Cusack, Debi Mazar, Michael Madsen, Benicio Del Toro, Michael Rapaport, Maury Chaykin, James Gandolfini, Fionnula Flanagan, Elizabeth Bracco, Ashleigh Dejon, Lenny Venito.

Based on a true story, this drama centers on a working-class man, Joey Coyle (John Cusack), who finds $1.2 million that has fallen off an armored truck and decides he wants to keep it. Michael Madsen plays the detective who is assigned to retrieve the money.

MORNING GLORY

Pro. Michael Viner for Dove Audio, Inc.; Academy Entertainment, Inc. *Dir.* Steven Hilliard Stern *Scr.* Charles Jarrott and Deborah Raffin; based on the novel by LaVyrle Spencer *Cine.* Laszlo George *Ed.* Richard Benwick *A.d.* David Hiscox *S.d.* Barry Kemp *Mu.* Jonathan Elias *MPAA* PG-13 *R.t.* 95 min. *Cast:* Christopher Reeve, Deborah Raffin, Lloyd Bochner, Nina Foch, Helen Shaver, J. T. Walsh.

Set in the Depression-era South and based on a best-selling novel, this drama stars Christopher Reeve as Will Parker, a former convict who answers an advertisement for a husband placed by a reclusive widow, Elly Dinsmore (Deborah Raffin), with two young children. Against all odds, the two slowly fall in love, only to have their relationship threatened when Parker is accused of murdering a local prostitute (Helen Shaver).

MOTORAMA

Pro. Donald P. Borchers for Proletariat Productions Corp. and Planet Productions Corp.; Two Moon Releasing *Dir.* Barry Shils *Scr.* Joseph Minion *Cine.* Joseph Yacoe *Ed.* Peter Verity *P.d.* Vincent Jefferds and Cathlyn Marshall *Mu.* Andy Summers *MPAA* R *R.t.* 90 min. *Cast:* Jordan Christopher Michael, John Diehl, Robin Duke, Meatloaf, Michael J. Pollard, Sandy Baron, Mary Woronov, Drew Barrymore, Dick Miller, Vince Edwards, Martha Quinn.

In this bleak statement about 1990's contemporary culture, a ten-year-old (Jordan Christopher Michael) from a dysfunctional home steals a car and sets out on an ultimately futile cross-country quest: He hopes to collect enough gas-station game cards to win a $500-million contest. Unfortunately, he falls prey to the greed and immorality of the adults he meets.

THE MUSIC OF CHANCE

Pro. Frederick Zollo and Dylan Sellers for American Playhouse Theatrical Films and Trans Atlantic Entertainment; I.R.S. Releasing *Dir.* Philip Haas *Scr.* Philip Haas and Belinda Haas; based on the novel by Paul Auster *Cine.* Bernard Zitzermann *Ed.* Belinda Haas *P.d.* Hugo Luczyc-Wyhowski *A.d.* Ruth Ammon *S.d.* Christina Belt *Mu.* Phillip Johnston *MPAA* R *R.t.* 98 min. *Cast:* James Spader, Mandy Patinkin, M. Emmet Walsh, Charles Durning, Joel Grey, Samantha Mathis, Christopher Penn, Pearl Jones, Jordan Spainhour, Paul Auster.

A down-and-out professional gambler, Jack Pozzi (James Spader), persuades an aimlessly wandering heir, James Nashe (Mandy Patinkin), to stake him in a poker game against two eccentric millionaires, Bill Flower (Charles Durning) and Willie Stone (Joel Grey). When Pozzi and Nashe lose, they are forced to work off their debt by building a stone wall on Flower and Stone's estate under the supervision of the menacing Calvin Murks (M. Emmet Walsh).

MY BOYFRIEND'S BACK

Pro. Sean S. Cunningham for Touchstone Pictures; Buena Vista *Dir.* Bob Balaban *Scr.* Dean Lorey *Cine.* Mac Ahlberg *Ed.* Michael Jablow *P.d.* Michael Hanan *A.d.* Charles Lagola *S.d.* John A. Frick, Jonathan Short, and Doug Mowat *Mu.* Harry Manfredini *MPAA* PG-13 *R.t.* 84 min. *Cast:* Andrew Lowery, Traci Lind, Danny Zorn, Edward Herrmann, Mary Beth Hurt, Austin Pendleton, Jay O. Sanders, Paul Dooley, Bob Dishy, Cloris Leachman, Paxton Whitehead, Matthew Fox, Libby Villari, Philip Hoffman.

A lovestruck teenager, Johnny Dingle (Andrew Lowery), plots a fake robbery in order to "rescue" the object of his affections, Missy (Traci Lind). Although the plot backfires and Johnny is killed, he returns as a people-eating zombie in order to keep his date for the prom.

MY LIFE

Pro. Jerry Zucker, Bruce Joel Rubin, and Hunt Lowry, in association with Capella Films; Columbia Pictures *Dir.* Bruce Joel Rubin *Scr.* Bruce Joel Rubin *Cine.* Peter James *Ed.* Richard Chew *P.d.* Neil Spisak *A.d.* Larry Fulton *S.d.* Anne D. McCulley *Mu.* John Barry *MPAA* PG-13 *R.t.* 112 min. *Cast:* Michael Keaton, Nicole Kidman, Bradley Whitford, Queen Latifah, Haing S. Ngor, Michael Constantine, Rebecca Schull, Toni Sawyer, Romy Rosemont, Lee Garlington, Mark Lowenthal.

Michael Keaton stars as an expectant father who, upon learning he has terminal cancer, decides to make a videotape about himself for his unborn child.

MY NEIGHBOR TOTORO (Japan, 1993)

Pro. Toru Hara for Tokuma Group; Troma Film Group *Dir.* Hayao Miyazaki *Scr.* Hayao Miyazaki *Ed.* Takeshi Seyama *P.d.* Yoshiharu Sato *A.d.* Kazuo Oga *Mu.* Jo Hisaishi *MPAA* G *R.t.* 87 min. *Voices:* Lisa Michaelson, Cheryl Chase, Greg Snegoff, Kenneth Hartman, Alexandrea Kenworthy, Natalie Core.

Two young sisters' affectionate bond is the subject of this captivating Japanese animated fantasy. The two cuddly girls, whose mother is recuperating from a mild illness, move with their professor father to rural Japan, where they meet the peaceful Totoro, a big-bellied and furry forest creature having magical powers, with whom they discover the joys of adventure.

NATIONAL LAMPOON'S LOADED WEAPON I

Pro. Suzanne Todd and David Willis for New Line, in association with 3 Arts Entertainment; New Line Cinema *Dir.* Gene Quintano *Scr.* Don Holley and Gene Quintano; based on a story by Holley and Tori Tellem *Cine.* Peter Deming *Ed.* Christopher Greenbury and Neil Kirk *P.d.* Jaymes Hinkle *Mu.* Robert Folk *MPAA* PG-13 *R.t.* 83 min. *Cast:* Emilio Estevez, Samuel L. Jackson, Jon Lovitz, Tim Curry, Kathy Ireland, Frank McRae, William Shatner, Whoopi Goldberg, F. Murray Abraham, Dr. Joyce Brothers, Bill Nunn, James Doohan, Charlie Sheen, Corey Feldman, J. T. Walsh, Erik Estrada, Larry Wilcox, Paul Gleason, Robert Shaye, Danielle Nicolet, Bruce Willis.

Emilio Estevez and Samuel L. Jackson attempt to parody the characters played by Mel Gibson and Danny Glover in their three *Lethal Weapon* films, in this send-up of the buddy-cop action genre. Although the film aims high, spoofing such hit films as *Basic Instinct* (1992) and *The Silence of the Lambs* (1991) and boasting star-studded cameo roles, *National Lampoon's Loaded Weapon I* tends to miss its mark.

NEEDFUL THINGS

Pro. Jack Cummins for Castle Rock Entertainment, in association with New Line Cinema; Columbia Pictures *Dir.* Fraser C. Heston *Scr.* W. D. Richter; based on the novel by Stephen King *Cine.* Tony Westman *Ed.* Rob Kobrin *P.d.* Douglas Higgins *S.d.* Dominique Fauquet-Lemaitre *Mu.* Patrick Doyle *MPAA* R *R.t.* 120 min. *Cast:* Max von Sydow, Ed Harris, Bonnie Bedelia, Amanda Plummer, J. T. Walsh, Ray McKinnon, Duncan Fraser, Valri Bromfield, Shane Meier.

Based on Stephen King's best-seller, this horror film revolves around the insidious machinations of a sinister antique-shop owner, Leland Gaunt (Max von Sydow), who is really the devil in disguise. Gaunt tempts the locals of a small town with his wares, turning the people against one another.

NEIL SIMON'S LOST IN YONKERS (also known as *Lost in Yonkers*)

Pro. Ray Stark for Rastar; Columbia Pictures *Dir.* Martha Coolidge *Scr.* Neil Simon; based on his play *Cine.* Johnny E. Jensen *Ed.* Steven Cohen *P.d.* David Chapman *A.d.* Mark Haack *S.d.* Thomas H. Paul, Mark Garner, and Marvin March *Mu.* Elmer Bernstein *MPAA* PG *R.t.* 110 min. *Cast:* Richard Dreyfuss, Mercedes Ruehl, Irene Worth, Brad Stoll, Mike Damus, David Strathairn, Robert Guy Miranda, Jack Laufer, Susan Merson.

Set in 1942, this Neil Simon semiautobiographical comedy-drama centers on two young boys (Brad Stoll and Mike Damus) who stay the summer with their dictatorial grandmother (Irene Worth) and become infatuated with charismatic gangster Uncle Louie (Richard Dreyfuss). The young boys' aunt Bella (Mercedes Ruehl) revolts against her mother's sterile authority and, through a tentative romance, learns to become satisfied with her life.

NEMESIS

Pro. Ash R. Shaw, Eric Karson, and Tom Karnowski; Imperial Entertainment *Dir.* Albert Pyun *Scr.* Rebecca Charles *Cine.* George Mooradian *Ed.* David Kern and Mark Conte *P.d.* Colleen Saro *A.d.* Phil Zarling *Mu.* Michel Rubini *MPAA* R *R.t.* 94 min. *Cast:* Olivier Gruner, Tim Thomerson, Merle Kennedy, Deborah Shelton, Marjorie Monaghan, Cary-Hiroyuki Tagawa, Brion James.

In A.D. 2027 Los Angeles, a fierce battle is raging between a band of cyborg terrorists and humans, led by the Los Angeles police. Veteran cop Alex (Olivier Gruner) is thrust into the center of the battle as he travels to exotic Shang-Loo, presumably to find a missing microchip. He is faced with his own mortality as he clashes with the evils of technology run rampant.

THE NIGHT WE NEVER MET

Pro. Michael Peyser; Miramax Films *Dir.* Warren Leight *Scr.* Warren Leight *Cine.* John A. Thomas *Ed.* Camilla Toniolo *P.d.* Lester Cohen *A.d.* Daniel Talpers *S.d.* Jessica Lanier *Mu.* Evan Lurie *MPAA* R *R.t.* 99 min. *Cast:* Matthew Broderick, Annabella Sciorra, Kevin Anderson, Jeanne Tripplehorn, Justine Bateman, Michael Mantell, Christine Baranski, Louise Lasser, Doris Roberts, Dominic Chianese, Garry Shandling, Ranjit Chowdhry, Tim Guinee, Bradley White, Greg Germann, Dana Wheeler-Nicholson, Bill Campbell, Katharine Houghton, Brooke Smith.

This romantic farce—despite its misleading title—describes the adventures of three New Yorkers who time-share an apartment in Greenwich Village on alternating days of the week. Since the three do not meet, written notes left in the apartment, fantasies, and switches in the time-sharing schedule lead to misperceptions about one another and to a delightul comedy of errors.

NOWHERE TO RUN

Pro. Craig Baumgarten and Gary Adelson; Columbia Pictures *Dir.* Robert Harmon *Scr.* Joe Eszterhas, Leslie Bohem, and Randy Feldman; based on a story by Eszterhas and Richard Marquand *Cine.* David Gribble *Ed.* Zach Staenberg and Mark Helfrich *P.d.* Dennis Washington *A.d.* Joseph P. Lucky *S.d.* Anne D. McCulley *Mu.* Mark Isham *MPAA* R *R.t.* 94 min. *Cast:* Jean-Claude Van Damme, Rosanna Arquette, Kieran Culkin, Ted Levine, Tiffany Taubman, Edward Blatchford, Anthony Starke, Joss Ackland, Allen Graf, Leonard Termo.

A fugitive (Jean-Claude Van Damme) turns into one family's knight in shining armor when he protects a widow (Rosanna Arquette) and her two young children (Kieran Culkin and Tiffany Taubman) from an evil land developer (Joss Ackland), in this weak action film.

ONCE UPON A FOREST

Pro. David Kirschner and Jerry Mills for Hanna-Barbera, in association with HTV Cymru/Wales Ltd.; Twentieth Century-Fox *Dir.* Charles Grosvenor *Scr.* Mark Young and

Kelly Ward; based on a story by Rae Lambert *Ed.* Pat A. Foley *P.d.* Carol Holman Grosvenor and Bill Proctor *A.d.* Carol Holman Grosvenor *Mu.* James Horner *MPAA* G *R.t.* 72 min. *Voices:* Michael Crawford, Ben Vereen, Ellen Blain, Ben Gregory, Paige Gosney, Elizabeth Moss.

Three furry friends—Abigail the mouse (voice of Ellen Blain), Edgar the mole (voice of Ben Gregory), and Russell the hedgehog (voice of Paige Gosney)—leave their forest home and embark on an odyssey to a distant meadow in search of rare herbs, when a chemical spill by humans leaves their friend Michelle the badger (voice of Elizabeth Moss) deathly ill. This animated adventure also features the voices of Michael Crawford as Michelle's uncle Cornelius and Ben Vereen as a gospel preacher.

112TH AND CENTRAL: THROUGH THE EYES OF THE CHILDREN
Pro. Jim Chambers, Vondie Curtis-Hall, and Hal Hisey; Flatfields, Inc. *Dir.* Jim Chambers *Cine.* John Simmons *Ed.* Michael Schultz *Mu.* Delfeayo Marsalis *R.t.* 108 min.

Intended as an educational film, this documentary presents children's and teenagers' views of the 1992 Los Angeles riots that followed the verdicts in the first Rodney King beating trial. The children, who are also the film's coproducers, genuinely speak about their rage, the gangs, and the Crips-Bloods truce.

ONLY THE STRONG
Pro. Samuel Hadida, Stuart S. Shapiro, and Steven G. Menkin, in association with Freestone Pictures and Davis Films; Twentieth Century-Fox *Dir.* Sheldon Lettich *Scr.* Sheldon Lettich and Luis Esteban *Cine.* Edward Pei *Ed.* Stephen Semel *P.d.* J. Mark Harrington *A.d.* Annabel Delgado *Mu.* Harvey W. Mason *MPAA* PG-13 *R.t.* 96 min. *Cast:* Mark Dacascos, Stacey Travis, Geoffrey Lewis, Paco Christian Prieto, Todd Susman, Richard Coca, Jeffrey Anderson Gunter, Roman Cardwell, Ryan Bollman.

Louis Stevens (Mark Dacascos), a U.S. Army Special Forces recruit trained in the Brazilian martial art called capoeira, takes on the gangs in his old Miami neighborhood by working with school administrators to train the twelve toughest students in this method of self-defense.

THE OPPOSITE SEX
Pro. Stanley M. Brooks and Robert Newmyer for Outlaw and Once Upon a Time; Miramax Films *Dir.* Matthew Meshekoff *Scr.* Noah Stern *Cine.* Jacek Laskus *Ed.* Adam Weiss *P.d.* Alex Tavoularis *Mu.* Ira Newborn *MPAA* R *R.t.* 86 min. *Cast:* Arye Gross, Courteney Cox, Kevin Pollak, Julie Brown, Mitch Ryan, Phil Bruns, Mitzi McCall, B. J. Ward.

This romantic comedy charts the course of the relationship of a young couple played by Arye Gross and Courteney Cox.

THE PICKLE
Pro. Paul Mazursky; Columbia Pictures *Dir.* Paul Mazursky *Scr.* Paul Mazursky *Cine.* Fred Murphy *Ed.* Stuart Pappe *P.d.* James Bissell *A.d.* Christopher Burian-Mohr and John Berger *S.d.* Dorree Cooper and Beth Kushnick *Mu.* Michel Legrand *MPAA* R *R.t.* 105 min. *Cast:* Danny Aiello, Dyan Cannon, Clotilde Courau, Shelley Winters, Barry Miller, Jerry Stiller, Chris Penn, Little Richard, Jodi Long, Rebecca Miller, Stephen Tobolowsky, Caroline Aaron, Ally Sheedy, Spalding Gray, Paul Mazursky, Linda Carlson, Kimiko Cazanov, Griffin Dunne, Isabella Rossellini, Dudley Moore.

Harry Stone (Danny Aiello), a middle-aged film director undergoing a midlife crisis, arrives in New York to see his picture's preview, a commercial science-fiction film for teenagers about a giant pickle launched into space by farm children. He regrets having worked on the film and takes out his frustrations on his loved ones.

THE PROGRAM

Pro. Samuel Goldwyn, Jr., for Touchstone Pictures and the Samuel Goldwyn Company; Buena Vista Pictures *Dir.* David S. Ward *Scr.* David S. Ward and Aaron Latham *Cine.* Victor Hammer *Ed.* Paul Seydor and Kimberly Ray *P.d.* Albert Brenner *A.d.* Carol Winstead Wood *S.d.* Harold Fuhrman and Kathe Klopp *Mu.* Michel Colombier *MPAA* R *R.t.* 114 min. *Cast:* James Caan, Halle Berry, Omar Epps, Craig Sheffer, Kristy Swanson, Abraham Benrubi, Duane Davis, Jon Maynard Pennell, Andrew Bryniarski, J. Leon Pridgen II.

A college football coach (James Caan) finds himself under the gun to win at any cost; his star quarterback, Joe Kane (Craig Sheffer), deals with family problems; and freshman tailback Darnell Jefferson (Omar Epps) vies for a starting position as well as the affections of the pretty Autumn (Halle Berry), in this sports drama.

RAIN WITHOUT THUNDER

Pro. Nanette Sorensen and Gary Sorensen for Taz Pictures; Orion Classics *Dir.* Gary Bennett *Scr.* Gary Bennett *Cine.* Karl Kases *Ed.* Mallory Gottlieb and Suzanne Pillsbury *P.d.* Ina Mayhew *Mu.* Randall Lynch and Allen Lynch *MPAA* PG-13 *R.t.* 87 min. *Cast:* Betty Buckley, Ali Thomas, Jeff Daniels, Carolyn McCormick, Frederic Forrest, Iona Morris, Linda Hunt, Robert Earl Jones, Graham Greene, Austin Pendleton.

Set in the future, this drama centers on the trial of a mother (Betty Buckley) and daughter (Ali Thomas) who attempted to go to Sweden to seek an abortion because such a procedure had been made illegal in the United States. Although the subject is highly controversial, the film itself tends to be tedious, as it concentrates on dialogue rather than on action.

THE REAL MCCOY

Pro. Martin Bregman, Willi Baer, and Michael S. Bregman; Universal Pictures *Dir.* Russell Mulcahy *Scr.* William Davies and William Osborne *Cine.* Denis Crossan *Ed.* Peter Honess *P.d.* Kim Colefax *A.d.* Paul Huggins *S.d.* Jonathon Short and Richard Charles Greenbaum *Mu.* Brad Fiedel *MPAA* PG-13 *R.t.* 106 min. *Cast:* Kim Basinger, Val Kilmer, Terence Stamp, Gailard Sartain, Zach English, Raynor Scheine.

Kim Basinger stars as a newly paroled master bank robber, Karen McCoy, who is blackmailed by a former associate (Terence Stamp) into committing one last heist when her young son is kidnapped. Val Kilmer plays her comic, bungling partner in crime.

RETURN OF THE LIVING DEAD III

Pro. Gary Schmoeller and Brian Yuzna; Trimark Pictures *Dir.* Brian Yuzna *Scr.* John Penney *Cine.* Gerry Lively *Ed.* Christopher Roth *P.d.* Anthony Tremblay *A.d.* Aram Allen Brennan, Christopher Nelson, and Wayne Toth *Mu.* Barry Goldberg *MPAA* R *R.t.* 97 min. *Cast:* Mindy Clarke, J. Trevor Edmond, Kent McCord, Basil Wallace, Sarah Douglas, Fabio Urena.

When the girlfriend, Julie (Mindy Clarke), of Curt (J. Trevor Edmond) dies in a motorcycle accident, he brings her back from the dead with a chemical he steals from his dad's lab on a military base.

RIFF-RAFF (Great Britain, 1991)

Pro. Sally Hibbin for Parallax Pictures and Channel Four; Fine Line Features *Dir.* Ken Loach *Scr.* Bill Jesse *Cine.* Barry Ackroyd *Ed.* Jonathan Morris *P.d.* Martin Johnson *Mu.* Stewart Copeland *MPAA* R *R.t.* 96 min. *Cast:* Robert Carlyle, Emer McCourt, Jimmy Coleman, George Moss, Ricky Tomlinson, David Finch, Derek Young.

This award-winning comedy-drama about the British working class centers on a London construction worker, Stevie (Robert Carlyle), with a criminal past. Stevie falls in love with an unambitious, untalented singer named Susan (Emer McCourt), who ridicules his dream of merchandising boxer shorts.

ROBIN HOOD: MEN IN TIGHTS

Pro. Mel Brooks for Brooksfilms, in association with Gaumont; Twentieth Century-Fox *Dir.* Mel Brooks *Scr.* Mel Brooks, Evan Chandler, and J. David Shapiro; based on a story by Shapiro and Chandler *Cine.* Michael D. O'Shea *Ed.* Stephen E. Rivkin *P.d.* Roy Forge Smith *A.d.* Stephen Myles Berger *S.d.* Ronald R. Reiss *Mu.* Hummie Mann *MPAA* PG-13 *R.t.* 102 min. *Cast:* Cary Elwes, Richard Lewis, Roger Rees, Amy Yasbeck, Mark Blankfield, Dave Chappelle, Isaac Hayes, Megan Cavanagh, Tracey Ullman, Eric Allan Kramer, Patrick Stewart, Mel Brooks, Dom DeLuise, Dick Van Patten.

One of the earliest masters of genre spoofing—Mel Brooks—attempts to deflate the pomposity of one of Hollywood's most recent "star vehicles," *Robin Hood: Prince of Thieves* (1991). Ironically, this uneven send-up does more justice to both the legend of yore and the buoyant style of Errol Flynn than the deadened Kevin Costner version.

ROBOCOP III

Pro. Patrick Crowley; Orion Pictures *Dir.* Fred Dekker *Scr.* Frank Miller and Fred Dekker; based on a story by Miller and on characters created by Edward Neumeier and Michael Miner *Cine.* Gary B. Kibbe *Ed.* Bert Lovitt *P.d.* Hilda Stark *A.d.* Cate Bangs *S.d.* Robert J. Franco *Mu.* Basil Poledouris *MPAA* PG-13 *R.t.* 104 min. *Cast:* Robert John Burke, Nancy Allen, Rip Torn, John Castle, Jill Hennessy, CCH Pounder, Mako, Robert DoQui, Remy Ryan, Bruce Locke, Stanley Anderson.

RoboCop (Robert John Burke)—part human, part machine—does battle with the evil corporation Omni Consumer Products and Japanese businessman Kanemitsu (Mako), who attempt to evict poor tenants from the inner city in order to build a futuristic development.

ROMPER STOMPER (Australia, 1993)

Pro. Daniel Scharf and Ian Pringle; Academy Entertainment *Dir.* Geoffrey Wright *Scr.* Geoffrey Wright *Cine.* Ron Hagen *Ed.* Bill Murphy *P.d.* Steven Jones-Evans *Mu.* John Clifford White *MPAA* NC-17 *R.t.* 92 min. *Cast:* Russell Crowe, Daniel Pollock, Jacqueline McKenzie, Alex Scott, Leigh Russell, James McKenna, Daniel Wyllie.

Extremely disturbing, this film of violence and gang warfare is set in Melbourne, Australia, and centers on a group of adolescent neo-Nazis. Led by Hando (Russell Crowe), fellow gang members Davey (Daniel Pollock) and Gabe (Jacqueline McKenzie), among others, wreak havoc on Vietnamese immigrants in their ongoing war of racial prejudice.

RUDY

Pro. Robert N. Fried and Cary Woods; TriStar Pictures *Dir.* David Anspaugh *Scr.* Angelo Pizzo *Cine.* Oliver Wood *Ed.* David Rosenbloom *P.d.* Robb Wilson King *S.d.* Martin Price *Mu.* Jerry Goldsmith *MPAA* PG *R.t.* 112 min. *Cast:* Sean Astin, Ned Beatty, Charles S. Dutton, Lili Taylor, Jason Miller, Robert Prosky, Jon Favreau, Greta Lind, Scott Benjaminson, Ron Dean, Chelcie Ross.

Based on a real-life story set in the 1960's, this drama centers on a young working-class man, Rudy Ruettiger (Sean Astin), who aspires to play football for Notre Dame against all odds.

THE SANDLOT

Pro. Dale de la Torre and William S. Gilmore, in association with Island World; Twentieth Century-Fox *Dir.* David Mickey Evans *Scr.* David Mickey Evans and Robert Gunter *Cine.* Anthony B. Richmond *Ed.* Michael A. Stevenson *P.d.* Chester Kaczenski *A.d.* Marc Dabe *S.d.* Judi Sandin *Mu.* David Newman *MPAA* PG *R.t.* 101 min. *Cast:* Tom Guiry, Mike Vitar, Patrick Renna, Chauncey Leopardi, Marty York, Brandon Adams, Grant Gelt, Shane Obedzinski, Victor DiMattia, Karen Allen, Denis Leary, James Earl Jones, Art La Fleur.

Set in the 1960's, this nostalgic comedy centers on a young boy, Scotty (Tom Guiry), who has just moved to a new neighborhood with his mother (Karen Allen) and stepfather (Denis Leary). He is promptly recruited into the local sandlot baseball team, through which he makes new friends and learns to overcome his fears.

THE SEVENTH COIN

Pro. Lee Nelson and Omri Maron for Orbit Entertainment and April Com Ltd.; Hemdale Communications, Inc. *Dir.* Dror Soref *Scr.* Dror Soref and Michael Lewis *Cine.* Avi Karpik *Ed.* Carole Kravetz *P.d.* Yoram Shayer *S.d.* Doron Shalem and Amir Kaplan *Mu.* Misha Segal *MPAA* PG-13 *R.t.* 91 min. *Cast:* Alexandra Powers, Navin Chowdhry, Peter O'Toole, John Rhys-Davies, Ally Walker.

An American teenager (Alexandra Powers) and an Arab thief (Navin Chowdhry) are pursued by the evil Emil Saber (Peter O'Toole) when they come into possession of a rare coin, in this adventure/romance set in Jerusalem.

SHADOW OF THE WOLF (Canada and France, 1993)

Pro. Claude Leger for Vision International and Mark Damon, in association with Transfilm, Inc., and Eiffel Productions S.A., with participation of Canal Plus; Triumph *Dir.* Jacques Dorfmann *Scr.* Rudy Wurlitzer and Evan Jones; adapted by David Milhaud and based on the novel *Agaguk*, by Yves Thériault *Cine.* Billy Williams *Ed.* Françoise Bonnot *P.d.* Wolf Kroeger *Mu.* Maurice Jarre *MPAA* PG-13 *R.t.* 108 min. *Cast:* Lou Diamond Phillips, Toshiro Mifune, Jennifer Tilly, Bernard-Pierre Donnadieu, Donald Sutherland.

A rebellious and white-hating young Eskimo hunter, Agaguk (Lou Diamond Phillips), sets out with the beautiful Igiyook (Jennifer Tilly) to live in isolation in the Arctic wilderness after having a falling-out his father (Toshiro Mifune) and killing a white trader (Bernard-Pierre Donnadieu). Unfortunately, the murder puts a Canadian mountie (Donald Sutherland) on his trail.

SIDEKICKS

Pro. Don Carmody for Gallery Films; Triumph Releasing *Dir.* Aaron Norris *Scr.* Don Thompson and Lou Illar; based on a story by Lou Illar *Cine.* Joao Fernandes *Ed.* David Rawlins and Bernard Weiser *P.d.* Reuben Freed *Mu.* Alan Silvestri *MPAA* PG *R.t.* 100 min. *Cast:* Chuck Norris, Beau Bridges, Jonathan Brandis, Mako, Julia Nickson-Soul, Joe Piscopo, Danica McKellar, John Buchanan, Richard Moll.

Daydreaming youngster Barry Gabrewski (Jonathan Brandis) is a sickly asthmatic outsider who is ridiculed by his classmates. He fantasizes about being the partner of his favorite hero, Chuck Norris, a dream that is realized when Norris himself appears at a karate tournament in which Barry is to fight a cruel schoolmate.

SNIPER

Pro. Robert L. Rosen; TriStar Pictures *Dir.* Luis Llosa *Scr.* Michael Frost Beckner and Crash Leyland *Cine.* Bill Butler *Ed.* Scott Smith *P.d.* Herbert Pinter *A.d.* Nicholas McCallum *S.d.* Leanne Cornish and Angus Tattle *Mu.* Gary Chang *MPAA* R *R.t.* 98 min. *Cast:* Tom Berenger, Billy Zane, J. T. Walsh, Aden Young, Ken Radley, Reinaldo Arenas, Carlos Alvarez, Roy Edmonds.

Two Marine snipers, one a seasoned professional (Tom Berenger) and the other a greenhorn (Billy Zane), penetrate the Panamanian jungle in order to assassinate a drug lord and a crooked politician.

SO I MARRIED AN AXE MURDERER

Pro. Robert N. Fried and Cary Woods; TriStar Pictures *Dir.* Thomas Schlamme *Scr.* Robbie Fox *Cine.* Julio Macat *Ed.* Richard Halsey and Colleen Halsey *P.d.* John Graysmark *A.d.*

Michael Rizzo *S.d.* Peg Cummings and Jim Poynter *Mu.* Bruce Broughton *MPAA* PG-13 *R.t.* 110 min. *Cast:* Mike Myers, Nancy Travis, Anthony LaPaglia, Amanda Plummer, Brenda Fricker, Debi Mazar, Phil Hartman, Charles Grodin, Steven Wright, Michael Richards, Matt Doherty, Mike Myers.

In this black comedy, a commitment-shy young man, Charlie Mackenzie (Mike Myers), thinks that he has finally met the woman of his dreams when he begins a relationship with a beautiful butcher, Harriet (Nancy Travis). No sooner are they married, however, than Charlie begins to suspect that his new wife may be a mass murderer whose gruesome deeds have been detailed in the supermarket tabloids.

SOFIE (Denmark, Norway, and Sweden, 1992)

Pro. Lars Kolvig; Arrow Releasing *Dir.* Liv Ullmann *Scr.* Liv Ullmann and Peter Poulsen; based on the novel *Mendel Philipsen and Son*, by Henri Nathansen *Cine.* Jorgen Persson *Ed.* Grethe Moldrup *A.d.* Peter Holmark *R.t.* 145 min. *Cast:* Karen-Lise Mynster, Erland Josephson, Ghita Nørby, Jesper Christensen, Torben Zeller, Stig Hoffmeyer, Henning Moritzen, Kirsten Rolffes, Lotte Herman.

Liv Ullmann makes her directorial debut with this critically acclaimed drama. Sofie (Karen-Lise Mynster), a single Copenhagen Jew in her late twenties, falls in love with an artist (Jesper Christensen) but, as he is a Gentile, her family encourages her to marry her shy cousin (Torben Zeller).

SON-IN-LAW

Pro. Michael Rotenberg and Peter M. Lenkov for Hollywood Pictures; Buena Vista Pictures *Dir.* Steve Rash *Scr.* Fax Bahr, Adam Small, and Shawn Schepps; based on a story by Patrick J. Clifton, Susan McMartin, and Peter M. Lenkov *Cine.* Peter Deming *Ed.* Dennis M. Hill *P.d.* Joseph T. Garrity *A.d.* Pat Tagliaferro *S.d.* Dena Roth *Mu.* Richard Gibbs *MPAA* PG-13 *R.t.* 95 min. *Cast:* Pauly Shore, Carla Gugino, Lane Smith, Cindy Pickett, Mason Adams, Patrick Renna, Dennis Burkley, Tiffani-Amber Thiessen, Dan Gauthier.

Rebecca (Carla Gugino) moves from her South Dakota home to attend college in Los Angeles. There she meets Crawl (Pauly Shore), a unique character who helps her cope with the change and whom Rebecca brings home for Thanksgiving break. It is a fish-out-of-water story as Crawl adapts to farm life, lending his unique insight to improving the lives of the characters he encounters.

SON OF THE PINK PANTHER

Pro. Tony Adams for United Artists, in association with Filmauro S.R.L.; Metro-Goldwyn-Mayer *Dir.* Blake Edwards *Scr.* Blake Edwards, Madeline Sunshine, and Steve Sunshine; based on a story by Edwards and on characters created by Edwards and Maurice Richlin *Cine.* Dick Bush *Ed.* Robert Pergament *P.d.* Peter Mullins *A.d.* David Minty, John Siddall, and Leslie Tomkins *S.d.* Peter Howitt *Mu.* Henry Mancini *MPAA* PG *R.t.* 93 min. *Cast:* Roberto Benigni, Herbert Lom, Claudia Cardinale, Debrah Farentino, Jennifer Edwards, Robert Davi, Anton Rodgers, Burt Kwouk, Graham Stark.

In this weak sequel to Blake Edwards' successful PINK PANTHER series, Italian comedian Roberto Benigni stars as Jacques, the illegitimate son of the original Inspector Clouseau (Peter Sellers). Like father, like son: Jacques bumbles his way into a case involving the kidnapping of a Middle Eastern princess (Debrah Farentino) that is being investigated by none other than the Clouseau-hating Commissioner Dreyfus (Herbert Lom) of the original series.

SPLITTING HEIRS (Great Britain, 1993)

Pro. Simon Bosanquet and Redmond Morris for Prominent Features; Universal Pictures *Dir.* Robert Young *Scr.* Eric Idle *Cine.* Tony Pierce-Roberts *Ed.* John Jympson *P.d.* John Beard

Mu. Michael Kamen *MPAA* PG-13 *R.t.* 87 min. *Cast:* Rick Moranis, Eric Idle, Barbara Hershey, Catherine Zeta Jones, John Cleese, Sadie Frost, Stratford Johns.

The plot of this English farce centers on Tommy (Eric Idle), who, as an infant in the 1960's, is accidentally abandoned in a restaurant by his careless parents, the fourteenth Duke of Bournemouth and his wife, Duchess Lucinda (Barbara Hershey), and is reared by Pakistanis. Years later, when the fourteenth duke dies and Tommy's friend Henry (Rick Moranis) becomes the fifteenth duke, Tommy finds out that he is the rightful duke and attempts to grab the aristocracy.

STRIKING DISTANCE

Pro. Arnon Milchan, Tony Thomopoulos, and Hunt Lowry; Columbia Pictures *Dir.* Rowdy Herrington *Scr.* Rowdy Herrington and Martin Kaplan *Cine.* Mac Ahlberg *Ed.* Pasquale Buba and Mark Helfrich *P.d.* Gregg Fonseca *A.d.* Bruce Miller *S.d.* Jay Hart *Mu.* Brad Fiedel *MPAA* R *R.t.* 101 min. *Cast:* Bruce Willis, Sarah Jessica Parker, Dennis Farina, Tom Sizemore, Brion James, Robert Pastorelli, John Mahoney.

Jaded and hard-drinking Pittsburgh River Rescue cop Tom Hardy (Bruce Willis) must find a serial killer nobody believes exists.

SUPER MARIO BROS.

Pro. Jake Eberts and Roland Joffé for Hollywood Pictures and Lightmotive/Allied Filmmakers, in association with Cinergi Productions; Buena Vista Pictures *Dir.* Rocky Morton and Annabel Jankel *Scr.* Parker Bennett, Terry Runté, and Ed Solomon; based on the Nintendo game concept and on characters created by Shigeru Miyamoto and Takashi Tezuka *Cine.* Dean Semler *Ed.* Mark Goldblatt *P.d.* David L. Snyder *A.d.* Walter P. Martishius *S.d.* Beth Rubino *Mu.* Alan Silvestri *MPAA* PG *R.t.* 104 min. *Cast:* Bob Hoskins, John Leguizamo, Dennis Hopper, Samantha Mathis, Fisher Stevens, Richard Edson, Fiona Shaw, Dana Kaminski, Mojo Nixon, Gianni Russo, Francesca Roberts, Lance Henriksen, Sylvia Harman, Desiree Marie Velez.

This film adaptation of a Nintendo video game features the Mario Brothers (Bob Hoskins and John Leguizamo) as two Brooklyn plumbers who enter a parallel dinosaur universe while in pursuit of the dinosaurs' reptilian leader, King Koopa (Dennis Hopper), and his young kidnapping victim, Daisy (Samantha Mathis), who possesses a magical meteorite fragment that can be used to join the dinosaur universe and the human universe.

SURE FIRE

Pro. Henry S. Rosenthal for Complex Corp.; Strand Releasing *Dir.* Jon Jost *Scr.* Jon Jost *Cine.* Jon Jost *Ed.* Jon Jost *Mu.* Erling Wold *R.t.* 83 min. *Cast:* Tom Blair, Robert Ernst, Kristi Hager, Kate Dezina.

A small-time real estate agent (Tom Blair) in rural Utah has big-time dreams of making money selling to wealthy Californians, but his shady business practices cause trouble.

SURF NINJAS

Pro. Evzen Kolar; New Line Cinema *Dir.* Neal Israel *Scr.* Dan Gordon *Cine.* Arthur Albert and Victor Hammer *Ed.* Tom Walls *P.d.* Michael Novotny *A.d.* Curtis W. Baruth *S.d.* Janis Lubin *Mu.* David Kitay *MPAA* PG *R.t.* 87 min. *Cast:* Ernie Reyes, Jr., Rob Schneider, Nicolas Cowan, Leslie Nielsen, Tone Lōc, Ernie Reyes, Sr., Keone Young, Kelly Hu, Tad Horino, John Karlen, Neal Israel, Olivier Mills, Phillip Tan, Romy Walthall, Rachel Kolar, Yoni Gordon.

When two California surfers (Ernie Reyes, Jr., and Nicolas Cowan) discover that they are really heirs to the throne of an obscure island nation, they travel to Patu San to battle its evil usurper (Leslie Nielsen), in this comedy adventure.

SWING KIDS

Pro. Mark Gordon and John Bard Manulis for Hollywood Pictures, in association with Touchwood Pacific Partners I; Buena Vista Pictures *Dir.* Thomas Carter *Scr.* Jonathan Marc Feldman *Cine.* Jerzy Zielinski *Ed.* Michael R. Miller *P.d.* Allan Cameron *A.d.* Steve Spence and Tony Reading *S.d.* Ros Shingleton *Mu.* James Horner *MPAA* PG-13 *R.t.* 112 min. *Cast:* Robert Sean Leonard, Christian Bale, Frank Whaley, Barbara Hershey, Kenneth Branagh, Tushka Bergen, David Tom.

Set in 1939 Germany, this musical drama centers on three teenage friends—Peter (Robert Sean Leonard), Thomas (Christian Bale), and Arvid (Frank Whaley)—who adore swing music and who are each forced to take a stand regarding the rising tide of Nazism.

TEENAGE MUTANT NINJA TURTLES III: THE TURTLES ARE BACK . . . IN TIME

Pro. Thomas K. Gray, Kim Dawson, and David Chan for Golden Harvest, in association with Gary Propper; New Line Cinema *Dir.* Stuart Gillard *Scr.* Stuart Gillard; based on characters created by Kevin Eastman and Peter Laird *Cine.* David Gurfinkel *Ed.* William D. Gordean and James R. Symons *P.d.* Roy Forge Smith *A.d.* Mayne Schuyler Berke *S.d.* Ronald R. Reiss *Mu.* John Du Prez *MPAA* PG *R.t.* 95 min. *Cast:* Mark Caso, Matt Hill, Jim Raposa, David Fraser, Elias Koteas, Paige Turco, Stuart Wilson, Vivian Wu, Sab Shimono, James Murray, Henry Hayashi, John Aylward, Travis A. Moon, Tad Horino, Glen Chin, Brian Tochi (voice), Tim Kelleher (voice), Corey Feldman (voice), Robbie Rist (voice).

Set in medieval Japan, this is the undistinguished third big-screen adventure of the Teenage Mutant Ninja Turtles. Leonardo, Raphael, Donatello, and Michaelangelo travel back in time to rescue their friend April (Paige Turco), fighting Samurai warriors along the way.

THE TEMP

Pro. David Permut and Tom Engelman; Paramount Pictures *Dir.* Tom Holland *Scr.* Kevin Falls; based on a story by Falls and Tom Engelman *Cine.* Steve Yaconelli *Ed.* Scott Conrad *P.d.* Joel Schiller *A.d.* Gordon W. Clark *S.d.* Kim Mackenzie Orlando *Mu.* Frederic Talgorn *MPAA* R *R.t.* 96 min. *Cast:* Timothy Hutton, Lara Flynn Boyle, Faye Dunaway, Dwight Schultz, Oliver Platt, Steven Weber, Colleen Flynn, Maura Tierney.

Young executive Peter Derns (Timothy Hutton) finds himself in a bind when his secretary suddenly takes two weeks off for family leave. His new temporary, Kris Bolin (Lara Flynn Boyle), saves the day but soon seems to use deception and murder to further her own meteoric rise up the corporate ladder.

THAT NIGHT

Pro. Arnon Milchan and Steven Reuther for Le Studio Canal Plus, Regency Enterprises, and Alcor Films; Warner Bros. *Dir.* Craig Bolotin *Scr.* Craig Bolotin; based on the novel by Alice McDermott *Cine.* Bruce Surtees *Ed.* Priscilla Nedd-Friendly *P.d.* Maher Ahmad *A.d.* Jeremy Conway *S.d.* Susan Kaufman *Mu.* David Newman *MPAA* PG-13 *R.t.* 88 min. *Cast:* C. Thomas Howell, Juliette Lewis, Helen Shaver, Eliza Dushku, J. Smith-Cameron, John Dossett.

Ten-year-old Alice Bloom (Eliza Dushku) idolizes beautiful teenage neighbor Sheryl (Juliette Lewis), who in turn is smitten with Rick (C. Thomas Howell). Because Sheryl's mother (Helen Shaver) does not approve, Sheryl meets Rick in secret, making Alice her confidante.

TITO AND ME (Yugoslavia and France, 1993)

Pro. Goran Markovic, Zoran Masirevic, Michel Mavros, and Zoran Tasic; Kino International *Dir.* Goran Markovic *Scr.* Goran Markovic *Cine.* Racoslav Vladic *Ed.* Snezana Ivanovic

P.d. Veljko Despotovic *Mu.* Zoran Simjanovic *R.t.* 110 min. *Cast:* Dimitrie Vojnov, Lazar Ristovski, Anica Dobra, Predrag Manojlovic, Vesna Trivalic, Voja Brajovic, Ljiljana Draguti-novic, Bogdan Diklic, Olivera Markovic, Rade Markovic.

Set in Yugoslavia in the 1950's, this comic drama centers on young Zoran (Dimitrie Vojnov) and his extended family, who all occupy a crowded apartment. Overweight, suffering unrequited love for an older girl, and obsessed with his hero—Marshal Tito—Zoran wins an essay contest about his idol and is sent on a "March Around Tito's Homeland."

TOM AND JERRY: THE MOVIE

Pro. Phil Roman for Live Entertainment and Turner Entertainment Co., in association with WMG and Film Roman; Miramax Films *Dir.* Phil Roman *Scr.* Dennis Marks; based on the cartoon characters created by William Hanna and Joseph Barbera *Ed.* Sam Horta and Julie Ann Gustafson *A.d.* Michael Peraza, Jr. and Michael Humphries *Mu.* Henry Mancini *MPAA* G *R.t.* 80 min. *Voices:* Richard Kind, Dana Hill, Anndi McAfee, Charlotte Rae, Tony Jay, Rip Taylor, Henry Gibson, Howard Morris.

In this full-length feature based on the well-known cartoon characters created in the 1940's by William Hanna and Joseph Barbera, cat Tom (voice of Richard Kind) and mouse Jerry (voice of Dana Hill) become friends and work to save a young girl from her evil nanny and lawyer.

TRUSTING BEATRICE

Pro. Mark Evan Jacobs and Cindy Lou Johnson for J.J. Films; Castle Hill Productions *Dir.* Cindy Lou Johnson *Scr.* Cindy Lou Johnson *Cine.* Bernd Heinl *Ed.* Camilla Toniolo *P.d.* Cynthia Kay Charette *Mu.* Stanley Myers *MPAA* PG *R.t.* 86 min. *Cast:* Irène Jacob, Mark Evan Jacobs, Charlotte Moore, Steve Buscemi, Nady Meas, Pat McNamara, Leonardo Cimino, Samuel Wright.

A hapless gardener (Mark Evan Jacobs) falls in love with a free-spirited illegal French immigrant (Irène Jacob) who comes to live with him and his barmy family.

TWENTY BUCKS

Pro. Karen Murphy for Big Tomorrow Productions; Triton Pictures *Dir.* Keva Rosenfeld *Scr.* Leslie Bohem and Endre Bohem *Cine.* Emmanuel Lubezki *Ed.* Michael Ruscio *P.d.* Joseph T. Garrity *A.d.* Rando Schmook *S.d.* Linda Allen *Mu.* David Robbins *MPAA* R *R.t.* 91 min. *Cast:* Linda Hunt, David Rasche, George Morfogen, Sam Jenkins, Brendan Fraser, Concetta Tomei, Melora Walters, Gladys Knight, Elisabeth Shue, Steve Buscemi, Christopher Lloyd, Kamau Holloway, William H. Macy, Diane Baker, Matt Frewer, Spalding Gray, Nina Sie-maszko.

Featuring an all-star cast, which includes Christopher Lloyd, Steve Buscemi, Gladys Knight, and Elisabeth Shue, this comedy follows the path of a twenty-dollar bill as it undergoes numerous transactions.

TWIST

Pro. Ron Mann, in association with Alliance Communications; Triton Pictures *Dir.* Ron Mann *Cine.* Bob Fresco *Ed.* Robert Kennedy *R.t.* 90 min. *Cast:* Hank Ballard, Chubby Checker, Cholly Atkins.

This documentary examines the revolutionary effects on society of the 1960's dance craze called the Twist, invented by Hank Ballard but made popular by Chubby Checker.

UNDERCOVER BLUES

Pro. Mike Lobell; Metro-Goldwyn-Mayer *Dir.* Herbert Ross *Scr.* Ian Abrams *Cine.* Donald E. Thorin *Ed.* Priscilla Nedd-Friendly *P.d.* Ken Adam *S.d.* James R. Bayliss *Mu.* David Newman *MPAA* PG-13 *R.t.* 89 min. *Cast:* Kathleen Turner, Dennis Quaid, Fiona Shaw,

Stanley Tucci, Larry Miller, Obba Babatunde, Park Overall, Tom Arnold, Ralph Brown, Jan Triska, Saul Rubinek, Jenifer Lewis, Michelle Schuelke.

Kathleen Turner and Dennis Quaid star as Jane and Jeff Blue, CIA agents and parents of an infant daughter. In the mode of a Nick and Nora Charles, they wage war on criminals, with their baby in tow.

THE VANISHING

Pro. Larry Brezner and Paul Schiff for Morra, Brezner, Steinberg, and Tenenbaum; Twentieth Century-Fox *Dir.* George Sluizer *Scr.* Todd Graff; based on the film *Spoorloos* (1988) and on the novel *The Golden Egg*, by Tim Krabbe *Cine.* Peter Suschitzky *Ed.* Bruce Green *P.d.* Jeannine C. Oppewall *A.d.* Steve Wolff *S.d.* Richard Yanez and Anne Ahrens *Mu.* Jerry Goldsmith *MPAA* R *R.t.* 110 min. *Cast:* Jeff Bridges, Kiefer Sutherland, Nancy Travis, Sandra Bullock, Park Overall, Maggie Linderman, Lisa Eichhorn, George Hearn, Lynn Hamilton.

When the girlfriend (Sandra Bullock) of a young man, Jeff (Kiefer Sutherland), mysteriously disappears, he begins an obsessive three-year search that culminates in his entrapment by her kidnapper (Jeff Bridges).

VEGAS IN SPACE

Pro. Phillip R. Ford; Troma Team *Dir.* Phillip R. Ford *Scr.* Doris Fish, Miss X, and Phillip R. Ford *Cine.* Robin Clark *Ed.* Ed Jones and Phillip R. Ford *P.d.* Doris Fish *Mu.* Bob Davis *R.t.* 85 min. *Cast:* Doris Fish, Miss X, Ginger Quest, Ramona Fischer, Lori Naslund, Timmy Spence, "Tippi," Freida Lay.

In this parody of the science-fiction genre, a starship travels to a female-only pleasure planet, where the male crew members undergo a sex change and pretend to be part of a touring lounge act in order to investigate a jewel robbery.

VISIONS OF LIGHT: THE ART OF CINEMATOGRAPHY (Japan and USA, 1993)

Pro. Stuart Samuels and Arnold Glassman for American Film Institute, NHK, and Japan Broadcasting Corp.; American Film Institute *Dir.* Arnold Glassman, Todd McCarthy, and Stuart Samuels *Scr.* Todd McCarthy *Cine.* Nancy Schreiber *Ed.* Arnold Glassman *R.t.* 90 min. *Cast:* Nestor Almendros, John Alonzo, John Bailey, Michael Ballhaus, Stephen Burum, Bill Butler, Michael Chapman, Allan Daviau, Caleb Deschanel, Ernest Dickerson, Frederick Elmes, William Fraker, Conrad Hall, James Wong Howe, Victor Kemper, Lazslo Kovacs, Charles Lang, Sven Nykvist, Lisa Rinzler, Owen Roizman, Charles Rosher, Jr., Sandi Sissel, Vittorio Storaro, Haskell Wexler, Robert Wise, Gordon Willis, Vilmos Zsigmond.

This acclaimed documentary centers on the photographic artistry of cinematographers throughout the history of filmmaking, incorporating interviews of leading cinematographers with excerpts from well-known films.

THE WAR ROOM

Pro. R. J. Cutler, Wendy Ettinger, and Frazer Pennebaker for Pennebaker Associates and Cyclone Films; October Films *Dir.* D. A. Pennebaker and Chris Hegedus *Cine.* Nick Doob, D. A. Pennebaker, and Kevin Rafferty *Ed.* Chris Hegedus, Erez Laufer, and D. A. Pennebaker *R.t.* 96 min. *Cast:* James Carville, George Stephanopoulos.

This candid and entertaining documentary centers on Bill Clinton's 1992 presidential campaign and on the two strategists who helped him win the election: the dynamic James Carville and George Stephanopoulos.

WARLOCK: THE ARMAGEDDON

Pro. Peter Abrams and Robert L. Levy for Tapestry Films; Trimark Pictures *Dir.* Anthony Hickox *Scr.* Kevin Rock and Sam Bernard; based on a story by Rock and on characters created by David N. Twohy *Cine.* Gerry Lively *Ed.* Chris Cibelli *P.d.* Steve Hardie *A.d.* John

Chichester *S.d.* David Koneff *Mu.* Mark McKenzie *MPAA* R *R.t.* 98 min. *Cast:* Julian Sands, Chris Young, Paula Marshall, Steve Kahan, Charles Hallahan, R. G. Armstrong, Nicole Mercurio, Craig Hurley, Bruce Glover, Dawn Ann Billings, Zach Galligan, Joanna Pacula.

Julian Sands returns in this sequel as a Warlock who appears in the twentieth century in order to collect six ancient Druid rune stones with which to summon Satan.

WATCH IT

Pro. Thomas J. Mangan IV, J. Christopher Burch, and John C. McGinley for Island World, in association with the Manhattan Project and River One Films; Skouras Pictures *Dir.* Tom Flynn *Scr.* Tom Flynn *Cine.* Stephen M. Katz *Ed.* Dorian Harris *P.d.* Jeff Steven Ginn *A.d.* Barbara Kahn Kretschmer *S.d.* Martha Ring *Mu.* Stanley Clarke *MPAA* R *R.t.* 102 min. *Cast:* Peter Gallagher, Suzy Amis, John C. McGinley, Jon Tenney, Cynthia Stevenson, Lili Taylor, Tom Sizemore, Terri Hawkes, Jordana Capra, Taylor Render, Lorenzo Clemons.

In this comedy, four male friends—Peter Gallagher, Jon Tenney, John C. McGinley, and Tom Sizemore—sharing a house in Chicago indulge in womanizing and playing cruel pranks on one another in a game they originated in their youth called "Watch It."

WAYNE'S WORLD II

Pro. Lorne Michaels; Paramount Pictures *Dir.* Stephen Surjik *Scr.* Mike Myers, Bonnie Turner, and Terry Turner; based on characters created by Myers *Cine.* Francis Kenny *Ed.* Malcolm Campbell *P.d.* Gregg Fonseca *A.d.* Richard A. Yanez *S.d.* Stephanie Gordon, Mark Poll, Gary Sawaya, and Jay R. Hart *Mu.* Carter Burwell *MPAA* PG-13 *R.t.* 94 min. *Cast:* Mike Myers, Dana Carvey, Christopher Walken, Tia Carrere, Ralph Brown, Kim Basinger, Chris Farley, James Hong, Michael Nickles, Larry Sellers, Ed O'Neill, Olivia D'Abo, Kevin Pollack, Drew Barrymore, Aerosmith, Lee Tergesen, Dan Bell.

Wayne (Mike Myers) and Garth (Dana Carvey) return—the dynamic duo who host a late-night cable-access television program from their Aurora, Illinois, home—this time to stage an ambitious concert, christened Waynestock, starring the likes of Aerosmith.

WE NEVER DIE (Hungary, 1993)

Pro. Sandor Simo for Hunnia Studio and Magic Media; Bunyik Enterprises, Inc. *Dir.* Robert Koltai *Scr.* Gabor Nogradi and Robert Koltai *Cine.* Gabor Halasz *Ed.* Mari Miklos *P.d.* Gyula Pauer *Mu.* Laszlo Des *R.t.* 95 min. *Cast:* Robert Koltai, Mihaly Szabados, Kathleen Gati.

A free-spirited wooden-hanger salesman, Uncle Gyuszi (Robert Koltai), takes his gangly adolescent nephew, Imi (Mihaly Szabados), with him on a sales trip that becomes an adventure, in this comedy set in the 1960's.

WEEKEND AT BERNIE'S II

Pro. Victor Drai and Joseph Perez for ArtimM; TriStar Pictures *Dir.* Robert Klane *Scr.* Robert Klane *Cine.* Edward Morey III *Ed.* Peck Prior *P.d.* Michael Bolton *A.d.* Eric Fraser *S.d.* Scott Jacobson *Mu.* Peter Wolf *MPAA* PG *R.t.* 89 min. *Cast:* Andrew McCarthy, Jonathan Silverman, Terry Kiser, Tom Wright, Steve James, Troy Beyer, Barry Bostwick.

In this sequel to the 1989 screwball comedy, Andrew McCarthy and Jonathan Silverman reprise their roles as insurance company office workers once again entangled with their dead boss, Bernie (Terry Kiser). Fired for their role in the original story, the two travel to the Virgin Islands with Bernie's corpse in tow, in search of funds embezzled by their dead boss. They are trailed by an investigator from their company (Barry Bostwick) and the mob.

WE'RE BACK: A DINOSAUR'S STORY

Pro. Stephen Hickner for Amblin Entertainment; Universal Pictures *Dir.* Dick Zondag, Ralph Zondag, Phil Nibbelink, and Simon Wells *Scr.* John Patrick Shanley; based on the book by

Hudson Talbott *Ed.* Sim Evan-Jones and Nick Fletcher *A.d.* Neil Ross *Mu.* James Horner *MPAA* G *R.t.* 72 min. *Voices:* John Goodman, Blaze Berdahl, Rhea Perlman, Jay Leno, Rene LeVant, Felicity Kendal, Charles Fleischer, Walter Cronkite, Joey Shea, Julia Child, Kenneth Mars, Yeardley Smith, Martin Short.

In this fantasy adventure, Captain NewEyes (voice of Walter Cronkite) travels to prehistoric times to bring dinosaurs to the twentieth century. With a special cereal, he transforms them into lovable, talking pets, who are befriended by a streetwise boy, Louie (Joey Shea). Unfortunately, Captain NewEyes' evil brother, Professor ScrewEyes (voice of Kenneth Mars), wants the dinosaurs for his own nefarious purposes.

WHEN THE PARTY'S OVER

Pro. James A. Holt, Ann Wycoff, and Matthew Irmas for WTPO; Strand *Dir.* Matthew Irmas *Scr.* Ann Wycoff; based on a story by Matthew Irmas and Wycoff *Cine.* Alicia Weber *Ed.* Dean Goodhill and Jerry Bixman *P.d.* John Gary Steele *A.d.* Merrie Okie *S.d.* Nancy Arnold *Mu.* Joe Romano *MPAA* R *R.t.* 115 min. *Cast:* Elizabeth Berridge, Rae Dawn Chong, Sandra Bullock, Fisher Stevens, Brian McNamara, Kris Kamm, Michael Landes.

Three young career women sharing a house in the Hollywood Hills experience multiple conflicts that come to a head at a New Year's party. Frankie (Elizabeth Berridge) is a social worker who is supervising a mural painting; M. J. (Rae Dawn Chong) is an ambitious stockbroker who is having an affair with Frankie's boyfriend, Taylor (Brian McNamara); and Amanda (Sandra Bullock) is an aspiring performance artist.

WHO'S THE MAN?

Pro. Charles Stettler and Maynell Thomas for New Line Cinema, in association with Tin Pan Apple, de Passe Entertainment, and Thomas Entertainment; New Line Cinema *Dir.* Ted Demme *Scr.* Seth Greenland; based on a story by Doctor Dre, Ed Lover, and Greenland *Cine.* Adam Kimmel *Ed.* Jeffrey Wolf *P.d.* Ruth Ammon *S.d.* Susan Raney *Mu.* Michael Wolff and Nic. tenBroek *MPAA* R *R.t.* 85 min. *Cast:* Ed Lover, Doctor Dre, Badja Djola, Denis Leary, Richard Bright, Cheryl "Salt" James, Jim Moody, Ice-T, Bushwick Bill.

Set in Harlem, this comedy stars Doctor Dre and Ed Lover as two inept barbers who become police officers against their will. Using their newfound authority, however, they solve a murder and save their neighborhood from unscrupulous investors.

WILD WEST (England, 1992)

Pro. Eric Fellner for Channel 4 Films, with the participation of British Screen and Initial; the Samuel Goldwyn Company *Dir.* David Attwood *Scr.* Harwant Bains *Cine.* Nic Knowland *Ed.* Martin Walsh *P.d.* Caroline Hanania *A.d.* Kave Naylor *Mu.* Dominic Miller *R.t.* 85 min. *Cast:* Naveen Andrews, Sarita Choudhury, Ronny Jhutti, Ravi Kapoor, Ameet Chana Bhasker, Lalita Ahmed, Shaun Scott.

This quirky British comedy centers on a London Pakistani country-and-western band that wants to make it to Nashville.

WILDER NAPALM

Pro. Mark Johnson and Stuart Cornfeld for Baltimore Pictures; TriStar Pictures *Dir.* Glenn Gordon Caron *Scr.* Vince Gilligan *Cine.* Jerry Hartleben *Ed.* Artie Mandelberg *P.d.* John Muto *A.d.* Dan Webster *S.d.* Leslie Bloom *Mu.* Michael Kamen *MPAA* PG-13 *R.t.* 109 min. *Cast:* Debra Winger, Dennis Quaid, Arliss Howard, M. Emmet Walsh, Jim Varney, Mimi Lieber, Marvin J. McIntyre, The Mighty Echoes.

Dennis Quaid and Arliss Howard star as estranged brothers Wallace and Wilder Foudroyant, who have the peculiar talent of being able to set fires telekinetically. In love with Wilder's wife, Vida (Debra Winger), Wallace flaunts his talent just as Wilder tries to hide his.

WRESTLING ERNEST HEMINGWAY

Pro. Todd Black and Joe Wizan; Warner Bros. *Dir.* Randa Haines *Scr.* Steve Conrad *Cine.* Lajos Koltai *Ed.* Paul Hirsch *P.d.* Waldemar Kalinowski *A.d.* Alan E. Muraoka *S.d.* Carlos Arditti and Florence Fellman *Mu.* Michael Convertino *MPAA* PG-13 *R.t.* 122 min. *Cast:* Robert Duvall, Richard Harris, Shirley MacLaine, Sandra Bullock, Nicole Mercurio, Marty Belafsky, Piper Laurie.

Robert Duvall and Richard Harris star as two aging and lonely men who meet and begin a tenuous friendship in a small Florida town. They have a series of small adventures together, during which each learns important lessons from the other about living and dying.

OBITUARIES

Don Ameche (May 31, 1908-December 6, 1993). Born Dominic Amici, Ameche was an actor who was a leading man in many Twentieth Century-Fox films of the 1930's and 1940's. Until the latter days of his career, he was most closely identified with the title role in *The Story of Alexander Graham Bell* (1939). Almost fifty years later, however, his role as the break-dancing oldster in *Cocoon* (1985), earned for him an Academy Award as Best Supporting Actor. He had a rich baritone voice that led to a career in radio as well as film and television. He was a versatile actor but specialized in light comedy. Fox often paired him with its leading ladies, and he appeared with Alice Faye in such films as *Alexander's Ragtime Band* (1938) and *In Old Chicago* (1938), and Betty Grable in *Down Argentine Way* (1940) and *Moon Over Miami* (1941). When his Fox contract expired in 1946, Ameche began making the transition to television, to which he devoted most of his energies after 1950. He returned to film in the 1980's, appearing in *Trading Places* (1983) and *Harry and the Hendersons* (1987), among others. Shortly before his death, he had completed filming on the Whoopi Goldberg vehicle *Corrina, Corrina*, as yet unreleased. His additional film credits include *Ramona* (1936), *The Three Musketeers* (1939), *Swanee River* (1940), *That Night in Rio* (1941), *Heaven Can Wait* (1943), *Slightly French* (1949), *Phantom Caravan* (1954), *Picture Mommy Dead* (1966), *The Boatniks* (1970), *Coming to America* (1988), *Things Change* (1988), and *Oscar* (1991).

Leon Ames (January 20, 1903-October 12, 1993). Born Leon Waycoff, Ames was a character actor who specialized playing avuncular or fatherly types. He was one of the original founders of the Screen Actors Guild in 1933. His film credits include *Murders in the Rue Morgue* (1932), *The Count of Monte Cristo* (1934), *Meet Me in St. Louis* (1944), *Thirty Seconds Over Tokyo* (1944), *The Postman Always Rings Twice* (1946), *A Date With Judy* (1948), *Peyton Place* (1957), *The Absent-Minded Professor* (1961), *On a Clear Day You Can See Forever* (1970), and *Tora! Tora! Tora!* (1970).

Andre the Giant (1946-January 27, 1993). Born Andre Rene Roussimoff, Andre the Giant was a 7' 4", 520-pound professional wrestler. He was featured as the gentle giant in *The Princess Bride* (1987).

Emile Ardolino (1943-November 20, 1993). Ardolino was a director who specialized in dance programming, in both television and film. After a distinguished television career with PBS that earned for him seventeen Emmy nominations, Ardolino made *He Makes Me Feel Like Dancin'* (1983), which won the Academy Award for Best Documentary. Moving into feature films, his *Dirty Dancing* (1987) also had dance as its theme. His biggest commercial success was *Sister Act* (1992). His additional film credits include *Three Men and a Little Lady* (1990) and *The Nutcracker* (1993).

Bill Bixby (January 22, 1934-November 21, 1993). Bixby was an actor who was best known for his starring roles in three television series, *My Favorite Martian*, *The Courtship of Eddie's Father*, and *The Incredible Hulk*. On screen, his most memorable moments came alongside Elvis Presley in *Clambake* (1967) and *Speedway* (1968). His additional film credits include *Irma La Douce* (1963), *Under the Yum Yum Tree* (1963), *Ride Beyond Vengeance* (1966), *The Apple Dumpling Gang* (1975), and *The Kentucky Fried Movie* (1977).

David Brian (August 5, 1914-July 15, 1993). Brian was an actor who worked extensively for Warner Bros., specializing in powerful, ruthless characters. He made several films with Joan Crawford, including *Flamingo Road* (1949), *The Damned Don't Cry* (1950), and *This Woman Is Dangerous* (1952). He also starred in the television series *Mr. District Attorney*. His additional film credits include *Intruder in the Dust* (1950), *Springfield Rifle* (1952), *The High and the Mighty* (1954), *A Pocketful of Miracles* (1961), *How the West Was Won* (1962), and *The Seven Minutes* (1971).

James Bridges (1935-June 6, 1993). Bridges was a director and screenwriter who made several highly successful films in the 1970's and 1980's. He wrote *The Appaloosa* (1966) and *The Forbin Project* (1970), at which point he was given the opportunity to direct his own screenplays. His second film, *The Paper Chase* (1973), was made into a television series; both productions starred John Houseman, who won an Academy Award for his portrayal as a crusty law professor. Bridges was nominated for an Academy Award for the screenplay of *The China Syndrome* (1979), which he also directed. His additional film credits include *The Baby Maker* (1970), *Urban Cowboy* (1980), *Mike's Murder* (1984), *Perfect* (1985), and *Bright Lights, Big City* (1988).

Hervé Bromberger (November 11, 1918-November 23, 1993). Bromberger was a French director best known for *Seul dans Paris* (1952) and *Les Fruits sauvages* (1954), films which have been called precursors of the French New Wave a decade later. His additional film credits include *Identité judiciaire* (1951), *Nagana* (1955), *La Bonne Tisane* (1958), *Mort—où est tâ victoire?* (1964), and *Un Soir à Tibériade* (1965).

Franco Brusati (1922-February 28, 1993). Brusati was an Italian director. He got his start as a screenwriter, collaborating on Franco Zeffirelli's *Romeo and Juliet* (1968). In the 1970's, he achieved international recognition with two films. *Pane e cioccolata* (1974; *Bread and Chocolate*) won a New York Film Critics Award, and *Dimenticare Venezia* (1979; *To Forget Venice*) was nominated for an Academy Award as Best Foreign-Language Film.

Raymond Burr (May 21, 1917-September 12, 1993). Burr was an actor who is best remembered for his starring roles in television's *Perry Mason* and *Ironside*. A heavy man with a smooth voice and expressive eyes, Burr worked in film for over a decade before *Perry Mason* made him a star. Frequently cast as a villain, his most prominent film roles came in Alfred Hitchcock's *Rear Window* (1954), in which he played a henpecked murderer, and *Godzilla, King of the Monsters* (1956), a Japanese film in which scenes featuring Burr were inserted when the film was released in the United States. After he became established in television, Burr focused most of his energies on that medium. His additional film credits include *San Quentin* (1946), *Walk a Crooked Mile* (1948), *Abandoned* (1949), *A Place in the Sun* (1951), *The Blue Gardenia* (1953), *Tarzan and the She-Devil* (1953), *You're Never Too Young* (1955), *Affair in Havana* (1957), *P.J.* (1968), and *Tomorrow Never Comes* (1977).

Sammy Cahn (June 18, 1913-January 15, 1993). Born Samuel Cohen, Cahn was a songwriter who specialized in lyrics. Best known for his work with composer Jimmy Van Heusen, Cahn wrote the lyrics to some of Frank Sinatra's best-known songs. He won four Academy Awards for his work, the first in collaboration with Jules Styne and the last three with Van Heusen. Those lyrics were the title song from *Three Coins in the Fountain* (1954); "All the Way," from *The Joker Is Wild* (1957); "High Hopes," from *A Hole in the Head* (1959); and "Call Me Irresponsible," from *Papa's Delicate Condition* (1963). Eighteen more of Cahn's songs were nominated for Academy Awards, including "It Seems I Heard That Song Before," from *Youth on Parade* (1942); "I'll Walk Alone," from *Follow the Boys* (1944); "Be My Love," from *The Toast of New Orleans* (1950); "The Second Time Around," from *High Time* (1960); "My Kind of Town," from *Robin and the Seven Hoods* (1964); and the title songs from *It's a Great Feeling* (1949), *Written on the Wind* (1956), and *Thoroughly Modern Millie* (1967).

Cantinflas (August 12, 1911-April 20, 1993). Born Mario Moreno Reyes, Cantinflas was a Mexican comic actor who was popular throughout the Spanish-speaking world. His characteristic image, with his pencil moustache, cocked hat, and drooping trousers, earned for him the nickname of "the Mexican Charlie Chaplin." His role as Passepartout in *Around the World in 80 Days* (1956) brought him temporary fame in the United States, though his follow-up feature, *Pepe* (1960), was a commercial failure. His additional film credits include *Ahí está el detalle* (1940), *Ni sangre ni arena* (1941), *Gran Hotel* (1944), *El bombero atómico* (1951), and *El patrullero 777* (1978).

Joyce Carey (March 30, 1898-February 28, 1993). Born Joyce Lawrence, Carey was a British character actress who specialized in playing upper-class roles. She worked extensively with Noel Coward on stage and also appeared in the film version of his *Blithe Spirit* (1945). Her additional screen credits include *Brief Encounter* (1946), *Cry the Beloved Country* (1952), *Greyfriars Bobby* (1961), *The V.I.P.s* (1963), and *The Black Windmill* (1974).

Janice Carroll (1932-September 10, 1993). Carroll was a dancer and an actress who is perhaps best remembered for her role as Susan Lewis in her first film, *Shane* (1953). She also appeared in *Daddy Long Legs* (1955), *How to Be Very, Very Popular* (1955), *The April Fools* (1969), and *The End* (1978).

Kenneth Connor (1916-November 28, 1993). Connor was a British comic actor best known for his featured roles in the bawdy "Carry On" series, where he played timid, nervous characters. His screen credits include *The Ladykillers* (1955), *Carry On Sergeant* (1959), *Carry On Nurse* (1959), *Dentist in the Chair* (1960), *Watch Your Stern* (1960), *Dentist on the Job* (1961), *What a Carve Up!* (1962), and *Carry On Cleo* (1965).

Eddie Constantine (October 29, 1917-February 25, 1993). Constantine was an American actor who starred as Lemmy Caution, the hard-boiled private-eye hero, in a series of French thrillers in the 1950's and 1960's. He is best known to American audiences through his work in Jean-Luc Godard's *Alphaville* (1965). His additional film credits include *Cet Homme est dangereux* (1953), *The Treasure of Santa Teresa* (1959), *Cleo from 5 to 7* (1964), *Lion's Love* (1969), *Beware of a Holy Whore* (1971), and *It Lives Again* (1978).

Cyril Cusack (November 26, 1910-October 7, 1993). Born in South Africa, Cusack was an Irish actor who had a long career on stage and in film. He occasionally won leading roles, as in Galileo (1968), but his small stature more often led to supporting roles. He made his first film appearance at the age of seven in *Knocknagow* (1917) and began appearing on-screen regularly after World War II. His additional film credits include *Odd Man Out* (1947), *The Elusive Pimpernel* (1950), *The Rising of the Moon* (1957), *The Spy Who Came in from the Cold* (1965), *Fahrenheit 451* (1966), *Harold and Maude* (1971), *The Day of the Jackal* (1973), *My Left Foot* (1989), and *Far and Away* (1992).

Mack David (1912-December 30, 1993). David was a lyricist whose work included best-selling songs and television themes, as well as music from films. Eight of his songs were nominated for Academy Awards, including "Bibbidi-Bobbidi-Boo" from Walt Disney's *Cinderella* (1950) and "My Wishing Doll" from *Hawaii* (1966), as well as the title songs from *The Hanging Tree* (1959), *Bachelor in Paradise* (1961), *Walk on the Wild Side* (1962), *It's a Mad Mad Mad Mad World* (1963), *Hush . . . Hush, Sweet Charlotte* (1965), and *Cat Ballou* (1965).

Don DeFore (August 25, 1917-December 22, 1993). DeFore was an actor who specialized in second leads in comedies. In addition to his film career, he worked extensively in television, first as Thorny, the neighbor in *The Adventures of Ozzie and Harriet*, and then as George Baxter, the head of the household in *Hazel*. His screen credits include *The Male Animal* (1942), *A Guy Named Joe* (1943), *The Affairs of Susan* (1945), *My Friend Irma*

(1949), *Jumping Jacks* (1952), *She's Working Her Way Through College* (1952), *Battle Hymn* (1957), and *The Facts of Life* (1960).

Curly Joe DeRita (1910-July 3, 1993). DeRita was a comic actor who was the last surviving member of the Three Stooges comedy team. DeRita was added to the Stooges' lineup in 1959, after the death of Joe Besser. DeRita never appeared in the Stooges' classic comedy shorts, but he did star in their feature films, including *Have Rocket Will Travel* (1959), *Snow White and the Three Stooges* (1961), *The Three Stooges in Orbit* (1962), *It's a Mad Mad Mad Mad World* (1963), and *The Outlaws Is Coming!* (1965).

James Donald (May 18, 1917-August 3, 1993). Donald was a Scottish character actor best known for his role as the doctor in *The Bridge on the River Kwai* (1957). He was also featured opposite Kirk Douglas as Theo Van Gogh in *Lust for Life* (1956). His additional film credits include *In Which We Serve* (1942), *The Pickwick Papers* (1953), *Beau Brummel* (1954), *The Vikings* (1958), *The Great Escape* (1963), *King Rat* (1965), *Cast a Giant Shadow* (1966), *The Jokers* (1967), *The Royal Hunt of the Sun* (1969), and *The Big Sleep* (1978).

Kenneth Englund (May 6, 1911-August 10, 1993). Englund was a screenwriter who specialized in comedy in a career that spanned three decades. His screen credits include *The Big Broadcast of 1938* (1938), *The Doctor Takes a Wife* (1940), *No No Nanette* (1940), *Here Come the Waves* (1944), *The Secret Life of Walter Mitty* (1947), *The Caddy* (1953), and *The Wicked Dreams of Paula Schultz* (1968).

Fritz Feld (October 15, 1900-November 18, 1993). Feld was a German-born character actor who specialized in playing eccentric foreigners in American films. His talents were employed frequently in minor roles by American filmmakers; it has been estimated that he appeared in more than four hundred Hollywood features. His acting credits include *The Last Command* (1928), *Tovarich* (1937), *Bringing Up Baby* (1938), *Artists and Models Abroad* (1938), *At the Circus* (1939), *The Secret Life of Walter Mitty* (1947), *The Errand Boy* (1961), *Promises! Promises!* (1963), *Barefoot in the Park* (1967), *Hello Dolly!* (1969), *Silent Movie* (1976), and *The World's Greatest Lover* (1977).

Federico Fellini (January 20, 1920-October 31, 1993). Fellini was an Italian director who is recognized as being one of the masters of the medium of cinema. His films were personal and featured striking, often surreal images that came to be known as "Felliniesque." Fellini kept the details of his early life obscure, and much of what is known about his childhood comes from his films. He was born into a middle-class family, but was a poor student and a troublemaker. Art was his only real interest, and he found early employment as a cartoonist. His friendship with actors led him into set design, acting, and ultimately screenwriting.

Fellini's work came to the attention of filmmaker Roberto Rossellini, who hired him to work on the script for the classic documentary *Roma, città aperta* (1945; *Rome, Open City*). Further work as a screenwriter led to his first attempt at directing, in *Luci del varietà* (1950; *Variety Lights*), which drew on Fellini's own experiences with a traveling acting troupe. Reaction to that film, as well as his next, *Lo sceicco bianco* (1952; *The White Sheik*), was tepid, but Fellini had found his vocation, and he persisted. His third film, *I vitelloni* (1953), another autobiographical film, this one about bored adolescents, was a huge success, and his career was established. Fellini's wife, actress Giulietta Masina, was often featured in his films, and she became an international star with the release of *La strada* (1954), which won an Academy Award as Best Foreign-Language Film. Fellini and Masina repeated their success in *Le notti di Cabiria* (1957; *The Nights of Cabiria*), which also won the Academy Award as Best Foreign-Language Film.

Fellini's next breakthrough was *La dolce vita* (1960), which introduced Marcello Mastroianni as Fellini's alter ego, and which marked a step away from the neorealism to a more exotic, occasionally surreal, style. The film's depiction of upper-class Roman decadence outraged the leadership of the Catholic Church in Italy, but their condemnation only enhanced Fellini's reputation. *Otto e mezzo* (1963; *8½*), his next significant work, continued his autobiographical explorations and starred Mastroianni as a filmmaker who was trying to make sense of his own life. This film earned for Fellini his third Academy Award for Best Foreign-Language Film. *Giwietta degli spiriti* (1965; *Juliet of the Spirits*) once more featured Giulietta Masina in an exploration of the fantasies of a woman who suspects her husband of adultery. Visually stunning, it was Fellini's first color film.

Fellini's next three efforts—*Fellini Satyricon* (1969), *The Clowns* (1970), and *Fellini's Roma* (1972)—were controversial among critics, who believed that the filmmaker was becoming self-indulgent, opting for style over substance. He returned to the top of his form with *Amarcord* (1973), a more personal film filled with childhood memories. *Amarcord* earned for Fellini his fourth Academy Award for Best Foreign-Language Film.

Over the last two decades of his life, Fellini made five more films, none of which reached the heights of his earlier efforts. Yet over the length of his career, Fellini ranked with Ingmar Bergman and Akira Kurosawa among the greatest filmmakers of his generation. In 1993, he was given a special Academy Award for his lifetime achievements in film. His additional screen credits include *Il bidone* (1955), *Boccaccio '70* (1962; the "Temptation of Dr. Antonio" segment), *Fellini's Casanova* (1976), *Orchestra Rehearsal* (1979), *City of Women* (1981), *And the Ship Sails On* (1984), *Ginger and Fred* (1986), and *The Voice of the Moon* (1990).

Daniel Fuchs (1909-July 26, 1993). Fuchs was a novelist and screenwriter. His film career was capped by his screenplay for *Love Me or Leave Me* (1955), which earned for him an Academy Award. His additional screen credits include *The Hard Way* (1942) and *Jeanne Eagels* (1957).

George Garvarentz (1931-March 19, 1993). Born in Greece, Garvarentz was a composer and songwriter who lived in France after the end of World War II. He worked often with French actor-singer Charles Aznavour, and his first film score was for *Un Taxi pour Tobrouk* (1965; *Taxi for Tobruk*), an Aznavour film. His additional film credits include *Triple Cross* (1967), *They Came to Rob Las Vegas* (1968), and *Triumphs of a Man Called Horse* (1983).

Penelope Gilliatt (1921-May 4, 1993). Gilliatt was a British-born novelist and film critic whose criticism appeared in *The New Yorker* from 1968-1979. Her screenplay for *Sunday, Bloody Sunday* (1971) was nominated for an Academy Award.

Lillian Gish (October 14, 1896-February 27, 1993). Gish was an actress who was one of the most popular stars of the silent era. She and her sister Dorothy began acting as small children to help support their mother. In 1912, Mary Pickford, a childhood friend, introduced the girls to director D. W. Griffith, who hired them on the spot and put them to work that same day in *An Unseen Enemy* (1912). Thus began an association with the great filmmaker that lasted for ten years and forty films. Gish became Griffith's idealized heroine, a seemingly fragile flower who was capable of great strength in times of crisis. She was featured in most of Griffith's major films, including *The Birth of a Nation* (1915), *Intolerance* (1916), *Broken Blossoms* (1919), *True Heart Susie* (1919), *Way Down East* (1920), and *Orphans of the Storm* (1922). During this period, she also directed one film, *Remodeling Her Husband* (1920), which starred her sister Dorothy.

Though devoted to Griffith—she entitled her 1969 autobiography *The Movies, Mr. Griffith & Me*—she eventually parted company with him in a salary dispute. She worked in a number of films throughout the 1920's, always with control over the scripts and directors. Her best roles during this period were in *Romola* (1924), *La Bohème* (1926), and *The Scarlet Letter* (1926). Her career was altered dramatically by the advent of sound films, and her final silent, *The Wind* (1928), was a commercial failure. By then, new talents such as Greta Garbo were emerging to challenge Gish's role as the leading lady of film, and the Victorian sensibilities of her earlier films were beginning to strike audiences as outdated. She made her sound debut in *One Romantic Night* (1930), but was unhappy with the new medium and left Hollywood for New York to return to the stage. Her last film lead was *His Double Life* (1933).

Over the ensuing decades, she appeared in character roles occasionally, in films such as *Duel in the Sun* (1947), *The Night of the Hunter* (1955), *The Unforgiven* (1960), and *The Whales of August* (1987). She was given an honorary Academy Award in 1970 for her lifetime achievements. Her additional film credits include *The Madonna of the Storm* (1913), *The Battle of the Sexes* (1914), *Enoch Arden* (1915), *Hearts of the World* (1918), *The White Sister* (1923), *Annie Laurie* (1927), *The Commandos Strike at Dawn* (1943), *Miss Susie Slagle's* (1946), *Portrait of Jennie* (1949), *Follow Me Boys!* (1966), *The Comedians* (1967), and *A Wedding* (1978).

Michael Gordon (September 6, 1909-April 29, 1993). Gordon was a director whose career was interrupted by the blacklist when he declined to cooperate with the House Un-American Activities Committee. After establishing himself through low-budget films such as *Boston Blackie Goes Hollywood* (1942), Gordon made his mark with respected dramas, including *Another Part of the Forest* (1948) and *Cyrano de Bergerac* (1950). Prevented from working in Hollywood by the blacklist, Gordon spent his time primarily in theater, directing several Broadway productions. He returned to film with *Pillow Talk* (1959), the first of several successful films which paired Doris Day and Rock Hudson. He concentrated thereafter on light comedies. Gordon's additional screen credits include *The Lady Gambles* (1949), *I Can Get It for You Wholesale* (1951), *Boys' Night Out* (1962), *Move Over Darling* (1963), *Texas Across the River* (1966), and *The Impossible Years* (1968).

Stewart Granger (May 6, 1913-August 16, 1993). Born James Stewart, Granger was a British actor who ranked with James Mason as the most popular British leading man of the 1940's, appearing in such films as *Secret Mission* (1942), *Waterloo Road* (1945), and *The Magic Bow* (1946). He came to Hollywood to star in *King Solomon's Mines* (1950) and eventually became an American citizen. In the 1950's, he starred in a series of swashbuckling costume epics, including *Scaramouche* (1952), *The Prisoner of Zenda* (1952), and *Beau Brummel* (1954). As his popularity waned in the 1960's, he took roles in European productions, as well as television. He was married for a time to actress Jean Simmons. His additional screen credits include *The Lamp Still Burns* (1943), *Captain Boycott* (1947), *Salome* (1953), *Bhowani Junction* (1956), *North to Alaska* (1960), *Requiem for a Secret Agent* (1966), and *The Wild Geese* (1978).

Nan Grey (July 25, 1918-July 25, 1993). Born Eschal Miller, Grey was an actress who was featured in many B films of the 1930's, including *Dracula's Daughter* (1936) and *The Black Doll* (1938). She retired from show business when she married singer Frankie Laine in 1950. Her additional screen credits include *Babbitt* (1934), *Crash Donovan* (1936), *Three Smart Girls* (1936), *Reckless Living* (1938), *Tower of London* (1939), *The Invisible Man Returns* (1940), and *The House of the Seven Gables* (1940).

Fred Gwynne (July 10, 1926-July 2, 1993). Gwynne was an actor best known for his comic roles. He starred in television's *Car 54, Where Are You?* and *The Munsters* in the 1960's. He reprised his role as Herman Munster in the feature film *Munster, Go Home!* (1966).

His additional film credits include *On the Waterfront* (1954), *The Cotton Club* (1984), *Ironweed* (1987), *Fatal Attraction* (1987), *Pet Sematary* (1989), and *My Cousin Vinny* (1992).

Ted Haworth (1916-February 18, 1993). Haworth was a production designer and art director who earned an Academy Award for his work on *Sayonara* (1957). He was nominated for Academy Awards in art decoration for *Marty* (1955), *Some Like It Hot* (1959), *The Longest Day* (1962), and *What a Way to Go!* (1964). His additional screen credits include *I Confess* (1953), *The Kentuckian* (1955), and *Invasion of the Body Snatchers* (1956).

Helen Hayes (October 10, 1900-March 17, 1993). Born Helen Hayes Brown, Hayes was an actress whose career spanned more than eight decades. Although she worked in film and television, winning two Academy Awards and an Emmy, she is best known for her stage contributions, where she earned the title of "the First Lady of the American Theater." Hayes began acting when she was five and made her Broadway debut at the age of nine. Her first starring stage role came in *Dear Brutus*, in 1918, by which time she had already appeared in two films. In 1928, she married playwright Charles MacArthur, and when he moved to Hollywood under contract to Metro-Goldwyn-Mayer, Hayes went with him. She won an Academy Award as Best Actress for her first film role, in *The Sin of Madelon Claudet (1931)*. *She was featured in several films in the early 1930's, including Arrowsmith* (1931), *A Farewell to Arms* (1932), and *What Every Woman Knows* (1934), but she felt temperamentally unsuited to motion-picture stardom and returned to Broadway, where she enjoyed a long and productive career. She continued to make films on occasion and earned her second Academy Award, as Best Supporting Actress, for her work in *Airport* (1970). She narrated the feature-length film autobiography *Helen Hayes: Portrait of an American Actress* (1974) and published three memoirs, the last of which, *My Life in Three Acts*, was published in 1990. Her additional film credits include *Jean and the Calico Doll* (1910), *Babs* (1920), *The Son-Daughter* (1932), *The White Sister* (1933), *Vanessa: Her Love Story* (1935), *My Son John* (1952), *Anastasia* (1956), *Herbie Rides Again* (1974), *One of Our Dinosaurs Is Missing* (1975), and *Candleshoe* (1978).

Audrey Hepburn (May 4, 1929-January 20, 1993). Born Audrey Hepburn-Ruston in Belgium, Hepburn was an actress who was a star in the theater as well as in film. Slender and beautiful, she projected a radiant elegance that won the hearts of audiences in the 1950's and 1960's. A fashion model in the early 1950's, she began appearing in small roles in films such as *The Lavender Hill Mob* (1951) and *Monte Carlo Baby* (1951). On the set of the latter film, she met the author Colette, who insisted that Hepburn play the lead in the Broadway adaptation of *Gigi*. Her stage success led to a featured role opposite Gregory Peck in *Roman Holiday* (1953), for which she won an Academy Award as Best Actress. Hepburn was nominated for Academy Awards four more times, for her work in *Sabrina* (1954), *The Nun's Story* (1959), *Breakfast at Tiffany's* (1961), and *Wait Until Dark* (1967). She is also remembered for her role as Eliza Doolittle in *My Fair Lady* (1964). By the late 1960's, Hepburn had cut back on her acting career, but she was featured in several films over the last two decades of her life, most memorably opposite Sean Connery in *Robin and Marian* (1976). From 1954 to 1968, she was married to actor Mel Ferrer. Hepburn was also known for her work on behalf of the international relief agency UNICEF. At the Academy Awards ceremonies in 1993, she was awarded the Jean Hersholt Humanitarian Award. Her additional film credits include *War and Peace* (1956), *Funny Face* (1957), *Love in the Afternoon* (1957), *The Unforgiven* (1960), *Charade* (1963), *How to Steal a Million* (1966), *Two for the Road* (1967), *Bloodline* (1979), *They All Laughed* (1981), and *Always* (1989).

Inoshiro Honda (1911-February 28, 1993). Honda was a Japanese producer and director best known as the creator of the monster Godzilla. Originally released in Japan as *Gojira* (1954), the film was reedited with additional scenes involving Raymond Burr for its American release as *Godzilla, King of the Monsters* (1956). Honda made a total of twenty-three monster films over the next two decades, including *Mothra* (1962), *King Kong vs. Godzilla* (1963), *Godzilla vs. the Thing* (1964), and *Godzilla's Revenge* (1969).

Cy Howard (September 27, 1915-April 29, 1993). Born Seymour Horowitz, Howard was a screenwriter and director who specialized in comedy. His *My Friend Irma* (1949), which marked the film debut of the comedy team of Dean Martin and Jerry Lewis, was based on the popular radio show of the same name that he had created. Howard wrote two more Martin and Lewis vehicles, *My Friend Irma Goes West* (1950) and *That's My Boy* (1951)—for which he served as associate producer. His second wife was actress Gloria Grahame. Howard worked extensively in television as a producer; he also directed two films, *Lovers and Other Strangers* (1970) and *Every Little Crook and Nanny* (1972)—which he also cowrote. His additional screenwriting credits include *Marriage on the Rocks* (1965) and *Won Ton Ton—The Dog Who Saved Hollywood* (1976).

Zita Johann (July 14, 1904-September 24, 1993). Johann was a Hungarian-born actress who emigrated to the United States as a child. She was a leading lady on Broadway, but also appeared in several films, most memorably opposite Boris Karloff in *The Mummy* (1932). She was married for a time to actor John Houseman. Her additional film credits include *The Struggle* (1931), *Tiger Shark* (1932), *The Man Who Dared* (1933), and *Grand Canary* (1934).

Aben Kandel (1896-January 28, 1993). Kandel was a novelist and screenwriter best known for his work on horror films such as *I Was a Teenage Werewolf* (1957) and *Horrors of the Black Museum* (1959). He also wrote the screenplay for Joan Crawford's last film, *Trog* (1970). His additional screenwriting credits include *The Iron Major* (1943).

Joel Kane (1921-April 20, 1993). Kane was a screenwriter best known for his work in television, where he worked on series as varied as *The Flintstones*, *Bonanza*, and *Columbo*. He earned an Academy Award nomination for his story for *The Tin Star* (1957).

Michael Kanin (February 1, 1910-March 12, 1993). Kanin was a screenwriter best known for his work on the Spencer Tracy-Katharine Hepburn film *Woman of the Year* (1942), for which he and collaborator Ring Lardner, Jr., shared an Academy Award. He often worked with his wife, Fay Mitchell Kanin, and their screenplay for *Teacher's Pet* (1958) was nominated for an Academy Award. He was the brother of director-writer Garson Kanin. His additional screenwriting credits include *They Made Her a Spy* (1939), *Sunday Punch* (1942), *Rhapsody* (1954), *The Opposite Sex* (1956), *The Outrage* (1964), and *How to Commit Marriage* (1969).

Ruby Keeler (August 25, 1909-February 28, 1993). Keeler was a Canadian-born actress, dancer, and singer who was best known for her work in Busby Berkeley musicals in the 1930's. Keeler worked extensively in Broadway musicals before making her film debut in Berkeley's *42nd Street* (1933). She was often cast as the hardworking chorus girl who got her big break when called upon to replace the star of the show at the last minute. Keeler was modest about her abilities, but her sincerity won over audiences, and she was featured in several Depression-era musicals such as *Gold Diggers of 1933* (1933), *Footlight Parade* (1933), and *Flirtation Walk* (1934). She had married actor-singer Al Jolson in 1928, and Jolson's feud with Warner Bros. prompted Keeler to leave the studio in 1937. She made one more film, the unsuccessful *Mother Carey's Chickens* (1938), before divorcing Jolson. After *Sweetheart of the Campus* (1941), she married again and retired from show business. Her final screen appearance was a cameo in *The Phynx* (1970). Her additional film credits include

Dames (1934), *Go into Your Dance* (1935), *Shipmates Forever* (1935), *Colleen* (1936), and *Ready, Willing and Able* (1937).

Charles Lamont (May 5, 1898-September 12, 1993). Lamont was a prolific director who got his start making comedy shorts in the silent era for Mack Sennett and Albert Christie. He is best known for his work on the popular Ma and Pa Kettle and Abbott and Costello films of the postwar era. His film credits include *The Lady in Scarlet* (1935), *Bulldog Edition* (1936), *Pride of the Navy* (1939), *San Antonio Rose* (1941), *Salome, Where She Danced* (1945), *Frontier Gal* (1945), *Ma and Pa Kettle* (1949), *Ma and Pa Kettle Go to Town* (1950), *Abbott and Costello in the Foreign Legion* (1950), *Abbott and Costello Meet the Invisible Man* (1951), *Ricochet Romance* (1954), *Ma and Pa Kettle at Home* (1954), *Abbott and Costello Meet the Mummy* (1955), and *Francis in the Haunted House* (1956).

Ely A. Landau (January 20, 1920-November 4, 1993). Landau was a producer who was known for the high quality of his films, often bringing theatrical productions to the screen. His films include *Long Day's Journey into Night* (1962), *The Pawnbroker* (1965), *The Madwoman of Chaillot* (1969), *The Iceman Cometh* (1973), *A Delicate Balance* (1973), *Luther* (1974), *Galileo* (1975), and *The Three Sisters* (1977).

Fernand Ledoux (January 24, 1897-September 21, 1993). Ledoux was a French character actor whose film career spanned six decades. He was a member of the Comedie Française from 1921 to 1943 and began his film career in the silent era, with *Le Carnaval des vérités* (1919). His best-known film role was in Jean Renoir's *La Bête humaine* (1938; *The Human Beast*). Ledoux's additional film credits include *Goupi Mains-Rouges* (1943), *Volpone* (1947), *Danger de mort* (1947), *Till l'Espiègle* (1956), *Les Misérables* (1958), *The Longest Day* (1962), *À chacun son enfer* (1977), and *Mille milliards de dollars* (1982).

Brandon Lee (February 1, 1965-March 31, 1993). Lee was an actor and the son of martial-arts star Bruce Lee. Brandon Lee died on the set of *The Crow* under mysterious circumstances, as a bullet from a gun believed to have been loaded with blanks struck him in the chest. Lee had acted on television and was also featured in *Rapid Fire* (1992).

Myrna Loy (August 2, 1905-December 14, 1993). Born Myrna Williams, Loy was an actress and leading lady of the 1930's. She went to high school in Los Angeles and began appearing in films shortly after graduation. She had a slightly exotic look that led to many vamp roles, and she was often cast as an Oriental temptress. She had appeared in more than sixty films by the time she was cast as Nora Charles, opposite William Powell in *The Thin Man* (1934). Her flair for comedy delighted the public, and her career was reborn. She made five Thin Man sequels with Powell; in addition, she was often paired with Clark Gable in such films as *Wife vs. Secretary* (1936) and *Too Hot to Handle* (1938). In 1936, she was named Hollywood's top female star. During World War II, Loy all but abandoned filmmaking to devote herself to Red Cross work but returned to acting with *The Thin Man Goes Home* (1944). Her work in the drama *The Best Years of Our Lives* (1946) earned critical praise, and she was also featured in comedies such as *Mr. Blandings Builds His Dream House* (1948) and *Cheaper by the Dozen* (1950). She continued to work through the 1950's, but thereafter limited her film appearances to cameos. She was awarded a special Academy Award for lifetime achievement in 1991. Her additional film credits include *The Cave Man* (1926), *The Jazz Singer* (1927), *What Price Beauty* (1928), *The Desert Song* (1929), *Body and Soul* (1931), *Arrowsmith* (1931), *After the Thin Man* (1936), *Libeled Lady* (1936), *Another Thin Man* (1939), *Love Crazy* (1941), *The Bachelor and the Bobby-Soxer* (1947), *Song of the Thin Man* (1947), *The Red Pony* (1949), *Belles on Their Toes* (1952), *From the Terrace* (1960), *Airport 1975* (1974), *The End* (1978), and *Just Tell Me What You Want* (1979).

Spanky McFarland (October 2, 1928-June 30, 1993). Born George Emmett McFarland, McFarland was a child actor who starred in the Our Gang comedy shorts of the 1930's, films which enjoyed a resurgence of popularity in the 1950's when they were broadcast on television as "The Little Rascals." McFarland was a chubby baby model; at the age of three, he was selected to replace Joe Cobb as the fat lead in the Our Gang series. *Bored of Education* (1936), in which McFarland was featured, won an Academy Award as Best One-Reel Short Subject. That same year, McFarland starred in the only feature-length Our Gang film, *General Spanky* (1936). In addition to the Our Gang series, he appeared in several features in juvenile roles, including *The Trail of the Lonesome Pine* (1936) and *The Woman in the Window* (1944). He retired from film in his early teens. McFarland's additional screen credits include *Free Eats* (1932), *Spanky* (1932), *For Pete's Sake* (1934), *Rushin' Ballet* (1937), *Practical Jokers* (1938), and *Captain Spanky's Show Boat* (1939).

Alexander Mackendrick (1912-December 22, 1993). Mackendrick was a Scottish director best known for the comedies he directed for Britain's Ealing Studios between 1949 and 1955. These included *Whisky Galore* (1949, released in the United States as *Tight Little Island*) and the Alec Guinness vehicles *The Man in the White Suit* (1951) and *The Ladykillers* (1955)—which also featured Peter Sellers. He also directed in the United States, most notably the drama *Sweet Smell of Success* (1957). His additional films include *Mandy* (1952, released in the United States as *Crash of Silence*), *The Maggie* (1954, released in the United States as *High and Dry*), *A High Wind in Jamaica* (1965), and *Don't Make Waves* (1967).

Joseph L. Mankiewicz (February 11, 1909-February 5, 1993). Mankiewicz was a screenwriter, producer, and director who made some of the 1950's most popular films. The younger brother of screenwriter Herman J. Mankiewicz, he joined his brother in Hollywood in 1929 and found employment working on scripts for Paramount. He earned the first of many Academy Award nominations for his screenplay of *Skippy* (1931). He also acted in *Woman Trap* (1929). By 1935, Mankiewicz knew that he wanted to direct, but studio boss Louis B. Mayer insisted that he work as a producer first. As a producer, Mankiewicz developed many successful films, including *The Three Godfathers* (1936), *Fury* (1936), and *Strange Cargo* (1940). His production of *The Philadelphia Story* (1940) was nominated for an Academy Award, and he followed this up with the first pairing of Katharine Hepburn and Spencer Tracy in *Woman of the Year* (1942).

By 1943, Mankiewicz was convinced that Mayer would never let him direct, so he left Metro-Goldwyn-Mayer and moved to Twentieth Century-Fox, where he wrote and directed *Dragonwyck* (1946), a gothic melodrama. He collaborated with screenwriter Philip Dunne on *The Late George Apley* (1947), *The Ghost and Mrs. Muir* (1947), and *Escape* (1948); then he directed his own screenplay of *A Letter to Three Wives* (1949). The film itself earned an Academy Award nomination as Best Picture, and Mankiewicz won two awards, for Best Director and Best Screenplay. The next year, his *All About Eve* (1950) won the Academy Award for Best Picture, and Mankiewicz repeated his sweep of the Best Director and Best Screenplay awards.

Mankiewicz's success continued throughout the decade. His scripts were known for their literacy and sparkling dialogue. He earned an Academy Award nomination for Best Director for *Five Fingers* (1952) and for the screenplay of *The Barefoot Contessa* (1954). His adaptation of *Julius Caesar* (1953), for which Marlon Brando was nominated for an Academy Award, was widely regarded as one of the best screen versions of a Shakespeare play. Other 1950's successes included *Guys and Dolls* (1955) and *The Quiet American* (1958). The 1960's, however, brought mixed results for the filmmaker. *Suddenly, Last Summer* (1959) was a success, but Mankiewicz ran into trouble on his next film. He replaced director Rouben Mamoulian on *Cleopatra* (1963) and added Richard Burton and Rex Harrison to the cast. The shooting was troubled by the controversial offscreen romance between Burton and Elizabeth Taylor, and the film cost the then-incredible sum of $40 million. Critics, reviewing the budget as well as the film, were unanimous in their disapproval, although the film was nominated for an Academy Award as Best Picture. Mankiewicz made only three more films, *The Honey Pot* (1967), *There Was a Crooked Man* (1970), and *Sleuth* (1972). In 1986, he was awarded the D. W. Griffith Award for lifetime achievement by the Directors Guild of America. His additional film credits include, as a writer, *Slightly Scarlet* (1930), *Sooky* (1931), *Million Dollar Legs* (1932), *Manhattan Melodrama* (1934), and *I Live My Life* (1935). Mankiewicz produced *Double Wedding* (1937), *A Christmas Carol* (1938), *The Feminine Touch* (1941), and *The Keys of the Kingdom* (1945). As a director, his films include *Somewhere in the Night* (1946), *No Way Out* (1950), and *People Will Talk* (1951).

Janet Margolin (July 25, 1943-December 17, 1993). Margolin was an actress perhaps best known for her first film role, that of an emotionally disturbed teenager in *David and Lisa* (1962). She also appeared in two Woody Allen films, *Take the Money and Run* (1969) and *Annie Hall* (1977). Her additional film credits include *The Greatest Story Ever Told* (1965), *Bus Riley's Back in Town* (1965), *Saboteur: Code Name Morituri* (1965), *Enter Laughing* (1967), *Buona Sera Mrs. Campbell* (1968), *The Last Embrace* (1979), and *Ghostbusters II* (1989).

Brenda Marshall (September 29, 1915-July 30, 1993). Born Ardis Anderson Gaines, Marshall was a leading lady in the 1940's. She specialized in adventure films, often set in exotic locales; and she is best remembered for her role opposite Errol Flynn in *The Sea Hawk* (1940). She was married for a time to actor William Holden. Her additional screen credits include *Espionage Agent* (1939), *The Man Who Talked Too Much* (1940), *South of Suez* (1940), *Singapore Woman* (1941), *Paris After Dark* (1943), *Whispering Smith* (1949), and *The Iroquois Trail* (1950).

Alexandre Mnouchkine (1908-April 3, 1993). A producer, Mnouchkine was born in Russia and emigrated to France as a child. A major figure in French cinema since the late 1940's, his best- known films include *L'Homme de Rio* (1964; *That Man from Rio*), *Un Homme et une femme* (1966; *A Man and a Woman*), *Satvisky* (1974), and *The Name of the Rose* (1986). Two of his productions, *Préparez vos mouchoirs* (1978; *Get Out Your Handkerchiefs*) and *Cinema Paradiso* (1988), won Academy Awards as Best Foreign-Language Film.

Carlotta Monti (1907-December 8, 1993). Monti was an actress best known as the companion of W. C. Fields from 1933 until the comic actor's death in 1946. Her chronicle of their relationship, *W. C. Fields and Me*, was made into a film in 1976 featuring Valerie Perrine as Monti. Her acting credits include *Ben-Hur* (1926), *The Merry Widow* (1934), and *One Night of Love* (1934).

Jeff Morrow (January 13, 1913-December 26, 1993). Morrow was an actor who worked extensively on stage and in television as well as in film. On screen, he is best remembered as the star of several science-fiction films of the mid-1950's, including *This Island Earth* (1955), in which he played an alien friendly to Earthlings, and *The Creature Walks Among Us* (1956), the last of the three "Creature from the Black Lagoon" films. His additional film credits include *The Robe* (1953), *Tanganyika* (1954), *Captain Lightfoot* (1955), *Pardners* (1956), *The Giant Claw* (1957), *The Story of Ruth* (1960), and *Harbor Lights* (1963).

Richard Murphy (May 8, 1912-May 19, 1993). Murphy was a screenwriter and director who was nominated for Academy Awards for his work on the screenplays of *Boomerang!*

(1947) and *The Desert Rats* (1953). He also worked in television. His additional writing credits include *Back in the Saddle* (1941), *Slattery's Hurricane* (1949), *The Last Angry Man* (1959), and *The Kidnapping of the President* (1980). He wrote and directed two films, *Three Stripes in the Sun* (1955) and *The Wackiest Ship in the Army* (1960).

Jean Negulesco (February 26, 1900-July 18, 1993). Negulesco was a Romanian-born director who worked successfully in Hollywood for three decades. Working for Warner Bros. in the 1940's, he was known for his skill in the melodrama genre, with films such as *The Mask of Dimitrios* (1944), *Humoresque* (1947), and *Johnny Belinda* (1948). He moved to Twentieth Century-Fox in the 1950's, where he specialized in lighter fare, including *How to Marry a Millionaire* (1953), *Three Coins in the Fountain* (1954), and *Daddy Long Legs* (1955). His additional film credits include *Singapore Woman* (1941), *The Rains of Ranchipur* (1955), *Boy on a Dolphin* (1957), *A Certain Smile* (1958), *The Best of Everything* (1959), *The Pleasure Seekers* (1964), and *The Invincible Six* (1970).

Walter Brown Newman (1916-October 14, 1993). Newman was a screenwriter who was twice nominated for Academy Awards—for *Cat Ballou* (1965) and *Bloodbrothers* (1978). His additional film credits include *Ace in the Hole* (1951; renamed *The Big Carnival*), *The Man with the Golden Arm* (1955), *The True Story of Jesse James* (1957), *Crime and Punishment USA* (1959), and *The Champ* (1979).

Rudolf Nureyev (March 17, 1938-January 6, 1993). Nureyev was a Russian-born dancer who appeared in two feature films. He was the leading dancer with the Kirov Ballet before defecting in Paris in 1961. His most frequent partner was Margot Fonteyn. Efforts to translate his popularity to film were unsuccessful, as both Ken Russell's biography *Valentino* (1977) and James Toback's *Exposed* (1983) were commercial failures.

Christian Nyby (1919-September 17, 1993). Nyby was an editor and director. Among the films on which he worked as an editor were *To Have and Have Not* (1944), *The Big Sleep* (1946), and *Red River* (1948); he was nominated for an Academy Award for his work on the latter film. He made his debut as a director with the science-fiction classic *The Thing* (1951). Thereafter, he worked most often in television. Among the feature films Nyby directed were *Hell on Devil's Island* (1957), *Young Fury* (1965), and *First to Fight* (1967).

Buddy Pepper (1922-February 14, 1993). Born Jack Starkey, Pepper was an actor and songwriter. Before World War II, he appeared in juvenile roles in such films as *Seventeen* (1940), *The Reluctant Dragon* (1941), and *Men of Boys Town* (1941). After the war, he turned to songwriting and served as composer and lyricist for Universal Studios. His best-known song was "Vaya Con Dios." He wrote the title songs for *Pillow Talk* (1959) and *Portrait in Black* (1960).

Mary Philbin (July 16, 1903-May 7, 1993). Philbin was an actress who was a star in the silent era. She is best remembered for her role as Christine opposite Lon Chaney in the original film version of *The Phantom of the Opera* (1925). She ended her film career with the advent of sound. Her additional screen credits include *The Blazing Trail* (1921), *Penrod and Sam* (1923), *The Temple of Venus* (1923), *The Gaiety Girl* (1924), *The Rose of Paris* (1924), *Stella Maris* (1925), *Drums of Love* (1928), and *The Shannons of Broadway* (1929).

River Phoenix (August 23, 1970-October 31, 1993). Phoenix was an actor whose death of a drug overdose outside a Hollywood nightclub earned for him posthumous tabloid notoriety. He was widely regarded as a sensitive actor who was willing to take on difficult roles. He first attracted notice in *Stand by Me* (1986) and played the young Indiana Jones in *Indiana Jones and the Last Crusade* (1989). He was nominated for an Academy Award as Best Supporting Actor for his work in *Running on Empty* (1988). His additional film credits include *The Mosquito Coast* (1986), *My Own Private Idaho* (1991), and *Sneakers* (1992).

Vincent Price (May 27, 1911-October 25, 1993). Price was an actor whose career was changed forever when he appeared as a crazed sculptor in the 3-D horror film *House of Wax* (1953). He proved so adept at horror roles that he rarely ventured outside the genre on film, although he continued to appear onstage in more conventional roles. His aristocratic looks and mellifluous voice earned for him leading roles in films such as *The Private Lives of Elizabeth and Essex* (1939) and *The House of the Seven Gables* (1940). He even made early ventures into the horror genre, starring in *The Invisible Man Returns* (1940) and *Abbott and Costello Meet Frankenstein* (1948). He rose to prominence, however, as the star of Roger Corman's series of films based on the works of Edgar Allan Poe, beginning with *The House of Usher* (1960). In addition to his acting career, Price was an authority on art and cooking, publishing several books on both topics. His additional film credits include *Tower of London* (1939), *Brigham Young—Frontiersman* (1940), *The Song of Bernadette* (1943), *The Three Musketeers* (1948), *The Ten Commandments* (1956), *The Fly* (1958), *Return of the Fly* (1959), *The Pit and the Pendulum* (1961), *The Raven* (1963), *Beach Party* (1963), *The Masque of the Red Death* (1964), *The Trouble with Girls* (1969), *The Abominable Dr. Phibes* (1971), *Theatre of Blood* (1973), and *Edward Scissorhands* (1990).

François Reichenbach (July 3, 1922-February 2, 1993). Reichenbach was a French documentary filmmaker. He is best known in the United States for *Arthur Rubinstein: L'Amour de la vie* (1970; *Arthur Rubenstein: Love of Life*), which won an Academy Award as Best Documentary Feature. His additional film credits include *Impressions de New York* (1955), *Au pays de Porgy and Bess* (1957), *L'Amérique insolite* (1960), *Grenoble* (1968)—codirected with Claude Lelouche—*Mexico Mexico* (1969), *La Caravane d'amour* (1971; *Medicine Ball Caravan*), and *Pele* (1977).

Claude Renoir (December 4, 1914-September 5, 1993). Renoir was a French cinematographer, the son of director Pierre Renoir and the nephew of director Jean Renoir, with whom he began his film career in films such as *Toni* (1935) and *La Grande Illusion* (1937). He is perhaps best remembered for *The River* (1951), shot in India and known for its sensual use of color. His film credits include *Monsieur Vincent* (1947), *Le Mystère Picasso* (1956; *The Picasso Mystery*), *Une vie* (1958), *Barbarella* (1968), *The Madwoman of Chaillot* (1969), *French Connection II* (1975), and *The Spy Who Loved Me* (1977).

Dorothy Revier (April 18, 1904-November 19, 1993). Born Doris Velegra, Revier was an actress whose starring role in numerous low-budget films in the silent and early sound eras earned for her the nickname "Queen of Poverty Row." She was often cast as the femme fatale and is best remembered for her role opposite Douglas Fairbanks in *The Iron Mask* (1929). Her additional acting credits include *The Broadway Madonna* (1922), *The Fate of a Flirt* (1925), *The Drop Kick* (1927), *Beware of Blondes* (1928), *Call of the West* (1930), *Anybody's Blonde* (1931), *Above the Clouds* (1933), and *The Cowboy and the Kid* (1936).

Davis Roberts (1917-July 18, 1993). Roberts was an African-American character actor whose career spanned half a century. He worked extensively in television, and his film credits include *Knock on Any Door* (1949), *Red Ball Express* (1952), *Phone Call From a Stranger* (1952), *All the Fine Young Cannibals* (1960), *The Great White Hope* (1970), *Westworld* (1973), and *To Sleep with Anger* (1990).

Sam Rolfe (1924-July 10, 1993). Rolfe was a writer and producer who was best known for his work in television, where he created such hits as *Have Gun, Will Travel* and *The Man From U.N.C.L.E.* He was nominated for an Academy Award for his screenplay for the James Stewart Western *The Naked Spur* (1953).

Richard Sale (December 17, 1911-March 4, 1993). Sale was a novelist, director, and screenwriter best known for light comedy. Many of his films, including *Campus Honeymoon* (1948), *Mother Is a Freshman* (1949), *Father Was a Fullback* (1949), and *Mr. Belvedere Goes to College* (1949), were set on college campuses. Sale wrote and directed such films as *I'll Get By* (1950), *The Girl Next Door* (1953), and *Gentlemen Marry Brunettes* (1955); he also coproduced the latter two films. His additional screenwriting credits include *Woman's World* (1954) and *Around the World in 80 Days* (1956).

Richard Schmiechen (1947-April 7, 1993). Schmiechen was a documentary filmmaker whose *The Times of Harvey Milk* (1984) won an Academy Award as Best Documentary Feature. His *Changing Our Minds: The Story of Dr. Evelyn Hooker* (1992), made in collaboration with David Haugland, was nominated for an Academy Award.

Dan Seymour (February 22, 1915-May 25, 1993). Seymour was a burly character actor who specialized in tough-guy roles in Hollywood films of the 1940's and 1950's. He is best remembered for his role as Abdul, the guard at Rick's casino in *Casablanca* (1943). He also appeared in two other Bogart films, *To Have and Have Not* (1944) and *Key Largo* (1948). His additional film credits include *Road to Morocco* (1942), *A Night in Casablanca* (1946), *Johnny Belinda* (1948), *Rancho Notorious* (1952), and *The Return of the Fly* (1959).

Irene Sharaff (1910-August 16, 1993). Sharaff was a costume designer whose work earned for her ten Academy Award nominations. She won the award for *An American in Paris* (1951), *The King and I* (1956), *West Side Story* (1961), *Cleopatra* (1963), and *Who's Afraid of Virginia Woolf?* (1966); she was nominated for *Brigadoon* (1954), *Guys and Dolls* (1955), *Porgy and Bess* (1959), *Flower Drum Song* (1961), and *Hello, Dolly!* (1969). Her additional film credits include *Madame Curie* (1943), *Meet Me in St. Louis* (1944), *The Best Years of Our Lives* (1946), and *Funny Girl* (1968).

Ray Sharkey (1952-June 11, 1993). Sharkey was an actor best known for his role in *The Idolmaker* (1980) and as star of the television series *Wiseguy*. He had a long history of substance abuse and died of AIDS (acquired immune deficiency syndrome) contracted through intravenous drug use. His additional film credits include *Paradise Alley* (1978), *Who'll Stop the Rain* (1978), *Willie and Phil* (1980), *Love and Money* (1982), *Scenes from the Class Struggle in Beverly Hills* (1989), and *Cop and a Half* (1993).

Anne Shirley (April 17, 1918-July 4, 1993). Born Dawn Evelyeen Paris, Shirley was an actress who began her career as a child star in silent films. Under the name Dawn O'Day, she made her screen debut at the age of four in *Moonshine Valley* (1922). She made the move to ingenue roles when she was cast in the title role in *Anne of Green Gables* (1934). Perhaps her most memorable performance was in *Stella Dallas* (1937), which earned for her an Academy Award nomination as Best Supporting Actress. She was married for a time to actor John Payne. Her additional screen credits include *Riders of the Purple Sage* (1925), *So Big* (1932), *Rasputin and the Empress* (1932), *Steamboat 'Round the Bend* (1935), *Anne of Windy Poplars* (1940), *The Powers Girl* (1942), and *Farewell My Lovely* (1944).

Alexis Smith (June 8, 1921-June 9, 1993). Born Gladys Smith, Smith was an actress who was featured in numerous films in the 1940's and 1950's. She specialized in romantic dramas, in which she often played the lead actress' rival. In addition to her film career, she also worked extensively on stage; she won a Tony Award for Best Actress in a musical for her work in *Follies* in 1971. Her film credits include *The Lady with Red Hair* (1940), *Dive Bomber* (1941), *Gentleman Jim* (1942), *The Constant Nymph* (1943), *The Horn Blows at Midnight* (1945), *Rhapsody in Blue* (1945), *Night and Day* (1946), *Here Comes the Groom* (1951), *Beau James* (1957), *The Young Philadelphians* (1959), *Jacqueline Susann's Once Is*

Not Enough (1975), and *Casey's Shadow* (1978).

Anna Sten (December 3, 1908-November 12, 1993). Born Annel Stenskaja Sudakevich, Sten was a Russian actress whose performance in the German film *Der Moerder Dimitri Karamasoff* (1931) attracted the attention of producer Sam Goldwyn. Goldwyn brought her to the United States in the hope that she would become another Greta Garbo or Marlene Dietrich and featured her in *Nana* (1934), but she never won large audiences and ultimately became known as "Goldwyn's Folly." Her film credits include *When Moscow Laughs* (1927), *We Live Again* (1934), *The Wedding Night* (1935), *Exile Express* (1939), *Chetniks* (1943), and *Soldier of Fortune* (1955).

Gerald Thomas (December 10, 1920-November 9, 1993). Thomas was a British director best known for the bawdy "Carry On" comedies, Britain's most successful comedy series. These films featured a stock cast and developed into a running parody of currently popular films and genres. His screen credits include *Circus Friends* (1956), *Carry On Sergeant* (1958), *Carry On Nurse* (1959), *Watch Your Stern* (1960), *Twice Round the Daffodils* (1962), *Carry On Cleo* (1964), *Carry On Emmannuelle* (1978), and *Carry On Columbus* (1992).

Ann Todd (January 24, 1909-May 6, 1993). Todd was a British actress best known for her role opposite James Mason in the romantic thriller *The Seventh Veil* (1945). She was married for a time to director David Lean, with whom she made *The Passionate Friends* (1949), *Madeleine* (1950), and *The Sound Barrier* (1952). Her additional acting credits include *The Ghost Train* (1931), *The Return of Bulldog Drummond* (1934), *The Paradine Case* (1948), *So Evil My Love* (1948), and *Time Without Pity* (1957).

Alexander Trauner (August 3, 1906-December 5, 1993). Born in Hungary, Trauner was an art director who worked extensively with European and American filmmakers in a career that spanned five decades. During the Nazi occupation of France, the Jewish Trauner went underground and worked anonymously on such films as *Les Visiteurs du soir* (1942) and *Les Enfants du paradis* (1945; *Children of Paradise*). His collaboration with Orson Welles on *Othello* (1952) led to numerous assignments on American films. His additional screen credits include *Hôtel du Nord* (1938), *Les Portes de la nuit* (1946; *Gates of the Night*), *L'Amant de Lady Chatterley* (1955; *Lady Chatterley's Lover*), *Land of the Pharaohs* (1955), *The Nun's Story* (1959), *The Apartment* (1960), *Irma La Douce* (1963), *La Nuit des généraux* (1967; *The Night of the Generals*), *The Private Life of Sherlock Holmes* (1970), *The Man Who Would Be King* (1975), *Coup de Torchon* (1981), and *Round Midnight* (1986).

John Truscott (1936-September 5, 1993). Born in Australia, Truscott was an art director and theater designer who worked extensively in the Australian National Theater. He worked in film during the 1960's and won two Academy Awards for his work on *Camelot* (1967), for costume design and for art direction (an award he shared with Edward Carrere).

Conway Twitty (September 1, 1933-June 5, 1993). Born Harold Jenkins, Twitty was a singer who had his greatest success in the country-music field, where he had more than forty number-one songs. He broke into music as a rock-and-roll singer in 1958 and appeared in two films that attempted to cash in on his popularity. His acting credits were *Sex Kittens Go to College* (1960) and *College Confidential* (1960).

Evelyn Venable (October 18, 1913-November 16, 1993). Venable was an actress who was featured in many films of the 1930's and early 1940's. She starred opposite Fredric March in *Death Takes a Holiday* (1934) and opposite Will Rogers in *The County Chairman* (1935). Venable was the model for the insignia of Columbia Pictures. Her additional screen credits include *Cradle Song* (1933), *Mrs. Wiggs of the Cabbage Patch* (1934), *The Little Colonel* (1935), *Alice Adams* (1935), and *Lucky Cisco Kid* (1940).

Sam Wanamaker (June 14, 1919-December 18, 1993). Wanamaker was an actor and director. A political leftist, he appeared in several American films, including the socialist-themed *Give Us This Day* (1949), before moving to England to avoid the reach of the House Committee on Un-American Activities. He was placed on the blacklist and worked primarily in theater throughout the 1950's. He began acting in films again in the 1960's, appearing in *Taras Bulba* (1962) and *The Spy Who Came in from the Cold* (1965), among others. In the late 1960's, he tried his hand at directing and made *The File of the Golden Goose* (1969), *Catlow* (1971), and *Charlie Muffin* (1979). His additional acting credits include *My Girl Tisa* (1948), *Mr. Denning Drives North* (1951), *Those Magnificent Men in Their Flying Machines* (1965), and *Warning Shot* (1967).

Frank Zappa (December 21, 1940-December 4, 1993). Zappa was a musician who made avant-garde rock and jazz music. He was also a prominent defender of the First Amendment, leading the fight against attempts to censor the lyrics of rock songs in the Reagan era. He appeared in the Monkees' feature film *Head* (1968) and directed *Two Hundred Motels* (1971), a nonlinear film that combined live action and animation.

Supporting Actress: Winona Ryder (*The Age of Innocence*)
Foreign-Language Film: Farewell My Concubine (Hong Kong)
Documentary: The War Room (R. J. Cutler, Wendy Ettinger, and Frazer
   Pennebaker)
The D. W. Griffith Career Achievement Award: Sean Connery

Golden Globe Awards
Best Picture, Drama: Schindler's List
Best Picture, Comedy or Musical: Mrs. Doubtfire
Direction: Steven Spielberg (*Schindler's List*)
Actor, Drama: Tom Hanks (*Philadelphia*)
Actress, Drama: Holly Hunter (*The Piano*)
Actor, Comedy or Musical: Robin Williams (*Mrs. Doubtfire*)
Actress, Comedy or Musical: Angela Bassett (*What's Love Got To Do with It*)
Supporting Actor: Tommy Lee Jones (*The Fugitive*)
Supporting Actress: Winona Ryder (*The Age of Innocence*)
Screenplay: Steven Zaillian (*Schindler's List*)
Original Score: Kitaro (*Heaven and Earth*)
Original Song: "Streets of Philadelphia " (*Philadelphia*: music and lyrics, Bruce
   Springsteen)
Foreign-Language Film: Farewell My Concubine (Hong Kong)

Golden Palm Awards (Cannes International Film Festival)
Palme d'Or: The Piano (Jane Campion) and *Farewell My Concubine* (Chen
   Kaige), tie
Grand Jury Prize: Faraway, So Close (Wim Wenders)
Actor: David Thewilis (*Naked*)
Actress: Holly Hunter (*The Piano*)
Direction: Mike Leigh (*Naked*)
Jury Prize: The Puppetmaster (Hou Hsiao-hsien) and *Raining Stones* (Ken Loach)
Grand Technical Prize: Jean Gargonne and Vincent Arnadi (*Mazeppa*)
Camera d'Or: The Scent of a Papaya (Tran Anh Hung)
Palme d'Or, Short Film: Coffee and Cigarettes (Somewhere in California) (Jim
   Jarmusch)

British Academy Awards
Best Picture: Schindler's List
Direction: Steven Spielberg (*Schindler's List*)
Actor: Anthony Hopkins (*The Remains of the Day*)
Actress: Holly Hunter (*The Piano*)
Supporting Actor: Ralph Fiennes (*Schindler's List*)
Supporting Actress: Miriam Margolyes (*The Age of Innocence*)
Original Screenplay: Harold Ramis and Danny Rubin (*Groundhog Day*)

Adapted Screenplay: Steven Zaillian (*Schindler's List*)
Original Score: John Williams (*Schindler's List*)
Best Foreign-Language Film: Farewell My Concubine (Hong Kong)
Short Film, Live Action: Franz Kafka's It's a Wonderful Life
Short Film, Animated: The Wrong Trousers
Alexander Korda Award for Best British Film: Shadowlands (Richard
    Attenborough and Brian Eastman)
Michael Balcon Award for Outstanding Contribution to Cinema: Ken Loach

MAGILL'S CINEMA ANNUAL

TITLE INDEX

DIRECTOR INDEX

461

DIRECTOR INDEX

SCREENWRITER INDEX

SCREENWRITER INDEX

SCREENWRITER INDEX

CINEMATOGRAPHER INDEX

471

CINEMATOGRAPHER INDEX

EDITOR INDEX

EDITOR INDEX

ART DIRECTOR INDEX

ART DIRECTOR INDEX

479

ART DIRECTOR INDEX

481

ART DIRECTOR INDEX

ART DIRECTOR INDEX

YATES, DIANE
  Free Willy   113

ZANETTI, EUGENIO
  Last Action Hero   191

ZARLING, PHIL
  Nemesis   424
ZEA, KRISTI
  Philadelphia   264
ZENKOV, VICTOR
  Ice Runner, The   415

ZHANG RUIHE
  Farewell My Concubine   100
ZIEMBICKI, ROBERT
  Dragon   408

MUSIC INDEX

487

PERFORMER INDEX

AARON, CAROLINE
  Pickle, The   425
  Sleepless in Seattle   334
ABERCROMBIE, IAN
  Army of Darkness   400
ABRAHAM, F. MURRAY
  By the Sword   404
  Last Action Hero   191
  National Lampoon's Loaded
    Weapon I   423
ACKLAND, JOSS
  Nowhere to Run   424
ADAMS, BRANDON
  Sandlot, The   427
ADAMS, JOEY LAUREN
  Dazed and Confused   77
ADAMS, MASON
  Son-in-Law   429
ADLER, JERRY
  Manhattan Murder Mystery   218
AEROSMITH
  Wayne's World II   434
AFFLECK, BEN
  Dazed and Confused   77
AH-LEH GUA
  Wedding Banquet, The   381
AHMED, LALITA
  Wild West   435
AHSAN, RAJU
  Masala   420
AIELLO, DANNY
  Cemetery Club, The   61
  Me and the Kid   420
  Pickle, The   425
ALBERT, EDWARD
  Ice Runner, The   415
ALDA, ALAN
  Manhattan Murder Mystery   218
ALDA, RUTANYA
  Dark Half, The   407
ALDREDGE, TOM
  Adventures of Huck Finn, The
    398
ALEXANDER, JASON
  Coneheads   406
ALEXANDER, KHANDI
  CB4   405
  Menace II Society   228
  What's Love Got To Do With
    It   389
ALLEN, GINGER LYNN
  Bound and Gagged   403
ALLEN, JOAN
  Ethan Frome   89
  Josh and S.A.M.   417
  Searching for Bobby Fischer
    311
ALLEN, KAREN
  King of the Hill   187
  Sandlot, The   427

ALLEN, NANCY
  Robocop III   427
ALLEN, ROSALIND
  Children of the Corn II   406
ALLEN, WOODY
  Manhattan Murder Mystery   218
ALLESSANDRINI, FABIO
  Ladro Di Bambini, Il   418
ALLEY, KIRSTIE
  Look Who's Talking Now   419
ALMENDROS, NESTOR
  Visions of Light   433
ALONZO, JOHN
  Visions of Light   433
ALTMAN, BRUCE
  Mr. Jones   421
  Rookie of the Year   295
ALVARADO, TRINI
  American Friends   399
ALVAREZ, CARLOS
  Sniper   428
AMECHE, DON
  Homeward Bound   146
  Obituaries   437
AMES, LEON
  Obituaries   437
AMIS, SUZY
  Ballad of Little Jo, The   29
  Rich in Love   288
  Watch It   434
AMOS, JOHN
  Mac   203
ANDERSON, KEVIN
  Night We Never Met, The   424
  Rising Sun   291
ANDERSON, RICHARD
  Gettysburg   126
ANDERSON, STANLEY
  Robocop III   427
ANDERSON, STEPHANIE
  Calendar Girl   405
ANDRE THE GIANT
  Obituaries   437
ANDREWS, NAVEEN
  Wild West   435
ANDREWS, SHAWN
  Dazed and Confused   77
ANGELOU, MAYA
  Poetic Justice   272
ANGLADE, JEAN-HUGUES
  Especially on Sunday   409
ANISTON, JENNIFER
  Leprechaun   418
ANN-MARGRET
  Grumpy Old Men   134
ANOTHER BAD CREATION
  Meteor Man, The   421
ANSLEY, ZACK
  This Boy's Life   360

ANTHONY, LYSETTE
  Look Who's Talking Now   419
ANTIN, STEVEN
  Inside Monkey Zetterland   415
ANUNCIATION, DEREK
  Mad Dog and Glory   207
ANWAR, GABRIELLE
  For Love or Money   411
  Three Musketeers, The   364
APISA, BOB
  Hard Target   413
APPLEBY, SHIRI
  Family Prayers   409
APPLEGATE, ROYCE
  Gettysburg   126
ARANDA, PILAR
  Like Water for Chocolate   199
ARCHER, ANNE
  Body of Evidence   402
  Family Prayers   409
  Short Cuts   322
ARENAS, REINALDO
  Sniper   428
ARGO, VICTOR
  Household Saints   157
  True Romance   374
ARIZMENDI, YARELI
  Like Water for Chocolate   199
ARKIN, ALAN
  Indian Summer   415
ARMSTRONG, JENNIFER
  Masala   420
ARMSTRONG, R. G.
  Warlock   434
ARNOLD, TOM
  Undercover Blues   433
ARQUETTE, PATRICIA
  Ethan Frome   89
  Inside Monkey Zetterland   415
  True Romance   374
ARQUETTE, ROSANNA
  Nowhere to Run   424
ARTURA, MICHAEL
  Amongst Friends   399
ASNER, EDWARD
  Happily Ever After   413
ASSANTE, ARMAND
  Fatal Instinct   409
ASTIN, SEAN
  Rudy   427
ATHERTON, WILLIAM
  Pelican Brief, The   256
ATKINS, CHOLLY
  Twist   432
ATKINSON, JAYNE
  Free Willy   113
ATKINSON, ROWAN
  Hot Shots! Part Deux   150
ATTENBOROUGH, RICHARD
  Jurassic Park   180

490

491

PERFORMER INDEX

PERFORMER INDEX

505

PERFORMER INDEX

507

PERFORMER INDEX

515

SUBJECT INDEX

The selection of subject headings combines standard Library of Congress Subject Headings and common usage in order to aid the film researcher. Cross references, listed as *See* and *See also*, are provided when appropriate. While all major themes, locales, and time periods have been indexed, some minor subjects covered in a particular film have not been included.

SUBJECT INDEX

SUBJECT INDEX

SUBJECT INDEX